THRESHOLDS IN FEMINIST GEOGRAPHY

THRESHOLDS IN FEMINIST GEOGRAPHY

Difference, Methodology, Representation

edited by

John Paul Jones III, Heidi J. Nast, and Susan M. Roberts

ROWMAN & LITTLEFIELD PUBLISHERS, INC.
Lanham • New York • Boulder • Oxford

ROWMAN & LITTLEFIELD PUBLISHERS, INC.

Published in the United States of America
by Rowman & Littlefield Publishers, Inc.
4720 Boston Way, Lanham, Maryland 20706

12 Hid's Copse Road
Cummor Hill, Oxford OX2 9JJ, England

British Library Cataloguing in Publication Information Available

The publisher gratefully acknowledges permission to reproduce the poem "Legal Alien" by Pat Mora which appears on p. 247. Pat Mora, "Legal Alien," *Chants.* Houston: arte Publico Press, 1985.

Library of Congress Cataloging-in-Publication Data
Thresholds in feminist geography : difference, methodology, and
representation / edited by John Paul Jones III, Heidi J. Nast, and
Susan M. Roberts.
 p. cm.
"Outcome of a workshop . . . sponsored by the National Science
Foundation and held at the University of Kentucky in 1995"—Pref.
 Includes bibliographical references and index.
 ISBN 0–8476–8436–9 (cloth : alk. paper).—ISBN 0–8476–8437–7
(paper : alk. paper)
 1. Feminist theory—Congresses. 2. Feminist geography—
Congresses. 3. Geography—Study and teaching—Congresses.
I. Jones, John Paul, 1955– . II. Nast, Heidi J. III. Roberts,
Susan M.
HQ1190.T57 1997
305.42′01—dc21   96–46790
                                                          CIP

ISBN 0–8476–8528–4 (cloth : alk. paper)
ISBN 0–8476–8529–2 (pbk. : alk. paper)

Printed in the United States of America

♾ ™ The paper used in this publication meets the minimum requirements of
American National Standard for Information Sciences—Permanence of Paper for
Printed Library Materials, ANSI Z39.48–1984.

In Memory of Glenda Laws

Teacher, Scholar, Friend

1959–1996

Contents

vii

Illustrations

Tables

Preface

Feminism, both in theory and practice, has long privileged relational modes of knowing, such as nonhierarchical interaction, mutual learning, and empathetic understanding. We can apply these relational principles not only to the feminist researcher's relation to her/his "subjects," but in all interactions with others. It is through this larger sense of relationality that we consider this text to have been a feminist production. In particular, it was nurtured through a relational process in which all authors were interconnected to the knowledges and understandings of other authors through a set of specific strategies.

Let us explain. The volume is the outcome of "New Horizons in Feminist Geography," a three day conference/workshop sponsored by the National Science Foundation and held in January 1995 at the University of Kentucky in Lexington. The first one-and-a-half days consisted of a conference open to the public, at which authors delivered presentations in three thematic areas: difference, methodology, and representation. For each, an introduction to key issues in the area was followed by six research papers. Rather than have each person present their own paper, we asked another person in the thematic area to give a lengthy summary; this was followed by a reply from the author. The format created intellectual and personal linkages among participants, while challenging us to internalize each other's work.

Thereafter, three groups of eight persons met for one-and-a-half days in workshops organized around the thematic areas. Each workshop included one of the coeditors, the six authors in the thematic area, and a facilitator (Audrey Kobayashi for difference, Susan Hanson for methodology, and Jan Monk for representation). The workshops were designed to produce roughly the equivalent of a seminar-length discussion of a single paper, and in the process to invest each of the eight persons in the production of each other's research. The discussions were thorough, sustained, intensive, collaborative, and supportive. Readers will judge whether these interconnections resulted in a volume that is more than a collection of edited chapters: namely, the product of a unique interactive process that produced relational knowledges among participants.

The authors in this volume engage a diversity of theoretical approaches and substantive topics, a diversity that reflects the vitality of feminist geography more generally. During our meetings, our collective enthusiasm for each others' work and for supporting different approaches within feminist geography outweighed attempts to arrive at a consensus as to what constitutes the subfield. Perhaps because of our differences, the workshop brought to the fore an interesting tension around the question, "what is feminist geography?" Some refused to align themselves with the term "feminist" in recognition of the historic neglect by "White" feminists of issues affecting women of color. In requiring that women of color identify their oppressions as first and foremost deriving from sexism rather than racism, some white feminists are seen to disavow women of color's *racialized* locations alongside men of color. Others expressed a reluctance to subscribe to a feminism that was perceived to privilege theory over experience, abstraction over concrete tactics for social change, or biology over the social constructedness of gender. Is it possible or desirable to forge a consensus? Or do these differences promote a tension that helps to ground us in political realities, which though not experienced equally by everyone, to some degree *do* belong to everyone in that they derive from the multilayered and sometimes contradictory social geographies of oppression (see Kobayashi, Introduction to Part 1)?

We think the conference/workshop pointed away from consensus, but not from the possibility of politics. In particular, we were encouraged by the differences provoked, differences that challenged us to think beyond the confines of what we understand feminist geography to be. Such differences erode the absoluteness of feminist geography's discursive and topical terrain, just as they point to re-identifications and re-alignments with groups whose political agendas may be located at the current margins of feminist geography. Through realigning with other self-identified "nonfeminist" struggles, many of us may find our positionings and identities transformed, leading us to confront an important threshold: the fact that feminist geography, while an important terrain of struggle, is not the only one. Our ability to place oppression *first* and gender second, while seemingly an anathema to some feminisms as we know them, is the only means for eventually working to overcome the discursive constraints of gender itself, allowing us to reimagine movements, identities, and languages beyond the linguistic confines of "male" or "female." Crossovers and realignments, then, are not necessarily treacherous, but are potentially productive and creative. Unlike anti-postmodernists who mourn the demise of immobile spaces and identities (which they see as dissipating the energies of those resisting oppression), we prefer to work with the creative possibilities that the mutabilities of space and identities make possible.

One measure of how much we *all* stand at a threshold of a diverse feminist geography was the absence of any African American participants in our conference/workshop, a fact raised forcefully by women of color participants at the meeting's concluding session. One might respond by stating that this results from the low level of participation of African Americans in geography as a whole. The Association of American Geographers (AAG) *Newsletter* of April 1996, tells us, for example, that in 1995 there were only 116 (self-identified) African American members of the AAG's over 7,000 person membership. But to place the blame on geography's "whiteness" would only displace our responsibilities as feminist geographers, who despite continued marginalization within the discipline, are—at least in the United States, Canada, and Britain—increasingly well positioned to promote social *and* institutional change.

In response to this absence, and upon the suggestion of Susan Hanson, the authors and editors decided to dedicate the book's royalties toward the establishment of a scholarship fund for minority students (inclusive of students male and female, undergraduate and graduate). Though we accept that in so directing the book's earnings we are complicit in the reinscription of the category of "race" that we find so problematic, we nevertheless maintain that, inasmuch as that category is a social demarcation with material effects, it is an appropriate site for intervention. This book thus initiates the AAG's "Fund for Underrepresented Students," politicizes in some small way its proceeds, and thereby implicates all those who purchase it and one major national geographical organization in promoting anti-racist social change. In this way we hope to make a bit more visible the racism that structurally undergirds socio-spatial relations in the United States and elsewhere.

JPJ, HJN, and SMR

Acknowledgments

This book grew out of a three-day workshop on feminist geography held at the University of Kentucky in January 1995. Primary funding was provided by the National Science Foundation (NSF 93-21163). Additional funding was provided by David Watt, vice-chancellor for research and graduate studies at the University of Kentucky.

Both the workshop and the compilation of the volume involved the concerted efforts of a number of colleagues at the University of Kentucky. We would like to thank Dick Ulack, former chair of the Department of Geography, for his advice and support throughout the project; Joyce Rieman, administrative assistant of the Department of Geography, for managing finances; and Susan Mains, research assistant, for providing a wide range of assistance. Additional support for the book project came from Robert Rotenberg, director of the International Studies Program of DePaul University, Mike Mezey, dean of the College of Liberal Arts and Sciences at DePaul University, and from the University Research Council of DePaul University. We are also grateful to Ron Abler and the Association of American Geographers for managing the Fund for Underrepresented Students toward which this book's proceeds are directed.

We appreciate the comments from a number of individuals. Both David Hodge, former director of the Geography and Regional Science Program at the National Science Foundation, and J. W. Harrington, the program's current Director, were very supportive and offered much valuable advice, as did the foundation's anonymous reviewers. The book manuscript has been improved by the editing of Rose Canon, the indexing of Jerry Martin, and by the careful and constructive comments provided by Gillian Rose, Susan Craddock, and several anonymous reviewers. Virginia Blum provided helpful feedback at various stages of this endeavor.

We have enjoyed working with Susan McEachern of Rowman & Littlefield, who throughout the process of publication has been receptive, enthusiastic, and supportive. Angela Martin, Eren McGinnis, and Rich Schein were also

there for us in many important ways, from the time we began the NSF proposal to the final stages of manuscript preparation.

Every edited volume is indebted to its contributors, but this one is especially
so. From the workshop, to draft stage, to finished product, all helped to make
the entire enterprise truly collaborative as well as memorable and enjoyable.
We are especially pleased that this volume contains the work of every participant in the workshop.

Last, we want to point out that the alphabetical order of the editors of this
book is just that, and in no way reflects a hierarchy of efforts. It is rare to find
colleagues who not only enjoy each others' company (even after all is said and
done), but who also, despite competing projects, genuinely commit similar
amounts of time and energy to a long project such as this one. We feel now an
almost nostalgic sadness as the completion of this book brings our lengthy,
intense, and altogether satisfying engagements to a productive end.

not previously considered in geography—for example, film, the body, and other visual images. In addition, our thinking about representations has been profoundly altered by the linguistic turn in the social sciences, with all its attention to discourse, by the recognition that all representations, including those that we produce as researchers, merely represent rather than mirror reality, and by theories that call into question the long held separation between theories of representations and theories of the material conditions of social life. With each rethinking, feminist geographers have opened new paths to social investigation—crossed new *thresholds*, one might say—and hence continually refashioned not only how geographers study places and people, but also what constitutes geography as a discipline. This book aims to engage and produce still newer thresholds among difference, methodology, and representation, and, in the process, open additional doors for students and researchers alike.

Though we hope this volume offers insights into new research opportunities and disciplinary agendas, we would be remiss in not also asserting another goal of the book, one that is of course shared by all who claim the label "feminist" namely, the social and political transformation of the world that feminist theories aim to understand. Yet, "feminist" is a highly contentious signifier. Within feminism, for example, the very category "woman," which initially served to crystallize both theory and politics, is now the site of productive debate. Nor can methodology provide the grounds for unifying "feminists," for feminists cannot claim a distinctive set of methods in social research—no single method has the analytical breadth capable of making it the umbrella for the broad range of research questions that feminists ask. Finally, there are disagreements within feminist scholarship in the social sciences and humanities over the role played by representational processes in social life and over the appropriateness and adequacy of our own representations of it. Despite these differences within feminism, there is substantial agreement among feminists that the world and theory do not exist separate from one another. Rather, theories of the world are shaped by our embeddedness within it—even if feminists would disagree as to how to theorize embeddedness. Likewise, feminists recognize that the world is produced and reproduced through both thoughts and actions that are themselves embedded within, and partake of, theoretical constructs. The recognition of this dialectical relation (i.e., between theory and the world) places an important responsibility upon feminist researchers, namely, to derive theories and to conduct research that emancipates rather than contributes to subjugation. Of course, by virtue of their theoretical differences, feminists have and will continue to have disagreements as to how emancipation is defined and can be realized, but at the very least feminists remain cognizant that their theories are part-and-parcel of ongoing reshapings of social relations and identities, of places and spaces, and of thoughts and actions.

This book, then, offers geographical perspectives on difference, methodology, and representation, with the goals of reshaping research agendas within both feminism and geography and of using the knowledge that results to reshape the world. Such goals, however, still leave open a question, one undoubtedly foremost in the minds of most nongeographer readers: how can geography contribute to the project of feminism more generally? It is to this question that we now turn.

The Possibility of Feminist Geography

We began this essay with a marker in time—1982—and one might expect that we would proceed by offering a chronology of feminist geography since that date. We have chosen, however, to pursue a different line of analysis, not the least because of the fact that many overviews have been done, some of them recently. Moreover, to recount the feminist literature within even a single subfield in geography today—especially in economic or urban geography—requires more space than even one chapter can provide. Finally, given the fact that feminist theories, research questions, and methodologies are now found in every subfield of human geography, defining feminist geography's boundaries has become increasingly problematic.

In place of a summative evaluation, we provide references to a number of key overviews of feminist geography in table I.1, each of which is tied to a specific research area. The list—a guide to guides—is suggestive rather than exhaustive. More important, although the left-hand side of the table shows research areas, feminism itself sees no clean separation between such spheres as "the economic" or "the political." Rather, these terms are conceived as having their own history of construction and deployment within various social and disciplinary enterprises. While in everyday language such terms may prove useful in thinking about social reality, that *reality* is relational: economic spheres of social life are intertwined with political ones. To give another example, the processes that produce what is designated "urban" and "rural" are not contained within the spaces that carry those designations—they cross both types of places in ways that thwart any easy separation of the two. What is more, the authors listed in table I.1 often recognize these complications and interconnections, and refuse to limit their analyses to traditionally defined subdisciplinary categories. Hence, some authors may well reject our characterizations of their work. In spite of these caveats, the table provides new readers of feminist geography with a guide to a diverse, unfolding literature.

If feminist geography cannot be maintained within a separate sphere of human geography, but is instead appropriate to all of human geography, and if feminist geography is critical of subdisciplinary divisions, then readers might ask, What is (the possibility of) feminist geography? For us, this question cannot be answered by asserting that the field combines feminist theory and research with geographical theory and research. Such easy addition is unhelpful given significant differences within feminist and geographic theory and research, both of which are dynamic literatures whose contours remain under debate. For example, some ten years ago it might have been sufficient to state that feminist geographers document and explain the spatial dimensions of

TABLE I.1
Feminist Geography: A Selective Guide to Recent Overviews.

Childcare and Children	Aitken (1994), England (1996), Fincher (1996), Rose, D. (1993)
Crime	Pain (1991), Valentine (1991), Wekerle and Rutherford (1994)
Built Environment/Landscape	Bowlby (1991), Bondi (1992b), Domosh (1995), Monk (1992), Nash (1996)
Development	Holcomb and Rothenberg (1993), Momsen (1991), Momsen and Kinnaird (1993)
Directions in Feminist Geography	Bondi (1990a, 1992a, 1993a), Bowlby, et al. (1989), Domosh (1996), Gruntfest (1989), Johnson (1994), *Journal of Geography in Higher Education* (1989), McDowell (1989, 1993a, 1993b), Monk (1994, 1996b), Penrose, et al. (1992), Pratt (1992, 1993), Rose, G. (1993b), Women and Geography Study Group (1984)
Disciplinary Critiques	Christopherson (1989), Domosh (1991), Hanson (1992), Massey (1994), Rose, G. (1993a)
Economic Geography	Gregson and Lowe (1994), Hanson and Pratt (1995), Kobayashi, et al. (1994), Massey (1989)
Environmental Geography	Nesmith and Radcliffe (1993)
Historical Geography	Rose and Ogborn (1988)
Housing and the Home	Dowling and Pratt (1993), Munroe and Smith (1989)
Identity	Bondi (1993b), Chouinard and Grant (1995), McDowell (1991), Pratt and Hanson (1994)
Methodology	*Antipode* (1995), *Canadian Geographer* (1993), Hanson (1993), Herod (1993), Katz (1995), Lawson and Staeheli (1995), McDowell (1992c), *Professional Geographer* (1994, 1995)
Pedagogy	Bowlby (1992), Johnson (1990), LeVasseur (1993), Mayer (1989), McDowell (1992b), Monk (1988, 1996a)

Planning	Little (1994)
Political Geography	Kofman and Peake (1990)
Postcolonialism	Blunt and Rose (1994), Mills (1996)
Postmodernism	Bondi (1990b), Bondi and Domosh (1992), McDowell (1992a)
Race	Kobayashi and Peake (1994), Peake (1993), Sanders (1990)
Rural Geography	Little (1986), Whatmore (1994)
Sexuality	Bell (1991), Bell et al. (1994), Bell and Valentine (1995)
Urban Geography	Fincher (1990), Hanson and Pratt (1988), Mackenzie (1989), Pratt (1989, 1990), Pratt and Hanson (1988), Winchester (1992)

NB: Ongoing sources of interest to feminist geographers include the journal, *Gender, Place and Culture*, and the regularly appearing reviews of the subfield published in *Progress in Human Geography*. An online Feminism in Geography bibliography is maintained through the Department of Geography at the University of California at Berkeley. For information, contact: http://www-geography.Berkeley.edu/WomenBiblio/geography + gender.html. In addition, the Department of Geography at the University of Kentucky maintains an active feminist geography internet discussion group. To subscribe, send a message to geogfem@lsv.uky.edu.

women's daily lives. Although this characterization remains central to the field, today's feminist geographer might question equating "women" with "feminist," believing this to elide important differences between the two while failing to problematize the term "woman"; analogously, s/he might note that the way in which "space" is defined and deployed in research is highly variable and contested, and is in no sense limited to the project of mapping. Perhaps a better strategy is to resist rigid categorizations of feminist geography. In so doing, feminist geographers can continue both to rework other subdisciplinary endeavors in human geography and to enhance connections with allied disciplines, thereby developing more novel subject matters and lines of analysis.

Our unwillingness to fix the borders of feminist geography should not be taken as a reluctance to insist upon the importance of *geography*—of space and place, of borders and transgressions, of the local and the global, of environments both built and "natural"—in contributing to feminist research more generally. Indeed, nearly twenty years of feminist geography has demonstrated that to ignore space in feminist research is to impoverish one's understandings and explanations, proving that feminist researchers outside geography would do well to consider spatiality—in all its forms—as one of *their* primary thresholds. We examine some of the questions posed by spatiality below, and in the process tentatively respond to the question "What is (the possibility of) feminist geography?".

We begin with "location," an apparently innocent concept at face value. Location specifies the place of a *thing* (a factory or home, a book or a film, a piece of clothing or machinery), *practice* (whether working or relaxing, reading or writing, or listening or speaking), or *person* (or group of persons). In the language of methodology, these are *objects of analysis*, all of which have locations. By providing a basis for mapping these objects of analysis, the concept of location permits feminist researchers to specify the place-based character of objects and to examine the spatial relationships (distance, connectivity, presence/absence) between them. These relations can be interrogated in concrete, material ways (thus, the question "Who works *where?*" helps to better ground feminist inquiry than the question "Who works?"). With this understanding of location, geographers contribute to feminist research by raising "where" questions about things, practices, and persons; by interrogating the spatial relationships among these objects of analysis; and by investigating how the different mappings of and relations among these objects affect the places within which they are located.

These projects, though based on a fairly straightforward conceptualization of location, already suggest how a geographic perspective may enrich feminist study. To further complicate matters, we can raise questions that fracture location's face-value conceptualization. We can ask, for example, whether objects of analysis exist as discretely bounded entities independent of space-as-location, thus making interrelationships among them specifiable only in terms of simple causality, one object impacting and changing another? Or, should we conceive of things, practices, and persons as woven into places, and places as woven into things, practices, and persons, such that their separation cannot be maintained? In addressing this second question from a dialectical understanding of space, one would hold that things, practices, and persons are constitutive of places *and* constituted by them. A co-constitutive understanding rejects the view that objects and locations exist as separate entities, even though we may find it easier to adopt such conceptions in everyday language. It asserts instead relational, process-oriented conceptions of places, things, practices, and persons. In this sense, places exist in and through things, practices, and persons, while things, practices, and persons exist in and through space. In discarding simplistic notions of location and static mappings of objects of analysis, the research task becomes much more complicated: One now needs ways of understanding the constitutive processes within which things, practices, persons, and places are all embedded.

We can reserve the term "context" for the interrelationships among things, practices, persons, and places. To the extent that feminist geographers call attention to the gendered and sexed spatial interrelationships in this array, they can be said to offer a *feminist contextual* approach to research. When attention to gender and sexuality is integrated with the study of other social relations of power with which they are codeterminant, such as "race" and class, researchers construct ever more complex and concrete understandings of how context is defined and how it matters. Although researchers will often disagree as to how such social relations should be theorized, at a minimum a feminist contextual approach will seek to understand how these relations work differently across space, as well as how space is produced and reproduced as a gendered and sexed context that mediates these relations (differently, we would add).

Such an understanding of context not only augments space-as-location (and hence mapping), it also allows feminist geographers to raise questions concerning the universality of research findings derived outside of a contextual approach. In this way, feminist geographers grapple with the contextual character of the very theories and concepts they bring to bear on their objects of analysis. They do so for two reasons. First, if contextuality is constitutive of the objects of feminist research, then our theories and concepts must be modified to take context into account. For example, a feminist contextual analysis of patriarchy would be "spatialized" by understanding how patriarchal practices and discourses are differentially embedded in and work through different spaces and cultural settings. Second, in recognizing that researchers are also embedded in contexts, feminist geographers make positionality geographic by understanding how the spaces of our lives influence the knowledges we have of places, things, practices, and persons.

These complexities, when applied to the person of a researcher, are related to discussions of "reflexivity," a term used by feminists to mark their own contexts in relation to those they research. Here we are made aware of our gendered, sexed, and emplaced positions as researchers, and of the resulting contextuality of our thinking, reading, writing, and speaking about the world we research. In summary, we can map two relations of feminist contextuality: those that exist between gendered/sexed objects of analysis and the places within which they are found, and those that exist between our own thoughts and practices as researchers and the complex gendered/sexed geographies within which we live and work.

These movements toward relational geographies come with the recognition that contextuality cannot be contained *within* any particular space. Rather, interrelations among places, things, practices, and persons cut across place; processes always work through space to exceed any "local." Hence, objects of analysis in feminist research are not simply constituted by and constitutive of their "own" space. Instead, they are contextually embedded in other spaces by virtue of constitutive relations they share with other places, things, practices, and persons. The extension of these relations is of course uneven: objects of feminist geography share contextuality to different degrees with contexts that are, and are not, their "own." Take for example the global fashion industry. It is dependent upon and reproductive of gender relations across the globe, from the fashionable Park Avenue shops where consumption (and identities) take place, to the *barrios* of Manila where production (and identities) are made. By recognizing the uncontainability of context, feminist geographers can "deconstruct" space so as to comprehend the interconnectedness and difference that weave together and separate—both socially and spatially—all objects of their analysis.

Difference

In the above discussion we indicated that one "object of analysis" in feminist research is the "person," but we left unexamined the range of different identities this "object" takes, as well as the social processes by which identities are constructed. We begin this volume with the topic of difference precisely because identity is central to feminist research. The "person" raises questions concerning how the social relations of gender and sexuality operate and intersect with (or, "map onto") class, "race," ethnicity, nationality, and so on. By understanding identities as socially constructed out of these relations, and in recognizing that their intersections can produce a complex map of identification positions, the researcher concerned with difference faces the task of investigating how, when, and where—that is, in what contexts—difference matters.

Much of feminism's critical development can be traced to the above issue. In responding to the complex matrix of social relations within which women's experiences are structured, feminists have been led to examine an ever increasing proliferation of identity positions within the category "woman." Radical and socialist feminists have focused attention on the intersections of class and gender; researchers in lesbian studies have decentered the presumptive heterosexuality that exists in some feminist theory and empirical research; Black, Latina, and other feminists of color have theorized how "race" underpins normative social constructions of gender and sexuality and how racisms permeate all social life; and Third World and postcolonial feminists have challenged the cultural biases and presumed centeredness of the "West" in "White" feminist writings and research. In so complicating women's lives in both theoretical and empirical terms, researchers have become cognizant of multiple, intersecting experiences and consciousnesses.

The proliferation of identity positions has enriched feminism at the same time that it has prompted other questions concerning the possibility and desirability of constructing a unified political movement across a diverse spectrum of differences. Is the political potential of feminism at risk of dissolution given the number of potential coordinates around which social action might be structured? How does one link together diverse feminist struggles? Can we acknowledge the futility of defining an "essential" woman, while nonetheless holding on to a strategic form of essentialism in order to ground politics? Or should all identity positions and the categorical imperatives they rely upon be recognized as constructions of social power and resisted accordingly, and if so, then how does one avoid the dissipation of political power that might inhere in these positions? These are by no means simple questions, but as Audrey Kobayashi argues in her introduction to Part 1, it may be more productive to deconstruct oppositions based on rigid, binary categories of *difference* (for example, White/Black or straight/lesbian) so as to focus on linking across categories the tangential connections of *diversity* that characterize subjects.

In different ways, each of the chapters in this section of the book raise spatial questions concerning difference. The authors show that identities are not only social constructions, but spatial ones as well. Difference is constituted by (and constitutive of) the concrete contexts within which bodies and identities are located, as well as the contexts with which they are coextensive. Thus, in Laura Pulido's research (chapter 1) on/with environmental activists in South Central and East Los Angeles, we see how both the spatiality of racism and the social relations constituting these particular places work to marginalize and crystallize identities. While White feminists may represent these activists as "women," the activists choose instead to prioritize other aspects of their identities (as mothers, as African Americans) in representing themselves. Representations of poor people that link essentialized notions of "race," gender, and poverty to particular places (e.g., the inner city) are challenged by Melissa Gilbert in chapter 2. Her research on poor women's survival strategies demonstrates that while the intertwined processes of women's economic and racial marginalization are spatial, that spatiality can also provide the basis for networks of mutual support. Glenda Laws (chapter 3) takes up an often neglected category of difference, that of age, and interrogates how public policies variously affect the mobility of women of different ages. In addition to showing how the state controls the spatial mobility of gendered and aged bodies, she argues that the regulation of mobility is part and parcel of the construction of social identities. In chapter 4, Gill Valentine explores the ways in which some lesbians, in establishing separatist, nonheteropatriarchal communities, have sought to maximize their identity as lesbians. However, she also demonstrates that the spatial strategy of separation can give rise to tensions among community members over subsumed but significant differences in identity that exist along lines of sexuality, class, and "race." That space and identity are related but not homologous, is further considered by Sherry Ahrentzen (chapter 5), whose study of the diversity of meanings of the home takes into account the variety and fluidity of women's experiences. Through her study of middle class homeworkers, she links work, home/place, and identity, showing how their meanings are mutually constitutive. This section ends with Karen Nairn's (chapter 6) examination of space and identity in the classroom. In her investigation of why many female students remain quiet, she examines the subtle interplays of power geometries in the classroom, including the room's physical layout, the juxtaposition of students, and the structure and content of lessons.

Methodology

As we have emphasized, feminist theory is not monolithic: instead of stasis we find dynamism; in place of fixity we find flux; and rather than imposed systems of understanding we find feminist theory continually producing new understandings. Debates within feminist theory—over various ontological, episte-mological, and substantive-conceptual issues—undermine in turn any attempt to specify a distinctly "feminist" methodology. This is so because of methodol-ogy's position in the linked chain of "theory-methodology-method." Inas-much as methodology links theoretical concerns to method's technical, "how to" ones, the middle link in the chain remains as dynamic and contested an area of inquiry as feminist theory itself. And given that different theoretical positions underpin different methodological stances, it follows that both in turn influence how specific methods are used in concrete research.

Despite these caveats, it is possible to think through some general coordi-nates of feminist theory in an effort to derive a set of expectations about what feminist methodology should *be able to do*. We expect first that, whatever its form, feminist methodology should be able to understand and explain a gen-dered and sexed social world. It should be flexible enough to adapt to the range of objects in that world, guiding investigations of how gender and sex categories infuse our norms and expectations, our thoughts and fantasies, our practices and performances, our books and films, and our architecture and language. In adopting a relational, interdependent understanding of a world represented in starkly binary (and, some would add, masculinist) terms such as male/female, heterosexual/homosexual, White/Black, feminist methodology should be able to grasp how processes of exclusion normalize binary relations as well as how those relations work in everyday life. In light of various femi-nisms' concern to elucidate difference, feminist methodology should help re-cover specificity among, rather than impose generality upon, research subjects. And, given feminist theory's critique of the separation of theory and practice, feminist methodology should strive to make everyday life both a politically and practically important site of research. Though our understanding of posi-tionality makes impossible the construction of a level field of power between researcher and researched, to the extent that it is possible we can expect that feminist methodology work toward creating nonhierarchical methods that break down barriers between researcher and researched, barriers constructed through differential power relations. Feminist methodology should empower research subjects by providing forms of knowledge that can help subvert proc-esses of oppression. At the same time, we should expect that feminist method-ology resist imposing the researchers' "created" knowledges upon the research subjects.

Importantly, these expectations of feminist methodology crisscross through a wide range of "techniques" in social research. Though most feminists tend not to use quantitative approaches precisely because of the difficulties involved in applying them in ways that are consistent with the above expectations, this reluctance should be understood as a contingent rather than a necessary condi-tion: counting, classification, descriptive statistics, and more advanced meth-ods of data analysis are far too powerful (in both the research and social senses) to leave in the hands of nonfeminists. As decades of research using interviews, surveys, ethnographies, interpretative and participatory methods of social research have demonstrated, not all uses of qualitative methods are consistent with feminism. Rather than view techniques as "quantitative" versus "qualitative" and then judge their applicability on this basis alone, feminist researchers would do well to determine whether or not the methods under consideration have the capacity to understand a gendered and sexed world in relational terms; whether or not the complexities of difference in everyday life can be elucidated; and whether or not the hierarchical and oppositional forms of power (between researcher/researched and theory/practice) in research can be subverted.

What then of geography and feminist methodology? As a discipline that has both laid claim to a unique "spatial perspective" and claimed as its own various objects of analysis (for example, cultural landscapes, built environments, nature-society relations, spatial variations, regions/places/localities, etc.), geography has witnessed considerable debate over how to draw its own methodological contours. Though most geographic debate over methodology has taken place outside of feminist geography, more recently feminists within the field have begun to engage feminist methodology more directly. As Susan Hanson argues in her introduction to the methodology section, they have done so both in an attempt to tailor feminist methodology in general to the types of questions geographers ask, and in an attempt to foreground feminist research questions within geographic methodology in particular. The result is, on the one hand, a "spatialization" of some of the central issues under discussion in feminist methodology. For example, with positionality understood as both a spatial and social location, issues of reflexivity take on a specific geographic character. On the other hand, feminism itself has proven useful within geography by cultivating methodological questions that previously laid fallow. Thus, we find the gender and sex constitution of places, landscapes, and built environments to be an especially rich area of contemporary research.

The authors in the methodology section of the volume are reflective of all of the diversity raised in the above discussion. Giving weight to the claim that a feminist perspective can be used to enrich quantitative methods, we first find Vidyamali Samarasinghe (chapter 7) arguing that the standard economic models of large development institutions such as the World Bank need to be rethought—from the ground up—to better account for the contribution that women make to the aggregate social product. The result, she argues, would transform both the results from and the policy uses of much applied research in development studies. In chapter 8, Karen Falconer Al-Hindi shows how feminists can harness the analytic power of critical realism while avoiding some of its tendencies to engage in rational abstractions that might have us lose sight of women's daily lives. She illustrates her arguments with an example drawn from her research on women engaged in telecommuting. Like Karen, in chapter 9 Ann Oberhauser pushes us to think about the intersection of the economy and home, and of methodological implications arising from the interpellation of the two in contemporary capitalism. Her empirical example demonstrates the special role of the home as a "field" site for feminist research, one that is both a site of power for her subjects and a node in a regional-to-national economic network. Similarly, Isabel Dyck examines the power invested in research sites (e.g., doctor's offices), which concretize and complicate researcher and researched interactions in her study of the delivery of health care to immigrants in Canada (chapter 10). She negotiates an anti-essentialist perspective with a recognition that difference cannot be assumed away as a "mere" social construction; such constructions must instead be accounted for in any study of the concrete socio-spatial contexts within which "raced" women live their lives. Richa Nagar, in chapter 11, puts additional light on the socio-spatial complexities of positionality, and on her own reflexive negotiation of these in her study of the Asian community of Dar es Salaam, Tanzania. In her ethnographic fieldwork, difference proliferates into a complex matrix of social spaces, each with its own space/identity configuration. Finally, Mona Domosh, in chapter 12, provides us with an example of how to read a traditional object of geographic inquiry—a cultural landscape—from a feminist perspective. Adopting an anti-essentialist perspective informed by the work of historian Joan Scott, Mona derives new ways of reading material landscapes that will be of interest to geographers and nongeographers alike.

Representation

Representation has long been of central concern to feminists, especially in the humanities and particularly with respect to the gendered and sexed codes deployed in literature, language, and the visual arts, including film, television, painting, sculpture, and photography. The textual and intertextual character of these codes have implications for the production of meaning within "representations." Textual or representational analyses are predicated on the understanding that, as social products, literature, language, and the products of the visual arts are both reflective and generative of the wider social contexts (including other texts) within which they are produced and received. From such a frame of reference, one that recognizes the mutual interpellation of text and context, there arise three key questions concerning representations: (1) who has the (social) power to represent?; (2) what is the form and content of the representation?; and (3) what are the reception contexts—or "readings"—of the representation, including the intended and unintended social outcomes? It is in all three questions that we find that feminist scholars do not simply analyze texts for their intrinsic value as "art," but understand them as sites through which gendered and sexed social relations are produced and reproduced within society at large.

In recognizing that the production of meaning in texts is inherently political and fraught with implications beyond the text "itself," feminist social scientists have come to place significant attention on representations and representational processes in their research. Feminist researchers interested in such diverse issues as gender divisions of labor in a factory, the organizational strategies of a women's social movement, and the funding of research on AIDs can incorporate into their analyses the study of advertising, political discourse, and photographic imagery, to use just three examples. These researchers could be interested in examining how gender and sex are textually coded in these objects, and how this coding enters into the wider social sphere under investigation.

Related to questions of representation are theoretical issues, often expressed within feminism as the differences among socialist/radical feminists, materialist feminists, and poststructuralist feminists, over the still prevalent epistemological and ontological dualisms of representation/nonrepresentation and discursive/nondiscursive. Some feminists fear that an emphasis on issues of textuality and discourse may cause us to lose sight of the coordinates of oppression grounded in material life; others are concerned to elucidate the interconnections between the objects and processes that comprise the dualisms; while still others work to deconstruct the oppositions so as to draw attention to the always intertextual and mediated (through representation and discourse) character of all objects of feminist analysis (from landscapes and houses to bodies and their performances). Whatever the theoretical and substantive impulses, feminists who examine "texts" are in agreement that, to the extent that representation is a social process, it is a gendered and sexed process as well.

The chapters in this section of the book work to demonstrate how feminist geography can bring a *spatial* imaginary to the study of representations. In general terms, this imaginary can take many forms. For example, in recognizing that power is always grounded in and emanative from geography—including the context of social relations, the surveillance and maintenance of borders, and the disciplining of practices and persons in space—geography helps concretize the question "Who has the (socio-spatial) power to represent?". Feminist geographers can also direct interpretive strategies toward the "spaces" represented, thereby adding a geographic dimension to questions of the form, content, and intertextuality of "texts." In re/de-coding the spatialities of representation, researchers can explore the concealed, revealed, withdrawn, juxtaposed, and interposed geographies that inhere in "texts" of all sorts. Finally, feminist geographers can examine the geographies of reception, demonstrating that it is not just a social process (that is, with "readers" who are classed, "raced," gendered, and sexed), but a spatial one as well ("readers" are *positioned* in and across spatial contexts and simultaneously *relocated* through their engagements in a representational world).

Such are the concerns traced by the contributors in the final section of the book, which deals with representation. In her introduction to this section on representation, which is itself an experiment in new forms of representation, Jan Monk reflects upon the social and scholarly practices of feminist geographers and explores the representational politics of those practices. She raises numerous concerns over the disciplinary regulation of representation, including problems related to claims to authority and the process of gatekeeping; the Anglocentric character of much feminist geography, and the appropriate representational forms for feminist geography's diverse audiences. In chapter 13, Nikolas Huffman offers a critique of mapping as a traditionally masculinist representational practice. He then argues for an explicitly feminist theory and practice of cartographic visualization: a theory/practice that situates mapping within wider social practices and that re-claims and redefines the cartographic enterprise in a much expanded and transformative manner. Reflecting upon her research on Galways Mountain, a former plantation site in Montserrat, Lydia Pulsipher (chapter 14) considers the question "Who has the sociospatial power to represent?". For example, in discussing issues of representational authority surrounding a Smithsonian exhibit on Galways, she demonstrates how, at various phases of the project, different bodily scriptings (of Montserratians, and of herself) in terms of "race," gender, and location, disrupted or reproduced dominant representational orders. Continuing the analysis of bodily practices, Patricia Meoño-Picado (chapter 15) traces the praxis of Las Buenas Amigas, a Latina lesbian group in New York City, which, in concert with other organizations, protested against a Spanish-language radio station for its homophobic and racist broadcasts. Patricia, in drawing a distinction between the liberal bourgeois and oppositional public spheres, shows not only the territorial dimension of the protests, but also how body/space tactics redefine the spaces of the city. Turning to the contextuality of representation, Bronwen Walter, in chapter 16, focuses on how the Irish have been, and continue to be, depicted in the United States and Britain. Through an examination of representations and discourses, she shows how Irish identity has been gendered and racialized differently across national contexts, provoking racialized assimilation in one country and continued racialization-as-difference in another. In chapter 17, Jeanne Kay challenges us to think differently about representations of nature, in particular about the alignment of Nature/Woman, which feminists have variously valorized and interpreted as hegemonic. From an analysis of the diaries of Mormon women in the nineteenth century, she explores a different, and possibly agendered way of thinking about the Nature/Woman linkage, one that revolves around how Nature is scripted as a stage for, or arm of, God's will—mapping its godly presence onto women's bodies. In the concluding chapter to this section (chapter 18), Francine Watkins examines how idyllic representations of the English rural village within one particular village work to define difference through practices of exclusion. Using data from interviews with a variety of village women, she shows how representations of the village that bind it to ideals of femininity and home serve to marginalize or exclude men and women defined as different.

Conclusion

Our discussion of difference, methodology, and representation has pointed to only a few of the ways that geography can contribute to feminist research and, in the chapters that follow, the authors examine many more geographies among the three thresholds. We leave it to readers to interrogate these "spatialities" and to judge their usefulness in constructing their own research and political practices. Before we end this introduction, however, we want to follow up on two points, the first theoretical, and the second organizational.

First, readers would do well to keep in mind that none of the three thresholds that we used to organize the book are in practice separable. Rather, questions of difference, methodology, and representation all intersect with one another in complex ways—sometimes contradictory, sometimes reinforcing: issues of difference overlap with those of representation, and both in turn hold implications for methodology. A single example will suffice to make this point: as Richa Nagar (chapter 11) explores how to tailor her research strategies to account for the variety of social differences existing in Dar es Salaam, she also faces ethical issues about how to represent her subjects; at the same time, she realizes that she is being "textualized" by those she interviews, her own body being the representational material through which her subjects engage her difference. Thus, readers should keep in mind that the thresholds examined here lead to interconnected pathways, ones that can be explored by reading across thresholds.

Second, note that the introductions to the sections do not include point-by-point reviews of the chapters within them. Instead, Audrey Kobayashi, Susan Hanson, and Jan Monk were asked to raise what for them are significant issues surrounding the section's topic. It is to our conclusion that the reader can look for further contextualization of the chapters. There, perhaps uncharacteristically, we re-cover the ground traveled in individual chapters by reading *across* the original conceptual divisions of the book to tease out new conceptual terrains or thresholds. We hope our conclusion helps to subvert readings of the chapters predetermined by the book's formal divisions, while also demonstrating how still *other* thresholds might be recovered in the chapters.

Acknowledgment

We would like to thank Susan Hanson, Audrey Kobayashi, Susan Mains, and Jan Monk for their help with this chapter.

References

Aitken, S. 1994. *Putting children in their place*. Washington, DC: Association of American Geographers Resource Publication.

Antipode. 1995. Symposium on feminist participatory research. 27: 71–101.

Bell, D. J. 1991. Insignifcant others: Lesbian and gay geographies. *Area* 23: 323–29.

Bell, D. J., and Valentine, G., eds. 1995. Introduction: Orientations. In *Mapping desire*, D. Bell and G. Valentine, eds., pp. 1–27. London: Routledge.

Bell, D. J.; Binnie, J.; Cream, J.; and Valentine, G. 1994. All hyped up and no place to go. *Gender, Place and Culture* 1: 31–47.

Blunt, A., and Rose, G. 1994. Introduction: Women's colonial and postcolonial geographies. In *Writing women and space: Colonial and postcolonial geographies*, eds. A. Blunt and G. Rose, pp. 1–25. New York: Guilford.

Bondi, L. 1990a. Progress in geography and gender: Feminism and difference. *Progress in Human Geography* 14: 438–45.

Bondi, L. 1990b. Feminism, postmodernism, and geography: Space for women? *Antipode* 22: 156–67.

Bondi, L. 1992a. Gender and dichotomy. *Progress in Human Geography* 16: 98–104.

Bondi, L. 1992b. Gender symbols and urban landscapes. *Progress in Human Geography* 16:157–70.

Bondi, L. 1993a. Gender and geography: Crossing boundaries. *Progress in Human Geography* 17: 241–46.

Bondi, L. 1993b. Locating identity politics. In *Place and the politics of identity*, eds. M. Keith and S. Pile, pp. 84–101. London: Routledge.

Bondi, L., and M. Domosh. 1992. Other figures in other places: On feminism, postmodernism and geography. *Society and Space* 10: 199–213.

Bowlby, S., guest editor. 1991. Women and the designed environment. *Built Environment* 16.

Bowlby, S. 1992. Feminist geography and the curriculum. *Geography* 78: 349–60.

Bowlby, S.; Lewis, J.; McDowell, L.; and Foord, J. 1989. The geography of gender. In *New models in geography*, Volume 2, eds. R. Peet and N. Thrift, pp. 157–75. London: Unwin Hyman.

Canadian Geographer. 1993. Feminism as method. 37: 48–61.

Chouinard, V., and Grant, A. 1995. On being not even anywhere near "the project": Ways of putting ourselves in the picture. *Antipode* 27: 137–66.

Christopherson, S. 1989. On being outside "the project." *Antipode* 21: 83–89.

Domosh, M. 1991. Toward a feminist historiography of geography. *Transactions of the Institute of British Geographers* 16: 95–106.

Domosh, M. 1995. Feminism and urban imagery. *Urban Geography* 16: 643–48.

Domosh, M. 1996. Feminism and human geography. In *Concepts in human geography*, C. Earle, K. Mathewson, and M. S. Kenzer, eds., pp. 411–27. Lanham, MD: Rowman & Littlefield.

Dowling, R., and Pratt, G. 1993. Home truths: Recent feminist constructions. *Urban Geography* 14: 464–75.

England, K. 1996. Introduction: Who will mind the baby? In *Who will mind the baby? Geographies of childcare and working mothers*, K. England, ed., pp. 3–19. London: Routledge.

Fincher, R. 1990. Women in the city. *Australian geographical studies* 28: 29–37.

Fincher, R. 1996. The state and childcare: An international review from a geographical perspective. In *Who will mind the baby? Geographies of childcare and working mothers*, K. England, ed., pp. 143–66. London: Routledge.

Gregson, N., and Lowe, M. 1994. *Servicing the middle classes: Class, gender, and waged domestic in contemporary Britain*. New York: Routledge.

Gruntfest, E. 1989. Geographic perspectives on women. In *Geography in America*, eds. G. L. Gaile and C. Willmott, pp. 673–83. Columbia, MD: Merrill.

Hanson, S. 1992. Geography and feminism: Worlds in collision? *Annals of the Association of American Geographers* 82: 569–86.

Hanson, S. 1993. "Never question the assumptions" and other scenes from the quantitative revolution. *Urban Geography* 14: 552–56.

Hanson, S., and Pratt, G. 1988. Reconceptualizing the links between home and work in urban geography. *Economic Geography* 64:299–321.

Hanson, S., and Pratt, G. 1995. *Gender, work and space*. London: Routledge.

Herod, A. 1993. Gender issues in the use of interviewing as a research method. *The Professional Geographer* 45: 305–16.

Holcomb, B., and Rothenberg, T. 1993. Women's work and urban household economy in developing areas. In *Women's lives and public policy: The international experience*, eds. M. Turshen and B. Holcomb, pp. 51–68. Westport, CT: Praeger.

Johnson, L. C. 1990. New courses for a gendered geography. *Australian Geographical Studies* 28: 16–28.

Johnson, L. C. 1994. What future for feminist geography? *Gender, Place and Culture* 1: 103–13.

Journal of Geography in Higher Education. 1989. The challenge of feminist geography. 13: 85–121.

Katz, C. 1995. The expeditions of conjurers: Ethnography, power, and pretense. In *Feminist dilemmas in fieldwork*, D. L. Wolf, ed., pp. 170–84. Boulder: Westview Press.

Kobayashi, A., and Peake, L. 1994. Unnatural discourse. "Race" and gender in geography. *Gender, Place and Culture* 1: 225–43.

Kobayashi, A., Peake, L., Benenson, H., and Pickles, K. 1994. Introduction: Placing women and work. In *Women, work, and place*, A. Kobayashi, ed. Montreal and Kingston: McGill-Queen's University Press

Kofman, E., and Peake, L. 1990. Into the 1990s: A gendered agenda for political geography. *Political Geography* 9: 313–36.

Lawson, V., and Staeheli, L. 1995. Feminism, praxis and human geography. *Geographical Analysis* 27: 321–38.

LeVasseur, M. 1993. *Finding a way: Encouraging underrepresented groups in geography—An annotated bibliography*. Indiana, PA: National Council for Geographic Education.

Little, J. 1986. Feminist perspectives in rural geography. *Journal of Rural Studies* 2: 1–8.

Little, J. 1994. *Gender, planning and the policy process*. London: Pergamon Press.

Mackenzie, S. 1989. Women in the city. In *New models in geography*, Volume 2, eds. R. Peet and N. Thrift, pp. 109–26. London: Unwin Hyman.

Massey, D. 1989. Spatial divisions of labour in practice: Reflections on the debate: Thoughts on feminism, Marxism, and theory. *Environment and Planning, A* 21: 692–97.

Massey, D. 1994. *Space, place, and gender*. Minneapolis: University of Minnesota Press.

Mayer, T. 1989. Consensus and invisibility: The representation of women in human geography textbooks. *The Professional Geographer* 41: 397–409.

McDowell, L. 1989. Women, gender and the organization of space. In *Horizons in human geography*, eds. D. Gregory and R. Walford, pp. 136–51. Totowa, NJ: Barnes and Noble.

McDowell, L. 1991. The baby and the bath water: Diversity, deconstruction and feminist theory in geography. *Geoforum* 22: 123–33.

McDowell, L. 1992a. Multiple voices: Speaking from inside and outside "the project." *Antipode* 24: 56–72.

McDowell, L. 1992b. Engendering change: Curriculum transformation in human geography. *Journal of Geography in Higher Education* 16: 185–97.

McDowell, L. 1992c. Doing gender: Feminism, feminists and research methods in human geography. *Transactions of the Institute of British Geographers* 17: 399–416.

McDowell, L. 1993a. Space, place and gender relations: Part I. Feminist empiricism and the geography of social relations. *Progress in Human Geography* 17: 157–79.

McDowell, L. 1993b. Space, place and gender relations: Part II. Identity, difference, feminist geometries and geographies. *Progress in Human Geography* 17: 305–18.

Mills, S. 1996. Gender and colonial space. *Gender, Place and Culture* 3: 125–47.

Momsen, J. 1991. *Women and development in the Third World.* London: Routledge.

Momsen, J., and Kinnaird, V., eds. 1993. *Different places, different voices.* London: Routledge.

Monk, J. 1988. Engendering a new geographic vision. In *Teaching geography for a better world*, J. Fein and R. Gerber, eds. pp. 92–103, 114–96. Edinburgh: Oliver and Boyd.

Monk, J. 1992. Gender in the landscape: Expressions of power and meaning. In *Inventing places: Studies in cultural geography*, eds. K. Anderson and F. Gale, pp. 123–38. New York: Wiley.

Monk, J. 1994. Place matters: Comparative international perspectives on feminist geography. *Professional Geographer* 46: 277–88.

Monk, J. 1996a. Partial truths: Feminist perspectives on ends and means. In *Understanding geographical and environmental education: The role of research*, ed. M. Williams, pp. 274–86. London: Cassell Education.

Monk, J. 1996b. Challenging the boundaries: Survival and change in a gendered world. In *Companion encyclopedia of human geography: The environment and humankind*, I. Douglas, R. Huggett, and M. Robinson, eds., pp. 888–905. London: Routledge.

Monk, J., and Hanson, S. 1982. On not excluding half of the human in human geography. *The Professional Geographer* 34: 11–23.

Munroe, M., and Smith, S. 1989. Gender and housing: Broadening the debate. *Housing Studies* 4: 3–17.

Nash, C. 1996. Reclaiming vision: Looking at landscape and the body. *Gender, Place and Culture* 3: 149–69.

Nesmith, C. and Radcliffe, S. A. 1993. (Re)mapping Mother Earth: A geographical perspective on environmental feminisms. *Society and Space* 11: 379–94.

Pain, R. 1991. Space, sexual violence and social control: Integrating geographical and feminist analyses of women's fear of crime. *Progress in Human Geography* 15: 415–31.

Peake, L. 1993. "Race" and sexuality: Challenging the patriarchal structuring of urban social space. *Society and Space* 11: 415–32.

Penrose, J.; Bondi, L.; Kofman, E.; McDowell, L.; Rose, G.; and Whatmore, S. 1992. Feminists and feminism in the academy. *Antipode* 24: 218–37.

Pratt, G. 1989. Reproduction, class and the spatial structure of the city. In *New models in geography*, Volume 2, eds. R. Peet and N. Thrift, pp. 84–108. London: Unwin Hyman.

Pratt, G. 1990. Feminist analyses of the restructuring of urban life. *Urban Geography* 11: 594–605.

Pratt, G. 1992. Feminist geography. *Urban Geography* 13: 385–91.

Pratt, G. 1993. Reflections on poststructuralism and feminist empirics, theory and prac-
tice. *Antipode* 25: 51–63.
Pratt, G., and Hanson, S. 1988. Gender, class and space. *Society and Space* 6: 15–35.
Pratt, G. and Hanson, S. 1994. Geography and the construction of difference. *Gender,
Place and Culture* 1: 5–30.
Professional Geographer. 1994. Women in the field: Critical feminist methodologies and
theoretical perspectives. 46: 54–102.
Professional Geographer. 1995. Should women count? The role of quantitative methodol-
ogy in feminist geographic research. 47: 426–66.
Rose, D. 1993. Local childcare strategies in Montréal, Québec. In *Full circles: Geogra-
phies of women over the life course*, C. Katz and J. Monk, eds., pp. 188–207. London:
Routledge.
Rose, G. 1993a. *Feminism and geography: The limits of geographical knowledge*. Minne-
sota: University of Minnesota Press.
Rose, G. 1993b. Progress in geography and gender. Or something else. *Progress in
Human Geography* 17: 531–37.
Rose, G. and Ogborn, M. 1988. Feminism and historical geography. *Journal of Histori-
cal Geography* 14: 405–9.
Sanders, R. 1990. Integrating race and ethnicity into geographic gender studies. *The
Professional Geographer* 24: 228–30.
Valentine, G. 1991. Women's fear and the design of public space. *Built Environment*
16: 288–303.
Wekerle, G. R., and Rutherford, B., eds. 1994. *Safe cities*. New York: Van Nostrand
Reinhold.
Whatmore, S. ed. 1994. *Gender and Rurality*. London: D. Fulton.
Winchester, H. P. M. 1992. The construction and deconstruction of women's roles in
the urban landscape. In *Inventing places: Studies in cultural geography*, eds. K. Ander-
son and F. Gale, pp. 139–56. New York: Wiley.
Women and Geography Study Group of the IBG. 1984. *Geography and gender: An
introduction to feminist geography*. London: Hutchinson.

Part 1

Difference

Introduction to Part 1

The Paradox of Difference and Diversity (or, Why the Threshold Keeps Moving)

Audrey Kobayashi

No issue has provoked greater discussion or deeper intellectual and moral dilemmas for feminists than that of defining "difference." The concept of difference is now widely viewed as the root from which stems virtually universal forms of prejudice, discrimination, and oppression, based on gender, "race," sexuality, age or class. The concept of difference allows the social creation of categories of people subordinate to a dominant norm, and allows the continuation of cultural practices that reinscribe difference as differential values placed upon human life. The chapters in part 1 explore various ways in which difference has been invoked as a basis for oppression, as well as ways in which women, in particular, have overcome differences in order to bring about social change through political action.

To invoke the concept of difference, however, is to embark upon a slippery slope of ironies that not only define the conditions of social life, but also pose difficult and controversial issues for social theorists. Difference—or its putative opposite, sameness—is an inevitable ontological condition that is never completely achieved. The most exciting feminist scholarship in recent times has caught the challenge of this paradox, and seeks to explore both the processes through which difference is socially constructed, and the political contradictions that inevitably result.

As a marker for social identity, difference is often constructed as dichotomy, as Sherry Ahrentzen points out in chapter 5. That is, something is either different, or not different, in which case it is, according to some standard, same. One is man or woman. One is White or not White. One is Christian and in a state of grace or not. Faith in dichotomous difference has been one of the leading tenets of human history, and has provided both moral and intellectual justification for most exclusionary prejudices. Such prejudicial categories create

3

a rationale for normative human values that set boundaries and divisions between people, and that inform social practices meant to maintain such boundaries as an inexorable social divide. To thus place limits to difference is to pronounce who stands within, and who without, the moral shelter of the same.

The conceptual challenge of this section is to refashion the notion of difference so as to challenge dominant norms, thereby furthering understanding of women's lives and of how their lives might change. The papers as a whole, therefore, are concerned with "shifting the center and reconstructing knowledge" (Anderson and Collins 1995) in order to document ways in which people have excluded and been excluded on the basis of socially constructed categories. All of the writers fashion their chapters around the paradoxical tension between processes of exclusion (racism, sexism, etc.) and processes of identity formation that allow resistance to develop through common cause.

It has become popular to invoke postmodern metaphors of spatial reordering in order to depict the ideological ordering of human relations through which difference is expressed. This language describes historic relations of sexism, racism, and colonialism in terms of a dominant center and subordinate margins, and urges political resistance and transformation through recentering power: to allow previously unheard voices space to be heard, and to encourage a diversity of expressions within a discourse that is liberatory rather than confining. To recognize and to value diversity over difference involves a repudiation of totalizing meta-theories, or theories that propound universal explanations (thus supporting the norm of the same), in favor of a plurality of theories that address specific circumstances and times and, moreover, that contain a program for emancipatory politics. To do so in spatial terms is to recognize that the social map results from plotting difference and diversity, and their actual outcomes.

The movement toward diversity, however, has itself been deeply riven, both theoretically and politically. For some, diversity is an unmitigated condition, which dictates that justice will occur once there is separate but equal representation of social groups defined according to their historical status. This position maintains that White men, and even White women will never on their own cease practices that marginalize women of color, and it places responsibility upon the group for its own destiny. The group, however, is defined according to essential characteristics, whether such characteristics are deemed to be biological (as immutable traits carried by sex or skin color) or historical. In its more extreme variants, essentialism leads to a doctrine of separation, such as that recently put forward by Louis Farrakhan. Although Farrakhan's views may be considered by most as extreme, the issue of essentialism is in the forefront of the current debate on the future of minority communities. The view, for example, that African Americans must gain and maintain control of their own resources, including education, is a direct legacy of Malcolm X (1970), now rapidly gaining ground, couched in terms of identity politics that provide a rationale not only for emancipation but for survival. The fact that all forms of essentialism contain the seeds of normative and exclusionary practices fades into insignificance against the exigencies of racism in the 1990s.

Those who eschew essentialism, however, seek alternate routes. For some, it is nonetheless politically expedient to engage in "strategic essentialism" to develop the full impact of people working together toward a common goal, a pragmatic response that has much in common with Gill Valentine's (chapter 4) observance of "minimizing" and "maximizing" social outcomes. Radical feminists, for example, argue that only by a separation of women and men can women overcome the bonds of patriarchy (Rich 1980). Others applaud the development of women-centered spaces, which can develop only through cultural separation (Mandell 1995, 15), and which depend upon a female identity that is not only assumed, but also cultivated as distinct. Such an "unmodified feminism" (MacKinnon 1987) is seen by many as the basis for a transition of power.

Across the conceptual divide stand those for whom any form of essentialism represents both a moral and intellectual slippage because the notion of difference, or otherness, leads inevitably to new forms of oppression (Spelman 1988). Identity politics, because it depends upon monolithic group solidarity, not only reinforces difference, but also can easily lead to oppressions based on intragroup difference. This is because "the violence that many women experience is often shaped by other dimensions of their identities, such as race and class" and therefore "they relegate women of color to a location that resists telling" (Crenshaw 1995, 333). As Angela Harris argues:

> MacKinnon's essentialist approach re-creates the paradigmatic woman in the image of the White woman, in the name of "unmodified feminism." As in the dominant discourse, black women are relegated to the margins, ignored or extolled as "just like us, only more so." But "black women are not white women with colour." (Omolade 1980) Moreover, feminist essentialism represents not just an insult to Black women, but a broken promise—the promise to listen to women's stories, the promise of feminist method. (Harris 1995, 163)

Furthermore, to give in to any sort of essentialism, even of the strategic sort, confounds a deeper understanding of the difficult process of social construction and, therefore, provides no clear path for imagining social change (Kobayashi 1994). By examining the full ramifications of social construction, as several of the chapters in this part do, construction itself is clarified as not one option among many, but the as the whole of social life (see Vance 1992). Formations of "race" and gender, therefore, are relational, confrontational, often contradictory, irrespective of genetics, and historically contingent (Haney-López 1995). The social construction of whiteness and of masculinity need to be problematized in this way (Bonnett 1996; Frankenberg 1993; Kokopeli and Lakey 1995), so that the normative and naturalized "same" becomes "un-natural" (Kobayashi and Peake 1994), unreasonable (Ignatiev and Garvey 1996), deracinated.

Politically, the task remains difficult, even if the conceptual demon of essentialism is exorcised. Social constructions are, afterall, immensely durable and powerful, and they set in motion processes that are difficult to conceive of as anything but inexorable. Anti-essentialism carries little weight in inner city neighborhoods and among single mothers for whom life above the poverty line is an impossible dream, or even among middle-class school children who are already strongly conditioned in their social responses (Nairn, chapter 6 of this volume). Privilege continues, despite our deep and vaunted understanding of its power, to create more privilege (Wildman and Davis 1995). There is a strong moral compulsion for groups to secede from those circumstances that cause their oppression (Buchanan 1991). Gender and "race" matter (Lorde 1984, 114–23; West 1993). Difference is a fact and diversity a passionate hope.

That passionate hope now leads some scholars to encourage a "post-identity politics" (Danielsen and Engle 1995) that would transcend the difficulties of identity politics while eschewing the postmodern nightmare of a world in which there is nothing but diversity, undifferentiated, individuals isolated by their personal constructions, unable to connect to others or to make authentic representations, even of themselves, because each of us lives a shifting multiplicity of selves. This slippery slope to solipsism is as unrealistic a journey as that which navigates between absolute dichotomies. Nonetheless, the conceptual trap of undifferentiated otherness needs to be resisted by researchers who engage with people on the ground, in the circumstances of their lives, amid the shifting constructions of difference that occur as social relations are imagined and reimagined. Several roads to resistance are illustrated in these chapters.

Postidentity politics start with a serious recognition of human experience, all experience, as political, which is to say, connected to other human beings in a way that involves power. It is inevitable. Difference and sameness, then, are always relative and mutually transformative. It is therefore only at the intersection of sociospatial and political constructions of the different and the same that momentous political events occur (Young 1993).

Postidentity politics (or all politics for that matter) occur on the ground, in ways that are explicitly spatial. Postidentity social and political changes, therefore, require not only a thorough and theorized understanding of the many ways that "social change and spatial change are integral to each other" (Massey 1994, 23), but also of the ways in which "space" has been used to consolidate difference, as subordination is rendered through separation and unequal access. Difference is based on boundaries (Anthias and Yuval-Davis 1992), which as often as not are articulated as streets, tracts, and no-go areas, clearly demarcated as public and private. As Glenda Laws shows in chapter 3, not only is spatial mobility integral to the expression of difference, but also the political, demographic, and economic factors that influence mobility are negotiated in complex ways, and need to be explored as both "enabling and constraining possibilities."

Such a project requires imagining the possibilities for new kinds of spatial existence, in which the territorial imperatives associated with racist, sexist, and colonial forms of human relations are challenged, in short, a "de-territorialization" of social relations based on challenging commonsense notions of who belongs where (Santos 1995). This process is as important in the classroom where social relations are instigated (Nairn, chapter 6) as on the streets where long-established spatial rituals are challenged (Pulido, chapter 1).

Another strategy of recent feminist theory is to explore the vast implications of paradox in making sense of the terrible irony that difference and sameness make up an impossible but inescapable dualism. Recognizing "paradoxical space" (Rose 1993, chapter 7) allows feminists to reimagine a world in which the masculinist gaze has shifted so dramatically that notions of same and other, center and margin, here and there, are destabilized, and so, new possibilities for spatial existence emerge. The fact that many of us have begun to accept, even to celebrate, the state of paradox does not make things any easier for us intellectually, however, and politically it sometimes makes our choices next to impossible, our failure that of imagination rather than will. If nothing else, to embrace paradox is to shed all remnants of idealism.

A loss of idealism was necessary to get through what has been perhaps the most exciting but painful crisis in feminism, the debate over essentialism. The monumental paradox here is that abandoning essentialism has meant challenging the powerful constructions of human difference that have allowed inequality and subordination to occur, while at the same time using those categories as ciphers for social change. As Rose (1993, 150–55) suggests, we've had to be "here" and "there" at the same time, buying into established notions of difference in order to refute them. And this paradox is more than a nice intellectual puzzle; it conditions the ways that marginalized women face sociospatial contradictions in their daily lives and constrains possibilities for increased mobility and new situations. Push the process too quickly or shift the ground too far, and there is potential for enormous failure, as learned by so many social movements that have ended in defeat and frustration. As Gill Valentine shows, this is especially true for lesbian women, who must depend on the category "woman" and its identity. Redefining their place too drastically may result in losing rather than gaining ground. Conversely, as Laura Pulido shows, only by reimagining the impossible can grassroots change take on political force.

Perhaps part of the means of mapping a way through the irony and paradoxes through which we sometimes compulsively move is to see difference as a basis for establishing the same, or vice versa, and then to begin to analyze why it is that, while all social formations are contingent and subject to change, some are more durable and some more fleeting than others. We need to focus, therefore, on the *effects* of difference, but also on the seemingly inevitable process of differenc*ing*, and the specific representations through which we construct myths about ourselves in order to engage in identity politics. Or about the ways we continue to make choices that lead to paradoxical outcomes; shifting places, everywhere.

Events occur at real places, not just moments on the postmodern metaphorical map. It helps us to get beyond diversity as an empty philosophic ideal if we actually can watch its crystallization, its *appearance* or taking place, in the landscape. Diversity, like place, is never undifferentiated. Geographers have the ability to make things time/place specific, relevant to location, and to the differentness or sameness of the viewer. Location need not be in relation to a center or a periphery, but may also be multifocal, with a kind of coalescence of movement that is not unlike the coalescence of ideologies that produce "race" and gender as significant historical constructions. To overcome the tyranny of space, then, and the power of geographical exclusion, we need to apply the same antiessentialist interrogation of space that occurs in Melissa Gilbert's chapter, which takes us several steps toward the threshold of change (chapter 2).

Approaching that threshold, we might hope to follow a feminist journey from the difference/sameness dichotomy to the paradox of diversity. We do so, inevitably, in bodies, and it is through bodies that we encounter and give place to geographical reality. Bodies express human differentiation and the spatial extensions of whatever selves we choose to construct. They are the primary sites of feminist struggle.

References

Andersen, M., and Collins, P. H., eds. 1995. *Race, class and gender: An anthology*. 2nd ed. Belmont, CA: Wadsworth.

Anthias, F., and Yuval-Davis, N. 1992. *Racialized boundaries: Race, nation, gender, colour and class in the anti-racist struggle*. London and New York: Routledge.

Bonnett, A. 1996. "White Studies": The problems and projects of a new research agenda. *Theory, Culture and Society* 13:(2), 45–155.

Buchanan, A. 1991. *Secession: The morality of political divorce*. Boulder, CO: Westview Press.

Crenshaw, K. 1995. Mapping the margins: intersectionality, identity politics and violence against women of color. In D. Danielsen and K. Engle, eds. *After identity: A reader in law and culture*, 332–54. New York and London: Routledge.

Danielsen, D. and Engle, K., eds. 1995. *After identity: A reader in law and culture*. New York and London: Routledge.

Frankenberg, R. 1993. *White women, race matters: The social construction of whiteness*. Minnesota, MN: University of Minnesota Press.

Haney-López, I. f. 1995. The social construction of race. In R. Delgado ed. *Critical race theory: The cutting edge*, 191–203. Philadelphia: Temple University Press.

Harris, A. 1995. Race and essentialism in feminist legal theory. In R. Delgado, ed. *Critical race theory: The cutting edge*, 253–66. Philadelphia: Temple University Press.

Ignatiev, N. and Garvey, J., eds. 1996. *Race traitor*. London: Routledge.

Kobayashi, A. 1994. Colouring the field: gender, "race" and the politics of fieldwork. *The Professional Geographer*, 46: 73–80.

Kobayashi, A. and Peake, L. 1994. Unnatural discourse: "Race" and gender in geography. *Gender Place and Culture* 1:(2) 225–44.

Kokopeli, B. and Lakey, G. 1995. More power than we want: masculine sexuality and violence. In M. L. Andersen and P. H. Collins eds., *Race, class and gender: An anthology*. 2nd ed., pp. 450–55. New York: Wadsworth.

Lorde, A. 1984. *Sister outsider*, Freedom, CA: Crossing Press.

MacKinnon, C. A. 1987. *Feminism unmodified*. Cambridge, MA: Harvard University Press.

Malcolm X. 1970. *By any means necessary: Speeches, interviews and a letter*. G. Breitman ed. New York: Pathfinder Press.

Mandell, N., ed. 1995. *Feminist issues: Race, class and sexuality*. Toronto: Prentice Hall.

Massey, D. 1994. *Space, place and gender*. Minneapolis, MN: University of Minnesota Press.

Rich, A. 1980. Compulsory heterosexuality and lesbian existence. *Signs* 5, pp. 531–60.

Rose, G. 1993. *Feminism and geography: The limits of geographical knowledge*. Cambridge: Polity Press.

Santos, B. de S. 1995. *Toward a new common sense: Law, science and politics in the paradigmatic transition*. New York and London: Routledge.

Spelman, E. 1988. *Inessential woman: Problems of exclusion in feminist thought*. Boston: Beacon Press.

West, C. 1993. *Race matters*. Boston: Beacon Press.

Wildman, S. M. and Davis, A. D. 1995. Language and silence: making systems of priviledge visible. In R. Delgado, ed., *Critical race theory: The cutting edge*, 573–79. Philadelphia: The Temple University Press.

Vance, C. S. 1992. Social construction theory: problems in the history of sexuality. In H. Crowley and S. Himmelweit, eds. *Knowing women: Feminism and knowledge*, 132–45. Cambridge: Polity Press and the Open University.

Young, I. M. 1993. Together in difference: transforming the logic of group political conflict. In W. Kymlicka, ed. *The rights of minority cultures*, 155–78. New York and Oxford: Oxford University Press.

1

Community, Place, and Identity

Laura Pulido

Gayatri Spivak's essay, "Can the subaltern speak?" (1988), poses a critical question to all those engaged in politically committed research, including feminist geographers.[1] Spivak identifies several reasons why the subaltern cannot speak, such as the heterogeneity of the "other," the role of local elites, and the fact that academics are only one of the many "receiver[s] of any collectively intended social act" (1988, 287). I am not so interested in investigating if indeed the voices of the subaltern can ever be fully recovered, as in examining one instance in which dominant feminist categories and frameworks have represented the experiences and identities of highly marginalized groups in problematic ways. Specifically, I explore to what extent the category of "woman" resonates with the identities articulated by low-income women of color involved in environmental justice struggles.

The destabilization of the category "woman" has been a necessary intervention with serious repercussions both in academia and in other political arenas. At the heart of the matter is a vexing set of political questions: How salient are the commonalities of multiple feminine identities? Is there a sufficient basis for meaningful political action? Who would benefit from such actions? Gillian Rose has summarized well some of the difficulties posed by attempting to dismantle a unitary femininity: "In its denial of all Woman-ly qualities it is difficult to know what could unite women as feminists: it is a strategy that dissolves the possibility of struggle by women as women . . . abandoning woman entirely for the diversity of women can be politically disabling because it removes any common ground for alliance and struggle" (1993, 12).

For academics, one of the central questions to emerge from Rose's observation is, how do we represent those who have historically been invisible, especially in light of geography's legacy of colonization? As feminist geographers, are we complicit in contributing to a consolidated feminism by systematically imposing our own constructs?[2] As Peter Jackson has noted, "Spivak's work

11

raises profound epistemological problems for those who seek to articulate a politics of representation. How can we, who have a professional interest in 'representing the Other,' carry out our work without imposing a form of 'epistemic violence' on the subject of our research" (Jackson 1993, 208)?

The problem of representation becomes increasingly difficult when studying identity formation and collective action. Instead of simply studying passive objects, we are faced with a situation where individuals are consciously articulating and acting upon identities that they have carefully chosen. To what extent should these identities be respected? What alternative insights or material gains might be derived from alternative frameworks? These questions have become increasingly pressing for feminist geographers not only as they have tried to expand their research agenda by focusing on less-privileged women, but also as 'Third World' and nonwhite women are making their presence felt within the discipline (no matter how slight). In the quest to build a united, feminist geographic community, both in terms of actors and as a subject of inquiry, scholars have at times misread the actions of certain females by casting them as "woman," while downplaying other forces and identities that actors choose to emphasize in constructing their lives.

This chapter addresses how the categories of "woman" and "feminist research" are used to situate the experiences of women of color (African American and Latina) environmental justice activists in Los Angeles. I examine whether the category of "woman" (let alone feminist) actually illustrates the realities and identities of these women, or, whether such political representations reflect the priorities of dominant writers, and thus further serve to reproduce the subaltern in our own image and likeness. While the lives of environmental justice activists are highly gendered, I argue that the category of "woman" as used to describe them is at times applicable and useful, but less so at other times (Seager 1995). Alternatively, place and the social relations that constitute it may rise to the surface and play a forceful role not only in producing everyday life, but also in understanding how people choose to identify and mobilize.

Because of the social relations in which Black and Latina community activists are embedded, their relationships to men are different from those typically conceptualized by Anglo feminists, and they must contend with the spatiality of racism, both differences that may undermine the applicability of the category "woman" to the self-definitions espoused by these activists. Recent scholarship, primarily by nonwhite women, has emphasized that the experiences of women of color cannot be seen as a choice between "race" or gender, but rather the forces of racism and sexism must be seen as creating a specific reality (Hill Collins 1991; Anzaldua 1990). While fully concurring, the fact remains that this may not be the way in which the women in question interpret their experiences or choose to identify. Thus, although we can demonstrate the specific ways in which gender relations and racisms constitute a particular reality, this doesn't mean that women choose to adopt and act upon such interpretations.

Because I wanted to see how female environmental justice activists defined themselves and their struggles, much of the data for this paper are drawn from six years of participant observation. During this time I have not tried to impose any frameworks on the discourse, but have listened, watched, and assisted however I could.[3] In the course of this activity, I have found that space and place are critical to understanding the activists' identities and subsequent mobilizations. Although a gendered identity is articulated in some instances and in varying ways, it is not the dominant identity espoused by activists, contrary to the practices of feminist scholars. This paper will first briefly outline some of the general themes of ecofeminism, including the environmental justice movement and how it seeks to build a consolidated "woman." Second, I present the stories of Concerned Citizens of South Central Los Angeles and the Mothers of East L.A. I then consider how the activists have defined themselves and their communities, and in particular I examine the roles of racism and space in creating these formations. Finally, I conclude with the political implications of such findings and how they might have an impact on feminist geography.

Feminism and Nature-Society Relations

Ecofeminism

The study of the relationship between women and the environment has been the purview of a number of disciplines, but has been most fully developed in an interdisciplinary body of work known as ecofeminism (Diamond and Orenstein 1990). Ecofeminism is a wide-ranging body of thought that encompasses such themes as the gendered nature of resource use and agriculture (Townsend 1995; Carney 1993; Schroeder 1993; Carney and Watts 1991), international development (Shiva 1987), landscape studies (Norwood and Monk 1987; Kolodny 1984), science and nature (Haraway 1991; Merchant 1980), the gendering of nature and nature-society relations (Warren 1990; Griffin 1978) including militarism (Seager 1993), and the environmental justice movement (Brown and Ferguson 1995; Hamilton 1994; Di Chiro 1993; Krauss 1993). In short, it examines the gendered construction of nature, how women interact with nature and the environment, and also how those relations are structured by patriarchy and how women choose to resist oppressive practices or celebrate their unique relationship to nature.

While ecofeminism is largely restricted to theory production (Di Chiro 1993, 112–13; Epstein 1993), some limited activism has been associated with it. For example, in the 1970s and 1980s, middle-class women actively made links between peace, antinuclear, and antimilitary activism, and the environment. Perhaps, however, the element of ecofeminism that has attracted the most attention (and controversy) is the spiritual connection between women and the environment. Nesmith and Radcliffe point out that for some, the common heritage of oppression by patriarchy experienced by women and nature is taken as a common bond, and others, in an inversion of historic gendered notions of nature, choose to celebrate the perceived unique connection between women, the earth, and its life forces, or a natural alliance between feminism and ecology, certain ecological feminists articulate an alternative conception of nature-culture relations, and male-female interactions. (1993, 383)

Though many reject such essentialized relations, other forms of essentialism have been suggested to explain the heavy involvement of women in the environmental justice movement. This argument focuses on women's roles as mothers and caretakers, as the guardians of home, family, and by extension, the larger community (for a critique of this argument, see Brown and Ferguson 1995). Indeed, one commentator has written, "Women of color are logical leaders of this dynamic movement to bring a people's agenda forward and provide clean alternatives necessary for the survival of Third World communities, in the United States and abroad" (Gauna 1991, 4–5). A number of writers have readily seen the parallels between the plight and struggles of women in both the First and Third World, as they seek to resist an increasingly insane global economic system and protect their homes and families. By focusing on the category of "woman," analysts are able to link a wide array of ideas and practices among all sorts of women.

> Women, especially those whose health and survival have always been particularly affected by ecological deterioration because of gender inequalities, are rapidly becoming more politicized each year, whether as low-income residents living near a toxic-waste site or incinerator or as workers in unsafe conditions that affect their reproductive capacities. . . . Women in Third World countries seek to protect natural resources necessary for survival through movements such as the rural Chipko in India. In most societies, gender influences women's social and economic position more generally, making women especially vulnerable to diseases. Their experience, based on the consequences of their socioeconomic position, has led them to play an initiating and leading role in many direct action movements for a peaceful, nuclear-free society, fighting ecological destruction and calling attention to health effects through protest, research, and public education. Mothers of East Los Angeles, a Latino American group that successfully fought against a toxic-waste incinerator, is a good example. (Hofrichter 1993, 3)

It is precisely this tendency to focus on the category of "woman" that must be interrogated in terms of environmental justice activists.

The Environmental Justice Movement

The environmental justice movement began in the 1980s in the United States in response to various communities' exposure and vulnerability to pollution. The uncontrolled hazardous waste fiasco known as Love Canal (in New York state) was the pivotal event that made "toxics" a household word (Szasz

1994). This movement has been welcomed and embraced by many as it has challenged conventional attitudes and practices of mainstream environmentalism (Heiman 1990; FitzSimmons and Gottlieb 1988). For one, environmental justice activists have rejected the staid attitudes of mainstream environmentalists toward large polluters by refusing to negotiate concessions, insisting instead that the offending polluter respond to community demands, be that a cessation of polluting activities or greater public oversight. Lois Gibbs, executive director of Citizens' Clearinghouse for Hazardous Waste, an organization formed in the aftermath of Love Canal, assists local communities opposing toxic threats. She describes the movement in the following way, "Our movement is about taking back what is ours. It is about no longer allowing others to say it is acceptable to pollute any community, give cancer to a certain number of people or send our polluting industry and jobs across the borders to take advantage of those who live there" (Gibbs 1993, 2). Indeed, Brown and Masterson-Allen characterized the movement as "implicitly strik[ing] at the heart of capitalist and technological rationality" (1994, 280).

While the goals of the movement are clearly significant, so too are its demographics. In contrast to the White, middle-class leadership of the mainstream movement, the grassroots movement for environmental justice is distinguished by a membership and leadership which is comprised largely of women, nonwhites, and other marginal groups. "In local communities across the country, disenfranchised poor, people of color, women, farmers, migrant farm workers, and industrial workers are making common cause with each other, and with civil rights, peace, and women's health groups" (Hofrichter 1993, 1–2). The subtext of such statements is the hope that these various constituencies will recognize their commonalities and come together in some broad, counterhegemonic movement. The significance of female and nonwhite involvement is attested to by the articles, conferences, media presentations, and other forms of work that focus on the identities of the victims and activists. Consider for a moment, "Black, Brown, Poor and Poisoned" (Austin and Schill 1991), "Blue Collar Women and Toxic Waste Protest" (Krauss 1993), "The People of Color Environmental Leadership Summit," and "Unsafe for Women, Children, and Other Living Things" (Gauna 1991).

While the above titles indicate an emphasis on both the nonwhite and female membership of the movement, the political currents surrounding the environmental justice movement have produced a more complex picture. Specifically, environmental racism has become the dominant organizing framework that has reduced the emphasis on gender (Pulido 1995). As Barbara Epstein notes, "A growing recognition of the particular exposure of communities of color to toxics has prompted a shift toward concern with environmental racism; in recent years people of color have made up the most rapidly growing section of the movement" (1995, 6). Capek (1993), writing within the context of environmental justice, has pointed out that *how* an issue or problem is framed is critical to the subsequent mobilization. In this case, emphasizing racism has led large numbers of nonwhites to engage in environmentalism.

Thus, despite the fact that activists are emphasizing a highly racialized identity and understanding of the problem, many scholars stress gender. "Although grassroots women activists have not necessarily seen themselves as descendants of prior movements, especially the women's movement, they follow in the steps of generations of women activists who fought for occupational health and safety concerns throughout this century and who more recently have become involved in the women's health movement" (Brown and Ferguson 1995, 146).

Consequently, the female involvement and leadership have been celebrated by many voices (including academics), who hope and anticipate what such political mobilizations might lead to: perhaps, a deeper feminist consciousness among marginalized women? A strengthening of links between feminist, antiracist, and working-class initiatives? A direct challenge to private production decisions? One writer makes explicit her hopes, "Though there are racial and gender-based tensions in the movement, the fact that its various constituencies are able to come together on a common terrain inspires hope in the possibility of a progressive politics in the U.S." (Epstein 1995, 1). These sentiments are widespread, although rarely voiced so forcefully:

> The Movement for Environmental Justice comprised of the people who have suffered the most—the women and children, the poor and people of colour—are stepping forward to demand a change. These women, often ridiculed as "hysterical housewives," recognize that environmental hazards . . . are killing children and others in our communities. It is no longer a question of how much pollution is acceptable; the demand is that there be no more pollution (Newman 1994, 43).

> Calling themselves the "new environmental movement," these grass-roots protesters bear little resemblance to the more middle-class activists who are involved in national environmental organizations. This movement attracts a diverse constituency that cuts across race and class lines, including working class housewives and secretaries, rural African American farmers, Navajo Indians, and low-income urban residents. According to the Citizens Clearinghouse for Hazardous Wastes (CCHW), an organization created to meet the needs of grass-roots activities, 80 percent of the leaders of grass-roots protests are blue-collar women.
>   The grass-roots activities of these women challenge both traditional assumptions of the policy-making process and left perspectives on social change (Krauss 1993, 107).

Both quotes not only emphasize the role of women in the movement, but clearly situate them as part of subordinated groups. By bringing such struggles and forms of activism under the feminist title, the positions of environmentalists and feminists, both of whom have suffered from charges of elitism, are enhanced. Nesmith and Radcliffe (1993), referring specifically to indigenous environmental concerns, appreciate the possibilities of this new articulation: "As feminism has been accused of being exclusionary and generally derived from a white middle-class perspective, this incorporation of aboriginal concerns can enhance the broadening of feminism which is already taking place" (386). They also note, however, the political pitfalls associated with this strategy: "In this way, environmental feminists risk making the move recognized from other strands of feminism . . . of appropriating other women's struggles as part of Western Feminism, as a monolithic and unproblematic category" (1993, 387).

This tendency of appropriation is potentially problematic because, although there is a large body of work on ecofeminism, it has, until recently, neither connected nor resonated with marginalized women.

> In the mid-1980s ecofeminists put forward a vision of a movement made up largely if not entirely of women, certainly led by women, that would bridge issues of the environment and militarism, and would be infused with feminism. The current grass-roots environmental movement does not look like this, nor is it likely to in the near future; the only point of overlap is the significant role of women in environmental groups, and their large and probably growing role in the leadership of the movement. (Epstein 1993, 150)

Thus, the question becomes, do the environmental justice struggles of non-white women belong to the heritage of ecofeminism? According to whom? For what purposes? Giovanna Di Chiro (1993) in her study of female activists notes the tenuous but potential link between ecofeminist theory and grassroots activists.

> Many ecofeminist writings construct theories as to why women would organize as women, in their struggle for socio-environmental change. Such theories . . . suggest that women possess unique knowledges about the connections between human health and survival, the environment, and the ever-increasing destruction by the capitalist-militaristic-patriarchal complex. These theorists claim that by virtue of these "innate" or experiential knowledges, women come together in political solidarity. . . . In the 90's, there is no visible, active, explicitly "ecofeminist" movement in the U.S. Instead, the ecofeminist efforts to theorize and strategize around a "women and environment" connection has remained almost exclusively within the realm of the production of theory. On the other hand, the movement for environmental justice, widely recognized as being driven and energized by women, *yet not marked as a "women and environment" movement,* continues to expand and develop its strategies, organization, and commitment to the grass roots. (1993, 111, 112–13, emphasis added)

Di Chiro makes explicit some of the problems between ecofeminist theory (predicated on a unitary idea of "woman") and the contrasting and fragmented reality of marginal women's practice. But as she herself points out, for the activists in question, their actions are not "marked," or defined as "woman." Nevertheless, this problematic approach is operative in a wide range of projects (Shiva 1994; "Women and the Environment" 1993; Krauss 1993; United Nations 1993). Carolyn Merchant illustrates this contradiction in her discussion of the environmental activism of Third World women. She writes, "while some might consider themselves feminists, and a few even embrace ecofeminism, most are mainly concerned with maintaining conditions for survival" (1992, 201). Given the subjects about which she is writing and the social relations in which they are embedded, it is entirely plausible that they *are* preoccupied with survival. While it is true that greater involvement in one arena (the environment) might inspire a heightened feminist consciousness and a challenge to patriarchal relations in the home, community, and workplace, we must consider the motives and usefulness of such a framework. Does such a framework match the identities espoused by activists, and if not, what identities do they articulate? And more important, why do they choose particular representations over others? To what degree are they part of a larger emancipatory project, and for whom is it geared?

Environmental Justice Activism in Los Angeles

Los Angeles has emerged as an important center of organizing for environmental justice as activists have faced two attempts to place incinerators in low-income, nonwhite communities (Russell 1989). Moreover, the city has also been the site of a major clean air initiative that has raised important issues of social justice (Mann 1991). The pivotal event that first put Los Angeles on the environmental justice map and raised the issue of women of color as the movement's leaders was an effort in the early 1980s to place an incinerator in the then largely African American community of South Central. In response to what was initially a secretive proposal, a large number of local women united and formed Concerned Citizens of South Central Los Angeles (CCOS-CLA) (Hamilton 1990). Through their collective efforts, a group of working-class women with low levels of formal education transformed themselves into experts on the incineration process and, after years of organizing, defeated the Los Angeles City Energy Recovery project (LANCER). A few years into the LANCER struggle, a hazardous waste incinerator was planned for Vernon, an industrial municipality adjacent to the Latino community of East L.A. The Mothers of East Los Angeles (MELA, or *las madres*) had been formed in the early eighties to combat a proposed prison for the community (Gutierrez 1994; Pardo 1990). Once MELA learned of the incinerator, it directed its efforts toward its defeat. After several years of struggle, with some assistance from CCOSCLA, they too were victorious.

Subsequent to overcoming the incinerators, both groups of activists not only emerged as "poster women" of the environmental justice movement, but also broadened their agendas to include community development, housing, antigraffiti projects, and scholarship programs. This led many to commend the activists for espousing such a broad, or ecological conception of the environment. "We got a focus on the environment which includes everything. We don't say the environment is just ecological. It's social, political, economical, the whole gambit . . . we get the community's consensus, and we do that" (member, CCOSCLA). Because of their gender, nonwhite status, and environmental and social justice credentials, both groups of women are accorded a high degree of moral authority by local residents, environmentalists, and community leaders alike.[4] As examples of their widespread recognition, MELA has been the subject of a special piece in the *New York Times,* and of a British film on environmentalism. Similarly, members of CCOSCLA have been invited across the country and to international gatherings on the subjects of environmental justice and women and the environment.

Not surprisingly, MELA and CCOSCLA have attracted the attention of feminists, who have been eager to publicize their remarkable achievements and in this way, broaden the scope and legitimacy of ecofeminism. Such readings have inevitably stressed that the activists are nonwhite, working class, and women. A closer investigation into CCOSCLA and MELA, however, reveal uneven and differing adoptions and articulations of a female identity. By listening to the words and actions of the activists, it appears that members of MELA and CCOSCLA, although they live highly gendered lives, often choose *not* to emphasize their female identities, but rather define themselves in terms of "race" and place.

Community, Identity, and Place

Before delving directly into the nature of MELA's and CCOSCLA's identities, it is necessary to consider briefly the relationship between place and identity. Drawing on the work of Massey (1994; 1992), Soja (1989), and others, I understand space not as a container or empty playing field, but rather as constituted by social relations. This would include such things as patterns of capital investment, class struggle, agency, and racism, to name but a few. Place can be seen as the articulation of a specific set of relations at a given time. South Central L.A. can thus be seen as a "ghetto" place that is constituted by capital disinvestment, white flight, and residential discrimination.

People who are part of places develop complex place-based identities. These identities are not inherently progressive or reactionary but can serve any number of ideological purposes. The politics of a particular place-based identity are a function of both the various subject-positions of the actor as well as the larger political objectives in which one is engaged. Like any other identity, place-based identities are not static or unitary, but are multiple and changing. They are drawn from the material at hand, but also inform a place.

Such a view of place challenges any possibility of claims to internal histories or to timeless identities. The identities of place are always unfixed, contested and multiple. And the particularity of any place is, in these terms, constructed not by placing boundaries around it and defining its identity through counter-position to the other which lies beyond, but precisely (in part) through the specificity of the mix

of links and interconnections *to* that "beyond." Places viewed this way are open
and porous.

　　All attempts to institute horizons, to establish boundaries, to secure the identity
　　of places, can in this sense be therefore seen to be *attempts to stabilize the meanings*
　　of particular envelopes of space-time. (Massey 1994, 5, emphasis in original)

Such efforts to stabilize places can be either an attempt to reinforce dominant
power relations or acts of resistance on the part of the subordinated. The latter
is certainly the case in terms of both CCOSCLA and MELA. In both instances
activists have appropriated and subverted maligned place-based identities as an
act of resistance and mobilization. These actions can be seen in two distinct
but linked and complementary ways.

　　First, such acts of resistance are highly ideological and have profound consequences. Both East L.A. and South Central have long been negatively racialized. By reclaiming a denigrated place, activists were able to attract a large
number of followers (both residents and extra-locals) who relished the opportunity to boast proudly that they were "from the 'hood' " or "the barrio," the
subtext of which was community struggle. In effect, activists were able to
change the meaning of a place, which not only has led to pride, but to a flow-
ering of activism.

　　The second implication of this appropriation of place has been to immediately protect the community from a potential threat, in this case to protect
specific places and people from pollution. Most activists interpreted the forces
undermining their community as racism, in particular, a spatialized racism.
Since both South Central and East L.A. have long suffered from poor infrastructure and service delivery, the placement of pollution is a spatialized collective form of racism. Thus, place becomes one of the vehicles through which
racism is experienced.

　　Among the two groups, CCOSCLA has been far more reticent to adopt a
gendered identity. Instead, both leaders and rank and file members continually
refer to themselves as "Blacks" and stress the fact that they are from a particular
place, South Central L.A. Because of the highly segregated nature of Los
Angeles and its sociospatial patterns of racism, South Central is known as the
heart of the African American community (Hamilton 1990). However, parts
of South Central are now 50 percent Latino (Turner and Allen 1991), due
both to Black outmigration (Johnson and Roseman 1990) and Latino immigration. The fact that South Central remains inscribed with Blackness demonstrates an effort on the part of African Americans and the larger dominant
society to put forth a unitary and hegemonic identity of South Central.[5] Because activists appeal directly to it, they are, in effect, reproducing it. They do
this by invoking nostalgia and seeking to portray South Central as a Black
place.

　　That they do so is entirely understandable. The African American population of Los Angeles has been devastated by economic restructuring, the inter-
nationalization of the economy, and a resurgence of racism. As a marginalized

group, they are seeking to hold on to at least a place-based identity, despite the fact that they are "losing" the place to Latino immigrants. For this reason, CCOSCLA is as much about protecting their space as they are about projecting a positive and viable image of South Central. One CCOSCLA member said this: "They think that just because we're South Central they can come and do whatever they want. Them forget that people live here. But we're used to getting the short end of the stick. We've learned how to organize and we've showed them that South Central can't be walked on."

The attack on their physical community, as witnessed through the LANCER project, inadequate schools and infrastructure, and limited housing funds, is one of the most readily identifiable forms of racism experienced by activists. For this reason, the formation of their community organization, CCOSCLA, and the collective identity behind it were heavily rooted in the spatial dimensions and practice of racism. In this instance, racism was not so much experienced through the individual, the body, or a gendered identity, but rather through a spatially and socially defined community.

Furthermore, much of their interaction with the mainstream environmental movement was also articulated through a lens of racism. Activists maintained that their organization and efforts remained marginalized because of racism. A CCOSCLA member commented:

> We don't believe they [mainstream environmentalists] are being inclusive, you know. Even like in all of their organizations they may have this minority program, or whatever. And that's just what it is, it's a component. It's like off to the side, "We're not going to put much priority on it." After all these years working with the mainstream, we still haven't seen any of our issues become the primary issues they're addressing. Like the siting of polluting waste in Black and Latino communities.

It is important to point out that CCOSCLA is composed almost entirely of African American women. Its seventeen-person board is all female, and almost all Black. Although there are men who participate in the block clubs (the group's organizational structure), and are employed by the organization, there are no men in positions of leadership. Yet, regardless of these highly gendered patterns, members and leaders rarely, if ever, refer to themselves as women or even articulate a gendered identity. One possible reason why activists appear to cling to a unitary "Black" identity is because of the existence of an array of structural and social forces seeking to undermine inner-city African American communities (Gray 1993). These women, like many other African American women, face tremendous challenges every day, including the daunting task of surviving with/without the African American male, who has been criminalized by the dominant society.[6] Indeed, it is difficult to have a conversation with these women without talk arising of a troubled son, nephew, brother, or husband. The criminalization of Black males is seen by many as part of a larger conspiracy to destroy the Black community. Accordingly, activists respond in a like manner, by proactively defining themselves as spokespersons representing a consolidated South Central Black community.

The situation of MELA is somewhat different from that of CCOSCLA. While Black men in South Central are facing 50 percent unemployment, mitigated primarily by public-sector employment, Latinos "enjoy" a different form of poverty: Latino men have one of the highest attachments to the labor force in California (largely in the private sector, both formal and informal), but also face the highest rates of poverty (Ong and Blumenberg 1992). Thus, although Latino individuals and households are working multiple jobs, low wages keep the population poor. Simply put, the Latino population serves a different role from Blacks in the racialized economy of Los Angeles—even though both groups are highly marginalized (Waldinger 1995; Kirschenman and Neckerman 1991). Moreover, even though Latino males have also become criminalized, it is perceived not to be to the same extent as Black men. The end result is that among activists, there is a feeling that the community is under attack, but this does not translate into fear of losing a family member to the state (incarceration). Thus, even though members of MELA articulate a somewhat gendered identity (as mothers), they work very closely with the men of their community. Men are available in greater numbers in East L.A. and are seen as partners in community struggles.

The name "Mothers of East L.A." itself is important to understanding the activists' identities. The name of the organization was actually conferred by a local priest who organized the women by calling a meeting and suggesting that they form a group to combat the proposed prison. He chose the word "mother" not only because he thought it would resonate with the women's identities, but also because it was nonthreatening. Drawing on the experience of women's nonviolent protest in Latin America (*madres de los desaparecidos*), he hoped that the "mothers" would attract attention, but not be seen as too radical (Sagahuan 1989).

The label, the Mothers, or *las madres,* did indeed speak to the reality of these women who felt that the "Mothers of East L.A." readily conveyed their various identities. These activists articulated an identity that simultaneously recognized their role as mothers, residents of East L.A., and Chicanas/Latinas. Although an ethnic identity is not explicit in their organizational name, it is understood by everyone in southern California, and by many far beyond, that East L.A. is coded as Mexican. This is because, similar to the case of South Central Blacks, racism and segregation have created a situation whereby East L.A. is known as the principal site of the Chicano/Latino population. Thus, like CCOSCLA, a large part of their identity stems from the spatial expression of racist social relations. Attesting to how her organization is spatially and racially defined, one of the leaders of MELA recently described the group's motivation for getting involved, "We are tired of being the dumping ground of Los Angeles. East Los Angeles has the freeways, the pipeline, the incinerator, the trash dumps, the most polluted air. They think because we are Mexicans they can dump on us. We are here to say 'no more'! The sleeping giant has awoken!"[7]

Pardo (1990) noted how the members of MELA constructed an enhanced and broadened definition of "mother" by allowing any woman to join the group, as it was believed that *all* women shared a concern for children and the future of the community. Indeed, one activist (without children) expressed a highly essentialized rationale for the participation of women, *Madres tienen un amor sin interes* [Mothers have a love without special interest]. This was basically a mechanism for inclusion that served to expand the membership of the organization and offer a degree of legitimacy to nonmothers.[8] More recently, however, attesting to the constructed nature of the category, "mother" has once again been broadened to include men, particularly fathers, but also nonfathers. Over the years, more and more men have been drawn to the organization. Not only have the husbands of the activists become more visible (some have always participated), but as MELA has become a powerful force in cultivating and projecting a positive image of the highly stigmatized barrio, growing numbers of young people have sought to connect with MELA. The leaders of MELA welcome such diverse participation, as they worry that as they get older, there will not be a fresh crop of activists to replace them. Thus, although MELA continues to be led primarily by women, and women remain the spokespersons of the group, the actual membership includes all segments of the Chicano/Latino population. In the words of one MELA leader, "We are the original mothers, but we include everyone. Everyone can be a mother, even the men and boys. Our purpose is to fight for East L.A. and the Latino community." This destabilization of "mother" is a vivid example of how seemingly clear identities can in fact be quite ambiguous. Moreover, this quote also suggests the extent to which MELA has become an ethnically and spatially defined community with prominent female leadership articulating only a limited gendered identity.

The fit between place and identity is also more complex than a first glance would suggest—there is a disjuncture between ethnic group, identity, and place. As previously mentioned, parts of South Central are now 50 percent Latino, and there also exists a significant Latino population in the eastern part of the San Fernando Valley. Yet, MELA equates East L.A. with the region's Chicano/Latino population. Similar to the case of CCOSCLA, activists are drawing on nostalgia, going back to a time when *Mexicanos*/Chicanos were largely confined to East L.A. and when it was *puro Mexicano*. Although MELA often speaks to and for all Latinos, their constituency is clearly East L.A., and not Latinos in other parts of Los Angeles. One MELA activist once commented that "the Latinos in South Central are different. They have their own needs and concerns."

It should be apparent that efforts to reify place and promote consolidated place-based identities is a mixed strategy at best (Penrose 1994; Anderson 1994). But the fact is, there are only a limited number of strategies available to the subaltern, all of which serve to exclude others. And the exclusion of others, the setting of boundaries in order to achieve a particular objective, is precisely what identity politics are all about. As previously mentioned, identity politics aren't necessarily good or bad and always contain their own contradictions, but in this case, a place-based identity has made concrete difference in two highly marginalized communities, both in terms of blocking incinerators and encouraging greater activism. Although not all the subordinated within both places or racial/ethnic groups were able to participate in these emancipatory projects, given the fragmented nature of contemporary metropolises (Chambers 1994), they have accomplished quite a bit by strategically drawing on those identities that they feel will best help them in achieving their objectives.

Conclusion

This chapter has looked critically at representations of nonwhite female environmental justice activists by arguing that although their lives are highly gendered, some activists choose to emphasize place-based identities. These place-based identities are a function of both the spatiality of racism, and macroeconomic processes, such as economic restructuring and immigration, as well as agency. These combined forces have prompted activists to appeal to unitary identities that are predicated on a "fit" between a particular racial/ethnic group and place. This selective emphasis of particular identities has been described as the "maximizing and minimizing of difference" by Gill Valentine (this volume, chapter 4). In this strategy, activists seek to maximize their differences with a hegemonic feminist identity and framework, while simultaneously minimizing the differences within their respective communities. This is clearly seen in efforts to stress a united Black or Latino community, one not split by gender differences.

Despite these articulations, the female identities of these activists are commonly emphasized by scholars and other observers. While the movement is in fact led by women, a feminist analysis has not consciously informed the discourse and strategies of these activists. "The feminist movement plays a crucial role in the education of our movement by identifying how women are impacted by the issues we are involved in. Beyond that there really hasn't been much discussion of specifically feminist issues at the annual gatherings" (Moore in Almeida 1994, 45). This comment by a leader of the Southwest Network for Economic and Environmental Justice (SNEEJ), which has prominent female leadership, accurately characterizes the limited feminist identification among nonwhite, low-income activists.[9]

Thus, a critical question for feminists is, why do we persist in such representations? Even more fundamentally, what are the implications of this practice for feminist geography as a whole? Who is our subject and what are our goals? On what bases are various subjects incorporated into the feminist research agenda? And what happens when they resist? Clearly, these are difficult questions to which there are no easy answers, but they must be grappled with before we can be clear as to what constitutes feminist geography.

Notes

1. Subalterns are those who are highly marginalized both economically and socially. The term was originally developed within the context of colonial India to describe those whose entire lives were structured by domination. See Guha and Spivak (1988).

2. All social science seeks to impose order on a vast and fragmented reality. The difference is that feminists (among others) profess a political consciousness about their research, including the questions asked, the methods used, and the consequences of such research.

3. The quotes from activists are drawn from public speeches, conversations, and a series of interviews conducted in 1993. Because of the visibility of these activists within the environmental justice movement and the Los Angeles area, I have chosen not to disclose individual identities.

4. One of MELA's leaders, for example, recently won the Goldman Environmental Prize, which has been described as the Nobel Prize of environmental activism (Quintanilla 1995).

5. For many Whites, South Central remains a distinctly Black place because it is so intensely racialized, and because few venture into the community to see the changing demographics. Thus, their interpretation of South Central as Black is racist. For African Americans, their insistence that South Central is Black is partly a survival strategy.

6. Criminalization refers to the current process in the United States of imprisoning vast numbers of persons—in particular, young African American males. Criminalization develops by fomenting a rampant fear of crime, rendering illegal the activities of the poor and otherwise marginal, and prosecuting such offenders. Currently 25 percent of all African American males are involved in the criminal justice system (Maurer 1992).

7. Subsequent to its formation, MELA split into two different camps—one rooted in Resurrection parish, and the other in Santa Isabel. Although the division is geographical, it is also ideological and political. Strong leaders emerged in each parish who increasingly disagreed, thus leading to the split. Both still use the name Mothers of East L.A.

8. Within *Mexicano* and Chicano culture, it is often the case that a woman's status and worth is derived from motherhood. Consequently, women without children are sometimes pitied and the idea of choosing not to have children is not widespread. For examples of resistance to this and other patriarchal practices, see Castillo (1995) and de la Torre and Pesquera (1993).

9. The SNEEJ is a network comprised of nonwhite environmental justice groups in the Southwestern United States and Mexico. Both MELA and CCOSCLA are members of the SNEEJ, and CCOSCLA, in particular, has assumed a leadership role.

References

Almeida, P. 1994. The network for environmental and economic justice in the Southwest: Interview with Richard Moore. *Capitalism, Nature & Socialism* 5(1): 21–54.

Anderson, K. 1994. Constructing geographies: "Race", place, and the making of Sydney's aboriginal redfern. In *Constructions of "race", place and nation,* ed. P. Jackson and J. Penrose, 81–99. Minneapolis: University of Minnesota Press.

Anzaldua, G., ed. 1990. *Making face, making soul.* San Francisco: Aunt Lute Books.

Austin, R., and Schill, M. 1991. Black, brown, poor and poisoned: Minority grassroots environmentalism and the quest for eco-justice. *Kansas Journal of Law and Public Policy* 1: 69–82.

Brown, P., and Ferguson, F. 1995. "Making a big stink: Women's work, women's relationships, and toxic waste activism. *Gender & Society* 9(2): 145–72.

Brown, P., and Masterson-Allen, S. 1994. The toxic waste movement: A new type of activism. *Society and Natural Resources* 7: 269–87.

Cable, S. 1992. Women's social movement involvement: The role of structural availability in recruitment and participation processes. *Sociological Quarterly* 33: 35–47.

Capek, S. 1993 The "environmental justice" frame: A conceptual discussion and an application. *Social Problems* 40(1): 5–24.

Carney, J. 1993. Converting the wetlands, engendering the environment: The intersection of gender with agrarian change in The Gambia. *Economic Geography* 69: 329–48.

Carney, J., and Watts, M. 1991. Disciplining women? Rice, mechanization, and the evolution of Mandinka gender relations in Senegambia. *Signs* 16: 650–81.

Castillo, A. 1995. *Massacre of the dreamers: Essays on Xicanisma.* New York: Plume.

Chambers, I. 1994. *Migrancy, culture, identity.* New York: Routledge.

de la Torre, A., and Pesquera, B. 1993. *Building with our hands: New directions in Chicana studies.* Berkeley: University of California Press.

Diamond I., and Orenstein, G. 1990. *Reweaving the world: The emergence of ecofeminism.* San Francisco: Sierra Club Books.

Di Chiro, G. 1993. Defining environmental justice: Women's voices and grassroots politics. *Socialist Review* 22(4): 93–130.

Epstein, B. 1995. Grassroots environmentalism and strategies for social change. *New Political Science.* 32 (summer): 1–24.

———. 1993. Ecofeminism and grass-roots environmentalism in the United States. In *Toxic struggles,* ed. R. Hofrichter, pp. 144–52. Philadelphia: New Society.

FitzSimmons, M., and Gottlieb, R. 1988. A new environmental politics? In *Reshaping the U.S. left: Popular struggles in the 1980s,* ed. M. Davis and M. Sprinkler, 144–30. London: Verso.

Gauna, J. 1991. Unsafe for women, children, and other living things. Available from Southwest Organizing Project, Albuquerque, New Mexico.

Gibbs, L. 1993. Celebrating ten years of triumph. *Everyone's Backyard* 11(1): 2.

Gray, H. 1993. African-American political desire and the seductions of contemporary cultural politics. *Cultural Studies* 7(3): 364–73.

Griffin, S. 1978. *Woman and nature: The roaring inside her.* New York: Harper and Row.

Guha, R., and Spivak, G. 1988. *Selected subaltern studies.* New York: Oxford.

Gutierrez, G. 1994. Mothers of East Los Angeles strike back. In *Unequal protection,* ed. R. Bullard, 220–33. San Francisco: Sierra Club Books.

Hamilton, C. 1994. Concerned citizens of South Central Los Angeles. In *Unequal protection,* ed. R. Bullard, 207–19. San Francisco: Sierra Club Books.

———. 1990. Apartheid in America. Reprinted from the *L.A. Weekly,* December 1989. Available from the Labor/Community Strategy Center, Los Angeles.

Haraway, D. 1991. *Simians, cyborgs and women: The reinvention of nature.* London: Routledge.

Heiman, M. 1990. From "Not in my backyard!" to "Not in anybody's backyard!" Grassroots challenge to hazardous waste facility siting. *Journal of the American Planning Association* 56: 359–62.

Hill Collins, P. 1991. *Black feminist thought.* London: Unwin Hyman.

Hofrichter, R. 1993. Introduction. In *Toxic struggles,* ed. R. Hofrichter, 1–10. Philadelphia: New Society Publishers.

Jackson, P. 1993. Changing ourselves: A geography of position. In *The challenge of geography: A changing world, a changing discipline,* ed. R. J. Johnston, 198–214. Cambridge: Blackwell.

Johnson, J., and Roseman, C. 1990. Recent black outmigration from Los Angeles: The role of household dynamics and kinship systems. *Annals of the Association of American Geographers* 80(2): 205–22.

King, Y. 1989. The ecology of feminism and the feminism of ecology. In *Healing the wounds: The promise of ecofeminism,* ed. J. Plant, 18–28. Toronto: Between the Lines.

Kirschenman, J., and Neckerman, K. 1991. We'd love to hire them, but . . . The meaning of race for employers. In *The urban underclass,* ed. C. Jenks and P. Peterson, 203–32. Washington, D.C.: The Brookings Institute.

Kolodny, A. 1984. *The land before her.* Chapel Hill: University of North Carolina Press.

Krauss, C. 1993. Blue-collar women and toxic-waste protests: The process of politicization. In *Toxic struggles,* ed. R. Hofrichter, 107–17. Philadelphia: New Society Publishers.

Mann, E. 1991. *L.A.'s lethal air.* Los Angeles: Labor/Community Strategy Center.

Massey, D. 1994. *Space, place, and gender,* chapter 4. Minneapolis: University of Minnesota Press.

———. 1992. A place called home? *New Formations* 17 (summer): 3–15.

Mauer, M. 1992. Americans behind bars. *Criminal Justice* (winter): 12–18 and 38.

Merchant, C. 1992. *Radical ecology.* New York: Routledge.

———. 1980. *The death of nature: Women, ecology and the scientific revolution.* New York: Harper and Row.

Nesmith, C., and Radcliffe, S. 1993. (Re)mapping Mother Earth: A geographical perspective on environmental feminisms. *Environment and Planning D:* 11: 379–94.

Newman, P. 1994. Killing legally with toxic waste: Women and the environment in the United States. In *Close to home: Women reconnect ecology, health and development worldwide,* ed. V. Shiva, 43–59. Philadelphia: New Society.

Norwood, V., and Monk, J. 1987. *The desert is no lady: Southwestern landscapes in women's writing and art.* New Haven, Conn.: Yale University Press.

Ong, P., and Blumenberg, E. 1992. Income and racial inequality. Manuscript. Urban Planning, University of California, Los Angeles.

Pardo, M. 1990. Mexican American women grassroots community activists: Mothers of East L.A. *Frontiers* 11: 1–6.

Penrose, J. 1994. Reification in the name of change: The impact of nationalism and social constructions of nation, people and place in Scotland and the United Kingdom.

In *Constructions of "race", place and nation,* ed. P. Jackson and J. Penrose, 27–49. Minneapolis, Minn.: University of Minnesota Press.

Pulido, L. 1995. People of color, identity politics and the environmental justice movement. Manuscript. Department of Geography, University of Southern California.

Quintanilla, S. 1995. The Earth Mother. *Los Angeles Times.* 24 April: E1, E5.

Rose, G. 1993. *Feminism and geography.* Minneapolis, Minn.: University of Minnesota Press.

Russell, D. 1989. Environmental racism. *The Amicus Journal* Spring, 22–32.

Sagahuan, L. 1989. The Mothers of East L.A. transform themselves and their neighborhood. *Los Angeles Times* 13 August: B1, B6.

Schroeder, R. 1993. Shady practice: Gender, and the political ecology of resource stabilization in Gambian garden/orchard. *Economic Geography* 69: 349–65.

Seager, J. 1995. Making feminist sense of the environmental crisis. Paper presented at the University of Southern California, 17 February.

———. 1993. Creating a culture of destruction: Gender, militarism, and the environment. In *Toxic Struggles,* ed. R. Hofrichter, 58–66. Philadelphia: New Society.

Shiva, V. 1994. *Close to home: Women reconnect ecology, health and development worldwide.* Philadelphia: New Society Publishers.

———. 1987. *Staying alive.* London: Zed Books.

Soja, E. W. 1989. *Postmodern geographies: The reassertion of space in social theory.* New York: Verso.

Spivak, G. 1988. Can the subaltern speak? In *Marxism and the interpretation of culture,* eds., C. Nelson and L. Grossberg, 271–313. Urbana: University of Illinois.

Szasz, A. 1994. *Ecopopulism.* Minnesota: University of Minneapolis.

Townsend, J. 1995. *Women's voices from the rainforest.* New York: Routledge.

Turner, E., and Allen, J. 1991. *An atlas of population patterns in metropolitan Los Angeles and Orange Counties.* Occasional Publications in Geography no. 8. Northridge: California State University Northridge, Department of Geography.

United Nations. 1993. Special issue on women and environment. *Instraw News,* vol. 19.

Waldinger, R. 1995. Black/immigrant competition re-assessed: New evidence from Los Angeles. Manuscript, Department of Sociology, University of California, Los Angeles.

Warren, K. 1990. The power and the promise of ecological feminism. *Environmental Ethics* 12: 125–46.

Women and the environment. 1993. *Canadian Women Studies.* Special issue, 13(3).

2

Identity, Space, and Politics: A Critique of the Poverty Debates

Melissa R. Gilbert

Introduction

The day after the Republican realignment of Congress in the 1994 elections, a subdued President Clinton predicted that "welfare reform" was one area of his legislative agenda that could be accomplished with bipartisan effort. Despite the rancorous debate that followed, Clinton signed in August 1996 a welfare reform bill that ended poor people's guarantee of federal assistance. This historic event suggests that there was broad agreement among both parties about the nature and causes of poverty. The debate about poverty, which has now shifted to the state legislatures, was focused almost exclusively on how to restructure Aid to Families with Dependent Children (AFDC), more commonly known as welfare—the recipients of which were stigmatized as dependent and morally unfit. Underlying much of the poverty debates are essentialist conceptualizations of "race," gender, poverty, and space. In these debates, poverty is explained by, or reduced to, "race," gender, unemployment, and the urban environment.

Essentialist conceptualizations of "race," gender, and space underlie a powerful academic and popular analysis of poverty resulting in the current retrogressive proposals to reform welfare. The urban underclass thesis suggests that there is a culture of poverty, particularly among African Americans in inner-city neighborhoods, in which the explanation for poverty is to be found in the maladaptive nature of African American culture. Feminist organizations have attempted to counter this retrogressive political analysis by drawing upon the notion of a feminization of poverty, a term coined by some feminists to point out that it is mostly women and their children who are impoverished. This

29

argument has been less effective than it could be, however, precisely because it is aspatial and focused only on gender.

My purpose in this chapter is to argue that an effective feminist and antiracist critique of, and alternative to, the prevailing poverty debates requires an analysis based on nonessentialist conceptualizations of identity and space. I begin by first discussing nonessentialist conceptualizations of "race," gender, and space that provide the framework for my alternative analysis of poverty. Second, I critique the urban underclass and feminization of poverty theses. Last, I draw on my research on the survival strategies of working poor women in Worcester, Massachusetts, to demonstrate how nonessentialist conceptualizations of "race," gender, and space help to make sense of women's everyday experiences of poverty. By focusing on the strategies of working poor women, I can counter the dominant narratives about poverty (e.g., passive, ghetto, African American "welfare queens") in which the underclass thesis is embedded and which the feminization of poverty thesis cannot effectively critique.[1]

Nonessentialist Conceptualizations of "Race," Gender, and Space

Both feminist and anti-racist theory have demonstrated that gender and "race" are not determining biological categories; rather, they are socially constructed, historically and geographically specific concepts that have real effects on people's lives (e.g., Omi and Winant 1986; Jackson and Penrose 1993; Kobayashi and Peake 1994). Using a nonessentialist epistemology, we can most usefully understand "race" and gender as processes whereby people become racialized and gendered.[2] Furthermore, these processes are mutually constitutive. Ideologies of femininity and masculinity are highly racialized, and racialized identities are highly gendered (e.g., Collins 1990; Ware 1992; Brewer 1993).

Nonessentialist work on identity has been extended to rethink essentialist conceptualizations of space and place (e.g., Massey 1993; Keith and Pile 1993; Pulido chapter 1 of this volume). As opposed to conceptualizing space as existing independent of objects and, therefore, having independent causal powers, nonessentialist conceptualizations of space see space as existing through the interrelationships of objects. Like social structures, space is socially constructed although it has real effects on people's everyday lives. Social structures are constituted spatially, and geographers use the term "spatiality" to indicate that space and social structures are mutually constituted processes. Massey (1993) argues that a more progressive sense of place sees places as processes of social relations rather than as bounded enclosures, and as having multiple meanings and identities.

The "Urban Underclass"

In the mid–1960s, the civil rights movement and urban riots shifted discussions of poverty from a concern with rural, often White, populations to a concern with African American urban poverty (Katz 1989). Most of the attention to poverty is now directed at the urban underclass. The urban underclass concept is highly racialized and gendered, and is focused on place in that it has come to mean African American female welfare recipients and unemployed African American male youths living in inner-city neighborhoods, as symbolized by the powerful political rhetoric of "welfare queens" and "urban gangs." This political rhetoric is given credibility by academic research despite the existence of a substantial literature that critiques the underclass thesis (e.g., Katz 1993). The urban underclass is argued to be a subset of the poor who exhibit "pathological" values and behaviors including welfare dependency, female-headed households, teenage pregnancy, unemployment, and drug use.[3] Furthermore, as Wilson (1987) argues, the urban underclass is spatially isolated and concentrated in inner-city neighborhoods, leading to a concern with the effects of environment on behavior.[4]

The underclass literature focuses much attention on the relationship between family structure and poverty (e.g., Murray 1984; Wilson 1987). Underlying the discussion have been ethnocentric and patriarchal beliefs that the best or normal family structure is the "traditional" nuclear family with its attendant male and female roles (for critiques, see Brewer 1988; Miller 1993). The literature invariably focuses on teenage pregnancy, welfare dependency, and female-headed households as causes of poverty. There is little analysis as to *why* female-headed households are often impoverished (e.g., occupational segregation by sex and "race," lack of affordable child care, low-wage jobs with few benefits). Rather the problem is viewed in terms of women's dependence on the state, and the solution is seen to be women's dependence on men within the traditional nuclear family.

The focus of underclass literature on African American women's fertility, family structure, and use of AFDC is inscribed in the public discourse on the "welfare queen." The prominence of this powerful symbol, despite the fact that most women receiving AFDC are not African American, must be understood within an analytical framework that sees racism and sexism as mutually constitutive processes. As bell hooks has argued, "Race and sex have always been overlapping discourses in the United States" (hooks 1990, 57). Women's sexuality is racialized as well as gendered. Within white racist discourse, African American women are constructed as "oversexed" and, therefore, in need of control (West 1993; Collins 1990). In the welfare reform debates, there is considerable agreement among both liberals and conservatives that teenage women's sexuality must be controlled and "illegitimacy" punished.

> Portraying African American women as stereotypical mammies, matriarchs, welfare recipients, and hot mommas has been essential to the political economy of domination fostering Black women's oppression . . . These controlling images are designed to make racism, sexism, and poverty appear natural, normal, and an inevitable part of everyday life. (Collins 1990, 67–68)

Not only have ideologies about sexuality been racialized, but also notions of "women's work" have been and continue to be racialized. The ideology of the cult of domesticity was predicated on a radical separation of the public and private spheres whereby masculinity was associated with the former and femininity the latter. The ideal of true (White) womanhood was not constructed for, or attainable by, African American women either during or after slavery given the economic and political context of their labor (Jones 1985; Collins 1990). This explains the contradictory arguments of right-wing ideologues that demand "lazy welfare mothers" (assumed to be African American) be forced to seek employment, in part to ensure that they will not pass on a poor work ethic to their children, while middle-class women (assumed to be European American) are vilified for working outside the home and thereby endangering their children:

> In the grip of the recession, with political figures outdoing each other to shift the blame from the structural inadequacies of the political economy and its effect on all of the poor, most of the working class, and an increasingly large share of the middle class, the lines between real and cultural politics disappear in the creation of all-purpose scapegoats. (Lubiano 1992, 336)

The racist messages encoded in the discourse of the "welfare queen" ensure that African American women are the scapegoats for the changing political economy. But the racist discourse that allows poverty to be racialized ensures that welfare "reform" will hurt all poor women and will fail to address the economic and social consequences of the restructuring of the political economy, which has adversely affected many people.

The conceptualization of space primarily used within this underclass debate is one of abstract space, space as a container. Poor people are literally fixed in space as "underclass" people who live in "underclass" neighborhoods. Hughes (1989; 1990) has argued that the focus on "underclass" census tracts leads to the ecological fallacy in which people are defined literally by where they live. It is mistakenly assumed that people who live in the same place (census tract) have similar attributes and behaviors. By treating the inner city as a walled off or contained space, we neglect the connections between the inner city and the rest of society such as the processes that form residential segregation and poverty. This definition inevitably leads to an environmentally deterministic view of neighborhoods as having independent effects on people's behavior.

Our ideas about "race," gender, and poverty are not only socially constructed but spatially constructed. A particular conceptualization of space contributes to how we construct and represent difference. Racist accounts of poverty are partially made possible by the process of racialization of African Americans through our bounding of the ghetto.[5] What it means to be African American women and men in the United States is partially set through the social construction of the place, "the inner city." In popular discourse, the inner city is constructed as a place of immorality, crime, and poverty, being inhabited primarily by racialized minorities. The social construction of "race" and place results in further essentializing the category African American.

By fusing essentialist conceptualizations of "race," gender, and space, the urban underclass concept shapes contemporary racist and sexist discourse and policies. Furthermore, it severely limits our understanding of the causes, consequences, and remedies of poverty by neglecting the majority of the poor, including people from different "races," the working poor, and people living outside of inner cities, and the processes by which people move into and out of poverty. By focusing on the moral attributes of one "race" of poor people, it promotes cultural and/or behavioral explanations of poverty, thereby allowing structural processes to be ignored. Last, by promoting racism and defining poverty by unemployment, it obscures the connections among many poor people—connections that could form the basis for political action.

The Feminization of Poverty

The most visible feminist intervention in the public debates about poverty and welfare reform is in the form of the feminization of poverty thesis. While less pernicious in terms of its political implications than the urban underclass thesis, the feminization of poverty thesis, as Baca Zinn (1990) has argued, essentializes gender by not recognizing that different structures of inequality give rise to different kinds of constraints and survival strategies. The term "feminization of poverty" was coined by Diana Pearce (1979) to highlight the fact that poverty disproportionately affects women and their children. A number of explanations have been put forth to explain this trend, including family structure, the welfare system, and women's disadvantaged position in the labor force (for reviews see Kodras and Jones 1991; McLanahan et al. 1989; Goldberg and Kremen 1990). It is clear that women are disproportionately impoverished (McLanahan et al. 1989; Pearce 1990). Yet women's poverty cannot be explained solely by gender, but must take into account processes of "race" and class (Baca Zinn 1990). For example, African American women are likely to be impoverished regardless of marital status because of the disadvantaged position of African American men in the labor market (Baca Zinn 1990; Jones 1985).

The feminization of poverty literature has neglected the geographic variability of poverty (for a critique see Kodras and Jones 1991) and the way that socio-spatial processes contribute to poverty. Pearce (1990) does argue that minority women in particular are geographically isolated due to racial segregation of housing and gender and child discrimination in housing markets. This, I would argue, contradicts her conceptualization of the feminization of poverty. By focusing only on gender and ignoring the spatiality of poor women's lives, the feminization of poverty thesis cannot capture the reality or complexity of poor people's lives. In neglecting processes of "race" and space in conceptualizing women's poverty, the feminization of poverty thesis cannot provide an effective academic or political critique of the urban underclass thesis.

An Alternative Analysis: Women's Survival Strategies

Having critiqued the urban underclass and feminization of poverty as conceptual frameworks for understanding poor women's everyday lives—or, more
generally, poverty—and the workings of the political economy, I will now
draw on my research with working poor women in Worcester, Massachusetts,
to illustrate how a nonessentialist conceptual framework precludes reducing
poverty to "race," gender, or the urban environment.

In 1991, I conducted in-depth interviews with twenty-six African American
and twenty-seven European American low-waged women with children living
in Worcester. Worcester, a classic frostbelt city, continues to experience economic restructuring similar to other old industrial centers in the United States.
From 1960 to 1990 the percentage of manufacturing jobs in Worcester city
declined from 38 percent to 18 percent, and the percentage of service jobs
increased from 22 percent to 38 percent (Gilbert 1993).

These economic trends have numerous effects in Worcester including hurt-
ing families headed by women and African Americans. According to United
States census data, in 1989, 31 percent of families with children under the age
of eighteen in Worcester were headed by women, as compared to 11 percent
nationally; nearly 57 percent of female-headed households in Worcester in
1990 were below the poverty line. While only 5 percent of the population of
Worcester is African American, African American families are disproportionately affected by poverty; 33 percent of African Americans fell below the poverty line as compared to 16 percent of European American families (Gilbert
1993).

While much of the public and academic discourse about poverty is focused
on women receiving AFDC benefits, many employed women are no more
financially secure than they would be if they were on welfare. Furthermore,
half of all single mothers who spend time receiving AFDC during a two-year
period also participate in waged labor (IWPR 1995). How do working poor
women ensure the survival of themselves and their families? I address this
question through an analysis of the role of women's personal networks—
family, friends, neighbors, coworkers—as one aspect of women's strategies to
obtain child care, housing, and employment. I chose to focus on women's
networks for two reasons. First, by exploring the creation and use of networks
as part of women's survival strategies, I counter traditional beliefs that poor
women are passive or lazy. Second, by focusing on the role of place-based
personal networks in women's attempts to find a job, child care, and housing
solution in space, I can explore the spatiality of people's everyday lives.

Similarities in Survival Strategies of African American
and European American Women

Contrary to the urban underclass thesis, my research suggests that there are
many similarities in the daily struggles and survival strategies of African Amer-

ican and European American working poor women as a result of their participation in gender and class processes. Interestingly, these similarities are often
the result of the geographical constraints that poor women experience.

Women's survival strategies and the spatial boundedness of their everyday
lives are mutually constituted. Many women, regardless of the presence or
absence of a partner, must fulfill the multiple roles of employee, mother, and
family provider. Many women experience severe time and space constraints
in attempting to meet all of their responsibilities in a society that does not
acknowledge or support women's multiple roles. Two single parents' experiences are indicative of the time and space constraints poor women face in
attempting to ensure their economic survival. One African American woman
described her morning routine after she could no longer afford car insurance:
"I wait for the bus for her [a child in first grade] to get picked up. I call a taxi
from some place in that area to take the taxi to the daycare provider and from
there I would take a bus to work."[6] A European American woman described
her evening routine as follows:

> Well, it's [childcare one] just five minutes [from work], but in the wrong direction.
> So I go there and pick her up, and I have to go pick up the other kid which is
> maybe ten minutes from there [childcare one], and then from there [childcare
> two] going home is another five minutes. But it would take at least a half hour
> because you can't just go there and throw the kid in the car as you drive by slowly.
> You have to park the car, go up the stairs, dress the kid, bring her down the stairs,
> do the seatbelt, and do the same thing for the next kid.[7]

Many women strategize in response to the time and space constraints by
making their employment, child care, and housing decisions in concert. As
one African American woman with four children aged two to twelve years
said, "I wouldn't go too far [to work], I'm having trouble as it is. I need to be
there if something happens with the kids—15 minutes max—like where I work
now, it takes about 15 minutes to get to any school I might need to."[8] A
European American woman with one son explained how she had made employment and child care decisions jointly within the constraints of a bus route.
Her son was ten when she made the following decisions:

> I looked for the job particularly because it was within the bus route. . . . The
> crossing guard at his [her son's] school, took him after school. . . . She'd walk him
> to the bus stop and put him on my city bus. I would like walk up to the front of
> the bus and say, "o.k. I'm here" and I'd wave to her and he'd get on.[9]

When women cannot strategize in response to the time and space constraints they face in attempting to meet their multiple roles, the results can be
devastating. One African American single parent had to quit her job and receive AFDC because of child care problems. She took a bus to work at 6:30
a.m. in order to be at work by 7:00 a.m. The oldest child, only ten years old,
put the youngest children on the bus to the daycare. The bus driver reported

her to the Department of Social Services for having such a young child be responsible for the youngest children. Her employer would not change her hours, nor would the union support her. She described her frustration and anguish:

> it hurts . . . because when I stopped working, I had to go to welfare to get them to pay my electric bill and then pay my rent. . . . When I was working . . . I was saving, I had money and everything in the bank. Right now I don't have nothing. . . . She [the social worker] kept calling me telling me things are going to get better. I said, "things are not going to get better for me because you should be able to talk to the people for the daycare to come and pick my kids up at 6:00 a.m. you know if you want me to work." I'm the one who wants to work.[10]

Not only do the spatial patterns reflect women's survival strategies, they affect them too. The spatial extent of women's daily activities patterns affects women's job and child care opportunities. One way this occurs is through women's use of personal networks to find a job, child care, and housing solution in place. The nature and spatial extent of women's personal networks is closely tied to their restricted daily activity patterns. Such networks play a vital role in determining how women define employment, child care, and housing opportunities. Most women in both racialized groups relied heavily on personal contacts to link them to jobs, child care, and housing.

Personal networks can be both a resource and a constraint, often simultaneously, on women's economic survival. It has been well documented that women rely heavily on personal contacts to find employment (Hanson and Pratt 1991, 1995; Gilbert 1993). Hanson and Pratt (1991, 1995) have demonstrated that the channels of information through which people get jobs are highly gendered and spatially differentiated. Women, particularly women in female-dominated occupations, are likely to receive job information from other women, family, and community-based contacts, while men find job information from other men and work-based contacts. Furthermore, women in gender-typical occupations are more likely than women in gender-atypical occupations to learn about their jobs from personal contacts who are women and who are from the local neighborhood (Hanson and Pratt 1991, 1995; Gilbert 1993). Therefore, while personal networks help women to find jobs, the use of personal networks can contribute to occupational segregation by sex and connect women to jobs that have lower wages and fewer benefits.

That personal networks can be both a resource and a constraint on women's economic survival can also be illustrated through an analysis of how personal networks connect women to child care providers. Most women in my study found their child care providers through personal contacts, although some women used institutional contacts and the newspaper or yellow pages. Family members played an important role in connecting women to child care, and to a lesser extent, so did neighbors and community-based contacts. The method used to find child care affects women's economic survival because different types of child care differ in terms of cost and hours of provision. For example, personal contacts were most likely to lead women to informal child care arrangements. This could be advantageous, providing inexpensive and flexible child care, or disadvantageous, providing insecure child care that could not be subsidized by the state because it was not licensed.

Differences in Survival Strategies of African American and European American Women

Yet while there are striking similarities between African American and European American women in their survival strategies, there are also important differences that are the result of processes of "race" or racism. The differences in survival strategies are not the result of a "culture of poverty," but rather are a result of the way power and resources are unequally distributed in society on the basis of "race." Institutionalized and individual racism in the housing and labor markets are constraints on African Americans' economic opportunities, their strategies reflect these constraints.

African American women tended to rely more heavily on personal contacts to link them to jobs, child care, and housing than did European American women. In this way, they can sometimes avoid the possibility of encountering racism from the majority society. Personal contacts can perform a screening function by giving women information about employers, landlords, and child-care providers. Personal contacts can also help African American women, for example, by "vouching" for them to an employer.

The kind of personal contacts used by African American and European American women often differed. African American women tended to rely more heavily on kin and community-based networks, especially church-related contacts, than did European American women. While there has been much discussion of the supposed breakdown of the African American family, studies have shown that low-income African Americans rely heavily on the extended family (e.g., Stack 1974; Taylor 1985). In fact, the extended family and the church have historically been important institutions in mitigating the effects of living in an often hostile and racist society. The differences in African American and European American women's strategies to find jobs, child care, and housing can be seen in the spatial extent of their daily activity patterns. African American women were significantly more spatially limited in terms of the journey to work and child care than were European American women (see figures 2.1 and 2.2). The reasons for African American women's spatial boundedness lie in several mutually constitutive processes. These include residential segregation, the "racial" composition of women's networks, and the relationship between women's daily activity patterns and the nature and spatial extent of their networks. Most women make their employment and child care decisions from a fixed residential location. Because African Americans are spatially segregated in Worcester, these women make employment and child care decisions from a more spatially limited residential base than do European American women (see figure 2.3). Most African American women I interviewed (69 percent), like most African American women in Worcester more generally (64 percent),

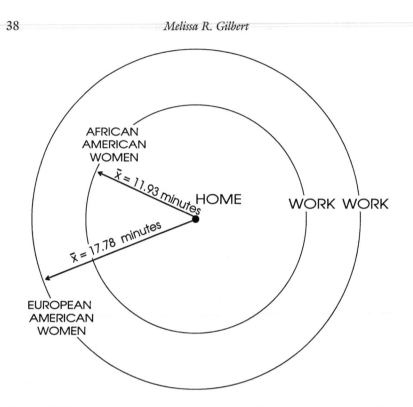

Fig. 2.1. Difference in mean travel time to work (all jobs) not involving child care trips for African American and European American women.

live in just thirteen census tracts. This does not mean that their activity spaces necessarily will be smaller than European American women's. The fact that most of their child care providers were other African Americans who were also residentially segregated, and that most of European American women's child care providers were other European Americans who were not as residentially segregated, does, however, partially explain the difference in the extent of activity space. Furthermore, African American women were more likely than European American women to use personal contacts to find jobs and child care, and personal contacts were more likely than other strategies to lead women to jobs and child care closer to home.

To understand how these differences play out in women's lives, I will present the stories of two women, one European American and one African American. Elizabeth Johns (a pseudonym) is a European American, twenty-eight-year-old, single mother with a four-year-old daughter and a nine-month-old son.[11] She earns under $10,000 per year as a preschool teacher in Grafton (an eastern suburb) working thirty-two hours per week with no benefits. She is laid off each summer and collects unemployment. Elizabeth searched for a job through newspapers, employment agencies, and personal contacts including

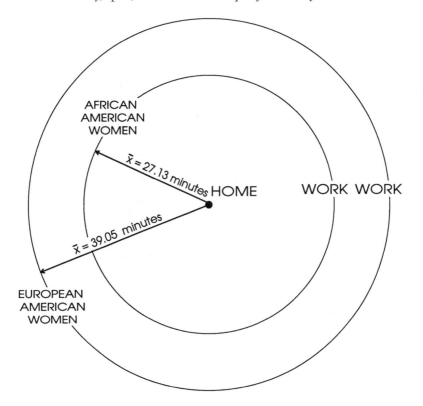

Fig. 2.2. Difference in mean travel time to work (all jobs) including child care trips for African American and European American women.

family and friends. She found her job through a European American woman friend that she met at childbirth classes who lives in Shrewsbury (an eastern suburb). Her friend's daughter had previously attended the preschool. Her friend saw an ad in the local paper where her mother lives and told Elizabeth about the job. Elizabeth called and applied for the job. Elizabeth travels sixty minutes from home to work including stops at child care. If she went directly from her home to work, it would take only twenty minutes.

Elizabeth's daughter attends a child care center at a local community college. Elizabeth had previously attended the college. If she needs more child care, a young woman who used to work in a convenience store across from Elizabeth's house, watches her daughter. Her son attends an unlicensed family day care run by a woman that she knew from high school. Another friend from high school had told her that this woman was a child care provider in Grafton, where Elizabeth works. She had also been calling places that she found in the yellow pages.

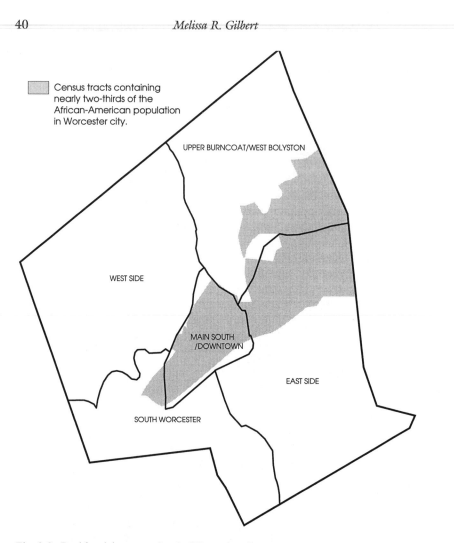

Census tracts containing
nearly two-thirds of the
African-American population
in Worcester city.

UPPER BURNCOAT/WEST BOLYSTON

WEST SIDE

MAIN SOUTH
/DOWNTOWN

EAST SIDE

SOUTH WORCESTER

Fig. 2.3. Residential segregation in Worcester city.

Elizabeth lives in an apartment in Grafton Hill on the east side of Worcester. She found her apartment through the newspaper. She had an extremely difficult time finding a landlord that would rent to her because she receives Section 8, a federal housing subsidy. She pays only $14 a month in rent.

Julie Clarkson (a pseudonym) is an African American, thirty-four-year-old, single mother of three children ages fifteen, four and one year.[12] She earns $29,120 as a full-time telephone operator for Massachusetts Electric on South-bridge Street in Worcester. She has worked there for years in different jobs. Her most recent job had been posted at her workplace, and she applied for it because it was more money and she was unhappy in her previous job. Her travel time to work is thirty minutes with child care trips and five minutes directly.

Julie owns a home in Main South that she bought with her mother. The house was a few doors down from a previous residence. Julie's mother did the household and child care responsibilities at no cost while Julie supported the family. After Julie's mother died, the children went to an aunt who ran a licensed family day care located in Main South. She now has her two youngest children in a formal daycare center located in an African American church. Although she does not attend that church, she found out about the center through her church and receives some help from her own church with child care costs. Julie prefers formal child care to kin-related child care despite her extensive use of the latter.

Julie's brother and one of his young children now live with her because he cannot afford to live on his own. Julie's brother helps with some of the bills, but does not pool income. Julie takes his child to and from child care, adding another twenty minutes to her journey to work.

These two women illustrate the differences in European American and African American women's job, child care, and housing strategies. We also see how the nature and spatial extent of women's personal contacts, the "racial" composition of their networks, and residential segregation result in African American women having more spatially limited daily activity patterns than European American women. Furthermore, we see how women's job, child care, and housing decisions are interrelated.

By examining the similarities and differences in strategies of European American and African American women, I have attempted to demonstrate that a nonessentialist conceptualization of "race" helps us to understand women's experiences of poverty and to challenge racist accounts of poverty. It is important, however, to examine the diversity of women's experiences within racialized groups. For example, I have explored elsewhere the ways that migration patterns affect the nature and spatial extent of women's networks as part of their survival strategies (Gilbert 1993). Migration is one of the most powerful processes affecting women's survival strategies. Quite expectedly, family plays a lesser role in these women's lives, especially in terms of finding jobs and child care. Women who had migrated to Worcester as adults were more likely to rely on neighbors or on work-based, and church-based contacts for the kinds of assistance that require proximity to people, such as finding a job or child care. Migrant women, did, however, rely on kin for financial and emotional support. Whether one had migrated to Worcester as an adult or had lived in Worcester her entire life inevitably led to quite different life experiences, problems, and solutions for women of the same racialized group.

Conclusion

The similarities and differences in the constraints and survival strategies of working poor African American and European American women can be understood within a theoretical framework that explores women's participation in gender, class, and "race" processes and conceptualizes these processes as mutually and spatially constituted. The constraints on all women's economic opportunities result from the gender division of labor in the family and labor force, the separation of "work" and "home," and the devaluing of women's work. Since neither employers nor the state are developing significant policies that recognize multiple roles, women's strategies are highly privatized. Thus, women's participation in class and "race" processes, and their resulting access to resources, become extremely important.

Much of the differences in constraints on working poor African American and European American women and their survival strategies are a result of "race" processes. Residential segregation, institutionalized racism in the labor market, and the racialized nature of the gender division of labor clearly affect African American women's strategies, while White privilege affects European American women's strategies.

Examining the everyday struggles of working poor women makes it impossible to maintain the essentialist conceptualizations of "race," gender, and space embedded in the urban underclass thesis. Furthermore, the limitations of the feminization of poverty thesis due to its aspatial analysis and privileging of gender become apparent. Poor women's survival strategies are varied and complex, attesting to their strength and ingenuity in extremely difficult circumstances shaped by their participation in processes of "race," gender, and class. The explanatory frameworks provided by these theses are at best inadequate explanations of the constraints on poor women or their struggles and are often politically retrogressive, providing the rationale for punitive social and economic policies.

The essentialist conceptualization of space underlying the urban underclass thesis has contributed to racist discourses about poverty. Our ideas about "race," gender, and poverty are not only socially constructed but also spatially constructed. Racist accounts of poverty are made possible partially by the process of racialization of African Americans through our bounding of "the inner city/ghetto." In so doing, it becomes possible to attribute independent causal powers to the "inner-city environment." The feminization of poverty thesis is less effective in countering the racist and sexist political agenda that follows from this reasoning than an analysis of poverty that examines the spatiality of gender, class, and "race."

An effective feminist and antiracist critique of the underclass thesis requires a geographical analysis based on, to borrow Massey's (1993) phrase, a progressive sense of place (and space). Clearly space and place play a role in the causes and consequences of poverty in women's everyday lives. However, place and space do not play the roles suggested by environmentally deterministic explanations of poverty that are based on conceptualizations of space as a container and place as a bounded enclosure. Rather, my research illustrates that the spatiality of women's lives is important, for example, in terms of the place-based nature of networks, residential segregation, and the time/space constraints women face in attempting to find a job, child care, and housing solution in places.

Nonessentialist conceptualizations of identity and space within an anti-racist and feminist theoretical framework provide an analysis of urban poverty that better explains women's everyday experiences than do either the urban underclass or feminization of poverty theses. They provide the basis for an effective, progressive political agenda that reframes the debate about "welfare reform" within the mutually and spatially constituted processes of the changing political economy, racism, and sexism and their effects on poor people.

Notes

This research was assisted by awards from the Social Science Research Council through funding provided by the Rockefeller Foundation and the National Science Foundation (SES–9103501). I would like to thank Heidi Nast, Sue Roberts, and John Paul Jones III for organizing the conference/workshop. I would also like to thank Sherry Ahrentzen, Glen Elder, Audrey Kobayashi, Glenda Laws, Karen Nairn, Laura Pulido, Sue Roberts, Chuck Rutheiser, and Gill Valentine for their helpful comments on earlier drafts of this paper, and Jeff McMichael for preparing the figures.

1. In the United States, the term "welfare queen" plays a crucial role in the representational politics of poverty. It is a pejorative term that encapsulates a particular narrative about women receiving AFDC benefits; recipients are believed to be lazy African American women with numerous children who are taking advantage of the generosity of the average tax payer.

2. A number of feminists have argued that accusations of essentialism have created a "chilly climate" in feminist debates because it is sometimes used to silence debate (e.g., Martin 1994; Schor and Weed 1994). Martin (1994) convincingly argues that European American feminist attempts to rectify their previous failures to theorize "race" and class (among others) has led to the pitfall of "false difference." These problems are not, I believe, inherent to nonessentialist theorizing. It is my intention that the following analysis will illustrate how a nonessentialist conceptualization of "race" and gender is an effective analytical and political tool for feminist and anti-racist research.

3. The emphasis is on behavioral patterns whether one is a conservative who believes government policies or, more recently, lower intelligence, cause poverty (Murray 1984) or a Social Democrat who believes labor markets and "concentration effects" cause poverty (Wilson 1987).

4. Wilson no longer uses the term underclass because of its pejorative overtones, but refers to the "ghetto poor" (Wilson 1991). This term, however, is a further example of the way space is essentialized in the underclass debates.

5. See Pulido (chapter 1) for a fascinating discussion of the racialization of South Central and East Los Angeles, and resident's challenge of, and participation in, this process.

6. Female, interview by author, tape recording, Worcester, MA., 27 August 1991.

7. Female, interview by author, tape recording, Worcester, MA., 9 August 1991.

8. Female, interview by author, tape recording, Worcester, MA., 13 August 1991.

9. Female, interview by author, tape recording, Worcester, MA., 5 August 1991.

10. Female, interview by author, tape recording, Worcester, MA., 26 August 1991.

11. Elizabeth Johns, interview by author, tape recording, Worcester, MA., 1 July 1991.

12. Julie Clarkson, interview by author, tape recording, Worcester, MA., 21 November 1991.

References

Baca Zinn, M. 1990. Minority families in crisis: The public discussion. In *Women, class and the feminist imagination: A socialist-feminist reader*, eds. K. Hansen and I. Philipson, 363–79. Philadelphia: Temple University Press.

Brewer, R. M. 1988. Black women in poverty: Some comments on female-headed families. *Signs: Journal of Women in Culture and Society* 13(2):331–39.

———. 1993. Theorizing race, Class and gender: The new scholarship of black feminist intellectuals and black women's labor. In *Theorizing black feminisms: The visionary pragmatism of black women*, eds. S. M. James and A. P.A. Busia, pp. 13–30. London: Routledge.

Collins, P. H. 1990. *Black feminist thought: Knowledge, consciousness, and the politics of empowerment*. London: Routledge.

Gilbert, M. R. 1993. Ties to people, bonds to place: The urban geography of low-income women's survival strategies. Ph.D. dissertation. Graduate School of Geography, Clark University, Worcester, MA.

Goldberg, G. S., and Kremen, E. 1990. *The feminization of poverty: Only in America?* New York: Greenwood Press.

Hanson, S., and Pratt. G. 1991. Job search and the occupational segregation of women. *Annals of the Association of American Geographers* 81:229–53.

———. 1995. *Gender, work, and space*. London: Routledge.

hooks, b. 1990. *Yearning: Race, gender, and cultural politics*. Boston: South End Press.

Hughes, M. A. 1989. Misspeaking truth to power: A geographical perspective on the "underclass" fallacy. *Economic Geography* 65(3):187–287.

———. 1990. Formation of the impacted ghetto: Evidence from large metropolitan areas, 1970–1980. *Urban Geography* 11(3):265–84.

Institute for Women's Policy Research. 1995. *Research in brief: Welfare to work: The job opportunities of AFDC recipients*. Washington, D.C.: Institute for Women's Policy Research.

Jackson, P., and Penrose, J., eds. 1994. *Constructions of race, place and nation*. Minneapolis, MN: University of Minnesota Press.

Jones, J. 1985. *Labor of love: Labor of sorrow*. New York: Basic Books.

Katz, M. B. 1989. *The undeserving poor: From the war on poverty to the war on welfare*. New York: Pantheon Books.

———. ed. 1993. *The "underclass" debate: views from history*. Princeton: Princeton University Press.

Keith, M., and Pile, P., eds. 1993. *Place and the politics of identity*. London: Routledge.

Kobayashi, A., and Peake, L. 1994. Unnatural discourse: "Race" and gender in geography. *Gender, Place and Culture* 1(2):225–43.

Kodras, J., and Jones, J.P., III. 1991. A contextual examination of the feminization of poverty. *Geoforum* 22(2):159–71.

Lubiano, W. 1992. Black ladies, welfare queens, and state minstrels: Ideological war by narrative means. In *Race-ing justice, En-gendering power: essays on Anita Hill, Clarence Thomas, and the construction of social reality*, ed. T. Morrison, pp. 323–63. New York: Pantheon Books.

Martin, J. R. 1994. Methodological essentialism, false difference, and other dangerous traps. *Signs: Journal of Women in Culture and Society* 19(3):630–57.

Massey, D. 1993. Power-geometry and a progressive sense of place. In *Mapping the futures: Local cultures, global change*, ed. J. Bird et al., 59–69. London: Routledge.

McLanahan, S. S., Sørensen, A., and Watson, D. 1989. Sex differences in poverty, 1950–1980. *Signs: Journal of Women in Culture and Society* 15(1):102–22.

Miller, A. 1993. Social science, social policy, and the heritage of African American families. In *The "underclass" debate: Views from history*, ed. M. B. Katz, 254–89. Princeton: Princeton University Press.

Murray, C. 1984. *Losing ground: American social policy, 1950–1980*. New York: Basic Books.

Omi, M., and Winant, H. 1986. *Racial formation in the United States: From the 1960s to the 1980s*. New York: Routledge.

Pearce, D. 1979. Women, work, and welfare: The feminization of poverty. In *Working women and families*, ed. K. W. Feinstein, 103–24. Beverly Hills: Sage.

———. 1990. Welfare is not **for** women: Why the war on poverty cannot conquer the feminization of poverty. In *Women, the state, and welfare*, ed. L. Gordon, 265–79. Madison, WI: University of Wisconsin Press.

Schor, N., and Weed, E., eds. 1994. *The essential difference*. Bloomington, IN: Indiana University Press.

Stack, C. 1974. *All our kin: Strategies for survival in a black community*. New York: Harper and Row.

Taylor, R. J. 1985. The extended family as a source of support to elderly blacks. *The Gerontologist* 25(5):488–95.

Ware, V. 1992. *Beyond the pale: White woman, racism and history*. London: Verso.

West, C. 1993. *Race matters*. Boston: Beacon Press.

Wilson, W. J. 1987. *The truly disadvantaged: The inner city, the underclass, and public policy*. Chicago: University of Chicago Press.

———. 1991. Studying inner-city social dislocation: The challenge of public agenda research. *American Sociological Review* 56:1–14.

3

Women's Life Courses, Spatial Mobility, and State Policies

Glenda Laws

My focus in this chapter is on how age and gender relations intersect to limit spatial mobility. Constraints on mobility restrict access to knowledge and power (Spain 1992). How do these restrictions affect the day-to-day lives of girls and women? And how do state policies institutionalize these restrictions? Unlike other forms of social apartheid, segregation on the basis of age is formally (under the rules of law) recognized and enforced in the United States and many other parts of the world. Children cannot begin school until a certain age. Young adults cannot enter the spaces of bars and taverns until they reach an age determined by state legislation. A driver's license similarly requires that the holder has reached a legally defined minimum age. Criteria for entry into some forms of housing are based on age. So, while we condemn discrimination on the basis of a whole range of characteristics, discrimination on the basis of age continues to be protected by state-sanctioned legal statutes that are both cause and effect of social attitudes toward people of different ages. These statutes place restrictions on where an individual can go and, in the case of driver's licenses, on how one might get there.

Particularly useful in considering the limits to women's spatial mobility are recent contributions to feminist theory that discuss the ways in which socially gendered bodies make a difference to the lives of men and women, including their experiences of the places in which they live and work. Feminist theory also reminds us that it is not too useful to talk about Woman or Man as though these categories were made up of homogeneous people. Rather, female and male identities and experiences are constructed by the intersection of gender and race, age, class, sexual orientation, and other attributes. In this chapter, I am particularly interested in how girls and women at different stages of their life course experience places and how their spatial mobility varies. My objectives in addressing these issues are to: (1) demonstrate how feminist geography can further illuminate an issue in which geographers have been long interested, namely spatial mobility; (2) show the importance of a consideration of sociospatial processes in the construction of women's identities, and therefore highlight the importance of geographical perspectives in feminist analyses; and (3) illustrate the gendered nature of state policies, focusing in particular on the ways in which they affect women's mobility. That is, I will explore both theoretical and substantive issues of concern to feminists within and outside geography.

Implicit throughout the chapter is the idea that social practices construct politically important differences between people across the life course. The income-maintenance programs discussed later in this chapter, for example, construct (usually young) single mothers as deserving of some (limited) forms of state support while older women are entitled to other forms of support via Social Security payments. In times of fiscal constraints, the differences *created by the state* between single mothers and those receiving pensions can become politically volatile. State policies clearly politicize the body at various stages of the life course. As a geographer, I am interested in the ways in which these state policies construct difference also by restricting people's spatial mobility. That is, state policies not only create categorical differences but also contribute to material differences (e.g., access to transportation, housing, jobs), which construct the recipient as different from the nonrecipient. These material differences are not only located in a spatial context, they are also at least partly determined by the spatial organization of society. It is thus important that feminists incorporate a spatial perspective into their analyses.

To understand why, and the ways in which, public policies can—and do—shape women's mobility, I will begin by drawing on several concepts that have only recently been introduced into geographic debates: first, the notions of "the body" and body politics, and second, "the life course." These are important ideas in understanding the range of experiences among women. They help us understand how human geographies, particularly the built and social environments that we inhabit, create varying opportunities for individuals and social groups and thereby contribute to the social construction of identities. I will then review the impact of income maintenance programs on women's mobility. Income-maintenance programs are particularly useful policies to look at since they vary across the life course and are therefore implicated in the construction of age-specific identities. In the conclusions, I draw out the implications of this argument for an understanding of how the spatial mobility of girls and boys, women and men, is shaped and reshaped. In doing so, I point to the advantages of a dialogue between feminism and geography and the contributions of feminist geography to these broader discourses.

Bodies and Life Courses: Why Geographers Are Interested

My concerns in this chapter fit with those of gerontologists and other social scientists interested in women's life courses and with broader concerns about body politics within feminist theory. Feminist geographers are also interested in these concepts. The essays collected by Cindi Katz and Jan Monk (1993), for example, focus upon how women's experiences of the spaces and places in which they live vary over their life course. Young women may find the nightlife of a downtown neighborhood particularly inviting, while an older woman may find it unwelcoming because (1) expectations of what an individual "should" be doing arise from social roles that correspond not just with gender but also roughly with stages in the life course, and (2) as we age we accumulate experiences that shape our own perceptions of places.[1]

A common question in geographic research agendas asks about the causes and consequences of spatial arrangements. Feminist geographers focus especially on the differential consequences of spatial arrangements for men and women and on the diverse experiences of groups of people distinguished on the basis of their age, race, class, sexual orientation, and other characteristics because geography matters to the construction of difference. The racialized landscape of North American suburbia, age-segregated retirement communities, and the inhospitableness of a city that is not wheelchair accessible are examples of spatial organizations that contribute to differentiation between social groups. Both as individual bodies and as part of the body politic, people express themselves and contribute to the social heterogeneity of places. But, as Doreen Massey (e.g., 1993) has noted, places (and space) are not simply the outcome of social practices; spatial organization—including the distribution of differentially constructed bodies—makes a difference to social practices.

Geographers need to attend to both the conceptualization and material construction of bodies because *our bodies make a difference to our experience of places:* whether we are young or old, able-bodied or disabled, Black or White in appearance does, at least partly, determine collective responses to our bodies (Dorn and Laws 1994). This is *not* to say that in any one instance, people will or will not treat someone in a particular way on the basis of their bodily appearances. Bodily differences open and close spaces of opportunity: because their bodies are sexed female and thereby subject to the threat of violence, many women will not travel alone at night; because they are old, some women will avoid certain parts of town; because of their skin color, some people find it difficult (if not impossible) to join certain clubs.

In this section, I discuss conceptualizations of bodies and life courses in order to introduce a vocabulary useful for thinking about *how people's spatial mobility is constrained by collective constructions of their bodies.*[2] Social theorists problematize the body and question its taken-for-granted status in academic work and in the politics of everyday experiences (Bordo 1993; Diprose 1994; Grosz 1994). Their message is that bodies (1) are socially constructed, (2) have material and discursive forms, and (3) are subjected to social control. Elizabeth Grosz has written extensively on the body. The following passage is a useful point of departure for reviewing the voluminous literature:

> The inscription of the body's insides and outsides is an effect of historically and politically specific signifying practices and representational systems that penetrate

it using a "social tattooing" system. Codes mark bodies and trace them in particular ways, constituting the body as a living, acting, and producing subject. In turn, bodies leave their trace in laws and codes. A history of bodies is yet to be written, but it would involve looking at the mutual relations between bodily inscription and lived experience. (Grosz 1993; 212, fn. 13)

The Social Construction of Bodies

Grosz notes that bodies are subjected to a process of social inscription or social tattooing. A much-publicized murder case in the United States illustrates this point. A young woman accused a "Black Man" of kidnapping her two children. The media picked up on this and reported it widely. It was later revealed that the woman had fabricated this story and that she had in fact killed her children. But her accusation of the wrongful doings of a Black Man were accepted—people drew on their own images of what a Black, male body was capable of doing, and many found no reason to question the woman (Lacayo 1994). Had the woman accused a White Man of kidnapping her children, we probably would have had a similar unquestioning reaction because of constructions of Man and Woman that portray Woman as caring and nurturing and therefore incapable of harming children. In its "embarrassment" at not having "seen through" the mother's account, the U.S. media went into a period of amateur psychology when it then reported on why it was so easy to accept the story and why the image of a Black Man was chosen. In these follow-up reports, the case of the construction of a Black male body as criminal was seen (to varying degrees) to be both plausible and acceptable. Because of a long history of racist images, many U.S. residents were able to accept that a Black Man would kidnap children. The Black male body, in the abstract, has been inscribed with certain attributes.

The idea that biologically sexed (male and female) bodies are marked by social codes of what those bodies can and should be like can usefully be extended to argue that biologically aged bodies are similarly socially encoded (see Laws 1995). Bodies are thus actively and socially constructed in discursive practices at a number of "sites of struggle" (e.g., state policies, the home, popular culture, or academic discourses) beyond biological and chemical processes. Media and medical attention has recently coalesced around discussions of when a woman can and cannot be a biological mother. The biological process of menopause is seen to be a marker of when a woman is "too old" to become full-time caregiver of a young child (i.e., a mother). Cases of post-menopausal women giving birth after surgical procedures have outraged many people and given rise to heated debates ("Too old to have a baby?" 1993; "Making babies after menopause," 1990). Several commentators argued that it was not right for a "middle-aged" woman to take on the responsibility of bringing up a dependent child. Yet, we routinely ask these same women to care for dependent elderly parents. Social norms thus shape what we think a body can and cannot do.

Material and Discursive Bodies

When society tattoos bodies to give them meaning, it creates constructions of bodies that are simultaneously part of and independent of bodily forms. Grosz notes this when she comments on the role of the representational systems that create bodies. In the case mentioned above, the discursive construction of Black Man played upon images independent of any particular body—there was in fact no material body that corresponded to the description given by the accuser, but millions of people knew exactly who she meant. One reporter noted that "a black man in a knit cap" fulfilled "everyone's most familiar image of the murderous criminal" (Lacayo 1994; 46). Consideration needs to be given then to the discrepancies between the material and discursive form. The majority of young Black men is not engaged in criminal activity. The notion of a frail elderly woman in need of supportive living arrangements is accurate in some cases, but the vast majority of older women live in their own homes. At the same time the social construction of Woman as nurturer and caregiver needs to be dispensed with; women participate in acts that undermine this image.[3]

The role of gendered representations is explored in the feminist literature concerned with the social location of embodied identities. In this literature, the metaphorical location and mobility of women is problematized. bell hooks's (1984) discussion of speaking from the margins and pushing toward the center is indicative of the arguments being made by Black feminists. Sandra Harding (1991) uses somewhat similar arguments when she describes standpoint epistemologies. The view "from below," of the oppressed, is different from that of those in the center of the science establishment. Betty Friedan and others have similarly criticized those feminist discourses that have pushed the lives of older women to the periphery (Friedan 1993). Both popular and social science literatures are thus implicated in the creation of public identities because they centralize some bodily images (the successful working woman or the happy mother) while marginalizing others (older women, single parents). Marginalization occurs in two broad ways. First, dominant discourses might ignore or exclude some bodily identities. Second, these same discourses might discuss some embodied identities in almost purely negative tones. Nancy Fraser and Linda Gordon (1992, 327) capture this second approach with the following example:

> postindustrial culture has called up a new personification of dependency: the black, unmarried, teenaged, welfare-dependent mother. This image has usurped the symbolic space previously occupied by the housewife, the pauper, the native, and the slave, while absorbing and condensing their connotations. Black, female, a pauper, not a worker, a housewife and mother, yet practically a child herself—the new stereotype partakes of virtually every quality that has been coded historically antithetical to independence. Condensing multiple, often contradictory meanings of dependency, it is a powerful ideological trope that simultaneously organizes diffuse cultural anxieties and dissimulates their social bases.

The verbal and visual language that we use to describe people not only reflects their embodied identities, but also constructs them.

Bodies, Social Control, and Spatial Mobility

The social construction of bodies in both their material and discursive forms is important to all types of social control. Constraints are placed upon what people can do on the basis of embodied identities. Racialized, gendered, and aged identities restrict the activities of individuals and social groups in both the short and long run. Society imposes control through a number of institutionalized mechanisms including the family, schools, church, and state. These institutions are called into operation when acts of transgression are perceived to be threatening to individuals or social order. For example, a family may restrict a young girl's movements out of genuine concern that her actions might result in her being harmed; in doing so, the family ensures that social images of women-as-vulnerable are reproduced. The welfare state disciplines unwed mothers, an increasingly visible class of transgressive bodies, by paying them below poverty-level benefits.

Central to social disciplining are restrictions upon spatial mobility (Foucault 1977). This is perhaps most obviously illustrated in the institution of prisons. The metaphor of a prison is often used to describe the restrictions faced by members of households in which an abusive parent or partner controls mobility. Dominant identities are constructed in relation to less-powerful ones and social positions are all important to the construction of power. Grosz (1992, 249) captures the essence of the arguments inspired by Foucault's analysis of bodies and social control when she writes: "As a hinge between the population and the individual, the body, its distribution, habits, alignments, pleasures, norms, and ideals are the ostensible objects of governmental regulations, and the city is a key tool." Urban geographies, and the body's mobility around these geographies, are key to understanding social control and discipline.

How do patriarchal social structures and institutions create embodied female identities, and how do these in turn limit women's spatial mobility? Iris Marion Young (1989, 62) writes that "if there are particular modalities of feminine bodily comportment and motility, then it must follow that there are also particular modalities of feminine spatiality. Feminine existence lives space as *enclosed* or confining, as having a *dual* structure and the feminine existent experiences herself as *positioned* in space." (emphasis in original)

Feminist geographers, with their focus on socio-spatial processes, can contribute to an understanding of the construction of the body since (male and female) bodies are constructed in space, bodies build spaces, and spaces imbue bodies with meaning. Consider as an example patterns of residential segregation. People who live in some parts of town have a certain public identity; those who live on "the other side of the tracks" have a different identity. Those people with the means choose to live in certain places because locations reflect social standing (usually determined by income levels) and public identities.

Our bodies are imbued with identity by virtue of where we reside. At the same time, we use the labor of our bodies to create identity in our residences. We can change our identity to some extent by moving—we establish independence from our parents by moving into our own home; as we become more financially secure, we may move from a rented apartment to an owner-occupied house; we might move from the inner city to a suburban location with a yard if we have children or pets. But Young's idea of feminine (and therefore masculine) spatialities should alert us to gender-differentiated identities associated with particular spaces. We must consider how these spatially constituted identities might be enabling—we should be careful of not essentializing the female experience as one of always-constrained mobility. Traditional geographic concerns with accessibility and movement must be recast in terms that will allow their gendered dimensions to be exposed.

How do bodies move through space and what constrains their movement? So-called time geography is perhaps the most explicit geographical approach to this issue. Time-space prisms show the spatial extent of an individual's movement through a certain time period (usually a day but the idea can easily be extended to a life course) (figure 3.1). My first exposure to this idea was that of a comparison between men's and women's daily activity paths. The diagrammatic representation showed that a woman traveled shorter distances during the day than a man because of her household responsibilities, which kept her tied to her home. This fitted well with my own upbringing because I had a stay-at-home mum who did not drive. This model fits less well, however, with the students I now teach, many of whom have two working parents each of whom has a car. The general question behind this model, nevertheless, still has utility: how are people's mobility patterns constrained by various social structures and roles?[4] People's freedom to move is constricted because of their gender, race, income, physical ability, mental ability, age, and stage of the life course. It is to the issue of the life course that I now turn.

Life Courses and Spatial Mobility

People are more spatially mobile at certain points in their lives than at others. Commonly, young middle-class adults in the United States move when establishing their first independent households, for example. These households also tend to have preschool-aged members, and so there is a relatively high degree of mobility among very young children and people in their twenties. This mobility is as much a function of the social clock as it is of the biological clock. Young adults may be expected to marry and/or go to college, both of which may entail new household formations away from the parental domicile. Another peak in residential mobility occurs around the retirement ages as people choose to move away from their workplace residence to a new home. This might be a distant move to another state, or it might be a local move into a smaller house more suitable for a family without young children. Geographers interested in spatial mobility have studied the migrations of peoples between

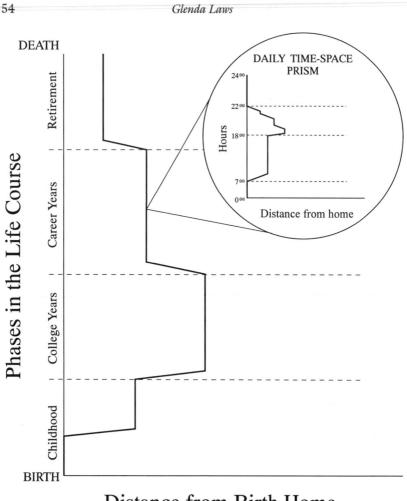

Fig. 3.1. Life course time-space prism.

different countries and regions, the residential choice behaviors of inter- and intra-urban movers, and the journey-to-work patterns of urban residents.

Feminist geographers are particularly interested in the ways in which people's socially ascribed gender roles make a difference to their mobility patterns. For example, Radcliffe (1993) notes gender-specific migration patterns among southern Andean peasant communities. The differences between men's and women's migration decisions are based upon the division of labor within households, under which women are more likely to find their way into waged labor markets than are men. Especially important are the opportunities for domestic work for women in urban areas. The mobility described in residential mobility studies (feminist and otherwise) is relatively largescale and relatively permanent. These studies do not describe small-scale movements, either in spatial or temporal terms. People's diurnal mobility patterns, captured in journey-to-work studies, also vary according to gender and stage in the life course. Johnston-Anumonwo (1992), among others, has demonstrated that women's mobility within urban areas may be restricted by the household responsibilities that keep them relatively close to home. Gill Valentine (1992) and Rachel Pain (1991) argue that women's fear of violence causes them to modify their spatial behavior (e.g., not going out after dark unless escorted). Biological and social "clocks" can work together to limit the spatial mobility of an older woman. If her health deteriorates, she may become less ambulatory; her social age may make her unwelcome in some places.To provide a comprehensive understanding of spatial mobility, geographers must therefore attend to various scales of movement (international, regional, and local), different temporal scales (long-term, short-term, and diurnal), differences in the motivations for and consequences of moves by men and women, and variations among men and women in their experiences of mobility. At the same time, researchers interested in the construction of women's embodied identities must acknowledge the importance of the spatiality of women's lives and the restrictions upon this spatiality. Doreen Massey (1993, 61) reminds us of this in her discussion of "power-geometry":

> For different social groups and different individuals are placed in very distinct ways in relation to these flows and interconnections [described in discussions of time-space compression]. This point concerns not merely the issue of who moves and who doesn't . . . it is also about power in relation *to* the flows and the movement. Different social groups have distinct relations to this anyway-differentiated mobility; some are more in charge of it than others; some initiate flows and movement, others don't; some are more on the receiving end of it than others; some are effectively imprisoned by it.

Income-Maintenance Policies and Constraints on Women's Spatial Mobility

The contemporary welfare state molds and is molded by women's actions. The dialectical relationships between human agency and social institutions like the state are part of what Grosz (1994, 144) has described as a "system of corporeal production." State policies inscribe bodies with social identities. Programs to which some groups are entitled while others are excluded draw upon and create particular embodied identities—indeed create difference—around who deserves and does not deserve state assistance. In this section, I begin a preliminary discussion of how state policies, especially those focusing on women's incomes, affect the mobility of women at different stages of their life course or at various socially constructed ages, and thus create and reproduce difference.

It is naive to think of the state as being gender neutral in either its evolution or its impacts. Policies are more and less explicit in their treatment of men and women. Often a universal citizen/body is assumed to exist, and thus there are no attempts to consider the different ways men and women might be affected by an initiative. This body is typed on the male experience of economy and polity. I do not, however, subscribe to the idea that there is a grand conspiracy at work against women. There are both intended and unintended consequences of policies. Again, it is worth listening to Grosz:

> Women are no more subject to this system of corporeal production than men; they are no more cultural, no more natural than men. Patriarchal power relations do not function to make women the objects of disciplinary control while men remain outside of disciplinary surveillance. It is a question not of more or less but of differential production. (Grosz 1994, 144)

Constraining or enabling the movement of bodies is one of the (intended and unintended) consequences of state policies. Few policies are as explicit in this regard as immigration laws. More often, state policies are more subtle in the ways in which they limit mobility. The intent of many income-maintenance programs, for example, is not to limit mobility, but the below poverty-level payments in fact ensure that the recipient is severely constrained in both short- and long-term moves. Since there are various programs for people at different stages of their lives, income-maintenance programs are particularly appropriate to my interests in how state policies might limit mobility over the life course. I do not want to imply that bodies move or do not move merely according to the dictates of state policies. Women (and men) work hard to have state policies shaped and reshaped, and they protest the outcomes of state policies.

I have been arguing that limits upon women's spatial mobility have implications for their acquisition of spatial knowledge/power, and thus can influence women's broader social roles. It is difficult to move over space without financial resources. It costs money to own a car, a necessary element of mobility in parts of the United States. It costs money to go to the cinema or to drive to a store. It costs substantially more to go on a long vacation, move to a new city, or buy a house. Just as money makes for social mobility, so too does it affect spatial mobility. While around 90 percent of U.S. households have access to at least one car, among households with a family income of less than $10,000 per year (in 1989), 48 percent did not have a car (table 3.1). Even if a car is available, women are less likely than men to have a license and the gender gap in licenses varies between age groups (table 3.2). Low-income women are the most likely to be limited in their use of private cars.

To examine the impact of government policies on incomes, it is best to consider several of the most politically visible and volatile income-maintenance

TABLE 3.1
Percentage of Car Ownership by Family Income, 1983 and 1989
($1989)

Family Income	1983	1989
< 10,000	50.5	51.6
10,000–19,999	83.2	82.1
20,000–29,999	93.3	94.4
30,000–49,999	97.0	95.5
> 50,000	96.4	96.8

SOURCE: *Statistical Abstract of the United States*, 1993, Table 751.

TABLE 3.2
Distribution of Licensed Drivers by Sex
Percentage in each age group, 1989

Age	Male	Female
UNDER 16	01.3	01.1
16–19	56.5	51.9
20–24	92.7	86.4
25–29	96.7	91.8
30–34	94.4	90.3
35–39	96.7	92.0
40–44	99.0	91.9
45–49	97.7	88.6
50–54	96.0	84.8
55–59	96.0	81.9
60–64	94.2	78.3
65–69	91.5	72.8
> 70	86.2	49.9

SOURCE: Federal Highway Administration, *Highway Statistics*, 1989, US Government Printing Office, p. 32.

programs in the United States.[5] My point here is that low incomes restrict women's mobility in a society that depends to a great extent on private transportation. Government policies that provide only a subsistence wage thus deny people opportunities to move freely through space. The two programs that I will focus upon are Social Security and Aid to Families with Dependent Children. Both of these were established with the passage of the federal Social Security Act in 1935. And both are the subject of heated debate in the U.S. Congress as the federal government seeks to slash public spending in an effort to reduce the budget deficit. These debates often draw attention to the position of recipients of aid along the life course: should teenage girls become mothers? should we spend money on older people (via Social Security) while the number of children living in poverty grows? Gordon (1994, 293) describes the gender-stratified system of social security in the United States under which there are "superior" and "inferior" programs, noting that the superior programs "are disproportionately white and male and they were designed to be so, because that was the dominant image of citizenship in 1925." Citizenship is an embodied concept, and those bodies that do not fit easily with this historically constituted image challenge the concept of social security and welfare.

Social Security benefits in old age are a function of contributions made during an individual's participation in the waged labor force. Working-age people "save" for their old age; a larger amount set aside during a person's working career will result in a larger pension. A substantial proportion of women do not have continuous careers because they take time out for child rearing. When they are employed, women earn less than men and have less opportunity for participation in private pension schemes (because of part-time work, etc.) (table 3.3). A woman's lower earnings at one stage of her life course have very real implications for her well-being at a later stage. A 1992 report by the American Association of Retired Persons (Smith 1992) showed that in 1990, a retired woman worker had a monthly Social Security benefit that was only 76 percent of a retired male's. And since women live longer than men, their minimal incomes and savings must go further. While 14 percent of all women over sixty-five are classified by the U.S. Census Bureau as poor, more than 23 percent of older women living alone are poor (U.S. Bureau of the Census 1991). Obviously this has implications for the mobility choices available to older, especially poor, women. It may be difficult for the older woman to move into a supportive living environment such as a retirement community or a nursing home. Federal Medicare can assist in the cases of the very poor if the woman requires nursing care.

Another problem for women arises in the case of divorce. Women raising children after a divorce are penalized relative to the children's fathers because of restrictions on claims upon a former husband's Social Security benefits. Nancy Folbre (1994, 208–9) describes the Social Security system as particularly unfair to mothers: "A male wage-earner who divorces his wife and contri-

TABLE 3.3
Pension Plan Coverage of Workers by Age and Sex, 1991
Percentage of workers with coverage

	Male	Female
Total	43	37
15–24 years	13	12
25–44	47	42
45–64	56	47
65 and over	21	22

SOURCE: *Statistical Abstract of the United States 1991*, Table 596

butes a negligible amount to his own children's expenses will receive far more income in old age through the Social Security system than the single mother who remains largely unemployed, or employed at low wages, because she devoted her time and money to raising children."

Social Security has undergone many changes since its inception in the mid-thirties, some of which have been gendered in their consequences. After reviewing the evolution of the Social Security Act, Abramowitz (1988, 254) concluded that "intentionally or not, the 1939 provisions presumed and supported the male breadwinner/female homemaker family model, encouraged women to choose traditional family life over work or alternative family forms, affirmed women's economic dependence on men, and otherwise enforced patriarchal arrangements that perpetuated the subordination of women." By the early eighties, this situation had changed somewhat so that working women were rewarded more by Social Security payments than nonworking women, and single women received slightly more in monthly payments than widowed or divorced women. Social Security rewarded those women who did not follow a traditional family path. But changes under the Omnibus Budget Reconciliation Act and the 1983 Social Security Amendments altered this state of affairs. Since 1975, there had been a guaranteed minimum grant for low-income and sporadically employed people. The majority of recipients were women, and so they were the most vulnerable when the program was abolished in early 1982 (Abramowitz 1988, 369–73).

While debates over Social Security are indeed important in contemporary politics, a more controversial program is public assistance to single mothers and their families through Aid to Families with Dependent Children (AFDC), a program explicitly geared toward women in their child-rearing years. Significantly less money is spent on this program than Social Security but it is a prime target for politicians advocating budget cuts. AFDC has become synonymous with the derogatory use of the term "welfare." Fraser and Gordon (1992, 46) note that receipt of "welfare" [read AFDC] is usually considered grounds for disrespect, a threat to, rather than a realization of, citizenship. The program serves women and their children, and thus women on welfare are not deemed citizens in the same way as those who work.

Although it has not reached the stage of policy formulation at the time of writing, the debate over welfare reform in the United States is an excellent example of how gender and age relations intersect in public thinking. There are many competing proposals, but one idea that has resurfaced in several iterations is the proposal that teenage girls be denied welfare benefits if they leave their parents' homes. Many conservative politicians argue that teenagers calculate the costs and benefits of early pregnancies and decide that AFDC payments are a route to spatial mobility, since they conclude that they can get their own apartment by having a child. Whether or not this is the case is unclear. But there may be strategic reasons why a teenage girl would need to leave her parental home (e.g., abuse), and the removal of AFDC payments might curtail these efforts. Regardless of the motivations of individual recipi-

ents, however, draconian welfare reforms of the sort being discussed deny the
teenager an identity independent of her own parents. This is an explicit denial
of a young woman's "right" to spatial mobility, at least, in terms of choice of
residence.

As retirees and widows in old age and as mothers in their younger years,
women play roles scripted by social institutions and practices. The text of state
policies creates discursive bodies that women resemble or imitate in their social
practices. At the moment, an unmarried woman of any age can apply for
AFDC if she is a legal resident in the United States. Current political discourses, however, portray unmarried teenage mothers who refuse to reveal the
identity of their child's father and/or who are immigrants as less deserving of
a share of the wealth accumulated by the body politic. Their status as deserving
citizens is challenged because they do not conform to dominant social practices
(e.g., delaying child birth until an "appropriate" stage of the life course, i.e.,
after marriage). For older women, the rewards of rearing a family and not
participating in the paid labor force are minimal Social Security payments and
the threat of a life in poverty. Those women who conformed to social expectations by marrying might be better off than someone who took a less-tradi-
tional path, since they might share in their spouse's private pension. Income-
maintenance policies that assume that women will play certain roles at various
stages of their life thus restrict opportunities for both short-term and longer-
term mobility.

Conclusions

Daphne Spain argues that women's limited access to particular spaces has circumscribed their acquisition of knowledge and their involvement in important
decision-making processes. It is not difficult then to see how limited spatial
mobility reinforces women's dependence upon men; if women are denied access to high-paying jobs, they become economically dependent upon men;
if they are denied independent access to downtown after dark, they become
dependent on (usually male) escorts. Constraints on spatial mobility are both
oppressive and controlling:

> Spatial segregation is one of the mechanisms by which a group with greater power
> can maintain its advantage over a group with less power. By controlling access to
> knowledge and resources through the control of space, the dominant group's abil-
> ity to retain and reinforce its position is enhanced. Thus, spatial boundaries con-
> tribute to the unequal status of women. For women to become more
> knowledgeable, *they must also change places*. (Spain 1992, 15–16, emphasis added)

To be mobile, women require access to resources and independence. This
chapter has suggested that women's freedom to move is severely curtailed by

the different roles they play across the life course and by state policies that institutionalize these roles.

Feminist discussions of the body and body politics demonstrate that comportment, mobility, and identity are socially defined and that spatial mobility is not simply a matter of voluntary movements. Feminist theory invites geographers to specify the bodies they represent by making clear whether, and how, the bodies are constructed male or female, Black or White, young or aged. Social roles make a difference to our experiences of places and more attention needs to be given to how social identities limit people's mobility—both in their individual lives and in their lives as a member of different social groups (see Massey 1993).

But this perspective does not imply that women (or other social groups) do not make choices about their mobility. People struggle against restrictive practices and develop strategies for changing their lives. And, important for political strategies, people's interests do vary across their life courses. While accessible day care may not seem of major importance to young women without children, at another time in their lives this may become an issue around which they are prepared to organize. Older women may enter political debates about conditions in long-term care facilities or about Social Security payments. The degree to which income limits a woman's mobility will vary during her life, and so she may be more or less involved in some struggles at different points. Other factors also limit a woman's mobility. Household responsibilities have been shown by several authors to limit a woman's activity spaces. Fear of violent attack also restricts women's movements. Both of these issues can be addressed by state policy. Programs that provide dependent care can release women from the home during the day (e.g., Fincher 1993). Efforts to create safe cities can likewise create opportunities for women (Werkele and Whitzman 1995).

But often stereotypes about gendered roles are reinforced in state policies. Public policies often assume an unpaid caregiver is available in the home. More often than not, that caregiver is a woman, and her responsibilities at home seriously limit her opportunities for work and leisure activities beyond the immediate neighborhood. The failure to provide reasonable incomes to women caring for dependent children forces them to live in poverty and limits their access to a range of opportunities including work, entertainment, housing, and medical and other social services. Perhaps most insidious here is the impact of the cutoff lines for eligibility for some services such that the working poor have less opportunities than the nonworking poor.

The variations in women's experiences across the life course, and thus the construction of difference among women, mean that we cannot assume that political actions to make movement easier for young women (e.g., providing affordable day care) will necessarily have the same effect for older women (who may need assisted transport services). Massey's (1993, 62) observation that "mobility and control of some groups can actively weaken other people. Differential mobility can weaken the leverage of the already weak" needs to be considered in terms of the differential treatment of women across the life course and the subsequent political construction of difference. Current debates about intergenerational equity and justice pit retirees against younger people as arguments are made that state policies are unnecessarily generous to well-to-do older people while poverty rates among children continue to increase. So, according to this line of reasoning, state policies are limiting the mobility opportunities of children of the poor while they maintain a comfortable life for some middle-class older people.

The degree to which state policies have these impacts varies according to the intersection of a number of social attributes including race, gender, class, ethnicity, age, sexual orientation and ability. The politics of mobility called for by Massey requires careful attention to how these attributes might structure the mobility of individuals and social groups in particular circumstances. It requires that we explore both the enabling and constraining possibilities created by state policies.

Notes

1. We need also acknowledge the importance of cohort effects. A woman in her seventies in the late 1990s was socialized in a different era than a woman in her twenties. That is, it is not only stage in the life course, but also cohort factors, which must be considered in understanding why some women are more or less spatially mobile than others.

2. Again, I think it is important to emphasize that I am discussing collective identities associated with particular bodies or stages in the life course. It is easy to come up with personal anecdotes that refute the general argument ("My old mum is really active and not afraid to go out at night"; "I don't stay at home at night simply because I am a woman"). Such anecdotal refutations do not, however, help us understand more general processes at work. Social scientists are interested in describing broad trends. While acknowledging individual experiences with which we may be familiar, it is important that we acknowledge that not all women (or men) fit into anecdotal characterizations (just as there are individual exceptions to social science "rules").

3. The correspondence between discursive and material bodies needs to be noted. In constructing particular embodied identities (e.g., mother, rebellious youth), social norms encourage people to fulfill certain roles in their day-to-day lives. As we will note below, these social and discursive constructions of female bodies have very real policy implications. Representations of women as the nurturing center of the nuclear family led to the so-called family wage and policies which encouraged stay-at-home moms (Folbre, 1994). Such policies impact differentially on women of different class standings. Women without the skills required by the prevailing job market may be forced into such low-wage jobs that they cannot afford child care. Instead they turn to public assistance programs which then stigmatize them as socially dependent and lazy.

4. Gillian Rose (1993) disagrees and criticizes this approach as being masculinist in that it assumes a space through which freedom is unrestricted and therefore draws on a

male-candor view of space. However, I feel that there is scope within time-geography to account for various constraints on people.

5. The discussion of policy debates reflects their status at the time this chapter was completed. The Editors decided not to alter or update Glenda's text after her untimely death in the summer of 1996.

References

Abramowitz, M. 1988, *Regulating the lives of women*, Boston: South End Press.

Bordo, S. 1993, *Unbearable weight: Feminism, western culture and the body*, Berkeley: University of California Press.

Diprose, R. 1994, *The bodies of women: Ethics, embodiment and sexual difference*, London: Routledge.

Dorn, M., and Laws, G. 1994, Social theory, body politics and medical geography: Extending Kearns' invitation, *The Professional Geographer* 46(1): 106–10.

Fincher, R. 1993, "Women, the state and the life course in Australia," in Katz, C. and Monk, J., eds. *Full circles: Geographies of women over the life course*, London: Routledge: 243–63.

Folbre, N. 1994, *Who pays for the kids? Gender and the structures of constraint*, London: Routledge.

Fraser, N. and Gordon, L. 1992, Contract versus charity: Why is there no social citizenship in the United States? *Socialist Review* 22(3): 45–68.

Friedan, B. 1993, *The fountain of age*, New York: Simon and Schuster.

Foucault, M. 1977, *Discipline and punish. The birth of the prison*, Harmondsworth: Penguin.

Gordon, L. 1994, *Pitied but not entitled*, New York: The Free Press.

Grosz, E. 1992, Bodies-cities, In Colomina, B., ed, *Sexuality and space*, pp. 241–54. Princeton, NJ: Princeton Papers on Architecture.

Grosz, E. 1993, Bodies and knowledge: Feminism and the crisis of reason, In Alcoff, L. and Potter, E., eds, *Feminist epistemologies*, 187–216. London: Routledge.

Grosz, E. 1994, *Volatile bodies: Toward a corporeal feminism*, Bloomington: Indiana University Press.

Harding, S. 1989, *Whose science? Whose knowledge?* Ithaca, NY: Cornell University Press.

hooks, b. 1984, *Feminist theory: From margin to center*, Boston: South End Books.

Johnston-Anumonwo, I. 1992, The influence of household type on gender differences in work trip distance, *The Professional Geographer* 44(2): 161–69.

Katz, C. and Monk, J., eds, 1993, *Full circles: Geographies of women over the life course*, London: Routledge.

Lacayo, R. 1994, Stranger in the shadows, *Time* November 14: 46–47.

Laws, G. 1995, Theorizing ageism: Lessons from postmodernism and feminism, *The Gerontologist* 35(1): 112–18.

Making babies after menopause, 1990, *Newsweek* November 5, 116(19): 75.

Massey, D. 1993, Power-geometry and a progressive sense of space, In Bird, J.; Curtis, B.; Putnam, T.; Robertson, G.; and Tickner, L., eds, *Mapping the futures: Local cultures, global change*, 59–69. London: Routledge.

Pain, R. 1991, Space, sexual violence, and social control: Integrating geographical and feminist analysis of women's fear of crime, *Progress in Human Geography* 15(4): 415–31.

Radcliffe, S. 1993, The role of gender in peasant migration: Conceptual issues from the Peruvian Andes, In Momsen, J., and Kinnaird, V., eds, *Different places, different voices: Gender and development in Africa, Asia and Latin America*, 278–87. London: Routledge.

Rose, G. 1993, *Feminism and human geography*, Minneapolis, MN: University of Minnesota Press.

Smith, M. 1992, *Statement of the American Association of Retired Persons on women and social security before the Subcommittee on Social Security, Committee on Ways and Means, U.S. House of Representatives, April 8*. Washington, DC: Association of American Retired Persons.

Spain, D. 1992, *Gendered spaces*, Chapel Hill, NC: University of North Carolina Press.

Too old to have a baby? 1993, *Lancet* February 6, 341 (8841): 344–45.

U.S. Bureau of the Census 1991, Money incomes of households, families, and persons in the United States: 1990, *Current Population Reports* P-60, 174, Washington, D.C.: Government Printing Office.

Valentine, G. 1992, Images of danger: Women's sources of information about the spatial distribution of male violence, *Area* 24(1): 22–29.

Werkele, G., and Whitzman, C. 1995, *Safe cities: Guidelines for planning, design and management*, New York: Van Nostrand Reinhold.

Young, I. M. 1989, Throwing like a girl: A phenomenology of feminine body comportment, motility, and spatiality, In Allen, J. and Young, I. M., eds, *The thinking muse: Feminism and modern french philosophy*, 51–70. Bloomington: Indiana University Press.

4

Making Space: Separatism and Difference

Gill Valentine

A rejection of grand universalizing theory has been at the heart of many feminist critiques of academia (e.g., Stanley and Wise 1983). In particular, feminists have challenged theoretical discourses that claim objectivity while articulating a masculinist position that excludes women as producers of knowledge (Barrett and Phillips 1992; Rose 1993). In the late 1980s and 1990s, poststructuralist and postmodern critiques of the "grand theories" of positivism, humanism, and Marxism have marked a more wide-sweeping and powerful attack on modern Western social theory (although often ignoring or undervaluing the original contribution of many feminists to this project). "Rather than stressing the essential 'sameness' of phenomena that allegedly arises because these phenomena are all expressions of the same centre, the same basic organising principles, post modernism urges a great sensitivity to 'differences' that exist between phenomena in all sorts of ways both obvious and subtle" (Cloke et al. 1991, 171). Many feminists have embraced or been sympathetic to these critiques. Consequently, between the 1970s and 1990s there has been what Barrett and Phillips (1992, 6) term an "almost paradigmatic shift" in feminist thought—away from essentialist conceptualizations of "woman" towards recognizing gender as a regulatory fiction (Fuss 1988; Butler 1990); and away from focusing on patriarchy as the source of all women's oppression toward recognizing the complex and historical intersection of gender, race, class, and sexuality (hooks 1984, 1991). In particular, feminism has been exposed as a "site of differences" (Rose 1993, 150). As Gillian Rose (1993, 151) argues: "The impact of black and lesbian feminism is evident in the recognition that everywhere all women are subject to constitution not only by gender but by sexuality and by class, and by race and by religion, and by a whole range of other social relations."

This has provoked painful divisions between feminists who have taken up different positions on the issue of difference. Some writers (Delphy 1992; Jackson 1992) claim that the deconstruction of the category "woman" ignores the material "realities" of patriarchy, and undermines the very project of feminism by denying "women" a position from which to speak. Jackson (1992, 31), for example, claims that "the logical outcome of post-modern feminism is post feminism." Others have responded to the development of postmodern feminist thought by viewing it as a positive retheorization that offers the possibility of destablizing the very "binary opposition between men and women that gives the category woman its meaning" (Barrett and Phillips 1992, 8). While other writers are picking a path between these camps—trying to acknowledge "difference" while not completely losing sight of the possibilities of collective political projects.

Whisman (1993) argues that while it is important to recognize that we all have a web of multiple identities that are shifting and contingent and a loyalty to a multiplicity of projects around which we construct fictions, sometimes we need "to maximize," to borrow Anne Snitow's (1990) phrase, a shared identity, to proclaim common needs and goals. One example is by mobilizing the identity "woman" in order to challenge male violence. Whisman also recognizes the danger inherent in this strategy, namely that the mobilization of a particular identity can lead to a sense of "groupness" or "unity" being constructed that ultimately privileges sameness over difference. She therefore reiterates Snitow's argument that while sometimes it may be politically expedient to maximize shared identities, at other times we need "to minimize" them by pushing against their boundaries, refusing to be controlled by them, and expanding ways of being.

This chapter uses the concept of maximizing/minimizing a shared identity to explore lesbian feminist attempts to produce non-heteropatriarchal space in rural areas (for a contrasting study of an attempt by lesbians to create an oppositional sphere in urban space, see Meoño-Picado, chapter 15 of this volume). Focusing on the attempts of some U.S. lesbian feminists in the 1970s and early 1980s to maximize their shared identities "woman" and "lesbian" through the spatial strategy of separatism, the chapter begins by exploring some of the ideals behind these movements. It then goes on to examine some of the tensions that arose in specific rural "lesbian lands" as a result of this privileging of sameness over difference. Using a range of examples, the chapter considers some of the different ways that "community" members began to refuse to be controlled by (or minimize) the identities "lesbian" and "woman" and to push against them by mobilizing performances of "other" identities in these places (for a very different consideration of the issues of identity and community in a rural space see Watkins, chapter 18, this volume).

Like much women's history, there is limited material recording lesbian separatist communities. One, if not the only attempt to document them is *Lesbian Lands* by Joyce Cheney (1985). This is a collection of chapters, each telling the story of a different womyn's project. Cheney (1985) began collecting material (letters, flyers, and so on) on women's communities in 1976 while living and working in one. In 1981, two years after her community dissolved, she set out to travel around other "lesbian lands" in order to record their experiences, and she organized two Lesbians on Land workshops. Cheney's (1985) research carried out in the early 1980s provides the main source of information for this chapter.

Maximizing a Lesbian Feminist Identity:
Spatial Strategies of Separatism

In the 1970s some radical feminists began to identify heterosexuality as the root of all women's (lesbian, bisexual, and heterosexual) oppression and to argue that separating from heteropatriarchal society was the only way of dealing with it. According to Faderman (1991, 207),

> Radical feminism propounded the behaviourist view of sexuality: as in a utopian socialist society where the individual could be conditioned to be nonviolent, noncompetitive, incorruptible, so too could women be conditioned to change their attitudes and desires. They could exit from the patriarchy through severing their relationships with men, which were seen as the cornerstone of the subordination of women, and they could learn not only how to make a new society with women, but also how to respond sexually to women.

In other words, heterosexual desire, like the institution of heterosexuality itself, was constructed and hence could be "undone." Feminism was the theory, lesbianism the practice (Abbott and Love 1972; Brown 1976). In this way, lesbian feminism tried both to fix lesbians as a stable minority group and to liberate the lesbian in every woman by encouraging women through consciousness-raising groups to choose not to be heterosexual. "Feminism provided the ideological glue which wedded these two sometimes contradictory impulses" (Stein 1992, 38).

In order to avoid maintaining or perpetuating patriarchy in any way and to enable women to construct a new society beyond the influence of men, some lesbian feminists adopted the spatial strategy of distancing themselves from mainstream society by establishing separatist communities that excluded all heterosexual and gay men. Although some women-only communities were established in urban areas, for example in Toronto, the aim of separatism was seen as best fulfilled in rural areas: first, because spatial isolation in the country meant that it was easier for women to be self-sufficient and purer in their practices than in the city, and second, because essentialist notions about women's closeness to nature meant that the countryside was identified as a female space. In contrast, the "man-made" city was blamed for draining women's energy. Faderman (1991) points out that this philosophy was reflected in women's fiction of this period. For example, in *Demeter Flower* (1980) by Rochelle Singer, male civilization is destroyed by nature, allowing women a new beginning. In Sally Gearhart's *The Wanderground* (1985), nature protects women, giving them the freedom to wander freely. In the 1970s, therefore, "many separatists established communal farms and became, as one of their 1970s journals called them, country women" (Faderman 1991, 238). This was an important social movement at the time and led to the establishment of a whole circuit of communal farms or "lesbian lands" in the United States. (Faderman 1991; Bell and Valentine 1995).

Separatists established land trusts to make land available to women forever. This control of space, they believed, was essential because it would give women the freedom to articulate a lesbian feminist identity, to create new ways of living, and to work out new ways of relating to the environment. These quotations from "lesbian land" residents testify to this experience:

> It feels very real in the city, not having enough women's space to go to. It's a constant struggle to have a space that we control. (Resident of A Woman's Place, in Cheney 1985, 23)

> We view our maintaining lesbian space and protecting these acres from the rape of man and his chemicals as a political act of active resistance. Struggling with each other to work through our patriarchal conditioning, and attempting to work and live together in harmony with each other and nature. (Resident of Wisconsin Womyn's Land Cooperative, in Cheney 1985, 132)

> Best of all, there is time and space for a total renewal of ourselves, our connections to each other and our earth. (Resident of Wisconsin Womyn's Land Cooperative, in Cheney 1985, 132)

These communities attempted to establish a lesbian feminist society in many different ways. Each attempted to establish nonhierarchical ways of organizing themselves and to be self-sufficient by developing their own economic institutions and skills, so that there was no need to go back into patriarchal society. Much energy was put into building new forms of dwelling and relearning old skills, such as firemaking, herbal medicine, and other survival skills. The communities also sought to articulate their identity by developing a women's culture (in terms of language, music, books, and herstories).

Many of these lesbian lands also had a strong spiritual dimension. In keeping with their identification with nature, many of the communities celebrated the full moon, equinox, solstice, and candlemas with ritual circles and used astrology and tarot readings (Warren 1980). As Faderman explains,

> Their idealized models were those ancient cultures, whether in myth or reality, in which women held secular power along with religious power. Lesbian-feminist spirituality was to resurrect the matriarchy, which would eliminate all of the destructive institutions of patriarchy— economic, political, sexual, educational, and return society to the maternal principle in which life is nurtured. (Faderman 1991, 227)

In particular, the emphasis was on goddess worship and on witchcraft, both traditions that were identified as women-centered and as symbolizing resistance against misogyny and patriarchy (Ruether 1975; Ehrenreich and English 1973). In this way, "separate feminist spirituality is not only linked to a personal search for meaning and greater inwardness but is often closely connected with the acceptance of social responsibility and political activism" (King 1993, 116). This is reflected in these quotes from residents of lesbian lands:

> We chant and sometimes share the names of our matrilineage. "I am Maryann, daughter of Mary, daughter of Mamie, daughter of MaryJane, daughter of Mary." (Resident of A Woman's Place, in Cheney 1985, 21)

> We do have a basic ritual. We open the circle with a blessing and a purification, similar to Dianic. We begin with the oldest to the youngest. Lots of the time we use the salt water purification. Each one cleanses the other woman and takes away her negative energy. (Resident of the Pagoda, in Cheney 1985, 113)

> Each spring we were directed to do a medicine walk upon our boundaries. We walk 129 acres up and down the sides of the mountain. . . . This encircles us and protects ourselves, our animals, our community, our children from any interference. (Resident of Arco Idris, in Cheney 1985, 31)

Separatist feminism therefore became synonymous with the creation of a woman-identified Jerusalem based on principles of "sharing a rich inner life, bonding against male tyranny and giving and receiving practical and political support" (Ross 1990, 75). Faderman (1991) argues that these attempts to maximize a lesbian feminist identity and to create new ways of living represented a coherent philosophy that was not only challenging sexism and homophobia but was also trying to create a unified alternative. She argues that it was intended that these "communities would eventually be built into a strong Lesbian Nation that would exist not necessarily as a geographical entity but as a state of mind and that might even be powerful enough, through its example, to divert the country and the world from their dangerous course" (Faderman 1991, 217).

Despite maximizing a lesbian feminist identity through proclaiming these common goals, Cheney's research suggests that separatist communes of the late seventies and early eighties actually established very diverse ways of living. Each lesbian land was a very specific place. Attempts to promote a sense of sameness or unity around the identities lesbian and feminist and to stake out a "collective identity" often exposed differences between women that were negotiated and contested differently in different places. The second part of this chapter, therefore, explores how particular separatist groups attempted to manage their differences.

Minimizing Identity: Lesbian Lands as Sites of Difference

Attempts to establish new ways of living required the women involved to define new ways of being and behaving. But this process of mutual identification automatically helped to generate homogeneity and to produce borders and exclusions (Young 1990). Perhaps the most significant debate faced by many separatists was how to define the sexuality of the space they were trying to create. It is generally assumed that separatism meant not only that lesbianism was "destigmatized" among radical feminists but also that it was "aristocraticized" (Faderman 1991). For some of the lesbian lands, this was certainly true. A desire for mutual identification or unity as lesbians led to the deliberate exclusion of heterosexual women and women with boy children because it was argued these women were implicitly contributing to the maintenance of patriarchy. Other lesbian lands wanted to be open to all women, recognizing that sexual identities are fluid and that many women go through stages of trying to redefine their sexuality and therefore welcomed heterosexual or bisexual women as long as they did not bring men with them.

Boy children were a major stumbling block for many of the lesbian lands. Ross (1990) documents how women with boy children were excluded from or made to feel unwelcome in the Canadian separatist community, LOOT (Lesbian Organization of Toronto). Similarly within U.S. lesbian lands, boy children were an important point of political cleavage. In one land, Kvindelandet, women with boys were turned away and the community even got rid of male foals and roosters in an attempt to create a "pure" women-only space (Cheney 1985). But in other lands, the exclusion of women with sons was actively contested as this comment illustrates:

> Although some questioned boys' rights to be at OWL Farm, others of us defended them. It was open women's land, to exclude women because they had boy children would not have been "open." Many of us called ourselves separatists (others didn't) but our separatism never went so far as to exclude boy children. (Resident of Nozoma Tribe, in Cheney 1985, 160)

Arco Idris allowed boy children and took a nonessentialist view of identity. As one woman explained:

> If a male child grows here and respects our ways and honours our ways and decides that he wants to stay here with us, at that time it would be taken before the womyn's counsel and decided upon. In my heart I feel that if that male child grew here and learned from us and our ways and decided he wanted to stay here, we would want him to stay here and be part of our community. (Resident of Arco Idris, in Cheney 1985, 38)

In Maud's land this was a fundamental debate through which the identity of the community was shaped.

> The male child issue has been the most painful one. We've all chosen to live without men, yet there are women now who are talking about having babies. This one has created not the most anger between us, but the most pain. We really have tried very hard not to go at each other. A lot of that anger or attack comes from fear; if she gets what she wants that means I may not be able to come here. (Resident of Maud's Land, in Cheney 1985, 88)

As this latter quote implies, the collective identities of many of these separat-ist groups were not always stable but rather were fluid, as women contested and (re)negotiated their mutuality and consequently the boundaries of their communities. In particular, many of the lesbian lands adopted changing posi-tions toward monogamy and nonmonogamy, experimenting with different ways of relating to each other. Redbird was one land documented by Cheney (1985) that (re)negotiated its identity around this issue, as this inhabitant ex-plains:

> We reasoned that one falls in love because of a lot of conditioning (e.g., tall and slender), that everyone is lovable, and that if one focuses on the specialness of each person, one can still love anyone. So, we decided to choose lovers by drawing names out of a hat, and then go about loving that person, until, after several months, we'd redraw and rearrange. I wouldn't recommend it. We tried. Oh, we tried. Some combinations were just too hard, and we rearranged pairings. We were practicing serial monogamy, one lover at a time. We thought we'd smash monogamy too by rotating through everyone in the collective until we had been with everyone and then having open sexual options within the collective. (Resi-dent of Redbird, in Cheney 1985, 120)

Such attempts to determine new ways of living and a sense of sameness or togetherness often produced tensions between women living on the land who made different choices. In particular, celibate women often felt marginalized by women who were able to mobilize their lovers to support them in commu-nity disputes. Others found it difficult to deal with relationships that had ended. Maximizing a nonmonogamous lesbian identity therefore often re-sulted not in unity, but in draining divisions and exclusions.

> Non-monogamy was politically correct. Monogamous couples felt an undercur-rent of criticism of their relationships. Many women had several lovers on the land. It was difficult to get away from relationships one might not want to witness. Sometimes dealing with our feelings around our multiple relationships took so much energy that we had little left for anything else. (Resident of Nozoma tribe, in Cheney 1985, 152)

Class, a charged issue in the lesbian community, also took on larger dimen-sions in lesbian-land environments. The land, while being a focus for unity, was also a source of division. Issues of ownership/co-ownership of sizeable investments such as the land itself, dwellings and "improvements" (wells, roads, electricity, fences, outbuildings), often exposed differences between women. In many cases the land on which communities were established was acquired with inherited money or bought by a few women with well-paying jobs or savings who were able to put down cash or take out a mortgage. In most cases, the "owners" would therefore have greater say in the direction of the community, with other women paying rent. The Arf community was one lesbian land organized in this way, as this woman explains:

There are two collectives, the living collective and the legal collective. The legal collective is the women who are on the deed. They have complete say over everything that has to do with the deed and the taxes, paying the money, how the money gets spent, and who else gets put on the deed. The living collective has complete say over what happens living here and how we work that out. That is made up of whosoever is living here. (Resident of Arf, in Cheney 1985, 14)

Other lesbian lands handled the issues of class and ownership differently. As Faderman (1991, 237) argues at this time, "working class was seen as superior to the middle class, at least partly by virtue of its poverty, which attested to its moral innocence in a corrupt society." Middle-class women bore a heavy burden of guilt. As a resident of Nozoma tribe recalls, "we played 'more oppressed than you.' " She explains how women manipulated each other to get what they wanted: "whoever hurt us was judged as 'middle class' and condemned" (Cheney 1985, 162). Another recalls some of the pressures this lead to:

One woman among us had a large inheritance that she was trying to deal with in a class-conscious way. . . . Eventually we decided to split the money 3 ways —$50,000 each to city women, country women and women of colour . . . we gave a small amount of money to the Oregon's Women's Land Trust. We could have completely paid off OWL farm with some of the money but didn't because of our white middle class guilt and pressure from other women that we should not use the money for "ourselves." (Resident of Nozoma Tribe, in Cheney 1985, 160)

While class was negotiated and contested within communities, lesbian lands also often came under pressure from outsiders who did not respect the boundaries of the communities and accused the residents of class privilege. One woman describes a bitter dispute her community had with a group of traveling women who tried to move in and appropriate the commune, claiming that "all property was theft": "There were some women who felt that we were elitist, capitalist, racist, classist snobs, taking our privilege with private land; they didn't respect private land" (Resident of Arf, in Cheney 1985, 15).

Claims of racism and a lack of tolerance of disabled women were other fissures of difference that split the fragile unity of lesbian land communities. Stein (1992, 36) argues that "lesbian feminism and the women's liberation movement in general drew heavily upon the images and symbols of Black Power and shared its commitment to authenticity, redefining and affirming the self, and achieving individual recognition via group identification." But despite this, few Black women were involved with White women in establishing lesbian lands.

Faderman argues that one explanation for this was that Black women "felt greater solidarity with 'progressive' minority men than with White lesbian-feminists who, it seemed to them, were denying that race could be as much a source of women's oppression as sex" (1991, 241). The evidence of Cheney's research (1985) is that many Black and Jewish lesbian feminists felt marginalized from communes because of the communities' inherent whiteness and their lack of consciousness about the specificity of oppression: a criticism shared by disabled women who often felt that lesbian lands were not set up for or would not respond to their needs. In particular, many of the communities emphasized a physical commitment to the land through shared physical labor. This emphasis on the "body" meant that many disabled women could not participate. Thus, by attempting to mobilize a lesbian feminist identity, the women involved in establishing lesbian lands often privileged their sameness over their differences, as these passages demonstrate:

> I do not want to define the Jewish struggle and I do not want to divide the womyn's movement into ethnic camps but I simply cannot sit by and let a group of white people reclaim my land. I also cannot sit silently by while white womyn compete with us for the little bit of validation we have received from the womyn's movement for being womyn of color. The Third World consciousness in the womyn's movement is relatively new, and the movement was dominated by white feminists for longer than we have enjoyed any validation for our struggle. (Resident of La Luz de la Lucha, in Cheney 1985, 69–71)

> One woman couldn't deal with seeing a disabled woman, because she had been disabled and didn't want that in her life unless I could somehow be happy. And I've not been at a place to do that. . . . There were those who would have preferred for me to take drugs in order for me to be more functional. I feel they had no caring for what happened to me tomorrow but only whether I was able to take care of myself and do physical work today. It's clearer to me now that I don't want to live with wimmin who have that kind of expectation of me, because it isn't what I choose to do with my life. . . . My rights as a disabled person to live on the land were not recognized . . . I wanted the country to be a healing place for me. The city had definitely been a place that made me more disabled. Golden was also a place that made me more disabled. The stress level and the constant pressure to push myself to the limits of my physical capacity have made my condition worse. (Resident of Golden, in Cheney 1985, 52)

While the emphasis on escaping patriarchy meant that many lesbian lands emphasized the residents' shared identities as women over their differences, not all separatist communities had the dominant aim of creating woman-centered space. Rather, some lesbian lands maximized other identities, with the aim of escaping disability oppression by making independent space for disabled lesbians, for example; others attempted to create nonracist environments. As one of the founders of Beechtree commune explains:

> I always had a dream of being in the country; I wanted to develop space for disabled people to live autonomously. There are a lot of care facilities of different levels, some apartments, but they all feel restrictive. . . . I began networking with disabled lesbians together, in an ableist-free environment. Maybe we wouldn't stay

together forever, but we deserved to live validated lives. There's no place I can feel
totally validated unless I'm with a lot of other disabled lesbians . . . I have a
disability; my culture is different, my herstory is different and my reality is different. (Resident of Beechtree, in Cheney 1985, 42)

Other communes were established by native American women and by women
of color. Arco Idris was a community specifically for womyn of color. White
womyn were only allowed to live there if they came with a womyn of color,
had biracial children, or were specially invited by womyn in the community.
Another example described in *Lesbian Lands* is La Luz de al Lucha (Cheney
1985).

Conclusion

Since the late 1980s and the 1990s, lesbian separatism has become the target
of heavy criticism, accused of naively promoting a transcendent lesbian identity and attempting to create a universal lesbian culture. According to Stein
(1992), "the 1980s and 1990s brought a retrenchment from the radical visions
of the previous decade. A triumphant conservatism had shattered previously
cohesive lesbian communities." From the evidence of Cheney's (1985) research, these critiques appear to be unfair. The histories of lesbian lands in the
1970s and early 1980s clearly demonstrate that lesbian separatism was never a
coherent, unified movement with a vision of a transcendent lesbian identity.
Certainly, many though not all of the communities appear to have attempted
to maximize the inhabitants' shared identities as women through the spatial
strategy of separating from heteropatriarchal society. However, there does not
appear to have been a common vision of how to create new ways of living and
new space. Each of the lands was a specific and unique place that defined its
own vision of how women should live together and establish their own collective identity. Some emphasize, for example, the creation of non-racist environments or space for the disabled to live independently, while others focused on
issues of monogamy or self-sufficiency. As Stein (1992, 37) has argued, "the
lesbian-feminist movement consisted of hundreds of semi-autonomous, small-
scale groups that were never centred."

Each lesbian land, by defining common new ways of living and new appropriate ways of behaving, constructed its own shared identity or groupness.
These desires for mutual identification or homogeneity simultaneously appear
to have generated boundaries and exclusions (see also Watkins, chapter 18, for
a discussion of the way that a desire for community can produce marginalization). As Iris Marion Young (1990, 301) argues, "A woman in a feminist
group that seeks to affirm her mutual identification will feel and be doubly
excluded if by virtue of her being different in race, class, culture or sexuality
she does not identify with the others nor they with her." As Cheney's (1985)
research shows, women felt excluded within lesbian lands for many reasons.

Some refused to be controlled by the dominant identities of the communities they were living in and pushed against their boundaries by mobilizing the performance of "other" identities. Others chose to leave one community and join or set up another. In this way, the lesbian lands were not stable communities but were fluid with new women coming and going as different identities were maximized and minimized. As a resident of Golden (Cheney 1985) explained, this was often a negative process.

> It made me feel guilty all the time to gang up on wimin. Yet in both cases, the wimin who were asked to leave were not fitting in with the existing group. This is a little bit of a different situation than I was in, where the wimin at the land basically split into two factions and one faction left. In the other cases it was one woman vs. the rest of the group. I don't know if that makes it any more justifiable. . . . I really encouraged a diversity, and thought diversity was something that would help us grow. Now I feel that, in a lot of ways, the diversity made it really hard. We were coming from so many different places, and had so many different goals, and were all so scarred as lesbians living in the patriarchy that we were bound to take some of that out on each other. Striving for good communication is about my first priority now. (Resident of Golden, Cheney 1985, 54)

As this woman clearly articulates, while some lesbian lands wanted to recognize and value diversity among the inhabitants of their communities, the reality was that in many lands, identities were not equally valued, rather, some were privileged over others. The tensions within these lands were not a product of diversity—the variety in women's experiences but were a result of difference, that is, the inequalities of power and hierarchies that were constructed between women. Rose (1993, 153) argues that the space of separatism clearly exposes feminism's "complex and divided self." The challenge facing feminism and implicitly feminist geography at the *fin de siècle* lies therefore, in learning how to negotiate our complex and divided selves in a way that acknowledges our webs of multiple identities and the multiplicity of projects around which we construct fictions, without creating hierarchies of power between these identities and projects.

Acknowledgments

I wish to thank Sue Roberts, Heidi Nast and John Paul Jones for organizing the excellent conference, New Horizons in Feminist Geography (and the accompanying workshop sessions), at the University of Kentucky, Lexington, where this paper was originally presented. I am grateful to all those in my workshop sessions, especially the facilitator Audrey Kobayashi, for their insightful comments which helped me to develop this chapter. Finally, I also wish to thank David Bell for finding Cheney's book *Lesbian Lands* and for his continued academic and personal support, and Angela and Rich for their hospitality and guided tours of Lexington.

References

Abbott, S. and Love, B. 1972. *Sappho is a right-on woman: A liberated view of lesbianism,* New York: Stein & Day.

Barrett, M. and Phillips, A. 1992. Introduction. In Barrett, M. and Phillips, A. eds. *Destabilizing theory: contemporary feminist debates* 1–9. Cambridge: Polity Press.

Bell, D., and Valentine, G. 1995. Queer country: Rural lesbian and gay lives. *Journal of Rural Studies* 11 (2): 113–122.

Brown, R.M. 1976. *A plain brown wrapper.* Baltimore: Diana Press.

Butler, J. 1990. *Gender trouble: Feminism and the subversion of identity.* New York: Routledge.

Cheney, J. 1985 *Lesbian lands.* Minneapolis: Word Weavers.

Cloke, P., Philo C., and Sadler, D. eds. 1991. *Approaching human geography: An introduction to contemporary theoretical debates.* London: Paul Chapman.

Delphy, C. 1992. "Mothers union?". *Trouble and strife* 24: 15–19.

Ehrenreich, B., and English, D. 1973. *Witches, midwives, and nurses: A history of women healers.* London: Writers and Readers Publishing Collective.

Faderman, L. 1991 *Odd girls and twilight lovers: a history of lesbian life in twentieth-century America.* Harmondsworth: Penguin.

Fuss, D. 1988. *Essentially speaking.* New York: Routledge.

Gearhart, S. 1985. *The wanderground: Stories of hill women.* London: Women's Press.

hooks, b. 1984. *Feminist theory: From margin to center.* Boston: South End Press.

hooks, b. 1991. *Yearning: Race, gender and cultural politics.* London: Turnaround Press.

Jackson, S. 1992. The amazing deconstructing woman. *Trouble and Strife* 25: 25–35.

King, U. 1993. *Women and spirituality: Voices of protest and promise.* Basingstoke: Macmillan.

Rose, G. 1993. *Feminism and geography: The limits of geographical knowledge.* Oxford: Polity Press.

Ross, B. 1990. The house that Jill built: Lesbian feminist organising in Toronto, 1976–1980. *Feminist Review* 35: 75–91.

Ruether, R. 1975. *New woman, new earth. Sexist ideologies and human liberation.* New York: Seabury Press.

Singer, R. 1980. *The demeter flower.* New York: St. Martin's Press.

Snitow, A. 1990. A gender diary. In Hirsch, M. and Fox, Keller E,. eds. *Conflicts in feminism.* New York, Routledge.

Stanley, L. and Wise, S. 1983. *Breaking out: Feminist consiousness and feminist research.* London: Routledge, Kegan Paul.

Stein, A. 1992. Sisters and queers: the decentering of lesbian feminism. *Socialist Review* 22(1): 33–56.

Warren, M.A. 1980. *The Nature of woman. An encyclopedia and guide to literature.* Inverness, CA: Edgepress.

Whisman, V. 1993. Identity crises: who is a lesbian anyway? in Stein, A. ed. *Sisters, sexperts, queers* 47–60. London: Plume.

Young, I.M. 1990 The ideal of community and the politics of difference. In Nicholson, L., ed. *Feminism/postmodernism,* 300–323. London: Routledge.

5

The Meaning of Home Workplaces for Women

Sherry Ahrentzen

Women's meanings and experiences of home are diverse and multivalent, unlike the narrow spectrum we often see in popular media and academic research. Much of this, as well as our residential architecture, is framed by an ideology that supports dichotomy rather than diversity—of a division of "home life" from "work life," of a private from public sphere. For example, some academicians celebrate the idea(l) of home, sometimes nostalgically (e.g., Rybczynski 1986; "Home: A Place . . ." 1991), while another cadre of scholars (e.g., Barrett 1980) claims home as the major site of women's oppression.

The dwellings and places we live in are as much psychological and social constructions as they are physical ones. Objects and spaces have cultural, social, and personal meanings. Psychoanalysts such as Carl Jung (1959) see the home as an archetype of people's psyches. Developers profit, in part, by marketing the image of home (Marcus, Francis, and Meunier 1986). Some architects, such as Charles Moore (Moore, Allen, and Lyndon 1974), embrace the traditional idea of home, while others such as Lars Lerup (1987) attack its cultural metaphor.

Yet psychologists, developers, and architects are not the only ones who have tried to understand what home means to the people who reside in dwellings. Social and behavioral researchers, with the tools of their trade, have also tackled this phenomena (see Després 1991 for review). I contend, however, that these investigations of home have only scratched the surface. While an ideology of home that encompasses privatization and domesticity is deeply embedded in our public policies, built landscapes, and research endeavors, this ideology is not always consistent with our lived experiences. Consequently, research working within such a framework presents a truncated understanding of the meanings of home. In a comprehensive review of the empirical research on the meaning of home, Carole Després (1991) argues that most of this literature defines home for traditional households living in single-family detached homes, and neglects the role of material aspects of housing and of societal forces in the production and reproduction of the meaning of home.

I want to expand upon these previous research efforts by demonstrating the diversity of home meanings to women, even among what may be considered—on the surface—a homogeneous cohort of women. In this chapter, I consider *diversity of meanings*—and demonstrate that such comes from a careful social analysis of the life experiences and situations of women. I am challenging the predominant research and popular perspective of a singular female view of home space, even among women of similar social positions of race and class. Yet my method of analysis is different from classical variants of individualism, which aim at abstraction from social context. Within this cohort, women express a variety of meanings of home, which are in part shaped by the interplay of social ideologies of gender, race, and class; their own particular life and living situations (personal, social, material); and their personal and material actions to confront, challenge, or accept the social expectations of "women's work in the home."

This research focus on the diversity of meanings rather than diversity of personal characteristics or social positions has important implications for the materiality of women's lives. For example, the narrow and selected components of a concept of home are used today to designate what is *not* home for some poor women (Watson and Austerberry 1986; Golden 1992). As Veness (1993, 319) convincingly argues: "Though definitions of home are comprised of an assortment of environmental and emotional components, which of the specific components of home are deemed essential depends on prevailing cultural ideals, social relations, and individual needs. Thus, when and where home is defined, who is given the power to prescribe and regulate home standards, and what purposes these standards serve are each important considerations." As she concludes (337), "established, conventional ideas about home often preclude discussions of alternatives and perpetuate policies that maintain the status quo."

In this chapter, I consider how various contemporary women experience home, but in a context often neglected by social researchers—when women use the dwelling as an occupational workplace. To better understand the meaning of their experiences, however, I also explore how these experiences of home are partially constructed by and reconstruct social ideologies of domesticity and work, and are further tempered by their social positions. I propose that women's experiences of home space reflect an interaction between socially structured opportunities, constraints, and expectations relevant to gender, class, age, and race, and women's active attempts to respond to these structures. Contradictions in these experiences are expected to occur because our lives within them, and the home's role in society, are complex and fluid. To understand what women feel about and do in their homes, we need to examine the meanings of their words and actions through the social frameworks in which they are embedded.

I first briefly present the domestic ideology that frames many of our building practices, social policies, cultural norms, and research perspectives of the meaning of home. In dominant cultural conceptualizations, home and work are often oppositions. Following the work of many scholars (e.g., Kanter 1977), I argue that the concepts and sites of home and work are often overlapping, and sometimes virtually the same, and that an understanding of this symbiosis leads us to new ways of visioning and envisioning space.[1] After presenting these frameworks, I describe how contemporary middle-class homeworkers use and experience the home as workplace.[2]

Home and Work

An underlying premise of my analysis is that women and men actively build and interpret their lives, in part, from the materials provided by a social structure.[3] As Margaret Atwood chillingly demonstrates in her novel *The Handmaid's Tale*, matters outside the walls of women's homes strongly shape the lives within them. Thoughts, values, and actions take meaning from the larger political and social reality surrounding them. Context matters (Dietz 1987).

One context in which our homes and home lives are embedded is the domestic ideology of the privatized home. This ideology upholds a sexually separatist system of public and private spheres—spheres physically, emotionally, and functionally separate. Women are identified with the private sphere, best exemplified by the domicile and domesticity, and men with the public sphere of labor and politics (see Kerber 1988 for review). Sociological theorists such as Talcott Parsons and many family historians proclaimed that this separation was essential for the functioning of society. But this position was later refuted by historians who felt that separation denigrated and subordinated women, enforced a class distinction, or was simply a tactic to buttress men's careers and status (see Pleck 1976).

Recent critics have challenged the actual existence of separate spheres for men and women, of public and private worlds (see Sharistanian 1987). Many individuals—noticeably among the working class, the poor, farm families, and immigrants—did not live in separate spheres. Women performed both paid labor and unpaid work at home. In the twentieth century, the distinctions between public and private blur as a consequence of mass media and women's increased labor force participation, among other factors. The myth of the privatized home is belied by the fact that the residence has always been and continues to be a space of reproduction *and* production, of nurturance, leisure, *and* work. Nonetheless, and contrary to all this evidence, the *social idea* of separate spheres continues to permeate residential development, public policy, and even our scholarship (for further elaboration, see Ahrentzen 1992).

Like the term "home," work is socially constructed. Employment is often

construed as the predominant and sometimes only form of work in contemporary Western society. In North American societies, whether or not one is being
paid for conducting an activity or service influences the social, and often personal, meaning of that activity. In this context then, what is the meaning and
value of the work of women? Unfortunately, the research addressing this question is largely limited to well-educated, Euro-American, middle-class women
raised in North American and Western European cultures. To these women,
like men, socially valued work affects their sense of personal work and value,
their sense of purpose and achievement, their capacity to contribute to the
wider society, and their independence from the control of others (Stewart
1990). But another important dimension of work to women, more so than to
men, is the fluidity of boundaries between work and personal life. Blending
and balancing work and personal lives are central and value-laden concerns of
many women today (Chester and Grossman 1990).

But understanding how women *feel* about their work must be considered in
light of society's view of that work. In Western countries, men's work is seen
as pivotal to the economy, to their families, and to their own sense of worth;
women's work is seen simply as supplementing the family income. In North
America, because men did not historically associate home with work, they also
failed to associate women with work (Cott 1977). This perception, as evident
in daily practice as well as national policy (such as the calculation of the gross
national product), devalues the unpaid work and skills homemakers perform
inside and outside the home.

Women's experiences of the home, then, as a place of work are influenced
not only by the setting, the nature of the task, or social exchanges within that
setting, but also by the activity defined within a social context. To develop a
portrait—or rather, a mural—of women's experiences of their homes as workplaces, we need to examine all types of work in the home, both paid and
unpaid.[4] Unfortunately, I cannot do this in a single chapter, although I clearly
acknowledge a more comprehensive definition and examination of women's
work in the home is necessary in painting the full mural. My focus in this
chapter is on occupational, or paid, labor in the home. I explore women's
experiences of their homes as workplaces, as derived from their actions in the
home, the material and social setting, as well as from the social ideologies of
domesticity and "women's work."

Today's Middle-Class Homeworkers

One of the most dramatic developments in the United States in the last three
decades has been the influx of women into the paid labor force—and the increasing number of women working for pay at home. The Bureau of Labor
Statistics estimates that in the mid–1980s, approximately four million women
work at least eight hours a week at home, as part of their primary, nonfarm
job. More than one million of these women work exclusively at home; on

average they are married, self-employed women of European descent, who work an average of twenty-seven hours a week (Horvath 1986). According to the National Center for Policy Analysis, more than 70 percent of businesses operating from the home are owned by women (Gonzales 1988). Of these women home-business owners, nearly 40 percent work in service occupations compared to 3 percent of male home-business owners who are more likely to have businesses in crafts, repairs, or sales.

Still, with these numbers, the social acceptance of homework as a credible work status is negligible. While at times homework is praised as an ideal work arrangement, many homeworkers still never obtain the professional credibility, economic standing, or legal rights of those working outside the house. As Beach (1989, 47) aptly claims, " 'home work' is a value laden term, not just a description of shared work and home space."

How is this setting, this "home space," of occupational work construed in the larger social context? As displayed in the popular media, homes are considered places of leisure, family nurturance, and domestic work—the picture of the idyllic, sanctified home. Work typically done at home—domestic or household work—is that which our culture views with low social status, economic dependence, repetitiveness, and a considerable lack of autonomy and control (Anderson 1988). As with working women outside the home, role conflict and overload for homeworkers is already a consuming and stressful factor of their daily lives. But it may assume an even more odious character when such demands are set in a social climate that economically and politically devalues domestic work and many forms of women's occupational work. But, as we will see, many women develop strategies to enable their homes to accommodate their complex lives and resist some of these demeaning characterizations.

I am basing my interpretation and analyses here primarily on my own empirical study of 104 homeworkers (Ahrentzen 1987, 1989a, 1990),[5] but also including those studies by Beach (1989), Christensen (1985, 1988), Costello (1988), Lozano (1989), Mackenzie (1986), McLaughlin (1981), Nelson (1988, 1990), and Pratt (1984). All of these researchers *interviewed* homeworkers. Except for Beach's research, all of these studies have moderate or large sample sizes. There are considerable differences, however, in the sample characteristics: some focus exclusively on women, others include both sexes; some focus on residents in one region, others are nationwide; one may focus on a single type of work, another may examine several different types. Generally, all include middle-class women, but some also include working-class women. While a few studies exist of low-income homeworkers of non-European ethnic backgrounds (e.g., Kelly and Garcia 1985), these studies do not address the meaning of home, and so were not used in the analysis here. In short, the research on contemporary homework focuses almost exclusively on middle-class men, and middle-class and working-class women, of European descent. The interpretations in this section are made in light of this research focus.

Identity and Misidentity

Home as a component of identity has traditionally revolved around two dimensions in the research literature. The social perspective, exemplified by the work of Donald Appleyard (1979), James Duncan (1985), and Erving Goffman (1971), views the home as a collective identification, but generally defined within the male's social position. The personal identification, best exemplified by the work of Clare Cooper (1974), emphasizes the connection between home and one's individual personality or a universal human. But both of these perspectives are expanded upon when we look at persons in the home with multiple and often conflicting social roles. Many homeworkers in my study felt their identification with their home had less to do with their own role behaviors than with the social interpretation of roles typically associated with the home or with one's personal interpretation, regardless of their own personal feelings of the situation.

Being visibly at work between 9 A.M. and 5 P.M. is an integral part of our cultural assumptions about work. Not being so can suggest that we are unemployed or "keeping house." Because of the strong cultural identification of the residence with domesticity, many homeworkers feel that others identified them with the domestic work nature of their homes, an identification that many of them found considerably frustrating. After completing a two-hour interview, a homeworker hesitated when I got up to leave. "I must tell you," she said, "working at home has made me a housewife."[6] While her occupational position and work activity at home is exactly the same as when she worked outside the home (a telephone sales operator), her husband and teenage children do not see her as "working" since she does not display the exterior signs of professional work, that is, she does not dress up and go out. And because her family sees her "at home" all day, they expect her to do all the housework. Likewise, when she tells friends she works at home, they exclaim that she now must be able to get all her household work done.

For some women, identification with the domestic role is desirable and hence nonconflicting. In Luxton's (1980) study of housewives in Flin Flon, Canada, who "took in" work to make ends meet, their paid work was usually an extension of their domestic role: providing for boarders meant making an extra lunch, cooking larger portions, washing more clothes and linens. Child care in the home meant watching an extra child. These activities fit into the existing domestic role pattern, and also reinforced their self-images of mother and homemaker.

But for women who are striving to establish separate careers, the domestic misidentification of their work by others can be disturbing. The lack of professional credibility associated with working at home is likely more serious for women than men because of the historical association of women in the home as mothers, wives, and housewives.[7] Their self-perception of identity and status conflicts with the perceptions of others. Christensen (1985) found that while women with word processing home businesses no longer thought of themselves as clerical workers but as professionals, their families and friends sometimes thought otherwise. Neighbors may ask them if they can drop off their children for a few hours while they go shopping or run errands. Family, friends, and neighbors drop by or call during the work day to talk about personal matters, presuming that their homeworking friends are not "really" working (Ahrentzen 1987; Christensen 1988; Costello 1988). In my study, I noted that this expression of misidentification often occurred for women with children at home—but only occasionally for men, regardless of whether or not they had children living at home.

There are also many women who synthesize and strengthen their professional and domestic roles at home. In my study, this was more noticeable among women than among men, regardless of their marital or family status. For many of these women, they assumed a more positive identification and attachment with the home. Home became a place that represented their multiple roles or what many homeworkers verbalized as "all of me" or "the whole." One married mother, a freelance writer, claimed, "My home now reflects my values, tastes, interests. My work allows me to express my values more than I would do with a washing machine." For another married woman, a writer and producer, home was now not only a place for family but also for her creative efforts. She said she liked her home more now than previously because "it incorporates all of me—the creative part and the other part." Another woman, a single parent working as a telephone sales operator, felt this greater expression of her social identification once she remodeled and converted the attic to her office. Another telephone sales operator felt more positively about her home because "I have something definite to do at home now." For a single mother involved in marketing research, home was "now my life—my work, son, friends, and myself." Her home was much more important to her than in the past because she worked (occupationally) at home—she said she would not have bought a house [a recent purchase] unless she could locate an office within it.

It is helpful to view these various feelings—the home as a domesticating emblem of one's self or as an enabling projection of the "integrative" self— along with the cultures and reference groups of these women. The rural families in Beach's (1989) study expressed a highly satisfying life and embraced this home life that integrated family and work quite fluidly. But, as Beach points out, this is partially due to the supporting rural culture in which these people live: an area traditionally valuing family life and independence, a low-consumption environment with few employment opportunities and low crime rates, and the historical presence and legitimacy of microbusinesses (e.g., cottage industries, one- or two-person service firms, artisans, and crafters). A culture, in short, that embraces homework as an honorable form of work and life.

From Isolation to Entrapment

Isolation is a common theme in journalistic accounts, anecdotes, self-help books, and scholarly inquiry of home-based work. But this professional or occupational solitude is not in itself undesirable, as often claimed by these accounts. Many women in Christensen's (1988) study liked the solitude of homework; nearly three-quarters of Pratt's (1984) sample of men and women claimed the amount of socialization was sufficient; and 80 percent of Beach's (1989) sample of rural homeworkers said they had a "nongregarious" nature, meaning they were able to work alone and not miss workplace socialization.

But while some homeworkers enjoy this solitude, for others the feelings can evolve into a sense of isolation within their homes. Family day-care providers talk about the loneliness of having little opportunity during the day to converse with adults (Nelson 1988). Many women feel cut off from a sense of community, of which the workplace has become a primary site in many people's lives today. Furthermore, while working at home, these women may be unable to keep abreast of trends in the marketplace or profession. Corporate-employed women in Pratt's (1984) study stressed that work at home was detrimental to their careers because they were no longer seen by their supervisors (an important condition, they thought, for promotion) and were less likely to hear about professional opportunities.

While the refuge quality of home—its distinction from the outside public world—is popularly touted in the research literature as well as the popular discourse on home, such "refuge" can become socially isolating (but see the following section in this paper discussing positive feelings of refuge within the home itself). Many women expressing this feeling do not live by themselves so, in effect, they are not truly alone in their homes. Yet, the sense of not being able to relate to a more public, social world permeates the experiences of many of these women. In fact, the clear majority of homeworkers in my study expressing this sense of isolation were women living with at least one other adult (spouse, partner, sibling, etc.) but with no children at home. Rarely would feelings of entrapment be expressed by men, by women living alone, or by single mothers. Their comments are sometimes couched in a discourse of power and powerlessness, so that the sense of isolation turns into one of entrapment. Many use the terms "chained" or "trapped." Living alone, a freelance writer claimed that her home was no longer a refuge because she could get "trapped here." In a similar vein, a married woman, also a freelance writer and scriptwriter, without children at home, used to feel her home was a sanctuary. She too said she now felt trapped because she was at home all the time. Another women, a systems trainer, said she felt "more chained" to the house because she was there so often. A single mother felt that the home became more of a refuge because she did not need to go out of the home as much. But because the home space was now the center of many activities, she felt much more vulnerable when she left it.

But most homeworkers do not simply resign themselves to being in an entrapping situation. Rather, they actively seek ways to mitigate these feelings. Some adjust by making sure they have regular social contact with people, either inside or outside the home. Many make efforts to get out of their homes for part of the day: on walks, runs, meetings with clients, luncheons, and so on. They establish "work breaks" in which they walk the dog or ride their bicycle in the neighborhood. Those living in close proximity to neighborhood shops and services, libraries, post offices, copy centers, and parks, use them almost daily as a means to establish social contact outside the home. One freelance writer, for example, said her neighborhood had become "much more critical" to her since working at home because in order to avoid feelings of entrapment, she would get out, walk around, and, as she called it, "extend" herself in the neighborhood. Several women homeworkers I talked with had formed business networks, often with other homeworkers of the same occupation living in the vicinity, with whom they met on a regular basis.

In a similar vein, women homeworkers in interior regions of British Canada and Ontario redesignated networks of friends and neighbors as "working" networks: drop-in centers, local play groups, local craft and arts councils, and informal trade or professional organizations (Mackenzie 1986). These networks acted as sources of contact, advice, and assistance. The household and the neighborhood became workplace and living space simultaneously. By doing so, these women altered not only the location of activities but also the social meaning and function of home, work, and neighborhood.[8]

Refuge within the Home

Homeworkers constantly make behavioral and social efforts to either blur or augment boundaries between the occupational and the domestic activities occurring in the home (see Ahrentzen [1987] for a description of the many ways in which this occurs, and the social conditions surrounding such). But some homeworkers also strengthen mental representations of the spatial boundaries surrounding these activities. They individuate spaces in the home differently from before, perceiving various areas as separated and differentiated.

Much of the research literature as well as popular imagery portray the home in its entirety as a haven or retreat from the world of work, or from the public sphere. Interestingly, many homeworkers experience a refuge quality of *part* of the home. That is, refuge is experienced within different spaces of the home, not the home ensemble separate from spaces outside of it (neighborhood, city, offices). One section of the home may become a retreat from the other areas of the house. Some women homeworkers feel that their workspace is now a haven within the home. But for others, the more traditional private areas of the home, such as the bedrooms, take on an increased refuge quality. While this reconceptualization of the spaces in the home is partly a factor of the changing social relationships occurring there, an examination of women's responses living in different household arrangements and structures reveals no consistent trends: single women living alone, single mothers, and married women with children all expressed experiencing a changing nature of refuge *within* the home. Among women living in households that were loosely organized, and for those living in highly organized household arrangements, there

again were no differences. It is feasible that this changing perceptual orientation is a result of the changing relationship of the self to work/domestic activities and to increased emotional and temporal commitments within the house
itself.

A single woman living alone who had a separate room in her apartment for
her office maintained that the office was her refuge. She did not like her friends
or other people to go in there. Likewise, a married woman with children at
home who worked as a data inputter claimed that her "workspace is more of a
haven, it needs to be, with having only four rooms in the house." A seamstress,
married and with children at home, likewise claimed that her "workspace is a
refuge for me from the rest of the house." A business writer, with a husband
but no children living at home, saw the office as "her space." She did not like
having her husband in there, even when she was not working. And she enjoyed
having a door to close the room off from the rest of the home.

For some women, other parts of the home took on a refuge quality. For
example, for a single freelance writer living alone, the bedroom became a retreat space. Previously, she used her bedroom as her workspace. But once she
converted another area outside the bedroom into her workspace, the bedroom's importance as a retreat space emerged. An accountant living at home
with her husband thought of all house space outside the office as "home" and
"refuge."

This mental separation of spaces in the home was sometimes reinforced by
the physical design of the home. For example, a freelance writer, living alone,
saw a distinction between her home and office. The mental separation, she
said, was partly due to the physical separation—the office was on a separate
floor in the home—but also because she actively tried not to let work and
home lives interfere with each other. Another business writer, one who lived
with another adult in the home, also envisioned this physical-mental separation. "The space above ground [her office was a converted basement] is
'Home'—friends, family, entertaining, good times. Below ground is 'Work'—
office, laundry, ironing, storage."

Vulnerability

For women homeworkers in particular, feelings of vulnerability may arise
when their work necessitates having clients or customers—often relative
strangers—enter the home. Because these women may be living alone or working alone for part of the day, they often meet unfamiliar clients alone in their
homes. Women talk about different strategies they use when an unknown cli-
ent is coming to visit them and they are alone: having a dog, leaving an item
of men's clothing draped around a chair, getting a neighbor to stop by and be
seen or at least heard (Lozano 1989; Ahrentzen 1987).

For women in American society, fear and vulnerability are entrenched in the social fabric. Women's fear of crime is greater than men's even though for most crimes, women are victimized less (Gordon, Riger, LeBailly, and Heath 1981). This fear directs their public and private experiences, their movements, their anger, their self-esteem. If not directly victims of crime, almost all women are victims, to some degree, of lost opportunity. This sense of vulnerability only reinforces the domestic ideology—the separate spheres for women and men—discussed previously. Ironically, the American home actually is *not* a safe space for many women, given the very high rates of domestic violence. According to the former U.S. Surgeon General, Dr. Antonia C. Novello, women are safer in the streets than in their homes ("Physicians begin . . ." 1991; see Weisman 1992).

But homeworking may bring a heightened sense of feeling of vulnerability to the confines of one's home. In some cases these feelings limit these women from expanding their businesses because they will only use clients referred by friends and well-known acquaintances. Thus, their potential business limits are established by social ties rather than market ones (Lozano 1989). As fear of public crime restricts women's use of public spaces, a fear of clients and customers in the home likewise restricts women's use of the home—hardly making home, for them, a place of privacy or control.[9]

Conclusion

The cacophony of voices and experiences described here should dispel the notion of a singular female view of home space. It does demonstrate a greater variety in women's experiences and meanings of home than the research literature often suggests. And these experiences are complex, derived from the sociospatial relations within the domicile as well as from reactions to social expectations of family, friends, and society about their and about women's position in both domestic and labor realms.

Acknowledging a diversity of (even contradictory) home experiences that derive from changing spatial, social, and economic conditions allows us greater freedom to reenvision what home is, and what home can be, for many women. Visions about the future of our built landscape are stifled if we limit ourselves to present myopic notions of what homes are. We then produce homes such as the *Family Circle*'s "Busy Woman's Dream House" (1990), which was designed in response to a survey finding that time is women's most precious commodity. The subsequent "Dream House" resulted in a computer and fax machine being placed in the kitchen/family area!

Instead, a richer understanding of the sociospatial geographies of our homes can lead to a greater diversity of forms of home and communities that better reflect, and support, the social experiences and desires of a diverse population. For example, the "pedestrian pockets"—the mixed-use communities—being developed and promoted by Peter Calthorpe (1988) counter conventional zoning and land use practices of typical suburban enclaves by creating communities that blend together domestic, public and commercial activities in a finer grain of the suburban fabric. Another increasingly visible alternative for a residential landscape is the hybrid housing development in which the residential structure contains both residential and business spaces and activities, where residents of that structure occupy and manage both spaces, and where such housing is intentionally designed to incorporate both spaces (Ahrentzen 1991). While many such hybrid houses are custom designed, single-family homes, an increasing number of spec homes and multifamily developments are being developed as hybrid housing, catering to artists, crafters, retailers, service providers, business entrepreneurs, telecommuters, and others. Another residential alternative is the cohousing development, which originated in Europe but has spread to the United States in recent years (McCamant and Durett 1989). Cohousing emphasizes a strong community focus in the design as well as social actions of residents. Here residents share common spaces and daily activities—such as preparing and eating dinner collectively in a "Common House"—as well as maintain their own private, self-contained residences. The common house in the cohousing development in Nyland, Colorado, even has a shared workspace for the homeworkers in the community. Many transitional housing developments for single parents have been developed to make support services—such as that for job training and child care, for example—integral in the spatial design of the housing complex. Flexible and adaptable floor plans in housing for low-income families have been developed by architects Christine Bevington, Michael Pyatok and Conrad Levenson that allow families to change and reconfigure the spaces in their homes differently as their circumstances and household members grow and change (see Ahrentzen 1989b; Franck 1994). All of these examples and many others (see Franck and Ahrentzen 1989; Fromm 1991; Hayden 1984) derive from a fundamental questioning of a singular or normative notion of how we live or should live in our homes—and challenge the conventional, singular ideal of home by rethinking and redesigning the physical form and layout of the home and community to better fit the daily life patterns and meanings of a diversity of families and households.

Ethnomethodologists argue that the best way to understand a social norm or construct is to investigate those instances in which it has been broken or is not operating: the resulting reactions provide clues to the structure and the meaning of the norm itself (Garfinkel 1967). My intention here has been to expand our understanding of the home concept within a segment of North American culture by considering those instances in which the domicile does not fit the ideological norm—in this case, when it is more than a place for domestic and family activities, but is also the place of paid labor for women. New interpretations of home are enabled by experiences elsewhere. "Elsewhere"—in this chapter—is the occupational position of home.

Notes

1. I do acknowledge that for certain individuals and conditions, the oppositional framework is appropriate.

2. I use the terms "homework" and "homeworking" to refer to remunerated labor done in the home. This distinguishes these terms from domestic and household labor.

3. This is premised on positions of sociological phenomenology and symbolic interactionism (e.g., Schultz 1967; Berger and Luckmann 1966), and also certain postcolonial, social, and contextual feminist positions (e.g., de Lauretis 1986; Epstein 1988; Ahrentzen, in press).

4. There is an extensive literature on the sociology of household work (see, for example, Cowan 1983; Strasser 1982) although little of this addresses women's attachments to their homes.

5. Of these, 74 percent were women. Also, 15 percent of the sample lived alone in their homes; 32 percent lived with another adult(s), usually spouse, partner, sibling, friend, but had no one under the age of 18 at home; 48 percent lived with at least one other adult *and* at least one child; and 5 percent had children at home but no other adults living there.

6. All quoted material in this section is from respondents in my study (Ahrentzen 1987).

7. Gottlieb (1988), however, with a small sample, found men also struggled with their public images when working at home.

8. This may be less feasible in many suburban neighborhoods where the majority of adults work outside the home, as such neighborhoods may be deserted during the day. In my field research in both urban and suburban settings, though, I frequently found several homeworkers working within a few blocks (or apartment floors) from each other.

9. Noticeably, the low crime rates in Beach's (1989) rural community freed women homeworkers of such concerns about personal danger and vulnerability.

References

Ahrentzen, S. 1987. *Blurring boundaries: Socio-spatial consequences of working at home*. Unpublished report. Milwaukee, WI: Center for Architectural and Planning Research, University of Wisconsin-Milwaukee.

———. 1989a. A place of peace, prospect, and . . . a p.c.: The home as office. *Journal of Architectural and Planning Research*, 6 4., 271–88.

———. 1989b. Overview of housing for single-parent households. In K. A. Franck and S. Ahrentzen, eds. *New households, new housing*. New York: Van Nostrand Reinhold.

———. 1990. Managing conflict by managing boundaries: How professional homeworkers cope with multiple roles at home. *Environment and Behavior*, 22/6: 723–52.

———. 1991. *Hybrid housing*. Unpublished report. Milwaukee, WI: Center for Architectural and Planning Research, University of Wisconsin-Milwaukee.

———. 1992. Home as a workplace in the lives of women. In I. Altman and S. M. Low, eds. *Place attachment*. New York: Plenum.

———. 1996. The F word in architecture: Feminist analyses for/in/of architecture. In T. Dutton and L. H. Mann, eds. *Reconstructing architecture*. Minneapolis, MN: University of Minnesota Press.

Anderson, K. 1988. A history of women's work in the United States. In A. H. Stromberg and S. Harkess, eds. *Women working*, 2nd ed. Mountain View, CA: Mayfield.

Appleyard, D. 1979. Home. *Architectural Association Quarterly*, 11/3: 4–20.

Atwood, M. 1985. *The handmaid's tale*. New York: Fawcett.

Barrett, M. 1980. *Women's oppression today: Problems in marxist feminist analysis*. London: Verso.

Beach, B. 1989. *Integrating work and family life: The home-working family*. Albany, NY: State University of New York Press.

Berger, P. and Luckmann, T. 1966. *The social construction of reality*. Garden City, NY: Doubleday.

Busy Woman's Dream House. June 1990. *Family Circle*, 103: 65–74.

Calthorpe, P. 1988. Pedestrian pockets: New strategies for suburban growth. *Whole Earth Review*, 58: 118–23.

Chester, N. L., and Grossman, H.Y. 1990. Introduction: Learning about women and their work through their own accounts. In H. Y. Grossman and N. L. Chester, eds., *The experience and meaning of work in women's lives*. 1–9. Hillsdale, NJ: Lawrence Erlbaum.

Christensen, K. E. June 1985. *Impacts of computer-mediated home-based work on women and their families*. Unpublished report. New York: City University of New York, Center for Human Environments.

———. 1988. *Women and home-based work: The unspoken contract*. New York: Henry Holt.

Cooper, C. 1974. The house as symbol of self. *Design and Environment* 3/3: 30–37

Costello, C. B. 1988. Clerical home-based work: A case study of work and family. In K. E. Christensen, ed. *The new era of home-based work: Directions and policies*. pp. 135–45. Boulder: Westview.

Cott, N. 1977. The bonds of womanhood: "Woman's sphere." In *New England 1780–1835*. New Haven, CT: Yale University.

Cowan, R. S. 1983. *More work for Mother*. New York: Basic Books.

de Lauretis, T. 1986. Feminist studies/critical studies: Issues, terms, and contexts. In T. de Lauretis, ed. *Feminist studies/critical studies*. Bloomington, IN: Indiana University Press.

Després, C. 1991. The meaning of home: Literature review and directions for future research and theoretical development. *Journal of Architectural and Planning Research* 8/2: 96–115.

Dietz, M. G. 1987. Context is all: Feminism and theories of citizenship. *Daedalus 116*, 1–24.

Duncan, J. 1985. The house as symbol of social structure. In I. Altman and C. M. Werner, eds. *Home environments*. New York: Plenum.

Epstein, C. F. 1988. *Deceptive distinctions: Sex, gender and the social order*. New Haven, CT: Yale University Press.

Franck, K. A. 1994. Questioning the American dream: Recent housing innovations in the United States. In R. Gilroy and R. Woods, eds. *Housing women*. London: Routledge.

Franck, K. A. and Ahrentzen, S., eds. 1989. *New households, new housing*. New York: Van Nostrand Reinhold.

Fromm, D. 1991. *Collaborative communities*. New York: Van Nostrand Reinhold.

Garfinkel, H. 1967. *Studies in ethnomethodology*. Englewood Cliffs, NJ: Prentice Hall.

Goffman, E. 1971. *Relations in public: Microstudies of the public order*. New York: Basic Books.

Golden, S. 1992. *The women outside: Meanings and myths of homelessness*. Berkeley: University of California Press.

Gonzales, M. 1988. Home sweet home. *American demographics*, 10/3: 18.

Gordon, M. T., Riger, S., LeBailly, R. K. and Heath, L. 1981. Crime, women and the quality of urban life. In C. R. Stimpson, E. Dixler, M. J. Nelson, and K. B. Yatrakis, eds. *Women and the American city*. Chicago: University of Chicago Press.

Gottlieb, N. M. 1988. Women and men working at home: Environmental experiences. In D. Lawrence, R. Habe, A. Hacker, and D. Sherrod, eds. *People's needs/planet management/paths to co-existence*. 149–154. Washington, D.C.: EDRA.

Hayden, D. 1984. *Redesigning the American dream: The future of housing, work and family life*. New York: Nortcon.

Home: A place in the world. *Social Research*, Spring 1991, 58/1: entire special issue.

Horvath, F. W. 1986. Work at home: New findings from the Current Population Survey. *Monthly Labor Review* 109: 31–35.

Jung, C. 1959. *The archetypes and the collective unconscious*. R. F. C. Hull, translator. New York: Pantheon.

Kanter, R. M. 1977. *Work and family in the United States: A critical review and agenda for research and policy*. New York: Russell Sage.

Kelly, M. P. F. and Garcia, A. M. 1985. The making of an underground economy: Hispanic women, home work and the advanced capitalist state. *Urban Anthropology and Studies of Cultural Systems and World Economic Development*, 14: 59–90.

Kerber, L. K. 1988. Separate spheres, female worlds, woman's place: The rhetoric of women's history. *Journal of American History*, 75: 9–39.

Lerup, L. 1987. *Planned assaults*. Montreal: Centre Canadien d'Architecture/Canadian Centre for Architecture.

Lozano, B. 1989. *The invisible work force: Transforming American business with outside and home-based workers*. New York: Free Press.

Luxton, M. 1980. *More than a labour of love: Three generations of women's work in the home*. Toronto: Women's Press.

Mackenzie, S. 1986. Women's responses to economic restructuring: Changing gender, changing space. In R. Hamilton and M. Barrett, eds. *The politics of diversity: Feminism, marxism and nationalism*. 81–100. London: Verso.

Marcus, C. C., C. Francis, and C. Meunier. 1986. Mixed messages in suburbia: Reading the suburban model home. *Places* 4/1: 24–37.

McCamant, K. M. and C. R. Durrett. 1989. Cohousing in Denmark. In K. A. Franck and S. Ahrentzen, eds. *New households, new housing*. New York: Van Nostrand Reinhold.

McLaughlin, M. M. August 1981. *Physical and social support systems used by women engaged in home-based work*. Unpublished Master's thesis, Cornell University.

Moore, C. W., G. Allen, and D. Lyndon. 1974. *The place of houses*. New York: Holt, Rinehart & Winston.

Nelson, M. K. 1988. Providing family day care: An analysis of home-based work. *Social Problems* 35, 1: 78–84.

———. 1990. Mothering other's children: The experiences of family day-care providers. *Signs*, 15, 3: 586–605.

"Physicians begin a program to combat family violence." 17 October 1991. *New York Times*, A16.

Pleck, E. H. 1976. Two worlds in one: Work and family. *Journal of Social History*, 10/2: 178–95.

Pratt, J. H. 1984. Home teleworking: A study of its pioneers. *Technological Forecasting and Social Change*, 25: 1–14.

Rybczynski, W. 1986. *Home: A short history of an idea*. New York: Viking.

Schultz, A. 1967. *The phenomenology of the social world*. Evanston, IL: Northwestern University Press.

Sharistanian, J., ed. 1987. *Beyond the public/domestic dichotomy: Contemporary perspectives on women's lives*. New York: Greenwood.

Stewart, A. J. 1990. Discovering the meaning of work. In H. Y. Grossman and N. L. Chester, eds., *The experience and meaning of work in women's lives*. 261–71. Hillsdale, NJ: Lawrence Erlbaum.

Strasser, S. 1982. *Never done: A history of American housework*. New York: Pantheon.

Veness, A. R. 1993. Neither homed nor homeless: Contested definitions and the personal worlds of the poor. *Political Geography* 12/4: 319–40.

Watson, S. and Austerberry, H. 1986. *Housing and homelessness: A feminist perspective*. London: Routledge & Kegan Paul.

Weisman, L. K. 1992. *Discrimination by design: A feminist critique of the man-made environment*. Urbana, IL: University of Illinois Press.

6

Hearing from Quiet Students: The Politics of Silence and Voice in Geography Classrooms

Karen Nairn

"Feminism, like other movements advocating social change, relies heavily on a politics of voice for achieving its goals. We aim to combat the effects of a patriarchal system which has kept us silent when we would speak, which devalues what we would say when we do speak, and which structures what we are able to say when the floor is finally ours."

—V. Hazel

The words of Hazel are an excellent summary of the key ideas that were my starting point for an exploration of the politics of silence and of voice in geography coeducational classrooms in Aotearoa/New Zealand. My research investigated why some students are silent in the public forum of class discussion and why a greater proportion of these silent students are female students in coeducational classrooms (Krupnick 1992). How are the effects of patriarchal relations in one particular place and time—Aotearoa/New Zealand in the early 1990s—played out inside geography classrooms? What keeps some female students silent, and what structures or strategies might provide a safer "floor" on which to speak? Other questions are even more complex: what keeps some male students silent, and would the same strategies encourage them to speak? You will notice from these rhetorical questions that an implicit dualism has already emerged: to speak or not to speak in public in the classroom. The politics of voice is no longer an unambiguous strategy to pursue; rather the politics of voice *and* of silence must be considered together.

The act of talking in the classroom has the potential to be empowering in two ways: it is an opportunity for students to practice their verbal skills *and* to shape curriculum content. Students are powerful whenever they make their own decisions to talk or not talk in the public verbal space of classrooms;

93

agency and context are the key to understanding whether silence represents a powerful or powerless position (Weiler 1988). For example, female students may resist a geography curriculum that is predominantly about men and men's activities (Nairn 1994) and resist appropriation of their ideas by remaining silent; in these situations silence is powerful. But if female students are silenced and disempowered by a geography curriculum that does not take account of women's traditional and nontraditional achievements, by the threat of being watched and judged, and by some male students taking up a disproportionate share of turns in classroom discussion, then this is an educational and social issue.

The politics of voice and of silence in one high school geography classroom in Aotearoa/New Zealand will be explored in this chapter. The research upon which this chapter is based was about the difference gender makes, as well as individual differences *within* gender groups, using the politics of silence as the guiding principle. The research was primarily concerned with the experiences of female and male students who were relatively silent in geography class-rooms. This chapter provides one space in which the experiences of these students may be "heard." But before we can listen to the quiet students, it is important to describe the broader context in which this research took place, to consider the theories that have informed it, to explain the rationale for choosing geography classrooms, and to introduce the concept of public verbal space.

The Research Context: Education and Employment in Aotearoa/New Zealand

The Status of Girls and Women in New Zealand Education and Training (Sturrock 1993) shows that the academic performance of female students is equal to or better than their male counterparts in all subjects including geography, but women are still disadvantaged in the labor market. Women are underrepresented in professional and technical occupations and in senior positions. Research has shown that quiet employees are less likely to be noticed for promotion (Krupnick 1992), and it could be argued that quiet individuals are less likely to be noticed for employment and/or training. Confidence and verbal skills are essential for students when they are interviewed for employment and/or access to tertiary (college) education in an increasingly competitive world. A greater proportion of quiet students in coeducational classrooms are female students, who may be disadvantaged in the postschool world where competency in verbal skills is one gatekeeping mechanism, determining access to labor and training markets.

Schools legitimate dominant groups in society by valuing the knowledge, language, and patterns of interaction—the cultural capital—used by the dominant groups (Weiler 1988). More specifically, it is Pakeha (White) male knowledge, language and patterns of interaction that are valued and legitimated in schools in Aotearoa/New Zealand (Alton-Lee and Nuthall with Patrick 1993; Newton 1988).[1] This Pakeha male knowledge and the way individual students deal with it, contribute to the cultural reproduction of unequal race, gender, and class relations in education and employment, as well as in other spheres. "The choice of particular content and of particular ways of approaching it in schools is related both to existing relations of domination and to struggles to alter these relations" (Apple 1991); teachers as well as students struggle to alter existing relations of Pakeha male domination in schools. Teachers who choose women-focused content are countering the domination of male knowledge in schools (see Alton-Lee, Densem, and Nuthall 1990). Female students who do not take part in a curriculum that excludes them may be resisting the domination of male knowledge in schools.

Why Geography Classrooms?

Student-teacher interactions have been widely researched at all levels of education and in subjects such as English, math, science, social studies, and home economics (see for example, Alton-Lee and Nuthall 1991; Grima and Smith 1993; Kelly 1988; Sadker, Sadker, and Klein 1991). What happens to students' public participation patterns in geography has not been explored. At the national scale, in Aotearoa/New Zealand high school geography is chosen by relatively similar numbers of female and male students, and a greater proportion of female students achieve success in geography (Sturrock 1993). Geography's gendered identity, on the basis of student choice, is fluid and dependent on location, time, level of education, and many other factors. For example, at one high school, geography may be a subject that mainly female students choose because it is timetabled against physics or chemistry, and perceived as a less-masculine subject than physics or chemistry. At another school, geography may be chosen by more male students because it is timetabled against art history and biology, and therefore perceived as a more masculine subject than art history and biology. In particular contexts, the gendered identity of geography shifts relative to the gendered identities of other subjects; this ambiguity may suggest an unexpected curriculum space for female students.

Spender (1981) explains how female experience is not articulated and validated in academic circles where the creation of knowledge is taking place. The teaching of geography is dominated by men at both the university (see Johnson 1994) and high school levels in Aotearoa/New Zealand (see Nairn 1991). This has a twofold effect on what is taught in high school geography. First, geography teachers are products of the gendered institutional context of their own educators, and this influences their own teaching. Second, female experience is not articulated and validated in high school geography courses either, so female and male students continue to experience geography as a gendered subject reflecting its position in more general male hegemony:

What geography is today is very much the product of those who have had their particular interpretation of the world accepted. It is therefore not surprising that the discourse of contemporary geography can, on the whole, be seen as a statement by white, middle-class, and middle-aged men about their environment (Longhurst and Peace 1993, 3–4).

Geography classrooms are one site where female and male students could practice talking in public. If the geography curriculum retains its male focus, however, talking in public may be problematic for female students: "Why should girls actively participate in a curriculum that largely excludes or devalues their experience?" (Alton-Lee and Densem 1992). Hence, I have formulated women-focused curriculum interventions and evaluated their impact on the gender distribution of student-teacher interactions in geography classrooms.[2] The rationale for incorporating women-focused curriculum interventions into the research discussed here was to go beyond description of students' public participation patterns to introducing a strategy for change and a means of evaluating the effectiveness of this strategy. Therefore, this research concerns the high school geography curriculum as well as selected geography classrooms in Aotearoa/New Zealand. At another level, it was about the microgeography of any classroom, the politics of voice and silence that operate in all classroom and curriculum spaces to include and exclude students on the basis of their gender, race, sexuality, class, and other characteristics. In other words, the research findings could relate to any classroom, not only to geography classrooms.

Strategic Feminism: Which Theories Are Given Voice?

The most important goal of the research was to make a contribution to positive change for female students in high school geography classrooms in Aotearoa/New Zealand. Achieving change for female students within the current educational system is considered to be a strategy of liberal feminism. It is not a simple process of naming feminist strategies, but of matching the strategies to the struggle and the desired outcomes. For this research, I chose from an eclectic collection of feminist strategies that have been influenced by liberal feminism and poststructuralism. Strategies were selected on the basis of their potential for social change rather than their academic status, and with disregard for real or imagined incompatibility of the respective feminisms. I call this "strategic feminism." The potency of contemporary feminist theory and research does not derive from its intellectual purity, but from the kinds of struggles it makes possible (Larner 1993). The politics of change is dependent on the most effective strategies to achieve stated political goals, rather than on what constitutes "more or less progressive feminist politics," which only achieves the *silencing* of other feminist politics (Larner 1993).

Underlying both the research and this chapter is a theoretical tension between the liberal feminist notion of every female and male student having equitable opportunities for publicly talking in her or his classroom, and the poststructuralist feminist challenge to dualisms such as talking and silence (see Hazel 1994) and the implicit valorization of public talking over silence (although I claim that silence can be empowering *if it is chosen*). My experiences as a high school geography teacher *within* the education system sustain my commitment to strategies that may be productive for quiet female and male students *in* geography classrooms, but these strategies and their effects must be carefully scrutinized, poststructuralist feminist theories provide other lenses with which to view the politics of voice and silence.

The importance of talking and the meaning of silence are cultural constructions that have gendered origins. Talking in public was and still is a male preserve; male and female students learn that this is the case from their experiences in (and out of) the classroom (Alton-Lee and Nuthall with Patrick 1993; Kelly 1988; Nairn 1991; Newton 1988; Sadker, Sadker, and Klein 1991; Spender 1982). I am arguing for female students to have fair access to opportunities for practicing their public talking in the public verbal space of the classroom so that they have the verbal skills to compete effectively in labor and training markets. A potential weakness in my argument is that it may be understood to mean that male public talking patterns are the yardstick by which female public talking patterns are measured and that the male way of talking is to be emulated. It means trying to improve female students' access in the existing system, without evaluating whether that system is good for female (or male) students (Dann 1992). Female students' achievement in the male system on male terms has contradictory and complex implications for girls and women. It may be empowering and provide access to status, money, and independence. At the same time, it may be disempowering because women are successful in a system that undervalues their gender.

Nevertheless, educational institutions cannot justify the continued dominance of the public verbal space of classrooms by particular male students. Female students' access to opportunities for talking is important for five reasons. First, talking is central to the learning process because through talking we "remake knowledge for ourselves" (Barnes 1976). Second, Alton-Lee and Nuthall with Patrick (1993) have shown that the students who talk aloud in class influence what gets taught. The third important function of talking in class is its relationship to the acquisition of new knowledge; students generate "knowledge constructs as they engage in the process of making meaning out of curriculum content" (Alton-Lee and Nuthall with Patrick 1993). This is problematic for female students because their new knowledge and understandings are being shaped by the male focus of the official curriculum and by the male students' experiences and opinions that are articulated during class discussions. Fourth, talking aloud provides one way in which a teacher can check a student's understanding at that specific time and correct any misunderstandings that have occurred. Finally, class discussions provide opportunities for female students to practice talking in public, an important skill for girls and women to gain so that they can talk with confidence in their workplaces, at the Department of Social Welfare, in their doctor's office, in their homes, and in local and national government.

My concept of strategic feminism involves taking action because "we do not need, and indeed never will have, all the answers before we act . . . it is often only through taking action that we can discover some of them" (Bunch 1983). Strategic feminism is grounded in a contextualized notion of agency: "a notion of agency born of history and geography" and anchored in the history of specific struggles (Mohanty 1991). It is about recognizing myself, students, and teachers as agents in our respective contexts within the broader social context of education in contemporary Aotearoa/New Zealand. Agency, action, and evaluation of action by those it directly affects are the elements of strategic feminism and therefore, of this chapter.

What Does Public Verbal Space Mean?

The public verbal space and the physical space (layout of seating, proximity to the teacher, characteristics of the back, front, center, and periphery of the room) are interrelational. Physical space influences what happens in the public verbal space, and the public verbal space influences what happens in the physical space of the classroom; "space is constituted through social relations and material social practices . . . [and] the social is spatially constructed" (Massey 1992, 70). The public verbal space and the physical space of the classroom are social and spatial constructions; the public verbal space of the classroom is constituted through the social and spatial relations of the students, the teacher, and myself, the researcher. In other words, the public verbal space exists as a space in which individuals do and do not speak, depending on their perceptions and experiences of the lived peer culture, the curriculum, the pedagogy, and the spatial arrangement of their seating positions. Participation and nonparticipation in the public verbal space of geography classrooms is also influenced by the gender, race, class, sexuality, age, and prior knowledge of the students. The conceptualization of the space of public talking, as public verbal space is shown in visual form in figure 6.1.

Figure 6.1 makes visible the audible and inaudible realms of public verbal space; the diagram has been constructed to take account of public talking and of silence. The left-hand side of the diagram shows public verbal space as one speech bubble to be "shared" by female and male students; this implies that female and male students are competing for an equitable "share" of finite public verbal space. The right-hand side of the diagram shows that some female

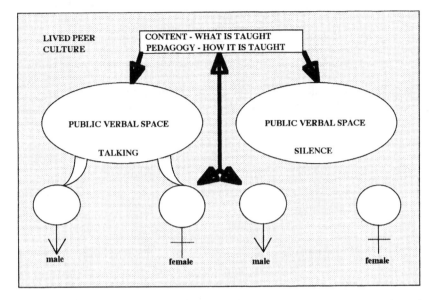

Fig. 6.1. Students' participation and nonparticipation in the public verbal space of geography classrooms.

and male students do not take part at all in the public verbal space; they are silent. The two sides of the diagram are not mutually exclusive. Students may take part in the public verbal space of one geography lesson and remain silent during another. Two factors that will influence individual female and male students' decisions about whether or not to participate in a lesson is the content and pedagogy of that lesson. The process of teaching content is not a one-way top-down process; students are influential in shaping the teacher's choice of content and teaching style before and during the lesson. This two-way process is indicated by the arrows.

Teaching and learning in the classroom take place within the sociocultural context of "lived [peer] culture," which "refers to [peer] culture as it is produced in ongoing interactions and as a terrain in which class, race, and gender meanings and antagonisms are lived out" (Apple and Weis 1983, 27). Each student's experience of the peer culture of particular classrooms will influence her or his decision to talk or remain silent. Lived peer culture is everywhere, inside and outside the classroom; it is invisible, and powerful in its positive and negative forms. The evaluations and the laughter of peers can be the most affirming and the most damaging experiences of an adolescent's life. The following section outlines the context of the selected geography classroom. The subsequent section is concerned with quiet female and male students' experiences of the public verbal space of this classroom.

Inside One Geography Classroom

They were lined up outside the classroom bursting with energy. . . . The class already sits in groups of four or five or six so it is very straightforward for groupwork to occur. . . . There was a great deal of noise, talking. Some students seemed lost; others worked well . . . Ms Lapresle said that my presence didn't seem to change things—they were behaving as they would usually . . . A positive learning atmosphere in the classroom; Ms Lapresle seemed relaxed.[3]

—K. Nairn

There were thirty students in this fifth form geography class—eleven female students and nineteen male students—and it was taught by a female teacher, Ms Lapresle. Students at this level in Aotearoa/New Zealand are usually aged fifteen to sixteen years. There was one Maori student in this class, the rest of the students were of Pakeha descent. The ethnic composition of the school was also predominantly Pakeha. This high school was located in a small town in a rural area. The physical space of the classroom was typical of many classrooms in Aotearoa/New Zealand; one wall of windows, two walls of noticeboards where students' work was displayed, and a whiteboard on the wall at the front of the room. The desks were arranged in groups of four to six. Therefore, students faced in different directions rather than the usual pattern where all students tend to face the front of the room.

Figure 6.2 shows where the quiet female and male students sat in the physical space of the classroom. Ten of these quiet students—seven female (including the Maori student) and three male—were each invited to a one-to-one interview. During the first round of interviews, I asked these students about how they chose where they sat in class; both female and male students related their decision to their friends' choice of location. Figure 6.2 also provides a diagrammatic summary of who (students, teacher, researcher) named particular students as quiet students. Amy, for example, was named by other students, the teacher, and the researcher as a quiet student, whereas Tammy and Kate were only named by the researcher as quiet students. All but three desks were occupied by students (see figure 6.2 for the location of empty desks).

The spatial pattern that is evident in figure 6.2 is the concentration of quiet students around the periphery of the classroom; it is almost as though they are on the edge looking in to a central public verbal space in which they seldom participate. Quiet students appear to group together mostly in same-sex pairs or groups. The largest "concentration" of quiet students is the group of five female students who sit together in the back right-hand corner of the classroom. The teacher usually stood in the central front area of the classroom when she was formally teaching and sat at her desk when carrying out administrative tasks; both these positions were central to the classroom, placing the quiet students in her peripheral vision rather than in her direct vision. Krup-

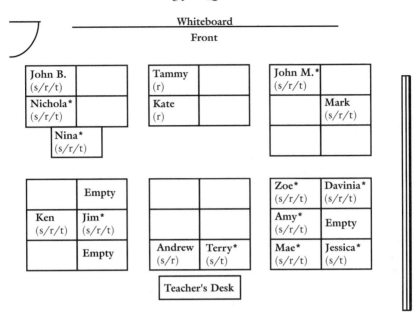

Key
s = named by other students as a quiet student
r = named by researcher as a quiet student
t = named by the teacher as a quiet student
* = interviewed by the researcher
Terry is a male student.

Fig. 6.2. Seat locations of quiet students and summary of sources of data about each student.

nick (1992) calls the areas where quiet students sit the "silence ghettoes"; the area of the room where the five female students sit is one example of a "silence ghetto." Soja (1985) observes, "As a social product, spatiality can be continuously reinforced or reproduced over time, presenting an appearance of stability and persistence. But it can also be substantially restructured and radically reconstituted, invoking again its origins and grounding in social practice."

The spatiality of silence in one geography classroom was captured at a certain time in figure 6.2, but this is not to deny that this pattern is transformable. One powerful example of the mutability of public verbal space is demonstrated in another geography classroom by a quiet female student, Lisa, who deliberately moves into the public verbal space. The experiences of the ten quiet fifth form students will be considered in detail in the following two sections of this chapter, and then I will return to the experience of Lisa.

"Hearing" from the Quiet Students

I have purposely devoted a greater proportion of the written space of the following section to the discussion of female students' experiences of the public verbal space of the geography classroom. The exploration of male students' silence has occurred in a relatively smaller written space for three reasons. First, a greater proportion of female students are quiet students in coeducational classrooms. In this particular classroom, nine of the eleven female students were quiet but only seven of the nineteen males. Twice as many female students were interviewed as male students. Second, hearing from the quiet male students was more difficult to achieve: one quiet male student declined the invitation to be interviewed, and another quiet male did not take seriously the questionnaires asking for his perspectives and threw them away. Third, the three male students who accepted the invitation to be interviewed said much less about themselves; they were relatively silent on the subject of their own silence. Therefore, I remain less knowledgeable about male silence. All of these factors contribute to the relative silence of this chapter on the subject of male silence.

Paradoxical Space: Quiet Female Students' Experiences of Being at the Center and at the Margin

The classroom is one of the most evaluative public spaces that exist; the academic and social capabilities, appearance, dress, and behavior of each individual student have the potential to be evaluated by their teacher and their peers. At the same time, the classroom may be experienced by students as a relatively private space in which it is possible to accomplish friendship and conversations (see Alton-Lee and Nuthall with Patrick 1993). The classroom is therefore a paradoxical space, and students' experiences of the classroom are likely to be paradoxical.

Female students may experience the public dimension of classroom space as they experience other public space, in a way that is self-conscious and fearful. Paradoxically, the same female students may experience their private dimension of the classroom space—where they sit with another friend—as mutually interactive and supportive. In this way female students may experience the classroom space as "insiders" *and* as "outsiders": "inside" their friendship networks, yet "outside" the public verbal space.

Nichola (see figure 6.2) chose a seating position that placed her at the margins of the classroom, yet provided her with a central viewing position of everyone in the room:

I like the wall at the back of me rather than being stuck in the middle and people are behind me . . . I feel more comfortable against something, when I rearrange my room I always have my bed against the wall, I wouldn't put it in the middle, I wouldn't feel safe (Nichola, first interview by author, tape recording, Aotearoa/ New Zealand, 27 May 1993).

Nichola and Nina both used the word "safe" in their respective interviews to explain the physical lay-outs of classrooms in which they felt safe and unsafe:

Some teachers have got their room and it is set out in a circle, all the desks in a circle, and that is a wee bit easier cos you are actually safe from everyone and you can see everyone and that makes you feel more comfortable. . . . (Nina, first interview by author, tape recording, Aotearoa/New Zealand, 28 May 1993)

The teacher's position is central to the web of public student-teacher interactions and Mae explains how it was easier to interact publicly with her science teacher because she was positioned close to the teacher. This contrasted with her experience in geography where there was a discernible gulf across which she had to reach from her physical location at the edge of the web. Mae conveyed a sense of physical distance and of occupants in that physical space as constraining factors to her participation in the public verbal space of the geography classroom:

It's easier because you are sitting up the front you can just sort of tell the teacher what the answer is . . .whereas if you are near the back, you are saying it across the room and . . . the class is in between you and the teacher and . . . it makes it harder because of that. (Mae, second interview by author, tape recording, Aotearoa/New Zealand, 12 August 1993)

Mae is a drama student and therefore is familiar with performance and voice projection, yet she is self-conscious about taking up public verbal space in this particular subject. This is one example of how students may lead double lives: a student may appear to lack confidence in her or his verbal skills inside the classroom, yet the same student is confident and competent in his or her verbal skills in a range of arenas outside the classroom.

Being Watched and Judged: Quiet Female Students' Experiences

For some women, there is no greater fear than that of making a spectacle of herself . . . much of the buffeting and bruising, the confinement and stumbling, of women's experience of space is part of a self-consciousness about being noticed: women watching themselves being watched and judged. (Rose 1993, 145)

Rose's description was echoed by some of the quiet female students:

> You don't feel comfortable in maybe other classes when you think people are looking at you . . . if I had my way I would sit down the back, most of the other classes I am down the back or against a wall. (Nichola, second interview by author, tape recording, Aotearoa/New Zealand, 15 July 1993)

Nichola articulated the experience of being watched. Nichola chooses seating positions that enable her to watch others in case they are watching her, another student cannot watch her unnoticed. Nichola went on to articulate the experience of being labeled, of being judged: "I hate people putting labels on anyone. . . . I really hate that, so that is something you are conscious of." The labels Nichola was most concerned about were to do with her physical appearance and her intellectual abilities:

> Probably skinny labels, or . . . I was sort of top of every class . . . and you sort of immediately got the label of brain box, or nerdy, boring person . . . you can't just . . . be yourself. (Nichola, second interview by author, tape recording, Aotearoa/New Zealand, 15 July 1993)

In contrast to Nichola, Mae prefers to sit near the front of the room and the teacher, so that she does not have to watch other students watching her and because it minimizes the distance across which she must project herself:

> I think at the front you feel more confident about saying the answer to something because everybody is behind you and they are not all turning around to look at you while you are trying to talk to the teacher. (Mae, first interview by author, tape recording, Aotearoa/New Zealand, 10 June 1993)

The experience of being watched and judged, so clearly articulated by Nichola and Mae, is one of the most objectifying processes to which the body is submitted (Young 1990). There is a sense of these two female students being "outside" their bodies watching themselves being watched and evaluated. Nichola evaluates herself as she perceives others would. Nichola and Mae construct themselves as objects both in their experiences of physical and evaluative space, and in their articulation of those experiences. Nichola wants to know who is watching her, Mae does not. This self-consciousness suggests that these two female students see themselves as located in space, a space that is not their own (Young 1990); "Women see their bodies as objects placed in space among other objects . . .Women's sense of embodiment can make space feel like a thousand piercing eyes; 'location is about vulnerability' " (Rose 1993, 146). Nichola's and Mae's words have conveyed the vulnerability of their location in the geography classroom, and the strategies they adopt to minimize vulnerability.

This vulnerability was experienced by other female students in the class, as the fear of being laughed at. The laughter and humor of peers can be a powerful controlling mechanism in the classroom; laughter can be a particularly intense form of evaluation:

People are just sort of scared . . . just the fact that if you are wrong you know you are going to get laughed at and be embarrassed, I guess it comes down to it. (Amy, first interview by author, tape recording, Aotearoa/New Zealand, 15 June 1993)

Amy went on to name the students that she thought were most likely to laugh out loud, two female and three male students, "especially Nicholas B. and Paul," who both sat at the neighboring group to Amy's. In response to the interview question, "Has it happened very much . . . how many times . . . roughly?", Amy was able to quantify the number of times she had been laughed at by "Paul and co." during the four months of geography prior to her first interview in mid-June:

Quite a few, but sometimes you just don't know whether that's what they are laughing at or they're laughing cos they laugh. Oh, I suppose about thirty. Because sometimes you just don't know. (Amy, first interview by author, tape recording, Aotearoa/New Zealand, 15 June 1993)

The teacher said that Paul directed his laughter and comments at female students. Amy's experience of his (and other students') comments and laughter were enough to silence her, even when she was not sure whether it was directed at her or not. Male students' laughter and humor in the public verbal space of the classroom not only takes up finite public verbal space and teacher attention, but operates as a form of peer evaluation that can silence female students. Even when this laughter is not directed at a particular female student, the implied threat of generalized laughter keeps some female students quiet.

Getting the Answer Wrong: Quiet Female and Male Students' Experiences

Six of the seven female students and two of the three males said that they were likely to get their answers to the teacher's questions right. Other factors negate the effects of being confident about giving correct answers, however, and these constrain female and male students from volunteering to answer the teacher's questions. Some of the factors that silence female students have already been highlighted—self-consciousness about being watched, judged, and laughed at. This section will look specifically at female and male students' experiences of getting an answer wrong.

The ten interviewed students' responses to the questions: "how do you feel if you get an answer wrong? what do the other students do?" provide some insight into how the risks of getting it wrong far outweigh any benefits of getting it right for some of these students. In the previous section, which considers laughter as a particularly intense form of evaluation, Amy has already explained that if you are wrong, "you know you are going to get laughed at."

Other quiet female students talked about their experiences of getting it wrong in terms of the effects on their self-confidence:

> Quite often I think of an answer and I don't say it and it ends up being wrong so you don't want to answer the next one . . . I'd much rather people tell me what to do and what happens rather than me having to tell them what I think happens and then being told you are wrong, cos that takes you back a notch. (Nichola, first interview by author, tape recording, Aotearoa/New Zealand, 27 May 1993)

For Nichola, the risks of getting it wrong mean that she would rather forgo any opportunities for independent decisionmaking in the classroom setting. In the second interview, Nichola went on to say how getting an answer wrong "sort of undermines your confidence." Both Jessica and Zoe used language that described how their bodies felt when they got an answer wrong:

> Oh sometimes I feel really stupid and then sometimes I don't really care, if I give a really stupid answer I feel really thick. (Jessica, first interview by author, tape recording, Aotearoa/New Zealand, 3 August 1993)
> Really stupid and very small, and you just like to shrink really, you don't want anyone to talk to you . . . you don't want to talk again. (Zoe, second interview by author, tape recording, Aotearoa/New Zealand, 20 August 1993)

Getting an answer wrong was articulated by Zoe in a way that showed her "intense self-awareness about being seen and taking up [too much] space" (Rose 1993). Both Jessica's and Zoe's experiences of *feeling wrong* about an incorrect answer that they gave, "dissolves the split between the mind and body by thinking through the body, their bodies" (Rose 1993).

In contrast, the following six students—three female and three male students—were relatively less concerned about getting an answer wrong. Nevertheless, there are still hints at discomfort in the following quotes. The quotes have been arranged so that the three female students are speaking first, followed by the three male students, so that the differences between the genders as well as within the genders will be more obvious.

> I'm not sure. I've never had a few answers wrong in geography before. You feel a bit stupid I think but then again people wouldn't really . . . notice if you got it wrong, they'd be looking it up in their books to find the right answer. (Mae, first interview by author, tape recording, Aotearoa/New Zealand, 10 June 1993)
> In geography I don't think I would feel stupid, Ms Lapresle doesn't make you feel silly . . . no-one has ever said anything to me that's awful or anything . . . I don't think I'd let it worry me. (Nina, first interview by author, tape recording, Aotearoa/New Zealand, 28 May 1993)
> I don't mind if I get it wrong, I mean, I don't think it's much of a big deal . . .I don't really worry about it too much . . . because sometimes, you know, I do get it right. (Davinia, first interview by author, tape recording, Aotearoa/New Zealand, 2 June 1993)

Well, usually a bit silly. I try not to get answers wrong really. I'm usually pretty sure of most of the answers because I do listen to what the teacher is telling us about. Seem to be quite good at remembering all the information in geography and other subjects. (Terry, first interview by author, tape recording, Aotearoa/ New Zealand, 4 June 1993)

It doesn't really worry me much. It's not really that much of a big deal. (John M., first interview by author, tape recording, Aotearoa/New Zealand, 8 June 1993)

I've never been in a situation where I've got an answer wrong and the whole class has been roaring with laughter, so

Author: How do you actually feel if you do get an answer wrong?

Well, I just got it wrong, I just have to find the right answer, I suppose. (Jim, first interview by author, tape recording, Aotearoa/New Zealand, 3 June 1993)

The arrangement of these quotes represents a continuum of experiences of getting an answer wrong in the public space of this geography classroom. One male student said he would feel "a bit silly" but that he was unlikely to get an answer wrong (Terry). There were female and male students who suggested that the experience of getting it wrong was no "big deal" (Nina, Davinia, John M., and Jim); Davinia does not worry if she gets an answer wrong, "because sometimes . . . I do get it right."

It was the experiences of female students such as Davinia and Nina that disrupted my expectations and generalizations by demonstrating that not all the quiet female students experienced giving the wrong answer in negative terms. The description and analysis of patterns and exceptions are important because they give voice and therefore visibility to the diversity of quiet female and male students' experiences of the evaluative climate of the public verbal space in geography classrooms.

Another important exception is Lisa, a quiet student who decided to take up more public verbal space *independently* of this research[4]:

Yeah, more so now than I did in the first term . . . because I feel better talking when I am up the front than I do . . . talking, way at the back. (Lisa, first interview by author, tape recording, Aotearoa/New Zealand, 21 July 1993)

Lisa was a powerful agent. She made a conscious decision to move away from where her peer group was sitting and *into* the public verbal space. I have in-cluded Lisa's words because they contain the essence of my ideal for quiet female and male students:

Well I said to them if they wanted to stay there that that's okay, but I'm moving up because I can't hear very well . . . I think if you are at the side or say if you are at the back, if people are talking it is sort of like a block between you and the teacher . . .the best place I'd go to the middle, for concentration . . . I think I understand the work a lot better because I am closer to it and I can check with things a lot better like it's not distorted, or like things getting broken, *like it's clear all the way through.* (Lisa, first interview by author, tape recording, Aotearoa/New Zealand, 21 July 1993, my emphasis)

The Women-Focused Lesson

I wrote the women-focused curriculum intervention to fit the *Prescribed Common Topics: Population Studies* currently taught in fifth form geography in Aotearoa/New Zealand. The women-focused lesson was centered around a video, *The Price of Marriage* (A Woman's World Series, ca. 1986), in which Daslima, who lives in Dacca, Bangladesh, tells her story about the decision she made not to marry. Daslima is a young woman of a similar age but of a different "race" and class than the students in the geography class. The video presenters are women of color; nevertheless, the politics of filming others for television and video consumption globally, compounded by the use of this video by myself as the basis for a women-focused lesson for a group of students in Aotearoa/New Zealand, turned out to be problematic. It raises issues about how and why "Western" feminists such as myself re-present others (who have already been re-presented in the process of filming) to "Western" students. Have I as a "Western" White feminist written a lesson that is about a different woman from a different country, inadvertently encouraged the students to conceive of Daslima as a typical Third World woman, as representing "*all* Third World women*"? (See Mohanty 1988.)

Two strategies were utilized in the pedagogy of the women-focused lesson: (1) the provision of an activity that enabled students to bring their prior knowledge to the lesson and (2) turn taking. The first strategy was achieved by a timetable activity that required students to write their own "typical" timetable alongside a "typical" timetable for Daslima. Starting with the student's own ideas and experiences is an important pedagogical principle (Alton-Lee and Densem 1992), but the risk of this particular activity is that the students' own experiences become the implicit yardstick against which Daslima's experiences are measured. My good intention of encouraging the students to recognize Daslima's paid and unpaid work may have had unplanned negative consequences because the activity may have reinforced "the 'third-world difference'—that stable, ahistorical something that apparently oppresses most if not all women in these countries" (Mohanty 1988).

The second strategy—turn taking—facilitates the public participation of all students in a class. This minimizes the relative risks for each individual student because everyone is participating within a similar set of evaluative conditions. The following steps were adopted to minimize the risks of public participation. First, everyone had the opportunity to think of and discuss with their neighbors what they thought the main message of the video was; in other words, there was preparation time. Second, everyone had the opportunity to present their point of view without interruption or response from other students, on a topic for which there was no right or wrong answer. Third, it was possible to decline; one male student decided not to take his turn in this lesson.

Both strategies have spatial elements: the women-focused curriculum intervention is concerned with devoting curriculum space to women-focused content on a small-scale and the turn-taking strategy is an attempt to equitably distribute access to the public verbal space to all students under similar conditions of risk. The quiet students were interviewed on a one-to-one basis *after* the women-focused lesson and were asked questions about the content and about the turn-taking strategy.

The Quiet Students' Perspectives of the Women-Focused Content

Four of the seven quiet female students said that they had participated more than usual during the women-focused lesson; the remaining three female and three male students said they had participated the same as usual. Two common themes emerged in the female students' explanations for their increased participation; they had found the video interesting and/or relevant to their own experiences. Mae's explanation extends the concept of participation; Mae said that she had participated more "because I watched it more . . . because I found it interesting. I was thinking about what they were saying about her life and what she does." Watching and thinking about the content of the lesson is participating in the content; Mae has highlighted the importance of this hidden dimension of classroom participation, a dimension that would be difficult to capture quantitatively.

The following comments reveal what two other female students thought about the content of the video:

> They didn't make it all seem really bad . . . like she seemed quite happy some of the time when she was talking with her friends and that, like some videos might just show all the negative sides of living where she was, but it showed both sides. (Nina, second interview by author, tape recording, Aotearoa/New Zealand, 23 July 1993)
>
> I thought they would be really conservative. And the way she sort of said well the rest of the family can do this or this, that's Daslima, and the mother agreed. If she'd had a father I don't think he would've agreed, I think she would have ended up getting married. (Nichola, second interview by author, tape recording, Aotearoa/New Zealand, 15 July 1993)

Nina has identified the positive nature of female friendship, and Nichola speaks of Daslima making decisions that are supported by her mother. For some of the female and male students who watched the video, however, what they initially noticed were the negative aspects of Daslima's and other women's lives in Bangladesh:

I thought it was pretty disgusting really, that the women get taken advantage of, especially the young girls, and that they get married off to somebody they don't even like. (Amy, second interview by author, tape recording, Aotearoa/New Zealand, 27 July 1993)

It is important that a women-focused lesson present women as agents in their worlds, who make decisions; if it does not do this, it feeds the myth that all women passively accept their "fate" of powerlessness. If the content of the video/lesson feeds this myth, then it does not contribute to female students' sense of themselves as agents in their own worlds. In spite of Amy's initial negative frame of reference, she did recognize Daslima as an active agent. "I can't really think of much that was positive except for the fact that she decided that she wasn't going to marry, and goes to work, that was good."

Terry found the women-focused lesson interesting, yet it would be impossible to deduce from his comments that it was women focused; Terry reverted to gender-unspecified language in his comments about the lesson. Jim and John M. both considered the experiences of Daslima within a negative framework. Jim pointed out that "girls could be sold off by their parents," and John M. felt "sorry for the girls like what they have to put up with," which suggests a somewhat patronizing concern. There was no recognition of the positive elements of Daslima's existence.

The negative frame of reference that Jim and John M. have constructed around Daslima's existence is not likely to affect their sense of themselves, but if these two (and other) male students equate women's existence with negativity, this may influence their perceptions of and interactions with girls and women in general. If male students perceive girls and women as powerless and feel sorry for them, this contributes to and becomes part of the evaluative climate and the lived peer culture of the classroom. In other words, male students' expectations of female powerlessness may become self-fulfilling prophecies and may affect the quality of the interrelationships between female and male students. These potential negative effects must be weighed against the identified positive effects of the women-focused content for female students that have already been discussed earlier in the section.

Developing women-focused content to empower female students is a complex task; content must realistically portray the positive and negative aspects of women's existence, and it must value women's traditional (often unpaid) achievements as much as their nontraditional achievements. Some of the female and male students of this geography class experienced the women-focused lesson in negative terms; they were upset about how women in Bangladesh were treated. Other female students recognized the positive elements of Daslima's existence—her friendships and her mother's support for her decision. The development of curricula about women to empower young women should include opportunities for dialogue, debriefing, and evaluation.

The Quiet Students' Perspectives
of the Turn-Taking Strategy

The quiet female students spoke positively about their experiences of the turn-taking strategy. These female students seldom participated in the public verbal space of their geography classroom, yet all of them were positive about being put on the spot to speak during the turn-taking segment of the women-focused lesson. Some of their comments follow:

> It was quite good because I had something to say for once. Yeah it was quite good, what I said. (Jessica, first interview by author, tape recording, Aotearoa/New Zealand, 3 August 1993)
>
> Yeah I thought that was good . . . because everybody got a chance to have their say and because everybody had to say it they were all sort of equal and nobody could . . . disagree with their answer because they could just say their own thing as well. (Mae, second interview by author, tape recording, Aotearoa/New Zealand, 12 August 1993)
>
> It was quite good I thought . . . because that way people get used to saying it and they are not really as worried about it and also if you are asking everyone to do it, you don't think oh I'm going to be the only one, if you are not used to calling out or something. (Nina, second interview by author, tape recording, Aotearoa/New Zealand, 23 July 1993)

Both Jim and Terry were positive about the turn-taking method; however, they did not speak about their own experiences of the strategy. Jim enjoyed the strategy "because everybody was trying to think of something that someone else hadn't said beforehand so we had a lot of different ideas," and Terry spoke in terms of how the strategy "makes people participate in it." John M. was the only one of the three male students who talked in terms of his own experience of the strategy—"I didn't really like it"— but reassured me that being put on the spot "didn't worry me." John M. was clear about his preference for the status quo where he could remain silent/uninvolved, and explained his silence—"I don't really like geography that much."

John M.'s point of view reinforced the rationale behind the curriculum intervention: if students find geography interesting (and therefore relevant), they are more likely to want to be involved in the class discussions. John M. says that he is not interested in geography even though it is concerned predominantly with male activities; this challenges the assumption that all male students will automatically be interested in male-focused content just as it challenges the assumption that all female students will automatically be interested in women-focused content. Male hegemony, however, makes it possible for male students to enjoy male knowledge, whereas it often renders female students' enjoyment of female knowledge problematic.

The content of a lesson and how it is taught are interrelated. It is not enough to introduce women-focused content and expect female students to automatically begin participating in public. The structure that facilitates public participation must be changed to provide minimal risk opportunities for quiet female students to take up and gain confidence; turn taking provides one such structure.

Silence and Voice—Some Conclusions

The experiences of quiet female and male students in geography classrooms are diverse. There were differences and similarities between and within the gender categories. During the interviews, female students talked easily about why they did not talk in class, and the male students remained relatively silent on the subject of their own silence. Therefore, I have written far more about female silence than I have about male silence.

The differences between and within the gender categories were the most clearly demonstrated by what quiet students said about their experiences of getting an answer wrong in class. A greater proportion of the female students and one male student were concerned about getting it wrong, yet there were female and male students for whom it was "no big deal." Some of the quiet female students' words suggested a greater level of fear of getting it wrong— "scared" (Amy), "I feel really stupid" (Jessica)—compared with the male students" words—"usually a bit silly" (Terry).

The concept of paradoxical space (Rose 1993) was used to explore and to understand the diversity and ambiguity of quiet female students' experiences of the classroom space. It meant that the classroom could be conceived of as being a space in which quiet female students may be simultaneously "insiders" *and* "outsiders." Female students talked with their friends in localized private spaces where they sat and were physically located inside the geography classroom, contributing to their sense of being insiders. At the same time, these female students were outside the public verbal space of the geography classroom. They were the listeners, *and* they were located on the periphery of the classroom's physical space—they were spectators of a central area dominated by the performance of two or three male students.

Two female students said that they would not feel safe or comfortable in particular seating arrangements. Their use of the word "safe" indicates how intensely the evaluative dimensions of classroom spaces are experienced by some female students. Seating arrangements and positions where they could see everyone else in the classroom—in a circle and at the back of the classroom—were considered to be safe, more comfortable. Comfortable spaces were also the shared private spaces at the groups of desks where female students sat—"I don't think it makes any difference *where* you are sitting . . . it makes a difference *who* you are sitting with." (Nina, my emphasis)

The experience of being outsiders was intensified for some female students, who were already self-conscious about potential evaluation of their physical appearance and intellectual abilities, by the evaluative climate of the classroom. Some of the female students articulated a sense of being "outside" their bodies—watching themselves being watched and evaluated. This process locates female students in the classroom space, a space that is not their own (Rose 1993). Nichola evaluated herself—"you . . . immediately got the label of brain box, or nerdy, boring person"—as she perceived others would; the evaluative climate was internalized to become this student's own evaluative process (Alton-Lee and Nuthall with Patrick 1993). Evaluations were experienced bodily and spatially—"[you feel] really stupid and very small, and you just like to shrink really . . ."(Zoe). For girls and women:

> Being in space is not easy. Indeed at its worst this feeling results in a desire to make ourselves absent from space; it can mean that "we acquiesce in being made invisible, in our occupying no space. We participate in our own erasure." (Rose 1993:143)

This desire to be absent from space occurred at the material level because female students were more likely than male students to be absent from geography classes (Nairn 1994), and at the auditory level because female students were more likely to be silent.

This research shows that female students have very good reasons for not participating in the public verbal space of geography classrooms. Silence is one self-protective strategy to manage the risks of evaluation. Silence, though, was not the answer to the problem. They were aware of being watched, judged, and laughed at even when they did not speak. These female students made conscious decisions to be silent; they were not *naturally* silent.

Silence in and absence from the geography classroom by female students is like a vote of no confidence in the current geography curriculum. It is problematic to expect female students to speak in the public verbal space of geography classrooms without making changes to the content and pedagogy of the geography curriculum. When they got women-focused content that was interesting and relevant to talk and think about, female students talked more, watched more, and wanted more. Altering the content on *one* occasion inspired some female students to talk more. It is the responsibility of the geography education community to make it worthwhile for female students to take part in our classes. Taking part is used in the broadest sense to include talking, watching, listening. This means creating curriculum content and participation structures with female students' needs and interests in mind. Creating spaces for female students in geographical education does not end here; my geographical imagination is already thinking beyond this written space to . . .

Notes

1. "Pakeha" is the Maori term for White New Zealanders. The term is used as a mark of respect for the right of the indigenous people to name those who came after them (Alton-Lee and Nuthall with Patrick 1993).

2. The term "women-focused curriculum/lesson" is used to refer to content that is primarily about women.

3. The names of the teacher and the students have been changed.

4. Lisa was in the seventh form geography class involved in the research; students at this level are usually aged 17–18 years.

References

Alton-Lee, A. and Densem, P. 1992. Towards a gender-inclusive school curriculum: Changing educational practice. In *Women and education in Aotearoa* 2, ed. S. Middleton and A. Jones, 197–220. Wellington, NZ: Bridget Williams Books.

Alton-Lee, A. and Nuttal, G. 1991. Understanding Learning and Teaching Project. Phase Two. *Final Report to the Ministry of Education*. University of Canterbury: Education Department.

Alton-Lee, A., Densem, P., and Nuthall, G. 1990. "I only think of the men . . .I don't think of the women." *Set Number 2* Item 16:1–8.

Alton-Lee, A., Densem, P. and Nuthall, G. with Patrick, J. 1993. Reframing classroom research: A lesson from the private world of children. *Harvard Educational Review* 63, 1, Spring: 50–84.

Apple, M. 1991. The culture and commerce of the textbook. In *The Politics of the Textbook*, ed. M. W. Apple and L. K. Christian-Smith, 22–40. New York: Routledge.

Apple, M. and Weis, L. 1983. Ideology and practice in schooling: A political and conceptual introduction. In *Ideology and practice in schooling*, ed. M. Apple and L. Weis, 3–32. Philadelphia: Temple University Press.

Barnes, D. 1976. *From communication to curriculum*. Middlesex: Penguin.

Bunch, C. 1983. Not by degrees: Feminist theory and education. In *Learning our way: Essays in feminist education*, ed. C. Bunch and S. Pollack, 240–53. New York: St Martin's Press.

Dann, C. 1992. Ecofeminism, women and nature. In *Feminist voices: Women's studies texts for Aotearoa/New Zealand*, ed. R. Du Plessis, 338–53. Oxford: Oxford University Press.

Grima, G. and Smith, A.B. 1993. The participation of boys and girls in home economics. *Gender and Education* 5, 3:251–68.

Hazel, V. 1994. Disjointed articulations: The politics of voice and Jane Campion's *The Piano. Women's Studies Journal* 10, 2:27–40.

Johnson, L. 1994. What future for feminist geography? *Gender, Place and Culture* 1, 1:103–13.

Kelly, A. 1988. Gender differences in teacher-pupil interactions: A meta-analytic review. *Research in Education* 39: 1–23.

Krupnick, C. 1992. Foreign correspondent television programme screened in New Zealand 4 June.

Larner, W. 1993. "Difference down under": Geography and feminism in New Zealand. Paper presented to the Canadian Association of Geographers, Carleton University, Ontario.

Longhurst, R. and Peace, R. 1993. Lecture theatre to classroom—feminist geography. *New Zealand Journal of Geography* October Issue:16–19.

Massey, D. 1992. Politics and space/time. *New Left Review* 196:65–84.

Mohanty, C. 1991. Cartographies of struggle. Third World women and the politics of feminism. In *Third World Women and the Politics of Feminism,* ed. C. Mohanty, A. Russo and L. Torres, 1–47. Bloomington: Indiana University Press.

———. 1988. Under Western eyes: Feminist scholarship and colonial discourses. *Feminist Review* 30:61–88.

Nairn, K. 1994. Quiet students in geography classrooms. M.A. Thesis. University of Canterbury: Geography Department.

———. 1991. Geography and gender in the secondary school classroom. *New Zealand Journal of Geography* April:14–15.

Newton, K. 1988. Teacher-pupil interaction—does it affect equity? *National Education* August: 127–29.

Rose, G. 1993. *Feminism and geography. The limits of geographical knowledge*. Minneapolis, MN: University of Minnesota Press.

Sadker, M. Sadker, D. and Klein, S. 1991. The issue of gender in elementary and secondary education. In *Review of Research in Education* 17, ed. G. Grant, 269–334. Washington, D.C.: American Educational Research Association.

Soja, E. 1985. The spatiality of social life: Towards a transformative retheorisation. In *Social Relations and Spatial Structures,* ed. D. Gregory and J. Urry, 90–127. New York: St. Martin's Press.

Spender, D. 1982. *Invisible women: The schooling scandal*. London: Writers and Readers.

———. 1981. *Men's studies modified: The Impact of Feminism on the Academic Disciplines*. New York: Pergamon Press.

Sturrock, F. 1993. *The status of girls and women in New Zealand education and training*. Wellington: Learning Media, Ministry of Education.

Weiler, K. 1988. *Women teaching for change: Gender, class and power*. London: Bergin and Garvey.

A Women's World Series. ca. 1986. *The Price of Marriage*. New Internationalist. Video.

Young, I. 1990. *Throwing like a girl and other essays in feminist philosophy and social theory*. Bloomington, IN: Indiana University Press.

Part 2

Methodology

Introduction to Part 2

As the World Turns: New Horizons in Feminist Geographic Methodologies

Susan Hanson

> For all my background in history, I had been thinking lately that stories
> were pretty useless. The first scientists, way back, in pre-Socratic time,
> figured out that if they were going to understand anything they would
> have to discard narrative in favor of empirical methods. The Creation
> myths explained, after a fashion, who and why, but science would tell how
> and what.
>
> —Jane Hamilton

In Jane Hamilton's novel, *A Map of the World* (1994), Howard and Alice
Goodwin try to make sense of a world that is spinning out of control. The
Goodwins are a young couple who have chosen to run a small dairy farm in
Wisconsin; sometime in the early 1990s they suddenly find their routine and
circumscribed lives untethered, and their marginal livelihood disrupted, by a
series of unforeseen events. In the quotation above, Howard struggles to understand what has happened and is happening, so that he can decide on a
sensible course of action. The narratives he and Alice had constructed, however loosely, to comprehend and, in turn, to shape their world had completely
unraveled.[1]

Jane Hamilton has spun a tale in which the questions, "What is real?" and
"How do we know what is real?" figure prominently. As examples, one thread
of the story concerns allegations from several children that Alice, who has a
part-time, off-farm job as the school nurse, had sexually abused them—she had
not, although she had swatted one of them in a moment of anger. Another
thread leads to the revelation that Alice's main childhood contact with her
mother was listening to a recording of a story her mother had taped as she was
dying of lung cancer when Alice was four. The title metaphor, a map of the
world, is telling. As a child, Alice would retreat from the "real" world to create
and recreate her own map of the world. At a pivotal point early in the novel,

119

when something tragic and undeniably real is happening a few yards away, Alice is searching for her swimsuit and happens upon her map of the world:

> I yanked the drawer open to the chaos of old shoes, pens and bolts, masking tape, and moth-eaten sweaters and my map, my map of the world. I hadn't thought about my map for years. I took out the sheaf of papers and knelt down, spread them on the floor, ran my fingers over the lime-green forests, the meandering dark blue rivers, the pointy lavender mountain ranges. I had designed a whole world when I was a child, in secret. I had made a series of maps, one topographical, another of imports and exports, another highlighting mineral deposits, animal and plant species, another with descriptions of governments, transportation networks, and culture centers. My maps had taken over my life for months at a time; it was where I lived, the world called Tangalooponda, up in my room, my tray of colored pencils at my side, inventing jungle animals, the fish of the sea, diplomats and monarchs. Although there were theoretical people in my world, legions of them, all races and creeds, when I imagined myself in Tangalooponda I was always alone, composed and serene as an angel in the midst of great natural beauty.

The maps and the imagined world they represented were more real to Alice than the world outside her room. The maps also clearly raise issues of power and control, issues that I want to take up later in the context of feminist methodology. In Tangalooponda, Alice is all powerful; it is a world—unlike the one outside her room—that is fully under her control.

What do these ruminations on *A Map of the World* have to do with methodological frontiers in feminist geography? What do they have to do with the title of a soap opera, *As the World Turns*? To say that Howard and Alice are leading charcacters in a soap opera would be to trivialize a serious book. Nor do I drag Alice and Howard into this because their ways of knowing are exemplary; in fact, they are not. Much of the novel turns on the consequences of the ineffectiveness of their ways of making sense of the world. But Howard and Alice prompt reflection on the various ways that people go about making sense of the world. Howard weighs the pros and cons of narrative and science as paths to understanding and rejects narrative in favor of science. Alice's touchstone is the map. Each of these ways of knowing is necessarily partial. Soap operas like *As the World Turns* are a fitting metaphor for this partiality: while purporting to represent full lives in all their complexity, they permit only partial glimpses of those various (and inevitably intertwined) lives. With each turn of the earth, only part is visible while part remains hidden. An important part of my argument is that new methodological horizons—and new questions and new understandings—are to be found through combining several different approaches to understanding, each of which alone affords only limited insights.

Hamilton's story of Howard and Alice prompted me to reflect on the two strands of our identity as both feminists and geographers and on the methodological implications of those identities. What is it that we as feminist geographers are trying to understand? In the most general sense, we are drawn to questions at the intersection of gender, space, and place—questions of how gendered identities, and the unequal power relations embedded in those identities, shape distinctive places and how, in turn, gendered experiences and identities are molded by space, place, and geography. Unlike Howard (sympathetic character though he is), we as *feminists* are not inclined to abandon narrative, nor are we inclined to separate the who and why (his "narrative") from the how and what (his "science"). The science/narrative dualism is simply one of many methodological dualisms (including quantitative/qualitative and general /specific) that feminists have inverted.[2] As *geographers*, we are interested in how geography, including geographical metaphors such as Alice's map of the world, can inform feminist methodologies. How can a heightened geographic awareness strengthen feminist approaches to understanding the world?

The chapters in this section self-consciously reflect upon how our identity as feminist geographers affects how we go about making sense of gender, space, and place. They shed light not only on how we approach the research process but also on how a feminist geographic methodology is changing what we know of the world, changing our map of the world, changing our understanding of how the world turns. These chapters illustrate how feminist geography can inform a range of methods and methodologies, from the design of a census (Samarasinghe) to critical realism (Falconer Al-Hindi), from semi-structured interviews (Oberhauser, Dyck) to ethnography (Nagar) and narratives of landscape (Domosh). In what follows, I consider the chapters in this section first as they illuminate *feminist* methodologies (Feminist Turns) and then as they begin to suggest the power of a feminist *geographic* methodology (Geographic Turns). Although separating these two strands of our identity as feminist geographers may seem artificial, I take up each thread by itself in order to make my central point: new methodological horizons in feminist geography are to be found where our expertise as geographers explicitly informs our feminist approaches to understanding the world. The chapters in this section begin to shed light on these new horizons. I conclude with some thoughts about new directions in feminist geographic methodologies.

Feminist Turns

Several years ago, a student came to tell me that she did not need to take our departmental research methods course, which was required of all majors. She explained that she had learned all about methods from her roommate, who had taken a similar course in the government department the previous year, and as far as they both could see, "it was all just plain common sense." It may be true that much of what we teach in research methods is indeed common sense, but it is also evident from recent developments in, and expositions of, feminist methods and methodologies—most of which cannot be found in those hefty methods texts—that what is one person's common sense is another person's "Eureka!" and that what makes sense in one time and place may not make sense in another.[3] Feminist methodologies and feminist methods *are* different from standard textbook fare, in emphasis if not in kind, and they *do* change what we are able to learn about the world.[4] If "it's all just common sense," then why weren't these methods part of the methodological canon long ago?

Feminist methodologies and methods have received considerable attention in the recent geographic literature. Collections of articles on the subject have appeared in *The Canadian Geographer* in 1993 under the rubric "Feminism as Method," in *The Professional Geographer* in 1994 ("Women in the Field: Critical Feminist Methodologies and Theoretical Perspectives"), and again in *The Professional Geographer* in 1995 ("Should Women Count? The Role of Quantitative Methodology in Feminist Geographic Research"). Taken together, these three groups of articles, along with the overview pieces that accompany each collection, provide an excellent, accessible introduction to feminist approaches to understanding how the world turns.[5] It is not my intention here to review in detail all of the points raised or concerns aired in these collections or to provide some kind of metaoverview of the literature on feminist geographic methodologies; instead, I simply wish to outline a few of the main features of what has come to be considered feminist methodology and to draw upon the chapters in this section of the book to illustrate these features.[6] This discussion lays the groundwork for the next portion of this chapter, which considers feminist *geographic* methodologies; for whereas the *CG* and *PG* collections convey to geographers how feminists approach the research process, they offer little guidance as to how geography informs feminist methodology.

At the core of feminist methodology is the open acknowledgment that the knowledge born of the research process is a joint, yet always unequal, creation of both the researcher and the research subjects, sometimes referred to as the researched. (I have had an aversion to using the term "researched," precisely because of the distancing and objectifying pall it throws over those with whom researchers participate in the creation of knowledge. As Gilbert [1994] has persuasively argued, however, some degree of distancing and objectifying is probably inevitable; in its jarring associations, the term, I have come to see, is actually apt.) This frank recognition that what we know depends on the relationship between the researcher and who or what we are studying spawns a heightened awareness of several aspects of the research process.

First, feminist investigators, like Ann Oberhauser and Isabel Dyck in the following chapters, are sensitive to the ways that the unequal power relations between researcher and researched can influence knowledge creation. In her interviews with Appalachian women homeworkers, Oberhauser, for example, sought to minimize this power imbalance and to create a less hierarchical relation between herself and the homeworkers, in part by choosing to interview women in their homes and in part by stressing their common identities as working women, wives, and mothers. Dyck, likewise, aimed to put investigator and research subject on an equal footing by matching the ethnicity of the interviewer with that of the research participant. Underlying these efforts is the assumption that reducing the power differential between researcher and researched will put the latter at greater ease, thereby inducing subjects to reveal more about their lives; the knowledge thus created will enable a richer and more complex understanding of the diversity of women's lives.

Second, feminists' sensitivity to power relations in the joint creation of knowledge by researcher and researched heightens an awareness of the multiple and shifting identities of both parties in the research process. Richa Nagar describes how members of the different Tanzanian Asian communities with whom she spoke perceived her differently (sometimes emphasizing perceived similarities between themselves and her; sometimes emphasizing differences) and how their varying perceptions affected what they revealed to her about their lives. Similarly, Dyck relates how the knowledge that emerged from her research interactions reflected the fact that both researcher and research subjects constructed themselves differently in different circumstances, sometimes stressing their roles as wives or as workers, other times emphasizing their position as mothers or as immigrants.

Third, feminists' sensitivity to the multiple and fluid layers of identity and the ways these can affect the creation of knowledge leads feminists to question many taken-for-granted categories and to search for new ways of conceptualizing categories. Nagar, for instance, takes apart four normative categories used to describe Tanzanian Asians (Sikh, Goan, Hindu, Ithna Asheri), showing how each label emphasizes language, religion, and/or region of origin. Domosh argues that historical geographers' focus on authorship has led to an uncritical use of the category "woman." Likewise, Vidyamali Samarasinghe proposes rethinking two taken-for-granted categories, work and the household.

Finally, many feminist research strategies are overtly linked to the researcher's engagement in social and political change.[7] In their selection of research questions, their choice of conceptual categories, and their judgment of what constitutes relevant data, feminists often design research with the aim of changing social, political, and economic structures so as to improve the life circumstances of women. Certainly, Samarasinghe's proposal to use time budgets to measure work has as a goal the explicit recognition, by both scholars and policymakers, of women's contributions to household survival. Part of Oberhauser's research involves establishing a network of Appalachian homeworkers; Dyck's research was motivated in part by her interest in improving immigrant women's access to Canada's health care system.

Like the articles in *The Canadian Geographer* and *The Professional Geographer* collections, the chapters in this section on methodology start to move us beyond statements *that* feminist methods and methodologies differ from other methods in particular ways and toward a demonstration of *how*, in the contexts of their own research questions, these differences affect what we learn. The next six chapters illustrate, for example, *how* the creation of knowledge is shaped by the unequal power relations between researcher and researched, by the multifaceted and fluid identities of researcher and researched, by the categories that research participants use to describe the world, and by a commitment to improving women's lives. In addition, the methodological diversity evident in this section underscores feminists' commitment to combining a variety of approaches in the quest for understanding. Where these chapters scout out new horizons is in suggesting how geography can inform these feminist methodologies.

Geographic Turns

A geographic turn of mind can in fact enrich each of the elements of a feminist methodology I touched upon in the previous section. The geographer's sensitivity to location (space-time context), to scale, and to connections in place and across places can strengthen feminist methodologies in useful ways: what we know depends on the relationship between the researcher and who or what is being studied, *and* that relationship depends on the relative locations of the research partners.

In conducting their fieldwork, both Oberhauser and Dyck were concerned to reduce the power inequalities between researcher and researched, and they describe how geographic strategies can be used to achieve this objective. Believing that interviewing women in their homes (which were also their work locations) gave research subjects more power, Oberhauser selected women's homes as the sites for data collection. Dyck analyzes two points in the research process where geography affected power relations in her studies. One was the site of recruitment of subjects into the study; she observes, for example, that the clinic, a place the immigrant women did not control, tended to exacerbate the power differences between researcher and researched. The other was the site of the interviews, whether in the clinic, the subject's home, or elsewhere. Dyck recognizes the impact of these locational decisions on the resistance of the subjects to the interview; in settings where subjects felt especially exposed, powerless, or ill ar ease, they tended to withold information. Dyck makes a good case for finding safe places for interviewing.

The fact that the knowledge that emerges from interviews depends in part on where the interviews take place reflects not only the relationship between location and power but also the relationship between location and identity. The chapters by Dyck, Nagar, and Domosh are particularly good illustrations of how multifaceted identities are constructed through interactions in different sociospatial contexts and how these identities affect the research process. Dyck exposes the difficulty of incorporating different women's voices and experiences into feminist theory when these different voices are constructed through interactions in various contexts, including the interview process itself. Nagar explores how identities are both constructed and challenged in a variety of socio-spatial contexts. Mona Domosh's critical exploration of traditional methodologies in historical geography also highlights the contingencies between identity and place. Ann Oberhauser's and Karen Falconer Al-Hindi's in-home interviews with home-based workers allowed the researchers to see several facets of the women's identities. In all of these examples the socio-spatial context of the research encounter—whether in a home, a particular neighborhood, or on a bus—shaped the knowledge outcome.

The ways that different locations and contexts highlight different identities points to the transitory nature of many categories: meanings are often context-specific. Domosh demonstrates this point in her arguments about the gendering of particular spaces. The point that meanings are often context-specific stands in contrast to the general a-contextuality of mainstream social science. Several of the chapters in this section illustrate how a contextual perspective is of necessity more attuned to everyday life. Samarasinghe, for example, argues that census forms must be contextualized and that census measurements must be specified at the regional level because they have different meanings in different regions. Falconer Al-Hindi draws attention to the tension between the specific and the abstract in constructing analytical categories and suggests that a solution lies in "maintaining the inherent spatiality of objects." A good example is her proposal to think of the category "home" not as a static, fixed place, but as a relational space, conceptualized in relation to other places. This kind of geography-based category stresses linkages more than boundaries.

Finally, and quite simply, geography must inform feminist research strategies designed to improve women's lives. As Falconer Al-Hindi notes, "oppression . . . varies with spatial context"; research aimed at eliminating oppression must recognize the causal role of spatial context in the process of oppression. Each of the papers in this section demonstrates this point.

New Turns, New Horizons

I conclude with some thoughts about possible new methodological turns that might open up new horizons in feminism and feminist geography. In this vein I would like to pose several questions—questions about surprise and control, questions about audience, and questions about teaching.

I would like to see us devise methods and methodologies that maximize the chance that we will see things we were not expecting to see, that leave us open to surprise, that do not foreclose the unexpected. I would like to see us avoid designing research processes that will lead to "discoveries" that simply affirm what we already believe. Pursuing this goal is likely to entail a letting go, a conscious attempt to relinquish control over the research process. I promised to come back to Alice, her map of Tangalooponda, and the question of control. Although Alice loved her map of the world because it was the one place in her childhood where she felt she was in control, her map did not serve her well as a map. Because Tangalooponda bore so little resemblance to the world Alice found herself in as an adult and because the map was a rigid and static representation, it did not really help her to find her way or to understand how the world turns. Alice and her map of the world suggest to me—perversely perhaps!—some ways that we might build into our methodologies the possibility of being surprised.

One way is to involve multiple voices, multiple viewpoints—in short, to engage "difference"—throughout the research process, from the design stage onward. Many, perhaps even most, research projects engage more than one person in carrying out the research, especially if primary data collection is involved; often the research collaborators are students, who can bring fresh insights to the process.[8] Rarely, however, is a variety of approaches and strategies actively sought out in the early phases of research and incorporated into the research design.[9] Doing so is likely to result in a research strategy that includes several different methods, which is one strategy for maximizing surprise. A research team that incorporates diversity is also probably more prone, than is a single investigator, to finding surprises in the data generated through any one method. In addition, banning hubris and cultivating humility help to make researchers receptive to insights they were not consiously seeking.

When the subject of study involves people, one set of voices to include from the outset should be those of the people we are studying. Including the researched in this way will not only open up chances to be surprised and to understand, in new ways, how the world turns; it also raises the question of audience: what is the purpose of better understanding how the world turns? Why do we deploy this methodology or that method? If it is, as most feminists avow, to effect change in the world so that women have more power over their own lives, then who is the audience for whom we write when we write about our research? Too often, it seems to me, the audience is confined to us—a small group of feminist geographer researchers who use a language that permits communication with only other feminist geographers or perhaps feminist academics. Our research methodologies, including the ways we choose to communicate about our research, must, I believe, be opened up to a far broader audience.

Of course, one captive audience we regularly communicate with is our students. What would I like for us to communicate to them? Ideally, questions of research methodology and research method would not be confined to methods courses. Instead, issues of method would permeate our teaching, and we could convey the central message everyday that what we know depends on how we come to know it (Ewick [1994] provides a good discussion of this idea, along with some concrete suggestions for implementing it). How much more powerful, too, if students could discover this message for themselves (rather than by having teachers pronounce it), through solving problems and conducting their own research. Perhaps then research methods truly would become "common sense," in the sense that they would not stand apart from the rest of learning but be part of each student's everyday work of understanding how the world turns—methods would then simply be part of the "native good judgement" that the *American Heritage Dictionary* uses to define common sense. And because communication is never only one-way, those of us who teach will also learn and in so doing will stand a good chance of being surprised by learning something truly new.

Understanding that *how* we come to know fundamentally shapes *what* we know underlines how partial knowledge inevitably is. Perhaps our feminist methodologies will never allow us to understand more than the fragments of the world captured on Jan Monk's postcards (see the introduction to part 3). Because each method and each methodology provides only a partial glimpse of the world as it turns, everyone must, as Hamilton seems to be saying to her readers through Alice and Howard, learn to accept and to live with partial understandings. Why not, however, increase the chances of being surprised by new insights by seeking understanding through multiple methods? Why not combine narrative and science and geographic thinking? Feminist *geographic* methodology, especially one that incorporates multiple voices speaking from multiple locations, holds out the hope of allowing us to understand more than one fragment at a time.

Notes

My thanks to J.P. Jones for his insightful comments on an earlier draft of this chapter.

1. By the very structure of the book, in which the story is told first in Alice's voice and then in Howard's, Hamilton makes clear that Howard's and Alice's narratives were not the same.

2. As have others. One example is Jacob Bronowski's *The Abacus and the Rose,* which I frequently use early in my research methods course to provoke students into heated debate over how fundamental the differences are between the sciences and the humanities. At the conclusion of the debate, students usually see far more similarities than they had at the outset—and more similarities than differences.

3. Feminists are not alone in suggesting changes to the methodological canon, but we have been an important source of methodological critique and innovation.

4. I am following the usual distinction between method and methodology, outlined by Eyles (1994, 50): "method [is] a technique for gathering evidence and methodology [is] a theory of research procedure."

5. Of course there are other pieces in addition to these, including Herod (1993), McDowell (1992), and Pratt (1993).

6. Because perhaps the most prominent trait of an explicitly feminist methodology is self-conscious reflection on the research process, methodological issues infuse all the chapters in this volume.

7. Sibley (1995) provides an interesting historical example of this linkage—and its adverse consequences for women's academic careers—in his description of women sociologists at the University of Chicago in the 1920s and 1930s.

8. Hanson and Pratt (1995, chapter 3) discuss the important impacts that students had on the data collected as part of the Worcester Expedition.

9. An exception is a project recently underway and directed by Jan Monk, "Building

across Borders: Gender and Health on the U.S. and Mexican Border." This is a joint project involving el Colegio de la Frontera Norte, el Colegio de Sonora, and the Southwest Institute for Research on Women. The consortium will "foster, conduct, and disseminate transnational, interdisciplinary research and action projects related to the border region."

References

Bronowski, J. 1956. The abacus and the rose. In *Science and Human Values*. NY: J. Messner.

Ewick, P. 1994. Integrating feminist epistemologies in undergraduate research methods. *Gender and Society* 8:92–108.

Eyles, J. 1993. Feminist and interpretive method: How different? *The Canadian Geographer* 37:50–52.

Gilbert, M.. 1994. The politics of location: Doing feminist research at "home." *The Professional Geographer* 46:90–96.

Hamilton, J. 1994. *A map of the world*. New York: Anchor Books.

Hanson, S. and Pratt, G. 1995. *Gender, work, and space*. New York: Routledge.

Herod, A. 1993. Gender issues in the use of interviewing as a research method. *The Professional Geographer* 45:305–17.

McDowell, L. 1992. Doing gender: Feminism, feminists and research methods in human geography. *Transactions of the Institute of British Geographers* 17:399–416.

Pratt, G. 1993. Reflections on poststructuralism and feminist empirics, theory, and practice. *Antipode* 25:51–63.

Sibley, D. 1995. Gender, science, politics and geographies of the city. *Gender, Place and Culture* 2(1):37–50.

7

Counting Women's Work: The Intersection of Time and Space

Vidyamali Samarasinghe

> The androcentric fallacy, which is built into all mental constructs of Western civilization cannot be rectified by simply adding "women." What it demands for rectification is a radical restructuring of thought and analysis which once and for all accepts the fact that humanity consists of equal parts of men and women and the experiences, thoughts and insights of both sexes must be represented in every generalization that is made about human beings.
>
> —Gerda Lerner

As Lerner noted ten years ago, it has become increasingly evident that gender equality cannot be ensured simply by "adding women" to the already established socioeconomic and political structures of the contemporary world. As a plethora of feminist literature illustrates, the fundamental issue is that the system of production and reproduction has a well-entrenched masculinist structure that has in place a built-in mechanism that ensures a dominance and visibility of men and a relative invisibility of women. Sandra Harding (1983) argues that this system, which perpetuates male dominance, appears to "[l]imit and create opportunities within which are constructed the social practices of daily life, the characteristics of social institutions, and all of our patterns of thought" (312). The two Marxian categories of human labor, production and reproduction, have both a dominant spatial component as well as a gendered dimension. Production is associated largely, though not exclusively with space outside the domestic arena, and with males, and is defined and counted as "work," the value of which is manifested in monetary terms. Reproduction is spatially in the domestic arena, associated with women's role as wives and mothers, and lies outside the definition of "work" that is counted (see Ahrentzen, chapter 5, this collection). In this chapter I argue that activities in the reproductive sphere are also "work" that should and can be counted by pene-

129

trating the mantle of invisibility thrown over the reproductive sphere. I thereby arrive at a justified and realistic evaluation of women's work.

Like McDowell (1983), I note the importance of erasing the false and over-simplified dichotomy between the public and the private, work and home, and I stress the urgent need to use appropriate analytical tools that will enable us to identify processes that bind the two spheres. Focusing primarily on rural subsistence agricultural societies of South Asia, we proceed to untangle the tightly woven strands of the so-called reproductive sphere of activities and propose a model for a more realistic count of women in national economic statistics. This involves reconceptualizing "work" so that statistics capture human activities that contribute toward economic survival of the household, in all its gendered diversity. It also involves building a methodology that erases the misnomer that is called "women's invisibility."

Time, Work and Space

Interaction of time, work, and space in relation to human activity is central to this study. Within the capitalistic productive sphere of activities, time spent on a job defines a bottom line in value measurement, as reflected in monetary remuneration. In general, differentials in monetary remunerations are based on the nature and type of activity, the performer, and the sophistication of training and skills. Closely associated with the "time-value" of productive activities is the explicit need for clear identification of activity types and task differentiation. Since monetary remuneration is not involved in the reproductive sphere, time plays no significant role in the evaluation of activities therein, and clear definitions of activities are not even deemed to be necessary. Consequently, work that clearly is part of economic survival strategies is hardly ever counted as such. It is this reality in rural agricultural societies that prompted Elise Boulding (1977) to note that female workers in the Global South contribute a significant amount of productivity, much of it discounted, providing a cushion for modernization that enable planners and policymakers to make poor allocation decisions without causing the economy to collapse.[1]

In contrast, I define "work" as the activities that make up all contributions towards household survival. This is an important distinction since women's so-called invisibility is a product of the continuing preoccupation of counting mostly remunerated work done by men in the productive sphere. Such work is clearly open to more institutional scrutiny and regulation and therefore easy to value and to count. Hence, a reconceptualization of work helps disclose what is done by women in rural subsistence societies, most of whose tasks are lumped together as "reproductive" and as noted earlier, not counted as work in economic statistics. By moving away from the dichotomy that divides work into private and public spheres, I bring the household into the center of our analysis.[2] The contention of this chapter is that the household forms the most appropriate "place" of analysis, firstly, to obtain a more accurate, comprehensive, and just perspective of gendered contributions to the economic survival of the members; second, to get a better understanding of the mutually supportive exchange value and use value activities that are often artificially categorized into a universally male public sphere and a specifically female private sphere; and third, arrive at a more accurate understanding of the gendered dimension of time allocation in household survival strategies.

Counting Work—Officially

Household survival strategies encompass all activities that contribute toward the well-being of its constituent members. These include both direct economic activities as well as support activities. "Forward Looking Strategies," adopted in Nairobi in 1985 at the United Nations (UN) Conference on Women, noted with concern the fact that contributions by women to agriculture, food production, reproduction, and household activities are ignored by state and private agencies. Consequently, among the recommendations of the conference was that efforts be made to measure and reflect these contributions to national accounts and economic statistics (UN 1986). The 1995 draft document of the UN Women's Conference, *Platform for Action*, clearly states the need to "devise suitable statistical means to recognize and make visible the full extent of the work of women and all their contribution to the national economy, including their contribution in the unremunerated and domestic sectors, and examine the relationship of women's unremunerated work to the incidence of their vulnerability to poverty" (UN 1995, 29). Despite the efforts of the past decade by individual researchers and world bodies such as the UN and its affiliates, including the United Nations Development Fund for Women (UNIFEM), the International Labor Organization (ILO), the International Research and Training Institute for the Advancement of Women (INSTRAW), and the United Nation's Development Program (UNDP) in devising appropriate methodologies to count women's work, the UN Technical Report of 1993, *Methods of Measuring Women's Economic Activity*, shows that there has not been much success in this sphere. Such lack of success points to the many difficulties involved in making women's work matter—economically, politically, and culturally.

One fundamental flaw in those efforts has occurred in how official macrolevel data are enumerated. Specifically, all agencies use the classification "economically active population," which does not capture the efforts of all those who work to contribute to human economic sustenance. Specifications of standards used for measuring the labor force have been developed to be compatible with the United Nations System of National Accounts (SNA). Accordingly, a labor force is defined as: persons of either sex, above a certain age limit, who work or seek to work for the production of goods and services in (1) market production or (2) nonmarket production (ILO 1986). Producers for the market are relatively easy to count. As for nonmarket production of goods and services, the international standards specify that within the boundaries specified in the SNAs, only those persons engaged in certain types of nonmarket production are counted as members of the labor force. These include persons engaged in such activities as production of primary products for own consumption, processing of primary products for own consumption by the producers of these items, production of fixed assets for own use, and production of other commodities for own consumption by persons who also produce them for the markets (ILO 1990). However, many activities that are done in the household mainly by women, such as child care, water and firewood procurement, and house maintenance, contribute to the economic sustenance of the household but still lie outside this system (Bose 1989).

The SNA procedures use the household as a basic accounting unit for measuring work. However, they rely on a predetermined framework for measuring human labor, which seems to define the household only as a place of residence, and only as a point-location for identifying the subject of the enumeration. Unfortunately, this methodology does not capture accurately human labor in the subsistence sector in the Global South since work often forms a continuum from the so-called productive sphere to the sphere of reproduction. Human activities in the reproductive sphere also do not lend themselves to neat categorizations, and the absence of a methodology to count such activities relegates reproductive activities to further insignificance. In addition, given the much more common practice of pooling gendered labor resources in the household to achieve subsistence, sharp gendered divisions of labor are not easily discernible. In contrast, in the production process of a name brand shoe, for example in the Export Promotion Zone in Sri Lanka, although components are made separately, credit for labor is given to all who perform tasks in the production process. Similarly, in garment manufacturing centers, assembly lines ensure that economic credit is given for individual workers, each of whom will be responsible for turning out only one component of the final product.

In subsistence-level rice farming, however, there are no task separations that are similarly recognized and credited. Methodologies adopted for enumeration of labor recognize only the male farmer, hired labor, and those who are recognized as unpaid workers. In the absence of a method to capture who does what in the nonmarket production of goods and services, women in the household do not get economic credit for the tasks that they actually do. The SNA revisions of 1993 incorporated a few additional items into national accounts, such as carrying water and production of food for own consumption. But the bulk of household work, including time spent on child care, cleaning, cooking, and voluntary community work remain excluded from national accounts (UNDP 1995, 89).

The need for recognition of the regionally specific perspective on women's work is well illustrated not only by omissions in the SNA measurements but also by errors of commission. The category "homemaker" or "houseworker" of the ILO falls under the broad classification of those "economically inactive," explicitly excluding "housework" from economic activity on the assumption that homemakers' activities are reproductive and do not contribute to "economic productivity." The seriousness of this misclassification can be clearly understood when one compares national aggregate statistics on studies based specifically on locating women's work in a given society. An attempt was made in the context of Sri Lanka to review gender-specific national aggregate data to locate women's productivity on a regional basis (Samarasinghe 1989). The study revealed that in the regions of irrigated rice farming, where the practice of intensive multiple cropping demands a high component of female household labor, the "economically inactive" houseworker category was as high as 50 percent of adult female population. This seems to be an obvious misrepresentation of facts, since these are the regions that have been highly impacted by the Green Revolution, which brought in its wake a high demand for farm labor throughout the year. While such labor demands could also be met by hired labor, in the Sri Lankan case, several microlevel studies undertaken in the same rice farming regions show a high level of household-level female labor not only in the main rice farming operations but also in homestead gardening activities (Lund 1978; Sirisena 1986; Wickramasinghe 1993). Hence, it is plausible to surmise that classification of such a high percentage of rural women as "economically inactive" houseworkers in national statistics is due to a flawed methodology, which by pushing women into the reproductive domestic sphere, could ignore women's contribution to economic survival of the household.

Anker, Khan, and Gupta (1988) point out the need to expand on the SNA labor force categories in order to measure more accurately women's contribution to economic survival among the rural subsistence sectors. In a field-based sample survey in Uttar Pradesh in India, they use four types of labor inputs, ranging from the narrowest definition of waged labor to broader definitions that incorporate women's household reproductive work, to tease out the different types of work that women do. The sampling test they used showed that while the proportion of women engaged in wage and market oriented activities was low, women in the study area nonetheless spent a considerable amount of time in activities related to economic sustenance of their households, most of which would not have been captured if existing SNA measurements were used. The UNDP *Human Development Report* (1995), which is devoted in its entirety to the gender issue, also notes that the SNA in its current form is still not comprehensive enough in its definition of economic activity. It reports that women in developing countries carry on average 53 percent of the burden of work. But in SNA's measurement, men's work made up 75 percent of the total workload. Accordingly, it is men who unfairly receive the larger share of associated income and recognition for their economic contribution, while women's work remains largely unpaid, not recognized, and undervalued (UNDP 1995, 88). The report reiterates what Beneria (1992) noted, namely, that underestimation of women's work has been observed particularly in four areas: subsistence production, informal paid work, domestic production and related tasks, and volunteer work, all of which significantly contributes to the household economy.

Locating Women—Household as the Base

Classifications of "human activity time" for the purpose of constructing national accounts typically assume a monetary/nonmonetary binary scheme. When census enumerators use the household unit as the basis for collecting data on activity time, this binary distinction is reproduced throughout the varied and interrelated activities found within households. An example from Sri Lanka shows how the totality of work that contributes toward the economic survival of the household is missed since the methodology adopted in census enumerations continues to rely on the market as the key basis for counting labor inputs.

In 1984, the Department of Census and Statistics in Sri Lanka conducted a *Survey of Household Economic Activities* (Department of Census and Statistics 1989). Noting that household activities are "usually unorganized, scattered, numerous and often seasonal in character," it presumably proceeded to inventory economic activities using the base unit of the household (1989, 1). One would expect that unless women were completely invisible, this sample survey would capture women's work within the household. Because the survey used the same framework as in the official national census surveys, however, women relegated to the economically inactive houseworker category in the census, remained so in this survey. Using the household as an accounting unit made no difference since the sampling frames were not changed to capture those who contributed to the economic survival of the household. While the Sri Lankan survey was expected to reduce "an area of deficiency in the national accounts by obtaining more comprehensive data at the household-level," (1989, 2) what it achieved was merely a more detailed and inflated account of male self-employed workers who had already been classified as "economically active." Again it completely ignored the contribution of women in households, because they were classified as "economically inactive houseworkers" for purposes of obtaining national-level statistics.

In the subsistence societies in the Global South, the household is not only a residential unit, but also, and more importantly, an operational unit ensuring the economic survival of its members. As Blumberg (1991, 21) eloquently makes the point, there is an "internal economy of the household" that needs to be studied carefully so as to differentiate the gendering of economic activity. In this respect, it is important to bring into census discourse the "household," not only as a unit of accounting but also as a vital functional unit of human activity.

Reconceptualizing the Household—
Context of Space and Place

As noted by Soja (1989, 80), space in itself may be primordially given, but the organization, and meaning of space is a product of social translation, transformation, and experience. Falconer Al-Hindi (in this collection, chapter 8) discusses the many dimensions and facets of space and place in the geographic literature, specially in the context of feminist realism. Oberhauser (in this collection, chapter 9) observes that a place, such as the household, is of particular importance to feminist geographer's analysis as it "provides an important context for understanding everyday events and their connection to broader structures" (169). Hence, fundamental to an understanding of the functional characteristic of the household, a central theme in this chapter, is the need to tease out the relational dimensions of its gendered activities.

Gary Becker's new home economics model (1981), based on the premise that the household is a unit where both production and consumption takes place, provided an initial impetus behind looking at households as basic units of analysis in order to understand the functional nature of household behavior patterns in resource allocations. Although many contentious issues have been raised in relation to the mechanisms of interaction among individuals within a household as reflected in the Becker model, the usefulness of the concept of the household in understanding the dynamics of labor and income allocation has now been well recognized in the literature (Binmore and Dasgupta 1987, Sen 1990). A series of studies undertaken by the World Bank during the 1980s titled "Living Standard Measurement Studies" (LSMS) attests to the increasing importance of household-level analysis in socioeconomic policymaking (World Bank 1980–1992). However, in many of these early resource allocation studies, reproductive activities were virtually left out, leading to a serious omission of women's work. As Elizabeth Katz (1991) shows, the household unit can be a meaningful basis of analysis of human behavior only if gender is made central. Katz argues that a "feminist model of the household must specify the actual mechanisms whereby household members are mobilized to work in various productive and reproductive activities" (46). Beneria and Roldan's (1987) study of home workers in Mexico City illustrates how "decomposing the household unit," can uncover the gendered mechanisms of household-level survival strategies (110–13). Such findings have prompted researchers to advocate strongly the adoption of an approach that includes reproductive activities as a fundamental component of human activity in development practices (Samarasinghe 1994). Work that contributes toward household sustenance is performed externally to, *and* internally within, the household. The reconceptualization of work has to come from a fundamental change in valuing the household as the ultimate receiver of the output of human labor. By dismantling the screen that hides most of household-level activity, we remove the invisibility of household-level reproductive work as well. If the outcome of household-level activities is economic sustenance and the well-being of household members, the first step is to give comparable value to all activities that contribute toward that goal. This requires the plethora of work done in the domestic sphere to be unscrambled from the heap of nonmonetized reproduction.

Unscrambling Women's Work— Time as a Measurement of Value

It is my contention that female labor contributions hidden in the reproductive sphere will continue to be ignored unless the household is used as the basic accounting unit of labor inputs from all its members. A method that has been used quite extensively to untangle women's work in the reproductive sphere is the "time allocation" survey method (Dixon-Mueller 1985). I use it in this chapter to show, first, that women are certainly not inactive and that their time is devoted to activities that are essential to maintaining the economic survival of the household unit. Second, time-use studies clearly show the need to acknowledge task separation within a given occupation in subsistence societies in the Global South. Third, it brings into sharp focus the need to value time in order to measure labor inputs from women in the reproductive sphere. By focusing on the time dimension, we are forced to identify the *production process* of goods and services, taking into account who does what for any given process, bringing us closer to analyzing interrelationships between what is defined separately as the productive and reproductive spheres.

Time-Use Analysis

Dixon-Mueller (1985), using a combination of values in task specialization and the time-use budgets of women in agricultural societies, devised a method by which the percentage of those in the "inactive houseworker" category dramatically dropped, while female labor participation increased. Acharya (1985) demonstrated how female labor force participation rates in ten Asian countries increased using the Dixon-Mueller method. The root cause for the low original count of women as workers lay with the tendency to use the "houseworker" category as the "lender of the last resort," an accounting unit for married women in subsistence sectors in the Global South who do not fall neatly into predetermined categorizations of national accounting frameworks.

Dixon-Mueller's study clearly demonstrates how the use of time allocation analysis captures more effectively women's tasks that contribute toward economic survival of households in societies of the Global South. Likewise, a number of other studies have established the utility of time allocation studies in dispelling the myth of women's "invisibility" in production processes (Momsen and Kinnaird 1993; Goldschmidt-Clermont 1987; Mies 1986). They also bring into feminist discourse the "multiple use of a unit of time," which is defined as use of a given unit of time to perform multiple tasks (Gold-schmidt-Clermont 1987; Floro 1994). Multiple use of a unit of time becomes necessary when tasks are many and time is scarce. To ignore multiple uses of time by women also undervalues women's use of time. In a Colombian case study of a new colonized settlement, it was noted that "peasant women carry out a diversity of tasks during the day, some more visible than the other, all of them frequently interrupted by another activity. One working day is not just one job for women but a permanent combination of tasks and allotment of attention and energy." (Meertens 1994, 263). Again, in Else Skjonsberg's study based in an African village, a researcher, Agnes Bande observed that she could not record all activities of a village woman named Tisalare because she (Tisalare) was busy doing so many things (Skojonsberg 1989).

Time allocation studies bring into focus a basis for disaggregating human activity itself. By recognizing female components of human activities, women are made statistically visible. The studies, moreover, demonstrate the great importance of female activities in the domestic sphere in sustaining the social and economic structures of society. Last, by focusing on time, studies show that women's work lies along a continuum between productive and reproductive spheres. By effectively mapping out women's work trajectories, time allocation studies show not only the critical need to reconceptualize gender dimensions of work but also that the divisions "production" and "reproduction" in the subsistence societies in the Global South misrepresent how labor tasks are carried on spatially and in terms of gender. The time dimension therefore affords a window through which a better unpacking of gendered work patterns at the household level could be achieved.

Operationalizing the Methodology

I advocate "time allocation" methods in *national*-level data-gathering exercises, specifically to identify work tasks. Time-use studies are already considered reliable methods to study leisure time (UN 1993, 54). However, recently it has been noted that time-use studies could serve a much wider purpose by measuring not only time spent in leisure, but also time spent in work currently not considered economically active (Goldschmidt-Clermont 1987). A similar observation is made in the context of the Indian census enumerations of 1991, where, for the first time, attention was paid to ways and means of capturing female labor force contributions in the rural subsistence sector (Krishnaraj 1993). Since the 1985 UN Conference on Women in Nairobi, when policymakers were alerted to the serious omission of women in national-level statistics in countries of the Global South, efforts have been made to rectify such omissions. Many new categories have been added to census frames in an effort to include women's hidden work in the subsistence sector, but there has not been a major revision of data-gathering methodologies, only an expansion of pre-existing categories and questions.

I propose to go beyond the existing use of time-use studies, particularly where they are used only to supplement or complement other methods of national data-gathering procedures. I suggest that the structures and frameworks derived from microlevel time-use survey-based studies be used to restructure national frameworks in region-specific terms. The challenge is to make conceptual use of time allocation studies to arrive at task differentiations, within realistic, nationally applicable categories.

My reconceptualizing of "work" is based on the premise that household-level analysis is the most appropriate way to capture the totality of activities that are required to sustain the household. The focus on the time dimension of work illustrates the deficiencies of earlier methodologies that were not structured to capture task differentiations in subsistence societies. It helps untangle the different types of work done at the household-level, so as to provide a workable method that can be used to gather data at a macro level. To do this a number of practical matters need to be addressed: (1) developing means of imputing value to work hitherto not given a monetary value, (2) separating out the multiplicity of women's and men's tasks, taking into account not only the type of work and seasonality, but also the tasks within a given unit of time, and (3) making surveys simple and unamenable to enumerator bias.

Imputing Values to Household-level Work

Goldschmidt-Clermont (1987) and Beneria (1992) have shown different means for imputing value to household-level work done by women, currently defined largely as reproductive. Beneria notes that the most accepted operational criterion is that of third person principle, whereby domestic production is defined as unpaid activities that can be performed by a third person in a remunerated form. To impute actual monetary value, two main methods have been used: (1) the input-related method involving a valuation of labor time and, (2) assigning market prices to goods and services produced in the domestic sphere (Goldschmidt-Clermont 1987; Beneria 1992). For each method, three ways of estimating are used, including the "global substitute," the "specialized substitute," and the "opportunity cost".[3] While admittedly such methods need contextualized refinement, giving monetary values to reproductive tasks previously considered a natural extension of "wifely" or "motherly" duties is an important step in eliminating women's invisibility. It draws them into the mainstream of legitimate human activity despite the fact that it poses problems of acceptance in patriarchal societies.

The method I propose combines time allocation with task differentiation. First, the twenty-four-hour period of a day is divided into three periods: sunrise to noon, noon to evening, and evening to night, with the actual clock alignment to be arrived at by a world body such as the ILO based on consultations with member countries of the UN. Second, task differentiation should be controlled by the seasonality of agricultural and subsistence practices.

Third, initial categorization of tasks in the *production process* should incorporate an explicitly gendered dimension of tasks performed and may be classified into three major groups: "leading economic activity," "other economic activities" (to include such activities as homestead gardening, vending, etc.), and "household maintenance." The leading economic activity would be locality/region specific and should be categorized in relation to the different tasks that are required to produce the goods. For example, if rice farming is identified as the leading activity of a Sri Lanka household, a time-use study would show that the tasks include: (1) preparation of the field, (2) transplanting, (3) weeding, (4) harvesting, (5) cleaning and winnowing, (6) drying and storing, and (7) preparation of food. A similar method called the "division of labor module" was tested in Kenya using an integrated rural survey that focused on the agricultural cycle. Four activities were identified for a selected list of crops: planting, weeding, harvesting, and marketing (UN 1993, 55).

Similarly, task separation can be undertaken for the other two classifications of the production process. The second category, "other economic activities," could include such tasks as homestead gardening, livestock rearing, and tasks in vending and trading. The third category, "household maintenance," should incorporate such tasks as cooking, cleaning, food processing, and fetching water and firewood. I advocate using task differentiations within each category and sub-category to frame national data-gathering exercises.

One of the most troubling aspects of macrolevel data-gathering exercises based on the household is the inaccuracies resulting from male enumerator bias and from patriarchal social norms entrenched in society that inhibit women from participating fully in census or national sample surveys. Women are generally ignored unless the interviews specifically focus on them or a woman is a head of the household. In order to eliminate bias, a comprehensive list of tasks to be used by the enumerator should be predetermined. Input for these should be obtained from country and region specific sample surveys, such as the thirty-one studies used for the UNDP study (1995) or the Anker, Khan, and Gupta study (1988). While the main purpose of using the time dimension is to untangle work processes in a gendered way, the value input used would give visibility to *all* work processes having an impact upon household economic survival.

Data Gathering and Analysis

In adopting my method of gathering data, I suggest a two-stage data collection and analysis process. In the initial field-based data-gathering stage, the survey design would be defined using categories of "production processes." As discussed earlier, these categories would be determined by a careful study of the diverse activities that are necessary to sustain the economic survival of the household. This would require careful thinking, but as noted earlier, the data that continue to be accumulated from micro-level studies could be used to classify work processes. Interviewer bias would be largely avoided since the interviewer/enumerator would be required to record who does what under the predetermined task differentiations, according to female/male classifications and village or region.

At the stage of analysis, work value inputs will be arrived at in accordance with the analysis done by those who designed the frameworks for the survey. Since time is used as the main basis for measurement, it will be the task of the census data analyst, and not the enumerator, to measure and value the time used (multiple use and single use) by men and women within any given spatial unit. Logistically, the two stages identified here are no different from what is already done in census enumerations and national sample surveys. The difference is in the methodology adopted to identify "work," which necessitates the use of task differentiation and the time-value measurement of those tasks, a practice already in place in enumerating work in industrial societies.

My contribution to feminist analysis is a reconceptualization of the gendering of work using a time-space analysis. It focuses on disaggregating activity patterns in an attempt to measure the actual contribution of women's labor. Time geography, which attempts literally to map out the temporal-spatial structuring of social life, has been used so far in feminist geography mainly, if not exclusively, to trace out and analyze either space-time paths in relation to Western suburban "housewives" activity trajectories or to understand the tensions and pressures faced by women who combine domestic work with outside wage work (Rose 1993). In the rural subsistence sector in South Asia, women's spatial interaction is centered in the household space, although their activity pattern is not rigidly entrenched within the physical confines of home. The field, homestead garden, sources of water and firewood, and centers of community activities are main points of spatial interaction. A multitude of tasks women are expected to perform flow from one task to the next and are meshed together, and a time-space path analysis would be a useful analytical tool for untangling such female work trajectories.

My model makes use of the time-space paths to propose a practical model for evaluating more realistically the actual contribution of women to household sustenance in a large number of countries of the Global South. It advocates the use of value inputs to all work acknowledged as contributing to the socioeconomic well-being of the household. The method I propose for census enumerations is designed to help eliminate the so-called invisibility of women relegated to the "reproductive" sphere, and to show that women in the rural subsistence sectors in the Global South are not mere "add ons" to the labor force.

Conclusions

This chapter focuses on rural agricultural societies of the Global South. The hidden dimension of women's work in the household is certainly not isolated to such societies. Nonrecognition of household activities as work that contributes toward the economic sustenance of the household is a problem faced by women globally. However, in the Global South, among subsistence households, nonrecognition assumes a larger dimension because of the nature of women's activities in such societies. Data gathered at the national aggregate level has failed to capture women's contribution to economic survival in the rural subsistence sector due to the continuous use of a methodology based on flawed conceptualizations of "work." In short, it does not define the totality of work and is unable to untangle the different tasks performed in the domestic sphere; it therefore fails to recognize women's continuing contribution to the economic survival of the household.

In an effort to include and value the many activities that form a continuum of women's work, I suggest that the household unit not merely be considered as an accounting unit, but as a processing unit; the household is the receiver of inputs from the totality of work of its members. All work members do, inside and outside the physical space of the unit, gets counted. By integrating time into my analysis, a refinement of task differentiations and the gendered work processes is achieved. Such a methodology would show very clearly that the "economically inactive houseworker" category, which accounts for a high percentage of women in rural subsistence sectors of the Global South, is a myth, a serious misclassification with damaging repercussions for women. The myth leads policymakers, primarily guided by national-level aggregate data, to ignore women when formulating plans for development. While I recognize the fact that under-renumeration of women has captured the attention of world bodies such as the UN, ILO, and World Bank, I find that no fundamental reconceptualization of women's work has been brought to bear on the problem. The methods these bodies advocate are geared toward adding women to pre-existing categories without acknowledging that the categories they use are inappropriate and need to be transformed, a transformation requiring far-reaching methodological change.

As Maracek notes (1989), feminist research should strive to move beyond refining and revisiting existing concepts and reconceptualize the terms of the debate itself. In this chapter, I reconceptualize women's work so as to help change the rules by which work is valued. Moreover, I devise a methodology that would give hardworking women in subsistence societies of the Global South long due recognition. The methodology I offer makes time and place central to the analysis of the gendered definitions and divisions of work. The methods I propose do not make for a neatly bundled model, but then again women's work in subsistence societies of the Global South is not bundled neatly either.

Notes

1. The term "Global South" is chosen to capture post-Cold War spatial relations between the industrialized North and the postcolonial South, and is preferred over the term, "Third World."

2. The degree of overlap between household and family continues to be a basis of debate among scholars. Family groups that are based on kinship ties are often members of a household, but sometimes they are not. In this chapter, I use a definition of the household from Boulding (1991). "In all its diversity, as the primary living units of human beings, where the species is reproduced and nurtured, the base from which individuals participate in the whole range of tasks that shape and change society. Looking at people in households means seeing each member as an individual, a source of production and reproduction." (xii).

3. Global Substitution uses the cost of hiring a domestic worker to carry out the tasks, whereas specialized substitution uses the cost of a specialized worker to do specific tasks. Opportunity costing is based on wages that the person may receive for doing market-oriented activity (Beneria 1992, 1554).

References

Acharya, S. 1985. Comparative studies in Asia: Background information report. Submitted to the UN University Project on Family Studies. Tokyo: UN University. Mimeo.

Anker, R., Khan M. E., and Gupta, R. B.1988. Women's participation in the labor force: A method test in India for improving its measurement. *Women, Work and Development* 16. Geneva: ILO.

Becker, G.. 1981. *A treatise on the family*. Cambridge: Harvard University Press.

Beneria, L. 1992. Accounting for women's work: The progress of two decades. *World Development* 20(11): 1547–1560.

Beneria, L., and Roldan, M. 1987. *The crossroads of class and gender: Industrial homework, subcontracting, and household dynamics in Mexico City*. Chicago: University of Chicago Press.

Binmore, K. and Dasgupta P., eds. 1987. *The economics of bargaining*. Oxford: Blackwell.

Blumberg, R. L. 1991. Introduction: The "triple overlap" of gender stratification, economy and the family. In Blumberg, R. L., ed. *Gender, family and economy: The triple overlap*, pp. 7–34. Newbury Park, CA: Sage Publications.

Bose, A. V. ed. 1989. *Limited options: Women workers in rural India*. Geneva: ILO.

Boulding, E. 1977. Dualism and productivity: An examination of the economic roles of women in societies in transition. In W. Lahore and J. Powelson, eds. *Economic Development, Poverty and Income-Distribution*, pp. 161–91. Boulder: Westview Press.

Boulding, E. 1991. Prologue. In Eleanor Masini and Susan Stratigos, eds. *Women, Household and Change*. Tokyo: UN University Press. 1991.

Department of Census and Statistics. 1989. *Survey of household economic activities— 1984–1985: Sri Lanka. Final Report*. Colombo, Sri Lanka: Department of Census and Statistics.

Dixon-Mueller, R. 1985. *Women's work in third world agriculture: Concepts and indicators*. Women, Work and Development Series. Geneva: ILO.

Floro, M. S. 1994. Work intensity and time use: What do women do when there isn't enough time in the day? In G. Young and B. Dickerson, eds. *Color, class and country: experiences of gender*, pp. 152–67. London: Zed Publications.

Goldschmidt-Clermont, L. 1987. *Economic evaluation of unpaid household work in Africa, Asia and Oceania. Women, Work and Development Series*. Geneva: ILO.

Harding, S. A. 1983. Why has the sex/gender system become visible only now? In S. A. Harding and M. B. Hintikka, eds. *Discovering reality: Feminist perspectives on epistemology, metaphysics, methodology, and philosophy of science*, pp. 311–26. London: D. Riedel Publishing Company.

International Labor Office (ILO). 1990. *Surveys of economically active population, employment, unemployment and underemployment: An ILO manual on concepts and methods*. Geneva: ILO.

————. 1986. *Statistical sources and methods*. Vol. 111. Geneva: ILO.

Katz, E. 1991. Breaking the myth of harmony: Theoretical and methodological guidelines to the study of rural third world households. *Review of Radical Economics* 23 (3) and (4): 37–56.

Khrishnaraj, M. 1993. Women's work in Indian census: Beginnings of change. *Economic and Political Weekly* December 1–8, pp. 2663–672.

Lerner, G. 1986. *The creation of patriarchy*. New York: Oxford University Press.

Lund, R. 1978. *A survey of women's working and living conditions in a Mahaveli settlement area with special reference to household budgets and household surplus*. Colombo: People's Bank Publications.

Maracek, J. 1989. Introduction. *Psychology of Women Quarterly* 13: 367–377.

McDowell, L. 1983. Towards an understanding of the gender division of urban space. *Environment and Planning D: Society and Space* 1: 59–62.

Meertens, D. 1993. Women's roles in colonization in the Columbia rain forests. In J. Momsen and V. Kinnaird, eds. *Different places, different voices: Gender and development in Africa, Asia and Latin America*, pp. 256–69. London, New York: Routledge.

Mies, M. 1986. *Indian women in subsistence agricultural labor*. Women, work and development series. Geneva: ILO.

Momsen, J. and Kinnaird, V., eds. 1993. *Different places, different voices: Gender and development in Asia, Africa and Latin America*. London: Routledge.

Rose, G. 1993. *Feminism and geography: Limits of geographical knowledge*. Minneapolis: University of Minnesota Press.

Samarasinghe, V. 1989. Women and geographic space: A regional analysis of women's well-being and productivity in Sri Lanka. In *The hidden face of development: Women, work and equality in Sri Lanka*, pp. 17–47. Colombo: Center for Women's Research (CENWOR).

————. 1994. The place of WID discourse in global feminist analysis: The potential for a 'reverse flow.' In G. Young and B. Dickerson, eds. *Color, class and country: The experiences of gender*, pp. 199–217. London: Zed Publications.

Sen, A. K. 1990. Gender and cooperative conflict. In I. Tinker ed. *Persistent inequalities*, pp. 123–49. New York: Oxford University Press.

Sirisena, W. M. 1986. *Invisible labor: A study of women's contribution to agriculture in two traditional villages in the dry zone of Sri Lanka. Modern ceylon studies* 2(2): 117–37.

Skojonsberg, E. 1989. *Change in an african village: Kefa speaks*. Hartford: Kumarian.

Soja, E. W. 1989. *Postmodern geographies: The reassertion of space in critical social theory*. NY: Verso.

United Nations 1995. *Draft platform for action. Fourth world conference on women. Beijing, China*. New York: UN.

————. 1993. *Methods of measuring women's economic activity: Technical report*. New York: UN.

————. 1986. *The Nairobi forward looking strategies for the advancement of women*. New York: UN.

United States Agency for International Development. 1989. *Making the case for gender variable: Women and wealth and well-being of nations*. Compiled by R. L. Blumberg for the Office of Women in Development. Technical Reports in Gender and Development. PNC-ABC-454. Washington: United States Agency for International Development (USAID).

United Nations Development Programme. 1995. *Human Development Report*. Oxford: Oxford University Press.

Wickramasinghe, A. 1993. Women's roles in rural Sri Lanka. In J. Momsen and V. Kinnaird, eds. *Different places, different voices: Gender and development in Africa, Asia and Latin America*, pp. 159–175. London: Routledge.

World Bank. 1980–1992. *Living standard measurement studies* (LSMS). Working Papers. Washington: World Bank.

8

Feminist Critical Realism: A Method for Gender and Work Studies in Geography

Karen Falconer Al-Hindi

Geography's traditional boundaries, both topical and methodological, are being eroded by contemporary research agendas. On the one hand, standard substantive categories such as economic geography and social geography no longer adequately describe research areas such as, for example, "gender and work." On the other hand, traditional research methods, which are often quantitative, and the implicit scientific epistemology they are based upon, are coming under greater scrutiny than ever before. Those who question these methods frequently do not reject them wholesale but adapt them for application in new ways (e.g., Rocheleau 1995).

Perhaps, as Pickles and Watts argue, geography has entered an era in which "disciplinary practice and concepts appear . . . to have broken loose from any notion of disciplinary closure and unitary coherence" (Pickles and Watts 1992, 301). If this is the case, then the idea of incommensurable paradigms is obsolete, leading geographers to search for methodological frontiers in the gaps or, conversely, in the intersections between different research frameworks. This chapter pursues one such area of methodological and substantive overlap, that found between critical realism and feminism.

Both feminism and realism came into geography in the wake of earlier critiques launched against spatial science, including those developed by humanists (e.g., Buttimer 1976) and Marxists (e.g., Slater 1975). Feminist geography emerged as the women's movement brought greater numbers of women into the academy in particular and into the paid workforce in general. Research on gender and work is a direct outgrowth of these trends, and has been among the most prominent themes in feminist geographical research. Such scholarship examines the reciprocal relations among paid and unpaid

145

work, gender, and space. Feminist geographers, drawing upon critiques of mainstream social science methods, have emphasized approaches that place women's lives and knowledge at the center of their agendas. Recent book publications attest to the vibrance of this research area, in which epistemological as well as methodological traditions are frequently challenged (e.g., Kobayashi 1994b; Gregson and Lowe 1994; England 1996).

Critical realism has engaged geographers largely through Andrew Sayer's work (1984, 1985a, 1985b, 1992, 1993). Realism offers a methodological strategy for analyzing concrete social events in terms of both contingent and necessary relations. Critical realism has proven popular with economic geographers, among others (e.g., Warf 1988). Questions concerning this philosophy and method continue to generate considerable interest and debate (e.g., Sayer 1993; Jones and Hanham 1995; Pratt 1995).

Both methodological and substantive commonalities provide a basis for productive engagement between feminism and critical realism. Critical realism emphasizes the importance of intensive methodologies, such as case studies, which lead to understanding how contingent conditions combine to produce outcomes in concrete settings (Sayer 1985b, 1992). Feminist explorations of the everyday lives of women similarly focus on complex social and spatial contexts, and often use case study approaches (e.g., Mackenzie 1989). Both have focused on work as a key aspect of social life and geographical relations in contemporary society (e.g., Sayer and Walker 1992; Greed 1992; Hanson and Pratt 1995). While my focus here is on gender and work studies, I believe that a feminist critical realism can contribute to the study of gender and space in other research arenas as well.

To introduce the subject of feminism and critical realism, I first outline their respective critiques of positivism and their epistemological bases. Next, I analyze the methodological implications of an approach that combines them, with special attention to the potential pitfalls of the method for feminist analyses. I then examine three distinct contributions of this method to feminist theory and geography. This is followed by an example of feminist realist research from my investigation of women telecommuters. Finally, I emphasize the need for a critical yet ecumenical stance toward new research strategies.

Critical Realism and Feminist Geography

Feminist Epistemologies

While feminist geographers have drawn inspiration from various theoretical influences, four have emerged as especially important: feminist empiricism, socialist feminism, standpoint theory, and feminist poststructuralism (Mattingly and Falconer-Al-Hindi 1995). The development of these feminist research philosophies has followed critiques of mainstream, usually positivist, social inquiry. Positivism has an old and complex history (Kolakowski 1993), the detail of which is beyond the scope of this chapter. However, contemporary interpretations focus on five principles: observation is more important than theory, observations must be repeatable (that they are is guaranteed by adherence to the scientific method), verified hypotheses are accepted as laws, these laws focus on combinations of events (in the form: if a, then b), and such laws accumulate over time into a monolithic Truth (Gregory 1994a). The following paragraphs discuss each feminist epistemology's critique of positivism, and its principal tenets. While the necessarily linear narrative implies both a temporal sequence and successive progress, the different perspectives are better thought of as overlapping in chronological as well as substantive development.

Feminism's empiricist critique focuses on the gender bias evident in much mainstream inquiry. Feminist empiricists are distinguished from others by their insistence on gender as an important analytical category; they maintain that the failure of nonfeminist science is its blindness to gender (Harding 1987, 1991). Thus, these scholars take issue with the way in which science is often practiced. This orientation calls for more strict adherence to principles of scientific rigor in the belief that this will reduce or eliminate sexism. A feminist empiricist orientation informs "gender geography" scholarship in such works as *Her Space, Her Place* (Mazey and Lee 1983), the goal of which is to make women visible as geographical subjects. Feminist empiricism also undergirds much of the research on women in the "welfare geography" tradition (Pratt 1994).

Socialist feminism developed concurrently with feminist empiricism. Building upon the Marxist rejection of positivism, which focused on the latter's failure to apprehend social structures and to recognize the political nature of knowledge (Harvey 1984), socialist feminists assert that classic Marxism, with its class-biased economic determinism, is inadequate to analyze intersections of gender and class (Vogel 1983). In addition, many argue that the broad, abstract categories of Marxist analysis obscure rather than illuminate women's lives. Materialist feminists, who draw upon Marxist methods of analysis and critique but stress feminist concepts and research questions (Hennessy 1993), emphasize knowledge and political struggle grounded in women's everyday experiences (e.g., Kobayashi et al. 1994).

Feminist standpoint theory originated with socialist feminists who wished to ground feminism's authority: "who it speaks for, and the forces of oppression and exploitation it contests" (Hennessy 1993, 67). Standpoint theorists maintain that a particularly clear vision of social relations is achieved through the experience of gender-based oppression (Harding 1991). Thus, they argue the knowledge gained by those oppressed (by, for example, sexism) is more useful than that held by those individuals who benefit from others' subordination. Moreover, Harding argues that a positioned objectivity is epistemologically stronger than that claimed by positivism: rather than asserting "objectivity" through the false presumption of distance between researcher and researched, standpoint objectivity is achieved through the hard work of first seeing and then acting against oppression directed at oneself. Extending the work of feminist epistemologists seeking to valorize subjugated people as knowledgeable agents, Haraway (1988) suggests that those who claim to know should epistemologically position themselves with respect to their objects of research, and in so doing, limit their knowledge claims.

While standpoint theory has been accused of essentializing "woman" and reproducing a collective subject (Hennessy 1993), feminist poststructuralists recognize multiple axes of difference among women, and even contradictory positions along such axes within the same person. Feminist poststructural theory highlights the relational nature of identities including gender; such categories are always under construction (e.g., Lawson 1995). The possibility of universalizing women's experiences, much less their subject positions and identities, has been brought into serious question by critiques from feminists who do not identify with middle-class, White, Western academics (e.g., Mohanty 1991b). Poststructuralist theory informs recent research on gender and work, as when, for example, questions of difference among women are explored in the context of the social and spatial relations of occupational segregation (Pratt and Hanson 1994).

As this brief review illustrates, many feminisms inform geographic scholarship. However, as McDowell (1993) has argued, many feminist geographers are united by the understanding that differences between women may contribute to shared or divergent political interests, and by the intent to make sense of gendered conditions in the material world. This orientation:

> insists on coming to terms with the actually existing . . . world, while recognizing its cultural construction, and demands a theoretical analysis of differences, building up an understanding of the mutual interrelations of gender (as a symbolic system, a set of social relations and an individual identity), of sexuality, household and family structures and the political economy of domestic and workplace relations within and between places (McDowell 1993, 315).

This definition is inclusive rather than exclusive; elements of each of the preceding four feminist epistemologies can be identified within it. In keeping with McDowell's own substantive research, this stance is consistent with that of many who conduct research in the gender and work arena.

Critical Realism

While critical realism is more readily characterized than feminism, it must be distinguished from naive realism. The latter describes the "common sense geographer," who believes that one's everyday grasp of reality—that which can be perceived directly—is all that exists (Gibson 1981). In contrast to this implicitly positivist view, the critical realist recognizes that much that is important about understanding the "real" world cannot be perceived directly. Both critical realism and positivism acknowledge various levels of reality, including the realms of experience, events, and "the real." But whereas positivism attempts to collapse the different levels of reality into one, the realm of experience, critical realism maintains their depth in its analysis (Bhaskar 1975, in Cloke et al. 1991). Thus, critical realism can theorize social structures such as patriarchy (at the "real" level), whereas positivism, with its lack of ontological depth, cannot do so. One result of the collapse of ontological levels in positivism is "causal confusion," which refers to the tendency to confuse empirical regularities with causal relationships. As Sayer (1992) notes, what causes something to happen has nothing to do with the number of times that thing has happened, and the same event can have different causes under different circumstances. Causal confusion arises from positivism's failure to account for the internal characteristics of objects and the mechanisms that activate these characteristics or properties under specific conditions (Sayer 1992).

As philosophy and as methodology, critical realism moves from the concrete realm of experience to successively higher levels of abstraction to reveal the necessary causal properties of social structures that are realized under specific (contingent) conditions (Gregory 1994b). Through this process, called "retroduction," the causal powers of social structures can be separated from the "unnecessary" or contingent circumstances under which those powers are realized (Sayer 1992). "Mechanisms" that bring the necessary powers into play can also be identified. At the highest level of abstraction are social structures such as gender relations and the capital-labor relation. The identification of structures, mechanisms, and necessary and contingent relations should not proceed linearly from the most concrete to the most abstract, but theorization should be conducted recursively among the levels of abstraction (Pratt 1995).

The phenomenon of renting property is an event that geographers may wish to explain, and can be used as an example. At the most abstract level, the institution of private property must exist in order for a landlord to offer an apartment for rent, so this is a necessary condition. Whether or not property is rented depends upon contingent factors that bring renters and landlords into contact. One such contingency might be the parental expectation that children establish their own homes (usually in rented apartments) at a particular age. This age might be expected to vary contextually, thus bringing further contingencies into play.

A distinction between intensive and extensive research is also central to critical realist epistemology. Intensive research focuses on the elucidation of causal relationships among phenomena, while extensive investigation discovers how widespread a phenomenon is. For example, an *understanding* of the production of a particular gendered division of household labor necessitates investigation of the necessary and contingent properties of factors that may contribute to it. Such intensive research requires study participants who are necessarily related to one another—that is, they interact—in ways that bear upon the phenomenon at hand. An extensive inquiry would reveal the frequency of the same phenomenon, using research participants who share certain characteristics but are not causally connected to one another (Sayer 1992). While both research approaches are worthwhile, Sayer emphasizes the importance of understanding events, rather than documenting their extent, through intensive realist inquiry.

In the following sections I draw upon these sketches of feminism and critical realism to address difficulties and strengths that become apparent when they are employed together.

How Abstract a Feminist Critical Realism?

As geographers learned in the 1980s, using critical realism to investigate feminist geography's questions may be problematic. I refer here to a well known realist-informed debate in the pages of *Antipode* between Jo Foord and Nicky Gregson (1986) and Linda McDowell (1986) concerning the relative importance of capitalism and patriarchy to women's subordination (also see Cloke et al. 1991; Pratt 1994). Foord and Gregson (1986) argued that both are important to understanding women's subordination, but that they must be separated for analytical purposes. Of the four necessary and internally related relations between men and women that they identified—biological reproduction, heterosexuality, marriage, and the nuclear family—Foord and Gregson determined that marriage and the nuclear family are contingent, while biological reproduction and heterosexuality are universally necessary. They also identified gender relations as a general object, and patriarchy as its specific form.

In her counter to Foord and Gregson's argument, McDowell contended that patriarchy and capitalism are inseparable, since "women's oppression is located in the relationship of child-bearing to the appropriation of surplus labour in a class society" (McDowell 1986, 320). While Foord and Gregson identified capitalism as a contingency intermediate between patriarchy (a structure) and empirical concrete events, McDowell argued that class relations and gender must be analyzed together and that "gender relations can only be analysed as part of the capital-wage relation" (McDowell 1986, 314). Neither side disputed the existence or importance of patriarchy or capitalism. Rather, the levels of abstraction and their positions within the abstraction schema were contested (Allen 1987).

I wish to examine some of the published commentary on the original two articles in order to highlight potentially troublesome areas when realism is used in feminist analyses. In particular, I will argue (*contra* Gier and Walton 1987) that the difficulties in these analyses flow not from problems inherent in realist method, but from the way realism was employed.

The primary criticism leveled against Foord, Gregson, and McDowell was that they relied on an overly abstract conception of theory. First, Johnson wrote that Foord and Gregson's highly abstract theory and their call for one theoretical framework and object of analysis for feminist geography reflected a "patriarchal conception of what theory is" (1987, 211). The concern is that such abstract theory may leave behind the real gendered geographies feminists seek to illuminate (Hanson 1992; Berg 1993). Second, Gier and Walton (1987) argued that Foord, Gregson, and McDowell marginalized gender through their use of realism's method of retroduction:

> any epistemology which marginalises epiphenomena can only serve to deprive gender, gender relations and patriarchal gender relations of a large and all-important part of their meaning. Gender does not exist outside its specific "locus." It can only be contemplated in the context of the conditions and circumstances of a particular time and place. (Gier and Walton 1987)

While Johnson was concerned that Foord and Gregson had subscribed to the dominant masculinist model of highly abstract theory, Gier and Walton suggested that critical realism had been selected "off the peg" (1987, 58), and maintained that reductionism is inherent in realism's method.

These reactions show that realism, though designed to aid investigations of real-world events, carries a danger of abstraction that may be at odds with feminist methodology. Realism relies upon retroduction to distinguish between the necessary and contingent relationships that combine to produce specific outcomes. If retroductive abstraction proceeds linearly, moving successively farther away from the concrete realm, it can seem to leave behind social and spatial relations that feminist geographers consider crucial to their work. Alongside this loss of context, realism's necessary relations may be accused of harboring masculinist, and exhaustive, knowledge impulses (e.g., Johnson 1987). While abstract social theory can be valuable, feminist scholars emphasize the need for theory closely tied to women's everyday lives in specific geographical settings.

In my view, critical realism's retroduction method can be useful for theorizing systems of disadvantage for women, but it is important to keep critical realist analysis focused on material, gendered geographies. This requires conscious recursivity as the researcher employs realism's method. Retroduction is not a one-way procedure in which successively higher levels of abstraction are achieved, but a circular one, in which movement from the abstract to the concrete should make as much sense as movement from the concrete to abstract. Women's (lack of) status and power can only be explained with reference to specific situations. A factor that contributes directly to women's subordination in one context may be contingent in another; that is, an adequate explanation of the phenomenon in one case requires the factor, while in another it does not. A realist-based approach to understanding gendered oppression grounds feminist theorizing in concrete situations, and retains feminism's political and empirical dimensions. Had the *Antipode* debaters, following Sayer (1985b, 172), employed a "handful of case studies" and explicitly located their discussion within these, the discussion (and the subsequent critique) might have taken on a very different character. In short, it is important for researchers to develop theory in a way that incorporates, and accounts for, the material realities of women's lives.

A Feminist Critical Realist Methodology

Concern for the empirical realm leads us to consider the question of methodology for critical feminist realist investigation. Studies of gender and work emphasize the utility of case study approaches in which research begins from women's experiences (e.g., Kobayashi 1994). Frequently such research focuses on women's interpretations of their lives and work as articulated through focused communication with the researcher (e.g., Moss 1994). Such intersubjective knowledge also has an important place within intensive realist investigations. Sayer has argued in favor of semistructured, in-depth interviews because such a "heretical method" is more likely to produce useful knowledge than, for example, the traditional survey questionnaire (1992, 246). Are case studies and in-depth interviews, then, keys to feminist critical realist research? In keeping with the open stance toward methods espoused by both realists and many feminists, I would argue that a variety of methods may prove valuable. For example, A. C. Pratt (1995) urges that the potentials of discourse analysis for realist investigation be explored, and some feminist researchers are open to this method as well (e.g., Pratt 1993).

Extending the arguments developed above, critical engagement between feminism and critical realism makes three distinct contributions to understanding gendered social life. First, building upon investigations of the necessary and contingent linkages among women's subordination and resistance, their spatial and temporal contexts, and large-scale social structures, critical realism can help to uncover what is necessary and what is contingent in feminist standpoints. As Harding (1987, 1991) insists, feminist standpoint is an achievement, a product of acting against oppression directed at oneself. Most important, oppression—and opposition to it—varies with spatial context. For example, as Massey and McDowell (1984) have shown, capitalism and patriarchy operated differently across nineteenth-century British regions. While women were disadvantaged throughout the country, understanding their lack of status and long workdays demands explications of different combinations of capitalism and patriarchy from one regional economy to the next. Just as feminist standpoint generates understandings of such hierarchical social relations from "below," critical realism can elucidate the contingent and varied nature of different standpoints.

Second, achievement of a standpoint may enable feminists to claim "strong objectivity" (Harding 1991). As mentioned above, explicitly positioned knowledgeable agents have better epistemological grounds for their insights than do those who anchor their assertions in the subject-object separation characteristic of positivism. In contrast, strong objectivity:

> increases the objectivity of the results of research by bringing scientific observation and the perception of the need for explanation to bear on assumptions and practices that appear natural or unremarkable from the perspective of the lives of men in the dominant groups. (Harding 1991, 150)

Feminist theorists have traced the implications of standpoint epistemology for the researcher's knowledge claims, and in so doing have produced a more nuanced understanding of the researcher-researched relationship than Sayer has done for critical realism. While Sayer (1992) recognizes that researcher and researched are bound in a relationship defined by the double hermeneutic, neither he nor other advocates of critical realism have problematized the inherently political nature of this relationship. That is, the realist researcher's epistemological position remains unexamined. Thus, Cloke et al. (1991, 137) were moved to comment that realism has been accused of arrogantly claiming to "know the world as it really is," as has positivism. Sayer might argue that the alternative is relativism, but feminist standpoint theory as well as feminist poststructuralism demonstrates that this is not necessarily true. Politically informed research that positions the researcher in relation to the researched guards against relativism by making clear the grounds upon which knowledge claims are based.

Third and finally, I wish to consider the implications of critical feminist realism for how geographers think about space and place. While Sayer (1985a) argued that space matters in realist analyses only at the contingent and concrete levels, and that at their most abstract, social relations can be theorized aspatially, others maintain that space must be kept in at every conceptual level (Cox and Mair 1989). In response to these and other critics, Sayer has recently conceded that "abstract theory ought to have some spatial content, in order to register the necessary spatial properties of social structures" (Sayer 1992:149). Such reluctant acknowledgment of geography's constitutive role in social life suggests that Sayer does not accept the full impact of arguments, such as Soja's (1980), for the inseparable and dialectical relationship between society and space. However, Sayer's emphasis on intensive realist research—which requires participant groups composed of related individuals situated in causal relations to one another—implies that space conceived in relational terms is not only consistent with critical realism, but also can aid in the development of fully spatial realist abstractions.

Drawing upon work by Mohanty (1991a) and others, McDowell (1993) has introduced a notion of relational space to which feminist critical realism can contribute:

> Place . . . is neither a categorical nor territorial concept but is defined in relational terms, that is places are constructed from alliances and oppositional struggles to lines of power. This is a provocative and useful definition because it leads us away from a spatially fixed, bounded notion of either place or community, based on mutual co-residence, biology or culture and instead suggests a political basis for defining our object of study (McDowell 1993, 313).

McDowell's interpretation of relational space builds upon previous articulations, such as those of Harvey (1973) Pred (1984), and Massey (1992) that emphasize the spatial relationships constituted in and through objects. Mc-

Dowell focuses on the specifically human social relations with which human geography is concerned. Such a dynamic and political notion of place enables us to link a variety of spatial scales and to trace the connections between places as well as among social relations.

The example of how geographers think about the home illustrates the possibilities for a relational conception of place. Home was long regarded as outside the purview of mainstream geographic research, not least because it was regarded as the locus of domestic activities and the sphere of women (Rose 1993). Marxist-informed analysis forced a reconsideration of home and social reproduction upon which the "sphere" of paid work depends; however, home was still regarded as a somewhat static site or place. Humanistic interpretations illustrated the emotional and social importance of home (e.g., Tuan 1974), but continued to treat it as spatially fixed and territorially bounded.

The value of the notion of home as a relational space is illustrated when we consider interviewing women in their homes as a feminist critical realist method of research (also see Oberhauser, chapter 9, this volume). Rather than a static site, home may be conceptualized in relation to other places (for example, offices), and the social relations appropriate to different places analyzed in terms of power and authority. For many women who are primarily responsible for the reproductive work of housecleaning and child rearing, home may be one of the few places where they can assert authority. Entering women's homes levels the playing field, so to speak, and may reduce the otherwise hierarchical relationship between researcher and researched. In such a situation, the researcher is not only "supplicant" in search of knowledge from the woman who is the expert on her own life (England 1994), but she enters the home in the role of "guest." The researcher may be welcomed as an ally into the participant's home, where lines of power (such as patriarchy) may actively contribute to spatial differentiation. This conception of relational space means, for a feminist critical realism, that spatial relations are integral to the social relations and structures that are our objects of analysis. This being the case, space is integral to realist abstraction. As Cox (1994) has recently argued:

> Obviously in order for our conceptualization of the causal significance of space to be meaningful, social objects have to have necessary *spatial* properties; properties, that is, that make a difference to what they have to do/what they can do. Their needs, for instance, must include needs for access to other objects. Workers and firms have to make themselves accessible to each other, children to schools, businesses to material inputs and so on. On the other hand, and as Sayer has argued, these needs can be satisfied by a wide variety of different spatial configurations. (Cox 1994,19)

In other words, Cox is arguing that objects *would not be what they are* without their spatial aspects. These necessary properties, then, must not be lost during the abstraction process. Maintaining the inherent spatiality in objects of feminist critical realist analysis facilitates the production of politicized notions of relational space, such as that given here for home.

Using such a methodology, its methods, and the conception of space described above ensures that the aspects of gendered society (such as, for example, patriarchal attitudes among household members), which Gier and Walton (1987) feared were left behind in Foord and Gregson's (1986) process of realist abstraction, are kept in and in fact made central to feminist realist theorizing. The next section illustrates feminist critical realism in practice.

An Example

I now turn to an example of this approach from my research on women telecommuters (Falconer 1993). Telecommuters are employees who substitute the use of telecommunications technology (computer modem, facsimile machine, and so on) for their commute to work during at least part of the regular workweek.[1] Both men and women telecommute, but their rationales for doing so are different: many men wish to be *around* their homes and families while they perform paid work, but many women desire telecommuting work arrangements so that they can be the primary caregivers for their children, or accomplish their unpaid domestic work more easily. Thus, while men's telecommuting is located primarily in the productive realm, women's telecommuting positions them in both the realms of production and social reproduction.

My research examines two questions: (1) how can women's telecommuting be understood as an outcome of a specific juncture in social, spatial, and economic relations? and (2) does telecommuting liberate women from the space and time constraints of productive and socially reproductive work (as promised in much popular literature), or does it trap them in the domestic realm and their domestic role, with the additional burden of paid work? In the following, I show how feminism and critical realism can productively interact to address these questions.

Contributions from critical realism include an operationalization of the dialectical relationship between agency and structure and a methodology for understanding this gendered phenomenon in ways that can inform emancipatory action. While structuration theory successfully articulates the process through which individuals reproduce or contest social structures at the ontological level, critical realism enables the researcher to draw theoretical insights from empirical evidence and to develop theoretical frameworks in which the agency-structure process is made clear.

In this study I acknowledged that patriarchy and capitalism are powerful "deep structures" that affect the households and companies in which women telecommute. Rather than attempting to determine which (patriarchy or capitalism) was more important, however, I directed my efforts toward the contingent and concrete levels of analysis (in light of my discussion above concerning

Foord and Gregson [1986] and McDowell [1986]). The questions driving the research concerned outcomes at the concrete level, where answers could be the most useful to women who telecommute. This is consistent with a feminist orientation that is less abstract and more concerned with peoples' daily lives (Kobayashi et al. 1994). It is also consistent with critical realism, which is concerned to produce explanations under specific circumstances. This means that, unlike some other research orientations, one can derive understandings from which to develop liberating explanations.

In this case, my research identifies social reproduction as the culprit behind the women telecommuters' long workdays (typically eighteen hours). Data collected during the study show that, while the relationship of women tele-commuters to the paid economy is highly variable, their time spent on domes-tic responsibilities is static. Whether she works part-time or full-time, each woman in the study spends forty to forty-eight hours per week on domestic work and child rearing. Likewise, paid household help does not reduce the number of hours spent on social reproduction. Instead, paid help enabled sev-eral women to perform additional services, such as baking bread or taking children on outings. Since their long workdays are due to the demands of social reproduction rather than to production, one must look first to the for-mer rather than to the latter for change.

But critical realism alone would have been inadequate as a methodology for this research. Feminist theory supplied the rationale for an approach that gives a central place to women's experiences and their own interpretations of them. In contrast, mainstream approaches accord primacy to the views of those in power, that is, supervisors or business owners, who are often male. Feminist researchers have frequently used in-depth semi-structured interviews to en-courage intersubjective understanding between researcher and participant (Reinharz 1992; e.g., Gilbert 1994). The questions I asked the participants in this research reflected the feminist political concern to empower women through the research process, and focused on those aspects of telecommuting that women are likely to value, such as telecommuting's impact on child-rear-ing arrangements. Follow-up interviews with the women telecommuters built on the rapport established during earlier interviews, and permitted previously discussed topics to be revisited after the participants had time to reflect upon them. In addition, time-space logs (e.g., Palm 1981; Dyck 1990) revealed the women's tight schedules and negligible leisure time. Finally, self-reports of domestic chores (after Hanson and Pratt 1990) demonstrated the gendered division of household labor.

Conceiving of the social and the spatial in relational terms compels one to consider methods that draw upon relationships among people and phenomena and that preserve these in the data they produce. Just as feminism has under-gone a transition from thinking about gender categories as given to thinking about them relationally (Rose 1993), contemporary geographical theorizing about space sees it not as a container or stage upon which social life is acted out, but as a simultaneously social and spatial relation (Soja 1980; McDowell

1993). I theorized women telecommuters as located (physically and meta-phorically) in the intersection between the spaces and responsibilities of social reproduction and production (see figure 8.1). This position is constituted on a daily basis through interaction with other people. I therefore wanted to learn about women's telecommuting from the points of view of other individuals involved in the phenomenon: the women's spouses and their supervisors. Spouses provided an additional window on the home and how it is affected by telecommuting, while supervisors spoke from the perspective of the office and of capitalist social relations more generally.

Duffy (1987, in Leedy 1993) distinguishes between data triangulation, in which observations are collected using a variety of sampling strategies, and methodological triangulation, where two or more methods of data collection are employed within a single study. Triangulating procedures are routinely used in qualitative studies (Walker 1985) to "double-check findings by exam-ining them from several vantage points" (Reinharz and Rowles 1988, 15). In this research project, however, triangulation was called for at the theoretical level as well as the level of method. Only through interviews with participants who were positioned differently in relation to the telecommuting phenome-non was it possible to gain the necessary insight into the multiple social and spatial relations that enmesh women telecommuters.

Both critical realism and feminism support the inclusion of participants' ideas in research design and their intervention in the research process itself. Participants shaped the process of this telecommuting study by including other family members in interviews that I had planned to conduct with them alone. Family members would not have been as easily included had interviews been conducted anywhere but in participants' homes. Standard interviewing proce-dure requires that individuals be interviewed alone when potentially sensitive issues such as the division of household labor are discussed. In one case, it was apparent that the couple had decided before my arrival that I would not inter-view the man by himself. Sensing that this was the situation (although not

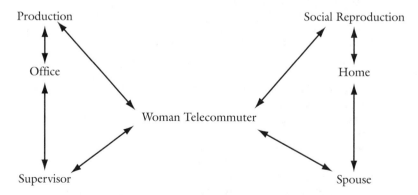

Fig. 8.1. Triangulating women's telecommuting.

knowing why), I interviewed him with his female partner. The primacy normally accorded the researcher in a dialogical interview was subverted. During the interview they occasionally lapsed into conversation with each other, and so generated illuminating insights. I was similarly displaced when I joined another woman telecommuter and her three children for lunch in their home. By involving me in their family lives, the participants gained control over the interviews and denied me the possibility of viewing their lives as anything less than highly complex.

I wanted to develop a theoretical framework reciprocally with empirical evidence, so that the deepening theorization of women's telecommuting would frequently be refreshed by the participants' interpretations. This approach required constant movement between the more abstract and more concrete theoretical levels, and indeed focused on the development of a meso-level understanding of spatially specific contingencies. I determined that the theoretical framework must contain the realms of social reproduction, production, and space, separated only for analytical convenience, since in reality they are inseparable. Next, following Sayer (1992) as well as geographers who have employed realism in their work (e.g., Greed 1992), I created horizontal rows for the concrete, contingent, and abstract levels. Drawing upon the relevant literature as well as insights gained through interviews, one by one each of the row and column intersections was filled.

The theoretical framework, while based initially on my review of the pertinent literature, depended upon contributions from the research participants. The telecommuters' supervisors, for example, contributed to theory as they described their rationales for employing telecommuting workers and the contingent factors that contributed to the success (and frustrations) of this labor process. Each participant and I worked together to produce knowledge based on that participant's position relative to the process; that is, knowledge was an outcome of the development of shared meanings between us.

Critical realist retroduction can be consistent with feminism's focus on women's experiences. This is achieved, in part, by refusing to ignore the spatial content of social relations. For example, one woman telecommuter emphasized the importance of being available when her children arrived home from school; when she explained to me why "a mom should be there," I realized how important being at home was to her identity and self-definition as a good mother (also see Ahrentzen, chapter 5). Her concern to be at home for her children is recognized in the theoretical framework at the concrete level in the reorganization of domestic work (see table 8.1). As one moves up the framework, however, "number and ages of children" and "patriarchy" are recognized at the contingent level, and at the structural level, the high value placed upon mothering is accounted for in the social construction of gender. These abstractions retain their spatial content, first, through dependence on geographic scale (Cox and Mair 1989) at the household level. Second, building upon the feminist notion of relational space advanced in the previous section, both spatial relations and social structures are "constructed from alliances and

TABLE 8.1
A Critical Realist Theorization of Women's Telecommuting

	Production	*Space*	*Social reproduction*
Abstract	Capital–Labor \ / Technology	Collapsing two spheres	Social construction of gender
Contingent	*Segmented labor* –by gender and race –by occupation –by union status *Firm differentiation* –by size –by sector –by technology employed –by organization culture –by supervisor gender-awareness	*Urban differentiation* –by residential location –by business location –by commuting times –by economic base	*Household differentiation* –by level of patriarchy –by number and ages of children –by housekeeping standards –by internal class issues
Concrete	*Telecommuting* –option, or part of formal labor process –extent –which workers	*Spatial reorganization* –of home space –of work space –of office location –of residential location –of commuting times	*Reorganization/negotiation of* *domestic work and child care* –by gender –by paid v. unpaid labor

oppositional struggles to lines of power" (McDowell 1993, 313). In other words, the *social* construction of gender is equally constituted *spatially*. Thus, women's everyday experiences, space, and place are "kept in" even at relatively high levels of abstraction.

Finally, this methodology is consistent with the goal of feminist social science to produce knowledge that is understandable to and useful for women who are not necessarily part of the academy. It is clear that the participants in my study care little whether patriarchy, capitalism, or some combination of the two is to blame for their harried lives, but they care very much how other telecommuting women manage their home and work lives and what factors (contingencies) seem to make a difference. This focus on the concrete, rather than on the development of abstract social theory, can also be consistent with realist methodology and epistemology.

Conclusion

Feminist geographers have used critical realism to great advantage in their studies of gender and work, yet some have been criticized for their highly abstract, decontextualized theory. I have shown how these problems may be avoided when feminism and critical realism meet, but those who explore such methodological innovations must be attuned to their difficulties as well as their advantages. I have argued that a union between realism and feminism in geography offers much to guide researchers, particularly those interested in gender and work. I do not, however, suggest that realism is appropriate for all feminist geography investigations or that it should become feminist geography's paradigm. If geography has indeed entered a postparadigmatic stage (Pickles and Watts 1992), then such an argument would take feminist geography backward, rather than forward. Foord and Gregson (1986) argued that "what feminist geography need[ed]" was one theoretical orientation and object of study. I believe the time for arguing in favor of one object of study and one theoretical orientation is past. The challenge is to explore new research philosophies, methodologies, and methods and to critically examine possibilities for combinations among existing ones.

Notes

My thanks to Susan Roberts, Heidi Nast, and John Paul Jones III for organizing the conference "New Horizons in Feminist Geography," where an early version of this chapter was presented. Additional thanks are due John Paul for his encouragement and painstaking criticism of drafts of the chapter, and to Musa Al-Hindi, Isabel Dyck, Diane Jacobs-Malina, and Ann Oberhauser for helpful comments on drafts. The text also benefited from a presentation to the Department of Geography at the University of Nebraska-Lincoln in December 1995.

1. The term "telecommuter" was coined in 1973 by Jack Nilles to designate an individual whose use of telecommunications technology substitutes, in part, for the daily commute to a workplace (J. H. Pratt 1984; Nilles 1988).

References

Allen, J. 1987. Realism as method. *Antipode* 19:231–40.

Berg, L. 1993. Between modernism and postmodernism. *Progress in Human Geography* 17:490–507.

Bhaskar, R. 1975. *A realist theory of science*. Leeds: Leeds Books (Reprinted 1978, Brighton, UK: Harvester).

Buttimer, A. 1976. Grasping the dynamism of lifeworld. *Annals of the Association of American Geographers* 66:277–292.

Cloke, P.; Philo, C.; and Sadler, D. 1991. *Approaching human geography: An introduction to contemporary theoretical debates*. New York: Guilford Press.

Cox, K. 1994. Concepts of space, understanding in human geography, and spatial analysis. Paper presented at the annual meeting of the Association of American Geographers, San Francisco, CA, April.

Cox, K., and Mair, A. 1989. Levels of abstraction in locality studies. *Antipode* 21: 121–32.

Duffy, M. E. 1987. Methodological triangulation: A vehicle for merging quantitative and qualitative research methods. *IMAGE: Journal of Nursing Scholarship* 19:130–33.

Dyck, I. 1990. Space, time, and renegotiating motherhood: An exploration of the domestic workplace. *Environment and Planning D: Society and Space* 8:459–83.

England, K. V. L. 1994. Getting personal: Reflexivity, positionality, and feminist research. *The Professional Geographer* 46:80–89.

———, ed. 1996. *Who will mind the baby?: Geographies of childcare and working mothers*. London: Routledge.

Falconer, K. 1993. Space, gender and work in the context of technological change: Telecommuting women. Ph.D. dissertation, University of Kentucky, Lexington.

Foord, J., and Gregson, N. 1986. Patriarchy: Towards a reconceptualisation. *Antipode* 18:186–211.

Gibson, E. M. W. 1981. Realism. In *Themes in geographic thought*, ed. M. E Harvey and B. P. Holly, 148–62. London: Croom Helm.

Gier, J., and Walton, J. 1987. Some problems with reconceptualising patriarchy. *Antipode* 19:54–58.

Gilbert, M. 1994. The politics of location: Doing feminist research at "home." *The Professional Geographer* 46:90–95.

Greed, C. H. 1992. The reproduction of gender relations over space: A model applied to the case of chartered surveyors. *Antipode* 24: 16–28.

Gregory, D. 1994a. Positivism. In *The dictionary of human geography*, ed. R. J. Johnston, D. Gregory, and D. M. Smith, 455–57. London: Blackwell.

———. 1994b. Realism. In *The dictionary of human geography*, ed. R.J. Johnston, D. Gregory, and D.M. Smith, pp. 499–503. London: Blackwell.

Gregson, N., and Lowe, M. 1994. *Servicing the middle classes*. London: Routledge.

Hanson, S. 1992. Geography and feminism: Worlds in collision? *Annals of the Association of American Geographers* 82: 569–86.

Hanson, S., and Pratt, G. 1990. Geographic perspectives on the occupational segregation of women. *National Geographic Research* 6:376–99.

———. 1995. *Gender, work and space*. London: Routledge.

Haraway, D. 1988. Situated knowledges: The science question in feminism and the privilege of partial perspective. *Feminist Studies* 14: 575–600.

Harding, S. 1987. Conclusion: Epistemological questions. In *Feminism and methodology*, ed. S. Harding, 181–90. Bloomington: Indiana University Press.

———. 1991. *Whose science? Whose knowledge? Thinking from women's lives*. Ithaca, NY: Cornell University Press.

Harvey, D. 1973. *Social justice and the city*. London: Blackwell.

———. 1984. On the history and present condition of geography: An historical materialist manifesto. *The Professional Geographer* 36:1–11.

Hennessy, R. 1993. *Materialist feminism and the politics of discourse*. London: Routledge.

Johnson, L. 1987. (Un)realist perspectives: Patriarchy and feminist challenges in geography. *Antipode* 19:210–15.

Jones, III, J. P., and Hanham, R. Q. 1995. Contingency, realism, and the expansion method. *Geographical Analysis* 27:185–207.

Kobayashi, A. 1994a. For the sake of the children: Japanese/Canadian workers/mothers. In *Women, work, and place*, ed. A. Kobayashi, 45–72. Montreal: McGill-Queen's University Press.

———, ed. 1994b. *Women, work, and place*. Montreal: McGill-Queen's University Press.

Kobayashi, A.; Peake, L.; Benenson, H.; and K. Pickles. 1994. Introduction: Placing women and work. In *Women, work, and place*, ed. A. Kobayashi, ix–xlv. Montreal: McGill-Queen's University Press.

Kolakowski, L. 1993. An overall view of positivism. In *Social research: Philosophy, politics and practice*, ed. M. Hammersley, 1–8. London: Sage.

Lawson, V. 1995. The politics of difference: Examining the quantitative/qualitative dualism in post-structuralist feminist research. *The Professional Geographer* 47:449–57.

Leedy, P. D. 1993. *Practical research: Planning and design*, 5th ed. New York: Macmillan.

Mackenzie, S. 1989. Restructuring the relations of work and life: Women as environmental actors, feminism as geographic analysis. In *Remaking human geography*, ed. A. Kobayashi and S. Mackenzie, 40–61. Boston: Unwin Hyman.

Massey, D. 1992. Politics and space/time. *New Left Review* 196:65 84.

Massey, D., and McDowell, L. 1984. A woman's place? In *Geography matters: A reader*, ed. D. Massey and J. Allen, 128–47. Cambridge: Cambridge University Press.

Mattingly, D. J., and Falconer-Al-Hindi, K. 1995. Should women count? A context for the debate. *The Professional Geographer* 47:427–35.

Mazey, M. E., and Lee, D. R. 1983. *Her space, her place: A geography of women*. Washington, D.C: Association of American Geographers Resource Publication.

McDowell, L. 1986. Beyond patriarchy: A class-based explanation of women's subordination. *Antipode* 18:311–21.

——. 1993. Space, place and gender relations: Part II. Identity, difference, feminist geometries and geographies. *Progress in Human Geography* 17:305–18.

Mohanty, C. T. 1991a. Cartographies of struggle: Third world women and the politics of feminism. In *Third World women and the politics of feminism*, ed. C. T. Mohanty, A. Russo, and L. Torres, 1–50. Bloomington: Indiana University Press.

——. 1991b. Under western eyes: Feminist scholarship and colonial discourses. In *Third World women and the politics of feminism*, ed. C. T. Mohanty, A. Russo, and L. Torres, 51–80. Bloomington: Indiana University Press.

Moss, P. 1994. Spatially differentiated conceptions of gender in the workplace. *Studies in Political Economy* 43:79–116.

Nilles, J. 1988. Traffic reduction by telecommuting: A status review and selected bibliography. *Transportation Research A* 22A:301–17.

Palm, R. 1981. Women in nonmetropolitan areas: A time-budget survey. *Environment and Planning A* 13:373–78.

Pickles, J., and Watts, M. 1992. New paradigms for inquiry? In *Geography's inner worlds: Pervasive themes in contemporary American geography*, ed. R. F. Abler, M. G. Marcus, and J. M. Olson, 301–26. New Brunswick, NJ: Rutgers University Press.

Pratt, A. C. 1995. Putting critical realism to work: The practical implications for geographical research. *Progress in Human Geography* 19:61–74.

Pratt, G. 1993. Reflections on poststructuralism and feminist empirics, theory and practice. *Antipode* 25:51–63.

——. 1994. Feminist geographies. In *The dictionary of human geography*, 3d ed. ed. R. J. Johnston, D. Gregory, and D. M. Smith, 192–96. London: Blackwell.

Pratt, G., and Hanson, S. 1994. Geography and the construction of difference. *Gender, Place and Culture* 1:5–30.

Pratt, J. H. 1984. Home teleworking: A study of its pioneers. *Technological Forecasting and Social Change* 25:1–14.

Pred, A. 1984. Place as historically contingent process: Structuration and the time-geography of becoming places. *Annals of the Association of American Geographers* 74:279–97.

Reinharz, S. 1992. *Feminist methods in social research*. New York: Oxford University Press.

Reinharz, S., and Rowles, G. 1988. *Qualitative gerontology*. New York: Springer Publishing Co.

Rocheleau, D. 1995. Maps, numbers, text and context: Mixing methods in feminist political ecology. *The Professional Geographer* 47:458–66.

Rose, G. 1993. *Feminism and geography: The limits of geographical knowledge*. Minneapolis: University of Minnesota Press.

Sayer, A. 1984. *Method in social science: A realist approach*. London: Routledge.

——. 1985a. The difference that space makes. In *Social relations and spatial structures*, ed. J. Urry and D. Gregory, 49–66. London: Macmillan.

——. 1985b. Realism and geography. In *The future of geography*, ed. R. J. Johnston, 159–73. London: Methuen.

——. 1992. *Method in social science: A realist approach*, 2d ed. London: Routledge.

——. 1993. Postmodernist thought in geography: A realist view. *Antipode* 25:320–44.

Sayer, A., and Walker, R. 1992. *The new social economy: Reworking the division of labor*. London: Blackwell.

Slater, D. 1975. The poverty of modern geographical enquiry. *Pacific Viewpoint* 16:159–76.

Soja, E. 1980. The socio-spatial dialectic. *Annals of the Association of American Geographers* 70:207–25.

Tuan, Y-F. 1974. *Topophilia: A study of environmental perception, attitudes and values*. Englewood Cliffs, NJ: Prentice-Hall.

Vogel, L. 1983. *Marxism and the oppression of women: Toward a unitary Theory*. London: Pluto Press.

Walker, R., ed. 1985. *Applied qualitative research*. Hants, England: Gower Publishing Co.

Warf, B. 1988. Regional transformation, everyday life, and Pacific Northwest lumber production. *Annals of the Association of American Geographers* 78: 326–46.

9

The Home as "Field": Households and Homework in Rural Appalachia

Ann M. Oberhauser

Locating Lydia's house in rural McDowell County had been a challenge. We finally stopped at a small post office to ask directions and were directed to a house across a nearby stream. As we reached our destination, a dozen chickens, two goats, and several puppies greeted us in the front yard. Lydia stepped onto the side porch and invited us inside. "Be careful on the stairs," she warned, "my husband still hasn't fixed them rotten boards." Upon entering a small kitchen, Lydia showed us some pictures of the children in her home-based day care. In the living room, a coal-burning stove was sending off welcome heat on that cold November morning (figure 9.1).

Thus began my interaction with one of eighty-two homeworkers who participated in research on gender and household economic strategies in rural Appalachia.[1] The multiple dimensions of this fieldwork confirm the complexity of the household, both as a crucial methodological component of the "field," and as a site of income-generating activity. This research employs a feminist methodology to explore the intersection of production and reproduction in women's home-based economic activities, and presents the household as the strategic "site" of analysis. Methodologically and analytically, the social and spatial construction of the household is an important component of this research. Positioning the home as the "field" challenges masculinist assumptions about the household as a private sphere outside the public purview and analyzes it as an important site for feminist geographic research.

This chapter examines how feminist methodology can uncover otherwise hidden activities which are of strategic importance to household production and reproduction. First, I focus on the significance of everyday life and the feminist challenge to the unequal power relations often established between the researcher and participant in traditional scientific research. Second, I demonstrate that the home is often a place where household members engage in strategic economic activities. In many cases, the domestic sphere is a site of income generation and productive work along with activities surrounding social reproduction. Accordingly, women engaged in home-based work must constantly negotiate their time and space to accommodate various activities and their multiple roles in the household. Finally, the methodological discussion and reconceptualization of home is applied to research on women's home-based economic activities in rural Appalachia. Semi-structured, qualitative interviews with more than eighty women reveal the complex social dimensions of the household and the significance of homework to many West Virginia households.[2] It is argued that feminist methodology can go beyond the boundaries of conventional masculinist research to highlight the household as an economically strategic place having a significant impact on women's lives and on the research process.

Reflexivity and Research in the Home

Feminists view the world through a different lens than their masculinist counterparts. The latter's focus on objectivity and rational scientific knowledge contrasts with the emphasis in feminist research on subjectivity and knowledge stemming from everyday experiences (Mascia-Lees et al. 1989; McDowell

Fig. 9.1. View of Lydia's backyard in rural McDowell County. She and her two children and husband live in this house in a wooded hollow. They burn coal for heat.

1992a; Roberts 1981). Feminist research in particular has examined how marginalized people, particularly women, negotiate the social and spatial aspects of their daily lives to overcome oppression. In order to uncover the significance of these negotiating strategies, some feminist researchers have employed qualitative, ethnographic methods to assess people's everyday experiences ("Feminism as Method in Geography" 1993; Nast 1994). These methods are couched within a framework that attempts to reveal otherwise hidden household gender dynamics in a way that reduces the hierarchical power relations often found in masculinist research. Feminist methods, therefore, position the *participant* as someone who informs the researcher about the processes and relations under study, in contrast to the situation where the *researcher* is viewed as the expert on a separate critical plane from the subjects of study (Fonow and Cook 1991; Stanley and Wise 1993). In this instance, participants and the researcher develop a reciprocal relationship, sharing knowledge and information about key issues of concern. England (1994) examines the reversal of hierarchical power relations in her attempt to study lesbian networks in Toronto: "Fieldwork for the researcher-as-supplicant is predicated upon an unequivocal acceptance that the knowledge of the person being researched . . . is greater than that of the researcher" (England 1994, 82). According to England, the use of intersubjectivity in feminist research produces a dialogical process in which the research is structured by both the researcher and the participant. Part of the feminist project, therefore, is to challenge masculinist assumptions surrounding knowledge and power in the research process and, in some cases, to shift a significant portion of power to the researched.

Additionally, efforts to overcome hierarchical relations between researcher and participant include employing reflexivity, or "the tendency to reflect upon, examine critically, and explore analytically the nature of the research process" (Fonow and Cook 1991, 2). Through reflexivity one constantly assesses and reevaluates one's positionality and assumptions as a researcher (Stanley and Wise 1993). This process requires amending and fine-tuning the objectives and script of the research project in response to unexpected outcomes or situations (England 1994). Likewise, attempts to overcome or at least acknowledge asymmetrical power relations underlying field-based research demand critical examination of the researcher as "outsider."

Addressing the positionality of the researcher has been a major issue in feminist methodological discussions, particularly in regard to the effect of gender on the research process (Herod 1993; Hondagneu-Sotelo 1988; McDowell 1992b), but also in regards to "race" and ethnicity (Kobayashi 1994; Peake 1993) and sexuality (England 1994; Valentine 1993). Although differences inevitably exist among women, they experience similar types of oppression in the household, the workplace, and society at large. Once these differences and similarities are recognized, a reflexive researcher—one sensitive to both her and her participant's positionalities—can establish a certain rapport with the subject. Attempts to establish a reciprocal relationship, however, can be problematic, and may lead to hesitancy or outright rejection on the part of the person being approached to participate in the research. England (1994), for example, interprets her own experience with the lesbian community she attempted to research as rejection and a "failed" project. In contrast, one can build on one's experience as a marginalized outsider within the dominant culture, as is the case with Kobayashi (1994) in her research on and with Japanese Canadians.

Finally, in many areas of feminist research, the field is viewed as a political arena where a researcher meets and interacts with research participants. Approaching the field as a place of potentially contentious interaction highlights one's position as a subjective researcher (Eyles 1993). Katz raises similar issues in her discussion of "the artificiality of the distinctions drawn between research and politics, the operations of research and the research itself, the field and the 'not field' " (1994, 67). She illustrates how attempts to define the field and draw boundaries entail wielding power as a researcher. In cases where the home is the site of fieldwork, the household becomes a strategic, or politically situated location for both researcher and researched. This situation encourages reflexivity by the researcher who is forced to negotiate the space of the researched and thus become more aware of her own economic and social position vis-à-vis the subject. In addition, the home as "field" reworks power dynamics between parties in that the home is the terrain of the researched, putting into play multiple power relations anchored in the spatiality of the subject. The investigation of household economic strategies requires reconceptualizing the dualisms constructed between home and work and a redefinition of what constitutes a field of research.

In sum, feminist research critically examines relations between researcher and participant, and exposes the political contexts of the field. Feminist methodology challenges conventional masculinist research with its androcentric assumptions about societal processes to yield a better understanding of economic and social strategies employed by people in everyday life. Additionally, feminist methodology questions power relations within the research process, attempting to reduce the otherwise hierarchical relation between researcher and the researched. The discussion that follows draws from the methodological premises outlined above to analyze income-generating strategies employed by women in the household. Exploring the multiple dimensions of domestic space reveals how the household is an important locale for both productive and reproductive activities. Examining this dual function of the home helps rework feminist methodological frontiers, thereby pushing towards new horizons in feminist research.

Linking the Household to Productive Labor

One of the strengths of feminist analysis is its ability to connect everyday life, particularly among women, to broader political-economic change and societal structures. Fonow and Cook (1991) stress the significance of women's everyday lives because these lives help sustain gender inequality. By overlooking gender dynamics at the household scale, conventional analyses neglect the connection between household economic strategies and local, regional, or international economic structures and change. This neglect of crucial household dynamics contributes to gender biases in policies aimed at economic development and reinforces wage inequality, uneven employment levels, and occupational segregation.

In contrast, feminist analysis show that the gendered social economy of the household holds a strong but reciprocal relationship with different economic scales (Hanson and Pratt 1988; Pahl 1988). Globally, for example, women are entering the workforce in greater numbers as more households require multiple sources of income in order to survive. The ensuing shift in the composition of the labor force affects production processes, consumption patterns, and economic restructuring processes at local, regional, and international scales. Likewise, social relations and divisions of labor at the household scale are affected by restructuring at these scales as well as at the household level (Mackenzie 1986). Therefore, a locale or place such as the household provides an important context for understanding everyday events and their connection to broader structures. Examining the intersection of these different scales of socioeconomic change leads to a more comprehensive and less gender-biased understanding of economic development.

Several theoretical debates about the general categories of production and reproduction address how patriarchy and capitalism affect gender relations and economic strategies both within and outside the home. With industrial capitalism came the increased physical separation of home and work, although reproductive activities in the domestic sphere remain closely integrated with productive activities in the workplace (Pahl 1988; Redclift and Mingione 1985). Marxian analyses of the impact of industrialization on households recognize the importance of reproductive work but fail to conceptualize the link between consumption and reproduction in the household and production in the workplace (Castells 1983). In particular, Young's work on dual systems theory argues that Marxist feminists' attempts to make Marxism more explanatory of gender wound up adding preexisting Marxian categories onto those of gender, creating a dual systems model (Young 1980). Other feminists have critiqued the analytical separation of production and reproduction and, by extension, the domination of capitalism and patriarchy over production and reproduction respectively (Mackenzie and Rose 1983; McDowell 1986). These analyses demonstrate the integral connection between activities in the home and the workplace, arguing that the home is a site where capitalism and patriarchy intersect (McDowell 1986; Women and Geography Study Group 1984). Moreover, as gender relations continue to change, outcomes of struggles between women workers, male workers, capital, and the state will not only be determined by capitalism, but by relations between women and men in the domestic sphere (Peake 1994). For example, feminists challenge the image of the home as a safe haven and a private space in part by documenting violence and abuse towards women in the home (Pain 1991; Valentine 1992) and the role of the state in reproductive rights, property rights, and immigration and naturalization.

The simultaneous and often contentious nature of the household as both a private sphere of reproduction and a public sphere of productive activities is highlighted in women's homework (Ahrentzen 1990; Boris and Daniels 1989; Mackenzie 1987). Women's home-based economic activities bridge private and public domains, reproductive and productive work, and the domestic arena and the workplace. For homeworkers, the household is a site where goods and services are produced and sometimes sold in addition to it being a private sphere of reproductive activities. The simultaneous nature of productive and reproductive activities in the domestic sphere is evident in research outlined below on women homeworkers in rural West Virginia (Oberhauser 1993, 1995).

Exploring the Home as a Strategic Research Site

This section explains the methods used to engage these women in the research process and to understand the multiple roles and income-generating strategies used by women in the household. This type of research necessarily involved developing trusting relationships with participants to allow entry into their homes. As researchers, we were outsiders to these women, often separated from them by our education, socioeconomic status, and geographic background. Entering a stranger's home could be seen as an invasion of privacy and a potential threaten to personal safety. Being female, and in some instances being with my children, reduced their suspicion of us, but did not necessarily alter the fact that we were outsiders entering their private space.

Additionally, our topic of research required considerable explanation as most women had never participated in a research project. Many women questioned our interest in their home-based businesses and household economies: some were curious about our motives, expecting queries about the legality of their activity, while others viewed us as experts and asked questions about how to produce or sell their goods more effectively. After learning more about the project, most women were pleased and even flattered that we showed an interest in them and their activities.

Despite our differences, most women accepted our presence in their households.[3] In chapter 8 in this volume, Falconer Al-Hindi also demonstrates how entering women's homes can redefine the relationship between researcher and researched in a way which creates a positive rapport. Likewise, our interacting with these women in their homes leveled the playing field, so to speak, and prevented a unidirectional power relation from developing. Their general acceptance of our presence was apparent not only in some of the participants' willingness to share their experiences, but also in their generosity during our visits. One woman who runs a catering service, for example, prepared a huge table of food for us. Moreover, most were happy to show us quilts, baskets, clothing, and other goods they made. Our discussions with these women often became more than just an interview and entailed personal interactions such as meeting family members or sharing concerns about work, children, or husbands.

Oakley (1981) argues that sharing personal experiences with the research participants is an effective way to overcome the hierarchical relations that often occur between the interviewer and interviewee. Despite the differences mentioned above, as a mother, wife, and working woman, I shared certain roles and experiences with many of these women. These commonalities were particularly evident when I was accompanied by my two young children. Different studies address the advantages of combining parenting and fieldwork (Cassell 1987; Hondagneu-Sotelo 1988). In most instances, the presence of children facilitates entree and helps to establish a rapport and trust between the researcher and the researched. Consequently, women were not as likely to be suspicious of my research motives and perhaps felt more comfortable participating in the research. One woman was actually relieved when she learned I was going to bring my children because she was concerned that her own children would disturb our interview. In contrast, a disadvantage of combining parenting and fieldwork is the practical issue of keeping the children occupied to minimize disruption during the interviews. In most cases, however, the presence of my children was an advantage because, in addition to being a university researcher, I was seen as a mother, sharing concerns similar to many of the participants around juggling child care and paid work.

I identified women's homes as the site of research in this project for both practical and strategic reasons.[4] First, it was more convenient for many of the participants to remain at home for interviews because of domestic responsibilities, the most common being child care. One woman needed to be home with her disabled son and her mother-in-law with Alzheimer's disease. She is a member of a knitting cooperative, which allows her to do her work at home while caring for these family members. Second, by interviewing these women in their homes, we were able to learn more about their daily lives. We observed the physical space where homework activities take place and how the activities fit into the overall household setting.

It was also revealing to see how women negotiate their responsibilities as homeworkers and wives, mothers, and daughters. Their time is often spent doing domestic chores and homework activities simultaneously. For example, during our interview with Terry, a mother of three who does word processing and other home-based office services, we were interrupted several times by the phone and her children. In response to a question about the challenges of running a home-based business on top of her domestic responsibilities, she commented,

> That's very difficult. Even things like when the phone rings and you have toddlers, you have to be able to teach them that if Mommy is on the business phone, they

can't be screaming in the background. You have to put up a business-like front. I know of people who have even purchased tape recordings of typing sounds that will make them sound more professional on the phone.[5]

Observing and talking to Terry in her home setting provided insights into the multiple dimensions of her everyday life as a homeworker that would not have been evident had we interviewed her in another setting. Additionally, some women talked about the invasion of privacy that they felt from having home-based economic activities. For example, some activities involved clients who would enter these women's homes to purchase goods or pay for their services. These situations challenge the myth of the home as haven and as a private space where only reproductive activities occur.

Home interviews also revealed how homework activities are related to women's local communities and surrounding economies. Each woman talked about her employment options and the economic situation in her area. Many women live in remote areas where few jobs are available, day care is limited, transportation is difficult to access, and there are few options for female employment outside the home. Consequently, women in rural West Virginia face considerable barriers to formal employment, thus are more apt to engage in home-based income-generating strategies. According to one woman who owns a greenhouse in a rural area of the state,

> It's not economically viable to take a job in town, between the cost of the gas to get there, what the child care would be, and the area in West Virginia . . . the unemployment rate here is 25 percent, I believe. If you get a job, it would be minimum wage and you'd be working to pay child care and pay your taxes. That would be it.[6]

In cases like these, women have no option but to generate income through a home-based activity.

In sum, approaching the home as "the field" raises important methodological issues in our research on women and home-based work, in part by interacting with participants in places where lines of power are redrawn and the means of communication are more reciprocal. Interviewing women in their homes affects the research process itself, particularly our approach to participants and the multiple dimensions of our interactions in the household. During the interviews, we not only talked about income-generating activities, but were able to observe their everyday lives and be a part of their surroundings. We did not intend to be outsiders, or academic voyeurs, but people who share somewhat similar dilemmas and experiences in their work and personal life. We approached the fieldwork and these women not just to observe, question, and then leave, but to engage with them on their own terms, in their own space.

Exploring the Home as a Strategic Economic Site

In addition to critically analyzing the home as the site of research, this study examines the economic and social contribution of home-based activities to the household and the homeworker. Women gained both material and emotional benefits from their homework, despite the difficult negotiating strategies they were often required to employ to overcome the cultural and physical barriers to their participation in income-generating activities. Four elements of homework are outlined below to show the outcomes and efforts required to engage in home-based income-generation. These include examination of the activities encountered, the contribution of these respective activities to household incomes, the spatial negotiations needed to combine domestic responsibilities and homework, and the personal advantages and disadvantages of engaging in homework.

The most tangible outcome of homework for women is the production of goods and services to sell outside the household. Table 9.1 indicates the types of homework among the women interviewed for this project and figure 9.2 their location in West Virginia. The categories of crafts, services, and agricultural goods represent the major types of goods and services produced. Fifty of the eighty-two women interviewed produced craft goods. Quilting is a common activity among Appalachian homeworkers, representing just over one-fifth of the women we interviewed. A majority of quilters work in organized groups, the largest of which is Cabin Creek Quilts (CCQ), located near Charleston. Items made by women around the state are sold in the main shop and through a national catalog. This cooperative has approximately 250 members. As indicated in figure 9.2, the members of CCQ interviewed for this project are clustered in a few areas of the state. Our sample also includes fourteen members of a knitting cooperative, Appalachian by Design, which was established in the late 1980s and has successfully produced and marketed knitwear for national and international markets (figure 9.2 and table 9.1).

Services make up nearly a third of the homework done by women in this study and include a wide variety of activities. Finally, seven women engage in the production of agricultural goods. The one agricultural production and marketing network operating among this sample of homeworkers is the Appalachian Flower Network (AFN). The AFN is a group of approximately thirty people who work together to grow, dry, and arrange flowers and who market their products both individually and collectively throughout the state (figure 9.2). Approximately one half of the homeworkers interviewed work alone in the production and marketing of their goods and services. These women often market their items in craft fairs and farmers' markets, or on an individual basis. In contrast, some homeworkers developed networks with other people to produce or sell their goods. In many small rural communities, women have gotten together to set up quilting guilds, craft cooperatives, or other types of networks. Overall, collaborative organizations serve as important support groups, increase production efficiency, and can effectively market goods beyond the state level (Oberhauser 1996).

Home-based income generation frequently involves other family members in a variety of ways. Children or husbands often help homeworkers prepare, transport, and sell goods at craft shows or in other marketing outlets. Addi-

TABLE 9.1
Types of Homework Activities Among Selected West Virginia Women

Activities	Number of Women Homeworkers N = 82	Percentage of Total Homeworkers*
Crafts		
Weaving	1	1.3
Quilting	16	22.7
Pottery	5	6.1
Knitting	14	17.1
Silk goods	2	2.4
Sewing	3	3.7
Ceramics	2	2.4
Basketry	1	1.3
Misc. crafts	6	7.3
Total Crafts	50	61.0
Services		
Day car/preschool	4	4.9
Catering/baking	3	3.7
Office services	5	6.1
Housecleaning	2	2.4
Real estate	1	1.3
Catalog marketing	2	2.4
Gift baskets	2	2.4
Pet training	1	1.3
Costume rental	1	1.3
Bed and Breakfast	1	1.3
Music lessons	1	1.3
Hair care	1	1.3
Psychological svs.	1	1.3
Total Services	25	30.5
Agricultural Goods		
Beekeeping	1	1.3
Growing farm produce	4	4.9
Other	2	2.4
Total Agricultural Goods	7	8.5

SOURCE: Personal Interviews, West Virginia, 1993–1995
*Percentages may not add up to totals because of rounding

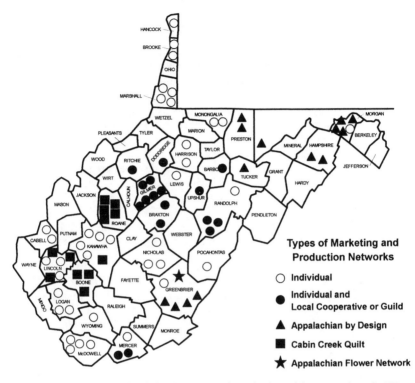

Fig. 9.2. Marketing and production strategies of selected homeworkers in West Virginia.

tionally, household members will assist with tasks normally done by the woman such as cleaning, cooking, or performing child care. Problems sometimes arise, however, when homework interferes with "normal" household operations. The following comments indicate that family members do not always support and sometimes even resent homework activities undertaken by their mothers or wives.

> I pile stuff on my kitchen table. My kids have come to the point where they kind of look over and they say, "Are we going to eat tonight or do I have to make a bowl of cereal?"[7]
>
> I hate to say this, but my husband, he's not real encouraging, because he feels that it's a kind of a waste of time. You know, that I should be doing other household chores.[8]

These quotes reflect the negative attitudes among some family members toward women's involvement in home-based work, disclosing the fact that homeworkers' "economic" work is deemed secondary to being a mother or wife.

Our study indicates that earnings from homework activities contribute to household income in various proportions. More than one-half of the eighty-two homeworkers interviewed contributed less than 20 percent of their total household income from their home-based activities and nearly one-third contributed between 20 and 40 percent. Although the majority of homeworkers do not solely support their households, their earnings provide crucial sources of income during periods of transition such as when the primary breadwinner is laid off, loses a job, becomes disabled, or retires. For example, one woman's earnings from housecleaning and quilting supported their household during periods when her husband was on strike and laid off from his coal mining job. These earnings are especially important to the household because they are almost always spent on domestic needs such as clothing, car payments, or other household expenses.

Women's contributions to household incomes from homework also fluctuates with changing domestic responsibilities, especially child care. Terry's explanation of why she cut back on typing services is typical of many women with young children.

> He [husband] is finally making enough income so I don't have to feel that I have to work as I have done in the past. This was intended to be a rest period and a time to concentrate on the children. So I've picked up school activities and I maintain my word processing and my computer skills by typing for the school.[9]

During childbearing years, women tend to be less involved in homework, whereas older women whose children have left home increase their homeworking activity.

The spatiality of where and how women perform homework activities can be problematic. Spatial constraints and limited resources often make it difficult for many of them to negotiate demands on time and household space. Although many homes were well maintained, some housing was substandard, making it difficult to imagine how women manage to run a business when electricity is unreliable, water is unsafe to drink, and windows leak cold air in the winter. Lacking any separate space for their work, women often use central areas within the household for homework activities, setting up their sewing machine on the kitchen table, storing materials in a bedroom closet, or dealing with clients in their living rooms. Figure 9.3 illustrates one way that domestic space is used for homework activities. The knitting machine and workplace for this knitter occupy the family room. In contrast, some women have separate spaces for work, such as an office, a garage, a workroom, or a workshop in the backyard. The ability to physically separate their domestic space and workplace tends to increase productivity and alter perceptions of themselves as working women. For example, Linda complained to us about the disadvantages of trying to run her sewing and costume rental business out of her home.

> If I had a different home, they [my customers] could have an outside entrance into my basement and I'd have an area there for them to try on costumes. Now

Fig. 9.3. The family room serves as work space for the knitting machine and other sewing activities of this homemaker.

> they've got to go into my son's room to try them on. It feels like I don't have enough privacy and the kids have to move out. I want to be more professional, so I have them [the children] go with my husband somewhere.[10]

Linda is concerned about establishing a professional appearance despite the spatial limitations of her workplace and the difficulty trying to accommodate her customers while maintaining family responsibilities.

In contrast to the physical constraints and other problems outlined above, many women receive intangible personal benefits from their involvement in home-based work. Our conversations with women revealed that many experience an increase in self-esteem and confidence as they succeed in producing and selling goods and services. Even those who generated small amounts of money became more confident and were apt to change their attitudes toward themselves as capable women. One woman conveyed this feeling in the following comment:

> I needed something to feel good about. I felt bad because I didn't go to college or didn't have some kind of degree. I've always felt kind of inferior because of that, and this [homework] has kind of brought me up.[11]

Given the widespread traditional attitudes toward women in rural West Virginia, these women are moving beyond their primarily reproductive role as they engage in productive activities that generate income.

Finally, the marketing strategies used by many homeworkers in part reflect limited outlets for their goods and a general undervaluing of their work. Women who sell their goods or services at the local scale often undervalue their products, either giving them away or selling them below market prices. One woman justified the low prices she charged for typing by calling attention to the local economy.

> There's a lot of people up here out of work and when you are going to be doing resumés for people, 90 percent of the time those people don't have a job, so I don't want to soak them on a resumé. Those are the same people who come back to me. A lot of them are in school at the same time.[12]

Many women claimed that they *liked* quilting, making baskets, or caring for elderly people, and therefore did not feel comfortable charging people a lot for these goods or services. Due to the lack of financial resources, bartering is also common among women with friends or family. Overall, limited resources and inadequate markets often decrease the overall success and economic potential of homework in this study region.

In sum, this analysis demonstrates that the household is a common, yet potentially contentious place where women perform multiple types of productive and reproductive work. Engaging in home-based income-generation means that women often perform homework activities while taking care of children or elderly family members, cooking meals, cleaning house, and maintaining other domestic responsibilities. Thus the overlapping spaces of home and work challenge conventional ideas about the separation of reproductive and productive activities. Moreover, the simultaneous demands on women performing home-based work require significant juggling of resources and time. The scale and types of activities observed in this research vary tremendously, from small hobbies to extensive regional and international businesses. Women's contributions to household income also fluctuate alongside economic constraints, domestic responsibilities, and personal goals. In most cases, however, homework results in both personal benefits and sacrifices for women who help financially support their households while also maintaining their domestic roles.

Conclusion

It is said that Appalachian people have strong ties to home ("Holding onto Home" 1989). In Lydia's case, she has lived in the same hollow all her life and strongly identifies with the place and its people (figure 9.1). These ties have kept many people from leaving the state, despite the lack of well-paying jobs. Given this situation, home has acquired an increasingly significant meaning as a locale where women can undertake economic activities alongside their domestic responsibilities.

This chapter examines the home as a methodological frontier in feminist research and as a site for income generation. As the location of interactions between researcher and participant, the home presents complex interviewing challenges. Identifying the home as the field involved gaining women's trust in order to enter their domestic space and discuss their homework activities. Employing a feminist methodology in this field-based research allowed me to critically examine and shift the hierarchical power relations between researcher and researched. Although I entered their homes as an outsider, I shared some common experiences with these women as a mother and working woman. The relationship between myself and the participants, however, required constant reflection and evaluation of my role as a researcher.

This project challenges masculinist notions of the home as a private space where primarily reproductive activities take place. Masculinist analyses dismiss important household activities and strategies or see them as irrelevant to economic restructuring (see Samarsinghe in this collection, chapter 7). Marxian analyses also overlook the integral relationship between production and reproduction, and capitalism and patriarchy, in addition to the ways in which these categories affect gender relations in the household and workplace. Drawing from the example presented in this study, women's home-based work is frequently overlooked in conventional analyses of economic restructuring. Consequently, attempts to enhance women's employment opportunities and reduce poverty ignore the household level because it is seen as lying outside the economic sphere of productive activities and disconnected from other scales of economic activity. This separation of home and work is typical of economic development programs where patriarchal attitudes toward gender roles are carried over into policy implementation. In contrast, the analysis of home-based, income-generating activities in this study yields a different picture of the home as a strategic economic locale where productive activities occur alongside reproductive activities. In these situations, women creatively negotiate their time and domestic space with often limited resources. The household economic strategies at the center of this analysis are often critical to household survival, especially during periods when the primary source of income is eroded or in transition.

Finally, and perhaps most importantly, home-based income-generating activities often result in women gaining confidence and self-esteem as they develop their skills and financially contribute to their households. Many women homeworkers have not been active in the formal labor force, or have held menial jobs. They therefore benefit from being able to develop strategies to produce and market their goods and services. The research thus illustrates a methodological threshold in feminist fieldwork, namely, the economic and social dimensions of homework as an income-generating strategy. These women, and many others like them, play crucial roles in their communities and households as they strive for economic and social empowerment.

Notes

1. Funding for this project was supported by the National Science Foundation (Grant SRB-9309275) and the West Virginia University Regional Research Institute.

I would like to thank my graduate research assistants, Urmilla Bob, Tammy Core, Toni Hickey and Anne-Marie Turnage for their unfailing support during the interviews and other phases of this research project. All of the names of the homeworkers quoted in the text have been changed to maintain confidentiality.

2. Home-based work, or homework, is broadly defined as the production of goods or services in the household for monetary exchange or barter. Due to the wide variety of home-based economic activities taking place in this part of Appalachia, I have included both formal and informal activities in my definition.

3. It is difficult to determine the refusal rate of this study since the targeted population was contacted through various avenues. In some cases, we acted through an intermediary who approached a homeworker or homeworkers about participating in the project. In other cases, we contacted them directly and they either refused altogether or agreed to participate. Overall, most people we contacted were willing to talk once they understood the general purpose of the project.

4. Although most of the interviews took place in women's homes, some interviews took place in an office or other "neutral" location. In some instances, it was more convenient for us to interview several women in one place such as a local extension office.

5. Terry, interview by author, tape recording, Greenbank, WV, 19 June 1995.

6. Nancy, interview by author, tape recording, Williamsburg, WV, 19 June 1995.

7. Cindy, interview by author, tape recording, Elkins, WV, 16 Sept. 1994.

8. Cathy, interview by author, tape recording, Normantown, WV, 23 May 1994.

9. Terry, interview by author, tape recording, Greenbank, WV, 19 June 1996.

10. Linda, interview by author, tape recording, Dunbar, WV, 6 June 1994.

11. Iris, interview by author, tape recording, West Hamlin, WV, 20 June 1994.

12. Karen, interview by author, tape recording, Moundsville, WV, 18 Feb. 1994.

References

Ahrentzen, S. B. 1990. Managing conflict by managing boundaries: How professional home-workers cope with multiple roles at home. *Environment and Behavior* 22(6):723–52.

Boris, E., and Daniels, C. R., eds. 1989. *Homework: Historical and contemporary perspectives on paid labor at home*. Urbana, IL: University of Illinois Press.

Cassell, J., ed. 1987. *Children in the field: Anthropological experiences*. Philadelphia: Temple University Press.

Castells, M. 1983. *The city and the grassroots*. London: Edward Arnold.

England, K. 1994. Getting personal: Reflexivity, positionality and feminist research. *The Professional Geographer* 46(1):80–89.

Eyles, J. 1993. Feminist and interpretive method: How different? *The Canadian Geographer* 37:50–52.

Feminism as method in geography. 1993. *The Canadian Geographer*. Special section. Vol. 37(1): 48–61.

Fonow, M. M., and Cook, J., eds. 1991. *Beyond methodology: Feminist scholarship as lived research*. Bloomington, IN: Indiana University. Press.

Hanson, S. and G. Pratt. 1988. Reconceptualizing the links between home and work in urban geography. *Economic Geography* 64(4):299–321.

Herod, A. 1993. Gender issues in the use of interviewing as a research method. *The Professional Geographer* 45:305–17.

Holding onto Home. 1989. Special Report. *Charleston Gazette*. December.

Hondagneu-Sotelo, P., 1988. Gender and fieldwork. *Women's Studies International Forum* 11(6):611–18.

Katz, C. 1994. Playing the field: Questions of fieldwork in geography. *The Professional Geographer* 46(1):67–72.

Kobayashi, A. 1994. Coloring the field: Gender, "race," and the politics of fieldwork. *The Professional Geographer* 46(1):73–80.

Mackenzie, S. 1986. Women's responses to economic restructuring: Changing gender, changing space. In *The Politics of Diversity*, ed. R. Hamilton and M. Barrett, pp. 81–100. London: Verso Press.

———, 1987. Neglected spaces in peripheral places: homeworkers and the creation of a new economic centre. *Cahiers de Géographie du Québec* 31(83):247–60.

Mackenzie, S., and Rose, D. 1983. Industrial change, the domestic economy and home life. In *Redundant Spaces in Cities and Regions*, ed. J. Anderson, S. Duncan and R. Hudson. London: Academic Press.

Mascia-Lees, F. E., Sharpe, P., and Cohen, C.B. 1989. The post-modernist turn in anthropology: Cautions from a feminist perspective. *Signs: Journal of Women in Culture and Society* 15:7–33.

McDowell, L., 1986. Beyond patriarchy: A class-based explanation of women's subordination. *Antipode* 18(3):311–21.

———, 1992a. Doing gender: Feminism, feminists and research methods in human geography. *Transactions of the Institute of British Geography* 17:399–416.

———, 1992b. Valid games? A response to Erica Schoenberger. *The Professional Geographer* 44:212–215.

Nast, H. J. 1994. Women in the field: Critical feminist methodologies and theoretical perspectives. *The Professional Geographer* 46(1):54–66.

Oakley, A., 1981. Interviewing women: A contradiction in terms. In *Doing feminist research*, ed. H. Roberts, pp. 30–61. London: Routledge and Kegan Paul.

Oberhauser, A., 1993. Industrial restructuring and women's homework in Appalachia: Lessons from West Virginia. *Southeastern Geographer* 33(1):23–43.

———, 1995. Gender and household economic strategies in rural Appalachia. *Gender, Place and Culture* 2(1): 51–70.

———, 1996. Flexible production networks in rural Appalachia: Locating gender in regional economic networks. Paper presented at the 28th International Geographical Congress, The Hague, Netherlands, Aug. 4–10, 1996.

Pahl, R. E. 1988. *On work*. New York: Basil Blackwell.

Pain, R. 1991. Space, sexual violence, and social control: Integrating geographical and feminist analyses of women's fear of crime. *Progress in Human Geography* 15(4):415–31.

Peake, L., 1993. "Race" and sexuality: Challenging the patriarchal structuring of urban social space. *Environment and Planning D: Society and Space* 11:415–32.

———, 1994. Engendering change: Women's work and the development of urban-social theory. In *Women, work, and place*, ed. A. Kobayashi, pp. 3–26. Montreal: McGill-Queen's University Press.

Redclift, N., and E. Mingione, eds. 1985. *Beyond employment*. London: Blackwell.

Roberts, H., ed. 1981. *Doing feminist research*. London: Routledge and Kegan Paul.

Stanley, L. and Wise, S. 1993. *Breaking out again: Feminist ontology and epistemology*. London: Routledge.

Valentine, G. 1992. Images of danger: Women's sources of information about the spatial distribution of male violence. *Area* 24(1).

———, 1993. (Hetero)sexing space: Lesbian perceptions and experiences of everyday spaces. *Environment and Planning D: Society and Space* 11:395–413.

Women and Geography Study Group. 1984. *Geography and Gender: An introduction to feminist geography*. London: Huthchinson.

Young, I. 1980. Socialist feminism and the limits of dual systems theory. *Socialist Review* 10(2/3): 169–88.

10

Dialogue with Difference: A Tale of Two Studies

Isabel Dyck

The category "woman of color" is of particular concern in feminist theories dealing with dimensions of difference in women's experiences. In the process of deconstructing a universalizing notion of woman through the inclusion of a diversity of women's voices, "race" and ethnicity are identified as key axes of difference to be explored. But while Black feminist theoretical literature has mounted a challenge to the dominance of White, Western feminist interpretations of women's experiences of subordination, the lives and voices of women of color remain largely hidden from view. This is particularly so for women immigrants in Western countries. In this chapter, I report my experiences, as a White woman involved in health and health care research, of the research processes of two studies concerned with the perspectives and experiences of first generation, Indo-Canadian women living in British Columbia, Canada. In addition to being "women of color," these women are mothers, daughters, wives, and workers, and some live with chronic disability.

One objective of comparing the processes of the two studies is to interrogate the notion of woman of color by exploring how multiple dimensions of women's identities become apparent and how they influence the construction of knowledge in the intersubjective context of interviewing. I view the research situation as one context, among others more common in everyday life, in which women's identities shift and are negotiated. I reflect on the question of whether, in focusing on a particular ethnocultural group, the researcher unintentionally contributes to the construction of the "other" by fixing a dominant identity. My second objective is to explore the efficacy of in-depth interviewing—a research method compatible with the principles of feminist inquiry—across cultural groups and different social and material settings. In doing so I consider the intertwining of identity and geography in the women's lives, as evidenced first in the actual interview dynamics, and second through my momentary insertion in their lives as a researcher, as played out in the sites of access and interviewing. I am particularly interested in power relationships in the analysis; as Harding (1991) points out, researchers are agents of knowledge in the same critical plane as those they study, enmeshed in social relations of power and bringing their own cultural values and interests to research.[1] My reflection on the studies suggests that the differential social positioning of researcher and "researched" is also intimately tied to the respective relationship of each to a particular place, as experienced through specific sociospatial settings of local geographies.

At the onset, I wish to emphasize that this is my version of the story of the two studies. Other stories from the study participants' viewpoints also exist but are not accessible to myself or the reader. In my rendering of events, I focus on the issue of "difference" and the associated concern of how social categories used by researchers in framing research, such as woman of color, or Indo-Canadian, influence what knowledge is constructed. The dynamics of the field research indicated that the challenge of including diverse voices in feminist theories, particularly in cross-cultural research, is a complex matter involving both local and nonlocal relations. In the first section of this story, I identify the academic narrative that forms the context of my discussion, including the tensions between feminist standpoint epistemology and poststructuralist approaches in studying "difference." In the second section, I present an account of two studies conducted with women from the Indo-Canadian community of Vancouver, identifying further discursive contexts within which the research was conceived and designed. Examination of the dynamics of the field methods show that both gender and "race" were important dimensions of identity in the joint construction of the women's accounts (by researchers, research assistants, and study participants). However, negotiations of power in the research process showed their relevance to vary according to each interview situation. In the final section, I reflect on what the two studies can suggest with regard to the use of in-depth interviewing in feminist research across cultural groups, and how the experience of using this method can inform our understanding of the constitution of identity "in place." I also discuss the implications of the research experience for a poststructuralist understanding of difference.

"Reading" the Research Process: Deconstructing or Remaking Difference?

Academic Narratives

Research is located in an ongoing academic narrative in which researchers define rules and procedures, negotiate types of admissable evidence, establish paradigms, and construct and contest theories. As academics, we carry theories and concepts of the world that give us some power to define that world, whether or not such conceptualizations are contested. We bring these to the interview encounter in the process of framing and responding to questions. We are also carriers of accepted research methods that are legitimized and given authority in the course of debate within our discipline, and through the peer review process of publication. Feminist scholarship, in the struggle to legitimize its knowledge, has launched powerful critiques of dominant "ways of doing" research, particularly in the realm of science, through nuanced accounts of how knowledge is produced and comes to hold authority. Debate within feminist discourse on methods and theories of difference informed the studies discussed here (e.g., Barrett 1987; Collins 1991; Fonow and Cook 1991; Harding 1987; hooks 1992; Reinharz 1992; Spivak 1990; Weedon 1987; Young 1990). In the analysis I employ a Foucauldian understanding of the exercise of power through discursive and material practices, along with a sensitivity to the possibilities of resistance to dominant discourse and practices.

It is now commonplace to observe that the diversity of women's experiences modifies the claims of feminist theory, which has, in the main, been constructed by Western, White women. Such experiences are considered central in challenging the fixity of the notion "woman," for without them the subject is removed from the generative process of research, and conventional categories cannot be transformed. There are, however, tensions over how and by whom the voices of difference among women can be, and should be, incorporated into theory building. These tensions are located within a discourse in feminism that engages the claims of standpoint epistemology with a poststructuralist critique based on an understanding of the discursive construction of difference. Feminist standpoint epistemology refers to an "engaged vision," which is achieved through the experience of living as a woman in a particular social positioning (see Harding 1991). The methodological implication is that an approach to knowledge is advocated that centers these experiences in the understanding and explanation of women's worlds. Women may have common experiences, for example, through their standpoint as mother, by virtue of their position in a gendered division of labor, or through the particularities of oppression as a Black woman (see, for example, Collins 1991; Hartsock 1987; hooks 1992; Ruddick 1989; Smith 1987). It is from these diverse experiences of women's lives that claims of the situatedness of knowledge are grounded. For some feminists, particularly within Black and Third World feminism, claims to the specificity of Black women's oppression and ways of expressing their experiences has tended to lead to a concern about the appropriation of the voices of women of color by White feminists who cannot fully appreciate this experience.

The valorization of experience has met with critique, however, as feminists have also pointed to a fragmentation of identity, sometimes contradictory, with women drawing on and performing different scripts in the particular situations of their everyday interaction (Bordo 1992; Butler 1990; Grosz 1994). The notion of the embodied subject is central to understanding difference, but whereas standpoint epistemology tends to view the body as a locus of experience, poststructuralism interprets the body as "text," or a surface of inscription. This anti-essentialist view understands the body (in its corporeality *and* the meanings ascribed to this corporeality) as culturally constructed in the context of historically specific discourses and relations of power (Grosz 1994). The pervasiveness of discursive inscriptions tends to naturalize difference, for example according to the idea of "race" (Miles 1993). Furthermore, difference logically only comes to have meaning in social interaction, for it is the inscription of the body as "other," within oppositional categories, that subjectivities are constituted. Identity is thus set against shifting contexts, where different power relations may be operating.

Barrett (1987) claims that feminist standpoint epistemology, as "a theory of knowledge based on the social positioning of women," presupposes "a social world that exists outside our knowledge of our discourse about it," and shows "optimistic confidence" in ontological reality and empirical method. If accepted uncritically, such a viewpoint may encourage essentialist notions, even while remaining cognizant of diversity. So while the inclusion of experience may be integral to the production of accounts of how women make sense of and act in their worlds, such accounts need to be sensitive to the significance of context, local knowledge, and the discursive construction of subjects. Experience, then, is not unproblematic and cannot be relied on exclusively in understanding women's various social and spatial positionings (McDowell 1991). Poststructuralist feminism suggests that there will be a range of interpretive schema from which women can draw in living "woman," so that inquiry needs to focus on how and where meaning is acquired and resisted within the subtle interplays of power that legitimize and control certain definitions and bodies of knowledge.

Although an alternative theory of knowledge may challenge standpoint epistemology, dilemmas remain in research that claims to construct knowledge about a certain group. This is of central concern in cross-racial research where typically researchers from a cultural majority and in a privileged subject position construct and represent a minority "other." As such constructions enter ways of talking about the "othered," it is important not to reproduce dominant definitions which may serve to naturalize socially constructed categories and so be party to processes of racialization (Bhavnani 1993). Feminist methodological discussion, however, suggests this is not an easy task in pointing to the complexity of the process of knowledge construction and the situatedness and partial nature of all knowledge (Haraway 1988). As McDowell (1992, 214) states, feminist social scientists "recognize the intersubjectivity of the relations between a researcher and her subjects and that as a consequence, the knowledge that is acquired is contextual and interpersonal." In addition, social processes invisible in the face-to-face contact of the interview are involved in how and what knowledge is constructed (Nast 1994; Bhavnani 1993). In my research with women from minority population groups, these issues were of central concern. In the rest of the chapter, I explore the layering of contextual dynamics of two studies, particularly with regard to my positioning in the research and the negotiation of the category "woman of color" that occurred in the interview process. In discussing this layering I suggest that there is a spatiality to knowledge production that feminist methodology debates have not fully explored.

Studying The Other: Further Discourses of Difference

The two studies both concerned the experiences of first generation Indo-Canadian women. The first dealt with cultural change, particularly in relation to women's organization of their domestic and wage labor. My interest in this topic derived from an earlier study concerned with the tensions between these types of labor for women living in family-oriented suburbs (Dyck 1989, 1990). This prior research, which did not include women of color, found that women developed assistive social networks during the course of their mothering work that were integral to how they interpreted and managed the conflicting demands of home and wage labor. I was interested in the strategies Indo-Canadian women used in dealing with these issues, in the context of the economic and social changes they would experience through the processes of immigration. The omission of experiences of women of color in the earlier study and the perception of health professionals that isolated Indo-Canadian women formed a significant proportion of the caseload of acute care psychiatric services in the city stimulated and informed the research.

In the second study, I was part of an interdisciplinary team of researchers, comprised of two White women and one woman of color.[2] I draw on this distinction of color because it became integral to our discussions of the research. Following from earlier work of one of the team members that explored the social circumstances that act as barriers to immigrant women's access to health care as they manage chronic illness (Anderson 1986; Anderson, Blue, and Lau 1991), we designed a further study to investigate how practices at different sites where women seek help for and manage chronic illness influence their acquisition and use of professional health care knowledge. Women were observed as they met health professionals in clinic settings as well as being interviewed about their everyday lives.

While these were the immediate rationales for carrying out the studies, it is also useful to locate them in the wider context of the research. By doing this I aim to show that the studies, in addition to being forged within feminist academic discourse, were closely connected to our positioning as researchers within a particular geographical setting, the city of Vancouver, where the issue of "cultural difference" took on local significance according to the ongoing transformation of the social geography of the city in the context of international migration. In other words, the choice of substantive issues to be addressed in the research, and their perception as important, were due to their embeddedness in contemporary processes of social displacement and the re-identification of peoples as reflected in Canada's changing immigration patterns.

Since the Immigration Act of 1976, the profile of new immigrants in Canada has shifted from a largely European-based population to one of greater diversity in terms of countries of origin. During the period from 1981 and 1991, for example, 60 percent of immigrants to Canada were born in Asian and Middle Eastern countries (Badets and Chui 1994). Hong Kong and India have consistently been among the top five source countries during this time and, in Vancouver, people of Chinese and South Asian heritage continue to form the two largest "minority populations" in the city. Residential clustering has signaled the existence of identifiable Chinese and Indo-Canadian "communities." While inaccurate, the term "immigrant" in popular usage has come to indicate the visibly different, fostered by rapid demographic changes that challenge dominant conceptions of a "White" Canada.

The concept of "visible minorities" is thus a relatively recent phenomenon in Canada, associated with changing immigration patterns, and applied to immigrant groups rather than native or First Nations people. Coming to terms with this difference, or cultural diversity, has involved practical concerns surrounding settlement within Canada's ethic of equality. The Multiculturalism Act of 1988 encourages Canadian institutions and health services to be responsive to the multicultural reality of the country, with sensitivity to and respect for an increasing diversity of values, experiences and language. Its intention is to promote equal participation in society for Canadians of all ethnic backgrounds, and it adopts an antiracist stance. Cultural sensitivity in health care is considered important within this multicultural ethic, given the observation that groups at high risk for health problems include ethnic minorities, with youth, the elderly, and women from "traditional cultures" being particularly vulnerable (Multiculturalism and Citizenship Canada 1989). The concept of culture, however, is frequently used unproblematically in health care research and practice. It is often conflated with ethnicity and "race," and used as a static, descriptive category (Ahmad 1993; Stubbs 1993). This usage tends to essentialize difference and racialize groups, and fosters a perceived linkage between biology and culture which may be drawn on in constructing explanations of the health problems of minority groups.[3]

Two factors shaped the interest in cultural difference in both studies: first, the larger context of the "problem" of culture in Canada, and, second, its specific interpretation in the health care arena. The latter was of concern because all of the researchers are involved in teaching students in health care professional programs. My specific interest in the situation of Indo-Canadian women derived from my familiarity, although very limited, with India. I had worked and traveled there for a short period, and because of these personal experiences and library work I had carried out on Fiji, I felt more affinity with this group than other minority populations in Vancouver.[4] In addition, my sense of the huge diversity of India suggested that the notion of a homogeneous Indo-Canadian community in Vancouver was misleading and that research was necessary to understand the diversity within such an imagined community. The problem of stereotypical views and simplistic understandings of culture, tend-ing toward essentialism in health care, also drove the concerns of the studies. Before the studies began, we were therefore already working with theoretical ideas about difference—in particular, the cultural shaping within Canada of social identities based on a collision of biological visibility and cultural "attributes" such as language, and perceived differences in values and customs. The women participants did not use the terms "Indo-Canadian" and "woman of color" to identify themselves. They might refer to themselves as East Indian or Indian (in situations with Whites) or other terms, according to whom the interaction is with and the particular context. While the constitution of social identities had not been the key purpose of either of the studies, the methods used uncovered the importance of identity in research and exemplified the notion of the researcher as being on the same critical plane as the "researched," as discussed below (see also Nagar, chapter 11, this volume).

Methods and Difference

Smith's (1987) concept of institutional ethnography informed both studies, in that we considered the way women talked of their experiences as a starting point to discovering the social relations organizing their day-to-day lives, including their responses to living in a "new country" (in the first study) and to health problems (the second study). From a geographical perspective, I was interested in how place mediated such social relations, contributing to ongoing action and influencing the meanings given to everyday experience. The women's experiences were understood to be context dependent, and therefore inseparable from the full range of local social practices. Both studies employed qualitative strategies and relied primarily on in-depth interviewing, although the second study included observation of the women's clinical encounters. Debate on feminist methodology, particularly that concerning the interactive interview, also influenced the projects. We accepted the notion that methods for feminist research should be ones in which knowledge is constructed through researcher and study participants talking together *as women* about the topic at hand.

A model of interactive interviewing has influenced feminist researchers ever since Oakley's (1981) recommendation that this is the most likely form of social interaction to gain detailed experiential accounts of women's lives. The private accounts produced through open exchange in a situation of trust have been contrasted with the public accounts gained when interviewees are on guard and sensitive to the power relation of the interview (Cornwell 1984). The narrative accounts produced through interviewing are also understood to be a joint construction of researcher and study participant as meanings are negotiated and consensus reached (Mishler 1986). Both interviewer and interviewee come to the interview situation with their own purposes and expectations, but the outcome is not purely either's story. Questions guiding the development of the story, however, are largely informed by the theoretical interests of the researcher. Interviewing is therefore not only highly dependent on intersubjective relations, but also imbued with concepts from theory that sensitize the purpose and content of the researcher's questions.

While the in-depth, interactive interview is viewed as compatible with feminist aims of breaking down hierarchical relations in research encounters, there is a lack of consensus on its efficacy. For instance, the interview has been critiqued as a method reflecting a focus on the individual that is consistent with White feminism, but may not be appropriate in other research situations where cultural emphasis is laid on collectivity (Jackson 1993). The interview is also described as a site in which power relations operate in complex ways, with the social positioning of interviewers and interviewees—based on class, status, age, "race" and sexual orientation, et cetera—influencing interview dynamics as well as a study's theoretical underpinnings (Cotterill 1992; Edwards 1990; Finch 1984; Nast et al. 1994; Ramazanoglu 1989; Ribbens 1989). Caste and religion are other, although less-recognized axes of difference, influencing researcher-"researched" relations (see Nagar, chapter 11). The dynamics of power relations in research have been of particular concern in cross-racial research, where structural inequalities underlie the differing subject positions of women of color and White women. It is in this context that standpoint epistemology has been drawn on in defining the politics of research, although White women's accounts of their experiences of interviewing Black women show variation in the stories made available to them (Edwards 1990; Rhodes 1994).

With these points in mind, the research projects were designed to provide conditions conducive to open exchange. The women were to be interviewed in their own homes in the language of their choice. The research assistants who assisted with interviewing were chosen so that the study participants could talk to women with whom they were likely to have some common experiences and language. They possessed specific language skills, and like the women they interviewed, were immigrants to Canada associated with the broad Indo-Canadian grouping in Vancouver. In addition to conducting interviews, the research assistants participated in the interpretation of the interview dynamics and the analysis of the transcripts. They alerted the researchers to culturally specific terms, nuances in conversation, and common cultural practices.

The women for the first study, concerned with cultural change, were recruited through two channels. These were service agencies, publicly funded and set up to enhance integration of immigrants, and the research assistant's own contacts that she had developed as a multicultural worker aiding the resettlement of immigrants of Indian descent. Through this method, fifteen women, all from Punjab, participated in the study. They were between twenty-six and forty years old, and had lived in Canada between one and ten years. The second study, due to its concern with women receiving treatment for chronic illness, recruited women through medical clinics and hospitals. Sixteen women, most in their fifties and sixties, participated in the study. Length of residence in Canada was between two and thirty-one years. Seven of these women were from India (all but one from Punjab), seven from Fiji, and two from African countries (Tanzania and Uganda). The age differences of the two groups directly reflected the topics of the two studies, one concerned with women with young children and the other with women with arthritis or diabetes, which usually begin in middle or later adulthood. The length of time the women had been in Canada reflected patterns of immigration from these countries, especially in the context of immigration policy, which has encouraged family reunification (Proudfoot 1989). There was diversity among the women according to education level, ranging from elementary school to university levels of education in the women's home countries. Some women spoke English well, others not at all or minimally.

The women in the two studies therefore differed in their degree of homogeneity. In the first, the women were from the same region of India (the numerically dominant group in Vancouver), engaged in social networks based on this regional affiliation, and had used service organizations designed for "multicultural minorities." In the study that recruited through disease definition and the health care system, participants reflected more of the diverse origins of those composing the Indo-Canadian community in Vancouver.[5] The diversity found among the women was not unexpected, but it was less clear how this would effect the research process. As might have been anticipated from other researchers' documentation of their experiences, however, the interview dynamics indicated a complexity of interpersonal relationships and subtle shifts of power. Just as other researchers had found that gender was not enough to establish an intimate, open exchange, neither was color. Nor did the attempt to culturally match research assistants and study participants guarantee a setting characterized by equality, negotiation, and consensus. While there were successes, as defined in terms of the detailed stories of Cornwell's (1984) "private" accounts, there were other women who divulged little.

In both studies, women interviewers and interviewees drew on various dimensions of identity and experience to "place" each other and establish grounds for negotiating knowledge. Most commonly, motherhood and position in the family as a wage-earner were reference points from which both parties to the interview described experiences and concerns. In some instances common geographical origins was an important point of connection between the research assistant and interviewee. Several women, particularly in the chronic illness study, drew on perceived common ethnicity with the research assistant (for example, "we Punjabis"), or oppositional racial categories as when women described their doctor as "White." [6] In my interviews in the first study, the women took the opportunity to compare with me—as a worker outside the home and as a mother—ways of negotiating home and work, and some expressed concern about what they saw as conflicting notions of child rearing in White and Indian culture. These women spoke of their experiences at some length. Yet in interviews with the Indo-Canadian research assistant in this study, they were more guarded, despite common regional and ethnic affiliation. It is possible that the research assistant's authority and wide-ranging contacts as a community worker might have acted as a constraint on communication. [7] Age and length of residence in Canada did not have a clear effect on the degree of open exchange in either of the studies.

Although interpersonal styles may have had some affect on communication, how the interviews worked out suggested there were other dynamics at work. The examples above, of the ways in which differences and commonalities were drawn on during interviews in the two projects, alerted me to the complex interweaving of experience and identity. Rather than fixed, identities shift according to both the social positionings of researcher and "researched" and the particular topics pursued in a research project. The interview dynamics also indicate that the power relation of "expert" knowledge, represented by the institutional practice of research, is neither unidirectional nor uniformly accepted or contested. The research project is also positioned in a place-specific context. Next, I will consider resistances to interviewing in the context of research power relations as experienced in the multicultural "reality" of Vancouver.

Method and Resistance

The diversity in the interview dynamics in the two studies is open to different interpretations. There is evidence of a fragmentation of identities, strands of which may become more or less salient as both interviewers and study participants construct meanings and knowledge during an interview. The interview played a role in the women's negotiation of their own identity and situatedness in local social relations, as well as its more usually understood role as a text through which a researcher may interpret these issues. "Unsuccessful" interviews may represent resistance to power differentials in an interview, as the privileged and subordinated subject positions of researcher and researched meet. But which power relations are most significant in cases of resistance? Is it the interview as a specific, and often unfamiliar, research method that constitutes some aspects of women's resistance? Or is the overarching framing of the research within postcolonial relations, together, in the case of the second study, with its location within biomedical knowledge and institutional practice, the most significant power relation? To what extent are points of access and the sites of interviews significant? Reflection on the two studies, for example, suggests that the geographical and social dimensions of access to study participants are closely linked to the ongoing social construction of social identities of "self" and "other" as predominant understandings of local social geographies are destabilized and re-made.

In the study concerning cultural change and women's management of home and wage labor, gaining access to study participants involved negotiating entry to the social networks of women who fit the study's inclusion criteria. I began with the personal contacts of an Indo-Canadian colleague active in the community, and with White women working with various immigrant services.

Through these initial contacts I then reached bilingual Indo-Canadian multi-cultural workers employed by school boards, health clinics, and municipalities providing services to women immigrants. While the White directors of services acted as initial gatekeepers, active negotiation of access to study participants took place through multicultural workers. These latter women acted as bridging points between the "White world" and women's usual participation in primarily Indo-Canadian social networks. The multicultural workers perceived the study as having some value in identifying specific needs of immigrants from India, and they actively worked to arrange meetings for me with the groups they were coordinating. They also translated for me as I explained the study to different groups. Recruitment settings included a preschool, a support group for mothers, and an English language class for senior women (with a request to take the information home for their daughters or daughters-in-law). The research assistant also introduced the study to women participating in a parenting class. Women began talking in general about mothering and health topics during my initial meetings with them, and they often interjected questions. While interested in the study, they were cautious about participating, and insisted in checking with other family members before making a decision. In most cases women did not volunteer. In some instances women initially showed interest, but later canceled interview appointments.[8]

From these settings, six women eventually agreed to take part in the study, one from the preschool, the rest from the mothers' support group. The woman from the preschool was interviewed there at her request, with a research assistant translating. In the case of the mothers' support group, women volunteered to participate after I had visited the group twice to talk about the study. The women spoke English, but they directed most of their responses and questions through the multicultural worker, who facilitated the group's activities, in their first language. They expressed a preference for filling in a questionnaire or having their group facilitator conduct the interviews, but agreed to talk to me if necessary. They preferred that I did the interviews rather than the research assistant, who was another multicultural worker in the community known to them. Our various positionings vis-à-vis the women and their everyday worlds appeared to be more important than personal characteristics in this matter. The multicultural worker, who facilitated their mothers' group on a routine, ongoing basis and appeared to engender a high degree of trust, or myself, as an outsider to the community, were most acceptable to the women as interviewers. Nine further women, however, were recruited through the research assistant's own connections in the Punjabi community as a multicultural worker and she carried out the interviews in the women's first language.

In this first study, therefore, access to study participants was gained through the research assistant's own social network, which was based on both her work in the Indo-Canadian community and migration linkages connected with region of origin in India, and through other non-White spaces where I had received temporary access. These spaces were created to address social adjustment concerns of Indo-Canadian women in areas of the city where there was clustering of families from India, particularly Punjab, and were organized by women of the community.

The process of access in the other study was quite different. As we wanted to observe women's encounters with health professionals, as well as talking to them about their illness management, we recruited through medical settings. We followed guidelines provided by the clinics, which typically involved a health professional introducing the research assistant to a potential study participant when she came to a clinic for treatment or assessment. Several women spoke little English and were accompanied by a family member, who usually encouraged the woman to participate. There was much less resistance to recruitment in this second study, where women were approached in settings they did not control and that were separate from those of their routine activity. They were also spaces imbued with power relations of biomedical knowledge and practice, within which the women were positioned through their illness. This is not to suggest that women were unwilling to participate. Ethical procedures were followed carefully to avoid any sense that participation was required, but the exigencies of their positioning within the research was quite different from those women in the other study. The latter had more opportunity, particularly when meeting as a group, to resist participation in spaces designated as theirs, rather than those primarily defined through White relations.

Interestingly, however, the mode of access did not necessarily differentiate between interviews that flowed easily and those that were stilted. As I pointed out earlier, the intersubjective relations and negotiation of power within interviews were complex. In the clinically based study, for example, the initial casting of the study within biomedical concerns was often decentered during the interviews as women talked of the concerns of their day-to-day lives and their use of a plurality of remedies (including traditional medicines) in the management of their illness. But spaces of access did play a part in issues of control, and in some cases they were significant as to how the interview, as a social practice embedded in a particular research philosophy, was later negotiated and resisted, as I now go on to describe.

Resistance to research may be expressed through nonparticipation or the decision to limit the content and detail of narrative accounts, but choice of interview site and modification of interview practice can also be part of a study participant's resistance to a researcher's access to their private lives; as Rhodes (1994, 549) comments, "opening a window onto another's social world depends not only on the language and forms of communication but on the respective parties' willingness to grant access." Many qualitative researchers view conducting interviews in the subject's home as facilitating such access. It is a space where study participants will usually feel comfortable and the researcher may also gain contextual information useful in interpreting interview transcripts. Furthermore, using the home as an interview site is compatible with the aim of reducing power differentials between researcher and researched. Feminist researchers alert to power imbalances in conversations involving men and women further qualify the parameters of home interviewing, preferring that women be interviewed on their own to avoid silencing by others in the household, such as a male partner or husband (see Reinharz 1992, for further discussion of interviewing issues). In both studies the aim was to interview women in their own homes, but although many women agreed to this, some did not. In other situations, interview conditions were redefined, for example through the presence of other people at the interview.

In the first study, interviews conducted by the research assistant took place in women's homes, but none of the women I recruited through the mothers' support group agreed to be interviewed in their home. Instead, we used a small office in the building where the group met weekly. The building was located in the core of a predominantly Indo-Canadian neighborhood, where there were a variety of commercial and service outlets catering to the local population. It housed a variety of neighborhood activities, was familiar to the women, and was occupied by them as active participants of a group defined through their positioning as immigrants from India. It was thus tied to the women's social identity and its activities were usually away from a White "gaze."[9] My entrance to the women's worlds was managed at this boundary, and their homes remained secure and private, safe from my intrusion or scrutiny.

A research assistant interviewed women participating in the second study following observation of their encounter with health professionals in the clinic. As in the first study, not all women chose to be interviewed at home. Some chose alternative sites such as their workplace or the clinic. In the cases of home interviews, the research assistant often found other family members or visitors present. Sometimes such additional people sat quietly in another part of the room, but in a few cases they took an active part in the interviews. This modified interview dynamics, perhaps reflecting ways of talking that are more familiar than that involved in individualistic one-to-one interviews. It may also be an active strategy on the part of some family members to monitor the researcher's access to private information. Or is it a method to protect an older woman from the unknown procedures of a research interview? Does talking as part of a group disturb the power of the researcher's "expert" knowledge? These are all possibilities, and are likely to vary with the particularities of household relationships, and perhaps also with specific household members' familiarity with and relationship to both Indo-Canadian and predominantly White institutions and workplaces.

The interview site is also a space within which a woman is making and remaking her own knowledge of her social positioning. For instance, women I interviewed did not usually converse with White women in the course of their day-to-day life. Four were divorced or separated, and they talked of their marginal positioning in both Indo-Canadian and White "communities," and of their need to develop marketable skills to support themselves by paid employment. Just as I was defining the women I interviewed as "different," they were relating to me as an "other" in a context in which they were resituating themselves. The women in the clinic-based study were informed that they were sought out because of their positioning in society as immigrants whose issues in accessing the health care system were likely to differ from those of the majority White population. In this way, research practice brought the women's positioning as "different" into focus as they experienced the institutional practices of biomedicine. In the two studies, therefore, the sites of access and interviewing were part of the process in which researchers, research assistants, and study participants were all involved in constructing different "others" in relation to themselves, both with regards to the specificity of the research project and in the broader context of a culturally heterogeneous city. As Nast (1994) comments, the researcher (and research assistants as her representatives) occupies a "field" that straddles academia and sites of data collection, so that both are integral to the fieldwork process.

Reflection on the interconnections between the field and the research processes of both studies suggest that the context—both spatial and social—of the studies was emplaced well before the drawing board stage of designing the project. Prior to the initiation of the research, both researchers and researched were embedded in a network of inscribed identities and sociopolitical contexts operating at national and local scales. Moreover, a priori boundaries were drawn around the women as "women of color" and as part of an imagined Indo-Canadian community of Vancouver, however much we intended to overturn characterizations that suggest a homogeneity of interests or experience. In both studies, the "marking" of the study participants as "other" according to their cultural background (as equated with their region of origin), was, in retrospect, an exemplar of how dominant strands of social identities are imposed within particular sets of social relations and taken on board in a way that may or may not correspond with self-identification. Paradoxically, by including diversity of experience and difference into the aims of our research, we may also play a part in the inscription of the women as the subordinate "other." In our attempts to understand and represent the realities of difference we need to be thoughtful about how the social identities of marginalized groups are constituted through different positionings of researchers and research participants within the social practices and discourses of research. The purpose and control of any interview may be negotiated and resisted, but this does not necessarily transform larger power relations within which the research is situated.

Conclusion: An Ongoing Story

Poststructuralist theories view subjectivity as socially produced and in flux as a result of material and discursive shifts that provide alternate ways of interpreting our experiences (Butler 1990; Grosz 1994; Hekman 1991; Weedon 1987). The Canadian context of multiculturalism provides one such material setting and discourse, intended to celebrate difference and provide social equality regardless of cultural background. Academic discourses, including feminist standpoint epistemology and poststructuralism, are also discursively at work in constructing "difference." As researchers we also come with our own culturally situated and discursively constructed views and experiences as we represent others in particular ways that may contest—or reaffirm— dominant ways of thinking about difference. Working with categories of the "other" therefore takes the researcher into complicated territory. The notion of "women of color," for example, like other social categories, is socially constructed and historically situated, and can be drawn on in different ways.

This chapter is therefore intended to provide a cautionary tale; as observers of difference, we are also at risk of being its creators. On the other hand, we are also in a position to reshape interpretations. The studies referred to here were predicated on the significance of difference, particularly that of "women of color" (in opposition to White women), suggesting that this dimension of difference has the most salience for the experiences of women. In these studies, the women's descriptions of their day-to-day lives are indeed compatible with work that documents processes of racialization, including the social fixing of the identity of "immigrant woman." But what then of the fragmented identities of women? Reflection on the studies suggests that the links between experience and cultural and biological markers drawn on in inscribing difference are complex and situational. Power relations of difference are negotiated and given meaning through everyday social practices, including, in the context of the two studies, those of feminist academic inquiry and institutional practices of medicine. As the notion of culture or "race" is negotiated in these situations, difference becomes real. The critical question remains as to whose "reality" gains dominance and legitimacy.

The purposes of presenting a particular reality is of concern here. Debates within feminism, for instance, indicate the importance of including diversity in understanding women's lives, with class, "race," and sexuality being among the most important dimensions of such diversity. Antiracist thought in the health field is also concerned with representation of the "other" in interpretations of health problems. Researchers are critical of studies that distort and make exotic minority group cultures, yet they also acknowledge that silences can contribute to unmet health needs (Ahmad 1993; Stubbs 1993). The incipient effects of "racial" discourse, predicated on constructions of "others" by dominant groups, are of primary concern. In my own work, I attempt to avoid reproducing divisions that are ascribed on the basis of "culture" or "color," particularly in view of my position in educating health care professionals who are engaged in a field of practice and research that has, for the most part, not problematized culture, ethnicity, and "race." How then, in research and writing, are we to approach the problem of diversity, given its construction through everyday interaction and discourses, including those of the academy?

Standpoint epistemology tends to rely on the experiential basis of categories such as "woman of color," which as representations of specific experiences of oppression are placed in opposition to dominant, usually White constructions of reality. Such an approach suggests a tendency toward essentialism, although such homogenizing, socially constructed categories of difference have also been used strategically in identity politics to assert common cultural experience in resistance to dominant power relations (Brah 1992; Spivak 1990; Young 1990). While there may be common experiences the studies discussed here suggest that these are dependent on the specificities of context, socially, geographically, and politically. The field research described here draws upon and supports anti-essentialist theories of difference and fragmented identities. People experience multiple identities simultaneously, although the saliency of specific strands vary according to the situation. Rather than forming a unitary standpoint, identities are negotiated, constituted, and imposed by others within shifting sets of relations.

By distancing itself from essentializing tendencies, poststructuralism enables an exploration of how microprocesses of power, operating through discursive and material practices, constitute particular people with particular capacities for action (Grosz 1994). The ongoing but never fixed geographical shaping of such constitutions, while grounding abstract categories, opens up spaces for identity alliances based on shared local meanings but having wider relevance. Attention to the diverse ways and contexts in which identities come to have meaning and are used in ordering social interaction, can provide more nuanced accounts of relations of oppression.

To create the conditions for effective social action, we first need to understand how social difference is created, including an awareness of the ways that context shapes our research agendas and practices. Research methodology is integral to representations of both the "other" and ourselves, and is part of the larger process by which identities are inscribed. Methods may be chosen with the intention of giving voice to "subordinated others" and gaining legitimacy for their knowledge, but my comparison of two studies indicates the considerable complexity of dynamics in the field. In beginning the chapter, I noted that the women in the studies were mothers, wives, daughters, and workers in both the home and the wage labor force. The interview and the layers of context of research within which it is nested comprise a process in which such identities are performed, negotiated, and constituted in conditions of some uncertainty and instability.

As researchers, our identities are also multidimensional and performed in the course of research, although it is not clear who or what we represent to those we study. The researcher may represent, for instance, relations of oppression, the "expert" knowledge of an academic institution, a woman with children with some common interests, or a person with whom concerns can be talked about in a safe environment beyond the networks of local knowledge. The in-depth interview is useful in uncovering diversity and in involving the study participant in the deconstruction of taken-for-granted concepts, but is itself constructed through such relations of difference and performative acts of identity. The comparison of the studies also suggests that methods are not geographically neutral; the sociospatial context of research will affect what the researcher will find according to the different subject positionings of all of those involved in the specific playing out of various social relations in a particular place. The power relation of "expert" knowledge in research is not fixed, as illustrated in this chapter. How we can most effectively engage with difference in our methods remains unresolved.

Notes

The research was supported by a U.B.C Humanities and Social Sciences Research Grant and funding from the Secretary of State, Canada, Multicultural Directorate. I wish to thank John Paul Jones III, Heidi Nast, Sue Roberts, and participants of the New Horizons in Feminist Geography Workshop, University of Kentucky, January 1995, for encouragement and stimulating ideas and support that benefited the writing of this chapter.

1. Harding distinguishes here between weak and strong reflexivity, with the latter explicitly considering a researcher's interests and values, and the cultural situatedness of a research project.

2. This study was conducted with Joan Anderson and Judith Lynam of the School of Nursing, University of British Columbia. It concerned barriers to health care for immigrant women, and focused on women from the Chinese and Indo-Canadian populations (the two largest groups of immigrants recorded in the 1986 Census). For purposes of comparison in this paper, I draw only on that part of the research conducted with women of Indian descent.

3. See Donovan (1984, 1986) and Pearson (1986) for critiques in medical geography of the use of culturalist approaches, and Jackson and Penrose (1993) for discussion of the concept of racialization.

4. See Dyck, I. (1973) for an examination of interethnic relations in Fiji.

5. These studies are reported in Dyck (1993, 1995).

6. For a more detailed discussion of the research assistants' participation in the study concerned with women with chronic illness, see Dyck, Lynam, and Anderson (1995).

7. Informal conversations with various researchers and community workers suggest that the relative smallness of ethnocultural communities and the possibility of private information spreading through existing social networks, or being relayed to state agencies, makes some women feel vulnerable in research situations.

8. The multicultural workers had warned that access would be difficult among recent immigrants; they explained family loyalty is very important and that people are cautious about talking about themselves or their family to others. Also, there is sometimes suspicion and fear of unfamiliar situations involving White people, such as participation in a research project.

9. The "gaze" in the Foucauldian sense is not merely part of a process of control, but is also constitutive of social identities.

References

Ahmad, W. I. U. 1993. Making Black people sick: "Race", ideology and health research, In *"Race" and health in contemporary Britain*, ed. W. I. U. Ahmad, pp. 11–33. Buckingham: Open University Press.

Anderson, J. M. 1986. Ethnicity and illness experience: Ideological structures and the health care delivery system. *Social Science and Medicine* 22:1277–83.

Anderson, J. M. ; Blue, C. ; and Lau, A. 1991. Women's perspectives on chronic illness: Ethnicity, ideology and restructuring of life. *Social Science and Medicine* 33:101–13.

Badets, J. , and Chui, T. W. L. 1994. *Focus on Canada: Canada's changing immigrant population.* Catalogue No. 96–311E. Scarborough, ONT: Prentice Hall.

Barrett, M. 1987. The concept of "difference," *Feminist Review* 26: 29– 41.

Bhavnani, K-K. 1993. Tracing the contours: Feminist research and feminist objectivity. *Women's Studies International Forum* 16: 95–104.

Bordo, S. 1992. Postmodern subjects, postmodern bodies. *Feminist Studies* 18:159–75.

Brah, A. 1992. Difference, diversity and differentiation. In *Race, culture and difference*, ed. J. Donald and A. Rattansi, pp. 126–145. London: Sage.

Butler, J. 1990. *Gender trouble: Feminism and the subversion of identity.* New York: Routledge.

Collins, P. Hill 1991. *Black feminist thought: Knowledge, consciousness and the politics of empowerment.* New York: Routledge.

Cornwell, J. 1984. *Hard-earned lives: Accounts of health and illness from East London.* London: Tavistock.

Cotterill, P. 1992. Interviewing women: Issues of friendship, vulnerability, and power. *Women's Studies International Forum* 15: 593–606.

Donovan, J. 1984. Ethnicity and health. *Social Science and Medicine* 19: 663–70.

———. 1986. *We don't buy sickness, it just comes: Health, illness and health care in the lives of Black people in London.* Aldershot: Gower.

Dyck, I. 1973. An examination of inter-ethnic relations in Fiji, with particular reference to the distribution of land. MA thesis, Department of Sociology and Anthropology, University of Manchester, England.

———. 1989. Integrating home and wage workplace: Women's daily lives in a Canadian suburb. *The Canadian Geographer* 33: 329–41.

———. 1990. Space, time and renegotiating motherhood: An exploration of the domestic workplace. *Environment and Planning D: Society and Space* 8: 459–83.

———. 1993. Health promotion, occupational therapy and multiculturalism: Lessons from research. *Canadian Journal of Occupational Therapy* 60:120–29.

———. 1995. Putting chronic illness "in place:" Women immigrants" accounts of their health care. *Geoforum* 26: 247–260.

Dyck, I.; Lynam, J. M; and Anderson, J. M. 1995. Women talking: Creating knowledge through difference in cross-cultural research *Women's Studies International Forum* 18: 611–626.

Edwards, R. 1990. Connecting method and epistemology. *Women's Studies International Forum.* 13: 477–90.

Finch, J. 1984. "It's great to have someone to talk to": The ethics and politics of interviewing women. In *Social researching: Politics, problems and practice*, ed. C. Bell and H. Roberts, pp. 70–85. London: Routledge.

Fonow, M. M. and Cook, J. A. eds., 1991. *Beyond methodology: Feminist scholarship as lived research.* Bloomington: Indiana University Press.

Grosz, E. 1994. *Volatile bodies: Towards a corporeal feminism.* Bloomington: Indiana University Press.

Haraway, D. 1988. Situated knowledges: The science question in feminism and the privilege of the partial prespective. *Feminist Studies* 14: 575– 95.

Harding, S. 1987. *Feminism and methdology*. Bloomington: Indiana University Press.

———. 1991. *Whose science? Whose knowledge?* Ithaca, NY: Cornell University Press.

Hartsock, N. C. . M. 1987. The feminist standpoint: Developing the ground for a specifically feminist historical materialism. In: *Feminism and methodology* ed. S. Harding, pp. 157–80. Bloomington: Indiana University Press.

Hekman, S. 1991. Reconstituting the subject: Feminism, modernism, and postmodernism. *Hypatia* 6:44–63.

hooks, b. 1992. *Black looks: Race and representation*. Toronto: Between the Lines.

Jackson, E. M. 1993. Whiting-out difference: Why U. S. nursing research fails Black families. *Medical Anthropology Quarterly* 7: 363–85.

Jackson, P. , and Penrose, J. , eds. 1993. *Constructions of race, place and nation*. London: UCL Press.

McDowell, L. 1991. The baby and the bathwater: Difference and diversity in feminist geography. *Geoforum* 22: 123–33.

———. 1992. Multiple voices: On being inside and outside the project. *Antipode* 24: 56–72.

Miles, R. 1993. *Racism after "race relations."* London: Routledge.

Mishler, Elliot, G. 1986. *Research interviewing*. Cambridge, Massachusetts: Harvard University Press.

Multiculturalism and Citizenship Canada. 1989. *Operation of the Canadian Multiculturalism Act*. Annual Report 1988/1989. Ottawa, On: Ministry of Supplies and Services Canada.

Nast, H. J. 1994. Opening remarks on "Women in the field." *The Professional Geographer* 46:54–66.

Nast, H. J.; Katz, C.; Kobayashi, A.; England, K. V. L.; Gilbert, M. R.; and Staeheli, L. A., and Lawson, V. A. 1994. Focus: Women in the field: Critical feminist methodologies and theoretical perspectives. *The Professional Geographer* 46: 54–102.

Oakley, A. 1981. Interviewing women: A contradiction in terms. In *Doing feminist research* ed. Helen Roberts, pp. 30–61. London: Routledge and Kegan Paul.

Pearson, M. 1986. The politics of ethnic minority health studies. In *Health, race and ethnicity*, ed. T. Rathwell and D. Phillips, pp. 100–16. London: Croom Helm.

Proudfoot, B. 1989. The setting of immigration levels in Canada since the Immigration Act, 1976. *British Journal of Canadian Studies* 4: 233–56.

Ramazanoglu, C. 1989. Improving on sociology: The problems of taking a feminist standpoint. *Sociology* 23: 427–42.

Reinharz, S. 1992. *Feminist methods in social research*. New York and Oxford: Oxford University Press.

Rhodes, P. J. 1994. Race-of-interviewer effects: A brief comment. *Sociology* 28:547–58.

Ribbens, J. 1989. Interviewing: An "unnatural situation"? *Women's Studies International Forum*. 12:579–92.

Ruddick, S. 1989. *Maternal thinking*. New York: Ballantine

Smith, D. 1987. *The everyday world as problematic: A feminist sociology*. Boston: Northeastern University Press.

Spivak, G. C. 1990. *The post-colonial critic: Interviews, strategies, dialogues*. New York: Routledge.

Stubbs, P. 1993. "Ethnically sensitive" or "anti-racist"? Models for health research and service delivery. In *"Race" and health in contemporary Britain*, ed. W. I. U. Ahmad, pp. 34–47. Buckingham: Open University Press.

Weedon, C. 1987. *Feminist practice and poststructuralist theory*. Oxford: Blackwell.

Young, I. M. 1990. *Justice and the politics of difference*. Princeton: Princeton University Press.

11

Exploring Methodological Borderlands through Oral Narratives

Richa Nagar

Discussions of the politics of fieldwork and representation have recently acquired a new meaning in feminist geography. By situating "fieldwork" in the multiple contexts in which we, as politically engaged women, academics, and ethnographers operate, Katz (1994), Nast (1994), and other feminist geographers have not only highlighted how the role of the researcher is constituted in "spaces of betweenness;" they have also helped us to recognize that fieldwork can be a form of resistance to dominant ways of acquiring and codifying knowledge.

In this chapter, I seek to contribute to this discussion on the basis of my own "fieldwork" experience in Dar es Salaam. Specifically, I discuss how feminist ethnography has enabled me to explore issues of multiply juxtaposed social identities and their connectedness with social places.[1] I also emphasize the importance of relationality and reflexivity in my work by illuminating how my social and spatial situatedness with respect to different communities and individuals defined my relationships with them, and thereby, the "knowledge" that we produced. Finally, I show how my own attempts to expose power relations through my research, and to overcome them in my personal life, affected what I saw, heard, probed, and wrote.

Identities and Narratives: The Focus of My Research

The fragmented nature of subjectivity and the contingency of social experience is captured well by Stuart Hall when he compares identity to a bus ticket: "You just have to get from here to there, the whole of you can never be represented in the ticket you carry but you have to buy a ticket in order to get from here to there" (quoted in Watts 1992, 124). Ethnic, gender, class, or sexual identities do not define a fixed profile of traits, but a fluctuating composition of differences, multiple intersections, and incommensurabilities (Lowe 1991) that are historically, politically, culturally, and contextually constructed (see Valentine, chapter 4, this volume), and constantly transformed in continuous plays of history, culture, and power (Jha 1991).

It is these complex and often contradictory constructions, expressions, and transformations of multiple and intersecting identities that I uncover in my study of Asian communities in postcolonial Dar es Salaam.[2] My work explores how Asian men and women experience, create, and modify their complex social identities and boundaries in the context of a rapidly changing political-economic environment and continuously shifting numbers and configurations of their communities in postindependence Tanzania.[3] In the course of this exploration, I examine essentializing descriptions based on race, gender, class, religion, sect, and language. I also highlight two other processes—namely, how individuals and organizations combine gender ideologies with race, caste, class, and religious ideologies to maintain or alter both social boundaries and gender relations; and the manner in which social places, such as community halls, clubs, beaches, mosques, and religious schools, reinforce existing identities and structures of power on the one hand, and become sites to challenge dominance on the other. Social places, communal organizations, languages, and various kinds of interracial, interreligious, and interclass relationships serve as multiple windows to reveal different facets of complexity and diversity associated with the lives of South Asian women and men. Throughout my work, I intersperse my own narrative with the narratives of men and women from different classes and religious, caste, sectarian, and linguistic backgrounds, some being "pures" and others being "half-castes," some respected and others shunned by their communities. This narrative challenges the dominant image of all Tanzanian Asians as exploitative male traders, and emphasizes how those in power (whether in state, communities, or organizations) try to shape racial and communal rhetoric, and how the less powerful internalize or challenge their ideas.

An important question that arises here is whether a focus on identity is the best way to examine the diverse experiences and the hierarchies of power among people. Margaret Somers's ideas illuminate why an "identity approach" is necessary to understand social action. An individual or a collectivity, Somers maintains, cannot be assumed to have any particular set of interests simply because one aspect of their identity fits into one social category such as class or race or gender. Rather than imputing interests to people on the basis of a social category, an identity approach to action focuses on how people characterize themselves. It recognizes that people are guided to act by the multiple relationships in which they are embedded, and that the patterns of their relationships continually shift over time and space (Somers 1992).

Identities are formed and challenged within numerous and multilayered narratives and social networks. As Somers (1992, 607) writes, "[n]arrative identities are constituted by a person's temporally and spatially specific 'place' in culturally constructed stories that comprise (breakable) rules, (variable) practices, binding (and unbinding) institutions, and the multiple stories of family, nation, or economic life." My research places the public and cultural narratives that inform people's lives in relation to spatial structures, institutional practices, organizational constraints, politics, and demography, all of which combine to shape the history and geography of social action. In this manner, Asians from different backgrounds can be located as characters in their social narratives within a temporally and place-specific configuration of relationships and practices.

Finally, excessive emphasis has been placed on race, class, and gender in much of feminist and identity-related literature. Although this emphasis may be pertinent in U.S. and British contexts, my study shows that race, class, and gender can, by themselves, be inadequate to understand experiences of peoples whose identities and social experience are defined just as saliently (if not more so) by religious, caste, sectarian, and linguistic affiliations. In the following discussion of the methodology of my research on "Asian" identity politics in Dar es Salaam, I show that identity theory needs to be geographically and historically contextualized, allowing the range of social multiplicities we consider as researchers to expand and alter according to the places and time periods we study.

Problematizing Categories

Identities are often defined in terms of normative categories that typically take the form of fixed binary oppositions, categorically asserting the meaning of masculine and feminine, White and Black, homosexual and heterosexual, and so on (Scott 1986). My study deals with normative categories based on race (African, Asian, Arab, half-caste), religion (Hindu, Muslim, Sikh), caste/sect (Ismaili, Ithna Asheri, Brahmin, Baniya), region of origin (Goan, Gujarati, Kutchi, Punjabi), class, gender, and language. I focus on four Asian communities of Dar es Salaam—the Hindus, the Ithna Asheris, the Sikhs, and the Goans. Although these communities distinguish themselves primarily along religious lines, their labels subsume other identities as well. *Sikh*, for example, is simultaneously a religious, linguistic, and regional category because it refers to followers of the Sikh faith from Punjab who speak Punjabi. The term *Goan* is generally used by Tanzanians to refer to Roman Catholics from Goa (even though more than 60 percent of the present population of Goa is Hindu), which was a Portuguese colony until 1961 and is now a part of India. The *Khoja Shia Ithna Asheris* of Tanzania are Shiite Muslims mainly from Kutch and Kathiawar regions of India. Tanzanian Asians use the term *Hindu* to refer mainly to people from Gujarat, Kathiawar, and Kutch who were born in any Hindu caste or subcommunity.[4] References to Hindus from other parts of India are generally qualified by terms such as *Hindu Punjabi* or *U.P. Hindu*.

Thus the labels *Sikh* and *Hindu* give primacy to religion, although regional and linguistic affiliations are also implied. The term *Ithna Asheri* gives primacy to a specific Muslim sect, but its regional origins are clear. The label *Goan* gives primacy to a region, but it has strong religious and sectarian connotations. There is no consistency, therefore, in the way names are applied to different groups. It is to highlight the inconsistent and unproblematized nature of these frequently used designations that I use the word "normative categories" in describing these communities.

I chose these four communities primarily to examine the too-often made distinction between Hindu, Muslim, Sikh, and Christian as if they are internally homogeneous, self-contained, separate, and disharmonious categories.[5] I challenge this simple classification of communities on the basis of religious affiliation by highlighting the manner in which social experience shapes and is shaped by various layers of social identities in different geographical and historical contexts.

While problematizing an automatic classification of people as Goan, Sikh, Hindu, and Ithna Asheri, simply because they were born in those particular communities, I simultaneously show how organizational, institutional and societal processes as well as ontological, public, and cultural narratives operate in people's lives over time and in different places to strengthen and reinforce their identity as members of these categories (see Nagar 1995).

Creating a "Feminist Ethno-geography" to Explore Social Boundaries

Over the years, the emphasis in feminist geography has slowly but surely shifted from "including women" and analyzing the structure of gender relations in particular geographical contexts, to exploring appropriate methods for feminist inquiry and for critiquing science and its ontological and epistemological foundations (Dyck 1993). As in other disciplines, feminist scholarship in geography has responded to the invisibility/distortion of women's experiences by developing theories not only to redress the omissions in mainstream, masculinist geography but also to create a new paradigm that aims to blend subjectivity with objectivity and knowing with doing (Moss 1993; D. Rose 1993). The ethnographic approach, generally understood to include intensive, qualitative methods such as participant observation and in-depth interviewing, has been increasingly recognized by scholars as particularly appropriate for feminist inquiry. This approach emphasizes the importance of human action and the continuous construction of meaning; it allows the "researcher" to describe women's activities and record women's own statements, perceptions, and attitudes; it identifies both researchers and subjects as active agents in knowledge production and underscores the importance of reflexivity in the research process (Dyck 1993). Using this kind of method, feminist geographers have highlighted the experiences of women in family, community, and workplace in order to create gender-aware explanations of geographical phenomena; explored interconnections between gender relations on the one hand and spaces, places, and landscapes on the other (G. Rose 1993); generated woman-centered knowledge; and sought to empower women by developing tools and knowledges to alter the social conditions of their oppression (Rose and Ogborn 1988; Dyck 1993; D. Rose 1993).

Although feminist scholarship has mainly focused on women and their narratives, women are not the only ones to be silenced by masculinist social science. Dominant paradigms in social science have largely excluded the experiences of subalterns from standard academic discourse and treated them as a residual category since they are not immediately visible participants in politics, trade, and matters of state (Ngaiza and Koda 1991). Through personal narratives of women and other oppressed peoples, oral and life historical research helps us understand the experiences of those who do not have access to means of publicity and whose feelings, thoughts, and actions get hidden behind the experience of the male middle class, which incorrectly acquires universal significance. The works of Behar (1993), Mbilinyi (1989), and Ngaiza and Koda (1991) show how oral narratives can make "private" oppressions of women and other subalterns more public and more shared, challenging dominant male definitions and the silencing of subalterns.

A critical awareness of relationality is central to any study of community and identity (Visweswaran 1994). Developing this awareness entails examining not only women's relationships with women and men, and men's relationships with men, but also relationships of wealthier with poorer, higher castes with lower castes, and one racial, linguistic, and/or religious group with another. Personal narratives, strengthened by participant observation, provide insights into the complexities of intersecting social relationships and the manner in which these construct communities and identities in different contexts.

In my research, I employed the ethnographic method, with a sensitivity to the role of place and space in constituting identities and communities as well as in the production of knowledge itself. Between 1991 and 1993, I spent a total of twelve months in Dar es Salaam, collected 58 life stories, and conducted 150 shorter interviews/conversations with Goan, Sikh, Ithna Asheri, and Hindu men and women from different backgrounds.[6] Shorter interviews centered on people's family and occupational histories, experiences of and opinions about various political events since 1960, participation in community activities, daily schedules and mental maps, as well as histories of communal institutions and organizations as narrated by both leaders and common people. Most life stories were the product of several long conversations with each informant over a period of time and involved (in addition to the topics mentioned above) discussions on family, marriage, and relationships; personal, economic, domestic, and/or other issues; race and gender relations; community politics; likes and dislikes toward individuals and groups; and analyses of informants' multiple and contextual identities. Additionally, I collected information from historical and contemporary newspapers, community records, and family archives.

Participant observation formed the core of my research and the heart of my experience in Dar es Salaam. There was no clear line of separation between my personal life and my research. I spent most of my time in the Asian-dominated city center with friends and acquaintances from different communities in temples, mosques, clubs, halls, playgrounds, beaches, religion classes, and community houses; in weekly communal gatherings; at celebrations of secular/ religious festivals and weddings; and in people's homes where I frequently spent time or lived as a guest, friend, researcher, or "adopted" family member. There was hardly any street in the city center that I did not know intimately. Many Asian families welcomed me as one of their own and gently insisted that if they ever found me paying for a meal they would be offended. Although I was totally cut off from Asians when I lived at the University of Dar es Salaam, once I entered the Asian area, I ate all my meals in people's homes, participated in family and neighborhood gossip, and caught up with everyday events in the communities. My presence in Asian residential and communal places gave me an opportunity to experience and identify the rifts and alliances along the lines of religion, class, caste, race, and gender that defined these places.

Dar es Salaam became a kaleidoscope of social sites for me, as I traversed its segregated gendered, classed, raced, and communalized spaces in the course of my daily life. With every turn of the kaleidoscope, I was conscious of my changed position, both geographically and socially. Not only did I behave differently in each situation, people in each place "textualized" me differently, and dialogical processes between me and my informants in different places continuously shaped the structure and the interpretations of the narratives that were produced in the course of my work.

My methodology attempted to infuse feminist ethnography with a geographical understanding and can be defined as a "feminist ethno-geography." A combination of oral narratives, observations, shorter interviews, mental maps of informants, and newspaper/archival sources helped me construct "life-historical geographies" that combined a geographical approach with a historical sensibility, made available elements of lived culture and subjectivity, and revealed how individuals were positioned within complex social relations in time, place, and space.

Reflexivity and Intersubjectivity in a Geography of Positionality

My research topic and methodology made reflexivity and intersubjectivity central to my work.[7] At the heart of both reflexivity and intersubjectivity lie issues of positionality. Understanding positionality entails an analysis of the locations of the researcher and the "researched," and of their relationship with each other. As Visweswaran (1994, 48) aptly notes, "the relationship of the knower to known is constituted by the process of knowing. Conversely, the process of knowing is itself determined by the relationship of the knower to known."

My exploration of the politics of communities and social identities is thoroughly intertwined with the complex ways in which my own identities and background situated me in relation to my informants. An examination of these intricate positionings in the following pages reveals how my aim to analyze normative categories through my research did not preclude people from labeling me and putting me into categories to which they directly or indirectly related. The way I was perceived by individuals or by a whole community, for example, shaped the degree to which they accepted me and the kind of thoughts and experiences they shared with me. These positionings were profoundly affected by place- and space-specific phenomena and processes, an aspect often overlooked by ethnographers.

Reflexivity also necessitates that I analyze my own personal and political commitments with respect to my informants and my research project. Such an investigation on my part can be defined as "an effort at accountable positioning, an endeavor to be answerable for what I have learned to see, and for what I have learned to do" (Visweswaran 1994, 48).

A number of scholars (Geiger 1986, 1990; Mbilinyi 1989; Mirza and Strobel 1989; Personal Narratives Group 1989; Popular Memory Group 1982; Warren 1988) recognize that an engagement with issues of reflexivity, intersubjectivity and positionality is essential in order to:

1. identify that both social analysts and their subjects are positioned and to be explicit about our partnerships, interests, and feelings;
2. examine how we and our subjects are situated with respect to the knowledge that is produced, which involves an exploration of the social experience of both the researcher and the researched;
3. develop a reflexive understanding of the gendered, aged, classed, and other complexities of the relationship between the knower and the known.

How Communities Perceived Me

Let me begin with my impressions of how I was perceived by the communities in which I was working. Some things about me were quite apparent to almost every Asian with whom I interacted—I was a single woman in her midtwenties, from a lower-middle-class Hindu family in India, doing Ph.D. research in Dar es Salaam. Other aspects of my background I revealed in diverse ways, depending on the context, and different things were perceived as important by different communities. Despite these differences, however, I never felt that the desire to build relationships with the communities was onesided. From the very beginning, all the communities sought common ground with me on which to build a foundation for our relationship. People's imagined and symbolic connections with geographical regions—whether it be the United States, the Indian states of Gujarat or Uttar Pradesh, or the city of Lucknow—and the manner in which they placed me with reference to those places, played an important role in defining their attitudes toward me.

Gujarati speakers, who formed about 90 percent of the Asian population of Dar es Salaam, easily guessed my Gujarati ethnic origins by my knowledge of the Gujarati language. My Hindi accent, however, often required me to clarify that although my family has retained a "Gujarati" identity in the state of Uttar Pradesh (where my ancestors migrated from Gujarat centuries ago), my first language is Hindi/Urdu, and I was born and raised in the city of Lucknow, the Muslim heart of Uttar Pradesh.[8] My "Gujaratiness" as well as my "Hinduness" and "Brahmanness," (which the Gujarati Hindus and Muslims were able to guess by my name) were always questionable however, and possibly "fake" when I was interacting with people in Dar es Salaam who considered themselves "more Gujarati" or "more Hindu" than I. At the same time, the doubtful state of my "Hinduness" allowed me to come closer to non-Hindus, particularly Muslims.

In the Hindu community, I was recognized as a "Gujarati" even though my family has had no contact with Gujarat for more than a century. Although I consider Hindi/Urdu as my mother tongue, my ability to speak and read Gujarati was appreciated as "respect toward my own mother tongue." Nobody ever openly questioned my "Hinduness" or asked about my beliefs or habits— often it was assumed that I was a "believer," a "vegetarian," and that I felt "uncomfortable" eating or living with Muslims, or with low-caste Hindus who ate meat. The upper-caste Hindus who did find out that I was not religious, ate meat, and had close relationships not only with low-caste Hindus and Asian Muslims, but also with Africans, often called me "a young, overenthusiastic radical," but even this assessment never seemed to have any outward affect on my personal relationship with these people. In lower caste homes, my willingness to eat nonvegetarian food with them often evoked expressions of pleasant surprise and contributed to making me more welcome in their homes by collapsing socially constructed barriers between high and low castes.

The Ithna Asheris were often impressed that my hometown was Lucknow since Lucknow is a major religious center of the Shias. Although my knowledge of Gujarati made communication with informants easy, they were fascinated by the fact that I could speak Urdu since Urdu is the language in which religious gatherings are held. Many times I was complimented for my familiarity with the Shia culture and religion by statements like: "When I saw you in the mosque, I thought you were an Ithna Asheri"; or "I was surprised to know that you were not an Ithna Asheri—you look like one." My "Hinduness" was also questioned by many Ithna Asheris on the grounds that I ate nonvegetarian food with them, lived with Ithna Asheri friends, and visited the mosque. I was often told in a tone of approval that I did not "act like a Hindu" and that I would "make a good Ithna Asheri." Thrice, I was also asked by some leaders whether my interest in their community and religion meant that I was going to convert to the Ithna Asheri faith. At such points, I never tried to deceive anyone and clearly stated that I was similarly trying to understand the Hindu, Sikh, and Goan communities.

Despite my warm acceptance by both Hindu and Ithna Asheri communities, however, I was often aware of being looked upon as an "oddity." In an environment where people's religious identities were generally quite strong, my informants often assumed that I was a practicing Hindu and seemed perplexed by my participation in the religious ceremonies of non-Hindus, especially of Ithna Asheris and Goans.

In the Sikh community, my being perceived as a "Hindu" did not raise any doubts as it is quite common for Hindus in Dar es Salaam to attend Sikh religious events, and vice versa. Culturally, I shared many things with the Sikhs. Most Sikh men and women I met in Dar es Salaam were fluent in Hindi and our conversations were, therefore, in my first language, not theirs. A large proportion of Sikhs in Dar es Salaam, especially women in their thirties and forties, immigrated to Tanzania in the last twenty years. These women developed an instantaneous affinity with me the moment they discovered that I was from North India. I was seen by the Sikh men and women as a sister or daughter "from our region" due to the physical proximity of the states of Punjab and Uttar Pradesh. I was often warmly invited to weekly gatherings and to people's homes: "This is your home. Come over whenever you miss your own food or people." I was often pampered by elderly Sikh women who fed me, gave me advice about looking after myself in Dar es Salaam, and urged me to get married before I got too old.

My connection with the "prestigious" United States seemed to matter more in the Goan community than anywhere else. I was often introduced by Goans to other Goans as "a scholar from the U.S. who wants to study our community." There was also an expectation that I would dress in a "trendy Western style" and would know all about "Western dancing," and some people seemed disappointed when I appeared in "traditional" Indian clothes or when I said I didn't know much about "Western dancing." Quite a few Goans had relatives in Canada and said that they could relate to my life and environment in the United States based on what they had seen or heard about Canada. Some others were thinking about migrating to the United States or Canada and were therefore eager to know about my life in the "West." My familiarity with Bombay and Poona, which are not far from Goa and where quite a few Goans have received their education or have relatives or friends, also brought me close to them in some ways.

Except in the Goan community, I introduced myself as a scholar from a U.S. university only when I interacted with businessmen, professionals, and housewives from the upper classes, and with university students and faculty. To most others, my affiliation with the United States did not matter in the first instance and only became clear when we talked about ourselves and our lives in greater detail. Some of my lower class informants who had assumed that I was a student from India, felt distant and uncomfortable once I disclosed my affiliation with the United States. This made me cautious about when and how I revealed this connection.

My living situation significantly influenced my relationship with the various communities. My attempts to build connections within each community frequently took me to those who were well known in their communities. These included the families of a Hindu lawyer, an Ithna Asheri journalist, a Sikh dentist, a Goan businesswoman, and a Hindu architect. We quickly built good personal relationships, I often shared meals or spent my weekends with them, and in one case I lived with the family for more than a month. During this close interaction, I visited community centers, temples, and mosques with my hosts and they introduced me to friends, acquaintances, and leaders of community organizations as someone who was "like a family member." Making my first entry into communal spaces from the homes of well-known members of those communities proved invaluable for me, and the communities invited me in with their doors wide open. I was always received warmly and often felt overwhelmed by the confidence that many people placed in me, unquestioningly and instantly. It was as if my trustworthiness had already been tested within their communities, and they did not have to worry about me anymore. At the same time, I was always aware of being looked upon as a "Hindu." While this made me feel completely free to argue, disagree, or agree with Hindus in discussions around communal issues, it also made me feel burdened with the weight of being looked upon as a Hindu "other" in non-Hindu communities. No matter how close I felt to people in the Goan, Ithna Asheri, and Sikh communities, I was careful not to do or say anything that could be construed by them as overstepping my limits as someone who did not follow the same faith.

Ethnographic Research and Betrayal

For me, fieldwork in Dar es Salaam was, in many ways, like knitting a large familial net. Differences, whether religious, political, or ideological, were part of the same multitextured, multicolored net where threads did not always match perfectly. Amid my many friends, "mothers," "aunts," "uncles," "sisters," "brothers," and "grandparents," I never felt that Dar es Salaam was not my home. At the same time, however, some of these very individuals who trustfully told me their stories, fed me regularly, showered affection on me, and received my affection in return, might disapprove of the manner in which I have used their words in my academic work. The dilemma that this situation has posed for me has been excellently articulated by Lila Abu-Lughod (1993, 41):

> Does using my knowledge of individuals for purposes beyond friendship and shared memories by fixing their words and lives for disclosure to a world beyond the one they live in constitute some sort of betrayal? As someone who moves

between worlds, I feel that confronting the negative images I know to exist in the United States toward Arabs is one way to honor the kindness they have shown me. So is challenging stereotypical generalizations that ultimately make them seem more "other." Yet how will my critical ethnography be received? This is the dilemma all those of us who move back and forth between worlds must face as we juggle speaking for, speaking to, and . . . speaking from.

The task I undertook in my research involved challenging the negative imaging and stereotyping of Asians not only in the West and among Africans, Arabs, and Europeans inside Tanzania, but also *within* the Asian "community" among people of differing religions, languages, classes, castes, and sects. This second challenge created a major ethical quandary. The communities that I studied were heterogeneous not only in terms of "race" and class, religious, sectarian, regional, and linguistic affiliations, but also in terms of their access to power. An understanding of the structures and hierarchies of power and the struggles around them in these communities necessitated that I engage with the privileged and the deprived, the dominant and the dominated. For example, wealthy businessmen, traders, professionals, and their spouses had as much to do with my study as did taxi drivers, shoemakers, street vendors, school teachers, seamstresses, and middle-class housewives. On several occasions, I felt a real tension between my ties of affection with particular people and my commitment to certain political beliefs, and was forced to reconcile two kinds of ethical commitments—the ethics associated with my political beliefs and the ethics of respecting the trust that each of my informants had placed in me. I tried to maintain my commitment to my informants by accurately representing their words and opinions and by respecting the need of many of them to remain anonymous. At the same time, my political commitment to expose relations of power and the struggles of the less powerful against the more powerful in communities and homes required me to use the words of several community leaders, husbands, and wealthy women and men in contexts where they might not have liked them to be used.

Reconciling "Political Correctness" with "Cultural Correctness"

The dilemmas that I confronted in connection with this research were not confined to the issue of betrayal, however. The biggest difficulty that I faced in the "field" was reconciling my antiracist commitment and my ideas about sexual relationships with the need to accept and respect my informants' opinions on these issues, particularly when I spent time in their homes like a family member. Having lived most of my life in a lower-middle-class extended household in a religiously mixed, old neighborhood of Lucknow, I felt perfectly at home in middle-class homes of Hindus, Muslims, Sikhs, and Christians. I had a good sense of what was "proper" or "improper" to talk about before elders, men, or women; when to avoid wearing jeans and tight clothes, when to cover my head, take off my shoes, sit on the floor, or help in the kitchen. But my ability to adapt myself to the homes and environments of my informants, also led them to think that I fitted their definition of a "good girl," that being unmarried I had not had any sexual experience, and that I "kept away from homosexuals." In a way, this situation was no different than the situation that I had faced in my hometown in India—where my need to respect elders superseded my need to shock them. In Dar es Salaam, therefore, I resorted to the same option that I do in Lucknow—I stayed silent except before those who I knew would understand me. With the exception of three women friends and their families, no one knew about my involvement with a white man with whom I had been living for some time in the United States.

My position as a young woman also caused me agony sometimes. There were times, especially in families that I was close to, when I was seen as someone who was too young to take care of herself in a "harsh place like Dar es Salaam." I often got advice about what I was supposed to do or not do, how it was important for me not to venture alone into African areas, who I should be interviewing, and who I should not be wasting my time with. I frequently had to resolve this agony by direct confrontation, or by ignoring what I was being ordered to do.

The racist attitudes of most Asians toward Africans caused me to make a bigger adjustment, however. When I first started my fieldwork, I spent almost all my time living, working, and socializing in the Asian section of town segregated from African residential areas. With the exception of African domestic servants in Asian homes and African workers in Asian shops and offices, I had no chance to interact with Africans. This situation did not allow me much opportunity to improve my Kiswahili so that I could communicate with working-class Africans. Although living in the Asian area allowed me to collect a lot of information, its racist environment stifled and angered me. As a result, two months after I started my fieldwork, I moved to the university campus, which was far from the Asian-dominated city center. In fact, many Asians were even scared to go there alone because it was "a totally African area." I commuted back and forth between the university and town, mostly by local buses or *dala-dalas*. Asians, whether rich or poor, rarely used *dala-dalas* and perceived them as "dangerous" because they are "full of lower class Africans." Asian girls and women, supposedly because of their relative inexperience and vulnerability as compared to Asian men, were especially warned against venturing into African areas on *dala-dalas*. When I did what other Asian women were not supposed to do, however, it was attributed to my being "Westernized," as people from the West were thought to "like to mix with the locals and do things like climbing on *dala-dalas*, which they can't do in their own countries."[9]

But choosing to commute to the town instead of living in it did not really take me away from racism. It showed me, sometimes through deep personal pain, the other side of the same coin. Here is an excerpt from a letter in which I tried to express my anguish (Nagar 1993):

> At times it pains me so much to have brown skin here. I take the bus everyday to town and most of the times I am the only Asian riding in the bus. Sometimes I am greeted sarcastically, "Kem Chho?" [Gujarati for "how are you?"]. I feel angry . . . because I can hear and feel the resentment against the brown skin in the voice that is greeting me. And I feel like screaming: "I am not an exploitative, racist, . . . *Muhindi* (Asian) from here. Don't look at me like that. I have nothing in common with them!" Being resented like that gives me some sense of what an antiracist white person must feel like in a black Chicago neighborhood. But then my position here as an Indian student from India is not quite the same as a radical *Muhindi* from Tanzania either. My problem is that I am a foreigner here, and at times I want to be recognized as such. But anyone who does not know me thinks that I am just an arrogant and aloof *Muhindi* who does not know enough Kiswahili in spite of having lived in Tanzania all her life. It hurts me so much to be resented here . . . And what really frustrates me is that the nature of my research keeps me away from the *Waswahili* and I just don't have enough time to get absorbed in their culture because I am too busy trying to get absorbed into the Asian communities.

In Dar es Salaam, where the divide between African and Asian residential areas is very sharp, the shift in my spatial location from the Asian-dominated city center to the African-dominated university significantly changed my lifestyle and the politics of fieldwork. It affected what I saw, what I considered important, and the manner in which I perceived things. The politics around multiparty elections had made the racial situation between Africans and Asians very tense at the time when I started living on campus. Living with African students and commuting for several hours on buses as a sole Asian made me acutely aware of the fury that many ordinary Africans felt against Asians. More important, however, living on campus provided me many opportunities to discuss with several faculty members the contemporary racial politics and how these politics were related to political economic changes in the country.[10] These discussions oriented me to some useful literature that enabled me to identify several important trends in how raced, classed, and gendered political discourse developed in Tanzania in different political and economic contexts since independence. Members of the Women's Research and Documentation Project at the University of Dar es Salaam gave me much helpful and critical feedback on my research ideas through both group and individual discussions, and emphasized the importance of situating my study in the context of Asian African "realities" as well. My previous research focus around Asian communal politics, shifted as a result of these interactions to encompass issues related to the politics of race and how they affected political discourse and social attitudes of those living in Dar es Salaam. While so far I had seen Asians simplistically lumping all Africans together, it now became clear to me that many Africans, including some educated ones, did not know or acknowledge the complexities of the Asian communities.

Dressing for Ethnography?

One issue that consistently posed a problem for me and that I was unable to satisfactorily resolve for myself throughout my stay in Dar es Salaam was the question of appropriate dress. In her "Sari Stories," Kamala Visweswaran (1994, 14) describes how a gendered body is "(ad)dressed" intimately by history, place, culture, age, and class. She observes:

> Nothing could be more "ordinary" for many South Indian women than wearing a sari, yet the stories underscore my own confrontations with this most unremarked activity: getting dressed. Of course, the idea of "dressing up" has a history in feminist ethnography, for what we female (as opposed to male) ethnographers wear has some bearing on how we are received as social actors and as anthropologists.

Feminists from Beauvoir (1973) to Butler (1987, 1990) have drawn attention to the body as a locus of cultural inscription. The body is a material reality that has already been culturally located and defined within a social context, and it is also the site that "receives" cultural interpretations (Butler 1987, 133). Through the act of dressing, the gendered body becomes a textualized site for the construction, imposition, and reception of preexisting identities and cultural meanings on the one hand, and for challenging the dominant categories and meanings on the other.

My confrontations with dressing were continuous. Public dress codes and gendered communal identities were intimately related among Asians in Dar es Salaam. Although *salwaar kameez* (loose fitting pants worn with long shirts) and Western dress were popular among the Hindu women in their young and middle ages, it was only a *sari* or a *bindi* (dot) on the forehead that automatically branded a woman as a Hindu. Most Goans saw both *sari* and *salwaar kameez* as "old fashioned" or "too Indian" and the majority of Goan women wore Western-style dress. Among Sikhs and Ithna Asheris, *salwaar kameez* with a *dupatta* (long and wide scarf to drape over head and chest) was the most popular dress although *hijaab* (veil) was practiced in public places by most Ithna Asheri women.

On a day-to-day basis, *salwaar kameez* was the most practical dress for me in the Asian neighborhoods even though it made many Goans and most Hindus of my age group think that I was "too old fashioned to be studying in America." It was a dress I had worn all my life, it was considered respectable in all the communities without making me an "insider" to a particular one, and it allowed me to interact spontaneously with Muslims and with Hindus and Sikhs of all ages without fearing that my clothes would offend anyone's sentiments. I was always aware of how easily many Ithna Asheris, Sikhs, and elderly Hindus granted me trust and respect on the basis on my being dressed "properly" in a *salwaar kameez*. I never wanted the same people to feel cheated by me if they spotted me in the streets in a pair of jeans or in anything that "inappropriately" revealed my arms or legs. Thus I had to bear the distaste of being looked upon as "old fashioned" by some to avoid being seen as "disrespectful" or "phony" by others. But even this balancing act did not work entirely because *salwaar kameez* always made me "the odd other" in the homes and communal places of the Goans.

Wearing a *salwaar kameez* also made me acutely aware of my Asianness when I commuted across the racially marked social spaces between the university and town. I tried to resist everything that would encourage an African to categorize me as an Asian from Dar es Salaam. As a part of my struggle to challenge assumptions, I often tried to disrupt dress codes by wearing Western-style shirts with my *salwaar* or long skirts with loose, long-sleeved tops. This was easier for me to do when I spent most of my day in the newspaper archives rather than talking to the people and walking from street to street. While this way of dressing discouraged Africans from looking at me as a "regular *Muhindi*," it also made me "too odd" an Asian to be able to move freely in the streets of the downtown area among Asian acquaintances.

Sometimes, negotiating between these conflicting expectations and needs made things quite complicated for me. For example, when I initially met my first Goan life-historian, he commented on my *salwaar kameez*, saying, "We Goans are far more westernized and progressive than most Indians. You will find no Goan woman in Dar es Salaam wearing a dress like yours." His judgmental tone troubled me so much that I wore my American pants, teeshirt, and tennis shoes when I went to see him for our second interview appointment. But dressing according to the codes of one community left me inappropriately attired for a gathering I was to attend in a different communal (and classed) space. That same evening, I wanted to attend a big Hindu celebration and my upper-class hosts had told me that none of my cotton *salwaar kameezes* would do because it was going to be a "nice gathering." So, I had to walk all day on the streets with a heavy bag that carried not only my tape recording equipment and papers but also a silk *sari*, a matching blouse and petticoat, a *bindi*, and another set of footwear. Before entering the Hindu communal space, I had to go to the house of a Hindu woman and undergo the necessary transformation of appearance in order to become a part of the gathering.

The question of dress, therefore, intimately linked the gendered body with the everyday politics of communal, class, and race identities in social spaces. My need as a researcher to associate simultaneously with different communities without being seen as solely identifying with only one of them, compelled me to negotiate the gendered dress codes without showing disrespect toward people and without making undesirable compromises. Such a negotiation, however, was not easy. It required me to deal with contradictions and complications associated with my social and geographical position throughout my stay in Dar es Salaam.

Situatedness and Social Relationships in the Making of Life-stories

Life-stories are an essential tool to understanding how social actors characterize themselves, and how those characterizations are constructed in specific social and geographical contexts. Far from being the creation of a single individual, a life-story results from a collaboration between two individuals, "often an insider speaking about herself and her society and an outsider asking questions from her own frame of reference" (Mirza and Strobel 1989, 1). From the start, a life-story embodies the agendas, purposes, and interests of the narrator and the interpreter, both of whom are socially and spatially positioned subjects (Rosaldo 1989) and whose positions not only influence their perspectives but also their relationship with each other. The mutual situatedness of these positioned subjects has a profound influence on the shape of a narrative. For instance, my study of multifaceted, contextually constructed identities is itself shaped by the complex identities of those who participated in the production of life histories. Every brief or long-term relationship that was established with each informant was characterized by the multiple and complex intersections of our personal histories and geographies, which in turn influenced who or what we talked about and in what way. To further explore this point, let me discuss the process by which life-stories of two individuals, Francis and Nargis (not their real names), were produced.

In terms of the normative categories described initially, Francis is a married Goan man in his forties, Tanzanian by nationality, a motor mechanic and school bus driver by profession, and a resident of Dar es Salaam since birth. I can describe Nargis as a divorced Ithna Asheri woman, also in her forties, who was born in Dar es Salaam in a wealthy business family, but spent more than a decade in Britain where she acquired British citizenship. She returned to Dar es Salaam with her father a few years ago to fight a case against the illegal acquisition of his property by his relatives. But these sketchy descriptions by themselves reveal very little about why the stories of Francis and Nargis took the particular forms that they did. In order to understand that, one has to consider how I, as a positioned subject, shaped their narratives.

Francis and Nargis were introduced to me by an intimate friend who thought that both of them would be good informants for my research. Nargis and I had some long conversations. We often disagreed on race-related issues but agreed on many matters, particularly those related to gender and religious communalism. We soon developed respect and affection for each other, and became good friends. A few months after we were introduced, Nargis was shattered by the death of her father, who lived with her, and she invited me to stay with her. I lived with Nargis for more than two months and her life story was the end-product of many long and short conversations that we had in a variety of social and personal contexts.

The life-story of Francis, in contrast, was obtained in one short meeting of about half an hour followed by a long one of about five hours the next day. For the first interview, I met Francis in the lounge of the YWCA, which I found to be a safe public space to chat with male informants whom I did not know well. The second conversation took place in Francis's home and was more casual in nature, although my presence as a visitor with a tape recorder and a notebook clearly established the terms of our relationship: Francis was the narrator, I was the researcher, and each of us was an "outsider" to the other person's life, both spatially and socially.

Despite his racist and sexist ideas, I was impressed by Francis's openness and his well-formulated perspective on many social issues that I was interested in. I was aware that his ideas and experiences would greatly enrich my study of social identities. The Goans whom I had interviewed before Francis were those who were considered important in the community and who supposedly "knew all there was to know about Goans." Francis was different. No Goan was ever likely to send me to him, and no Goan did. In fact, when a Goan community leader found out that I had spoken to Francis, he chided me for wasting my time on a taxi driver who knew nothing. I felt that I had a lot to learn from Francis but unfortunately, our relationship could not develop much. At the end of our long conversation, Francis directed at me what I considered to be improper sexual remarks, and I chose to bring our relationship to an end.

Until Francis made overt sexual remarks, I felt safe with him. His position as a married man in his midforties, who saw himself as a "working-class person" and who was introduced to me by a close friend, encouraged me to ask him intimate and sensitive questions about his family life and about issues such as prostitution, interracial relations, and Asians' involvement in underground economic activities, such as smuggling. Francis's response to my questions was significantly influenced by my position as an unmarried, twenty-four-year-old woman who was seen as an Asian but who was simultaneously perceived as "Westernized" because of her connection with the United States. The assumption that I was Westernized led several men, including Francis, to think that they could openly discuss their personal, intercommunal and interracial sexual relationships with me, a topic they would have felt uncomfortable to discuss if I had come directly from India instead of the United States to do the same research. For example, when I asked Francis if he and his wife were planning to have more children, he responded by telling me about his extramarital relationships with three women, two of whom had to have abortions. My status as an "outsider," both geographical and socially, encouraged Francis to criticize and discuss people openly. For instance, he did not mind my knowing that he disliked his neighbor, Linda (an alias), because he considered her as a bad influence on his wife. He not only mentioned Asian prostitutes and their clients by name, but he also told me about his ex-boss who was once engaged in smuggling. He freely discussed his love affairs and his differences with his wife because he was aware that I did not know his wife and was not likely to know her if he did not want that to happen.

In Nargis's case, the distinctions between my status as an "insider" and "outsider" became increasingly blurred with the passage of time. At the beginning, we were both "outsiders" to each other in several ways. While Nargis freely talked about her community and her life to me and I shared some of my experiences with her, our relationship remained quite formal, and both of us were aware of my position as a researcher who did not belong to Nargis's home or communal space. While discussing communal issues, we both avoided mentioning people by name, and I was careful to not disclose to her anything about my other interviews. When I started living with Nargis, however, all the spatial barriers of public/private and home/community that previously existed between us collapsed. As the sites of our conversations shifted from formal spaces of the living room and dinner table to informal spaces of Nargis's kitchen, bedroom, and neighborhood streets, our conversations became too personal and sensitive to be tape recorded or jotted down verbatim. Although I continued to be a social outsider for Nargis at times when she observed religious fasts or participated in religious mourning, in most other spheres, we became "insiders" to each other's lives. We discussed with each other everything that happened in our lives on a day-to-day basis. She talked about the developments of her court cases, as well as her relationships with relatives, community leaders, lawyers, and friends. I talked to her about the people I met and the interviews I did, and we spent a considerable amount of time discussing issues such as Asian-African relations in the context of multiparty politics and the social and political issues specific to the Ithna Asheri community.

As in the case of most of my other informants, my "Asianness" often allowed me to be considered an "insider" by both Francis and Nargis, particularly in the context of discussions around race. Both felt free to voice their prejudices and racist sentiments against Africans before me because they assumed that like most Asians, I shared those opinions. Although such views always made me angry, I reacted quite differently in each case. In Francis's case, beyond posing some questions to challenge his position, I did little to voice my anger. First, the nature of my brief relationship with him did not allow me to risk offending him. Moreover, being unfamiliar with Francis's social milieu, I wanted to know as much as possible about his family background, his work, social relationships with Asians and Africans, his perspectives on gender, race, and class relations among Goans and non-Goans, his attitude and stereotypes about people of different communities and regions, and his perceptions of "Goanness," "Indianness," and "Africanness."

With Nargis things developed quite differently. In the beginning, when I interviewed Nargis for long hours, she shared with me many personal stories that she hadn't told anyone outside her immediate family before. At this time, our relationship was mainly that of "researcher" and "informant." I deeply valued the trust she had placed in me and even when I disagreed with her sometimes racist and homophobic ideas, I was careful not to say anything that might make her feel uncomfortable with me. Later, however, my close relationship with her, particularly at the time when I was living with her, allowed me to disagree and argue openly with her. Nargis's position as a "subject/informant" for my research took a back seat. She was first and foremost, a good friend, almost like an older sister, with whom I felt a need to communicate honestly without any barriers, and to make her understand my position on issues as I tried to understand hers. Also, once the barrier of formality between Nargis and myself was broken and we became an essential part of each other's daily lives, I felt responsible to decide in each instance whether a particular piece of information about her life was shared with me as a researcher, friend, or housemate.

Earlier in this chapter, I argued that in order to understand adequately the complexities of identity politics, we must be sensitive to the diverse and multiple social and geographical contexts in which those identities are constructed. The analysis of my relationship with Francis and Nargis goes a step further. It demonstrates not only that a contextualization of identity theory is crucial to our understanding of identities, but also that the narratives we as researchers produce in our work are themselves shaped by our own social and geographical positions with respect to the "subjects"/"informants" whose identities we study.

Conclusion

Identity theory, which has largely focused on the politics around race, class, gender, and sexuality, proves inadequate when we look beyond U.S. and British contexts, particularly at postcolonial societies. The above discussion underscores the point that in order to be of greater social relevance, identity theory needs to be geographically and historically contextualized. As researchers, our consideration of the social multiplicities that shape people's experiences must broaden and change in accordance with the places and time periods we study.

This chapter also illustrates that a keen understanding of the geography of positionality is crucial to feminist ethnography. The preceding discussion underscores how reflexivity and relationality enable us to understand more fully the ways in which the politics of social identities are played out in our everyday lives and spaces, and the manner in which they influence the knowledge we produce. The above analysis reveals me as positioned subject, situated in specific ways, with respect to the communities and people that I studied. Francis and Nargis, like all other informants who participated in my research, are positioned subjects, and their positionings must be analyzed with respect to my own in order to grasp how their life-stories came into being and how I have created academic knowledge on the basis of their stories. To conclude in Prell's (1989, 254) words: "In the life history, two stories together produce one. A hearer and a listener ask, respond, present, and edit a life . . . One must know oneself through and in light of the other. The subject-subject relationship is itself a reflexive event in which a self is presented with a full knowledge of reporting, or constructing itself."

Notes

This research was funded by an award from the National Science Foundation (SES–9205409) and a Davis Fellowship from the Department of Geography, University of Minnesota. I would like to thank John Paul Jones III, Heidi Nast, and Sue Roberts for organizing the conference and workshops. I am also grateful to Mona Domosh, Isabel Dyck, Karen Falconer Al-Hindi, David Faust, Susan Geiger, Susan Hanson, John Paul Jones III, Helga Leitner, and Ann Oberhauser for their comments on earlier drafts of this paper.

1. Social places are constituted and reconstituted in a space that is formed by the co-existence of social interrelations and interactions at all geographical scales. A place, then, is made out of a particular set of social relations interacting at a particular location (Massey 1992a, b).

2. Throughout East Africa, the term "Asian" is commonly used to refer to people who originally immigrated from what are now India and Pakistan. In this paper, I have retained this usage.

3. By "social boundaries" I mean: fluid lines of demarcation which define the "in group" and "out group" in a given context. For instance, an endogamous Muslim caste of Sunni Potters will consider all non-Sunnis *and* non-Potters as an "out group" for the purpose of intermarriage, but an "in group" in the context of Id celebrations. By "identities" I mean: the symbols, labels and affiliations by which people define themselves in a particular context, and by which they are perceived by the "others" in a particular context.

4. It is common for African Tanzanians to use the term *Banyani* for Hindus of any region.

5. The Goan community is the oldest, biggest, and most prominent community of Asian Christians in Tanzania. Among the Muslims, there are many sects, but I chose the Ithna Asheris because as a community, their rise in social and economic spheres has been very significant in the last decade, and I was interested in studying the processes leading to this rise.

6. While life-stories took anywhere between five hours to several days, shorter interviews usually lasted less than three hours.

7. Reflexivity refers to the capacity of the self to reflect upon itself as well as on the underlying systems that create it (Prell 1989, 251). Intersubjectivity can be defined as the shared perceptions and conceptions of the world held by interacting groups of people (Johnston et al. 1986, 236).

8. By using the term "Hindi/Urdu," I attempt to avoid the artificially created divide between Hindi and Urdu.

9. Farida (not her real name), conversation with author, Dar es Salaam, 7 October 1992.

10. These faculty included Professors Louis Mbughuni, Patricia Mbughuni, Marjorie Mbilinyi, Zubeida Tumbo, Issa Shivji, Suleiman Sumra, Muhsin Alidina, Adolpho Mascarenhas, Ophelia Mascarenhas, and Abdul Sheriff.

References

Abu-Lughod, L. 1993. *Writing women's worlds*. Berkeley: University of California Press.

Beauvoir, S. 1973. *The second sex*. New York: Vintage Press.

Behar, R. 1993. *Translated woman*. Boston: Beacon Press.

Butler, J. 1990. *Gender trouble: Feminism and the subversion of identity*. New York: Routledge.

———. 1987. Variations on sex and gender. In *Feminism as critique*, ed. S. Benhabib and D. Cornell, 128–42. Minneapolis: University of Minnesota Press.

Dyck, I. 1993. Ethnography: A feminist method. *The Canadian Geographer* 37(1): 52–57.

Geiger, S. 1990. What's so feminist about women's oral history. *Journal of Women's History* 2(1): 169–82.

———. 1986. Women's life histories: Method and content. *Signs* 11(21): 334–51.

Jha, P. 1991. Writing the nation. Manuscript.

Johnston, R. J., et al. 1986. *The dictionary of human geography*. Oxford: Blackwell.

Katz, C. 1994. Playing the field. *The Professional Geographer* 46(1): 54–66.

Lowe, Lisa. 1991. Heterogeneity, hybridity, multiplicity. *Diaspora* 1(1): 24–44.

Massey, Doreen. 1992a. A place called home? *New Formations* 17: 3–15.

———. 1992b. Politics and space/time. *New Left Review* 196: 65–84.

Mbilinyi, M. 1989. "I'd have been a man." In *Interpreting women's lives*, ed. Personal Narratives Group, 204–27. Bloomington: Indiana University Press.

Mirza, S., and Strobel M., eds. 1989. *Three Swahili women*. Bloomington: Indiana University Press.

Moss, P. 1993. Focus: Feminism as method. *The Canadian Geographer* 37(1): 48–49.

Nagar, R. 1995. *Making and breaking boundaries: Identity politics among South Asians in postcolonial Dar es Salaam*. Ph.D. dissertation. University of Minnesota.

Nagar, R. 1993. Personal communication, June 4.

Nast, H. 1994. Opening remarks: Introduction to critical feminist methodologies and theoretical perspectives. *The Professional Geographer* 46(1): 54–66.

Ngaiza, M., and Koda, B., eds. 1991. *The unsung heroines*. Dar es Salaam: Women's Research and Documentation Project.

Personal Narratives Group, ed. 1989. *Interpreting women's lives*. Bloomington: Indiana University Press.

Popular Memory Group. 1982. Popular memory: Theory, politics, method. In *Making histories*, eds. Richard Johnson et al., 205–52. London: Hutchinson in association with the Centre for Contemporary Cultural Studies, University of Birmingham.

Prell, R. 1989. The double frame of life history in the work of Barbara Myerhoff. In *Interpreting women's lives*, ed. Personal Narratives Group, 241–58. Bloomington: Indiana University Press.

Rosaldo, Renato. 1989. *Culture and truth*. Boston: Beacon Press.

Rose, D. 1993. On feminism, method and methods in human geography: An idiosyncratic overview. *The Canadian Geographer* 37(1): 57–61.

Rose, G. and Ogborn, M. 1988. Feminism and historical geography. *Journal of Historical Geography* 14(4): 405–9.

Rose, G. 1993. *Feminism and geography*. Minneapolis: University of Minnesota Press.

Scott, Joan. 1986. Gender: A useful category of historical analysis. *The American Historical Review* 91(5): 1053–75.

Somers, Margaret. 1992. Narrativity, narrative identity and social action. *Social Science History* 16(4): 591–630.

Visweswaran, Kamala. 1994. *Fictions of feminist ethnography*. Minneapolis: University of Minnesota Press.

Warren, C. 1988. *Gender issues in field research*. Newbury Park, CA: Sage Publications.

Watts, M. 1992. Space for everything. *Cultural Anthropology* 7(1): 115–29.

12

With "Stout Boots and a Stout Heart": Historical Methodology and Feminist Geography

Mona Domosh

> Equipped now with maps, note book, stout boots and a stout heart the
> historical geographer is ready to pursue his investigations o'er fell, field
> and fen, down macadamed road, up cobbled street with eyes open and
> mind alert to see and appreciate the visible landscape as the present phase
> of an ever-changing pattern indissolubly linked to its past and irrevocably
> the foundation of its future.
>
> —J. B. Mitchell, *Historical Geography*

It was this type of sentiment and sensibility that originally inspired my own
forays into historical geography—trampling across, in my case, not cobbled
streets, but the muddy fields of late-autumn New England in search of eighteenth-century farm homes, stone fences, and pungent-smelling barns. In my
imagination I recreated the character of these places, situating people's lives in
these houses as I walked hurriedly to keep warm. It was this vividness, this
visualness, of fieldwork that convinced me to do geography instead of history—I enjoyed experiencing and seeing for myself, the places of past events.
I wanted the past made visible. Eventually, I made my way into the library,
conjuring up lives again between the words, maps, and pictures I found there.

The texts I read and the ones I finally created spoke little of women and
were completely silent about anything that might be construed as feminist. I
didn't even know if there were any women historical geographers. In fact, Jean
Mitchell's book on historical geography, written, it seems, as a type of textbook, makes no mention of the fact that the author is a woman (she uses her
initials, J. B.). But then, in the late fifties when the book was written, the social
context from which an author wrote was not thought to have anything to
do with the knowledge that author conveyed. The rigorous methodology of

225

fieldwork and archival research were thought to expose the truths of the past without subjective bias. Because of this, historical geography, like most other specialties within the discipline, presented a clear case of what Gillian Rose (1993) refers to as the masculinism of geographic thought—the narratives it produced, spoken of as universal and comprehensive, actively erased from past and present knowledges the world of women, as well as all those outside dominant discourses.

Most of this is not news to us, as the past twenty years have witnessed the intellectual deconstruction of notions of "truth" that inhere in the world, and with it the unraveling of a belief in "objective" knowledge. Instead, we envision knowledge as the creation of the hearts and minds of real people existing within their own social and cultural parameters. But historical geography has positioned itself outside these discussions, moribund, as Jeanne Kay (1990) and others (Rose and Ogborn 1988) have reminded us, in an antiquarian world aloof from the problematics of recent social and cultural theory.[1] As a result, both the epistemological and methodological assumptions of historical geography have not been seriously challenged. Those of us who have tried to reckon with these challenges and to formulate a historical geography of difference have found the task forbidding, at least in part, I will argue, because we have accepted traditional historical methodology. This is a serious impediment to those of us who are interested in developing a historical perspective for a feminist geography, a perspective that, as Linda Nicholson (1986) argues, is essential for the making of feminist theory and practice. What I want to suggest in this chapter is that a formulation of a feminist historical geography must begin with an examination of its methodological stances, because by accepting the assumptions of the more-traditional historical geography, even one that includes women, we only reinscribe the very categories we may want to dismantle. In other words, what I am calling for is not necessarily a shift in the object of study (women's spaces instead of men's spaces), but a shift in how we conceive of those spaces to begin with, and with this, a reformulation of methodology sensitive to the gendered construction of all landscapes.

I am basing much of my discussion on the work of feminist historian Joan Scott, particularly her critique of historians' assumptions that making the "experiences" of oppressed people visible is sufficient for a radical history (Scott 1992). In her critique, Scott argues that accepting the authenticity of women's experiences as foundational, and therefore defining the project of a radical history as that of making visible women's experience in historical narratives, "precludes critical examination of the workings of the ideological system itself, its categories of representation (homosexual/heterosexual, man/woman, black/ white as fixed immutable identities), its premises about what these categories mean and how they operate, its notions of subjects, origin, and cause" (Scott 1992, 25). For example, if we are investigating the identities of Victorian women, we are limiting ourselves if we accept that the identities and experiences of these women as relayed in their diaries are self-evidently given. This simply reaffirms the differences between Victorian men and women. Instead,

Scott argues that historians of difference need to examine the conditions under which the identities of these women were produced, the terms in which that difference was being constructed. As she states, "It is not individuals who have experience, but subjects who are constituted through experience" (1992, 26). Therefore, if we want to understand Victorian women's identities, we would analyze how subjects acquire and have ascribed to them identities (e.g., feminine) through the experiences they recount in diaries. In this sense, it is the various processes that together constitute experiences that become our object of investigation. All of those processes as well as the experiences and identities they constitute are spatial and social practices.

I argue that historical geographers of difference, by accepting the methods of orthodox historical geography, have also accepted the epistemological assumptions that confirm the experiences of women in the past as foundational to historical explanation.[2] This approach certainly makes women's landscapes and places visible, but this visibility only serves to reaffirm what we may want to dismantle, that is, the assertion that there are essential differences between men and women. What I want to suggest in this chapter is that Scott's nonessentialist perspective on experience has significant implications for our understanding and interpretations of past geographies. A landscape, like a diary, is inscribed with layers of past experiences and therefore relays to "readers" past identities, but identities and experiences that are not fixed. Interpretations of that landscape, therefore, must include the conditions under which those identities and experiences were being formulated.

I will try to explain what I mean by first briefly summarizing the methodologies we have inherited from historical and cultural geography, and by analyzing and critiquing the assumptions that lie behind those methods. I will then outline a methodology that is more sensitive to the nuances of gender identities and spatial politics.

Inherited Methods

Feminists looking for methodological guides to historical studies in geography can find them in two fairly distinct bodies of work: historical geography and cultural geography. In historical geography, attention is given to the interpretation of materials gathered in archives, and in that sense is most similar to the work of historians. Cultural geographers engaged in historical work often add another interpretative layer to the analysis since their attention is directed not only to the archives, but also to the visible landscape. The new interpretative methods suggested by landscape as an object of analysis—an object that is far more concrete than that offered by the archives, yet whose creation and construction and therefore "meaning" is far less direct than with written texts—open possibilities for methods for feminist historical geographies. Yet, as I will discuss later, even these possibilities have been limited by an emphasis on "authorship" and therefore have precluded much feminist analysis.

Like historians, historical geographers have focused many of their methodological discussions on the nature of source materials, comparing the relative
merits of census data, historical directories, historical maps, archival manu-
scripts, and others, and discussing how those sources can be most effectively
interpreted (Butlin 1993; Baker and Billinge 1982). Even though some historical geographers have accepted the idea that interpretation of sources is inevitably a subjective matter, the uncritical acceptance of the reliability of those
sources remains, as they are seen as crucial to determining the reality of past
lives and past geographies. As Butlin comments, "The establishment of the
relative accuracy and reliability of data and information sources, in addition to
their 'meaning' in the broadest possible sense, is an important process for the
historical geographer" (1993, 75). From these written sources, historical geographers piece together a viable narrative that explains past geographies.[3]

To those who tried to introduce women into this world, the challenge was
to find written sources that speak of women's lives. One of the more significant
results of this challenge was a broadening of the definition of reliable and
accurate source materials, in order to allow those without access to the formal
record to speak to us now as scholars in the late twentieth century. Through
these more "informal" accounts, such as diaries and oral histories, we have
heard other stories of past worlds, and those other stories have forced a recognition of the partiality and incompleteness of many historical narratives. For
example, many stories of the settlement of the American West have recently
been reconsidered after feminist historians and geographers have shown how
women on the frontier envisaged, encountered, and created landscapes differently from many of their male counterparts (Kay 1991; Kay, chapter 17, this
volume; Kolodny 1975).

Yet historical geographers do more than labor in archives; as Jean Mitchell
reminded us, we also put on our stout boots and venture into the field. But
theorization of what happens in that field experience is practically absent from
methodological discussions in historical geography. Feminist geographers
have engaged in this discussion, but most of their scholarship has been directed
to the contemporary world, and therefore methodological discussions have
focused on questions of power and knowledge formation where the research
object may be distant in space, but not necessarily in time. Many feminists have
looked to ethnography for discussions of issues concerning the relationships
between the researcher and the people being "researched," of who speaks for
whom, and of what constitutes the "field" and who defines it (Nast 1994; Katz
1994; Kobayashi 1994). Yet, as historical geographers, when we go into the
"field" in those stout boots, we encounter not only different cultures, but different landscapes. How do these ethnographic issues translate into a situation
where the field is constituted only of visible remains of material artifacts?

Here we can turn to work in cultural geography, where the definition of
landscape and how it can be interpreted are currently under debate. Many of
the "new" cultural geographers tell us that the artifacts that comprise a landscape can be thought of as a text, a text that is created out of the same nexus

of social/cultural/economic constraints and possibilities, of emotional impulse and rational consideration, as are paintings or poems or essays (Duncan and Duncan 1988; Cosgrove and Daniels 1988). As such, landscapes are to be interpreted in ways similar to literature, and the "new" cultural geographers have proposed methods for such interpretations that range from iconography to deconstruction (Barnes and Duncan 1992; Cosgrove and Daniels 1988).

For feminists engaged in such "readings," the initial challenge was to find landscapes that had been "authored" by women. This led to studies of women's spaces of the past, and how their particular historical conditions, specifically contemporary ideas about appropriate gender behavior, shaped that landscape. Hence, we began to see studies of what could be called "women's" landscapes, such as domestic gardens (Ford 1991), home interiors (Spain 1992; Hayden 1984), and women's clubs (Rappaport 1994), and the incorporation into those landscapes of historically specific gender and class ideologies. Yet, again, what I am suggesting is that by uncritically accepting the identities of the women creating these spaces, such studies may only assert essential differences between men and women, and, consequently, between men's spaces and women's spaces.

Assumptions and Obstacles

What I have presented so far are very cursory summaries of how feminists have tried to incorporate women and feminist analyses into historical geography, and I have suggested that the results of such attempts may in fact reaffirm categories of analysis that some feminists may want to subvert. My purpose in this section is to outline why this reaffirmation is occurring. Let me begin by examining some of the methodological assumptions of reading the lives and experiences of women in the past from written sources, before turning to a discussion of landscape as a historical source.

As several scholars have pointed out (Scott 1988, 1992; Shapiro 1994), the field of women's history derived its original strength and legitimacy by claiming a unique place for women's experiences in the past, albeit experiences that are interpreted from less-formal written sources, such as diaries. By documenting these heretofore invisible experiences, historians of difference have been highly successful in remedying partial accounts of history. In historical geography, we have found through an examination of women's travel diaries, for example, that the heroic narratives of the settlement of the American West or the exploratory myths of the British colonial empire have been created out of very partial ways of seeing landscape (Domosh 1991; Blunt 1994).

According to Joan Scott, however, one danger in the turn toward women's history, is that we "take as self-evident the identities of those whose experience is being documented and thus naturalize their difference" (1992, 25). In assuming an apparent authenticity of women's experiences as expressed in written texts, one may reinforce the differences between men's and women's lives. This overlooks that the identities of women are created out of a societal sorting of characteristics that separates masculine from feminine, and therefore, that women's identities necessarily implicate the identities of men. In other words, identities are formed in relation to their opposite, and no experience—and hence, no landscape—can be seen as totally feminine or masculine, without in some way including its opposite.

If we assume that the meaning relayed by words written by women is transparent, that women's experiences are a given that need not be examined, then we are, as Scott argues (1992), reproducing, rather than contesting the given ideological system. What we end up with is knowledge of the different ways women in the past have utilized space, or spoken about their homes and gardens, but not an understanding of the framework in which those practices and knowledges were constructed. For that, we need to examine the historically contingent conditions that constitute that experience, so that both the processes that constitute experience and the experiences themselves become the item under investigation, instead of being taken as the purveyor of facts about unmediated experience. As Scott explains, "To do this a change of object seems to be required, one which takes the emergence of concepts and identities as historical events in need of explanation" (1992, 33). For example, in his recent book *Gay New York*, George Chauncey demonstrates how and why the identity of "gayness" was created:

> The ascendancy of *gay* reflected, then, a reorganization of sexual categories and the transition from an early twentieth-century culture divided into "queers" and "men" on the basis of gender status to a late-twentieth-century culture divided into "homosexuals" and "heterosexuals" on the basis of sexual object choice. Each set of terms represented a way of defining, constituting, and containing male "sexuality," by labelling, differentiating, and explaining the character of (homo) sexually active men. (1994, 22)

"Gay" identity, then, was a creation of a particular time and place; it was a historically constructed object. So, too, the identity of a woman explorer, of a woman settler in the American West, or of a middle-class New York shopper—all are and were created out of particular conditions and for particular reasons, and therefore these identities cannot act as foundations of "authentic experience."

In a similar vein, the methods proposed for interpreting landscapes also reinscribe a fixed identity for women. First of all, most of these interpretive theories assume that the landscape results from the conscious creation of an individual or a group of individuals. Interpretation, therefore, focuses on the "creator" and her or his social context. In other words, since the landscape is seen as a text, the "author" is in the position of paramount importance. And even when interpretative stances attempt to dislodge the author and to examine the broader context of meaning, the position of the author still maintains its epistemological importance.

For feminist literary critics, many of the interpretative methods that center analysis on the author have proved successful as ways of highlighting the contributions of heretofore invisible women writers, and therefore broadening the "canon" to include "other" voices. Yet the translation of such methods to geography is difficult, at best, because it leads to an emphasis on "authorship" and therefore limits us to analyses of landscapes "authored" by women. Instead of questioning the underlying gendered constructions of landscapes, or the processes of shaping feminine identity, these methods often reinscribe essentialist assumptions about the nature of femininity and masculinity. With their focus on creators, these author-centered methods actively preclude much feminist work by limiting it to those few areas inscribed to be within the control of women, for example, home interiors, women's clubs, or gardens. This lends legitimacy to the belief that there are, essentially speaking, men's spaces and women's spaces. It also leaves no place for a feminist analysis of most of our historical landscapes that were created through complex social processes that only rarely included women as active agents.

Second, the epistemological assumption of such interpretive methods is that the experiences of the "author" are unproblematically translated into built form. For example, in one study (1989), I analyzed the construction of a skyscraper from the perspective of the owner and his architect. The owner of a large corporation considered the wishes and demands of his company and of himself, worked with an architect to design a building that fit those needs, and made decisions based on his social/cultural context as well as his own personal predilections. This owner acted within the constraints of his society, constraints that included prescriptions concerning appropriate masculine behavior, but the nature of a patriarchal society is that, in the end, this man was operating in a system that ultimately favored his position—a White middle-class man. In contrast, women, and other disempowered people, may in fact be responsible for creating a building, but they may be doing so under conditions and in a manner not of their own choosing, and in a system that does not favor their position. Many nineteenth-century women's clubs, for example, were constructed under the authority of women, but this does not say that those spaces spoke of emancipation for women, or that they in any way relayed meanings other than those prescribed by the dominant order. In fact, most of these clubs echoed their male counterparts in design and function. So, studying women's clubs using a traditional method may tell us something about the women who were involved in it, but very little about the patriarchal society that controlled aesthetic ideology and gender ideology.[4]

In conclusion, then, by following these methods in historical geography, we are saying that (1) there is some essentialized womanness that marks particular places and spaces, and (2) that womanness is foundational to the interpretation. Instead of examining how and under what circumstances the ideas of "women" and "women's spaces" were constructed, we are simply reiterating and confirming their presence.

Toward a Historical Geography of
Gender Identity and Experience

What sort of method would allow us to examine the circumstances in which gender identities and gendered landscapes are formulated? Some of the essential components would be

1. A way of interpreting landscape that does not establish authorship as the basis of meaning, but rather focuses on the social and cultural context in which that landscape is created, of which the particular gender structure and ideology form an integral part.
2. An understanding of "authors" as important, but not autonomous, actors. In Judith Walkowitz's words, "that individuals do not fully author their texts does not falsify Marx's insight that men (and women) make their own history, albeit under circumstances they do not produce or fully control" (1992, 9). Different people, however, experience those circumstances differently, depending of course on how they have been positioned in society.
3. An acceptance that women's (or men's) experiences have in themselves no explanatory power, but instead constitute the foci of what needs to be explained.

Let me illustrate what I mean. As feminist geographers, many of us are interested in examining the construction of the division between public and private space, and as historical geographers, we may want to ask under what particular historical conditions these spaces came to be seen as distinct. Jurgen Habermas's thesis as to the origins and significance of a public sphere has already been critiqued by feminists for its essentializing view of the categories of private and public, and for its exclusionary definition of the public. Nancy Fraser (1989, 1994), for example, has clearly shown how Habermas's conceptions of the distinctions between the public and private spheres are based on bourgeois, masculine assumptions that are both empirically and theoretically misleading, and that can lead to undemocratic political practices (see, also, Meoño-Picado, chapter 15, this volume). In the following analysis, therefore, I will be using Habermas's terms of "private" and "public," recognizing them to be categories defined in relation to each other and that are not essentially distinct. In fact, it is precisely in an attempt to understand under what particular historical circumstances these two spheres came to be seen as distinct, and how those distinctions were correlated to purported male and female "spheres," that I suggest historical geography can be particularly productive.

If we follow Habermas (1991), then we should be searching for the origins of the modern, public sphere in the coffeehouses of seventeenth- and eighteenth-century London—situations where private citizens met to discuss public affairs, often in the form of critiques of the reigning political order.[5] The political functions of the public sphere, to use Habermas's terms, arose under particular conditions in the last decades of the seventeenth century as groups of property-owning men, with newly gained economic power, began to challenge the political order by bringing their case into the public sphere. This public sphere had already been engaged in social issues as the new private citizens gained a sense of themselves as individuals with subjectivities that could be expressed in written form and therefore shared with the public. In Habermas's words, this "psychological emancipation corresponded to the political-economic one" (1991, 46). For Habermas, the idea of psychological emancipation refers to the belief that humans have qualities intrinsic to their humanness separate from any extrinsic laws, and this emancipation is located in the home, the site of the conjugal family. So men were free as humans in the home, separated from the exigencies of the economic realm, and that freedom was extended into the spaces of the city where citizens came to discuss the political order in a public way—the spaces of clubs and coffeehouses.

Habermas argues that these two senses of emancipation (freedom as property owners and freedom as rational subjects) were conjoined into one to create the bourgeois public sphere. If the space of political emancipation was the coffeehouse, the space of psychological emancipation was the home. And yet the freedom offered by the political and economic autonomy of the new class of bourgeois men was accompanied by the reassertion of control over the family:

> the independence of the property owner in the market and in his own business was complemented by the dependence of the wife and children on the male head of the family; private autonomy in the former realm was transformed into authority in the latter and made any pretended freedom of individuals illusory (1991, 47).

So the emancipation in the political realm was only for bourgeois men and was predicated on the dependence of women.[6] The coffeehouses of London, in fact, explicitly excluded women from entering. The sites of the public, political sphere were defined as avowedly masculine; they were part, therefore, of the bourgeois construction of masculine identity, an identity based on the exclusion of the feminine.

And where were these new, public, masculine sites within the city? In the 1650s, the first coffeehouses in England were located in the city, near Cornhill, but by the 1670s, they began to appear farther west, particularly along Fleet Street and the Strand (Allen 1967; Lewis 1952; Chancellor 1912). Since these coffeehouses served as meeting grounds for men of similar business and political interests, it made perfect sense for them to be located close to the new centers of such worlds—the emerging financial district close to Cornhill and Lombard Street, and the emerging publishing industry along Fleet Street. Equally so, Fleet Street and the Strand, as the streets that connected the city with Westminster, were foci of public activity and protest. Both legal and media institutions were situated there, creating a space that both literally and symbolically represented the modern, bourgeois, masculine, public life.

We could interpret the construction of these new "public" spaces by documenting women's and men's words and artifacts, deciphering patterns of prescribed thought and actions, and then proceeding to analyze how and why the identities of bourgeois women and men were being defined in relationship to particular types of spaces in the city. The people, presumably men, who were responsible for creating and inhabiting those spaces were doing so because in their particular contexts, ideas of masculinity and norms of bourgeois life must have come together in what was being called a new "public" space. If we could examine this mutual relationship between space and social structure and behavior, then we could begin to understand how landscapes are constitutive of gender and class identity, and how in turn those identities are formulated in space. Seventeenth- and eighteenth-century coffeehouses were defined as masculine and public spaces for, I presume, a set of reasons related to the functionings of the dominant economic and social order, and, as such, these new spaces became integral to the new definitions of bourgeois, masculine identity.

For example, coffee itself connoted the new status of the English bourgeoisie. Imported into Europe as a luxury drink for the nobility, its entry into the English market in the early seventeenth century was made possible by, and coincided with, the ascendancy of mercantilism and the new merchant classes. Through its association with nobility, then, coffee became popular with the rising middle classes, as they distinguished themselves from the working classes. Taverns and alehouses were still popular as social settings, but coffeehouses carried with them the connotations of the new, literate, politically active businessmen of the middle class. So the new coffeehouses were distinguished by the class associations of the drinks served, and by the exclusive maleness of their clientele. This development of a masculine, bourgeois, public space was happening at the same time that the western limits of London were under construction for new middle-class residential squares, where the autonomy of the husband prevailed over the women and children in the private space of the home. The "privacy" of the home provided the bourgeois man with at least the illusion of power based on his ascribed position, power that he was now denied in the "egalitarian" public sphere. Therefore, integral to the creation of the new masculine, bourgeois identity was its relationship to both what was being defined as the "public" space of the coffeehouses, and the "private" space of the new residential areas—both types of spaces were sites for the exercise of male, bourgeois autonomy and for the construction of a masculine identity.

An analysis of these relationships might lead us to an understanding of how and why men came to be associated with public spaces and women with private spaces, and of how these two categories of spaces came to be seen as distinct in the first place. We know, for example, that "public" activities such as those at the coffeehouses, were only possible because of domestic "private" help, and "private" activities in the household were conducted using goods and services provided by the "public" sector. It would also help us understand how particular historical sites were implicated in the construction of modern gender and class identities, and how those identities and hence those sites were defined relationally, often out of deliberate exclusions. If followed through, this would be a type of analysis that does not focus on "authorship" (if it did, then our story would begin and end with middle class men), that looks to the broad, structural contexts of the people and landscapes examined, and that calls into question the experiences and identities of those people and the worlds they created, examining how those identities were articulated in space.

This, of course, is only a very brief outline of how a possible feminist historical geography could proceed with methods that do not presuppose fixed identities of the authors of texts or landscapes. I have presented it only to suggest possibilities, not limit options, and because I think it is important to challenge ourselves to think beyond our assumed categories of analysis.

Conclusion

I still get nostalgic about my treks across the New England landscape, but now that nostalgia is framed by my recognition of how invisible women were as practitioners and participants in the field. I am heartened that women's lives and gender identities are now at least considered in historical geography, and that, unlike Jean Mitchell, we can identify ourselves as women and be straightforward about the politics of our feminist analyses. I think it is now time to pursue that politics with a set of methodological assumptions that do not fix us, or our objects of study, in a prescribed identity that reinforces difference.

Notes

I want to thank Susan Hanson, John Paul Jones, Richa Nagar, Miles Ogborn, and Rich Schein for their very helpful and constructive comments on earlier versions of this chapter.

1. I do need to qualify this sweeping statement since there are important instances where historical work in geography is directly engaged in social and cultural theory. See, for example, the work of Steve Daniels (1993), Derek Gregory (1994), David Harvey (1985), and Allan Pred (1990). What I want to suggest here is that, particularly in the American context, these works are considered outside the normal disciplinary borders. They are "exceptions" to the rule.

2. Some very recent work by feminist geographers indicates a shift toward examining the construction of women's identities through spatial expression, though, at this point, the work has focused on the archives and women's words, and has overlooked the material landscape. See the essays in *Writing Women and Space* (Blunt and Rose 1994).

3. For a critique of the use of narrative as a historical method, see Felix Driver (1988).

4. I do not want to suggest here that women's clubs were completely controlled by the hegemonic order. On the contrary, as spaces set aside specifically for women, these clubs were often the sites for women's organizing efforts, many of which contributed to the suffrage movement. In this sense, these clubs served a subversive function. What I am arguing against is a method that assumes that women's spaces are necessarily subversive, simply because women built them.

5. Coffeehouses were only one type of site of bourgeois, masculine identity formation. Seventeenth- and eighteenth-century London was constructed around flourishing sites of commerce and politics, all of which participated in the creation of new, masculine identities. See Barker-Benfield (1992) and Solkin (1992).

6. For a detailed examination of how and why Habermas defined the public sphere in masculine terms, see Nancy Fraser's essay in *Habermas and the Public Sphere* (1994).

References

Allen, R. J. 1967. *The clubs of Augustan London*. Hamden, CT: Archon Books.

Baker, A. R. H. and Billinge, M. D. eds. 1982. *Period and place: Research methods in historical geography*. Cambridge: Cambridge University Press.

Barker-Benfield, G. J. 1992. *The culture of sensibility*. Chicago: University of Chicago Press.

Barnes, T., and Duncan, J. 1992. *Writing worlds: Discourse, text and the representation of landscape*. New York: Routledge.

Blunt, A. 1994. *Travel, gender,and imperialism*. New York: Guilford Publications.

Blunt, A., and Rose, G., eds. 1994. *Writing women and space*. New York: Guilford Publications.

Butlin, R. 1993. *Historical geography: Through the gates of space and time*. London: Edward Arnold.

Chancellor, E. B. 1912. *The annals of Fleet Street*. London: Chapman & Hall Limited.

Chauncey, G. 1994. *Gay New York: Gender, urban culture, and the making of the gay male world 1890–1940*. New York: Basic Books.

Cosgrove, D., and Daniels, S., eds. 1988. *The iconography of landscape*. Cambridge: Cambridge University Press.

Daniels, S. 1993. *Fields of vision*. Cambridge: Polity Press.

Domosh, M. 1989. The New York World Building: A method for interpreting landscape. *Area* 21: 347–355.

———. 1991. Toward a feminist historiography of geography. *Transactions of the Institute of British Geographers* 16: 95–104.

Driver, F. 1988. The historicity of human geography. *Progress in Human Geography* 12, 4: 497–506.

Duncan, J., and Duncan, N. 1988. (Re)reading the landscape. *Environment and Planning D: Society and Space* 6: 117–126.

Ford, S. 1991. Landscape revisited: A feminist reappraisal. In *New words, new worlds: Reconceptualising social and cultural geography*, ed. C. Philo, 151–55. Lampeter, Wales: Department of Geography, St. David's University.

Fraser, N. 1989. *Unruly practices: Power, discourse, and gender in contemporary social theory*. Minneapolis: University of Minnesota Press.

————. 1994. Rethinking the public sphere: A contribution to the critique of actually existing democracy. In *Habermas and the public sphere*, ed. Craig Calhoun, 109–42. Cambridge, MA: MIT Press.

Gregory, D. 1994. *Geographical imaginations*. Cambridge, MA: Blackwell Publishers.

Habermas, J. 1991. *The structural transformation of the public sphere: An inquiry into a category of bourgeois society*. Cambridge: MIT Press.

Harvey, D. 1985. *Consciousness and the urban experience*. Oxford: Blackwell Publishers.

Hayden, D. 1984. *Redesigning the American dream*. New York: W.W. Norton & Co.

Katz, C. 1994. Playing the field: Questions of fieldwork in geography. *The Professional Geographer* 46: 67–72.

Kay, J. 1990. The future of historical geography in the United States. *Annals of the Association of American Geographers* 80: 618–21.

————. 1991. Landscapes of women and men: Rethinking the regional historical geography of the United States and Canada. *Journal of Historical Geography* 17: 253–67.

Kobayashi, A. 1994. Coloring the field: Gender, "race," and the politics of fieldwork. *The Professional Geographer* 46: 73–79.

Kolodny, A. 1975. *The lay of the land*. Chapel Hill: The University of North Carolina Press.

Lewis, W. S. 1952. *Three tours through London in the years 1748, 1776, 1797*. New Haven: Yale University Press.

Mitchell, J. B. 1965. *Historical geography*. London: English Universities Press Ltd.

Nast, H. 1994. Opening remarks on "Women in the Field." *The Professional Geographer* 46: 54–66.

Nicholson, L. 1986. *Gender and history: The limits of social theory in the age of the family*. New York: Columbia University Press.

Pred, A. 1990. *Lost words and lost worlds: Modernity and the language of everyday life in late nineteenth-century Stockholm*. Cambridge: Cambridge University Press.

Rappaport, E. 1994. At the crossroads of public and private: The Victorian women's club and the female city. Paper presented at the Florida Women's Studies Conference, October 1994.

Rose, G. 1993. *Feminism and geography*. Minneapolis: University of Minnesota Press.

Rose, G., and Ogborn, M. 1988. Feminism and Historical Geography. *Journal of Historical Geography* 14: 405–9.

Scott, J. W. 1992. "Experience." In *Feminists theorize the political*, eds. Judith Butler and Joan W. Scott, 22–40. New York: Routledge.

————. 1988. *Gender and the politics of history*. New York: Columbia University Press.

Shapiro, A.-L., ed. 1994. *Feminists revision history*. New Brunswick: Rutgers University Press.

Solkin, D. 1992. *Painting for money: The visual arts and the public sphere in eighteenth-century England*. New Haven: Yale University Press.

Spain, D. 1992. *Gendered spaces*. Chapel Hill, NC: University of North Carolina Press.

Walkowitz, J. 1992. *City of dreadful delight: Narratives of sexual danger in late-Victorian London*. London: Virago Press.

Part 3

Representation

Introduction to Part 3

Marginal Notes on Representations

Janice Monk

Dear Heidi, JP, and Sue:

I've been resisting writing this piece for you. I don't see myself as an expert on "representation," or on the literature in geography and feminist scholarship that uses the term. My ideas are fragmentary and often "outside the project" as it is being constructed. So, what should I write? What are important issues about representation for feminist geographers? Can I say anything that will not be marginal because it doesn't cite and regurgitate the emerging canon? —Jan

*   *   *

Call for Papers:
New Forms of Representation. Papers will explore how new theoretical and methodological perspectives can best be communicated. In addition, papers will explore questions raised by the development of alternative forms of and fora for, representing diversity and difference. Questions include: Whom are we writing and working for? In what media and through what channels are research findings best communicated? Who controls the final form of the narrative or "text"? Such explorations will not only have direct implications for the practice of pedagogic and scholarly communication but raise political and practical issues of control and access.

*   *   *

representation *n* **1:** one that represents as **a:** an artistic likeness or image **b** (1): a statement or account esp. of an opinion and made to influence opinion or action (2) : an incidental or collateral statement of fact on the faith of which a contract is entered into **c:** a dramatic production or performance **d :** (1) a usu. formal statement made against something or to effect a change (2) a usu. formal protest **2:** the act or action of representing or state of being represented

241

as **a** (1) : the action or fact of one person standing for another so as to have rights and obligations of the person represented (2) : the substitution of an individual or class in place of a person (as a child for a deceased parent) **b:** the action of representing or the fact of being represented esp. in a legislative body **3:** the body of persons representing a constituency—**representational**[1]

Since feminist scholarship challenges the nature of authority, it seems odd to turn to a dictionary for guidance. But rather than closing down meanings, the dictionary offers wider possibilities for thinking about "representation" than I am getting from the geographic literature.

*   *   *

For some time I have been collecting postcards with images of women working (and a few of women at play!). I kept coming back to them as I thought about this piece. A postcard allows for a short message, usually not very profound. The sender doesn't expect or receive a direct response. Without an envelope, it can be read by anyone. It provides a visual image as well as space for a verbal message—something generally lacking in the current feminist geographic contributions on representation where words are "privileged." My collection comes from around the world, bought on my own travels or sent by friends. It is widely representative, even if it makes me and the senders seem like escapees from a David Lodge novel. So, I decided to include in my chapter postcard-like messages directed to various feminist scholars, mostly the other contributors to this book, some reflections of my own, and fragments of the voices of others, including genres other than academic publications.[2] It may not "work." But at least it will be a different form of representation— something that is rare in a literature that calls for polyvocality, nonlinear styles, alternative ways of representing difference and diversity, but is predominantly conformist in presenting itself as articles and chapters in academic books and journals and read papers at conferences, increasingly in the literary style of postmodernism.

*   *   *

Dear Audrey and Susan: I gather we have been identified as "senior scholars" who will help to select papers and moderate discussions at the conference. At least some reviewers of the proposal that funded the event thought some such mechanism was necessary to guard against "in-crowdism." Why should our "seniority" be seen as validation (or at least, as justification for spending government funds)? Anyway, it's instructive to be identified for our usefulness in guarding against "in-crowdism." Does that mean we are part of the "out-crowd" or that we are open-minded, inclusive, eclectic. . . . ?—Jan

The requirement of gatekeeping is alive and well, even as we talk about being more inclusive and incorporating   )thers." Is that inevitable in academia, with its structures of rewards and status? Who can (will) take risks and survive?

Fig. I.3.1. "Shooting Pool," photo by Abigail Heyman. (Produced by Flashcards Photographic Postcards "One picture is worth a thousand words.") Postcard mailed by the late Henriette Verduin Muller to Janice Monk from Maartensdijk, The Netherlands, 9 July 1990. Bought in Basel, Switzerland, printed in Fort Lauderdale, Fla.

What censorship do we impose on ourselves and others in the processes of reviewing and editing? Doing feminist scholarship used to be a risky proposition. It also drew on whatever paradigms we knew (including logical positivism, "masculinist" quantification, Marxist perspectives, cartographic representation) even as we tried to think about better ways to represent women; feminist scholars crossed boundaries into community activism (or so we told ourselves). Now feminist scholarship is part of the establishment—it has its literature that must be cited and gurus whose names should be incanted in order for the writer to be validated as doing worthwhile and "cutting edge" intellectual work.

*　　*　　*

Dear Lydia: Your paper (now chapter 14) directly addresses issues of audience and accessibility. You demonstrate your longstanding commitment to using a variety of genres in order to communicate with diverse audiences. One person at the conference suggested you were not being intellectual. What do we mean by "intellectual"? I remember an article in which you cooperated with a food writer to bring your research to readers of a popular magazine. It appeared under his name. Such work comes at the expense of standard academic writing that advances your career. And it involves imagination, negotiation, and/or willingness to yield control over the text. What makes wider communication important for you?—Jan

My own contributions to media other than research or pedagogical publications include the occasional television or radio interview, representation of my words by journalists in city or campus newspapers, and collaboration in a documentary film project. I'd like to write about my experiences of negotiating with a British filmmaker in creating the film *The Desert Is No Lady,* but it's too long a story for this book. Some of the issues: where are the boundaries between creative control and/or scholarly interpretation? Who is funding this production? What are our obligations to them? Why did the director's rough cut give so much space to American Indian women at the expense of southwestern-born Mexican American women? How was I able to argue effectively that this was not an "appropriate" representation? Making the film also increased my sensitivity to the effects of simultaneous representation of the verbal and visual and to the effects on the viewer of different modes of documentary production.

Dear Debby[3]: In my workshop for your international curriculum transformation project I'd like to include clips from three films on Middle Eastern women, work and family. The filmmakers' styles (cutting, presence or absence of narrators, narrators' voices, music, etc.) are so different—I think they have important implications for the ways we use film in the classroom. Faculty in projects we have done at Arizona see film as useful in trying to help students develop empathy with women of other cultures, and more realistic visions (beyond romanticization, exoticization, or victimization), but we need to increase our skills in reading film styles if we are to use film to address students' values and attitudes.—Jan

We haven't been trained to use diverse forms of communication. The National Council for Research on Women's 1995 conference highlighted working with media. We practiced the body language that would give our messages "authenticity" and audience appeal on a TV screen. We struggled (not very successfully) to create a message about affirmative action that would translate academic-style language into an effective communication with a working mother in a representative "woman's job" (niche marketing—but we had trouble defining the niche, let alone the message). To whom do we speak? To whom should we speak if feminist scholarship is to make a difference in society? What media do we use to convey our messages?

Dear Pamela:[4] Thanks for the clipping of Deborah Pearce's column, "Close to Home," from *The Times Colonial* of Victoria, B.C. (deconstructing the column and newspaper titles is too easy) which previews my talks on campus and introduces feminist geography. I was pleased that she used part of my article

Fig. I.3.2. "Interieur met slapende man," painting by Wybrand Hendriks (1744–1831). From Frans Halsmuseum-Haarlem, postcard mailed to Janice Monk by the late Henriette Verduin Muller, April 1986, with the comment "Not a single reference to the women!!" Used courtesy of Frans Halsmuseum De Hallen, Haarlem, Netherlands

that deals with representations of male and female bodies in public monuments as expressions of power in the landscape and found her own local examples (of a male politician and of nude female figures cavorting with a dolphin). That helps connect with readers in Victoria. The headline—"Sir John eh? And who's the naked lady down the way?" must have caught readers who would never look at feminist geographic writing. What was your reaction? Is this what you wanted for press on feminist geography?—Jan

P.S. What response are you getting from feminist geographers to your call for participation in the PRAXIS/NEXUS conference? How to link research and action is on my mind in connection with a collaborative project with Mexican colleagues. We're trying to create a consortium for transborder research and action on women's health that involves crossing disciplinary, national, and

Fig. I.3.3. "Bust of Queen Nefertiti." "In spite of statements to the contrary, neither the origin nor the end of the historical Nefertiti is known. It is known, however, that she not only bore her husband Amenhotep IV/Akhenater six daughters, but also served actively by his side to accomplish his religious reforms. It appears Nefertiti even resided in her own palace during her later years." © *Bildarchiv Preußischer Kulturbesitz,* Berlin. Verein zur Förderung des Ägyptishchen Musuems in Berlin—Charlotteburg e V., Scholssstrasse 70, 1000 Berlin. Used by permission. Postcard mailed to Janice Monk by Maria Dolors García-Ramon from Berlin, Germany, 24 June 1991.

academic/community boundaries. In what ways can we involve community women's organizations in defining our work?

Dear Patricia: "Redefining the Barricades" (chapter 15)— where are our barricades? What are the boundaries between scholarship and activism? I think back to the days of Bill Bunge and the Detroit Geographical Expedition; to geographers' efforts in advocacy planning; to SERGE (Socially and Ecologically Conscious Geographers), a group that is now defunct. Do feminist geographers have skills to contribute to community action? What are the arenas for activism? Must we confine ourselves to analysis? Who defines the problems to address? What impact is feminist geography having/can feminist geography have on the burgeoning work in applied geography? So far there doesn't seem to be much dialogue between applied geography and feminism.—Jan

* * *

Dear Nik: I am really pleased to see you thinking about feminism and cartography (chapter 13). We need to question (or should I say "interrogate" these days?) this classic geographic form of representation—and also to figure out whether/how to use it more effectively ourselves for feminist ends. We have a few feminist atlases—but maps rarely appear in feminist geographic articles and books—only words. What do you think about recent advertisements in feminist newsletters offering "equal area" projections as politically correct views of the world?—Jan

* * *

Dear Patricia and Francine: For me your writing about Latinas (chapters 15 and 18) and about class distinctions among women in English villages raises questions of naming, (fluid) identity, and place. Here are some southwestern takes.—Jan

LEGAL ALIEN

Bi-lingual, Bi-cultural
able to slip from "How's life?"
to *"Me'stan volviendo loca,"*
able to sit in a paneled office
drafting memos in smooth English,
able to order in fluent Spanish
at a Mexican restaurant,
American but hyphenated,
viewed by Anglos as perhaps exotic,
perhaps inferior, definitely different,
viewed by Mexicans as alien,
(their eyes say, "You may speak
Spanish but you're not like me")
an American to Mexicans

a Mexican to Americans
a handy token
sliding back and forth
between the fringes of both worlds
by smiling
by masking the discomfort
of being pre-judged
Bi-laterally.
—Pat Mora[5]

The following excerpt from the script of *The Desert Is No Lady* offers a perspective on the potentially liberating power of place for women[6]:

INT.DAY MS CISNEROS I/V CAPTION SUPERED	03.05 CISNEROS I think for myself there was that split, there was that split, especially when I lived in the Midwest, of having this private language, the language one spoke at home, and then the public language that I was educated in, and the major I was educated in, was English.
EXT. DAY AERIAL H/A VLS BUILDINGS, TRACK R	03.25 CISNEROS V/O But when I moved to the Southwest, what I was given permission to do from living here was to incorporate the voices I saw around me, and those voices mixed Spanish and English a lot more than I'd ever heard in my life.
WS CAR OUTSIDE BARBERS MS GARAGE	I had grown up with Spanish and English but they were separate, and they were also private, and all of a sudden to see Spanish on billboards, and to go into a bathroom and see graffiti, half in English and half in Spanish, and to see it everywhere . . . alive and living around you. So I started borrowing from the mixture of phrases I found in this particular place, in this borderland region
INT. DAY MCU CISNEROS I/V SYNC	04.08 — and using it to inspire me in story titles, and especially to allow the characters themselves, who had never appeared in North American literature, to speak
FADE TO BLACK	04.21 CISNEROS V/O through my stories.

*   *   *

"Gregson and Lowe's study is published in the Routledge *International Studies of Women and Place* series, perhaps an odd decision as the book is firmly based in contemporary Britain. However, their choice is justified in the excellent quality of the product with its extremely clear text and the now-expected stunning black cover."

I have withheld the name of the writer of this review since what I am interested in are its implications, not in criticizing an individual reviewer. Is Britain normative, with other (more exotic—to whom?) places qualifying as "international"? What are the roles of image and design in the promotion and acceptance of scholarship?

Dear Dolores[7]: Did you see the feminist geography review article claiming that nobody is writing about European women? Well, who is nobody? The numerous publications and presentations you and other European feminist geographers have published in English (not only your writings in other languages) continue to be unacknowledged in "mainstream" reviews. Yet you know, cite, and teach the Anglo-American work. The monolingualism of native speakers of English impoverishes our understanding of the possibilities of feminist geography—but that's not all. I worry about the construction of intellectual hegemony in a field that advocates polyvocality and theorizes about diversity—Jan

Fig. I.3.4. "Un marché à Fort-de-France," Photo by Cliché P. Chareton. Postcard mailed to Janice Monk by Helène (Helen Henderson), July 1987.

Fig. I.3.5. "Farmers Market, Los Angeles, Calif." Caption reads "The world's finest produce in exotic displays—hours fresh from the farm" (Plastichrome by Colour-picture, Boston, Mass.). Purchased by Janice Monk in Los Angeles, Calif., October 1964.

Dear Ana[8]: I like your article on gender differences and use of space, particularly your examples that acknowledge the importance of diversity, but discuss it in a different frame of reference from that which is pervasive in the literature in English. It generally invokes "gender, race, and class" and sometimes sexuality, but doesn't often ask how our categories should be sensitive to the contexts we are studying. Your inclusion of family structure, religion, access to health resources, and so on, are responsive to global processes and variations. Your subsequent discussion of the family in southern Europe is a reminder to question our "northern" assumptions. It's also great to see a geographical chapter in an interdisciplinary collection—that's quite rare.—Jan

> **Diversidad**. El análisis de la diversidad implica conocer y reconocer las variaciones territoriales en las relaciones de género: aspectos tales como las estructuras familiares, las prácticas matrimoniales, la religión, el aceso a los recursos educativos y sanitarios ofrecen profundas variaciones sociales y territoriales a nivel mundial, y son determinantes para las relaciones de género, la division del trabajo entre hombres y mujeres y la utilizacion del espacio.[9]

Dear Janet and Vivian[10]: Did you see the review that criticizes authors in *Different Places, Different Voices* for being methodologically timid, failing to deal with diversity of ethnicity, class, etc., presenting empirical case studies without much attention to the theoretical literature . . .? What are the priorities and possibilities of those Asian and African authors you put at the heart of the volume? How is their writing shaped by context, by local intellectual traditions and visions that may not promote the theoretical perspectives that are currently being advanced in Anglo-American scholarship, by their senses of the needs of women in their societies? How does funding by international development agencies shape their research and writing? Is theoretical work always more important than empirical and applied? What categories of difference are appropriate in these settings? Geography matters—Jan

Fig. I.3.6. "Landbouwsberwerken de gron met hak (Rwanda)/Agriculteurs labourant à la houe (Rwanda). © Koninklijk Museum voor Midden-Afrik / Musée Royale d'Afrique Centrale, Tervuren (Belgium). Postcard mailed to Janice Monk by Myra Dinnerstein from Brussels, Belgium, 5 October 1988.

*   *   *

Dear Jeanne: Mormon women's diaries (chapter 17)—did they write them to be read by others? What form of representation is the diary? Is it a private communication or also intended by the writer for later readers? Scholarship on women's diaries indicates that the answers to that question aren't clear cut. We write now about power relationships in research, especially in interviewing—what are the comparable questions with other methodologies? Who donates diaries to archives? What materials are open or restricted? Who imposes the restrictions? I've been doing oral histories with women geographers and see generational differences in the discourse (especially around sexuality). Then there are the times the speaker asks me to turn off the tape, yet still wants to tell me the story.—Jan

*   *   *

Dear Bronwen: If we think context is an important influence on representation, then comparative analyses such as yours can highlight issues that might be overlooked when the study focuses on one place (chapter 16). But comparative work poses new challenges. What are the hazards of being (relatively) an outsider in one context and an insider in the other? How do we deal with critics who want more attention to diversity among women *within* contexts but don't seem very interested in differences between or among contexts? At what geographic scales should we attempt comparative work? How do we deal with the disparate nature, qualities, and accessibility of sources across contexts?—Jan

*   *   *

Dear Sue, JP, and Heidi: How have you experienced collaborative organizing and editing? What have been the costs and rewards? Collaboration used to be promoted as a feminist ideal—do you remember that *Geography and Gender* identified the authors as the "Women and Geography Study Group of the Institute of British Geographers"? I was at first surprised that all the papers you received were single authored. Does this reflect individualism or a realistic (or automatic) response to academic conventions in the social sciences that credit is awarded for sole authorship? It's interesting that the "masculinist" sciences have different collaborative conventions (though there may be teams that are competing). Some feminist geographers are still questioning authorship norms, however. Julie Graham and Kathy Gibson have taken to signing their coauthored works J. K. Gibson-Graham.[11] Susan Hanson and Gerry Pratt/Gerry Pratt and Susan Hanson reverse their order of authorship for various pieces (and their book *Gender, Work and Space* has an unusual discussion of the roles and reactions of research assistants in their project). In what order are you going to list yourselves on the cover?—Jan.

*   *   *

Dear Readers: You may be looking for a summary or conclusion to this introduction. Heidi's reading of the draft identified seven points. Since the draft I've added some ideas. But I've decided not to write a paragraph to tell you what I've told you. Indeed, sometimes when I read what others have seen in my articles I'm struck by the varieties of interpretations. So instead of writing my own conclusions, I'd like to know what you are thinking. Please send me a postcard.—Jan

Notes

1. *Webster's seventh new collegiate dictionary* (1965) (Springfield MA: G and C. Merriam Company).

2. My messages to the other authors relate to their conference presentations rather than to the published versions of their work.

3. Deborah Rosenfelt, Curriculum Transformation Project, Women's Studies Program and Department, University of Maryland, College Park, MD, U.S.A.

4. Pamela Moss, Department of Geography, University of Victoria, Victoria, B.C., Canada.

5. Pat Mora, "Legal Alien," in Pat Mora (1985), *Chants* (Houston, TX: Arte Publico Press).

6. *The desert is no lady*, Shelley Williams, Director/Producer, Janice Monk, Executive Producer. Feline Films and the Southwest Institute for Research on Women. Distributors, London: Arts Council of England / New York: Women Make Movies.

7. Maria Dolors García-Ramon, Department of Geography, Autonomous University of Barcelona, Spain (or should I say, Catalonia?): It's always problematic to represent your name. "Dolores" to your English-speaking friends; "Maria Dolors to your colleagues" in Barcelona; Garcia with or without an accent on the "i", depending on choice of Castillian or Catalan orthography (but García is the Castillian part of your name); to hyphenate García-Ramon or not (you wouldn't in Spain, but if we don't do it for an English language publication, you'll be alphabetized under "R").

8. Ana Sabaté Martinez, Department of Geography, Complutense University of Madrid, Spain.

9. Ana Sabaté Martinez, "Diferencias Territoriales y Análisis de Género: Un Enfoque Global," en *El Espacio Según El Género: Un Uso Diferencial* (1995) (Edición a cargo de Constanza Tobio y Conche Denche, Departamento de Humanidades, Ciencias Politicas, y Sociologia. Communidad de Madrid. Dirección General de la Mujer).

10. Janet H. Momsen, Department of Applied Behavioral Sciences, University of California, Davis, and Vivian Kinnaird, Department of Geography, University of Sunderland, U.K.

11. See, for example, J. K. Gibson-Graham "Beyond Patriarchy: Reflections on Political Subjectivity," in B. Caine and R. Pringle (eds) *Transitions: New Australian feminisms* (1995) (St. Leonard, NSW, Australia: Allen and Unwin).

13

Charting the Other Maps: Cartography and Visual Methods in Feminist Research

Nikolas H. Huffman

Cartography and visual methods historically have been vital aspects of the geographer's imagination and have served as powerful images and tools in creating and sharing geographical knowledge (Muehrcke 1981). While I shall argue in this chapter that traditional cartographic practice has been constructed as a masculinist enterprise, this chapter is deeply motivated by Susan Ford's (1991, 151) claim that "visual communication would seem too powerful an arena to be given up to men." Just as feminist geographers have done for theory in geography, I shall argue that cartography and other visual methods need not be written off as essentially masculinist in form. Instead, we should acknowledge that "women have different spaces, mapped on different grids than men" (Rose 1991, 160), and feminist geographers can engage new cartographic methods for representing women's geographies, spaces, and experiences through maps.

This chapter then initiates a feminist critique of cartography and maps in order to retheorize the boundaries of the cartographic enterprise, address the masculinist foundations of traditional Western cartography, and explore other cartographies and maps excluded by Western cartography. The goal of this paper is to ground an explicitly feminist cartographic practice that better addresses the concerns of feminist geographical, political, and epistemological theory and serves to recover the power and pleasure of maps to serve feminist interests by highlighting the role of vision and the gendered body in the production of cartographic knowledge.

Mapping Ambivalent Bodies

Since the 1980s, feminist geographers have contributed to the development of new cultural geographies, while also expressing serious reservations about these new perspectives, in part because they have continued to exhibit biases found in previous social theories, such as the implicit and explicit sexism in the geographical outlook, research questions, and writing of many geographers (Massey 1991). In 1991, Gillian Rose expressed her own ambivalence about this new direction in academic geography, arguing that while she was an active participant in this geographic discourse, she also felt herself to be fundamentally different from her male peers and excluded from (and by) this discourse because of its decided failure to address the interests and experiences of women (Rose 1991).

Within the field of cartography, women in organizations such as the International Cartographic Association have also begun to raise and grapple with the issue of masculinism within the discipline. Although primarily concerned with improving the status, number, and working conditions of women involved in cartography professionally, these groups have also questioned negative stereotypes about women's spatial skills in using maps and the lack of academic interest in women's and gender issues as suitable concerns for cartographic research and map content.

According to Rose, her experience of difference and exclusion as a woman in academia arises in part from the Western intellectual tradition in which the discourse on knowledge and the body has historically cast men and women as fundamentally different beings. Through numerous historical variations, this discourse has cast men as superior, rational beings engaged in a purified, disembodied intellectual project through the transcendence of the male body, while females were cast as wholly under the influence of their bodily emotions and desires, incapable of transcending their embodiment and thus irrational and inferior creatures.

Feminists have criticized these traditional scientific epistemologies, or ways of knowing, as "masculinist" because they are based on a fundamentally gendered understanding of knowledge and bodies that depends on the active denial of the male body. This disembodied knowledge is rooted in the privileged position of an autonomous, objective, and masculine knower: Donna Haraway's straight, White, bourgeois male "master subject" (1991, 192). By denying its own gendered embodiment, the master subject defines everything in reference to its disembodied and ungendered self, while simultaneously defining and differentiating itself against that which it is not, the embodied and gendered female other.

Rose (1993, 4) argues that traditional geography is also masculinist for claiming to be exhaustive while ignoring women and construing male experience to be synonymous with human experience. For instance, women's experiences of space as bounded and constrained are erased by the concept of unbounded space, which only White heterosexual men actually have the freedom to enjoy without fear and constraint. In contesting the masculinist vision of a universalized and transparently knowable space, feminist geographers have held up "the map" as the quintessential symbol of masculinist ways of knowing, the ultimate representation of masculinist space. For Pile and Rose

(1991, 131), "maps institutionalize a certain understanding of space, certain claims to objective world views" that are grounded in "space as an actual structure, a geometry, a grid, a matrix, its relationship to society fully theorizable."

On the other hand, Patricia Price-Chalita (1994, 243) points out that "the map" has been used as an epistemological metaphor that challenges the complete and transparent knowledge assumed by the traditional map (Price-Chalita 1994). Feminist theorists, such as Donna Haraway (1992), Katie King (1990), and Chandra Mohanty (1991), have argued for the need to draft new types of "maps," new forms of knowledge, that "can be used as fluid guides for re-working and resisting established power relationships" and that foster dynamic and nontotalizing epistemological values.

In this paper, I want to go beyond these metaphorical "maps" to look at maps per se: maps as real cultural artifacts and as objects of geographical knowledge: maps that can be found at gas stations, in magazines, or scribbled on napkins. Most important, I want to look at maps and graphics that are sketched out during the research process and published to support arguments visually. Expanding on feminist geographers' recent efforts to explore women's ways of writing spaces (Blunt and Rose 1994), I shall look at the production of cartographic images of women's spaces and experiences, and different ways that maps can be used in feminist research. I believe that cartography is a powerful visual method that is too important for feminist geographers to simply forsake, and argue for a feminist cartographic practice that offers new perspectives on maps and mapmaking that resist totalizing masculinist knowledge and explore other cartographies that will enable feminists to chart women's geographies on their own grids and maps.

To facilitate a feminist cartographic theory, it is vital to challenge the historical discourse on knowledge and gendered bodies and to address the role of the body in creating cartographic knowledge. Rose argues that feminist geographers need to sustain a "strategic ambivalence" between constructivist and essentialist theories of gender difference in order to counter the complex discourses of "masculinist" geography. Constructivist feminists argue that notions of femininity and masculinity are culturally produced. On the other hand, essentialist feminists start from the fundamental positioning of subjectively different bodies denied by the constructivists. For Rose, it is strategically necessary to maintain this ambivalence in order to introduce and emphasize gender as a category fundamental to understanding human experience, while also demonstrating that gender is not inherently natural but organized within complex social and power relations.

Additionally, "gender issues" should not be seen as simply equivalent to "women's issues," because gender constitutes the social relationships between men and women, and thus concerns both men and women. In this sense, I regard feminism as an inclusive perspective that acknowledges both women and men, placing men on par with women as equally embodied and gendered persons. This stands in contrast to the masculinism of modern science that has excluded women to the benefit of men through a disembodied, masculinist epistemology and scientific practice.

The explicitly feminist cartographic practice suggested in this chapter—based on politics rather than some "pure" feminist epistemology (Tuana 1989)—is derived from Harding's (1989) feminist methodology that engages the following three gender practices. First is the feminist's focus on gender and its consequences as a variable and analytic category in research. As a relevant concern in cartography, one can consider gender issues in map content, in map use, in mapmaking as a profession, and in the social construction of gendered spaces. Second, feminist methods commonly rely on women's experience as a resource for selecting research questions and providing explanations to phenomena that address women's concerns, thus countering the masculinist blindness toward women's experience and exploring and representing geographies of women in and through maps. Finally, feminist methods exhibit a gender-sensitive reflexivity that sets the researcher in the same critical plane as the subject matter under study and calls upon the researcher to place the entire research process under scrutiny, including the representation of gendered spaces on maps, as well as the relationship between knowledges and the gendered body.

Utilizing this feminist methodology, I shall explore the notion of cartography as a visual method for feminist research. I argue that feminist geographers can extend the boundaries of the map to include new cartographic methods that are responsive to the social, political, and epistemological concerns of feminist researchers. First, I outline a broad social theory of cartography that highlights the active production and inscribed spatial qualities of maps. Next, I present a critical feminist history of Western cartography that confronts the masculinist epistemology of disembodied knowledge that grounds modern cartography and reveals masculinist practices within the discipline of cartography. Finally, I argue for a feminist theory of cartographic visualization that draws its strength from acknowledging gendered subject positions and the perspectives of the observer through Haraway's epistemology of situated knowledge. This feminist cartographic theory and practice seeks to resist totalizing masculinist knowledge and offers new perspectives on maps and mapmaking for feminist research that explore other cartographies that will enable feminists to chart women's geographies, spaces, and experiences on their own grids and maps.

Cartographies and Other Maps

In this section, I argue that considering cartography from the perspective of contemporary social theory offers a more comprehensive theory of mapping that allows one to include many types of maps excluded by the classical Western definition of "the map." This is achieved by focusing on the general features that unite maps across a broad range of cultures, including the reflexive representation and production of social space, the social production of map images, and the role of visual technologies, such as cartographic media, spatial geometries, and map grids. Expanding the boundaries of what we acknowledge as maps is central to facilitating a feminist critique of masculinism in Western cartography, and to grounding a specifically feminist cartographic practice that acknowledges gendered bodies in mapping and explores new modes of cartographic representation.

In countering the essential Western definition of the map, I draw upon Haraway's idea of objects as "boundary projects" whose fluid meanings are mapped out by our efforts to understand and define them (1991, 201). According to MacEachren (1995, 150–62), the cognitive category of "the map" is an unbounded and fuzzy category, which sets the boundaries of the viewer's interpretation of a map-like object as a "map" in relation to a prototypical map along defining axes, such as physical scale and abstractness of the image. Liben and Downs (1986) consistently found the small-scale world political map to be the prototypical map among their (American) subjects of mixed ages and gender.

This map, however, is the common prototype exactly because we are inundated with such maps that make visible a global political world we recognize and understand. We respond almost exclusively to such images of the world as "maps" because they fit the Western model of the map: empirically surveyed scientific images of an objective, transparently knowable physical world. Because our categories derive from our experience with the maps we see around us and the ways we perceive and understand the world, we also fail to recognize as maps other images of the world that do not fit these strict scientific boundaries.

But recent scholarship has clearly shown that there are other maps in the world, other ways of knowing and looking at the world (Harley and Woodward 1987; Turnbull 1989). Different cultures have different social spaces, and produce very different kinds of maps. In fact, some researchers have come to believe that mapping is an innate environmental behavior exhibited in humans, and many animals as well (Blaut 1991). We have a natural awareness of our environment that we communicate to other people through actions, language, or graphics, however different societies have clearly produced mapping traditions of varying degrees of complexity.

In response, map scholars have posed new definitions of cartography that address how other cultures have viewed, conceived, and represented space through graphic images. Wood, on the other hand, has argued that maps are not mere images of our human worlds, but has questioned how all cultures have used maps in creating and understanding the social worlds around them. For Wood, the map is "a social construction of reality" (1993, 52) that serves to create the social and political spaces they represent by linking the territory depicted on the map with the social and spatial mandates that go with the map.

Similarly, Lefebvre has argued that "(social) space is a (social) product"

(1991, 26), and has proposed a "conceptual triad" that serves to explore the role of maps in the social construction of space by teasing out the complex interrelation between the experience and production of space through our ideas, actions, and experiences (Roberts and Schein 1995). The spatial practices of a society are composed of the physical and built environments, as well as the connections and relations that order and differentiate social space and interaction; representations of space are the conceptual and semiotic structures that order and organize space, and how spaces are understood and represented intellectually; and finally, representational spaces are the lived symbolic meanings of spaces experienced directly and unreflexively through the body immersed within the environment. Each aspect is constantly and inseparably intertwined with and reinforced by each of the others, and is subject to continual revision and renewal as the constitution of social space evolves. Together, these aspects constitute social space as a texture—as opposed to a transparently knowable structure—that is lived through the images, networks, and hierarchies that order space in a fluid and interactive way.

While Lefebvre's conceptual triad can be applied to understanding social spaces and images of space in general, here I use what I call Wood's "sociology of cartography" as a starting point for understanding maps and mapping specifically. For Wood, it is the specific act of inscription, producing a mark or a sign—a representation of space—that distinguishes mapping behavior from mental mapping, speech, or body language. Inscriptions are graphic images, not just in the visual sense, but, like tactile maps for the visually impaired, "graphic" in the sense of being written, tangible artifacts. Graphic production is fundamental to mapping: "the map is always inscribed" (Wood 1993, 51), whether it is lasting like a USGS topographic map or ephemeral like the outline of an island drawn in the sand and washed away with the next high tide.

Additionally, I argue that maps are representations of space that use the graphic spatial grid of the inscription to construct an image of (social) spaces. Space in the world is linked to the inscribed grid through geometries, or systems for organizing, describing, and measuring space. The familiar abstract Euclidean geometry used for measuring physical spatial relationships is not the only way of measuring and representing the world. One can also utilize relational geometries that measure space based on our personal experiences of space or other, non-Euclidean relationships between objects in space. For instance, Native American maps very accurately reflect the topology of river networks, and in the Marshall Islands, maps are based on the relationship between islands and ocean currents.

Wood makes a further distinction between maps and mappings based on the different ways inscription media are used in map production. For Wood (1993), mappings, such as sketch maps, are ephemeral images that share spatial information between people engaged in interpersonal communication, but whose meaning and utility evaporate upon leaving the communication setting. On the other hand, the map is a tangible, graphic record that has a stable presence of its own and is intended to bear its meaning beyond the immediate mapping setting through shared interpretable cartographic codes (Wood 1993, 82). Mapmaking differs from mapping because it allows one to consolidate the power of recreating spaces in the form of a map that can be carried away from the scene, manipulated, compared to, and integrated with other images and spaces.

This distinction carries over to the societies in general (Wood 1993). Mapping societies use, but don't rely on, consistent patterns of mapping to conduct and maintain their social lives. Mapmaking societies, on the other hand, engage in social, economic, and spatial practices that require the collection and maintenance of a variety of stable records to facilitate and manage social, political, and bureaucratic control over the society. These records tend to constantly produce new types of records, such as census lists and property deeds, as well as more complex graphic records such as maps. These map records are based on complex systems of graphic codes and visualization technologies, such as surveying and maps projections, that structure how maps are inscribed, interpreted, and utilized. Maps require shared sign systems to be broadly socially useful and we are all generally familiar with the various visual technologies of Western cartography. In our society, maps have become so common that we barely even notice them all around us, and there is such a diverse variety of printed, and now electronic, maps that we have become a "map-immersed society" (Wood 1993, 56).

In this section, I have outlined a definition of maps as images that are inscribed, spatial representations of space that use graphic grids to represent images of social space through a variety of cartographic grids, mapping media, and visual technologies. Understanding and focusing on these basic elements of mapping and mapmaking offers a broad theory of cartography that will facilitate a feminist critique of masculinism in Western cartography, as well as ground a more inclusive perspective on maps to begin the exploration of new modes of cartography for feminist research efforts to address gendered spaces, geographies, and experiences. In exploring a variety of cartographic images, one needs to address the personal, gendered, and cultural differences in the experience and representation of social space, the active production of map inscriptions, the different geometries and grids used to measure and map space, the variety of ephemeral and lasting media used to inscribe maps, and the many visual technologies used to construct maps.

Feminist Histories of Masculinist Cartography

Drawing upon contemporary social theory of cartography, in this section I propose a feminist critique of the masculinist foundations of traditional Western cartography that is built upon an abstract, disembodied, and "masculine" epistemology of objective knowledge. Bordo (1987) has argued that this masculinization of modern science was a gendered psychological and philosophical reaction to the emergence of abstract social space in early Modern Europe.

This masculine epistemology served as the basis for the institutionalization of a masculinist scientific and cartographic practice that systematically has acted to exclude women, which can be seen in the ensuing history of women in cartography, and how masculinity is reflected in maps as images of power and in the virtual silence about women in the disciplinary discourse of academic cartography.

Masculinization of Cartography

The analysis of the masculinization of knowledge and cartography is based on Bordo's (1987) psychocultural reading of the transformation of social space around the time of the Renaissance, which Lefebvre (1991, 234–48) describes as a shift from relational, absolute space to abstract space. According to Lefebvre, medieval societies lived immersed in absolute social spaces that were situated, perceived, and interpreted in terms of sacred spaces, such as the hierarchy of Catholic religious centers, and that were given meaning through representational spaces that are lived rather than conceived. Feudal and ecclesiastical domains existed as the hub of the social and political worlds that radiated from these sacred spaces. Medieval maps express this sense of absorption in an absolute ecclesiastical world through hierarchical and multi-perspectival geometries based on the relationships of meaning between people and places in a cosmology that ordered the world around Jerusalem and the Church.

Although socially extremely misogynous, the medieval natural world was viewed as a feminine maternal receptacle, a receptive materiality that was impregnated by the active and masculine spiritual world of Forms and Truth. Through the Renaissance there existed a set of epistemological values associated with "feminine consciousness" (Keller 1985, 102) that viewed people as an integral part of the world, mimetically and inseparably connected to it. This epistemology of sympathetic understanding posited a union between subject and object, which merged and mutually participated in the creation of meaning (Keller 1985).

In the late medieval period, this epistemology of sympathetic union ruptured as Western Europe underwent a profound transformation from within the absolute social spaces of the medieval world into the abstract "space of accumulation" of the modern world (Lefebvre 1991, 248–91). The birth of the modern world of abstract social space initiated a cultural "drama of parturition" (Bordo 1987, 5) which followed from an increasing sense of separateness from the ruptured medieval world.

Lefebvre's abstract social space emerged during the Renaissance as spatial practices and representations of space were reflexively linked through the abstract political authority of the new urban commercial classes and a powerful trend toward visualization underpinned by abstraction. The active production and reconstruction of urban space became the merchants' most powerful weapon in negotiating new relations of space and power between the feudal oligarchy and the merchant classes. Cities were conceived as independent abstract political entities and individual towns emerged as subjects, assuming abstract identities defined by representations of space and social spaces of power addressed to the intellect, whose meanings delineated the power and boundaries of the town.

The production of urban spaces was facilitated by the application of new abstract graphic representations of space for conceiving, ordering, and representing things within a universalized Euclidean space structured by the empirical measurement of physical spatial relationships. These representations of space were first conceived and represented graphically and then inscribed directly upon the urban social space through an architectural unity that linked visualization techniques, architecture-as-practice, and the spatial practice of the new, planned urban spaces.

The emergence of abstract social spaces and representations of space coincided with an increased recognition of the subjective locatedness of all knowledge claims. The techniques of perspective reminded viewers that all vision occurred from a specific point of view, while bodily sense perceptions became internal and unreliable sensory judgments, and knowledge of the New World underscored the point that truths are perhaps more deeply tied to cultural values than to any Truth in the world.

In her psychocultural reading of Descartes's *Meditations*, Bordo (1987) argues that there is a similarity between cultural and individual cognitive development. Children are born in a state of complete immersion in their perceptual worlds, unable to distinguish between their selves and the world. Through experience and interaction, they undergo "individuation" and isolate their perceptions of themselves from their perceptions of the world external to themselves. Similarly, Bordo argues that medieval societies were culturally immersed in their absolute spatial worlds. Bordo argues that the early modern world underwent a similar cultural individuation through the emergence of abstract social space. The philosophical individuation and development of inwardness and locatedness lead to the adoption of an epistemology of disembodied objectivity as a reaction to this increased cultural recognition of subjective locatedness of knowledge claims.

Locatedness describes the emerging sense of personal boundedness and presence in a distinct spatial position, such as that seen in Renaissance art that arranged images geometrically based on their specific physical locations rather than their symbolic relationships with other objects in the image. Inwardness describes the emerging belief in an internal, spiritual being or mind that separated internal thought from the external world and divided our experiences into interior and exterior worlds, as opposed to the prior belief in the insurmountable union of subject and object in the world.

The subsequent sense of separation and alienation from a previously undifferentiated world produced "separation anxiety" over the loss of unity with the world. Bordo argues that while writing the *Meditations,* Descartes was experiencing this separation anxiety on a cultural level as the emerging modern world alienated the knowing subject from the existing immersed world. Descartes's doubts about the validity of knowledge of the new world of objects can be read as a "reaction-formation," a pragmatic defense against the birth of the modern world and the loss of connection with the world. This anxiety was dealt with by making the separation of self and world the central key to knowledge in the modern world and by pressing this separation to its absolute limit, pure objectivity.

The Cartesian epistemic program for pure objectivity required the purification of the mind of the "detached neutral observer" through passive perception of the external world with complete and disinterested accuracy. This state of "clear and distinct perception" required the active transcendence of the body, and this disembodied intellect had to be continually on guard against the influences of bodily desires and emotions. The institutionalization of abstract representations of space and the Cartesian epistemology of disembodied knowledge helped entrench empiricism and the hegemony of physical, Euclidean geometry as the sole valid representations of (masculinist) space. Additionally, the rhetoric of scientific objectivity naturalized these abstract representations of space by claiming that the nature of concrete worldly objects corresponds directly with these objective images. In effect, this "rhetorically orchestrated denial of rhetoric" (Wood and Fels 1992, 115) reconstructs the world in the image of our representations of space, in turn giving scientific inscriptions the appearance of natural and objective images.

Bordo describes an "aggressive intellectual flight from the feminine" (100) as another aspect of early modern thinking, whereby philosophers dealt with their separation anxiety through an explicit "masculinization of thought" promoted through the Cartesian ideals of clarity, distinctness, and disembodied rationality, and the active repudiation of the feminine epistemological values, such as the empathy and union with the object associated with medieval epistemology. Coincident with this masculinization of knowledge came a concerted effort to gain mastery over the object of separation, the (feminine) material world, the epistemological denial that a union with that world had ever existed, and the cultural denial of the feminine soul of nature and its replacement by a mechanistic, nonliving material world (Merchant 1980).

These explicit metaphors of "masculine" and "feminine" knowledge were central to the debates over appropriate epistemologies for the scientific work, and the mechanistic and objectivist masculine epistemology was hailed by proto-scientists such as Francis Bacon as the only way to true knowledge (Keller 1985). Preliminary research by Dalia Varanka (1994) has shown that masculine epistemological claims were also part of the language sustaining and valorizing empirical, scientific cartographic practice. Thus, it is important to look beyond the masculine epistemology of cartography to consider how women have been systematically excluded from cartographic institutions, as well as how the research concerns of male scientists have subsequently and routinely ignored women's concerns and experiences.

Cartography and Masculinism

Bordo's arguments apply specifically to the masculine foundations of modern scientific epistemology, but other important arguments have been raised addressing masculinism in modern science in the form of women's exclusion from scientific institutions (Alic 1986) and misogyny in scientific practice (Schiebinger 1989). In this section, I look at some of the gendered consequences of masculinism in the history of cartography, in modern cartographic practice, and in the production of map images.

Surprisingly, within the discipline of geography, women have actually been best represented—which is not to say well represented—in the field of cartography (Monk 1994). The presence of women in cartography might be attributable to the fact that although scientific and military institutions actively excluded women, the emerging commercial mapping industry included many family-owned mapmakers and sellers, where women participated in and later inherited the business.

Whatever the reasons, there has been a significant historical presence of women in professional cartography, which is only now being revealed by map historians (Hudson 1989; McMichael Ritzlin 1989; Gilmartin 1990). As part of her ongoing archaeology of women cartographers, Alice Hudson has been uncovering historical maps that woman have played an integral role in (Hudson 1989), such as Virginia Farrar's map of the colony of Virginia. Such projects cast light onto the historical invisibility of women cartographers, but also question the role of gendered divisions in craft skills and artistic media, and whose labor and products are culturally valued, commercially rewarded, and critically evaluated. Women have produced a rich history of quilted and embroidered educational maps (Tyner 1994), which like other "women's" crafts have been denigrated in the academic art and design communities in favor of the more industrially inclined maps engraved and printed by men (Buckley 1989).

In his essay on "silences and secrecy" in cartography, Harley (1988) argues that what a statement—whether a map or a historical essay—does not say is as important and revealing as what that statement does say. Arising from the unspoken biases internal to a particular cultural system, Harley's "unintentional silences" are particularly revealing of the masculinist character of the cartographic discipline (Huffman 1995). The discipline's determined silence regarding women in the history of cartography is a manifestation of the exclusion of women from the profession, as those few women who succeeded as cartographers actively have been written out of the history as well (Hudson 1989).

In her analysis of the Paris Academy of Sciences, Terrall (1995) shows how science was institutionalized as a strictly male arena by actively excluding women from scientific practice, while allowing socially influential women and "uneducated" men to share in the fruits of science in the role of feminized spectators lead to truth by the heroic, masculine scientists. Women were believed to lack the capacity for disembodied masculine reason because their minds were too influenced by their frivolous and emotional feminine bodies. Systematic efforts to deny women access to rigorous scientific education and to exclude them from the primary institutions of science because of their sex have effectively constructed a gendered geography of scientific practice that has explicitly barred women from the sciences. This gendered geography of science, which follows from Bruno Latour's sociology of science (Latour 1987), has been produced by limiting women's access to the privileged spaces of science where knowledge is created, challenged, and consolidated: the universities, research laboratories, and field study sites, as well as the academic journals and meetings where knowledge is shared (Middleton 1964).

Furthermore, the absence of women in the profession is self-justifying and makes young women hesitant to join the field as a career in the absence of role models. The hesitancy toward maps and cartography has also been reinforced by cultural stereotypes about women's poor map skills, often supported by geographical and psychological research on such gender differences. However, Kumler and Buttenfield's review of this research area shows that there have been no conclusive and reliable findings demonstrating women's weaker spatial and map use skills (Kumler and Buttenfield 1995). Fausto-Sterling (1985, 1992) has criticized research on gender differences in other fields for its decided predisposition toward biological (essentialist) explanations, thus raising the argument that better explanations of these differences could be found with greater attention given to the socially reproduced (constructivist) differences in spatial abilities arising from women's different spatial practices and experiences.

Finally, recent feminist psychoanalytical critiques of landscape imagery in cultural geography offer the potential to extend the analysis of masculinism into the creation and reading of maps themselves. Rose (1993) discusses the White, heterosexual, masculinist "visual ideology" that structures the construction and analysis of landscapes in cultural geography, and Ford (1991) engages this structuring "male gaze" in an effort to address the possibility of "feminist spectatorship" and visual methods in feminist research. In a reading of landscape images that applies analogously to cartographic images, Ford draws on work by feminist film theorist Linda Mulvey (Mulvey 1975) to show how landscape images, in their construction and the manner in which they are used, represent masculine images of power that satisfy erotic and power desires for control and possession of the landscape and work to affirm and enhance masculinist social power structures.

Ford's primary concern is the feminist appropriation of the power and pleasure of visual imagery and she asks herself, "Can I, as a feminist geographer, politically and morally inhabit the 'male gaze'?" In the next section, I shall explicitly address this question, and investigate feminist maps that dress up in the power and pleasure of the Western map while establishing a critical feminist perspective, as well as new cartographic methods for feminist research that resist the masculinist spaces of the Western map.

Feminist Cartographies and Other Maps

Although critical social theory has raised important critiques of the social, cultural, and political aspects of cartography, mapmaking itself has remained tightly bound to its eminently practical geometric, empiricist traditions, yielding only a few new critical mapping projects and cultural cartographies to challenge our standard view of the map (Bunge 1969; Peters 1983; Kidron and Segal 1984). For feminist geographers, the exploration of new cartographic methods is important for appropriating tools that have long been part of the geographer's craft and participating in the game of science, which is vital for researchers interested in creating real knowledge, "enforceable reliable accounts" that matter in the power-matrices of society and academia (Haraway 1991, 188).

In this final section, I argue that feminist cartography is a viable and fruitful addition to the critical practice of feminist geography and its effort to address women's geographies, spaces, and experiences. Feminist geographers can recover the power and pleasure of maps through a feminist cartographic practice that works in opposition and resistance to masculinist Western cartography and explores other modes of cartographic vision that strive to make women's spaces visible. Feminist cartography grounds these other maps by adopting an epistemology of embodiment and working from a definition of cartography that acknowledges different modes of production and cartographic media, and a variety of graphic grids and geometries of experience, as well as addresses the role of both visual technologies and our gendered bodies in the production of cartographic images.

Haraway (1991, 193–95) argues that visualization can be resurrected from its abstract, disembodying practice by treating all vision and visualization as embodying practices that force us to acknowledge and account for the entire arena of visual production. She insists on the recognition that all vision implies a standpoint and a position, as well as the power to see. Drawing upon her epistemology of "situated knowledge," feminist cartographers should acknowledge the biology of human vision, the various visual technologies of mapping, the semiotic production of cartographic meaning, and the power to observe in our geographic and cartographic projects. Reconstructing the essential Cartesian metaphor of objectivity, Haraway's epistemology highlights the role of the body and visual production in creating knowledge, and means accepting responsibility for one's embodiment and vision, one's knowledge, and one's social practices.

The "scientific objectivity" of traditional Western maps can be repositioned

Fig. 13.1. (On following two pages) Job ghettos from *The Atlas of Women in the World*. This map subverts its own traditional Western style by representing women's geographies, fracturing cartographic grids, and encouraging readers to question the mapping process. (Courtesy of Myraid Publishing)

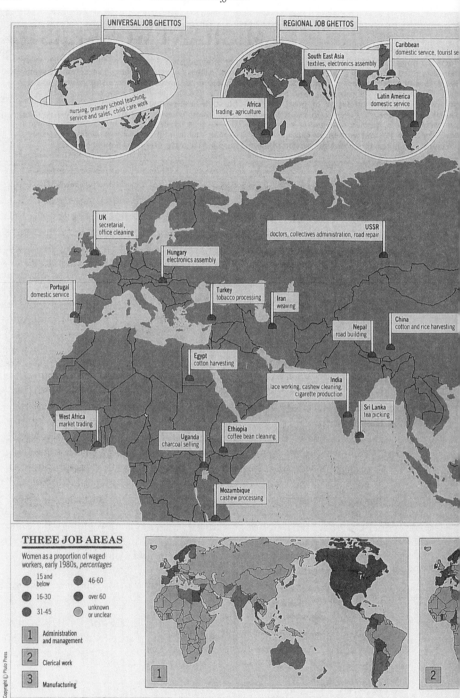

UNIVERSAL JOB GHETTOS

nursing, primary school teaching, service and sales, child care work

REGIONAL JOB GHETTOS

South East Asia
textiles, electronics assembly

Caribbean
domestic service, tourist se

Africa
trading, agriculture

Latin America
domestic service

UK
secretarial, office cleaning

USSR
doctors, collectives administration, road repair

Hungary
electronics assembly

Portugal
domestic service

Turkey
tobacco processing

Iran
weaving

Nepal
road building

China
cotton and rice harvesting

Egypt
cotton harvesting

India
lace working, cashew cleaning, cigarette production

Sri Lanka
tea picking

West Africa
market trading

Uganda
charcoal selling

Ethiopia
coffee bean cleaning

Mozambique
cashew processing

THREE JOB AREAS

Women as a proportion of waged workers, early 1980s, *percentages*

- 15 and below
- 16-30
- 31-45
- 46-60
- over 60
- unknown or unclear

1 Administration and management

2 Clerical work

3 Manufacturing

JOB GHETTOS 18

WORK

he range of jobs that women fill in the workforce is uch narrower than for men. And, in every country d every region of the world, there are jobs that are ecifically defined as 'women's work'. These are the bs that are filled almost exclusively by women – d are usually considered beneath men's station.

In some countries, almost all bank tellers and cretaries are women. In other countries, tea pick-g and cotton harvesting are considered women's work. In Latin America and the Caribbean, domestic service is almost entirely feminized, and up to 80 per cent of all women who earn wages work as servants. In South East Asia, textile manufacturing and electronics assembly rely heavily on female labour – and, especially, on a young, female workforce.

Although specifics vary, it is universally true that jobs defined as women's work carry low pay, low status, and little security: thus termed, 'job ghettos'.

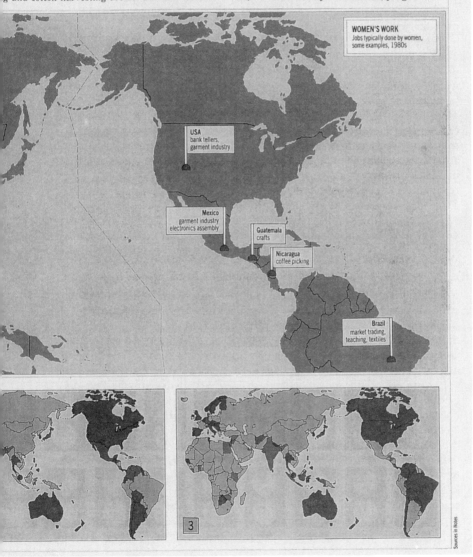

WOMEN'S WORK
Jobs typically done by women, some examples, 1980s

USA
bank tellers, garment industry

Mexico
garment industry electronics assembly

Guatemala
crafts

Nicaragua
coffee picking

Brazil
market trading, teaching, textiles

3

Sources in Notes

to address explicitly the impact of the observer's perspective and the visual technologies of mapping in the meanings of the map. It is important that traditional cartographic methods remain accessible to feminist geographers because they are the most familiar and powerful maps, but these maps can also be used subversively to challenge the masculinist epistemologies and perspectives of the "scientific" representation of space. Subversive feminist maps rely on the familiar elements of Western maps; they also employ representation of space that undermine the assumption of an objective and transparently knowable space. Similarly, by introducing women's experiences of space into cartographic images, subversive feminist maps challenge cartography's traditional masculinism.

Masculinist biases in geography have created a decided absence of thematic maps that represent women's spaces and experiences. However, in the last decade, there have appeared a group of feminist atlases that have mapped women's issues and experiences, while also exploring more appropriate representations of space (Gibson and Fast 1986; Seager and Olson 1986; Shortridge 1987). These atlases break the silence about women as subjects of cartographic inquiry by overtly focusing on women's and gender issues that subvert the more common apolitical historical and geographical emphasis of atlases. These feminist cartographers also employ a gender-sensitive reflexivity in actively trying to highlight problems of experience, data collection, and representation rather than hiding them behind the design. In Seager's, the use of a fractured basemap and overlapping projections and scales on the page subverts the traditional sense of cartographic accuracy while highlighting the various local, regional, and global concerns of women. The cartographers have created a series of comprehensive but critical statements that reveal both the extent and the limits of the available data, while giving a strong sense of the overlapping personal and political geographies of the labor markets open to women (figure 13.1). By employing a creative and colorful variety of relevant symbolization techniques throughout the book and by simply leaving holes on the map where data are missing, the designers help the reader contextualize this extensive look at women in the world, while also prompting the reader to critically analyze and question each data set as well as the book's own cartographic process.

Playing off traditional archeological drawings, Lydia Mihelič Pulsipher (1995) proactively uses the colonial landscape view to challenge the implicit objective view-from-nowhere of this perspective (figure 13.2). Similar to her work on Galways Mountain (chapter 14, this volume), she reflects on her own experience as a marginalized woman in academia and in the field, and turns that experience back onto her work by actively trying to subvert the processes by which she might be marginalizing the subjects of her own studies. Acknowledging that she cannot separate herself from her position as a White academic outsider, she engages such drawings as representational "means for negotiating discrete political agendas" (291). She critically engages the act of

Fig. 13.2. The Marin *Ohana* (Houseyard) of the 1830s. This image utilizes a traditional colonial representation, but undermines its marginalizing power through the author's critical production and her reflexive interaction with local people in shaping an image that allows both parties to benefit from her research. (Courtesy of Lydia Mihelič Pulsipher)

representing landscapes to create a more reflexive and accessible graphic archeological resource that forces her into a closer, more intimate reading of the data in order to uncover and reveal the presence of her subjects and to create a representational space for critically reflecting upon her own presence in the visual production of the image. Through her landscape images, the local people of her study area are encouraged to participate proactively in the process of representation, allowing them to access, engage, and partake in her academic research and their own histories.

In her work *Body Map Series* (figure 13.3), Irish artist Kathy Prendergast has used the borderland between art and cartography to explore the complex relations between cartography and the colonization and control of nations and gendered bodies. While Prendergast claims to resist feminist interpretations of her work in favor of the post-colonial, Nash (1994) points to the feminist implications of using cartographic themes to make connections between landscapes and female bodies. Using the traditional conventions of Victorian cartography, Prendergast maps a landscape that is clearly in fact a female body, but with the body parts identified as landscape features. Nash argues that map-

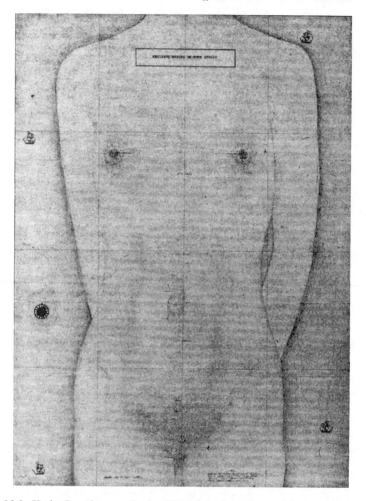

Fig. 13.3. Kathy Prendergast, *Enclosed Worlds in Open Spaces* (1983). Utilizing traditional cartographic conventions, the author has mapped a female body as a landscape in order to draw connections between the colonization of nations and gendered bodies. (Courtesy of Vincent Ferguson)

ping the female body as landscape disrupts the disembodied objectivity of the Western cartographic perspective and challenges us to reconsider this perspective in our geographical discourses of both landscapes and women. The body as landscape also destablizes the eroticization of female bodies and plays off the erotic and control fantasies of cartography. Other images in the series describe the processes of colonial exploration and control of landscapes and confront the viewer with the connections between the political control of landscape and control of female bodies.

Relying on conventional basemaps, the *Penn State Campus Night Map* and the *University of Oregon Guide for People with Disabilities* are traditional maps that address basic feminist issues of safety and access to public spaces (figures 13.4 and 13.5). These maps were designed to be efficient navigation tools for their target audiences and this purpose is graphically reflected in the map. For example, the night map uses bright yellow on a black background to highlight the well-lit, well-traveled paths and safe areas across campus, while the disabilities map uses bold blue lines to foreground the network of wheelchair accessible routes. More important, the production of these maps is directly linked to university and private efforts actively to alter the social space of the campuses, by making all campus spaces accessible to everyone and by improving the sense of nighttime security for women on campus. Both maps emerge from and directly represent these changes in the campus landscape by showing things like security stations, newly installed safety phones, curb cuts and elevators, as well as by providing relevant information about local and campus information resources.

On the other hand, these maps conceal negative information that might reflect poorly upon these universities and their efforts to improve campus spaces (and promote their efforts to do so). While providing information on campus accessibility, no mention is made of places that might be difficult, if not impossible, for a disabled person to access. Similarly, the campus night map provides information on safer public places, but says nothing about the domestic and dating spaces where the campus is most dangerous, and campus security the farthest removed.

Such maps might also be approached in another fashion, utilizing alternate geometries that reflect the experience of space from the perspective of the intended audience. The campus night map could be remapped onto a grid that represents the geometry of fear of someone walking across a dark and lonely campus. Walking distances in concealed, dark, and empty areas would appear exaggerated on the map as they are enhanced by the tension and fear of crossing them, while well-lit areas would appear foreshortened by feelings of relative safety. Similarly, highly accessible areas of campus would appear normal on a map based on a geometry of accessibility, while inaccessible areas would be enlarged by the sense of difficulty in gaining access to them. These other maps would better reflect the experiences of their audience, but this must also be balanced against the requirement that the maps function as viable navigational tools.

Computer mapping technology offers the potential to help bridge the gap between functional traditional maps and maps based on alternative cartographic grids and geometries of experience that would serve personal and research interests. While based on traditional, scientific cartographic approaches, analytical cartographic tools, such as GIS, also offer the potential to explore

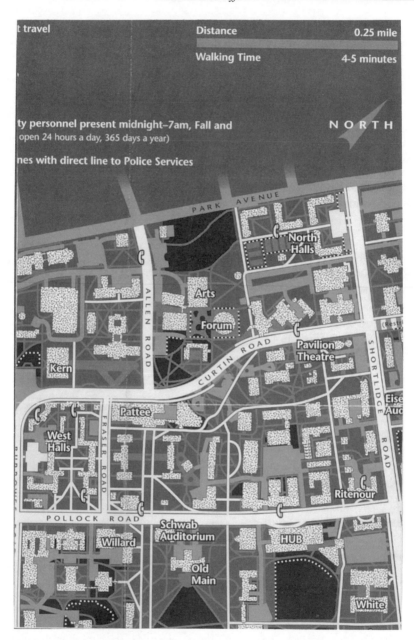

Fig. 13.4. The Penn State Campus Night Map. The light lines on this map appear bright yellow in the original and represent well-lighted, well-traveled walkways, as part of a university program to improve the safety of campus space for women. (Courtesy of the Deasy GeoGraphics Lab)

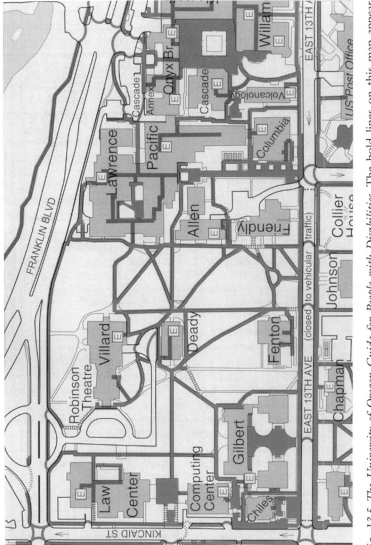

Fig. 13.5. The University of Oregon Guide for People with Disabilities. The bold lines on this map appear bright blue in the original, and represent routes that have been made accessible to people with disabilities. (Courtesy of the InfoGraphics Lab)

alternate geometries and to construct fluid and critical presentations while maintaining some common standards for comparison. By utilizing hypermedia software, these new cartographic systems constitute an inscription medium that allows one to create maps that are permanent and tangible digital records, but which are also fluid and ephemeral because they can be interactively manipulated by the user. Krygier (1995) argues that hypermedia mapping allows for the decentered and nontotalizing representations that new cultural geographers and feminist theorists have sought to bring out in other media.

However, although these new map analysis and production tools have expanded greatly the number and type of people who have access to cartographic tools today, like all other maps, computer cartography cannot be taken in isolation from the gendered social and political world around us. Hypertext, no matter how decentered, is still text that has defined limits and demands interpretative reading, and some of hypertext's strongest proponents have been criticized for their (now redirected) masculinist devotion to traditional literary canon and practice (Palattella 1995). Additionally, digital spaces are gendered just like every other social space (Stone 1991), and all computer media bear inherent problems related to the affordability of and access to the computer hardware and software necessary to participate.

Further emphasizing that Euclidean geometry is not the only way of ordering and measuring space, another alternative geometry that is used commonly in geography is the cartogram. Cartograms are based on traditional Western maps, but the map grid is deformed in relation to some (usually quantitative) attribute of the mapped space, such as a census cartogram that takes the basic census enumeration units and deforms them so that their size is relative to the population of the census unit, rather than its actual physical area (Dorling 1993). Woodward and Dorling (1994) have used this type of cartogram to explore changes in women's labor participation across deindustrializing Britain (figure 13.6), arguing that the cartograms allow the reader to actually see and compare the important social relationships between the census units better than maps that show the basically irrelevant physical area of the units. Cartograms are also an excellent example of how quickly people in our map-immersed society are able to accommodate and incorporate new cartographic systems and images.

Julie Nicoletta, in her study of Shaker drawings from the nineteenth-century American frontier (1993) has demonstrated how Shaker graphic practices were neatly divided along gender lines. The Shakers developed an extensive, and exclusively male, urban planning practice that mapped and produced the idealized, Euclidean social spatial arrangements of Shaker communities, while Shaker women created spirit drawings of the Shaker societies (figure 13.7). Some of these spirit drawings can be read as maps of the Shaker social and spiritual landscape, because they are based on a relational, spiritual geometry that situates members of the Shaker community and important historical figures within a spatial grid according to their position within the Shaker spiritual

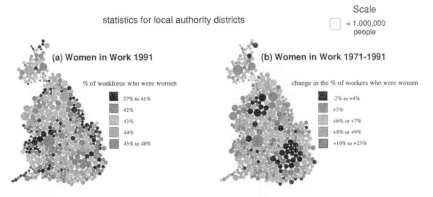

Fig. 13.6. The Geography of Women in Work, 1971–1991. The changing geography of British working women is mapped on a cartogram that shows census units proportional to their population rather than to their actual physical area. (Courtesy of Daniel Dorling)

hierarchy and in relation to significant Shaker religious places. These hierarchical, spiritual relationships, which for the Shakers were more important than their physical relationships, are expressed graphically and spatially on the spirit drawings.

In the next few maps, the role of the cartographer's visual production and the medium of inscription are brought to the fore in challenging the limitations of traditional cartography and forging new representations that better address the needs and concerns of feminist geographers. These alternative media offer feminist academicians and activists new ways to produce and publicly share knowledge that will bring feminist maps to new audiences and directly address important women's issues in the social spaces where they occur. In another form of spiritual geometry, artist and former cartographer Michelle Stuart has created 1:1 scale maps of the desert Southwest by laying out large sheets of paper and impressing the landscape directly onto the sheet by rubbing it with graphite sticks and rolling on it with her body (Duvert 1987). Stuart's style of visual production and use of the earth as a cartographic medium highlight her earth books as records of the artist's direct experience with the earth. They symbolize the earth's own natural history of geological and environmental rhythms recorded by the motion of the bodies of artist and earth together, and freed from the linear, written history of human progress and discovery.

One can also look at graffiti as a cartographic production technique that uses urban space as a medium for directly engaging social and political issues in their immediate spatial settings. In such cases, activists literally can produce critical mappings in social space with graffiti, which can be read as a territorial marker that works beyond the simple two-dimensionality of the printed map to inscribe maps directly onto the very social space of the city itself (Ley and

Fig. 13.7. An Emblem of the Heavenly Sphere (1854). This Shaker spirit drawing represents the spiritual space of the Shaker community by mapping the relational geometry of the Shaker social and religious hierarchy. (Courtesy of Hancock Shaker Village)

Cybriwsky 1974). In the predominantly gay Dupont Circle area of Washington, D.C., signs reading "A gay man was bashed here" have been spray-painted directly onto the sidewalk, marking the sites of antigay attacks in the area. Taken as a whole, these inscribed signs form a map of antigay violence that openly confronts each map reader, straight or gay, with the geography of violence that casts its shadow over this usually relatively safe neighborhood. Such graffiti maps have obvious applications for feminist projects, potentially turning the social space of the city into a map of its own dangers for women, and forcing people to acknowledge dangers they might not normally experience themselves in these same spaces, and perhaps would prefer to overlook.

Similarly, protest marches can also be read as critical mappings that confront social spaces directly using urban space as mapping medium. By taking mapping performance as a form of visual production, protests marches can be read as performed mappings that directly challenge the public representational space of the city with an alternative, critical vision of that social space. In her telling of a Latina lesbian organization's efforts to oppose antilesbian prejudice and hatred in New York City, Meoño-Picado (chapter 15, this volume) recounts how the group used public demonstrations to reveal and inscribe their presence onto the urban social spaces where they would normally be invisible. Demonstrating against a radio station that routinely used hate speech to boost its ratings, the group used the immediate performance of these marches to reveal the dominant heterosexual (and antilesbian) spaces of the city, while leaving behind ephemeral inscriptions that continued to bear witness to the presence of the lesbian spaces of the city.

The other maps discussed in this section form a feminist alternative to Western cartographic practice by utilizing a variety of production practices, non-Euclidean, relational geometries of experience, as well as different mapping media in the creation of cartographic images of gendered social spaces. I have also discussed numerous feminist maps that work subversively within Western cartographic tradition to challenge its masculinist epistemology and content. Together, these feminist maps engage the visual method of cartography by highlighting the role of vision and the gendered body in the production of feminist geographical knowledge that addresses issues of gendered space and experience.

Conclusion

Throughout this chapter, I have engaged feminist theoretical perspectives in order to explore the boundaries of the other map and to ground an explicitly feminist cartographic practice that addresses the concerns of feminist geographical, political, and epistemological theory. Feminist geographers can begin to realize the other maps of women's different spaces and cartographic grids by actively exploring new avenues of cartographic expression for representing women's geographies, spaces, and experience through maps. In this way, feminist geographers can ground a cartographic theory "that privileges contestation, deconstruction, passionate construction, webbed connections, and hope for transformation of systems of knowledge and ways of seeing" (Haraway 1991, 191).

For the discipline of cartography, the real challenge of feminism is to engage the masculinist discourse of cartography that serves to reinforce women's hesitancies toward maps and cartography, and to combat the social and intellectual exclusion and denigration of women. This will require the intellectual openness to acknowledge, rather than dismiss, claims on an expanded epistemological frontiers in cartographic theory, as well as the willingness to relinquish male privilege and accept women as social, professional, and economic equals. Maps are important and powerful representations of space in our discipline and our society, and I have tried to show that feminist cartography is a viable and important visual method that can harness the traditionally masculinist power of Western cartography for feminist causes, as well as explore, create, and promote new map forms for feminist geographers. In the end, we all stand to benefit from expanding and changing the practice of cartography and the kinds of maps we create.

References

Alic, M. 1986. *Hypatia's Heritage*. Boston: Beacon Press.

Blaut, J. M. 1991. Natural mapping. *Transactions of the Institute of British Geographers New Series* 16 (1): 55-74.

Blunt, A. and Rose, G. eds. 1994. *Writing women and space: Colonial and postcolonial geographies*. New York: Guilford Press.

Bordo, S. 1987. *The flight to objectivity: Essays on cartesianism and culture*. Albany, NY: State University of New York Press.

Buckley, C. 1989. Made in patriarchy: Towards a feminist analysis of women and design. In *Design discourse: History, theory, criticism*, ed. V. Margolin. 251–62. Chicago: The University of Chicago Press.

Bunge, W. 1969. *Field notes: Discussion paper no. 1: The Detroit geographical expedition*. Detroit: Society for Human Exploration.

Dorling, D. 1993. Map design for census mapping. *The Cartographic Journal* 30 (2): 167–83.

Duvert, E. 1987. With stone, star, and earth: The presence of the archaic in the landscape visions of Georgia O'Keeffe, Nancy Holt, and Michelle Stuart. In *The desert is no lady: Southwestern landscapes in women's writing and art*, eds. V. Norwood and J. Monk. 197–222. New Haven and London: Yale University Press.

Fausto-Sterling, A. 1992. *Myths of gender: Biological theories about women and men*. 2d., rev. ed., New York: BasicBooks.

Ford, S. 1991. Landscape revisited: A feminist reappraisal. In *New words, new worlds: Reconceptualising social and cultural geography in the department of geography, University of Edinburgh*, edited by C. Philo, 151–55. Lampeter, Wales: Department of Geography, St. David's University.

Gibson, A. and Fast, T. 1986. *The women's atlas of the United States.* New York and Oxford, England: Facts on File Publications.

Gilmartin, P. 1990. Mary Jobe Akeley's exploration in the Canadian Rockies. *The Geographical Journal* 156 (3): 297-303.

Haraway, D. 1991. Situated knowledges: The Science Question in Feminism and the privilege of partial perspective. In *Simians, cyborgs, and women: The reinvention of nature*, 183–201. New York: Routledge.

Haraway, D. 1992. The promises of monsters: A regenerative politics for inappropriate/d others. In *Cultural Studies*, eds. L. Grossberg, C. Nelson, and P. Treichler. 295–337. New York: Routledge.

Harding, S. 1989. Is there a feminist method? In *Feminism and science*, ed. N. Tuana. 17–32. Bloomington: Indiana University Press.

Harley, J. B. 1988b. Silences and secrecy: The hidden agenda of cartography in early modern Europe. *Imago Mundi* 40: 57-76.

Harley, J. B. and Woodward, D. eds. 1987. *Cartography in prehistoric, ancient, and medieval Europe and the Mediterranean. vol. one. The history of cartography.* Chicago: The University of Chicago Press.

Hudson, A. C. 1989. Pre-twentieth century women mapmakers. *Meridian* 1: 29–32.

Huffman, N. 1995. Silences and secrecy in the history of cartography: J. B. Harley, science and gender. *Proceedings of the 17th International Cartographic Conference.* Barcelona, 3–9 September 1995.

Keller, E. F. 1985. *Reflections on gender and science.* New Haven, CT: Yale University Press.

Kidron, M. and Segal, R. 1984. *State of the world atlas.* New York: Simon & Shuster.

King, Katie. 1990. Producing sex, theory and culture: gay/straight remappings in contemporary feminism. In *Conflicts in Feminism*, eds. M. Hirsch and E. F. Keller. 82–104. New York: Routledge.

Krygier, J. B. 1995. Geography and cartographic design. In *Cartographic design: Theoretical and practical perspectives*, eds. P. C. Keller and C. H. Wood. 19–34. London: John Wiley & Sons.

Kumler, M. and Buttenfield, B. 1995. Gender differences in map reading abilities: What do we know? What can we do? In *Cartographic design: Theoretical and practical perspectives*, eds. P. C. Keller and C. H. Wood. 125–36. London: John Wiley & Sons.

Latour, B. 1987. *Science in action.* Cambridge, MA: Harvard University Press.

Lefebvre, H. 1991. *The production of space.* Translated by D. Nicholson-Smith. Oxford, UK and Cambridge, MA: Blackwell Publishers.

Ley, D. and Cybriwsky, R. 1974. Urban graffiti as territorial markers. *Annals of the Association of American Geographers* 64 (4): 491–505.

Liben, L. S. and Downs, R. M. 1986. *Children's production and comprehension of maps: Increasing graphic literacy.* Washington, D.C.: National Institute of Education. Final Report NIE #G-83-0025.

MacEachren, A. M. 1995. *How maps work.* New York: Guilford Press.

Massey, D. 1991. Flexible sexism. *Environment and Planning D: Society and Space* 9 (2): 31–57.

McMichael Ritzlin, M. 1989. Women's contributions to North American cartography: four profiles. *Meridian* 2: 5–16.

Merchant, C. 1980. *The death of nature.* San Francisco: Harper and Row.

Middleton, D. 1964. *Victorian lady travelers*. New York: Dutton.

Mohanty, C. T. 1991. Cartographies of struggle: Third World women and the politics of feminism. In *Third World women and the politics of feminism*, eds. C. T. Mohanty, A. Russo, and L. Torres. 1–47. Bloomington: University of Indiana Press.

Monk, J. 1994. Personal communication.

Muehrcke, P. C. 1981. Whatever happened to geographic cartography? *The Professional Geographer* 33 (4): 397–405.

Mulvey, L. 1975. Visual pleasure and narrative cinema. *Screen* 16 (3): 6-18.

Nash, C. 1994. Remapping the body/land: New cartographies of identity, gender, and landscape in Ireland. In *Writing women and space: Colonial and postcolonial geographies*, eds. A. Blunt and G. Rose. 227–50. New York: Guilford Press.

Nast, H. and Kobayashi, A. 1996. (Re)coporealizing vision. In *Body space: Destabilizing geographies of gender and sexuality*, ed. N. Duncan. 75–97. New York: Routledge.

Nicoletta, J. 1993. Mapping the Shaker landscape: Spirit drawings and community planning. Paper presented at the Yale/Smithsonian Institution Maps as Material Culture Seminar. New York, 3–9 March 1993.

Palattella, J. 1995. Formatting patrimony: The rhetoric of hypertext. *Afterimage* 23 (1): 13–21.

Peters, A. 1983. *The new cartography*. New York: Friendship Press.

Pile, S. and Rose, G. 1991. All or nothing? Politics and critique in the modernism-postmodernism debate. *Environment and Planning D: Society and Space* 10 (2): 123–36.

Price-Chalita, P. 1994. Spatial metaphor and the politics of empowerment: Mapping a place for feminism and postmodernism in geography. *Antipode* 26 (3): 236–54.

Pulsipher, L. M.. 1995. Depicting the Marin ohana (houseyard) of the 1830's. Paper presented at the Society of Historical Archaelogy Meeting, Washington, DC, 6 January 1995.

Roberts, S. M. and Schein, R. H. 1995. Earth shattering: Global imagery and GIS. In *Ground truth: The social implications of Geographic Information Systems*, ed. J. Pickles. 171–95. New York: Guilford.

Rose, G. 1991. On being ambivalent: women and feminism in geography. In *New words, new worlds: Reconceptualising social and cultural geography in department of geography, University of Edinburgh*, edited by C. Philo. Lampeter, Wales: Department of Geography, St. David's University. 156–63.

Rose, G. 1993. *Feminism and geography: The limits of geographical knowledge*. Minneapolis: University of Minnesota Press.

Schiebinger, L. 1989. *The mind has no sex? Women in the origins of modern science*. Cambridge, MA: Harvard University Press.

Seager, J. and Olson, A. 1986. *Women in the world: An international atlas*. London and Sydney: Pan Books.

Shortridge, B. ed. 1987. *Atlas of American women*. New York: Macmillan.

Stone, A. R. 1991. Will the real body please stand up?: Boundary stories about virtual cultures. In *Cyberspace: First steps*, ed. M. Benedikt. 81–118. Cambridge, MA: The MIT Press.

Terrall, M. 1995. Gendered spaces, gendered audiences: Inside and outside the Paris Academy of Sciences. *Configurations* 3 (2): 207-232.

Tuana, N., ed. 1989. *Feminism and science*. Bloomington: Indiana University Press.

Turnbull, D. 1989. *Maps are territories: Science is an atlas*. Chicago: University of Chicago Press.

Tyner, J. 1994. Early geographic education of women: Westtown School in the Nineteenth Century. In *Abstracts of Association of American Geographers 90th Annual Meeting in San Francisco*. Washington, DC: Association of American Geographers.

Varanka, D. 1994. The manly map: The English construction of gender in early modern cartography. Unpublished typescript.

Wood, D. 1993a. The fine line between mapping and mapmaking. *Cartographica* 30 (4): 50–60.

Wood, D. 1993b. Maps and mapmaking. *Cartographica* 30 (1): 1–9.

Wood, D. 1993c. What makes a map a map? *Cartographica* 30 (2&3): 81–86.

Wood, D. with Fels, J. 1992. *The power of maps*. New York: The Guilford Press.

Woodward, R. and Dorling, D. 1994. The geography of women and work in Britain, 1971–1991. 1–28. Unpublished typescript.

14

For Whom Shall We Write?
What Voice Shall We Use?
Which Story Shall We Tell?

Lydia Mihelič Pulsipher

This chapter continues the exploration begun by others (such as Clifford and Marcus 1986; Duncan and Ley 1993; Gilbert 1994; Katz 1994; Keith 1992; Kobayashi 1994; Mascia-Lees et al. 1989; Nast 1994) of how as scholars we represent our research. I am particularly concerned with the creation and use of various "texts" that justify and interpret any given project (including the space occupied by the project itself) and how these texts in turn influence the research enterprise. I use as a case study research on Galways Mountain on the West Indian island of Montserrat, where for fifteen years, I (and many other colleagues both Montserratian and North American) have done interdisciplinary research on the history of ordinary people, in this case European and enslaved African settlers on one of the thousands of sugar plantations that once dotted Eastern Caribbean islands (figure 14.1). I will first briefly explain the Galways project and then how feminism has influenced my work there. A discussion of a selection of the various texts created to interpret the Galways research and site will complete the chapter.

Introduction to the Galways Study

The study of Galways Mountain began in 1980 at the behest of the Montserrat National Trust, which was addressing the then emerging government policy of promoting tourism as the island's primary economic development strategy.[1] After World War II, a rapidly declining plantation economy had left the island (which is still a British Crown Colony) without a sustaining economic base.

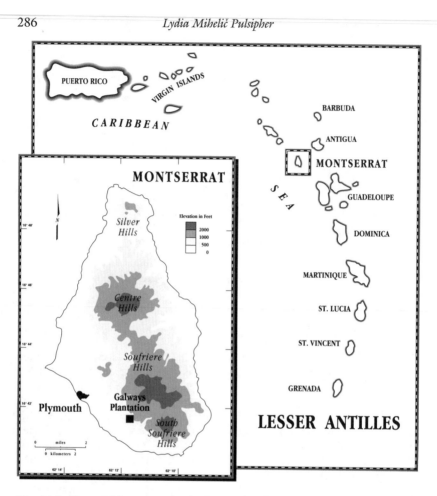

Fig. 14.1. Map of Montserrat in the Lesser Antilles (Courtesy of University of Tennessee Cartographic Services Laboratory).

The Montserrat National Trust promoted the idea that foreign currency earned with upscale tourism would provide the island with a means of support, enhancing the island's infrastructure while preserving what tourists might view as a quaint and charming place within an exotic environment. Such romantic renderings of the island were undoubtedly what had attracted European and North American seasonal retirees in the 1960s–70s. To compete in the upscale market, the trust thought Montserrat needed several properly researched and interpreted historic sites—sites that would set Montserrat apart from other islands where plantation ruins had been unreflectively turned into trendy hotels and bars. It was hoped that scientifically studied and interpreted sites would appeal to more educated, wealthy, and culturally sensitive tourists.

Among the most intriguing possibilities on Montserrat were the eighteenth-century Georgian ruins of Galways sugar estate situated high on the flanks of the Soufriere Hills and overlooking the sea far below (figure 14.2). Galways, though spectacularly situated and architecturally beautiful, is actually quite an ordinary sugar plantation like hundreds throughout the Caribbean. The descendants of those who once were indentured Irish and enslaved African labor-

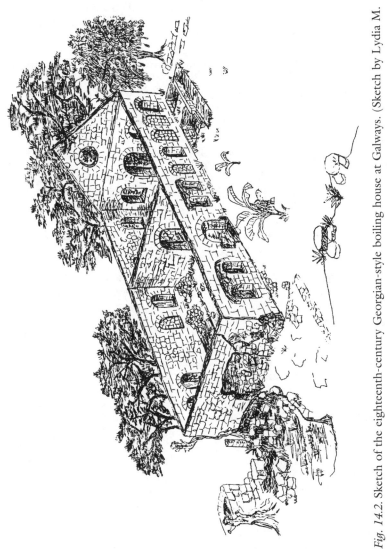

Fig. 14.2. Sketch of the eighteenth-century Georgian-style boiling house at Galways. (Sketch by Lydia M. Pulsipher)

ers at Galways live about 1,000 feet lower on the slope in the village of St. Patricks. Some, in return for minimal rents, use parts of the mountain for small tropical horticulture plots or for grazing goats and cattle; but these days much of the mountain lies unused and most of the villagers work at jobs in town or in tourism or are dependent on remittances from relatives abroad.

I was invited to direct the Galways project because I had just finished a historical geography study of the island as my Ph.D. dissertation. My mandate from the Montserrat National Trust (not necessarily from the people of Galways Mountain) was to learn what I could about the place and write a report that would aid in interpreting the site for visitors. Since I had to raise all the research funds myself, I was given the liberty to define the goals of the research to suit my academic needs. My interest in human adaptation to the New World tropics (1986) and in the lives and landscapes of ordinary people led me to seek at Galways the types of information that would illumine the role of plantations in the development of modern Caribbean Creole culture.[2] I chose modes of inquiry drawn from history, anthropology, geography, and archaeology.

The research at Galways, which began with archaeological surveys and excavations, soon captured the interest of all who came to watch us work. For a number of reasons, including how we represented ourselves and our work to the trust and the local community, the research momentum rolled on for the next twelve years. Galways Mountain was invaded seasonally by a cadre of interdisciplinary scholars and volunteers from across the globe as well as from Montserrat. The site became the setting for all the personal intrusions and technical entertainments that archaeology and related research can provide to local inhabitants, researchers, and tourists alike.[3]

Through it all, I and my eventual codirector, Mac Goodwin, questioned how and why the research should be done from a local perspective, tourism promotion being highly problematic in our view partly because of its tendency to trivialize and commodify Caribbean people and their ways of life. We reflected on the academic rationale and methodology of the study, on how it might positively or negatively affect the lives of the people of Galways Mountain, and on how and to whom the research should be addressed. As familiarity and respect between Montserratians and researchers developed, we all began to wonder if, in what ways, and for whom the slave plantation that once occupied Galways Mountain might best be interpreted as a historic landscape. Eventually, Mac and I chose to bring the politics of interpretation—the debate on who should tell which story to whom and why—to the Montserrat public by making it part of our casual discussions with individuals and part of our television and radio interviews and formal speeches. That conversation with the public, now held in a wider venue, continues to the present.

The Feminism in All This

Soon after the field study of the ruins of Galways Plantation began, the Montserrat Chamber of Commerce decided to fund ten secondary school students to work with us so they could learn, from close involvement with the Galways study, about little-known aspects of island history and about how research is conducted. When I requested that some of these students be female, the leader of the chamber initiative exclaimed, "Oh, do you think this would be a proper activity for girls?" He suddenly remembered that he was talking to the woman that headed up the project, grinned with embarrassment, and the moment passed. Then, on the first work day for the students, I began to explain what we were doing at Galways and why, and what the work day would consist of. One young man nudged his friend in the ribs and asked sarcastically in Creole, "She be de man now?" to which his friend replied, "Seems so!" This exchange apparently derived from the fact that after I wrote the first successful funding proposal, I acquired the assistance of a male archaeologist. A tall fellow with a commanding presence and a graduate student at the College of William and Mary (though actually the same age as I), he was then entirely unfamiliar with the Caribbean. Yet, although he was working for me, Montserratians, who had known me for a decade and him for only a few days, inevitably assumed that he was the director of the Galways project and I his junior, wifelike assistant. Thus began two odysseys in the "scholarship of difference." One, the more obvious, was the experience of discovering and telling the story of African/Irish-Caribbean people on Galways Mountain. The other was the reexamination for me and for Montserratians, of the notion of "women's work."

The experiences of being told during my doctoral program that my initial interests in women and development would forever marginalize me in academia and of having to squeeze my eventually more acceptable research agendas into painfully ill-fitting scientific paradigms meant that I naturally positioned myself in the field not as an academic authority figure—as I saw my male colleagues doing—but as a feminine, cheerful, helpful, inquisitive sojourner, one fascinated with Montserrat's past and present culture. Accordingly, I used my children as a representational foil. My little boys (and my discussed but absent husband) identified me, first and foremost, as a married mother. I continually and consciously cultivated this image (self-representation) so that I could talk to men of all ages without being sexualized by them.[4] Moreover, by representing myself as mother and wife, women would feel less threatened by and thus more comfortable with me. Once the Galways research began, however, my cultivated identity began to fail me. The size of the project and the management and negotiating skills necessary meant I had to find a new voice as that authority figure I had eschewed.

That is how gender comes into my work and into this chapter. The experience of being constructed and marginalized as a female "other" made me aware of the political force of representational practices—be these written or enacted. My need to validate my work, and my right as a woman to be in charge made me especially conscious of the differentiated hardships and experiences of ordinary people, of the need to design my research and to position myself within that enterprise carefully so that I myself was not guilty of devaluing or excluding. But then, remembering historiographer Hayden White's (1978) caution to pick up the threads of the story that don't necessarily fit my version, I must note that my male archaeologist colleague (he who was inadvertently so problematic to my identity as the project director) was every bit as troubled as was I over the politics both of our easy intrusion into the private space of Galways Mountain and of the ways we eventually would represent our findings to different audiences. Together we searched for culturally sensitive research questions and the methods to address them—questions that would reveal how ordinary people, in this case generations of indentured Irish and enslaved Africans, lived on Galways Mountain and passed their material and cognitive heritage to their common descendants. It was between us, male and female, that we worked out how to explain our research interests consistently but in different voices to the public in Montserrat or elsewhere and to our academic colleagues. Together we sought to explain to our Montserratian sponsors the inherently Eurocentric biases that adhered to plantation studies and that we wished to avoid. Throughout our years of field research, we struggled to interpret our accumulating data in ways that would shed new light on the proactive roles of slaves in creating viable resilient communities within the repressive plantation system—communities that underwrote so much of modern Caribbean culture. If we originated a unique stance, set of research tools, and modes of interpretation and representation in plantation studies (and we have reason to believe we did), this perspective grew not only out of my feminism but out of our joint recognition of the politics of our research enterprise and out of our desire to introduce our Montserratians and North American coworkers (through our own working relationship as codirectors and our relationships with them) to the idea that long-held gender and status roles could be amicably changed.

The Politics of Representation

"The form of the text is where it does its ideologically significant work."

—Hayden White

Several unconventional interpretive texts were created and used to represent the Galways research for different social and political ends. Each text was created for particular audiences who, directly or indirectly, affected the research enterprise, with text, audience, and research being thereby dialectically linked. By tailoring each representational form to a particular audience, the research was privately and publicly validated and promoted across a broad social spectrum. Most important, all "audiences" in our representational reach were encouraged to help rewrite or craft our stories. In other words, the actual (or anticipated) responses of laborers, the Montserratian public, our colleagues, our granting agencies, those who heard our speeches in Europe or North America or who attended the Smithsonian exhibit (discussed below) helped to "correct" our representations of the site, be these written, spoken, or performed. In this way, particular subjectivities were elicited and addressed; and as each mode of representation emerged, it interacted with the audiences and the research enterprise in a dialectic that molded both (Nast 1994, 60–62).

The form the representational text takes is an important indicator of the political ends being negotiated. Dominick LaCapra (1985, 11) has written that modern critical readings of documentary sources should be "premised on the conviction that documents are texts that supplement or rework 'reality' and not mere sources that divulge facts about 'reality.' " The same is true of the texts that scholars themselves produce (see also Clifford and Marcus 1986; Duncan and Ley 1993; Nast 1994). Far from being objective, representations are fashioned for particular ends; they are made to construct the world in particular ways for particular audiences.

The texts representing the Galways research, then, may be seen as means for negotiating discrete political agendas (White 1982, 300). Sometimes when we spoke to various work crews (especially those made up of young people from North America and Montserrat), we did so as archaeological "authority" figures in an effort to elicit their support and to secure their best efforts as workers. In other work situations, for example when collecting ethnographic information from elderly Montserratians, we spoke more as colleague to colleague. In contrast, when we gave public addresses to Montserrat audiences or to colleagues abroad, we tried to be entertaining and to sweep the audience up into our intellectual excitement over the emerging evidence. Last, when we wrote research proposals, we shaped our arguments in ways that might appeal to institutional agendas. In all cases, we sought explicitly to enter into dialogue with our audiences not only to "hear" their voice, but also to anticipate and address larger criticisms of our work that might impact the research negatively in future. It seems certain that at least some of the widespread acceptance and success of the project is due to the fact that we continually renegotiated our representations of the Galways project with the communities we worked with or addressed. Given that representational negotiations varied substantially, it should not be surprising that not all persons or groups interacted with particular representational forms in the same manner. For example, Montserratians were usually pretty matter-of-fact in their reactions to presentations on Galways (being generally positive, but only mildly curious), while North Americans were often emotionally touched by the prospect of learning about the everyday life of people in Galways past, and said so.

Representing Galways Mountain

A range of written, spoken, and "performed" representational forms were used to convey the results of the Galways research and to depict the site of that research. Although not exhaustive, the list of representational forms includes:

- explanations to, and conversations with, workers, volunteers, and colleagues about what we were doing and the meaning of that effort

- public addresses in Montserrat, the Caribbean, Europe, and North America
- research proposals and reports to funding agencies
- tourist brochures that explained the site to casual visitors
- popular newspaper and magazine articles
- a major exhibit at the Smithsonian National Museum of Natural History, including several dioramas
- an annotated fictional folk geography of Galways Mountain
- scholarly articles in academic journals and books
- a children's book
- the interpreted historic site, itself

Here, then, I deal with five of these ten types of "texts," choosing those I consider to be among the less explored, and/or more problematic examples of representational efforts. The five are (1) explanations to crew and colleagues in the field (especially during the early stages of the project); (2) theoretical discussions with the local community; (3) the Smithsonian exhibit, *Seeds of Change*, which ran at the National Museum of Natural History from October 1991 to May 1993; (4) the annotated fictional folk geography, *Here Where the Old Time People Be* (Pulsipher 1992); (5) and the children's book, *The Hidden Garden of Galways Mountain* (Pulsipher and Sims, forthcoming).

Conversations with Project Workers

Our conversations with workers verbally communicated information about the research effort primarily to Montserratian colleagues, but also to academic and volunteer colleagues from off the island. Besides verbal directives to crews at the site and discussions about theoretical directions, this representational form includes slide-based interactive discussions in local rum shops in which we (local laborers and cultural consultants, codirector Mac Goodwin, and I) reviewed and communally discussed the field season's experiences and research results.

The crew included several elderly women and men of Galways Mountain who had only limited opportunity to attend school, local secondary school students working for the project on chamber of commerce-funded summer internships, and junior academic colleagues and Earthwatch volunteers from North America. The latter included teachers, doctors, lawyers, and engineers. With the exception of the academic colleagues, all were new both to the fields of archaeology and geography and to the concept that the everyday lives of ordinary people could be the focus of academic research. Early in the mornings, we would gather by a particularly hospitable mango tree in the plantation yard, our Mango Tree Classroom (figure 14.3).[5] Some of the younger crew sat in the tree's large canopy, while the rest of us gathered beneath the tree in the shade. I would then explain the day's work. The following is an abbreviated

Fig. 14.3. The mango tree classroom. (Photo by Mac Goodwin)

version (translated into formal English) of the introduction I would give an assembled crew on the first morning of any particular field season.

> Good morning, everyone. Today we are beginning [continuing] the study of Galways Plantation, which we have been asked to do by the Montserrat National Trust. The idea is eventually to turn Galways into a park where Montserratians can come on special occasions and bring their visitors. As researchers we are interested in learning as much as possible about how this plantation operated as a colonial enterprise; but our primary goal is to learn about the everyday life of the

people who formed the labor force of the plantation, people who are the ancestors of those still living in Montserrat today.

I would then explain how we would survey and map the site, do a systematic surface collection, and selectively excavate, always keeping meticulous records. I would go on to explain that our ultimate goal was to discern the behavior (and the meaning behind that behavior) that had produced the landscape at this site and across the mountain—the buildings, landforms, soil stains, evidence of changing plant and animal life, and artifact assemblages and distributions. These patterns, "textual" traces of former material life, reveal how people organized and used the spaces around the site. I would explain that from interpreting or "reading" this material evidence in tandem with information gleaned from historical records and oral histories we would try to represent former lifeways over the past three hundred years on Galways Mountain and to discern the meaning people had attached to the material. At this time, also, anyone was free to pose practical or theoretical questions about our work. The classroom mode of introducing and representing ourselves, the site, and the research project served three purposes. First, it was an educational medium that brought the crew into a circle of inquiring minds. Second, but as important, our explanatory process helped Mac and me to verbally confirm our proposed layout of the work. Third, the classroom setting meant that our thoughts and agendas could be negotiated with our crew in an interactive, reflective way.

These sessions with our worker colleagues helped Mac and me to see our representations more concretely and thereby to continuously reevaluate the "research/representational" process, including the politics behind it. Initially, for example, we conscientiously mentioned our main local sponsors, the Montserrat National Trust, thinking it would lend us special legitimacy as outsiders to Galways Mountain. We hoped our local sponsorship would convey that we were not interlopers embarking solely on our own research agenda. While our North American colleagues were reassured, we later learned that most Galways Mountain people had never heard of the National Trust; and those who had, thought of it as an expatriate and hence somewhat suspect agency. We also very consciously mentioned Galways as "a future park for Montserratians" as a means of shaping the project along egalitarian lines—one geared for *local* consumption and *local* people. This representational choice was made to distinguish our efforts from those of developers interested primarily in attracting outside tourists. While our choice may seem odd given that the trust supported the project as a tourist-oriented one, we felt that the project's ends might be molded to suit more local (as well as some tourism) needs by promoting primarily local experiences at the place. As Haunani-Kay Trask (1993) and others have shown, tourism, especially in small island communities, is at least partially a neocolonial endeavor that often appropriates the space of rightful inhabitants and allocates it to an alien elite.

Theoretical Discussions with the Local Community.

The politics of representing the project to the crew members extended to the community at large. Such politics were made clear to us early on when it became apparent that the word "slave" was problematic. Initially we studiously avoided this word based on the understanding that Montserratians were reluctant to have their ancestors represented by what they felt was a dehumanizing term. White expatriates said so and, a little checking revealed that, indeed, until very recently, when Caribbean people had taken over from the British the writing of their school texts, the discussion of the role of slavery in the Caribbean past was rarely explicitly covered in school. It seemed that some Montserratians had adopted British constructions of slavery as having so disgraced the victims that the mere mention of slavery or of Africa should be avoided. For example, I was told by a geographer colleague originally from St. Patricks village that while his family often mentioned their Irish forebears, the fact that they also had African forebears was never discussed, though this was visually obvious.

Slavery was, however, one of the main foci of our research. We therefore set out to find ways of negotiating its representation with the Montserrat public. Accordingly, we discussed how the project was set up to critique slavery and would thus valorize slaves as human beings worthy of recognition. Not only would the project work to recognize the political inequality inherent in slave plantation systems, it would show the tremendous resilience of slaves in the face of oppression as well as the material and cultural forces slaves and their descendants were able to mobilize in shaping and creating Montserratian lifeways that persist up to the present.

Negotiating the project's emphasis on slavery additionally required that we representationally and politically rework our identity as "White" European-Americans. While we are "White," a social construction that is tied historically to European-instigated slavery and colonization, we contended that we had no wish to keep the Galways study a White-dominated project, hence our efforts to train local students who could one day take over our work. Also, in speeches, interviews, and private conversations, we openly questioned our own authority as European-American Whites to study African-Caribbean culture, thus encouraging a dialogue that continues. These rhetorical strategies vis-à-vis ourselves, our colleagues, and our research helped assuage the misgivings of critics while suggesting to our Montserrat constituents new ways of thinking about the past that validated the Galways study and everyone's participation in it.

Input from the community not only derived from misgivings about the word "slave." There were also the daily questions posed by the archaeology work crews and tourists that forced interactive reflection and negotiation. New crew members typically challenged the need for such meticulous work in view of the tedium, the heat, and the dust. The tourists, who passed through the site almost continuously, would often ask while gazing at huge stone ruins and piles of artifacts, "Have you found anything yet?" apparently expecting us to strike gold or treasure. After a few months of experiencing the pleasures of fitting archaeological evidence together, however, the crew members began to help each other accept the tedium of archaeological fieldwork; and, similarly, they accepted the role of explaining what we were doing to passing tourists, disabusing them of the idea that treasure was our goal (figure 14.4).

Interestingly, it was the assumption of this explanatory role that seems to have led Montserratian members of the crew to explore with each other just what particular artifact patterns might mean. Mac and I then realized that they, themselves, might be the answer to one of our most worrisome challenges: how were we, as cultural outsiders, to "read" the archaeological evidence? While the vertical layering and horizontal spatial arrangements of artifacts would suggest hypothetical ways in which the Galways site was used by its occupiers at various times in the past, how were we to understand and interpret the site and its artifacts as they actually had been experienced, culturally valued, and invested with meaning by those who had lived in this place?

When we realized that Montserratian crew members held important insights into both the material culture of the plantation and the cognitive processes of its inhabitants, we decided to begin extensive ethnographic and archival research in support of the Galways fieldwork immediately, instead of deferring it (as we had intended) to some time in the near future. After all, the plantation era had lasted into the 1960s! Montserratians not only helped us identify artifacts, they shared with us their subjective sense of the place as a physical envi-

Fig. 14.4. Screening for artifacts in the Galways village. (Photo by Lydia M. Pulsipher)

ronment with a particular array of resources, and as a venue for past and present occurrences and human relationships. Some of their families began participating in four studies that went a long way toward making the archaeological signature of the Galways slave village, and especially the role of women in that village, intelligible. These studies included an ethnoarchaeological examination of modern houseyards and domestic life (Pulsipher 1986b, 1993a, 1993b), the documentation of folk material culture (Pulsipher 1986c), human ecology studies of small-plot tropical horticulture (Berleant-Schiller and Pulsipher 1986; Pulsipher 1990, 1994), and a reconstruction of the folk geography of Galways Mountain (Pulsipher 1992). In these ways, representation of the research to various local audiences and the feedback that ensued created multiple opportunities to reshape and improve the research project and to extend local participation.

The Smithsonian Exhibit

In 1987, as we prepared to excavate the slave village, we were unexpectedly invited to Washington, D.C., to present our research findings to a small group of people at the Smithsonian National Museum of Natural History who were planning an exhibit marking the five hundredth anniversary of the arrival of Columbus and his entourage in the Western Hemisphere. The exhibit was to be called *Seeds of Change,* and its purpose was to educate the public on the many ways exchanges of plants, animals, diseases, people, and ideas, following in Columbus's wake, had affected human life all over the earth. Five items of intercontinental exchange were chosen to stand as illustrations: diseases, corn, potatoes, the horse, and sugar cane. After Mac Goodwin and I took five Smithsonian officials to Montserrat, the Galways site was chosen as the case study of how the introduction and cultivation of sugar cane had changed New World landscapes, fueled the slave trade, and inadvertently yet extensively influenced modern Caribbean culture (figure 14.5).

The concerted interdisciplinary character of the research at the Galways site revealed archaeological insights unavailable in other island communities. Information was now available at Galways, for example, on the physical infrastructure, geographic setting, and environmental impact of a sugar plantation. Most important, much information was also known about the daily life of enslaved laborers and about acculturation processes that they shaped. Over the years, our ethnohistorical and geographical research had revealed how Africans had assessed the tropical island environment, designed adaptive strategies, and devised and reproduced community life, all under a system of harsh forced labor and social surveillance. Hence, our study of one small and seemingly insignificant place made it possible to convey to the museum public the wide-ranging and layered effects of European expansion during the age of exploration.

As the level of our official participation in planning for the exhibit quickly escalated, the elation of being able to tell the Galways story to literally millions

Sugar: A Bittersweet Legacy

Sugarcane, also cargo on Columbus's second voyage, thrived in the American tropics. By the 1700s, lush Caribbean rainforest was replaced by the world's most productive sugar plantations. Once an expensive novelty, sugar became a necessity of the European diet, with millions of African slaves paying the price.

Despite the abuses of slavery, Africans forged new cultures in the Americas. The legacy of this experience is encapsulated in a video of life on the island of Montserrat, a former sugar colony. What happened on Montserrat, and throughout the Americas, is the true significance of 1492. From two hemispheres people, plants, animals, and customs came together and unknowingly formed the real New World.

Fig. 14.5. Galways as represented in the Smithsonian *Seeds of Change* exhibit brochure.

of museumgoers was tempered by the growing realization that despite our roles as directors and principal investigators of the Galways project, the power to fine-tune the message of the exhibit, indeed, the representation of our research, lay elsewhere—with museum officials, technical writing consultants, and exhibit designers.

Meanwhile, the dialectic between museum representation of the Galways research and the site of the research enterprise itself was unusually complex. First there was the matter of dealing with perceptions in Montserrat of what it meant for the Galways research to go into a major exhibit. Some Montserratians thought this meant Mac and I would become rich, while most had no experience and hence no conception of what a large museum was like, or of the size of the audience that would soon learn about Galways and Montserrat. Furthermore, the increased attention Montserrat received from the attendant publicity overpowered our careful efforts to establish an egalitarian and interactive research enterprise. Visiting Smithsonian officials made expansive promises to Montserratians that were never kept. Travel writers swarmed to the island, most failing to comprehend the scope and meaning of our work and some writing outrageously patronizing articles about our Montserratian colleagues. North American tour organizers flocked to the site, often when we were not on the island; and although the local Galways crew could have served as informed guides through the site, when we were not there to suggest them for this role (and source of income), inexperienced and uninformed tour guides were hired instead, giving out misinformation about the site and our purposes.

Representing the Galways research in the exhibit also was problematic. Smithsonian exhibits, which host millions of visitors from all over the world, must appeal to an unusually broad audience (in age, culture, and level of education). To ensure a steady flow-through of visitors, museum exhibits have to be designed so as to be absorbed in a short time. Hence, of necessity, they must be graphically interesting and selective in terms of artifacts, tableaux, and pictures. Little text can be accommodated because it would require time-consuming reading. In fact, the crowds at *Seeds of Change* were enormous and had to be moved through the exhibit especially quickly. All of this meant that the complex story of Galways could easily be misinterpreted either in its telling or in its comprehension. Furthermore, from some quarters came pressure to downplay the resilience, creative adaptation, and resistance of Galways people to slavery and to accentuate instead the more sadistic characteristics of slavery such as the victimization and defeat of slaves. This last pressure came indirectly from some apparently powerful White Washingtonians who were understandably nervous about the fact that Mac and I were White scholars dealing with Black history. They interpreted our research perspective as revisionist and elitist. This perception of our work undoubtedly stemmed from ignorance of the project's philosophy and practice and from the fact that our many Montserratian colleagues were not present in Washington. We could not convince the museum to finance their travel, and as a result, only a few were involved in the exhibit planning and opening. In the end, only about thirty people from Montserrat made the trip to see the exhibit, nearly all paying their own way. Eventually the Smithsonian SITES office sent a quite spare traveling poster version of the exhibit, which I hung in a public restaurant in Plymouth, Montserrat, for several months.

Ultimately the rather subtle and layered findings of our research were muted by the glossy and overly simplified exhibit design. Much detail that would have conveyed the texture of everyday life was eliminated. In terms of the politics of representation, then, the Smithsonian exhibit was partially a return to convention with representational authority taken away from Montserratians involved with the project and revested, to some extent, in Mac and me, but ultimately in museum officials, writers, and designers. Nonetheless, the overall representational goal of the exhibit—to show the massive and continuing effects of the conquest of the New World by the Old, with many of these effects frankly portrayed as very negative—was, for a large publicly funded museum, quite unconventional and commendable.

Description of the Seeds of Change Exhibit

Seeds of Change eschewed the usual fascination with the lifeways of the elite and emphasized instead the central role of ordinary people—Native American, European, and African—in the conquest and resettlement of the New World and the resultant cultural exchanges. The sugar part came last in the exhibit, just after a section on the effects of the introduction of the horse to the New World. Visitors were helped in making a bodily and mental transition to the story of sugar and slavery by having to stoop to enter the bowels of an audibly creaking and physically cramped slave ship. As people passed through, a male narrator dramatically read the eye-witness account of such a ship by Olaudah Equiano (1814), who was captured by slave traders as a child in Benin in the 1740s and eventually sold to a master in Montserrat. A back-lit panel showed contemporary illustrations of the interior of slave ships.

Visitors emerged into a large Z-shaped, dimly lit room to face a mural of Galways Mountain as it would have looked before the plantation era, clothed in a many-tiered tropical forest. In a few moments, this mural (actually a perpetually oscillating scrim) metamorphosed into a mural of the same landscape but this time with Galways Plantation having replaced the forest. In the foreground, slaves cut cane near their village; with plantation buildings looming in the mid-ground against dark green volcanic peaks. This mural represented the setting in which, over the course of three centuries, first Irish indentured servants, then hundreds of enslaved Africans, and finally, several thousands of their descendants of mixed African and European blood lived out their lives.

The visitors then passed by several displays that emphasized the fact that slaves were pro-active within the repressive system of slavery. One explained how slaves grew and marketed produce with such success that by the late eighteenth century they were the primary suppliers of fresh food to both White and Black populations in many West Indian islands. Another featured domestic artifacts found in the Galways village that we think were chosen and purchased by the slaves themselves with their garden profits: clay tobacco pipes, sewing thimbles, and the European and Chinese-made ceramic dishes that were the international trade goods typical of European working class tables in the period.

These ancillary displays channeled the visitor's attention to a life-size diorama of a house-site excavated in the Galways slave village (figure 14.6). The central figure was a woman cooking pepperpot stew over a three-stone fire pit, surrounded by features of village life discovered during excavations in the Galways village: several small wooden houses, a "water stone" (a large boulder chiseled to form a small catchment and basin to collect the nightly rains), a cassava press (used to process manioc), banana trees, chickens, pigs, and broken pottery sherds. Behind her was a landscape mural of Galways Mountain showing people cultivating and reaping the produce from their subsistence gardens. In order to breathe some life into this fairly static tableau, a fictitious Caribbean slave woman (rather unsuccessfully narrated by Whoopie Goldberg via audiotape) explained the role of gardening in her life. In this way, visitors were literally told how she had learned cultivation from her mother who was born in Africa; the joy it brought her to work in her garden; the usefulness of the produce in feeding her family; and the fact that she sold her surpluses to get cash to buy cups and bowls and pipes and tobacco. One result of this was that, unlike visual media, which anyone can access merely by looking, visitors

Fig. 14.6. Rough sketch (no photo is available) of the Galways village diorama, *Seeds of Change* exhibit. (Sketch by Lydia M. Pulsipher)

were placed in a less-powerful position. They had to wait and listen for the story to be told—hypothetically assigning the speaker (the Caribbean slave woman) greater narrative or textual power.

The next part of the exhibit explained the global sugar trade and the ways European culture had adapted to its use. The visitor was then brought back to modern Montserrat with a visit to the replica of the Top 'O The Cove rum shop in St. Patricks village at the bottom of Galways Mountain. The rum shop, which functions as a village "Stop 'n' Shop" in addition to a drinking establishment, was outfitted with the products typically sold in such a place: toilet paper, matches, laundry soap, tinned food, and cold drinks. Behind the bar, a television set continuously ran a sprightly video relating modern life in Montserrat to the themes of *Seeds of Change*, especially the idea that it is important to see modern culture in New World places as intimately related to post-Columbian diffusions of people, material culture, and ideas. Every New World place, no matter how small and remote, is an amalgamation of cultural elements borrowed from afar and acted upon in a new physical and cultural setting.

The representational format of the exhibit required becoming bodily enmeshed in the life-sized, three dimensional places and spaces of the slave ship and Galways Mountain. The museum visitor consequently performed the representation rather than just passively reading pictorial or written texts. The ideas (we can no longer recall who originated them) of beginning with the experience of the slave ship and ending with rural community life in a television-equipped rum shop effectively represented how African West Indians have transformed the experience of slavery in modern Creole society.

Two Fictional Representations of Galways Mountain

> The role of storytelling [is to overcome] the gulf between self and other,
> past and present, near and distant
>
> —G. Revill

Reconstructing past landscapes provides us with clues as to how past peoples have historically lived in and been constrained by their place (Cronon 1983; Jackson 1984; Meinig 1993; Brown 1968). Several persons have attempted to reconstruct Caribbean landscapes (Craton 1978; Olwig 1985; Higman 1988; Berleant-Schiller 1991; Pulsipher 1986a, 1991), though few, to my knowledge, have attempted to represent the meaning these past landscapes may have carried for their inhabitants.

At Galways, the decades-long experience of examining the past, meanwhile living and working with Galways people of the present, brought out in several of us a desire to go beyond the usual descriptive interpretation that characterizes most reconstructions of historic landscapes. Some Montserratians began to talk about spiritual connections to those whose belongings we were excavating.[6] The fact that our oral history and archival work revealed the names of real people at Galways in the 1820s and something of their life histories under slavery made us feel that we were coming to know these people. Furthermore, all of us began to feel at Galways Mountain what E. V. Walter calls the "haptic experience"—"the way the whole body senses and feels the environment" (1988, 134)—an encounter that led to thinking we in some way knew those who had preceded us in that place. This haptic experience of Galways Mountain has been available with minor variations to all who passed that way, from prehistory to the present, but just how this sensory experience may have registered in the consciousness of slaves and taken on cultural meaning for them in everyday life is more difficult to retrieve and represent. I am reminded of Michel Foucault's warning that we can never truly understand the experience of the other (1971, 153). But, on the other hand, anthropologist, Richard Price, in his book *Alabi's World*, one of several written by him and Sally Price on their Surinam research (1990, xvii), says that it is important to try.

Price writes that for a scholar long steeped in the culture examined, it is legitimate to try to interpret and represent how a particular place may have looked, smelled, and felt to those who lived in it in another time. And further, that it is legitimate to try to understand and convey "the meanings that those who lived in [a place] attached to [it]." A problem with such an effort—one that Price acknowledges—is that there may be a tendency to "read the present backward into the past." But this is a problem that plagues all historiography; as Price notes, any scholar's interpretation of the records of the past is "unavoidably colored by the present" (xvii). For me on Galways Mountain, this was especially so because so many of the clues as to how people in the past may have used and viewed the place came from trying to understand how their descendants experience the place in the present.

I chose, therefore, to experiment with fiction as one of the representational media through which to explore what it meant physically, spatially, and spiritually to live and work on Galways Mountain as a slave. To do this, I imagined myself living in the time and space, the social and physical setting that we had "scientifically" reconstructed. Such imaginings were informed by many individual Montserratians' stories of themselves and their ancestors as well as more "objective" data from archives and archaeological and geographical field research. While such imaginings are fictional, I would argue that these representations themselves are no less objective than more "scientific" accounts of macroscale features of the Galways landscape (Pulsipher and Goodwin 1982; Goodwin 1987; Pulsipher 1991). The difference is that fiction allows for the body and its sensory experiences to be represented and made significant to the story of slave life. Often it is not recognized that more conventional interpretations of landscapes require similar imaginative schemes because they are executed in ways and at scales that exclude the body. I would contend that it is particularly appropriate to focus on the bodily (the haptic) experience of the place, Galways Mountain, because in the context of slavery, the body is central.

By now I have used the fictional genre several times: first, in the Smithsonian exhibit catalog (Pulsipher 1991), then, for a scholarly symposium (Pulsipher 1992) where I defensively footnoted (2,500 words of fiction were documented with 25,000 words of footnotes), and most recently in a children's book I am completing (Pulsipher and Sims, forthcoming). It is significant to note here that, just like the previous representational media I have discussed, in creating fiction I have had to acknowledge a political tension between me, my audience, and my representation of life on Galways Mountain.

From my subjective point of view, fiction has proven to be the most effective (though precarious) method for combining all the evidence we collected—archaeological, geographic, ethnographic, and archival. This is because fiction not only imparts something of the minutiae of everyday life on Galways mountain, including the haptic experience of that place, but it also attempts to show how human relations and activities produce such archaeological traces as post holes, firepits, cultivation ridges, housesites, and artifact distributions. Fiction also allows one to imagine how landscapes reflect and influence the ideas and values—the cognitive frameworks—of the people who lived there.

Yet, for all the knowledge and familiarity with the place and its people that can be revealed through fiction, as Revill (1994) notes in his commentary on Carol Lake's book of short stories, *Rosehill: Portraits from a Midland City* (1989), whatever the level of my insight and knowledge, in storytelling I cannot "get it just right" nor elude the urge to appropriate and control the message. Revill's perceptive reference to the author's "unrequited empathy for the subject"—strikingly evokes the regret I feel that despite all my connections to the people of Galways Mountain, my attempt to tell their story in whatever form will inevitably remain inadequate. And yet, it seems important to try.

Below I have reproduced portions of fictional representations of Galways Mountain. I wrote the texts both for the people of Galways Mountain and for those who may never visit the place. The first excerpt was footnoted to prove to non-Montserratian, mostly academic, colleagues that every detail was backed up with archival, ethnographic, archaeological, and geographic research (1992). The second excerpt from a children's story (written with Billy Sims, forthcoming), is meant to help modern children see their connections with the historic "other" and to convey both historical and geographic information about a place. To date, various versions of this story have been critiqued by children in the Caribbean and the United States. For Montserratian children, the fictional trip that Nelly makes up Galways Mountain is a tale about their own place, and it can be relived any day they choose, because cultural and material life on that part of the island have not yet changed that much. For children who live elsewhere, the story is meant first to connect them with a child in another time and circumstance. It is also meant to teach them (and their parents) about the geography, ecology, and ambiance of a distant and different place. In both stories below, the names of the characters are those of people who lived on Galways Mountain in the early part of the nineteenth century. The personifications are inspired by the Montserratians I know and who worked with us in the study of Galways.

"Here Where the Old-Time People Be": The Fictional Annotated Folk Geography of Galways Mountain (Excerpt)

It is early on a Sunday morning in June of 1817.[7] The wind sighs through the crowns of the tall coconut palms, and dips down to rustle the leaves of the banana, pawpaw and cedar trees.[8] Finally, it stirs the cane-leaf thatch roofs of the small wood houses and animal pens nestled on informal terraces along the mountain slope (figure 14.7).[9] The sails of the windmill just above in the plantation yard can be heard straining against the tethers that tie them down on Sundays when, for a day, the processing of sugar cane is suspended. In the east the sky behind the mountains begins to turn pink and far below to the west, the ocean glints silver.

Garrick struggles up off his pallet[10] and stretches, filling the door frame of the tiny house with his shoulders. His head, covered with tight graying curls, juts out above the opening and brushes the cane-trash roof. He notices the calm sea and wishes briefly that some of his precious time today could be spent fishing.[11] The structure shudders a bit as he sits down heavily on the door sill and rests his feet on the boulder just outside.[12] He checks furtively over his right shoulder to see if

Fig. 14.7. Artist's concept of Galways village based on historical, archaeological, and ethnographic research. (Courtesy of Barbara Tipson)

Fagan, the estate manager, might be idly monitoring the early morning activity of the slaves from the boiling house windows. He sees no one and relaxes a bit, pleased that the thick foliage around the house shields them so effectively from observation.[13] Rummaging on a ledge inside the door for his white clay pipe, Garrick asks the boy, Quacou to interrupt his "Chiney Money" game[14] with Granderson from the next house and hand him an ember from the cooking fire so he can light the tobacco. The first draft of the homegrown stuff is raw and he gruffly suggests to his companion, Margaret, that she should buy him a bit of imported tobacco from the itinerant trader when she passes through Kinsale village today on her way to market in Plymouth town (figure 14.8).[15]

Margaret has just finished heating up last night's peppery stew of pigeon peas, plantains, and dasheen[16] in the heavy black clay cooking pot.[17] . . . [She] hands [Garrick] a calabash bowl full of the stew and offers the same to Quacou and Granderson. . . . While they eat, she finishes sweeping the area around the house with the bract that has fallen from Quacou's coconut tree during the night. She then tugs at a handful of loose fibers on the banana tree,[18] rips them down the length of the tree and ties together a large cloth bundle containing disks of cassava bread and other items to sell in town.[19] Leaving the bundle, she walks along the irregular terrace and past several other small houses, giving a quiet greeting to the residents.[20] After reminding a friend to save her sweet potato peelings for Garrick's pig,[21] Margaret stops to rinse the soil off her hands in the water stone;[22] and at a line of cedar trees just past the cassava press, Margaret takes her cutlass[23] and first cuts a huge leaf from the "chaney bush" plant growing in the crotch of one tree. Then, from the same plant she cuts a six-foot tendril, a "chaney string".[24]

Fig. 14.8. European clay pipes excavated in the Galways village. (Courtesy of Jean Howson)

The Hidden Garden on Galways Mountain[25] (Excerpt)

In the year 1820, the summer rains have finally come to Galways plantation. The sugar cane harvest is under way, and like other enslaved people on the Caribbean island of Montserrat, young Nelly Dyer[26] is hard at work. She finishes sweeping the dusty floor of the greathouse store room, and stands in the doorway, enjoying the misty breeze.

Unexpectedly, her great-Aunty Moth, who is the housekeeper of the greathouse, looks down from the porch above.

"Nelly Dyer! Time for idling, have you? Girl, I told you if you do good work for the Mistress, she keep you up here in de big house and you na' have to wield no hoe or cutlass in dem sugar cane fields.

"Finish there and fetch Cook another pail of water, Quick, now!"

At sunset, Nelly is allowed to go home. She walks slowly along the greathouse garden path in the soft twilight to where she has hidden a mango earlier in the day, hoping to sneak home with it.

As she reaches into a crevice in the garden wall for the mango, suddenly, in the shadows nearby she notices Lucy Fagan, the master's daughter, sitting and eating the mango herself.

"Jus' you be moving along," says Lucy Fagan smartly as she wipes bits of the sweet juicy fruit from around her mouth. "You know you're not allowed anythin' from my father's garden."

Not daring to reply, Nelly turns and runs toward the gray huts and glimmering cooking fires of the slave village.

Aunty Moth is hobbling around their fire stirring a savory pepperpot stew. Nelly joins Grandfather who is sitting on a large boulder just outside the door of their hut.

"You got a sad face tonight. What troublin' you, girl?"

After a while Nelly replies softly, "Lucy Fagan na let me have one mango from the big house garden. Why she so mean, Dada? Me work hard, hard in that garden."

Grandfather's shoulders sag. "Well, Nelly, that jus' how it be. Dem big-house people be in charge here. But you best forget worrying about that now."

After some thought, he leans close to her and lowers his voice to a whisper. "Nelly, Girl, high in those dark green mountains me have something to show you. Up there is a hidden place with something special for my little girl."

Nelly is astonished and the mango forgotten.

"A hidden place?" she whispers. "Where, Dada? Tell me!"

"Tomorrow be Sunday, our day off from plantation work, you can come with me and Boca on a trip up the mountain.

"Now, eat your food! God willing, morning bring a fine day." Grandfather's deep voice rings rich with promise.

Long before dawn the next morning, Nelly awakens wondering where Grandfather will take her. She slips into her clothes and sits on the boulder sipping a cup of chocolate tea as Grandfather prepares his donkey, Boca, for the trip. Then he settles her on Boca's back atop several folded hemp bags.

Quietly, they move out of the village, past the mill and the sugar cane fields, and into the forest. Tree frogs peep in the cool darkness as the first rays of the sun begin to glisten in the thick foliage overhead.

The way quickly grows steeper. Grandfather tells her the names of the places they pass. "Cinnamon, Hollup Ghaut, Golan."

Nelly, who has never been so far up the mountain before, is enchanted. But soon she hears the roar of rushing water, and a sudden breeze brings a foul whiff of sulfur making her cough.

"Better walk now," says Grandfather as he helps her down from Boca's back. "Follow me. We must cross the old volcano crater, and you walk your foot good now, 'cause the mud be boilin' hot!"

Conclusion

The three questions in the title of this paper occurred to me well before I began the Galways study. Although they are about representation, and were raised repeatedly during the project in the ways I have described, writing about how we worked out the answers has caused me to reevaluate the meaning and emotions of the entire research experience. The act of doing the Galways research has been one of personal liberation as a woman, as a scholar, and as a North American person with "White" skin. Together I and my colleagues, both Montserratian and North American, proved that we could study the history of a past place during a particularly difficult and contended era in New World social ("race") relations and find community and exhilaration in the process. Nonetheless, in the end it has not been possible for me to "overcom[e] the gulf between self and other, past and present, near and distant" of which Revill speaks (1994, 123). Though I may do my best to let the mountain and its people speak for themselves, my interpretive roles as writer and speaker cannot be separated from my roles as White North American, academic entrepreneur, fund raiser, adopted Montserratian (as I am often called there), teacher, vulnerable friend, pay master, project director, or woman. Not only are there many possible versions of the account from my pen, there are many others who could wield that pen. Yet I suspect Galways people would find all this agonizing "reflexivity" quite silly. Nelly Dyer, a chief provider of information for the study and now ninety years old, would say, "Oh Lord, Lyd, just sit down here on one of these stone chairs and tell the story" (figure 14.9).

One Sunday afternoon more than a decade ago, some people from St. Patricks village sat under the mango tree in the Galways yard and chatted about the ambiance of the place. It was already taking on a different look because two acres or more had been regularly cleared and the old Georgian ruins—the boiling house, windmill tower, cattlemill, and greathouse—were set off in a carpet of bright green grass. One said, "You know, this place is nice. You could bring your family here to relax." Another added, "We could have our fetes here, do a goat water." (Goat water, the Montserratian ceremonial meal for everything from weddings, baptisms, and family reunions to Emancipation

Fig. 14.9. Nelly Dyer, Galways Mountain, summer 1992. (Photo by Lydia M. Pulsipher)

Day, starts with butchering the goat on the site of the event.) A third suggested that one could bring a diesel generator and set up electronic instruments for music. But he was shouted down. "No, no, That wouldn't suit the place," several chided. "You would need the old time music—a string band." And so, the Galways Mountain people of today construct representations of the place, Galways Plantation, where once their forebears were enslaved. But there are many competing concepts of what the place should be: a thicket like it used to be, a park, a living history museum, a site for cultivation plots, a pasture, a housing development, an ecotourism haven. The question of "who represents Galways Mountain and for whom?" thus goes beyond my own personal framing of the dilemma. The debate is revealing; no one person or group is beyond the politics of representation.

In 1995 the Galways site is still a place becoming. It looks like a park but has never been so designated formally. There are some fences that fail to keep out wandering cattle, a sign that briefly explains the site to visitors, and lots of

Fig. 14.10. St. Patricks village people at a Galways goatwater fête, 1992. (Photo by Lydia M. Pulsipher)

blooming oleander bushes planted one spring by Clint, a young man from Tennessee (cattle won't eat oleander). In 1992 the site won an international award for research and restoration;[27] but beyond landscaping and some repair to the stone ruins after Hurricane Hugo, there has been little actual restoration. Some of us talk about building a replica of the slave village because for us that, not the industrial core, was the real heart of the plantation. But today the village remains a guava thicket and you have to slither under a barbed wire fence to visit the village places—the waterstone, the cassava presses, the house sites—places that to me whisper the stories of Margaret and Garrick, Quacou and Granderson, Nelly, and her grandfather. Instead, Galways people appropriate the old plantation yard and have their fetes under the mango tree, sometimes with electronic music, sometimes with a flute, a fiddle, and a boom pipe (figure 14.10). During field trips, school children clamber on the stone ruins of the boiling house or stand in the grand entrance of the windmill tower gazing thoughtfully out to sea. When the people leave at dusk, just as the evening winds rush down from the mountains to the east, the tree frogs take up their music and the cattle and goats come back to meander through the ruins.

Notes

1. The Montserrat National Trust began as a primarily expatriate organization interested in historic and natural preservation. Although the officers were Montserratian business and government leaders, much of the work, and indeed the policy formation of the organization was taken on by retired North Americans and British who always had as one of their goals the preservation of Montserrat as a stable place to retire. During the time of the Galways study (1980–1995), the National Trust has evolved into much more of a Montserratian-led organization, with officers now willing to ask difficult questions about the political, socioeconomic and environmental ramifications of any project they undertake.

2. Although definitions of creole culture are outside the parameters of this paper, briefly, I see creole culture as predominantly popularly based, being derived from an amalgam of New and Old World influences that are now difficult to untangle. Muted strains of African influences may include female-centered domestic life, performance-based social commentary, and food and linguistic patterns; but in all these categories and others as well, elements of both Native American (Pulsipher 1995) and European folk culture are evident (Berry 1995). Creole culture is in tension with, yet often is incongruently overlaid with, Eurocentric middle class values and patriarchal rules for behavior.

3. The Galways project (1980–present) is sponsored by the Montserrat National Trust and has been funded by grants from Earthwatch/Center for Field Research, John Carter Brown Library Fellowship Program, Skaggs Foundation, Wenner-Gren Foundation, Association of American Geographers, Boston University, University of Tennessee, Smithsonian Museum of Natural History, Smithsonian Associates Program, National Endowment for the Humanities Summer Fellowship Program, Fulbright-Hays Program, and numerous private contributions. The project is an interdisciplinary

study of the cultural ecology of plantation society in a specific place. Field research included extensive archaeological excavations of the plantation yard, the greathouse, the burying ground and the slave village. Ethnographic research with the descendants of Galways slaves was also conducted along with ethnoarchaeological research on slave domestic sites, archival research, and detailed landscape reconnaissance and mapping. Colleagues from many disciplines have participated in this study, most importantly, the archaeologists Conrad McCall Goodwin (now of the University of Tennessee) and Jean Howson (of New York University), without whom the Galways project would not have been possible.

4. In Montserrat culture, a woman in public is assumed to be (at least potentially) sexually available, and it is often necessary for a woman to reiterate explicitly that this is not the case. An ignored overture may not be sufficient to signal disinterest.

5. Mango (*Mangifera indica*) trees now symbolize prosperity and independence in Montserrat because, during slavery and after, their fruit was not often allowed to ordinary laborers. Rather the fruit was sold as an extra plantation cash crop. This tree, prominently positioned in the middle of the plantation yard, was planted at the birth of Eleanor Cassell some sixty years ago, long after the estate was abandoned. According to local custom, such trees are owned by the child so honored despite the fact that it might be growing on land held by others.

6. Rupert Pemberton, interview by author, Galways Mountain, July, 1987; Nelly Dyer, interview by author, St. Patricks Village, June, 1985, July, 1990).

7. The original of this fictional account was published in the *Seeds of Change* catalog (Viola and Margolis, 1991) and also used in a symposium paper (Pulsipher 1992).

8. Bananas (*Musa sapientum*) were brought to the Caribbean by the Spanish from the Canary Islands in the 1400s. They were quickly adopted by Native American cultivators and diffused throughout the Caribbean basin. They and coconut trees (*Cocos nucifera*), also introduced by the Spanish, were commonly depicted in pictures shading the houses of slave villages. Pawpaw (*Carica papaya*) is native to the New World tropics and was a common garden plant in Amerindian gardens that was then adopted by African and European settlers. Cedar trees (*Cedrela ordorata*) are native to Montserrat and are prominent in the forest assemblage. They regenerate quickly on cleared land, and a few are allowed along fencerows because they offer shade and a variety of products (leaves, bark) that are useful in crafts and folk medicine.

9. Archaeology in Galways slave village has established that the village was located on a series of terraces below the boilinghouse to the southwest. The houses were set up on posts (nogs) and hence were probably of wood with wood floors, much like still extant traditional houses. And, like today, many useful and/or valued items were stored under the houses, such as tools, work clothes, cooking utensils, and curiosities, all of which were identified archaeologically. The fact that roofing material was not present in the archaeological record indicates that, as documents and oral histories attest, the roofs were thatched with grass, probably sugar cane leaves. Animal keeping is known from many sources to have been an important part of the slave-managed subsistence economies of plantations. Animal remains and other evidence of animal keeping were found in the Galways village and on other plantation village sites (Howson 1987; Goodwin and Pulsipher 1983).

10. The furnishings in slave houses varied considerably. This pallet might have been a simple bed roll made out of old clothes, still used by some people in Montserrat; or

it may have been a locally made slatted mahogany bench like heirlooms passed down in Montserrat families. Such a bench would have been topped with a straw-stuffed mattress.

11. Fishing as a subsistence activity is often noted in descriptions of slave lifeways (Price 1966) and is a long, though not prominent, tradition in Montserrat, especially in the southwest, where it has typically been combined with smuggling. Steep cliffs would have facilitated covert access to the water, protecting fishermen and smugglers from detection. The fishing/smuggling connection between St. Patricks and Guadeloupe is celebrated in folk lore (Nelly Dyer, interview by author, July 1989) and folk music: "Run, Run, Ben Dyer, Run" (performed by the Emerald Community Singers, Baird Auditorium, the Smithsonian National Museum of Natural History, March 19, 1992).

12. Today people who live in traditional houseyards on Montserrat often joke about the stone furniture in their yards. "Hey Lyd, me gon' send one couple these fine stone chairs home on de plane wid you" (Dyer, interview by author, St. Patricks village, August, 1989). The Galways slave village has many volcanic boulders that were used as doorsteps, work areas, grinding stones, play sites, and water catchments.

13. Verbal and pictorial descriptions of slave villages almost always emphasize the foliage of gardens and trees that provided sustenance and set the village apart from the rest of the plantation core (Stewart 1823; Edwards 1793; Barclay 1826). Such foliage screens consisted of banana, pawpaw, coconut, cedar, soursop, sugar apple, guava, prickly pear, colita (*Sansavieria liberica*), croton, and hibiscus. Herbaceous annuals like herbs, peppers, onions, and shallots, and many useful wild plants would also have been found around houses. All were used for food, medicine, fiber, or building. They remain important features of houseyard gardens in Montserrat, today (Thomasson 1992).

14. Modern Montserratians can still describe a game called "Chiney Money" which is a sort of dice game; but the pieces are three disks, about the size of a U.S. penny or nickel, which are made by smoothing round the edges of broken pieces of pottery or china that have decoration on one side (often a Chinese landscape scene common on Chinese export porcelain or English transfer printed pottery, hence the name "Chiney Money." The three pieces are thrown on a table, and the arrangement in which they fall brings the thrower a score of 3, 17, or 18 (Rupert Pemberton, interview by author, Centre Square rum shop, July, 1987).

15. Shards of white clay pipes were found in profusion in the slave village and throughout the plantation yard. Tobacco is still one of the most often found plants in Montserratian houseyards; but it reportedly does not give a pleasant smoke, hence most smokers prefer to buy imported tobacco. Since early colonial times, itinerant traders filled a crucial niche in the informal economy of slaves and free laborers. Often described as dark and swarthy, or sometimes explicitly as Jews or Arabs, these traders brought in a variety of products needed or desired by people with little cash. They would barter and accept in-kind payment, hence they facilitated entrepreneurial activity on the part of slaves, and thereby brought down the disapproval of the planter class (who undoubtedly also used their services). Laws to control or eliminate their trade were often passed under another guise, such as laws that prohibited the ramshackle buildings they used as trading centers (Montserrat 1740). Itinerant traders of Middle Eastern origins, carrying suitcases of goods, still came to Montserrat in the 1960s (Colin Riley, interview by

author, Knoxville, TN, January, 1992; Nelly Dyer, interview by author, St. Patricks village, August, 1992; Reg Murphy, interview by author, Antigua, June, 1994).

16. None of these ingredients (dasheen [*Colocasia esculenta*], pigeon peas [*Cajanus cajan*], or plantains [*Musa paradisiaca*]) are native to the New World, yet they are very common in the diets of African Caribbean people, who may have been in part responsible for introducing them and for their diffusion in the Americas. Pigeon peas are African in origin, dasheen and plantains are originally Asian but were used in Africa before 1492.

17. Heavy clay cooking pots, sometimes called Yabas, were common throughout African America and are still preferred by some cooks. Reddish-brown, unglazed, unevenly fired sherds from such pots, often charred on one side, were the most common artifact collected in Galways village. Other clay vessels were used until the last several decades to store water, dried beans, condiments, and oil, and as griddles for baking cassava bread (Nelly Dyer interviews by author, St. Patricks village and Galways Mountian, 1988–1992).

The volcanic deposits of Montserrat offer numerous small caches of clay good for potting; several exist on Galways Mountain. A project is now underway to match the physical and chemical characteristics of these clay sources with those of the sherds found at Galways to determine if they could have been made locally (Locke-Paddon 1992). In some cases—determined by shape of vessel and color of the slip—red burnished sherds like the one Garrick found are thought to be of Amerindian origin; but differentiating these sherds as to those made by Africans or by contact-period or pre-contact Amerindians is often very difficult.

18. The vegetative material culture referred to in this paragraph should be noted: the calabash tree (*Crescentia cujete*), which produces round, hard-shelled, pulp-filled globes that can be cleaned out and carved into useful vessels and used for serving, storing, and even cooking for short periods, is native to the New World; several trees are still to be found on abandoned house sites on Galways Mountain. The coconut provides many useful products: food, fiber, containers, bracts; it can have some unexpected impacts on the landscape. The bracts, which are still used to sweep yards throughout the islands, have prongs that are extremely abrasive. The sweeping action results in the rapid erosion of the soil in the surrounding yard. Soon a residue bank of soil will develop under a house and the bottom of the supporting nogs will be exposed as the yard surface descends (Pulsipher 1986b). The coconut tree is referred to as Quacou's because a tree is (was) often planted at a child's birth and then became that child's possession even though the tree was growing on land owned by someone else (in this case, the plantation owner). (Such customs are ways of appropriating space from those in authority by those who have been rendered "spaceless" by colonial systems.) The banana is a common source of fiber used for tying packages, attaching plants to stakes, tying goats, etc.

19. Cassava (*Manihot esculenta*), a South American domesticate, was quickly adopted by New World Africans who may have first encountered the plant in Africa, where it became part of the Portuguese food supply network in support of the slave trade (Vansina 1990). Because the preferred bitter cassava requires elaborate processing before it is edible, this transaction between Africans and Native Americans remains one of the most interesting and obscure cultural exchanges of the colonial period. Cassava production was an important part of the informal economy of Galways village, as at-

tested to by archaeological evidence that a section of the village specialized in this activity. No doubt it was consumed in the village in large amounts, but also sold for profit. Cassava is still processed in the traditional way in Montserrat and sold in the market weekly (Pulsipher 1995).

20. Houses in Galways village were close together, often no more than four to ten feet apart. They measured about eight feet by sixteen, or ten by twenty, and were informally arranged on terraced west-facing slopes. As in modern houseyards, nearly all activities but sleeping and dressing must have taken place outside. Hence, people interacted nearly constantly, respecting or breaching the local norms governing privacy and communication. If someone either entered private space without permission or failed to speak when passing, explanations would be demanded.

21. This exchange illustrates two important components of the subsistence economy of slaves: reciprocal exchange and the keeping of pigs. Pigs were among the most common animals kept by slaves, as attested to by many contemporary pictures. Because they could destroy desirable plants quickly, pigs were usually penned, tethered, or watched by children. They were fed with surplus agricultural production, especially sweet potatoes, but also with household waste frequently contributed by neighbors who, depending on the size and regularity of their pig food contributions, would have the right to part of a butchered animal. Reciprocity was especially important in the food and agricultural economy but also extended to many other aspects of life, including child and elder care.

22. The identification of the "water stone" at Galways village by St. Patricks villager Susie Howson, (who remembered such stones from her childhood) opened important inquiries into slave water management; and water stones have since been identified all over the island. The Galways village stone consists of a large irregular boulder about ten feet by five by five. It has been carved into a sloping wedge-shaped catchment with a basin at the bottom. Since it rains almost nightly at Galways, the stone will catch a basin of fresh water every night, perfect for washing the baby or for boiling the morning tea. It should also be noted that the east side (down-slope) of the stone contains the carved notch (three inches in diameter, 18 inches off the ground) commonly used in setting up a cassava press, as does that of another nearby boulder. All three of these features were recognized and identified first by Montserratian archaeology laborers.

23. Many chroniclers and the artwork of the period attest to the fact that slaves regularly carried cutlasses and used them as multi-purpose tools—to prune and clear vegetation, to strip bark or other tree products for use, to carve and peal, to dig in the soil, to butcher, and occasionally to strike out at enemies. The power of this ubiquitous tool to enable humans to quickly change the landscape cannot be appreciated until seen. The remains of many cutlasses were found in the Galways village archaeological excavations.

24. There are two varieties of chaney bush (*Philodendron sagittifolium*) growing on Galways Mountain. "Hard leaf" is used to feed animals, "soft leaf" is used to wrap food for storing, carrying or even cooking. The tendrils that the plant sends down from its usual home in the crotch of a tree are tough and fibrous and are used for many purposes requiring a rope or a cord.

25. A version of this story is currently being illustrated for publication by Dial Press, New York City.

26. The name Nelly Dyer is that of an elderly woman now living in St. Patricks

village whose stories of her childhood companionship with her grandfather, James Dyer, and of her remembrances of her greatgrandmother, Rosetta Williams, born well before emancipation, were the inspiration for this story.

27. In 1992 Galways Plantation was the recipient of first place award for research and restoration of a Caribbean historic site awarded by the International Congress of Monuments and Sites (ICOMOS) and American Express.

References

Barclay, A. 1826. *A practical view of the present state of slavery in the West Indies*. London.

Berleant-Schiller, R., and L. M. Pulsipher. 1986. Caribbean subsistence agriculture. *Nieuwe West Indische Gids*, 60: 1–40.

Berleant-Schiller, R. 1991. Hidden places and creole forms: Naming the Barbudan landscape. *The Professional Geographer* 43:92–101.

Berry, V. 1995. The European influence on Montserrat's folk medicine. Dissertation proposal on file in the Department of Geography, University of Tennessee, Knoxville, TN 37996–1420.

Brown, R.H. 1968. *Mirror for Americans; Likeness of the eastern seaboard, 1810*. New York: Da Capo Press.

Clifford, J. and G.E. Marcus, eds. 1986. *Writing culture: The poetics and politics of ethnography*. Berkeley and Los Angeles: The University of California Press.

Craton, M. 1978. *Searching for the invisible man: Slaves and plantation life in Jamaica*. Cambridge: Harvard University Press.

Cronon, W. 1983. *Changes in the land: Indians, colonists, and the ecology of New England*. New York: Hill and Wang.

Duncan, J.S., and D. Ley. 1993. *Place/culture/representation*. London and New York: Routledge.

Edwards, B. 1793. *The history, civil and commercial, of the West Indies*. London: John Stockdale.

Foucault, M. 1971. Nietzsche, genealogy, history. In *Michel Foucault: Language, counter-memory, practice: Selected essays and interviews*, ed. D.F. Bouchard. Ithaca New York: Cornell University Press.

Gilbert, M. 1994. The politics of location: Doing feminist research at "home". *The Professional Geographer* 46:90–96.

Goodwin, C.M. 1987. *Sugar, Time and Englishmen*. Ph.D. dissertation, unpublished, Department of Archaeology, Boston University.

———. and L.M. Pulsipher. 1983. Little Bay Report, the Galways Project, on file at Department of Geography, University of Tennessee, Knoxville.

———. 1990. Outline of documented history of Galways Plantation, Montserrat, West Indies, through the mid-nineteenth century. On file, Department of Geography, University of Tennessee, Knoxville.

Higman, B. 1988. *Jamaica surveyed*. Kingston: Institute of Jamaica Publications.

Howson, J. 1987. Report of the 1987 Fieldwork at Galways Village, Montserrat, West Indies, the Galways Project, on file at Department of Geography, University of Tennessee, Knoxville.

Jackson, J.B. 1984. *Discovering the vernacular landscape*. New Haven: Yale University Press, 1984.

Katz, C. 1994. Playing the field: Questions of fieldwork in geography. *The Professional Geographer* 46:67–72.

Keith, M. 1992. Angry writing: (Re)presenting the unethical world of the ethnographer. *Environment and Planning D: Society and Space* 10:551–68.

Kobayashi, A. 1994. Coloring the field: Gender, "race," and the politics of fieldwork. *The Professional Geographer* 46:73–80.

LaCapra, D. 1985. *History and criticism*. Ithaca, NY: Cornell University Press.

Lake, C. 1989. *Rosehill: Portraits from a midlands city*. London: Bloomsbury.

Locke-Paddon, T. 1992. Field project on the potting clays of Montserrat. On file at the Department of Geography, University of Tennessee, Knoxville, TN 37996-1420.

Mascia-Lees, F. et al. 1989. The postmodernist turn in anthropology: Cautions from a feminist perspective. *Signs: Journal of Women in Culture and Society* 15:7–33.

Meinig, D.W. 1986, 1993. *The shaping of America*. 2 vols. New Haven: Yale University Press.

Montserrat Assembly. 1740. *Acts of Assembly 1668–1740*. London: James Baskett.

Nast, H. 1994. Women in the field: Critical feminist methodologies and theoretical perspectives. *The Professional Geographer* 46:54–66.

Olwig, K.F. 1985. *Cultural adaptation and resistance on St. John*. Gainesville: University of Florida Press.

Price, R. 1966. Caribbean fishing and fishermen. *American Anthropologist* 68:1363–83.

———. 1990. *Alabi's world*. Baltimore and London: Johns Hopkins University Press.

Pulsipher, L.M. 1986a. Seventeenth-century Montserrat. *Historical Geography Research (Monograph) Series No. 17*. Norwich, England: Geo Books.

——— 1986b. Ethnoarchaeology for the study of Caribbean slave villages. Presented in *Ethnohistory and historical archaeology in the Caribbean*, a symposium and workshop sponsored by the Program in Atlantic History, Culture, and Society, Johns Hopkins University.

———. 1986c. Folk material culture notes, on file at the Department of Geography, University of Tennessee, Knoxville, TN 37996–1420.

——— 1990. They have Saturdays and Sundays to feed themselves. *Gardens and Landscapes of the Past*, a special issue of *Expedition Magazine* 32:24–33.

———. 1991. Galways Plantation. In *Seeds of change*, ed. Herman Viola and Carolyn Margolis, 138–59. Washington: Smithsonian Press.

———. 1992. 'Here where the old time people be:' Reconstructing slave-made landscapes in the Caribbean. *The Lesser Antilles in the age of European expansion*, a symposium. Hamilton College, Hamilton, NY, Cornell University, Ithaca, NY.

———. 1993a. Changing roles in the life cycles of Women in traditional West Indian Houseyards. In *Women and change in the Caribbean*, ed. Janet Momsen, 50–64. Kingston: Ian Randle; Bloomington: Indiana University Press; London: James Currey.

———. 1993b. He won't let she stretch she foot. In *Full circles: Geographies of women over the life course*, ed. Cindi Katz and Janice Monk, 107–21. London: Routledge.

———. 1994. The landscapes and ideational roles of Caribbean slave gardens. In *The archaeology of garden and field*, ed. Naomi Miller and Kathryn Gleason. Philadelphia: University of Pennsylvania Press.

————. 1995. Ecological and symbolic roles of plants: The case of manioc. Paper presented at the Association of American Geographers annual meeting, Chicago.

Pulsipher, L.M. and C.M. Goodwin. 1982. The Galways plantation project, Montserrat, West Indies: Report of the 1981 field season. Department of Geography, University of Tennessee, Knoxville.

Pulsipher, L.M. and B. R. Sims. Forthcoming. *The hidden garden of Galways Mountain*. New York: Dial Press.

Revill, G. 1994. Reading Rosehill. In *Place and the politics of identity,* ed. M. Keith and S. Pile. London: Routledge Press.

Stewart, J. 1823. *A view of the past and present state of the island of Jamaica*. Edinburgh: Oliver and Boyd.

Thomasson, D. 1992. *The social ecology of kitchen gardens: Montserrat, West Indies*. M.A. Thesis, Department of Geography, University of Tennessee.

Trask, Haunani-Kay. 1993. *From a native daughter: Colonialism and sovereignty in Hawai'i*. Monroe, Maine: Common Courage Press.

Vansina, Jan. 1990. *Paths in the rainforests: Towards a history of political tradition in Equatorial Africa*. Madison: University of Wisconsin Press.

Walter, E.V. 1988. *Placeways: A theory of human environment*. Chapel Hill: The University of North Carolina Press.

White, H. 1978. *Tropics of discourse: Essays in cultural criticism*. Baltimore: The Johns Hopkins University Press.

————. 1982 Method and ideology in intellectual history: the case of Henry Adams. In *Modern european intellectual history,* ed. D. LaCapra and S.L. Kaplan, 280–310. Ithaca, NY: Cornell University Press.

15

Redefining the Barricades: Latina Lesbian Politics and the Creation of an Oppositional Public Sphere

Patricia Meoño-Picado

In this chapter I address practical problems faced by Latina lesbians in New York City as they actively participate in the formation of an oppositional public sphere.[1] Negt and Kluge suggest that the oppositional public sphere is a space of cultural and political representation where a subaltern group in contemporary capitalism may reclaim its daily life experience from the hegemonic definitional interests of the liberal bourgeois public sphere.[2] The subaltern group may then rearticulate in this space its daily life experience in terms more appropriate to its local exigencies. Crucial to Negt and Kluge's definition of an oppositional public sphere is the notion of transcending the universalist restrictions imposed by liberal ideals of, among others, representation, publicity, privacy, family, and community.[3] For Negt and Kluge, an oppositional public sphere is separate and different from the other liberal bourgeois publics, particularly those associated with the state.

While attempting to bring into public life, and hence to invest with a political dimension, those elements of cultural production usually deemed too frenzied to be displayed outside the confines of the home (or the gay bar), Latina lesbians must assess their cultural politics at different levels. At the level of modernity, as an aesthetic sensibility, the lesbian has served as one of the privileged personae onto which male desire concentrates its gaze—Buci-Glucksmann (1987) adds to this category the prostitute, the barren woman, and the androgyne. Thus, lesbians, rather than facing absolute invisibility in the public sphere, must confront with new strains of utopic sexual fantasy the already existing representational forms that are dictated by hegemonic male desire.[4] At the level of the larger women's movement, Latina lesbians must stress that, although their cultural and political interests in many respects overlap those of

the women's movement, contemporary society constructs the bodies of Latinas as sites of a specific kind of oppression. Within the women's movement,
in many instances our cultural heritage (usually incarnated as linguistic intona-
tion), ethnic roots (usually incarnated as epidermic difference), and sexual orientation serve as sources for discrimination. Similarly, within the lesbian
community at large, some of those same sources may be mobilized to overlay
the construction of the bodies of Latina lesbians with excessive desire, hence
turning them into exotic objects.[5] At the level of the Latino community itself,
Latina lesbians must face the contradictory manifestations of homophobia.
Ironically, the Latino community allows for the open display of androgyny in
its more hermetic popular practices. For example, in the religious practices
associated with spiritism and Santería, a certain degree of androgyny is permitted.[6] Nevertheless, in the case of its own public sphere, the Latino community
constantly attempts to either eradicate or deprecate any manifestation of lesbianism and homosexuality. In the latter case, the problem is not their complete
invisibility; on the contrary, there is an excessive presence of lesbian and homosexual images in Latino culture. The problem is that their presence is always used as a means to prop up heterosexual machismo. In sum, in the
creation of an oppositional public sphere, in addition to assessing their own
specific interests, Latina lesbians must take into consideration the contiguities,
overlaps, and disjunctures that exist between their own public sphere, the hegemonic liberal public sphere, and other publics, specifically, the Latino community and the lesbian and gay community at large.

In this chapter I trace how New York City Latina lesbians, under the aegis
of Las Buenas Amigas (LBA), have engaged in workshops, retreats, cultural
events, and marches with the purpose of constructing their own oppositional
public sphere. In particular, I examine the 17 November 1994 demonstration
against Spanish-language radio station MEGA WSKQ 97.9 FM. This demonstration is of special significance because in articulating the specifics of homophobia in the Latino community and in mobilizing and working with other
lesbian organizations, LBA had to engage with the often contradictory, elusive, and fluid elements characterizing any attempt to create an oppositional
public sphere.

The Oppositional Public Sphere and Geography

In their concern to scrutinize the possible interconnections between sexuality
and space, lesbian and gay geographies have assigned central importance to
notions of the public and the private (Adler and Brenner 1992; Bell 1991,
1994, 1995a, b; Brown 1994, 1995; Forest 1995; Geltmaker 1992; Knopp
1987, 1990a, b, 1992, 1994; Lauria and Knopp 1985; Valentine 1992,
1993a, b, 1995; Weightman 1980). This is not surprising if, as Sedgwick
(1990) argues, in modernity, a "closet"—with all its connotations of closure/
aperture, secrecy/disclosure, and ignorance/knowledge—serves as the organi-

zational principle whereby a heterosexual/homosexual dichotomy of subjectivities is defined. What is surprising is that in such a small number of contributions, lesbian and gay geographies evidence a multifarious number of positions.

In investigating their direct connection to the housing market mechanisms and the transformation of the state apparatus, Forest (1995), Knopp (1987, 1990a, b), and Lauria and Knopp (1985) stress the fixity and openness of gay neighborhoods. Adler and Brenner (1992) and Valentine (1993a, b, 1995), on the other hand, stress the fluidity and secrecy of the lesbian presence in the urban landscape to the extent that it is difficult to even talk about lesbian neighborhoods as such. Knopp (1992) argues about the relevance of class analysis in the study of gay and lesbian geographies by attempting to show that there are very clear connections between the transformation of capitalism and the restructuration of gender and sexuality. Valentine (1993b), on the other hand, demonstrates how difficult it is to pin down specific class positions to the manifestations of lesbian sexuality in space. Brown (1994, 1995) shows the advantages of working with the shadow state in the provision of services for people with AIDS and HIV-positive people. Geltmaker (1992) and Bell (1995a), on the other hand, stress how crucial it has been for gay organizations to present an oppositional front against the state apparatus.

But this apparent inconsistency of positions, rather than a problem of miscommunication among its practitioners, shows that lesbian and gay geographies in dealing with sexuality and space and, by implication, with the public and the private spheres, are tackling an object that resists easy classification. In this respect, a cursory examination of the context for discussions about the public and the private is illuminating.

Fraser and Nicholson (1989) find that, around 1980, gender studies went through a rupture in their conceptualization of the public and the private spheres. Before, the two were conceptualized as fixed, separate realms. To the public belonged matters of collective importance, the state apparatus, the economy, and maleness. To the private belonged matters of individual concern, the home, culture, and femaleness. After 1980, in part because of the encounter of gender studies and German critical theory (Fraser 1985, 1992; Hansen 1993; Hohendahl 1982, 1995; Schlüpmann 1988, 1990), this clearcut separation of the two spheres has been questioned. In this sense, Habermas's (1989) definition of the public sphere has been crucial: a discursive arena, separate from the state, where bourgeois private citizens meet to discuss matters of common interest.

In response to the question, where and when is the public sphere? Habermas's position has been fundamental. The public sphere is not a literal space; it is a process that under specific circumstances can invest a space with publicity—namely, a situation where the decision-making process is based on the equality of the members and the egalitarian nature of the discussions. And the public sphere only existed during the late 1700s, when the bourgeoisie was at the brink of grasping political power away from the feudal regime. Habermas then shifts his analysis toward the transformation and disintegration of the public sphere, which, he claims, is traceable to two interrelated processes. Politically, the public sphere changes and disappears with the birth of the bourgeois liberal state, particularly as the latter tends to encroach into the former. Culturally, the transformation of the public sphere is predicated on the organizational principle of modern society, that is, commodity exchange and its tendency to "internally colonize" the different facets of society, particularly the private sphere and the formation of subjectivity.[7] Still, Habermas believes that it is possible to reclaim the bourgeois public sphere provided the same discursive rules that governed it in the past are maintained in the present (Habermas 1984).

From the perspective of gender studies, Habermas's contribution has been crucial in that it has helped to remap the often contradictory manifestations of gender in the public and private spheres and in relation to the state (Fraser 1985). If there are any shortcomings in Habermas's conceptualization, they are with respect to the place he assigns to oppositional movements (Habermas 1992; Hansen 1993). In fact, for Habermas, for whom the liberal public sphere is a bourgeois form of publicity, the principles of public discursiveness are so intimately tied to the internal workings of bourgeois society that any room for opposition at all is due to the internal contradictions of capitalism proper and nothing else (Habermas 1975, 1984).

If we follow Habermas's argument, we may partially explain the inconsistency of positions evidenced by the practitioners of lesbian and gay geographies. The fixity and openness of gay neighborhoods, the clearly demarcated relationship between the transformation of capitalism and the restructuration of gender and sexuality, and the facile articulation of certain gay organizations with the shadow state are traceable to the internal workings of capitalism and the transformation and disintegration of the bourgeois public sphere.[8] But what about those gay organizations that present themselves in opposition to the state? What about the fluidity and secrecy of the lesbian presence in the urban landscape and the difficulty to pin down specific class positions to the manifestation of lesbian sexuality in space?

Negt and Kluge (1993) have contributed one of the most important critical encounters with Habermas's definition of the bourgeois public sphere.[9] First, they have pointed out several inconsistencies in Habermas's conceptualization and efforts to reclaim the bourgeois public sphere: (1) his attempt to reclaim a form of publicity that only existed momentarily is futile, and (2) he is strangely disingenuous in his oversight of the ideological elements of the bourgeois public sphere—namely, its mechanisms of exclusion, its existence in the service of the particular interests of a sector of society, and the founding of its legitimacy on the negation of the very basis of its own existence, that is, commodity production. Second, Negt and Kluge have stressed that, on a closer examination, the bourgeois public sphere is bound to fail because (1) it is chaotic, dysfunctional, and inefficient; and (2) it is fragmented, composed by an amalgamate of individual publics. Third, Negt and Kluge have proposed an alternative to the bourgeois public sphere. Despite its inherent problems, Negt and Kluge agree with Habermas, the bourgeois public sphere has a very important function in capitalist society. Through it, the dominant mode of daily life experience, following the model of commodity production, is articulated, but, because of its partiality in representing the interests of only some sectors of society, the bourgeois public sphere leaves out the daily life experience of other sectors. The solution then, Negt and Kluge have proposed, is for those unrepresented sectors of society to create oppositional publics.

Negt and Kluge address the question of how to create an oppositional public sphere by shifting the focus of their analysis to questions of representation, so that what had started out as a political problem is addressed in the cultural realm. This shift is particularly important if, as Spivak (1988) argues, there is no perfect continuity between political representation (having someone speaking in someone else's place in matters related to the state and the law) and cultural representation ("re-presenting in matters of art or philosophy" [275]). But whereas Spivak questions whether, in the face of postcolonialism, the subaltern can speak for itself, Negt and Kluge ask what voice will the subaltern use in speaking for itself in an oppositional public sphere. To answer this fundamental question, Negt and Kluge examine the ephemeral instances when "proletarian" oppositional publics have risen to rearticulate the daily life experience of the working class. In these cases, as Hansen (1993) stresses, there has been a juxtaposition of heterogeneous discursive practices, there has been room for the expression of fantasy, and there has been a strong resistance to the facile reduction of historical acts into linear narratives with closure.

Could it be then that the second part to the inconsistency of positions evidenced by the practitioners of lesbian and gay geographies may be explained in terms of oppositional publics? Could it be that disenfranchised homosexuals (especially those living in the HIV-positive, AIDS, sexual perversion continuum) must represent their interests in opposition to the state? Could it be that lesbians, compared to the more facile formation of distinctly gay neighborhoods, have a greater difficulty in making their presence in the urban landscape fixed, open, and clear, therefore opting for fluid, secret, and elusive forms of expression of their sexuality in space? In the next two sections, I examine the kinds of voices that Latina lesbians use in their attempts to create an oppositional public sphere.

Las "Buenas" Amigas

Las Buenas Amigas (LBA) was organized as a consensual collective in November 1986 by five Latina lesbians from the New York City metropolitan area. LBA's intricate territorial dimensions were clear since its inception. During the first year and a half, the group regularly met in private apartments, mostly located in Latino neighborhoods. The purpose of these meetings was to conduct internal discussions about the political issues affecting the lives of Latina lesbians and to address Latina lesbian subjectivity in a novel fashion. So, even when discussions were conducted within the realm of privacy, they were designed to integrate notions normally fragmented or disregarded by the liberal public society. For example, an assessment of the situation of Latina women in contemporary U.S. society—usually a matter of public, political interest—was coupled with a discussion of sexual repression within the Latino community and its possible connections with the high incidence of alcoholism in the lesbian community—usually matters of private, ethnic, and familial interest.

The roots of the involvement of these five Latina lesbians with LBA can be traced to the late 1970s and early 1980s. Other than organizations such as El Comité Homosexual Latinoamericano (COHLA)—a New York City-based lesbian and gay organization founded in 1977 and mostly composed of Latino gay men—and Salsa Soul Sisters—a New York City-based lesbian organization founded in the 1970s and mostly composed of African-American lesbians— Latina lesbians had mostly participated in White middle lesbian and gay organizations. Although these organizations provided a forum for the discussion of issues of interest for most lesbians and gays, issues of crucial importance for Latina lesbians—such as those associated with recent immigration, linguistic alienation, and economic, political, and cultural disenfranchisement—had been considered too specific and not generalizable enough as to deserve the whole group's attention. In the case of their participation in Latino lesbian and gay groups, these Latina lesbians had found that machismo was extremely pervasive and that there was little that they could do to circumvent their expected traditional role as subordinate caretakers.

Moreover, in November 1980, some of them, in association with Latina lesbians from other parts of the United States and Latin America, had organized a writers' collective (Colectiva Lesbiana Latinoamericana) with the purpose of compiling, editing, and publishing writings reflective of the Latina lesbian experience. Although the Colectiva dissolved in the mid–1980s, it mustered enough impetus to elicit contributions by at least forty-seven Latina lesbians from around the United States and Latin America. To publish a compilation of these writings and to secure funding from donating institutions, several of these Latina lesbians founded in 1986 the Latina Lesbian History Project. The end-result of these efforts, *Compañeras* (1994), came about through an artisanal mode of production whereby the Latina Lesbian History Project and LBA members, in the company of their friends and lovers, did all the work: transcription, typesetting, copy editing, proofreading, printing, securing of funds, and distribution of the book.

During this early phase, LBA's seeming retrenchment away from New York City's different publics was accompanied by efforts to nurture relations with other Latinas across the continental United States and Latin America. In principle, the purpose of these efforts was to search for a common cultural and historical ground on which to base a new kind of political movement. But LBA's experiences with both the lesbian and gay movement at large and Latinas from other places demonstrated that defining a common ground, especially on the basis of biology, kinship, or territorial proximity, was basically illusory. First, there was the tremendous diversity that pervades the Latino community—ranging from different dialects of Spanish to different religious practices to different racial categories. Second, notions of family and community brought to mind contradictory connotations, since the home and the barrio are where most Latina lesbians first encounter homophobia.[10] Third, in many instances, it had been easier to create meaningful ties with Latina lesbians who lived far away—for example, in Puerto Rico or Chile. Consequently, this new political movement needed to work with the assumption that in order to achieve any goals, diversity had to be recognized as an integral part of a Latina lesbian organization; that even when such organization was going to give priority to Latino issues, it was going to do so in opposition to the Latino community's stigmatization of lesbians and homosexuals; and that, territorially, it would privilege spatial disjuncture in order to achieve cultural and historical contiguity.[11]

Paradoxically, it was through LBA's contacts with Latina lesbians from outside New York City and, in particular, through attendance at the First Conference of Latin American and Caribbean Lesbian-Feminists and the Fourth Latin American and Caribbean Feminist Conference, held in Mexico in October 1988, that the group reassessed its orientation. By mid–1987, LBA had started to invite other Latinas to attend its meetings to promote their participation in these conferences. So, in early 1988, LBA—which by then included fifteen active members and many more collaborating members—moved its operations to New York City's Lesbian and Gay Community Services Center (the Center), located in Manhattan at the northern edge of Greenwich Village. With this move, the group began to directly engage with the specificities underlying any participation in the different public spheres of New York City. Besides providing a forum where Latinas could discuss their situation in society and gain consciousness about the need to struggle against all forms of oppression, LBA had to redefine its existence in terms of the creation of a visible space within the Latino and the lesbian and gay communities, and within the liberal public sphere.

In opening its doors to other Latinas, LBA also restructured its work into five interconnected levels. Bimonthly, Latina lesbians would meet at the Center to discuss, in a workshop style, issues dealing with their condition: homophobia and sexism in the Latino community, tokenism and racism in the lesbian and gay community at large, health provision for low-income lesbians, legal rights for new immigrants, domestic violence among lesbian couples, and so forth. The formation of coalitions with other local and national/international lesbian and gay groups, especially those composed of people of color, was to be actively pursued. Contact with a rapidly increasing number of Latina lesbians associated with LBA was to be maintained through mailings, telephone calls, and a regular newsletter. LBA would participate in public events designed to encourage gay pride and visibility, for example, the Puerto Rican Day Parade. And, more important, LBA members would continue to engage in the preservation of Latina lesbian history and stimulate the production of written forms, as had been the case with *Compañeras*.

By 1990, LBA's demographic structure had changed. At the beginning most LBA members were Latinas with a relatively high social-rank within both the Latino and the lesbian and gay communities—although the majority came from working class and low income backgrounds, most of them had graduate degrees or had distinguished themselves as writers or artists. By 1990, most LBA members came from a broader base, particularly blue collar occupations. While most early LBA members were in their middle to late thirties, by 1990, the group included Latina lesbians of all ages. While originally most LBA members were of Puerto Rican descent, by 1990, the group included lesbians from all Latin American backgrounds. Also, although LBA had continued to grow, to expand the diversity of its membership, and to exercise a more visible presence both in New York City and across the U.S. and Latin America, by mid–1991, it was obvious that the group was undergoing a crisis.[12] The results of an informal survey of forty LBA members conducted in the summer of 1991 showed that only five members were interested in political issues.[13] Most members wanted LBA to serve both as support group and facilitator of social activities so that Latinas could meet other Latinas. In addition, there were complaints that the group was "too leftist," that there was "too much bickering and aggression," and that "sometimes decisions [were] made by those who [hadn't] participated."

A new leadership, headed by Latina lesbians in their twenties and early thirties, took over LBA in October 1991 and immediately instituted two fundamental changes. Up to that point, decisions had been made by a direct democracy.[14] During each bimonthly meeting, in addition to a workshop on a predesignated topic, Latina lesbians discussed organizational issues until a consensus was reached. The new leaders instituted a steering committee, open to any member interested in participating, yet separate from the bimonthly meetings. The steering committee would discuss the organization's direction as a whole whereas the bimonthly meetings would be solely devoted to workshops designed to enhance LBA's role as support group. Moreover, the new LBA leadership redefined the political status of the group.

From its inception and perhaps in connection with the founding members' backgrounds, LBA's politics had been implicitly articulated in reference to dependency theory.[15] In making indirect reference to dependency theory, some LBA members had proposed that the struggle for the emancipation of Latina lesbians needed to be tied to the struggle against economic neocolonialism in Latin America. This position, however, as the results of the previously cited survey indicate, had in many instances been a source of divisiveness, especially for lesbians of Cuban background. Therefore, in place of dependency theory, some of the new LBA leaders informally adopted Santería's form of syncretism as a model to guide their political efforts. Santería (Cabrera 1968), rather than combining European saints and African deities into an even religious amalgamate, allows for the public worship of Catholic saints at the same time that the worship of African deities is performed in private. Thus, although people may present themselves in public as adherents of the mainstream, underneath, in their private spaces, they adhere to their supposedly displaced older traditions.

The informal adoption of Santería's form of syncretism did not necessarily mean that Latina lesbians would flaunt heterosexuality in public while living lesbianism in private. Neither did it mean that LBA would distance its politics from class analysis. It meant that some LBA members would make reference to Santería's long tradition of turning private places into public spheres, separate from the hegemonic public sphere, for the preservation of tradition and the contestation of hegemonic culture. It meant that some LBA members would explore the ways in which Santería questions the heterosexual/homosexual dichotomy—for example, the African Orisha Changó (an ambisexual deity) manifests as the Catholic Saint Barbara (a female saint). It meant that some LBA members would resort to Santería's sense of humor and irony following Orisha Eleguá's lead. Eleguá, the trickster, guards the door to the space where the religious ceremony is performed; he is the first Orisha to arrive; his coming is marked by jokes, turns, and surprises. In tandem with this new approach, LBA started to define visibility in terms specific to the local Latino modes of cultural representation, taking into account that it was necessary to reimage New York City's multifarious territories with a Latina lesbian aesthetic and political sensibility.

The first step in this new direction was to place emphasis on the local Latina population. This meant that networking with groups from outside the New York City metropolitan area was relegated to whatever efforts individuals undertook on their own.[16] It also meant that LBA had to acknowledge and work with the specific characteristics of the local Latino community. In contrast to many other U.S. communities, where people of Mexican, Central American, and South American descent predominate—the other exception is the city of Miami where there is a large concentration of White Cuban-Americans—New York City's Latino population is mostly from the Caribbean islands. Therefore, daily life experience is greatly mediated by a strong Afro-Caribbean cultural influence. In addition, most Latina women are economically and politically disenfranchised, highly unaware of lesbian and feminist politics, and in many instances, incapable of dealing with their own sexuality. Hence, LBA had to engage in a two-pronged approach. Instead of distributing flyers and newsletters in Greenwich Village—a traditional White, middle-class gay stronghold—LBA members would attend the gay bars located in Latino neighborhoods proper—for example, Jackson Heights. There, lesbians who had come together solely to display their virtuosity at salsa dancing would be confronted by other Latina lesbians who were equally dextrous yet had the extra appeal of being organized in a cohesive political group.[17]

The second step was the creation of a cultural space representative of the experience of Latina lesbians in U.S. society, but from a perspective that took into account, among others, the Latino sense of humor and irony. For this purpose, LBA revamped its newsletter from a calendar of events and short reports to a magazine featuring regular columns, poetry, and fiction by LBA members. The regular columns were of particular interest as they were designed to challenge mainstream definitions of lesbianism (e.g., "El diccionario lésbico"/"The Lesbian Dictionary" investigated the roots of Spanish words commonly used to denigrate lesbians) and to provide an alternative cultural experience (e.g., "La esquina de Erotiza Memaz"/" The Corner of Erotize Memore," an "advice column," turned irony into a political tool by poking fun at psychic advisers who prey on the Latino community). More than three hundred copies of each newsletter were mailed to LBA members and friends. In addition, members distributed by hand another five hundred copies to the other Latina lesbians on their own turf.

Another aspect of the creation of a cultural space was a series of projects designed to foster the cultural representation of Latinas in their own terms and in media other than writing. For example, forty Latina lesbians attended an educational retreat held in the Catskill Mountains in April 1994. There, LBA challenged them to produce alternative histories of the participation of Latinas in the 1969 Stonewall Rebellion. To equip these Latina lesbians with the appropriate tools to undertake such challenge, LBA organized workshops on writing, photography, music, and painting. The first product of this retreat came in the form of collaborative efforts with *Lesbian Central* and *Dyke T.V.*, two television shows that air on local access channels. Out of such collaboration, LBA members had the opportunity to produce, among others, television segments documenting the plight of lesbian domestic workers and exploring domestic violence among lesbian couples. The second product of the retreat was a photography exhibit held at the Center in April and May 1995 (Heines 1995). Since early 1993, LBA members had started to take snapshots at all sorts of activities with the purpose of preserving, as a kind of historical record, bits of their daily life experience. Inspired by the discussion at the retreat, several LBA members selected some of the snapshots and organized a formal display intended for the general lesbian and gay public.

"Pa'arriba, pa'bajo, la MEGA pa'l carajo"

On 17 November 1994, LBA joined forces with the Lesbian Avengers and African Ancestral Lesbians for Societal Change (formerly Salsa Soul Sisters) to protest against radio WSKQ 97.9 FM (MEGA KQ), the largest Spanish-language radio in New York City. Without a permit from the city and against the will of a massive police force, one hundred lesbians of diverse ethnic and religious backgrounds stopped traffic on 57th Street in Manhattan and marched to the headquarters of the Spanish Broadcasting System (SBS), owner of radio MEGA KQ. Besides banners and placards denouncing the station's use of homophobic, racist, and misogynist speech to boost its ratings, the lesbians carried a ten-foot long by four-foot wide piñata monster, depicting in black, red, yellow, and green a three-headed radio. Accompanied by loud drums, the lesbians chanted, among other things "Pa'arriba, pa'bajo, la MEGA pa'l carajo"/"Up and down, MEGA should go to hell." Once in front of the radio station, the lesbians decapitated the radio-piñata monster in a mock ceremony. After chanting a few more songs and arguing with several radio MEGA KQ employees who had come outside, the organizers of the march announced the location of the restaurant where the lesbians, immediately afterward, could meet for food and drinks and to celebrate.

Several events had motivated such clamorous display of cultural lesbian politics in public. Repeatedly, LBA members had complained that MEGA KQ's morning show "El vacilón de la mañana" engaged in continuous hate speech against lesbians, gays, East Indians, Jews, Africans, and the disabled. After discussing several strategies, LBA decided that to enhance its power against radio MEGA KQ, it had to traverse multiple territories. By protesting alone, LBA risked seeing its efforts completely privatized. That radio MEGA KQ could escape scrutiny of media watchdogs such as the Federal Communications Commission (FCC) and the National Association for the Advancement of Colored People (NAACP), indicated that, because of its linguistic difference, radio MEGA KQ had a very particular claim to the rights of privacy: after all, for the liberal hegemonic public sphere, a Latino public sphere is private. The specificity of these rights were confirmed by the fact that, whereas most English-language radio stations are held accountable under the FCC's regulations regarding the use of obscene language on the air, radio MEGA KQ seemed to elude sanctions. Almost every morning words such as "joder"/ "fuck" aired as part of the comedic skits of "El vacilón de la mañana." Worse yet, MEGA KQ's use of homophobia had escaped scrutiny of the Gay and Lesbian Alliance Against Defamation (GLAAD). When LBA confronted GLAAD for its apparent oversight, the latter alleged lack of resources to monitor a radio station that in any case aired its programming only to a portion of New York City's population.

So LBA decided to involve other lesbian groups in its fight against radio MEGA KQ, especially those with a long visible record of oppositional appearances against the liberal hegemonic public sphere.[18] In consultation with LBA, the Lesbian Avengers staged a series of direct actions against the radio station. In August, the Avengers briefly took over MEGA KQ's studios, momentarily interrupting its transmission of hate ("Crime in the City: Attack of the Lesbian Avengers and Other Crimes from the NYPD Files" 1994); this was followed by a demonstration in front of the station and letters of appeal to both the corporate sponsors and the station's owner. LBA doubled the Avengers' efforts with a series of letters directed to Raúl Alarcón, owner of SBS, and the DJs of "El vacilón de la mañana." Also members of LBA, the Avengers, and African Ancestral Lesbians pasted signs and stickers, denouncing radio MEGA KQ, in Latino neighborhoods and subway stations across the city. As a result of these actions, MEGA KQ removed most of the homophobia by firing the most vitriolic of the two DJs of "El vacilón de la mañana" and retiring those comedic skits evidencing direct attacks against lesbians and homosexuals. Nevertheless, the spread of hate against other ethnic groups, the disabled, and women continued. The 17 November march was meant to signify that as long as radio MEGA KQ disseminated any hate, lesbians remained targets of oppression.

One of the most significant aspects of the 17 November march is that it served as a means to recodify the presence of lesbians in liberal public society. The tone of the march was celebratory, meant in part to commemorate months of arduous work by the three lesbian groups. The presence of the radio-piñata monster, the noise coming from the chants and the drums, and the mock decapitation undoubtedly confused and destabilized any expectation that marks lesbians as objects of male gaze. According to several LBA members, the radio-piñata monster resembled a chicken with three heads. From a hermetic perspective, decapitation of the radio-piñata monster in front of SBS's headquarters could be read as a form of animal sacrifice, reminiscent of those performed in Santería's rituals designed to conjure evil against the enemy. But it could also be read more simply: lesbians can use their great sense of humor and irony as a political weapon. Besides, the fact that in their chants the lesbians used rough language—for example, "Radio Mega says that women like to be raped. Bullshit!!" or "Alarcón, cabrón; Alarcón, maricón"/ "Alarcón, cuckold or traitor; Alarcón, faggot or coward"—was a clear indication that the issue at hand was not obscenity per se.[19]

Despite numerous press releases announcing the 17 November march, most New York City mass media blacked out news about it. Those that reported the action obscured the details of its occurrence. For example, *El Diario/La Prensa* ("Protesta Contra Omega KQ" 1994) dedicated a photograph and a small blurb to the march, where the name of the radio station was misspelled to read radio OMEGA KQ instead of MEGA KQ. In a blurb that appeared in *Alerta* ("Las lesbianas y afeminados le declaran la guerra a MEGA 97.9" 1994), news of the march was couched in homophobic terms: "Lesbians and Fags Declare War to MEGA 97.9" (p. 19). Radio MEGA KQ countered efforts of the three lesbian groups by increasing the number of prize-winning gimmicks, launching a publicity campaign on the subway stations, and working in collusion with other Latino media to clear its public image. The week after the march, WXTV Channel 41, the local affiliate of Spanish-language network Univisión, ran a three-part series called "The voices of the radio," featuring one of the DJs of "El vacilón de la mañana." When asked about any complaints in the Latino community against this kind of programming, the DJ responded that if there were any, these came from "histéricos"/"hysterical people" who had no sense of humor.

Having predicted that the media itself would use its power to black out news as means to privatize lesbian politics, the lesbian groups responded with a bombardment of information about radio MEGA KQ's use of hate speech through alternative channels: in gay and lesbian publications ("Dykes Blast Mega-KQ" 1995), in the alternative press ("Lesbians Strike Back at Hate Radio" 1995; Stroud 1995), in liberal radio programs (interviews with *Alter-*

nativa Latina and *Latino Journal*, both on radio WBAI), and in television shows that air on the local access channels (*Homovisiones* and *Dyke T.V.*). In addition, members of the three groups participated in an informal educational campaign whereby thousands of flyers denouncing the radio station were distributed in Latino neighborhoods.

Epilogue

Two months after the 17 November march, LBA, the Avengers, and African Ancestral Lesbians abruptly ended cooperative work against radio MEGA KQ, according to LBA, because of the Avengers's efforts to privatize the interests of Latina lesbians (Stroud 1995). Within a year of the march, radio MEGA KQ increasingly returned to its homophobia, but without ever mentioning lesbians. In early 1996, SBS filed with the Securities and Exchange Commission a public offering to sell 7.5 million shares (at $10.00 each share). Parts of the proceeds were to be used in the purchase of another FM radio station in New York City, which would bring up to nine the number of AM/FM radio stations owned by SBS in Los Angeles, Miami, and New York City ("Spanish Broadcasting System Registers Initial Public Offering" 1996).

On numerous occasions, I have gone back to 57th Street and the headquarters of SBS in search of reminders of the 17 November march. As far as that street is concerned, the march never occurred. Instead, I find billboards in Latino neighborhoods and posters in the subways that loudly advertise Radio MEGA KQ. I have to go elsewhere in search of reminders: a few newspaper clippings, old copies of flyers, a copy of a television segment.

Despite the territorial dimensions of Latina lesbians' efforts to create an oppositional public sphere where they can represent their interests culturally and politically, the kinds of spaces they produce are contradictory, elusive, fluid, and ultimately, subject to erasure. This is not to say that Latina lesbians' efforts are superfluous. It simply means that they represent their sexuality in space in ways that often escape the cognition of the liberal bourgeois public sphere: by developing networks across contiguous and discontinuous space; by tapping into alternative forms of explanation, such as the use of Santería as a political and cultural strategy; by taking an oppositional stance vis-à-vis the different publics that form the liberal public sphere; and by taking the lack of closure not as a sign of defeat, but as an indication that the struggle must continue.

Notes

1. I have based this chapter on participant-observations from January 1992 through April 1995, when I was an active member of Las Buenas Amigas. In addition, I have relied on minutes of meetings, newsletters, descriptions of the organization attached to

grant proposals, flyers, pamphlets, responses to a survey conducted among LBA members in 1991, and interviews with several LBA founding members. Whereas most researchers of lesbian and gay geographies (e.g., Brown 1995; Knopp 1987, 1990a, b; and Valentine 1992, 1993a, b, 1995) have taken a more detached approach toward their object of study, I was an integral part of LBA's organization. Still, in my conversations with LBA members, I kept most of the concepts presented in this chapter to myself. For me, it was fascinating to discover that Latina lesbians' practical sense of geography, even when they lacked the right terminology, in many respects paralleled the theoretical debates of our discipline.

2. I use the terms "subaltern" and "hegemony" in the sense developed by Gramsci (1971) in his writings about civil society and the state. With these terms, Gramsci explores the mechanisms that allow for the subaltern (e.g., the working class) to internalize hegemonic ideals (e.g., those of the bourgeoisie) by means other than violence and coercion.

3. On occasion, I use the term "publicity" to refer to the discursive aspects of the public sphere and to remind the reader of the semantic difficulties we encounter in attempting to reduce to one word such a complex field; for a more detailed discussion of the difficulties encountered in the definition of the public sphere, see Habermas (1989) and Hansen (1993).

4. For a discussion of the different and complex forms of women's invisibility in modernity, see Wolff (1989).

5. It is only recently that gay and lesbian studies have begun to assess the relation between sexual desire and race. For an introduction to this difficult debate, see Bad Object-Choices (1991), De Lauretis (1994), and Longfellow (1993).

6. Santería is the admixture of Catholicism and Yoruba religious traditions practiced in Cuba and elsewhere (Cabrera 1968). In Santería, deities and spirits of the dead "mount" the living, oftentimes crossing gender lines (e.g., a male deity may "mount" a woman).

7. Historically, commodity fetishism, as an organizing principle that first manifested in the realm of the public economy (both in the areas of exchange and production), has progressively colonized other levels of society, threatening to become an integral part even of the most intimate aspects of the private sphere, such as childrearing and fantasy (Habermas 1984; Negt and Kluge 1993).

8. For a similar argument comparing different historical cases of gay visibility, see Chauncy (1994).

9. Negt and Kluge (1981, 1992, 1993) have contributed to the public sphere debate for the last three decades. Of these, *Geschichte und Eigensinn* (1981) is perhaps the clearest example of what an oppositional book may look like. Kluge, especially, has been the topic of special issues of *October* (Liebman 1988) and *New German Critique* (1990). See Strum (1994) for a comprehensive list of sources that include discussions about Habermas, Kluge, and Negt. See Schlüpmann (1988, 1990) for a discussion of Kluge's controversial encounter with feminism.

10. See New York City Gay and Lesbian Anti-Violence Project (1994) for an analysis of the proportionally higher incidence of violence against lesbians and gays in the Latino community.

11. See Young (1990) for a similar view on the formation of alternative communities outside the traditional boundaries of kinship and the neighborhood. See Morley and

Robins (1989) for a discussion of the effects of the new mass media on the formation of identity and communities.

12. LBA's visibility has resulted from several interconnected activities: (1) participation in local and national marches, for example, New York City's yearly Puerto Rican Day Parade and the 1987 and 1992 Lesbian and Gay Marches on Washington; (2) participation in national and international conferences, for example, the International Conference of Lesbians and Gays of Color—held in Mexico in 1988—and the First National Lesbian Conference—also held in 1988; (3) membership in networks, such as the Network of Latin American and Caribbean Lesbian Feminists, which included member organizations from seventeen countries, and New York City's Lesbian and Gay People of Color Steering Committee, which unites Latinos, Asian Americans, and African Americans; (4) sponsorship of cultural events, such as the New York Lesbian and Gay Film Festival; and (5) participation in ad hoc committees with other lesbian and gay organizations, such as the Latino Gay Men of New York. Undoubtedly, another important source of visibility has been Routledge Press's reprint of *Compañeras: Latina Lesbians (An Anthology)* (Ramos 1994).

13. The survey focused on LBA's governing structure, membership demographics, and direction of the group (e.g., social versus political activities). Results of the survey were published in an LBA newsletter dated June 1991.

14. According to LBA, membership is open to *any* Latina lesbian, irrespective of her background, who regularly attends meetings. Up to 1991, when the group was run as a consensual collective, LBA made a distinction between active and collaborating members. The former, besides their regular attendance, participated in the consensual formulation and execution of programs. The latter were Latina lesbians who occasionally attended meetings and other activities. After 1991, LBA started to distinguish between group membership, which was open to all, and participation in a steering committee, which was as well open to all, yet restrictive in that it assumed membership based on active and direct involvement in the consensual formulation and execution of plans. As of fall 1995, LBA has restructured its steering committee—now formed by fifteen to twenty formally nominated and elected members, who in addition must make a two-year commitment to the organization—and has created several working committees—political/advocacy, communications, fund-raising and development, finance, social/recreational, and cultural educational—which are partially open to any LBA member and should produce annual workplans. Both the steering and the working committees are now run by elected officers. Brown (1994) shows (although in reference to organizations involved in the provision of services to HIV-positive people and people with AIDS, and thus with the shadow state) the tendency for lesbian and gay groups to progress from the simplicity of grassroots structures toward the complexity of bureaucratic institutions. In the particular case of LBA, the recent decision to "bureaucratize" the organization has been articulated by some LBA members as a critique of one of the most serious problems inherent in any consensual collective, i.e., how to avert the division of a group into leaders and followers, and consequently, how to avert leaders' burnout and followers' apathy. Other LBA members, nevertheless, have interpreted this "bureaucratization" as a form of distancing LBA from the objectives of an oppositional public sphere.

15. For a discussion of dependency theory, see Brewer 1980. It is necessary to keep in mind that there is an abundance of popularized versions of dependency theory in the

regular lexicon of many Latinos. An important source has been Dorfman and Mattelart (1975), a book still widely read by college students in Latin America, which argues that the cultural relations between Latin America and the United States resemble the economic dependence of the former on the latter. In consequence, Dorfman and Mattelart describe the cultural interaction of the two areas as a form of acculturation, whereby North American culture displaces and eventually erases Latin American culture. Rowe and Schelling (1991), in a poignant critique against the limitations inherent in dependency theory and acculturation, propose the concept of transculturation. Transculturation also describes the interaction of two cultures in terms of an unequal distribution of power. But whereas dependency theory views that relation as one of aggressor versus victim, in transculturation, the culture that is subsumed under the more powerful one is not a passive victim that disappears completely. Out of the interaction of the two, a mestizo culture, evidencing elements of the two original cultures, is born. Furthermore, according to Rowe and Schelling, the process of transculturation varies across the different sectors of society in a decentered manner. A cultural practice that is publicly coded to signify submission in one sector of society may be privately coded to signify dissent in another sector. See Bartra (1987) for the examination of a Mexican case of religious transculturation, in which the Virgin of Guadalupe serves as the façade for Tonatzin, the Aztec deity. Paz (1988), in his unparalleled study of Sor Juana Inés de la Cruz, prefers to use the term "syncretism" to refer to the transcultural practices of the criollo Jesuits in New Spain during the Baroque period.

16. In its early years, LBA used some of its funds to support the travel expenses incurred by members attending conferences. These funds came from individual donations, fund-raising activities, and foundation grants.

17. For a discussion of salsa's roots in New York City's Latino neighborhoods, see Calvo Ospina (1995), Manuel (1994), and Schneider (1994). Nevertheless, in their discussion of the possible emancipatory aspects of salsa, these authors privilege the political realm, neglecting the more pleasurable aspects of salsa, which also have emancipatory value.

18. See Schulman (1994) for a history of the Lesbian Avengers's many oppositional demonstrations against the liberal public. See Pursley (1995) for a description of the Avengers's tactic in a rural setting.

19. "Maricón" means more than simply "faggot." Its root is the word "María," both a common woman's name and the name of the Virgin. Besides femininity, "maricón" implies cowardice, which makes it semantically similar to "cabrón." "Maricón" and "cabrón" rhyme.

References

Adler, S., and Brenner, J. 1992. Gender and space: Lesbians and gay men in the city. *International Journal of Urban and Regional Research* 16: 24–34.
Bad Object-Choices, ed. 1991. *How do I look?: Queer film and video*. Seattle: Bay Press.
Bartra, R. 1992. *The cage of melancholy: Identity and metamorphosis in the Mexican character*. New Brunswick: Rutgers University Press.
Bell, D. 1991. Insignificant others: Lesbian and gay geographies. *Area* 23: 323–29.

————. 1994. Erotic topographies: On the sexuality and space network. *Antipode* 26: 96–100.

————. 1995a. Pleasure and danger: The paradoxical spaces of sexual citizenship. *Political Geography* 14: 139–53.

————. 1995b. [screw]ing geography (censor's version). *Environment and Planning D: Society and Space* 13: 127–31.

Brewer, A. 1980. *Marxist theories of imperialism: A critical survey.* New York: Routledge and Kegan Paul.

Brown, M. 1994. The work of city politics: Citizenship through employment in the local response to AIDS. *Environment and Planning A* 26: 873–94.

————. 1995. Ironies of distance: An ongoing critique of the geographies of AIDS. *Environment and Planning D: Society and Space* 13: 159–83.

Buci-Glucksmann, C. 1987. Catastrophic utopia: The feminine as allegory of the modern. In *The making of the modern body*, ed. C. Gallagher and T. Laqueur, 220–29. Berkeley: University of California Press.

Cabrera, L. 1968. *El monte, igbo, finda, ewe orisha, vititi nfinda. (Notas sobre las religiones, la magia, las supersticiones y el folklore de los negros criollos y del pueblo de Cuba.)*, 2d ed. Miami: Rema Press.

Calvo Ospina, H. 1995. *¡Salsa! Havana heat: Bronx beat*, trans. N. Caistor. London: Latin America Bureau.

Chauncy, G. 1994. *Gay New York: Gender, urban culture, and the making of the gay male world, 1890–1940.* New York: Basic Books.

Crime in the city: Attack of the Lesbian Avengers and other true accounts from the NYPD files. 1994. *Spy*, November-December, 32.

De Lauretis, T. 1994. *The practice of love: Lesbian sexuality and perverse desire.* Bloomington: Indiana University Press.

Dorfman, A., and Mattelart, A. 1975. *How to read Donald Duck: Imperialist ideology in the Disney comics*, trans. D. Kunzle. New York: I. G. Editions.

Dykes blast MEGA-KQ. 1995. *Color Life!*, Winter, 9–10.

Forest, B. 1995. West Hollywood as symbol: The significance of place in the construction of a gay identity. *Environment and Planning D: Society and Space* 13: 133–57.

Fraser, N. 1985. What's critical about critical theory? The case of Habermas and gender. *New German Critique* 35: 97–131.

————. 1992. Rethinking the public sphere: A contribution to the critique of actually existing democracy. In *Habermas and the public sphere*, ed. C. Calhoun, 109–42. Cambridge: MIT Press.

Fraser, N., and Nicholson, L. 1989. Social criticism without philosophy: An encounter between feminism and postmodernism. In *Universal abandon? The politics of postmodernism*, ed. A. Ross, pp. 83–104. Minneapolis, MN: University of Minnesota Press.

Geltmaker, T. 1992. The Queer Nation acts up: Health care, politics, and sexual diversity in the county of angels. *Environment and Planning D: Society and Space* 10: 609–50.

Gramsci, A. 1971. *Selections from the prison notebooks of Antonio Gramsci*, ed. and trans. Q. Hoare and G. Nowell-Smith. New York: International Publishers.

Habermas, J. 1975. *Legitimation crisis*, trans. T. McCarthy. Boston: Beacon Press.

————. 1984. *The theory of communicative action. Vol. 2. Lifeworld and system, a critique of functionalist reason*, trans. T. McCarthy. Boston: Beacon Press.

———. 1989. *The structural transformation of the public sphere: An inquiry into a category of bourgeois society*, trans. T. Burger with F. Lawrence. Cambridge: MIT Press.

———. 1992. Further reflections on the public sphere. In *Habermas and the public sphere*, ed. C. Calhoun, pp. 421–61. Cambridge: MIT Press.

Hansen, M. 1993. Foreword. In *Public sphere and experience: Toward an analysis of the bourgeois and proletarian public sphere*, trans. P. Labanyi, J. Daniel, and A. Oksiloff, pp. ix-xli. Minneapolis: University of Minnesota Press.

Heines, C. 1995. Las Buenas Amigas launches exhibit April 18. *Center Voice,* April, p. 4.

Hohendahl, P. 1982. Critical theory, public sphere, and culture: Jürgen Habermas and his critics. In *The institution of criticism*, 242–80. Ithaca: Cornell University Press.

———. 1995. Recasting the public sphere. *October* 73: 27–54.

Knopp, L. 1987. Social theory, social movements and public policy: Recent accomplishments of the gay and lesbian movements in Minneapolis, Minnesota. *International Journal of Urban and Regional Research* 11: 243–61.

———. 1990a. Exploiting the rent gap: The theoretical significance of using illegal appraisal schemes to encourage gentrification in New Orleans. *Urban Geography* 11: 48–64.

———. 1990b. Some theoretical implications of gay involvement in an urban land market. *Political Geography Quarterly* 9: 337–52.

———. 1992. Sexuality and the spatial dynamics of capitalism. *Environment and Planning D: Society and Space* 10: 651–69.

———. 1994. Social justice, sexuality, and the city. *Urban Geography* 15: 644–60.

Las lesbianas y afeminados le declaran la guerra a MEGA 97.9. 1994. *Alerta,* 19 December, p. 19.

Lauria, M., and Knopp, L. 1985. Toward an analysis of the role of gay communities in the urban renaissance. *Urban Geography* 6: 152–69.

Lesbians strike back at hate radio. 1995. *The Progressive,* January, p. 17.

Liebman, S., ed. 1988. Alexander Kluge: Theoretical writings, stories, and an interview. Special issue of *October* 46: 1–218.

Longfellow, B. 1993. Lesbian phantasy and the other woman in Ottinger's Johanna d'Arc of Mongolia. *Screen* 34: 124–36.

Manuel, P. 1994. The soul of the barrio: 30 years of salsa. *NACLA: Report of the Americas* 28(2): 22–26, 28–29.

Morley, D., and Robins, K. 1989. Spaces of identity: Communications technologies and the reconfiguration of Europe. *Screen* 30: 10–34.

Negt, O., and Kluge, A. 1981. *Geschichte und Eigensinn*. Frankfurt am Main: Zweitausendeins.

———. 1992. *Massverhältnisse des Politischen. 15 Vorschläge zum Unterscheidungsvermögen*. Frankfurt am Main: S. Fischer Verlag.

———. 1993. *Public sphere and experience: Toward an analysis of the bourgeois and proletarian public sphere*, trans. P. Labanyi, J. O. Daniel, and A. Oksiloff. Minneapolis: University of Minnesota Press.

New York City Gay and Lesbian Anti-Violence Project. 1994. *Gay/lesbian-related homicides in the United States, 1992–1994: First national analysis and report*. New York: New York City Gay and Lesbian Anti-Violence Project.

Paz, O. 1988. *Sor Juana or, The traps of faith*. Cambridge: Belknap Press of Harvard University Press.

Protesta contra Omega KQ. 1994. *El Diario/La Prensa*, 20 November, p. 3.

Pursley, S. 1995. With the Lesbian Avengers in Idaho. *The Nation* 260: 90, 92–94.

Ramos, J., ed. 1994. *Compañeras: Latina lesbians (an anthology)*. New York: Routledge. (Originally published by the *Latina Lesbian History Project*, New York City, 1987.)

Rowe, W., and Schelling, V. 1991. *Memory and modernity: Popular culture in Latin America*. New York: Verso.

Schlüpmann, H. 1988. "What is different is good": Women and femininity in Alexander Kluge. *October* 46: 129–50.

————. 1990. Femininity as productive force: Kluge and critical theory. *New German Critique* 49: 69–78.

Schneider, C. 1994. Musica against drugs: Fighting AIDS with salsa. *NACLA: Report of the Americas* 28 (2): 26–27.

Schulman, S. 1994. *My American history: Lesbian and gay life during the Reagan/Bush years*. New York: Routledge.

Sedgwick, E. 1990. *Epistemology of the closet*. Berkeley: University of California Press.

Spanish Broadcasting System registers initial public offering. 1996. *The SEC Today*, 11 January, p. 1.

Special Issue on Alexander Kluge. *1990. New German Critique*. 49: 3–138.

Spivak, G. 1988. Can the subaltern speak? In *Marxism and the interpretation of culture*, ed. C. Nelson and L. Grossberg, 271–313. Urbana: University of Illinois Press.

Stroud, I. 1995. Your dream, their nightmare: Irene Elizabeth Stroud introduces the Lesbian Avengers and their less-talk-more-action activism. *Crossroads* 49: 9–11.

Strum, A. 1994. A bibliography of the concept Öffentlichkeit. *New German Critique* 61: 161–202.

Valentine, G. 1992. Negotiating and managing multiple sexual identities: Lesbian time-space strategies. *Transactions of the Institute of British Geographers, N.S.* 18: 237–48.

————. 1993a. Desperately seeking Susan: A geography of lesbian friendships. *Area* 25: 109–16.

————. 1993b. (Hetero)sexing space: Lesbian perceptions and experiences of everyday spaces. *Environment and Planning D: Society and Space* 11: 395–413.

————. 1995. Out and about: Geographies of lesbian landscapes. *International Journal of Urban and Regional Research* 19: 96–111.

Weightman, B. 1980. Gay bars as private places. *Landscape* 24(1): 9–16.

Wolff, J. 1989. The invisible *flâneuse*: Women and the literature of modernity. In *The problems of modernity*, ed. A. Benjamin, 141–56. New York: Routledge.

Young, I. 1990. The ideal of community and the politics of difference. In *Feminism/Postmodernism*, ed. L. Nicholson, 300–323. New York: Routledge.

16

Gender, "Race," and Diaspora: Racialized Identities of Emigrant Irish Women

Bronwen Walter

Exploration of multiple, shifting connections between place and identity is a central concern of feminist geography (Massey 1994). In this chapter, I contribute to debates about intersections of gender, "race," and nation by examining constructions of identities across geographical localities (Jackson and Penrose 1993; Kobayashi and Peake 1994). I will highlight constructions of difference by comparing representations of the Irish in Britain and the United States, focusing on emigrant Irish women. On the one hand, the Irish have historically been marginalized from hegemonic "White" British society through processes of representation that have cast them as a racial "other." The British still wield considerable representational authority over the Irish, as derived from their historical position as colonizer. On the other hand, in the United States, Irish identity has been representationally negotiated to recast Irishness as a favorable part of a larger "White" or "European" hegemonic whole. The study, then, both problematizes "color-based" definitions of "race," and challenges us to explore ways in which dominant ethnic/racial groups in Western societies have asserted their authority.

Migration is a neglected aspect of feminist geography, despite increasing interest in cross-cultural comparisons of women's lives (Katz and Monk 1993). Yet displacement across national boundaries adds a sharp political edge to constructions of gendered identities, raising issues of entitlement to citizenship and perceived threats to national security. The unusual mobility of Irish women over two centuries allows changing representations of their identities to be examined in a variety of spatial and historical contexts.

While gender is integral to national identities, it is rarely acknowledged as such in nationalist searches for unity, partly evident in the fact that women are marginalized in all national narratives (Anthias and Yuval-Davis 1992; Mc-Clintock 1993). In this chapter, however, I show how gender is central to all nationalism; how Irish women migrants move from the representational edge of their nation of origin to a new place on the margins of the "imagined communities" in which they settle.[1] Moreover, I shall show how it is through constructions of gender that larger political identities and agendas within and outside Irish immigrant communities are negotiated over time, across generations. Accordingly, the analysis explores how "public" domains are representationally cast as masculine arenas of nationalist struggle in ways that require and depend upon a separate and subordinate "private" sphere for women.

What's the Problem?

In January 1994 the popular British tabloid newspaper *The Sun* proclaimed "Funnyman Frank Carson reckons the £50,000 survey into racism against Irish people in Britain is 'a load of codswallop.' We agree with him." It proceeded to "prove the point" by listing forty-one "all-time greatest [anti-] Irish jokes" to "give the researchers a flying start." These were vitriolic representations of the stupidity of Irish people. Only one mentioned an Irish woman, a barmaid.

I am one of two researchers who conducted the above-mentioned survey assessing the extent to which Irish immigrants in Britain experience discrimination.[2] In Britain the Irish have been constructed as an alien and inferior homogenized "race" with inherited tendencies toward stupidity, violence, and drunkenness. These representations were transported to the United States in the nineteenth century, but over time their salience there declined sharply. In Britain, however, representations of the Irish as inferior are continually reenacted with the specifics of racialization changing to suit shifting agendas, especially with reference to the construction of British national identity. Paradoxically, popular British denials of the racialization of the Irish are accompanied by unchallenged, and strongly gendered, racist stereotyping (Hickman and Walter 1995).

In order to interrogate comparative representations of Irishness, I call upon notions of "diaspora," that is, communities created through large-scale migrational displacement. I shall also examine spatiality in social constructions of difference in individual women's day-to-day lives. In this way, my analysis brings together geographical ideas about constructions of identity through *displacement*—both metaphorical and material—at a global scale, with those of *placement* at the local level of migrants' work and settlement patterns (Pratt and Hanson 1994). The analysis consequently shows how representations of Irish womanhood are used historically in different ways and places to negotiate different nationalist ends.

Historical Geographic Roots of the Irish Diaspora: United States and Britain

Emigration from Ireland has been at extraordinarily high levels throughout the nineteenth and twentieth centuries. Between 1841 and 1961 the population of the island of Ireland (including both the Irish Republic and Northern Ireland after 1921) halved, from 8.5 to 4.2 million, despite much higher birthrates than the European average. Two-and-a-half million people left Ireland in the period 1846–55 alone as a result of the Great Famine and social changes in its aftermath (Fitzpatrick 1984). In the second half of the nineteenth century, a total of 4.5 million persons settled in America, 80 percent of all Irish emigrants. But during the 1920s, there was a sharp change in the direction of flow. By the second half of the decade, 80 percent of Irish emigrants were entering Britain (Kennedy 1973). While Irish emigration has typically been represented as a male phenomenon until recently (Walter 1989; O'Sullivan 1995), Irish women have outnumbered men in most intercensal periods, a demographic fact atypical of European migration flows. Moreover, most of the women have been unmarried, leaving independently between the ages of sixteen and twenty-four (Fitzpatrick 1984). In the second half of the nineteenth century, women left Ireland for reasons different from those of men. Following post-Famine impartible land inheritance patterns, for example, daughters and all but one son were displaced from the land.[3] Women were also progressively excluded from most areas of agricultural work (Lee 1978). By the end of the nineteenth century, their control of milk production had been seized by the creameries, and poultry raising had shifted away from the farmstead and out into the male territory of the fields (Bourke 1987; 1990).

Besides these agricultural factors, there were educational differences. Girls were educated to higher levels than boys, partly to provide them with skills that would make them better providers of remittances from abroad (Fitzpatrick 1986; Nolan 1989). Women were in this way encouraged to emigrate because they were seen as likely to secure regular employment, whereupon they could save money; women were also considered less likely to squander their earnings.

Restrictive and limited roles for women have been sanctioned since the Famine by the Catholic Church, which has portrayed married motherhood as the only acceptable status (Beale 1986). Women have rebelled against these disempowering representations, rejecting them most completely by permanent emigration throughout the nineteenth and twentieth centuries (*Mother Ireland* 1989; Kelly and Nic Ghiolla Choille 1990; Walter 1991). Apart from a slightly greater tendency for Irish women entering Britain in the nineteenth century to travel in family groups (Diner 1983), there is little reason to believe that their backgrounds were significantly different from those of Irish women who crossed the Atlantic to settle in the United States.[4]

Comparative analysis of Irish emigrants to Britain and the United States is inevitably complicated by the weighting of generations in the two countries.

Most Irish-Americans are currently fifth or sixth generation, while the largest number of Irish people recognized as belonging to the "Irish community" in Britain are Irish born or have Irish-born parents.[5] Moreover, while a much greater proportion of the British population than this has Irish ancestry, a more distant Irish connection is rarely claimed. This is because Irishness and Britishness are represented as incommensurable identities, making "Irish British" an uncomfortable contradiction. It is exactly these differences, however, that allow for transnational comparative analyses to be made.

Displacement: Concepts of Diaspora

In recent years, the term "diaspora" has often been used to describe Irish settlement overseas, both in single and multiple destinations (e.g., McCaffrey 1984). Its relevance and value, however, must be examined to assess ways in which its use structures meanings of Irish emigration. In the context of persons of African descent, the notion of diaspora has been embraced by Gilroy (1993). According to Keith and Pile (1993, 18), Gilroy uses the term to connote a "third space" which

> invokes an imagined geography, a spatiality that draws on connections across oceans and continents yet unifies the Black experience inside a shared territory. This experience is the source of difference and yet does not legitimate the elevation of "the Black experience" to an incommunicable cultural essence.

Gilroy's use of the term "diaspora" in some ways geographically extends hooks's (1990) claims that "Black" places of sociospatial marginality can simultaneously be political sites of cultural resistance. In particular, Gilroy formulates a *global* sense of shared marginality along common ethnic or racialized lines. His work offers possibilities, then, for *transnational alliances*, something that might prove similarly useful in addressing anti-Irish racism in different national contexts.

This chapter additionally explores ways in which constructions of gendered Irish identities have been representationally refracted within and across diasporic communities. Strong contrasts are evident in constructions of gendered Irishness in Britain and the United States. In Britain, Irishness is represented as male, even though in colonized Ireland, men were represented in feminized positions of dependence (Cairns and Richards 1988).[6] Consequently, Irish people are collectively named "Paddies" and "Micks," regardless of gender. The stereotype of violent, drunken stupidity is a male one, conjuring up the "navvy" drinking his earnings in the pub and mindlessly lashing out with his fists (figures 16.1 and 16.2). The Irish person is also seen easily to slip into inexplicable but genetically inherited tendencies toward political violence. In Britain it is popularly believed that these characteristics can be recognized by the voice—the Irish "accent" (see Meoño-Picado, chapter 15, this volume).

Fig. 16.1. The Irish in Britain are collectively stereotyped as building workers, or "navvies," which is in part evidence of the demand for Irish labor in Britain but used to confirm lack of education, poor verbal skills, dirtiness, and stupidity. In Britain this cartoon image would be immediately recognized as depicting the Irish by a number of clues. The apelike features of the man follow a long tradition of representing the Irish as subhuman (see also figure 16.2). In the nineteenth century, the Irish were racialized by physical appearance and claimed to be the "missing link" between apes and humans (Cohen 1987). Depiction as apes was common in cartoons in the magazine *Punch* in the later nineteenth century (Curtis 1971) and was revived in British newspaper cartoons after the escalation of the conflict in Northern Ireland in 1968 (Kirkaldy 1979). Other clues are the pint of beer in the worker's hand, associating him with drunkenness, and the, possibly ironic, inclusion of the "Brits not guilty" newspaper headline in his pocket, reflecting public denial of British responsibility for any aspect of hostilities in the Northern Ireland. This cartoon encapsulates the racialized stereotype of the Irish in Britain, emphasizing its homogenizing male character and its linkage of physical with cultural traits. The key features of violence, stupidity, and tendency to drunkenness are signaled very clearly to a British readership. (Jak cartoon, *Evening Standard*, 20 January 1978, p. 16, reprinted with permission of artist and publisher.)

THE FENIAN-PEST.

HIBERNIA. "O MY DEAR SISTER, WHAT *ARE* WE TO DO WITH THESE TROUBLESOME PEOPLE?"
BRITANNIA. "TRY ISOLATION FIRST, MY DEAR, AND THEN———"

Fig. 16.2. This *Punch* cartoon illustrates the paradox whereby the Irish *nation* is represented as a beautiful young woman seeking protection from the stern figure of Britannia, whereas the Irish *people* are represented by apelike men. The epithet "pest" reinforces the animal image. Again the Irish are racialized by physical appearance, ugly, dark, and wild, compared with white-skinned, white-clad Britannia. The threat of violence is very apparent, but there is no sign of its cause. Hibernia is portrayed as weak and helpless, the dreamy, unwordly Celt in need of protection from strong, rational Anglo-Saxon Brittania. This is the British view of a feminized Ireland and justifies the Act of Union between Britain and Ireland in 1800. Brittania is an ambiguous image, apparently female yet with the masculine attributes of military attire, large stature, clenched fists, and commanding gaze. Her response illustrates the British chosen stereotype as colonial rulers—fair-minded, tolerant, but maintaining order through violence. The Irish, by contrast, are simultaneously too weak and too uncivilized to govern themselves. (*Punch*, 3 March 1866, p. 90. Used with permission of the Syndics of Cambridge University Library)

While this demeaning of Irish voices works to homogenize men *and* women as "other," it ironically works against women with more frequency, given their greater numbers and likelihood of being employed in workplaces with British people (Walter 1995).

In America constructions of Irishness have both borrowed and transformed older British versions (Knobel 1986; Clark 1991). In the nineteenth century, there were remarkable similarities in the racist stereotypes of Irish men in both countries. In the United States, for example, "Pat" was similarly represented as unreliable and prone to violence (Diner 1983). Politically he was likely to challenge the status quo by involvement in un-American union activities, and his support for Irish nationalism cast doubt on his allegiance to the new nation (Miller 1990). He was a poor provider for his family, both because of his inability to obtain secure employment and his tendency to drink what he earned. Over the course of several generations, this stereotype lost its negative connotations such that today Irish men are typecast in positive terms, with cultural attributes of sociability and cheerfulness. In fact Irish identity is currently claimed by the largest number of "White" Americans of mixed parentage, in preference to other ancestry (Alba 1990).

In contrast, Irish women in America were often defined in opposition to Irish men (see Domosh, chapter 12, this volume). Irish women were most commonly stereotyped as "Bridget," the domestic servant, variants being "Nora," "Maureen," and "Mary." As a servant, Bridget was clumsy, had no manners, could not cook, and might leave at any moment; but she was also "lovable" (Diner 1983). Her behavior was ridiculed according to satire that differentiated women and men. Clark (1991, 39), for example, discusses Nast's cartoons in the 1870s, which "showed Brigid, the clownish Irish maid, enacting follies or having tantrums in domestic situations" whereas "the [male] Irish" were depicted as "ape-like, corrupt, violent and religiously depraved" (figure 16.3). Moreover Irish women who were mothers were represented as powerful figures, the "civilizers" of their large families (figure 16.4). Such women were commented on with approval as the prime agents in the move "from shanty town to lace curtain" for the Irish community as a whole (Diner 1983).

Irish women arrived in Britain and America with very similar backgrounds and entered similar types of occupations—overwhelmingly domestic service in large towns, followed by mill work in certain regions. Nonetheless women negotiated their work and home differently in the two nations in ways that altered both their own identities and those of the nation.

Placement: Local Constructions of Gendered Irishness

Workplaces: Employers' Homes

Domestic service has placed Irish women in a complex relationship to public and private worlds in Britain and the United States. Through interactions with

Fig. 16.3. This representation of Bridget Malony, a stereotypical name for an Irish domestic servant, is one of a series of sixteen cartoon portraits depicting recipients of valentines in "Valentines delivered in our street" published on 14 February 1856. Three are caricatures of ethnic minorities, Irish, German, and African American, each with exaggerated stereotypical physical and linguistic characteristics. It is significant that a female servant has thus been selected as the principal represention of the Irish, with a much smaller male figure ambiguously portrayed on her valentine.

A pan hanging on the wall and her apron place Bridget in the kitchen as a paid domestic worker. She is the only one of the five women caricatured not to be given the courtesy title of "Miss." Her appearance is rosy-cheeked and cheerful, a generally positive image, although her coarse features and use of dialect suggest low intelligence. She is shown as innocently, though foolishly, deceived by "Patrick." His apelike image was transported to America from Britain. In this cartoon, Irish men and women share a number of negative traits, but stronger racialization is directed at males. (Source: *Harper's New Monthly Magazine* 14 February 1856, p. 430)

"Here and there; or Emigration the Remedy": British woodcut, 1848
Bettmann Archives

Fig. 16.4. This woodcut, created in 1848, contrasts a family in Ireland at the time of the Famine with its changed fortunes after emigration to America. In the grouping before emigration, the mother is a shadowy figure, hiding her face in her bonnet, but she comes to the forefront in the American home, presiding over a large, well-ordered family. The title of the woodcut is "Here and there; or Emigration the Remedy" and shows that the success story is told in terms of family life, with well-fed and neatly clothed children as a goal. Whiteness and the cleanliness of the family is emphasized in contrast to the dirt and gloom of Ireland. The importance of the role of the Irish mother in providing for the well-being of emigrants is made very clear. (Source: British woodcut 1848, reproduced in Dale Knobel, *Paddy and the Republic* Wesleyan University Press, 1986. Used by permission of the publisher.)

their employers, they are directly exposed to majority nationalism, being judged by and exposed to middle-class values. At the same time, they remain ensconced within individual households where they are held accountable to other—marginal, yet also hegemonic "White" women.

Historically, emigrant Irish women entered domestic service in large numbers. In New York City in the 1850s, 80 percent of women in paid household labor were Irish (Diner 1983) and in London in 1861, 44.8 percent of Irish women were "in service" (Lees 1979). Domestic service held many benefits for Irish women. For single migrants, it provided board, lodging, and hence opportunities to save. It was less arduous and healthier than factory labor. Irish women's preference for domestic service made them increasingly popular among employers during the nineteenth century (Tebbutt 1983; Diner 1983), especially as office work tempted other "White" women into better-paid jobs (Mackenzie and Rose 1983; Lewis 1984).

Strikingly, Irish women's presence in Britain went largely unrecorded, a few references to Irish servants being buried within novels or employers' biographies. In America, however, Irish women were highly visible, largely because the quality of their domestic service was debated in public forums. As Diner (1983:86) writes

> Dozens upon dozens of statements, evaluations and judgments were offered during the last half of the nineteenth century about the merits—and mostly the demerits—of the Irish servant girl.

One reason for this representational contrast may lie in the ways in which a sense of the nation and of national belonging were constructed in each nation. In Britain national identity was represented almost exclusively through the middle-class notion of "breeding" (Cohen 1988, 64–71). An ideology of inheritance entitled only the ruling classes to be full members of the master race, and gave them the duty of carrying a "civilizing mission" to the rest of the population. Nationalism in the United States, however, is representationally mediated through the more egalitarian and inclusive concept of "citizenship," a concept born out of early "White" settlers' rejection of the British subject relationship (Marston 1990). Citizenship, in turn, emanated from Western representations of civil society as an economic marketplace, with individuals being cast as market competitors. Irish domestic servants, having been integrated into the market both as wage earners and paying consumers, were thereby much more easily absorbed into hegemonic "White" constructions of the nation.[7]

At the same time, Irish women in America were negatively typecast as domestic servants of Catholic working-class background. This identity was made in hierarchical distinction to, and was mutually constitutive of, representations of their employers as nonworking class. Such class-based and religious distinctions helped mediate dominant hierarchical constructions of "White" ethnicity within the nation. Thus, Irish servants who had become the "standard household servant class" in Philadelphia before 1850 simultaneously "were the subject of continuous complaint and criticism by Victorian matrons" (Clark 1982, 36). This is partly evident in the observation of a *London Times* correspondent in New York that "White" American-born girls refused to enter domestic service because of its negative associations with Irishness. In fact non-Irish "White" girls chose lower paying jobs as needlewomen or millworkers just so they would not be identified with the Irish (Diner 1983:81).

Nonetheless, by saving much of their earnings, Irish women in Britain and the United States provided many of their daughters with an education, enabling them to avoid domestic service (Hornsby-Smith and Dale 1988; Perlmann 1988). Such generational differences resulted in the fact that in 1900, less than 5 percent of all Irish-born women in the United States were "white blouse" workers, whereas more than 14 percent of the second generation were teachers, bookkeepers, accountants, and typists. The jump in upward mobility was far higher than that registered for other groups (Nolan 1989) or for Irish men (Diner 1983). New arrivals still entered domestic service, which continues to be the major source of Irish-born women's employment in both countries today. In the United States, a survey of the "new Irish" in New York in 1987–88 showed that the majority of young women "illegals" were working as nannies or companions in private homes (Corcoran 1993). Similarly in Britain, 34.6 percent of Irish-born women were recorded in the personal service category in 1991, compared with 12.8 percent of the total population (Office of Population Censuses and Surveys 1993). Domestic service, then, while apparently restricting Irish women to the "home," provided opportunities for their daughters' education and, hence, social mobility. Moreover, Irish-born wage-earning women in the United States were more easily absorbed into dominant constructions of the nation through the concept of "citizenship." In Britain, by contrast, movement out of the migrant niche of domestic service had to wait until the second generation with a concomitant erasure of linguistic difference.

Family Homes: Matriarchal Strengths

Wills (1993, 66) traces the growth of an unusually strong association between motherhood and femininity in Ireland during the nineteenth and twentieth centuries to Ireland's colonial status: the private sphere became associated with the nation-as-family in opposition to the alienated and bullish British state. Such oppositional colonial politics of representation may help to explain the symbolic importance and practical association of Irish women and the home.

Added to this political content of associations between women and the home were larger practical considerations. At the level of industrial capitalism, the strategic benefits of a well-ordered reproductive sphere were being recognized throughout European and American societies in the later nineteenth century (Mackenzie and Rose 1983). Within Irish immigrant communities, moreover, women were often controllers of households as well as managers. Industrial accidents disproportionately affected Irish men so that there were many widows, while some men left their families to seek work or to return to Ireland (Diner 1983; Lees 1979). Women also commonly worked in the home by boarding lodgers.

All of these factors resulted in a representational paradox. On the one hand, Irish women were expected in both British and American cultures to embrace and conform to passive and benevolent "angel of the hearth" ideals of femininity (Hall 1992), a construction in keeping with middle- and upper-class

"White" standards. On the other hand, the peculiar hardships and socioeconomic activities of emigrant Irish women required that they be anything but passive or dependent. In the United States and Britain, these paradoxical positions were representationally negotiated very differently. In the United States, Irish women were cast as pillars of family strength. Commentators contrasted Irish women's dedicated family support with men's distinctive cultural pattern of socializing within Irish male groups (Diner 1983). Whereas women were applauded for keeping nuclear families together and advancing their collective status, men were seen as a source of family disorganization.

In Britain, Irish women's various strengths were not celebrated or even commented on. If anything, they were represented as culturally aberrant. In northwest England, for example, Irish women and children had been directly recruited to mill work, giving them relatively greater earning power than in other regions (Walter 1989). In contrast, Irish men in Lancashire cotton towns could find only intermittent laboring jobs, and were often absent from home (Foley 1973). This gender division of socioeconomic labor was represented in denigratory contradistinction to Victorian patriarchal ideals of the male "breadwinner" and the dependent home-based wife (Mackenzie and Rose 1983). Music hall jokes in Manchester depicted Irish men in racist, sexist terms as weak and "henpecked," reflecting British anxieties over the tenuousness of dominant constructions of masculinity (Tebbutt 1983).

Neighborhoods: Catholicism and Irish Women's Sociospatial Roles

In the United States, by contrast to Britain, ethnicity of the nineteenth-century city was demarcated spatially through clearly defined neighborhoods that served to localize ethnically defined political and cultural activity (Marston 1988).[8] In Lowell, Massachusetts, for example, a tightly organized local community of Irish people existed that was centered on Catholic churches, charitable organizations, and cultural and social activities. These provided a base from which the Irish "developed an effective political consciousness that sought to challenge their disadvantage" (Marston 1988, 429).

Community political organization at the neighborhood level in the United States was, however, predominantly a male activity. It might even be said that the corollary to representing Irish emigrant women in terms of the home was the construction of "public" space and masculinity in terms of the street. Irish male voluntary associations provided Irish businessmen with contacts, thereby helping to transform an agrarian peasantry into citizens. Literary societies were also exclusively male, with such titles as the "Young Men's Catholic Lyceum" and the "Young Men's Catholic Library Association." Apparently, the only women's organizations were sodalities affiliated with particular Catholic churches (Marston 1988, 423).

Catholicism has been key in defining and negotiating Irish distinctions between public and private spheres. It has also mediated Irish emigrants' exclusion from or inclusion in dominant constructions of the nation in Britain and the United States respectively. British fear of invasion by its Catholic neighbors, France and Spain, helps to explain the fiercely anti-Catholic underpinnings of Englishness (Colley 1992). Religious-based distrust of the Irish was transported to America, where it was used as a political platform by the anti-immigrant Know-Nothing party in the first half of the nineteenth century (Miller 1985). This political grouping was strongly nativist and focused its campaigns particularly against the Irish. McCaffrey (1980) argues that Catholicism was seen as dangerous ideological European despotism, threatening Anglo-Saxon Protestant culture and liberty. The strength of this negative stereotype linking Irish identity to Catholicism obscured the reality that the majority of Irish-Americans were descended from Protestant settlers in the eighteenth century (Akenson 1993).

During the second half of the nineteenth century, however, a Catholic hierarchy of bishops transformed Catholic Irish emigrants in the United States into "Good Americans" by promoting a new middle class Catholic identity congruent with American values (Miller 1990). A similar elision of Catholicism and Britishness would have been out of the question in Britain, given the symbolic importance of the break with Rome under Henry VIII in defining English national identity from the sixteenth century onward. It was not until the Catholic Emancipation Act of 1829 that Catholics in Britain and Ireland could vote, enter Parliament, or fill the majority of civil offices for which they had social and economic qualifications (Colley 1992). They are still excluded from the throne. The Catholic Church repaid the British state for its widespread reinstatement by helping to detach religious allegiance from Irish national identification. This was accomplished primarily by placing second-generation Irish children in a Catholic education system devoid of Irish content (Hickman 1995). The potential danger of political Irish identification was thus controlled by replacing it with a less-threatening religious one. It is only recently that a second-generation Irish identity is being reclaimed (*Our Experience of Migration* 1984).

Although Irish women were historically denied access to formal Catholic Church structures, they have been indispensable to the more informal realms of religious practice. Not only have women been the most assiduous attendants, they have assumed responsibility for maintaining the faith of the next generation (Marks 1990). In the nineteenth century, for example, commentators in both the United States and Britain remarked approvingly on the religiosity of Irish women (Diner 1983; Tebbutt 1983). Such religiosity was thought to contribute to their reliability and honesty as servants, even though it confirmed their "otherness."

In Britain, Catholicism was excluded from dominant constructions of national identity, reinforcing the invisibility of Irish women. Interviews in Luton (in southeast England) in the 1970s show that Irish women, who had emigrated in large numbers in the 1950s and subsequently married, focused much of their lives around the Catholic parish. These religious, social, and cultural activities were hidden from the English population and never reported in the local press, despite much higher levels of attendance than in Protestant congregations (Walter 1986).

Women were also largely invisible in, though they helped facilitate, the informal social organization of Irish communities. Again this was an extension of their domestic roles within Irish culture as a whole. In a telling choice of images, Clark (1982, 38) describes the Irish woman boardinghouse keeper as being "in a position somewhat analogous to that of the priest and the saloon keeper in the Irish community," providing a wide range of economic services to single male lodgers.

> She aided lodgers by trusting them for rent payments until they got their start, lending them money to get to Scranton or Pittsburgh where relatives were, for example, or holding messages about their whereabouts when they migrated into the hinterlands for work. The boardinghouse manager was a fount of information about how to send money back to Ireland, where to find a doctor, or who to see about one's legal status as an immigrant . . . the landlady became an archetypal figure. She mothered greenhorns and gave them their first instructions about America.

Despite exclusion from the formal structures of Irish communities, therefore, and despite very limited public representation, Irish women have played key roles in the reproduction of emigrant Irish life. Evidence of the underpinning of community life by work within the home, both for family members and other countrywomen and men, provides powerful arguments about the need to uncover women's histories and geographies at the local scale.

Conclusion: Diaspora and Identity

In this chapter I have shown how the notion of diaspora is a useful one in discussing the different experiences of Irish emigrant communities. I have argued that the term might serve as a new form of representation for what have heretofore been considered as separate and homogeneously "White" communities. The notion is analytically useful in that it simultaneously unites and juxtaposes emigrant Irish populations.

Diasporic experiences are always gendered, but as Clifford (1994) points out, this is hidden in most accounts, which discuss them in unmarked ways. I have shown that women have played distinctive parts representationally in the Irish diaspora, but their role at the material level has also been central. Irish women have financed the migration of other family members, and been responsible for maintaining personal connections among scattered families between and within different national contexts. Women have "kept track" of relatives and maintained contact by letter and telephone. They have also integrated their children into the "private" family of past generations and more distant branches. Alba (1990) argues that "White" ethnic minority women in America give much greater weight to their ethnic background than men, 43 percent viewing it as important compared with 20 percent of men.

Connecting diverse experiences at a transnational scale allows for broader-based constructions and negotiation of ethnic identity to take place. At one level, my work shows that national identities are mediated largely through masculinist constructions of the public sphere. Despite the pivotal role of Irish mothers in securing the upward mobility of their children in the late nineteenth and early twentieth centuries, and the larger number of women entering white-collar employment, contemporary Irish-American political and economic successes are predominantly mythologized in masculinist terms, for example through narratives of the life of the late president John F. Kennedy. To the Irish in Britain, the myth suggests that Irish-Americans can achieve upward mobility without losing an Irish identity, a possibility that starkly contrasts with the practical and representational opportunities open to the Irish in Britain (Hillyard 1993; O'Flynn 1993). Thus, at another level, my work suggests that images of different histories of Irish settlement in the United States have had a strong impact on Irish migrants in Britain.

British imperialism in Ireland has resulted in a complexly textured diaspora that shares common features with other major displacements of population, but is also profoundly different. This study draws out key features of the specificity of the Irish experience of diaspora. But comparisons and contrasts can fruitfully be drawn with other diasporic experiences. While cautioning against simplistic connections between traditions that are themselves disparately derived and internally heterogenous, Gilroy (1993) nevertheless points to parallels in the experiences of people of African origin and Jewish populations. Themes of catastrophe, brutal dispossession, loss, exile, and journeying also underlie memories of the emigrant Irish, but again there are clear contrasts between Irish experiences and those of Jews and people of African origin. Perhaps most important, the Irish middle classes in the United States have been incorporated into an Anglo-Saxon hegemony. This highly significant transformation, in which women have played a central role through their early integration as wage earners and consumers, means that Irish people in the United States need not share "this experience of fear in all its radicality, which cuts across class and gender to the point of touching the bourgeois in the very isolation of his town houses or sumptuous apartments" (Jameson 1988, cited in Gilroy, 1993, 206). Instead they are placed centrally in a national narrative described by Toni Morrison in Gilroy (1993, 179): "We live in a land where the past is always erased and America is the innocent future in which immigrants can come and start over, where the slate is clean."

In postwar Britain, the Irish are also represented as being integral parts of a "White" hegemony, even though they are marginalized through racialized constructions. This apparent paradox is explicable in terms of nationalist constructions of a homogeneously "White" race endemic to the "British Isles" (Hickman and Walter 1995). That is, "race" is conflated with "the nation,"

making whiteness central to the "myth of British homogeneity." This confla-
tion is clearly evident in the notion of an "island race" whereby cultural and
biological concepts of the British nation are fused. The geographic logic of
this notion requires the inclusion of the whole island of Ireland. Racism in
Britain is therefore only *acknowledged* on the grounds of skin color. Miles
(1993) shows how silence about high levels of Irish immigration, including
its neglect as an object of study by geographers and sociologists, works to
strengthen a denial of Irish racialization. Such denial, however, does not di-
minish racist practices and the ongoing construction of English/Britishness
(rationality, tolerance, fairness) against Irishness (unpredictability, violence,
stupidity).

Irish men have received the full force of these derogatory racialized characterizations. In part, this reflects the masculinity of Britishness and the exclusion
of all women from English national identity. In the formative period for the
construction of this identity in the late nineteenth century, women were seen
as possessing "transnational characteristics" of domesticity and maternity
(Mackay and Thane 1987). Shared whiteness and Catholic "family values"
continue to assign Irish women to this ambiguous sphere, whereas women
racialized by skin color have been stereotyped as dangerously hypersexual
(Rattansi 1992; Mirza 1992). Boose (1994) relates these fears more fundamentally to anxieties expressed in the seventeenth century about unions between "White" men and "Black" women, which crucially undermined
patriarchal explanations of conception giving sole reproductive power to the
male seed. Children provided incontravertible evidence of women's genetic
contribution. As a result "Black" women were unrepresentable. She argues:

> In a resolution that allowed Britain to contain difference within the much nar-
> rower sphere of intra-White hatreds, White Racism—conceived on English
> shores—was shipped off to the colonies along with racial difference, thus leaving
> the land called "Albion" virtually untainted—for centuries, at least—by racist im-
> putations. To the Irish was left the job of playing out the English Other. (Boose
> 1994, 53)

Because whiteness obscured Irish women's share in reproduction, the threat
of miscegenation could be forgotten. Moreover, today's deepseated fears
bound up with blackness may reinforce intra-"White" ties now that ex-colonial
migrants and their descendents have settled in Britain.

The absence of representations of the Irish as sexually threatening may also
stem from specific feminized colonial representations of Ireland. In the nineteenth century, Ireland was represented externally to Britain as the pure, weak
"Hibernia" in need of protection by strong, masculine "John Bull" or the ambiguously gendered "Britannia" (figure 16.2). From within the nation, representations of "Mother Ireland" emphasized safe, maternal feminine qualities
of an ageing woman.

Today anti-Irish racism in Britain continues to be excluded from acknowledgment in the public realm. As evident in the opening quote taken from *The Sun*, keeping the Irish "in their place" is hotly defended as a means of maintaining British national boundaries.

Notes

Part of this research was supported by ESRC research grant R000234790. I am grateful to Heidi Nast, Michael O'Brien, and Mary Hickman for helpful comments.

1. Anderson (1991, 6) describes nations as "imagined communities" because "the members of even the smallest nation will never know most of their fellow-members, meet them, or even hear of them, yet in the minds of each lives the image of their communion."

2. Anti-Irish racism in Britain has a long history. It derives from ongoing constructions of a British/English national identity against an Irish "other." For a discussion of its changing forms over time see Cohen (1987), Curtis (1971), Curtis (1984), and Hickman (1995).

The project was a research initiative on the Irish community in Britain, funded by the Commission for Racial Equality, examining the extent and nature of anti-Irish discrimination. It was based at the Irish Studies Centre in the University of North London and the co-researchers were Mary Hickman and Bronwen Walter. The report was completed in March 1996.

3. Before the famine years of the 1840s, farms were divided between children on the father's death. This led to extreme fragmentation. Farming patterns changed dramatically after the Famine, accompanying a shift from tillage to livestock, and a single male heir was chosen by the father. Keeping "the name on the land" assumed great importance. For further details see Arensberg and Kimball (1968).

4. Studies at the urban scale suggest strong similarities in the occupational status of women in America and Britain. However, accurate statistics on the demographic and socioeconomic characteristics of Irish migrants in the two countries at a national scale are not available. Akenson (1993, 227) argues that "a *permanently invisible majority* of the Irish have been excluded from U.S. records." Although numbers of Irish-born women in Britain are available in Censuses since 1841, no additional details were published. Moreover, O'Grada (1973) estimates that between 1852 and 1910 a million Irish migrants to Britain were unrecorded.

5. A recent survey showed 17 percent of randomly sampled non-Irish-born people in Britain having Irish ancestry (Irish Post 1994). In 1980, 22 percent of U.S.-born "Whites" claimed Irish ancestry in the 1980 Census (Alba 1990, 33).

6. This parallels the masculinity of Britishness (Mackay and Thane 1986) against which the Irish have been constructed as "other" for centuries (Colley 1992; Hickman 1995).

7. The "public" identity of Irish women as citizens was thus indissolubly linked to their roles in the "private" sphere of domestic work, illustrating the problematic and contradictory nature of a binary divide between the two spheres (see Meoño-Picardo, chapter 15, this volume).

8. Although strongly Irish residential districts have been identified in British cities,

there is no evidence that they functioned as the basis of political life in the nineteenth century (Fitzpatrick 1989; Pooley 1989; Busteed, Hodgson, and Kennedy 1992).

References

Akenson, D. H. 1993. *The Irish diaspora: A primer*. Toronto: P.D. Meany.

Alba, R. 1990. *Ethnic identity: The transformation of White America*. New Haven: Yale University Press.

Anderson, B. 1991. *Imagined communities: Reflections on the origins and spread of nationalism*. Rev. ed. London: Verso.

Anthias, F., and Yuval-Davis N. 1992. *Racialized boundaries: Race, nation, gender, colour and class and the anti-racist struggle*. London: Routledge.

Arensberg, C., and Kimball, S. 1968. *Family and community in Ireland*. 2d ed. Cambridge, MA: Harvard University Press.

Beale, J. 1986. *Women in Ireland: Voices of change*. London: Macmillan.

Boose, L. 1994. "The getting of a lawful race": Racial discourse in early modern England and the unrepresentable Black women. In *Women, "race", and writing in the early modern period*, ed. M. Hendricks and P. Parker, pp. 35–54. London: Routledge.

Bourke, J. 1987. Women and poultry in Ireland. *Irish Historical Studies* 25: 293–310.

———. 1990. Dairywomen and affectionate wives: Women in the Irish dairy industry, 1890–1914. *Agricultural History Review* 38: 149–64.

Busteed, M.; Hodgson, R.; and Kennedy, T. 1992. The myth and reality of Irish migrants in mid-nineteenth century Manchester: A preliminary study. In *The Irish in the new communities Vol. 2, The Irish World Wide*, ed, P. O'Sullivan, pp. 26–51. Leicester: Leicester University Press.

Cairns, D., and Richards, S. 1988. *Writing Ireland*. Manchester: Manchester University Press.

Clark, D. 1982. *The Irish relations*. London: Associated University Presses.

———. 1991. *Erin's heirs*. Lexington: University of Kentucky Press.

Clifford, J. 1994. Diasporas. *Cultural Anthropology* 9:302–338.

Cohen, P. 1987. The perversions of inheritance: Studies in the making of multi-racist Britain. In *Multi-racist Britain*, ed. P. Cohen and H. Bains, 9–118. London: Macmillan.

Cohen, R. 1995. Rethinking "Babylon": Iconoclastic conceptions of the diaspora experience. *New Community* 21:5–13.

Colley, L. 1992. *Britons: Forging the nation 1707–1837*. London: Pimlico.

Corcoran, M. 1993. *Irish illegals: Transients between two societies*. Westport, Connecticut: Greenwood Press.

Curtis, L.P. 1971. *Apes and angels: the Irishman in Victorian caricature*. Washington, DC: Smithsonian Institution Press.

Curtis, L. 1984. *Nothing but the same old story: The roots of anti-Irish racism*. London: Information on Ireland.

Daniels, M. 1993. Exile or opportunity? Irish nurses and Wirral midwives. *Irish Studies Review* 5:4–8.

Diner, H. 1983. *Erin's daughters in America*. Baltimore: Johns Hopkins University Press.

Evening Standard. Jak cartoon. 20 January, 1978, p. 16.

Fitzpatrick, D. 1984. *Irish emigration 1801–1921*. Studies in Irish Social and Economic History 1. The Economic and Social History Society of Ireland.

———. 1986. "A share of the honeycomb": Education, emigration and Irish women. *Continuity and Change 1*. 2:217–34.

———. 1989. A curious middle place: The Irish in Britain, 1871–1921. In *The Irish in Britain 1815–1939*, ed. R. Swift and S. Gilley, pp. 10–59. London: Pinter.

Foley, A. 1973. *A Bolton childhood*. Manchester: Manchester University Extra-mural Department and Northwestern District of the Workers' Educational Association.

Gilroy, P. 1993. *The Black Atlantic: Modernity and double consciousness*. London: Verso.

Hall, C. 1992. *White, male and middle class*. Cambridge: Polity Press.

Harper's New Monthly Magazine. 1856. Valentines delivered in our street. 14 February, p. 430.

Hickman, M. 1995. *Religion, class and identity: the state, the Catholic Church and the education of the Irish in Britain*. London: Avebury.

———, and Walter,B. 1995. Deconstructing whiteness: Irish women in Britain. *Feminist Review* 50:5–19.

Hillyard, P. 1993. *Suspect community: People's experience of the Prevention of Terrorism Act in Britain*. London: Pluto Press.

hooks, b. 1990. Marginality as a site of resistance. In *Out there: Marginalization and contemporary culture*, ed. R. Ferguson, M. Gever, M. Trinh and C. West, pp. 341–43. New York: The New Museum of Contemporary Art and MIT Press.

Hornsby-Smith, M., and Dale, A. 1988. The assimilation of Irish immigrants in Britain. *British Journal of Sociology*, 36:519–43.

Irish Post. 1994. Irish in Britain: a formidable presence. November 26, p. 7.

Jackson, P., and Penrose, J. ed. 1993. *Constructions of race, place and nation*. London: UCL Press.

Keith, M., and Pile, S., ed. 1993. *Place and the politics of identity*. London: Routledge.

Kelly, K., and Nic Giolla Choille, T. 1990. *Emigration matters for women*. Dublin: Attic Press.

Katz, C., and Monk, J., ed. 1993. *Full circles: Geographies of women over the life course*. London: Routledge.

Kennedy, R. 1973. *The Irish: Emigration, marriage, and fertility*. Berkeley, CA: University of California Press.

Kirkaldy, J. 1979. English newspaper images of Northern Ireland 1968–73: An historical study in stereotypes and prejudices. PhD. thesis, University of New South Wales.

Knobel, D. 1986. *Paddy and the republic*. Middleton, CT: Wesleyan University Press.

Kobayashi, A., and Peake, L. 1994. Unnatural discourse. "Race" and gender in geography. *Gender, place and culture* 1:225–43.

Lee, J. 1978. Women and the church since the Famine. In *Women in Irish society: The historical dimension*, ed. M. MacCurtain and D. O'Corrain, pp. 37–45. Dublin: Arlen House.

Lees, L. 1979. *Exiles of Erin: Irish Migrants in Victorian London*. Manchester: Manchester University Press.

Lennon, M., McAdam, M., and O'Brien, J. 1988. *Across the water: Irish women's lives in Britain*. London: Virago.

Lewis, J. 1984. *Women in England 1870–1950*. Sussex: Wheatsheaf Books.

McCaffrey, L. 1980. A profile of Irish America. In *America and Ireland 1776–1976*, ed. D. Doyle, and O. D. Edwards. London: Greenwood.

———. 1984. *The Irish diaspora in America*. Washington: Catholic University of America Press.

McClintock, A. 1993. Family feuds: Gender, nationalism and the family. *Feminist Review* 44: 61–80.

Mackenzie,S., and Rose,D. 1983. Industrial change, the domestic economy and home life. In *Redundant spaces? Social change and industrial decline in cities and regions*, ed. J. Anderson, S. Duncan, and R. Hudson, pp. 155–200. London: Academic Press.

Mackay, J., and Thane, P. 1986. The Englishwoman. In *Englishness:Politics and culture 1880–1920*, ed. R. Colls, and P. Dodd, pp. 191–229. London: Croom Helm.

Marks, L. 1990. Working wives and working mothers. *Polytechnic of North London Irish Studies Centre Occasional Papers Series* 2.

Marston, S. 1988. Neighborhood and politics: Irish ethnicity in nineteenth century Lowell, Massachusetts. *Annals of the Association of American Geographers* 78:414–32.

———. 1990. Who are "the people"?: Gender, citizenship, and the making of the American nation. *Society and Space* 20:449–58.

Massey, D. 1994. *Space, place and gender*. Cambridge: Polity Press.

Miles, R. 1993. *Racism after "race relations."* London: Routledge.

Miller, K. 1985. *Emigrants and exiles: Ireland and the Irish exodus to North America*. Oxford: Oxford University Press.

———. 1990. Class, culture and immigrant group identity in the United States: The case of Irish-American ethnicity. In *Immigration re-considered: History, sociology and politics*, ed. V. Yans-McLaughlin, pp. 97–125. Oxford: Oxford University Press.

Mirza, H.S., 1992. *Young, female and black*. London: Routledge.

Mother Ireland. Derry Film and Video. 1988.

Nolan, J. 1989. *Ourselves alone: Women's emigration from Ireland 1885–1920*. Lexington: University Press of Kentucky.

O'Flynn, J. 1993. *Identity crisis: access to benefits and ID checks*. London: Action Group for Irish Youth.

O'Grada C. 1973. A note on nineteenth-century Irish emigration statistics. *Population Studies* 29:143–49.

O'Sullivan, P., ed. 1995. *Irish women and Irish migration*, Vol.4, *The Irish World Wide*. Leicester: Leicester University Press.

Office of Population Censuses and Surveys, 1993. Census, Britain. Ethnic group and country of birth tables, Table 14. London: HMSO.

Our experience of migration. 1984. Report of the first London Irish Women's Conference. London Irish Women's Centre.

Perlmann, J. 1988. *Ethnic differences: Schooling and social structure among the Irish, Italians, Jews and Blacks in an American city, 1880–1935*. Cambridge: Cambridge University Press.

Pooley, C. 1989. Segregation or integration? The residential experience of the Irish in mid-Victorian Britain. In *The Irish in Britain 1815–1939*, ed. R. Swift and S. Gilley, pp. 60–83. London: Pinter.

Pratt, G., and Hanson, S. 1994. Geography and the construction of difference. *Gender, Place and Culture* 1:5–30.

Punch. 1866. The Fenian-Pest 3 March, p. 90.

Rattansi A., 1992. Changing the subject? Racism, culture and education. In *"Race", culture and difference*, ed. Donald J. and Rattansi A., pp. 11–48. London: Sage.

The Sun. 1994. Paddy thought he was the world's best lover . . . 22 January, p. 9.

Tebbutt, M. 1983. The evolution of ethnic stereotypes: an examination of stereotyping, with particular reference to the Irish (and to a lesser extent the Scots) in Manchester during the late nineteenth and early twentieth centuries. M.Phil. thesis, University of Manchester.

Walter, B. 1986. Ethnicity and Irish residential segregation. *Transactions of the Institute of British Geographers* 11:131–46.

———. 1989. Gender and Irish migration to Britain. *Anglia Geography Working Paper* 4.

———. 1991. Gender and recent Irish migration to Britain. *Geographical Society of Ireland Special Publications* 6:11–20.

———. 1995. Irishness, gender and place. *Society and Space* 13:35–50.

Wills, C. 1993. *Improprieties: politics and sexuality in Northern Irish poetry*. Oxford: Oxford University Press.

17

Sweet Surrender, but What's the Gender? Nature and the Body in the Writings of Nineteenth-Century Mormon Women

Jeanne Kay

Some of the oldest, most widespread, and durable of metaphors for landscapes and Nature invoke the female body: land as the Great Mother in any of her many guises, wilderness as an enticing temptress available for the frontiersman's wooing or taking, or dangerous and uncontrollable Nature as hag or fury (Neumann 1963; duBois 1988; Kolodny 1975; Merchant 1980, 1989, 1995; Rose 1993).[1]

Some feminists have criticized the patriarchal, naturalizing implications of the metaphor of earth as female body (Ortner 1974); while Kolodny (1984), Monk and Norwood (1987) , Robertson (1990), and Norwood (1993) found in historical studies that some American female writers' own choice of landscape metaphors emphasized "naturally" feminine, even maternal concepts of new lands as prospective homes, gardens, or shared communities; or, alternatively, that wild landscapes symbolized women's extended sense of liberated, even erotic self.

Ecofeminists view patriarchal oppression of women and of nature as coincident (Merchant 1980, 1995). Some embrace the imaginative Nature/woman's body correspondence as a means of empowering women through goddess spirituality and environmental activism (Diamond and Orenstein 1990, Gaard 1993). Paradoxically, they often do so by glorifying traditionally feminine attributes such as the earth's and women's mutual reproductive capabilities, nurturance of others, and commensalism.

The shared assumption of these debates, however, is that Nature and space are best understood through metaphors of heterosexual female identity. Nature, it seems, is not multigendered, nonheterosexual, or asexual; seldom is it masculine. A physically challenging landscape may be an exclusive man's world, but that setting nevertheless is female, be she Aphrodite or Hecate. Gregory (1994, 129) summarizes a basically androcentric perspective on the feminization of Nature:

> It is a commonplace of feminist history that "Nature" has been coded as feminine within the Western intellectual tradition; and if concepts of space can be derived directly from concepts of nature . . . then it is scarcely surprising that socially produced space—spaciality—should have been coded in the same way: as a space to be mastered, domesticated and gendered.
> This is particularly intrusive in the sexualization of colonial landscapes, where . . . a rich and fecund virgin land is supposedly available for fertilization . . . [or where] a libidinous and wild land has to be forcefully tamed and domesticated.

I argue for an expanded interpretation of women and Nature by discussing religious variables that encouraged alternative metaphors. I address Nature and the female body as described by pioneer Mormon women in Utah and the American West during the period of circa 1847 to 1920, using samples of landscape representations in three ordinary women's autobiographical accounts.[2] This is not to place Mormon women's life stories in binary opposition to Mormon men's (or Man's), but simply to elucidate representations of Nature within a small selection of materials by writers who self-identified as Mormon women.[3]

I argue that the encoding of Nature as female body did not predominate in Mormon women's writings, largely because this metaphor was preempted by their church's construction of Utah and the West as Zion, a complex construction informed by the Bible and Mormon scriptures. This was land as sacred space, sculpted through Old Testament metaphors. Land was often described as their Christian God's handiwork, retributive instrument, or vineyard; but only infrequently and rhetorically or poetically as Mother Nature (cf. Kimball 1994).

My three principal subjects understood themselves in profoundly religious and traditionally feminine ways. Representations of feminized landscapes as locations of home and womanly domesticity (cf. Kolodny 1984) are strongly present in my subjects' autobiographical writings; however, they are fortified by the Latter-day Saint belief that creating communities in the wilderness was tantamount to preparing their Zion for the second coming of Christ. New lands were only occasionally places of self-valorizing liberation for women (cf. Monk and Norwood 1987) because both the Victorian Cult of Domesticity and Mormon theology emphasized women's role as mothers and demanded female obedience to figures of patriarchy. Women might self-select out of these ideologies, but then they effectively left the church.

The Nature/woman's body linkage was nonetheless present, but in a different form. My subjects were concerned with Nature's impact upon the human body. Suffering incurred from droughts and blizzards or remoteness from urban services, and the poverty endemic to pioneer life were seen as inscribing themselves on women's limbs, wombs, or faces; incurring pain, disfigurement, or even death; yet these marks became emblems of Christian refinement and redemption. Through Nature as both materiality and extreme events, the Father registers His power and provides a means of salvation through trial. Surrender to God's testing as one's own cross to bear, more than conquest and domination, becomes the principal motif and moral stance for Mormon pioneer women. There simply isn't much archival evidence that Mormon women's representations of harsh or dangerous Nature were encoded as female.

The study takes us into analytically treacherous "Geography of Women" territory, with its menaces of naturalized (even positively Amazonian) women, voyeuristic glimpses of life "among the Mormons," liberal and radical feminisms, places naively described as objectively real, absolutist erasures of Mormon women's differences, totalizing narratives, and "hegemonic readings of the body" (Rose 1993, 80). Here be dragons. Yet by exploring the religious ideology so apparent in Mormon women's life histories, the varied terrain between Nature and the prevalent female body metaphor for landscapes can be better understood (see also Townsend 1991). This revisioning is important for feminist geography because scriptural texts and beliefs frequently underlay other types of narratives (Frye 1982; Duncan and Duncan 1988; Nast 1996), particularly of religious women's imaginative and material landscape constructions.

Most premodern and recent antimodern religious environmental thought is based upon syncretistic and diverse conceptual frameworks and normative beliefs. Indeed a principal challenge for theologians is to reconcile apparently contradictory texts within their canon. Christian fundamentalists like the Mormons often sought to explain their experience through expounding phrases in the Bible, which offers few renderings of the earth as a female body, even where the earth is feminized through feminine nouns or metaphors. (Consider, for example, lack of earth-as-body-associations with the biblical Hebrew feminine noun *adamah*, or feminine metaphors of Nature in the Song of Songs. In the latter, it is the beloved who is described with landscape metaphors, not the other way around.) In contrast, the Bible frequently represents Nature as neuter divine handiwork, or as an epiphany of an explicitly masculine heavenly Father (for example, rainfall or the burning bush.) The Woman/Nature body connection in Renaissance or early modern literature, so extensively presented by Merchant (1980, 1995), owes far more to its pagan northern European and classical Graeco-Roman foundations than it does to the Christian Bible. Mormons related Eve's transgression in the Garden of Eden to environmental decay and to women's subordinate status; but again, there is little evidence that Mormon thought conferred female body imagery upon landscapes as a result.

For those reasons, I recommend a rethinking of Merchant's (1980) ecofeminist argument that male domination of women implies dominating attitudes towards a feminized Nature even where the Woman/Nature correspondence is not textually explicit:

> a given normative theory is linked with certain conceptual frameworks and not with others. . . . We cannot accept a framework of explanation and yet reject its associated value judgments because the connections to the values associated with the structure are not fortuitous. (Merchant, 1980, 5)

Some feminist or profeminist scholars have derived the Nature-female body correspondence principally through historical sources displaying hegemonic masculinist discourses of Nature or female identity that have been developed by "great men" of Western thought, and that thereby reinscribe a masculinist privileged intellectual status (Merchant 1980, 1995; Rose 1993; Gregory 1994). While acknowledging these scholars' significant contributions, as well as those of their historical sources, I attempt in this chapter to put forth a more populist approach to the Nature-body question. It seems to me that an exclusive focus on viewpoints of a dominant group's elite intelligentsia may reproduce and thus further reinscribe the very "othering" that feminists condemn, when it positions the "different" group principally as the object of the privileged writer. While my chapter may naively downplay the very dramatic gendered power relations within Mormon society, I also hope to avoid within my own text the patronizing implications of restricting Mormon women to a two-dimensional, no-exit collusion or resistance to dominant males. Fresh insights may be available from focusing on the writings of ordinary women, typically relegated to discursive margins.

Normative Mormon Identity

Said (1978) argued that representations of unfamiliar people-in-places typically reveal far more about the cultural biases of the observer than they do about the societies being described.[4] The danger is that a privileged White scholar-observer, may co-opt and demean a "marked" and textually subordinated populace through a mistaken belief in her powers of impersonal, objective, and rational description. To be sure, it is impossible to do much more than "tour" Mormon theology and culture without extensive study, religious conversion, and practice. However, the assumptions of the racialized or oppressed Other that are common to subaltern or postcolonial studies (cf. Blunt 1994, Walter 1997) are both helpful and problematic when applied to Mormon society.

As Walter has shown in this volume (chapter 16), white skin was not an undifferentiated category in the nineteenth-century United States. Like the Irish she describes, Mormons were often rendered marginal or even deviant by the non-Mormon secular or Protestant reporter's "gaze" and some were harassed, disenfranchised, or imprisoned for their religious beliefs. On the other hand, a White but non-Mormon (i.e., "Gentile" or "outsider") observer position is not superior within Mormon society (comprised, after all, of predominantly upwardly mobile Americans of northern European descent). Mormon doctrine has always taught that it is the one legitimate religious faith, and in their own writings, Mormons have often "gazed" back disparagingly at their critics and Gentile society. Non-Mormon scholars of Mormonism range from anti-Mormon (and thus open to charges of bigotry) to scholars in the unenviable position of attempting to write a balanced account of Mormon subjects who would interpret the scholars' own personal beliefs and social status as distinctly inferior to their own (Smith 1992).

What distinguishes Mormons from anybody else is not specifically race, ethnicity, gender, or class, but a complex set of religious beliefs and practices, including a tightly knit sense of community. Religion differentiated Mormons from their next-door Anglo-American neighbors, and gave Mormons of various ethnic or class backgrounds a degree of cohesion even where foreign-born converts could not speak the same language. Although Anglo-American primacy was taken for granted, the only passport to unearned superiority that whiteness carried for Mormon women who gave birth or buried their children while pushing handcarts across the Great Plains in the 1850s, for example, was the ability to assimilate or displace a small population of Native Americans. Most first-generation Mormon pioneers lived in a state of poverty and physical hardship. Any emblems of moral superiority conveyed by their fortitude hardly places them in the privileged position of, say, British travelers or civil servants in India or West Africa during the high colonial period (cf. Blunt 1994).

The Church of Jesus Christ of Latter-day Saints, or "Mormons" (also "saints," LDS) was established in upstate New York and the Middle West during the 1820s to 1840s as a small fundamentalist, millennial, prophetically based non-Protestant Christian denomination.[5] Expulsions at the hands of confrontational neighbors supported by government led the Mormons to isolate themselves in present-day Utah in 1847, from which they extended their settlements to much of the intermountain West. To outsiders, their faith was marked by a scandalous promotion of polygamy (abolished in 1890) (Hardy 1992), strong in-group cohesiveness enabled by their church's tight organizational structure, active global missionary activity, and adherence to uniquely Mormon religious texts and practices. Redacted by a literate, Anglo-American male core of leaders, the tenets of LDS faith appear in the Bible, in Mormon scriptures, and in ongoing and recorded revelation from the church president, believed to be a divinely appointed prophet.

Given these beliefs and origins, Mormon representations of landscapes unsurprisingly often explicitly or implicitly reference the Bible and Mormon scripture (Duncan and Duncan 1988; Kay and Brown 1985). The juxtaposition of Mormon history and doctrine generates a set of temporal and spatial tensions or competing discourses to be harmonized (Duncan 1990, 181) that resonate throughout Mormon writings. On the one hand, the faith promises a prophetic vision of the End of Days and the Kingdom of God, with an elaborate eschatology and scriptural geography. On the other hand, it is equally grounded in the recorded life histories of present-day Mormons' recent ancestors, such as the three "foremothers" cited below, for whom a chain of memorabilia links many contemporary Mormons with a 150–year-old religious heritage located in identifiable, everyday places. This tension between the world-to-come and this-world encouraged religious interpretations of mundane events and places. For example, church leaders offered practical farming advice in their sermons, or interpreted natural hazards like crop infestations as religious portents.

Particularly during the early years of Western settlement, an imbalance of attention on abstract doctrine at the expense of basic needs would have spelled starvation for Mormonism and Mormons. One intellectual challenge of the church, therefore, was to interpolate between the celestial and the terrestrial. The church has always stressed its practicality as a religion: Latter-day Saints express their faith in constructing a house to "build the Kingdom" or in raising a Mormon child, as much as in Bible study. A related challenge for Mormon teachings is to mediate between high sectarian standards of conduct and promises for godliness and the normal lapses, mediocrity, and disappointments of everyday life. Thus improvement and progress are highly prized values: improvement of the landscape through development, self-betterment through constant striving. Both are interpreted as God's work.

Mormon texts, both scriptural and historical, reveal an authoritarian viewpoint and ecclesiasticism. Questioning the tenets of the faith, particularly through prayer, is permitted, but must stop at the point of open criticism of church leaders or apostasy. Having established itself in the mid-nineteenth century as the most radical of Christian denominations, and having a firm belief in ongoing directives from a president as a living prophet, a tenacious conservative commitment is subsequently required to sustain its tenets.

Church members during the nineteenth century were largely of Western European extraction. By class, most would be described as working poor, although economic and social opportunity on the frontier offered significant upward mobility. Conventional Anglo nineteenth-century social mores pervaded much of Mormon social thinking, including racism toward people of color. Mormons, like most Euro-American settlers, were imperialist. Indigenous Ute, Paiute, and Goshute people were alternatively patronized, proselytized, or dispossessed of their lands by the Mormon influx.

Mormon Women's Identity

Mormon religious beliefs and social practice are demonstrably patriarchal. Men formulated the theology and ecclesiastical institutions. Only men could attain the religious ranks of the priesthood, conduct some important religious rituals, or independently attain more exalted stations in the afterlife. Women are instructed to be obedient to their church authorities and husbands. Mormon women diarists sometimes repeated religious sentiments or even quoted specific passages (see Tanner's remarks below) that would have come to them through their male church leaders or through the patriarchal Christian Bible.

Polygamy (practiced by perhaps a quarter of Mormon families in the nineteenth century) is often seen as a symbol of profound patriarchy. A woman's decision to enter a polygamous marriage (ca. 1840–90) was a shockingly submissive, even immoral act in the eyes of other white Americans. Mormon "sisters" nevertheless admonished one another to support polygamy and to obey their husbands and church leaders in this tenet, although a number of them privately admitted misgivings. Yet polygamy paradoxically generated many *de facto* female heads-of-household through men's frequent absences from home due to missionary work or visits to their other plural families. The church also placed an early practical emphasis on women's economic self-sufficiency, which became increasingly important when many legal marital separations were required by the abolition of polygamy in 1890 (Embry 1987; Hardy 1992; Iverson 1984; Van Wagoner 1992).

The mid-nineteenth century Cult of Domesticity, or Cult of True Womanhood, to which the chaining of bourgeois white women to lives of useless domesticity has been attributed (Welter 1966; Lerner 1980), was profoundly modified in frontier Utah by the perceived need for all of the faithful to be productively employed in the region's economic development. Utah was one of the earliest states to approve women's suffrage, and some Mormon women claimed that polygamy, with its assurance of child care provided by "sister wives," gave them liberty to pursue careers in law or medicine (Arrington 1984; Beecher 1981; Beecher and Anderson 1987; Foster 1991; Van Wagonen 1991).

Despite the sense of community and moral superiority fostered among Latter-day Saints, women's identities were often destabilized through a number of factors: conversion to a religious faith considered deviant by the mainstream and even by their unconverted friends and relatives, mandatory obedience to the person of the church president as a living prophet as well as to their husbands regardless of their temperaments, the prospect of adding a new and possibly disliked co-wife to one's family circle, a new language and culture for the foreign-born immigrants, frequent uprooting and moving when a "call" came to a family to establish a new frontier settlement, and occasional extreme privation. Social status was not secure: a woman who attained some measure of recognition in her community might find her circumstances reversed overnight if her husband died, apostatized, married a more favored wife, or terminated her plural marriage (post–1890). Illness or health and age of a woman or her family members made an enormous difference to her outlook and circumstances.

The body of Mormon women's writings studied suggests that their identities were—at a time when most of them married and raised children—most firmly anchored in motherhood and religion, with their attendant emphasis on suppression of their individual wants and self-expression to the higher good of service. Childless women were brought into this circle through assistance to other women, particularly to co-wives and children in need of foster care. The majority of women's writings that I have examined dwell on childrearing and poignantly address the empty nest syndrome. Faith in God, in the correctness of Mormon teachings, and in a divine plan that explained the vicissitudes of life as Christian trials provided a rationale through which to accommodate oneself to one's lot in life, however rewarding or unfortunate. Being a 'sister" among the Latter-day Saints provided a close economic and social welfare support network as well (Beecher 1982).

Writing Mormon Women's Lives

The historical records themselves afford only skewed glimpses into nineteenth century-Mormon womanhood. The valorizing quality of Mormon historical source materials is readily apparent, and it occurs for several reasons. One is the exclusionary, "faith-promoting" character of Mormon archives. Memoirs included in the extensive Daughters of Utah Pioneers or Relief Society collections, for example, are generally restricted to those judged to have served and died in the faith.[6] Gatekeeping by orthodox editors, even censors within sanctioned church publications, standardized the majority of published historical materials designated "Mormon" through deployment of typical narrative formats. Regardless of these women's own lived realities, their memoirs and biographical sketches generally describe in sequence their own or their parents' early conversion to the church; a difficult passage to Utah; ritual observances such as patriarchal blessings or temple marriages; trials and triumphs of home, home economics, and family; and death described together with one's testimony to the faith (Swetnam 1991). Genealogies and hardships encountered are emphasized, complaints about suffering are frequent yet firmly circumscribed within acceptable limits.[7] Outsiders are seen as persecutors of a true Christian minority. Some of these literary conventions seem peculiarly Mormon (that is, religious conversion), others seem common to Victorian values of the nation and era.

Few pioneer women letter-writers and diarists had the equivalent of a high school education. Their representations of Nature are only occasionally elaborated, normally they are implicit and expressed with an economy of words that characterizes nineteenth-century frontier autobiographical writing (Hampsten 1982, 47).[8] While this terseness suggests a lack of education or imagination, sometimes it is an explicit rhetorical strategy to signify the writer's fortitude and selflessness, as uncomplaining or stoic in the face of hardship.

Mary Jane Mount Tanner's (1837–91) pioneer letters and diary illustrate a number of the preceding aspects of Mormon women's identity. In the first excerpt she displays church-sanctioned womanly qualities of obedience to her husband and God as she copes with a family crisis. As a Latter-day Saint she overcomes her instinctive resistance to patriarchal authority through heroic, ultimately ennobling effort, in which her very terseness serves a rhetorical, valorizing function. (In all direct quotations I retain the original spelling and punctuation.)

> May 19. 1866, a change was made in our family by [husband] Myron marrying another wife . . . Of this I will say but little. It is a heart history which pen and ink can never trace. It was a great trial but I believed it to be a true principle, and summoned all my fortitude to bear it bravely. . . . I tried to be watchfull and prayerful striving to overcome every weakness that caused me unhappiness and live uprightly doing my duty before God and my fellow man. I sought to train my children properly and rear them in the "nurture and admonition of the Lord." (Ward 1980, 117, 120)

Tanner's identity as a Mormon wife and mother is even more striking in the following scriptural interpretation of her marriage and the deaths of three of her children (Ward 1980, 176). Here is a mental map not located in the Utah Valley but in the world-to-be.

> Provo Aug 6. 1879
> Woman was made for man and finds her life imperfect without the union . . . the instincts of our nature lead us to conjugal happiness and offspring is the natural results of healthy constitutions and gods blessing on those who are united in purity and truth. . . . I would rather bear children to die than not bear them, for I am laying up treasure in heaven where wealth nor rust doth corrupt, and some day they will be stars in my crown of glory . . . I have laid three little ones away, not lost but gone before.

These are extraordinary statements in the context of current Western secular interpretations of self. If the death of one's children and breach of one's marriage can be rationalized through the language of personal salvation, it is likely that landscapes will be similarly represented.

Landscape as Zion

It is in the engagement of Mormon theology with the Western lands they encountered that their imaginative landscapes are to be glimpsed. Despite the masculinist basis of orthodox Mormon belief, the predominant images of the land are not of a female body to be mastered: the most articulated beliefs simply extend the biblical allegory of Saints as the Children of Israel embarked on a lengthy Exodus and progression to the Promised Land. Utah figures most frequently in Mormon doctrine as Zion, or *Deseret*, a name taken from the Book of Mormon. The name Zion occurs frequently in Mormon sermons and hymns, and was often used to designate Latter-day Saints collectively, as in their nineteenth century "Gathering of Zion" mass immigration to Utah

(Stegner 1992). The designation "Zion" also has a geographical application, as in the location of home, community and Church for Latter-day Saints; and it also has an eschatological meaning as the location of the Second Coming (Kay and Brown 1985). Mormons are a clear example of a textual or scriptural society who projected their texts onto their environments (Duncan 1990, 22–23), and who used landscape "evidence" to validate those texts.

The duty of the faithful is to "build up the Kingdom" [of God]. If they are righteous and successful, the land will reward them with prosperity (Kay and Brown 1985). Development and improvement of wilderness become evidence of the rightness of the Chosen Peoples' beliefs and practice, a biblical form of the literary pathetic fallacy. Natural disasters and crop failures have two biblically derived interpretations: either the people have lapsed from their faith and must make a special effort to become more saintly in order to reverse Nature's deterioration; or alternatively, a harsh or disruptive landscape supplies the tests and trials necessary to the refinement of a true Christian.

Zion imagery appears in some of Mary Jane Mount Tanner's letters. Tanner represents the Wasatch Front landscape as sterile, lonely, and desolate: that is, desert in the Christian sense as a *deserted* place or latter-day Judaea; a foil against which the Saints' progress and improvement can be measured. Tanner implies the Zion metaphor through her allusion to Isaiah's vision that the Chosen People will occupy the barren desert and cause it to bloom like the rose. They rightfully displace the "unworthy" indigenes who have "forfeited" their right to the land, like the biblical Canaanites or Philistines (Kay 1991, 441). In one letter, Tanner (Ward 1980, 163) writes:

> "Provo [Utah] Jan 19, /[18]61
> Dear Aunt
> . . . Thirteen years ago this was a barren wilderness with only a few huts and an Indian encampment here and there to break the perpetual loneliness of the scene We have had no advantages of navigation and almost everything to oppose and discourage us The wonder is not that we are not more flourishing and intelligent but that we lived at all . . . The Indians are a continual expense to us both by their squalid wretchedness and depredations they are too Idle to work . . .

Twenty years later she reports much the same landscape imagery, with paraphrases from Genesis and Isaiah (Ward 1980, 190).

> Provo. July 16. 1882.
> He [Gen. Albert Johnston, an army officer sent to oversee the Mormons] thought the generel aspect of the country was poor [in 1857]. So it is, we have conquered the desert. The sage brush and the rabits. Our cities did not look rich and prosperous. Not in comparison with large cities in the East . . . He could not realize the bone and sinew and the sweat of the brow and hearts blood it has taken to fertilize this soil and populate this barren desert, and make it blossom as the rose. with beautiful orchards and fruitful fields, and stock upon the thousand hills. And our enemies are trying to wrench them from us.

To be sure, one can readily read a subconscious sexuality in Tanner's land-scape imagery of Zion, by noting her words, "conquered," "fertilize," "popu-lated," and "fruitful." But sexual glosses on an already explicit doctrinaire construction of Zion or this-world would by no means prescribe a simple heterosexual female body representation of the Great Basin. If Mormon Na-ture is sexualized, it certainly occurs in an equivocal fashion. For one thing, Tanner as a Mormon woman consistently identifies herself as one of the people doing the conquering, fertilizing, populating, and fructifying of the land sur-face. Mormons occasionally designated the earth or their habitats as "her" or "Mother Nature" in preference to neutered terms" impersonal and detached connotations. Yet one could equally make an argument for Mormon phallo-centrism in their landscape representations. For example, Saints are com-manded to "build up" the Kingdom, and to construct spired temples and tabernacles. Zion itself is the rational, orderly project of a Heavenly Father, His Son, male prophets, and priests. The earth is the male God's handiwork or manufacture, rewarding the faithful with material security; not the goddess of pagan belief, nor the temptress of Virginia's English explorers (Kay and Brown 1985, Kolodny 1975).

Landscape as Home

If Zion preempted feminized representations of Mother Nature, tempting vir-gin, or raging fury, alternative representations nevertheless link Nature and Mormon women in their autobiographical writing. Unsurprisingly, the princi-pal of these were the tiny portions of space and ground that constituted home and community (cf. Hampsten 1982). My three subjects wrote about their lives in agricultural villages. Within the Cult of Domesticity or of True Wom-anhood, home was woman's proper location. Most writers I studied, seldom described places beyond the borders of their own house and grounds: home-bodies, indeed.

To the extent that home is understood as an extension of oneself, home-scapes for rural Mormon women had several broad feminized zones of contact with Nature that eroded the dualism of Woman/Nature. This was not land-scape described or painted by men as a female body; but rather, a more eco-feminist concept of a rural household as an extension of or haven for the female self (cf. Valentine 1997).

Despite the small area that spatially constituted home, home implicitly linked women's bodies with Nature as the place where women were most "natural." It was the center of women's most biological of activities: eating, sleeping, coping with illness, conceiving, nurturing children, and (in the nine-teenth century) giving birth and dying. Public spaces like the church building were for more social and intellectual matters like attending services. Early homes were constructed of local natural resources: adobe or fired brick from community clay beds, or logs from nearby canyons linked one's home to one's ecological surroundings.

Home was more than a domicile for Mormon women, however. It was also the location of essential and productive outdoor work in the garden, orchard, poultry coops, and dairy. Many women expected to be largely self-sufficient in foodstuffs they produced on their irrigated one-acre house lots as well as to earn income through a cottage industry within its bounds, such as selling produce, weaving, or hat-making (Arrington 1984, Beecher 1981). Before these activities were well established, many women in new frontier settlements gathered wild berries and greens from local creek banks and canyons. Particularly before rail and improved road transportation made imported food and clothes affordable, rural Mormon families were closely dependent upon women's horticultural and small livestock-raising activities.

The image of woman and Nature that emerges from domestic descriptions was of a woman "planted" in her site, drawing upon its soil and irrigation water for sustenance, converting its nutrients into food and furnishings. Although a few women like Tanner (above) adopted the discourse of masculine conquest and domination of Nature, homemaking was more often described through the religious ideology of beautifying the earth, the practical need for economic security, or the general Victorian concern for improvement of one's personality and material circumstances.

Mormon women often represented their homes much like an organism whose skin or outer shell might be outgrown, that grew with the passage of time, and that constantly was to be "cultivated" or improved upon. They noted when wood floors replaced the original packed dirt, and later when they covered the wood floors with rag rugs; when curtains made from flour sacks or from outworn clothes were replaced with new fabrics.

Few diarists or letter-writers were eloquent on their autecology. Organicism is sometimes only implicit in descriptions of homegrown produce served upon the dinner table; or in records of improvements to the orchard, dairy, or garden. The writer's flower or vegetable garden (with implicit or explicit correspondence to the Garden) is an underlying theme. One can infer from these descriptions how rapidly the native sagebrush was replaced by order and "proper" foodstuffs. Such images perhaps draw upon the general nineteenth-century American—and explicitly doctrinaire Mormon—emphasis upon agrarianism and self-improvement. The ideology of Zion explicitly mandated building more substantial homes, more extensive planting of orchards and gardens.

Mary Ann Hafen, a Swiss immigrant, set up housekeeping in the new settlement of Bunkerville, Nevada, in 1891 as a young, former plural wife who was recently required to separate from her husband when the church terminated polygamy. Regarding her marriage as sanctioned, she never divorced her husband John, but lived as a single head-of-household for most of her adult life, as he lived in another town and visited her infrequently.

Hafen's detailed description of her site—a new home, garden, female-headed household, and pioneer fortitude—offer a rich landscape description, yet most of it is circumscribed within an acre or two of ground. Hafen as a single parent expected to feed her family of eight principally from the produce of her own lot and a "partly cleared" field of twenty-five acres outside of town to be tilled by her sixteen-year-old son. Implicit in Hafen's description is obedience to Brigham Young's admonition to the Saints to build up the Kingdom and to convert the desert through ornamental and food-producing trees and shrubs of various kinds. Although Hafen describes a geographic situation that is more tempestuous and unpredictable than Tanner's *desertum*, nowhere are those external dangers explicitly feminine (Hafen 1983, 73–76).

> It was a two-roomed adobe house with dirt floors and dirt roof. That did not look so inviting, but John promised that he would see that it was soon finished off with a good roof and floors, and probably would put a second story on the house to make more bedrooms.
>
> The big lot already had five or six almond trees growing, and a nice vineyard of grapes. But . . . there was only a makeshift fence of mesquite brush . . . [and] the lot was covered with rocks.
>
> [Son] Albert dug up three young mulberry trees from Mesquite and planted them around our shadeless house. Now, after forty-seven years of growth, those mulberry trees completely shade the old place.
>
> I remember how in those earliest years we were disturbed by the hot winds that swept over the dry bench lands from the south.
>
> From the first we found that the river dam [necessary for irrigation] was . . . unstable . . . Each flood that came down the river broke our Bunkerville dam . . . teams often stuck in the quicksand and had to be dug out. Range animals occasionally mired fast and starved to death in the sandy bars of the river.
>
> For a while John came down every month or so to help Albert and me to make small improvements around the place. But being Bishop at Santa Clara, and with his other three families, he could not be with us much. So I had to care for my seven children mostly by myself. He had provided us a house, lot, and land and he furnished some supplies. But it was a new country and we had a hard time to make a go of it.
>
> I did not want to be a burden on my husband but tried with my family to be self-supporting . . . I always kept a garden so we could have green things to eat. Keeping that free from weeds and watering it twice a week took lots of time. (79)

Yet "home" as a small portion of landscape was a secondary consideration to home as the location of the daily interactions with one's family, particularly with one's children (Hafen 1983, 85–86). Visits from grown daughters, having a granddaughter move into the house—these occur as significant events in the narratives of older women.[9]

Certainly women across the Mormon region glimpsed further horizons and drew upon widespread literary traditions, in greater frequency with the passing of the frontier, notably romantic images of sublime mountain scenery. The early generations of pioneer women, many from northern Europe, had traveled across the plains or from California to Utah. They extended their purviews through occasional wagon rides to nearby mountain canyons. Church work or midwifery drew some women throughout their community and sometimes beyond, as did gleaning wheat in the fields surrounding the agricultural towns. Some women reported long hikes afoot to round up stray cattle or to pick wild berries, but the overwhelming autobiographical narrative locus was home. The geometry of a Mormon woman's home as a single site or node, often interior, indeed contrasts with masculinist geography's preoccupation with extensive spaces and scenery. The Mormon mother's constricted domestic landscape projected an acceptable naturalized femininity that was familial, relational, and centered upon Woman as Mother and Caregiver.

Within the sheltering walls of home, unfortunate realities nevertheless collided. Many private journals (less so the memoirs and letters written for the eyes of other readers) also described the unrelieved drudgery of frontier housework, where everything was done by hand without appliances or electricity. The chores were exacerbated when occasional serious illness struck the writers themselves or a family member, or when husbands who were ideologized as protectors and bread-winners left home for months at a time, leaving wives to take up their secondary and somewhat contradictory roles as economically self-sufficient providers. Where incompatible or jealous plural wives lived together under one roof, home as a sheltered haven of refuge was out of the question. And often in the women's diaries, as Hafen indicates in her descriptions of desiccating wind, flash floods, rock, and wild brush; beyond the Garden a vast and unsympathetic wilderness intrudes.

A Wilderness Condition

Vast portions of the Great Basin and Colorado Plateau even today are unsettled. Only 2 percent of Utah's land surface is sufficiently level and watered to be classified as arable. An immense out-of-doors, often in an uncultivated state, and the intimate interface of one's body with its rocks, heat, cold, precipitation, and the like were immanent to male and female settlers on the Western frontier. They spent far more of their lives outside than is typical for Americans today: for example, any heating fuel or drinking water had to be fetched out-of-doors by hand. Early adobe and log homes provided, at best, permeable barriers from the elements. Many conveniences and technologies of the Industrial Revolution were left "back East." Mormon immigration to Utah initially was a 1,300–mile overland journey by wagon or on foot. Nature as scenery, as obstacle, as location for home, community, or economic activity is not easily ignored or taken for granted in either Mormon text or turf, as it might be in modern urban settings (Kay 1995; Limerick 1987).

The hardships residing within early frontierswomen's homes point to another important representational correspondence between women and Nature: the impact of Nature on women's bodies.[10] Home is not solely the cozy refuge of sanctioned maternal fulfillment, sequestered from hunger, cold, or pain, in the early settlers' records. Life in the midst of the Western wilderness brought with it isolation from medical care and creature comforts of civilization; uncontrollable climatic forces like droughts, flash floods, and blizzards; and the niggardly soils and precipitation regimes from which impoverished Saints attempted to wrest their livelihoods. The vast unsettled spaces encircle the homes and permeate their walls (cf. Ward 1980, 56, 67, 74–76, 94, 155, 168).

This is not Nature represented in terms of painterly scenery or rational scientific variables, but Nature as the executor of peoples' destiny or fate, operating in tandem with other personal misfortune or happenstance. Such adversity put the Mormon writer in a problematic position, since the Intermountain West was, after all, supposed to be the Promised Land. The Mormon woman's environment was therefore scripted to enact an omniscient personal God's plans for her moral development. The true Latter-day Saint meets its vicissitudes with courage, exertion, and testimonies to her faith. The suffering body, replicating Christ, ennobles and redeems the Mormon woman, provided she is constant in her faith.[11] Such narratives of women's surrender to adversity textually situate them as the Son, with wilderness hardships as their cross. Christian denominations throughout the nineteenth century indeed frequently interpreted severe trials and misfortunes as Providentially designed to sift out the elect: prayer, silent suffering, and redemption in death were acceptable responses.

Following are some samples from the diary of Eliza Partridge Lyman in the Salt Lake Valley in 1848–49. She is a woman of few words, but one reads between her lines the impact of a harsh Nature on her body and senses, as interpreted through belief in divine Providence.

Oct. 17th. Reached the place of our destination in the valley of the Great Salt Lake. I have been as comfortable on the journey . . . as could be expected under the circumstances [of a son born 20 August in a covered wagon en route.] Some of the time the weather has been very cold with rain and snow so that I could not be comfortable anywhere as I had no stove in the wagon; but I and my child have been preserved through it all, and I feel to give thanks to my Father in Heaven for His kind care over us . . .

18th. Moved into a log room. There are 7 of us to live in this room this winter . . . We are glad to get this much of a shelter, but it is no shelter when it rains, for the dirt roof lets water through and the dirt floor gets muddy which makes it anything but pleasant.

April 8th. During the past winter . . . My baby was very sick with whooping cough. Many children around us died with it . . . Baking the last of our flour today and have no prospect of getting any more till after harvest.

Thirty years later, Lyman's diary entries in southeastern Utah indicate that she has hardly any heat in her house in December due to inadequate shelter or fuel wood supply. Readers who bake their own bread can imagine the chilling sensation of kneading partially frozen dough, and the prospect of poor fare for Christmas because cold bread dough made without commercial yeast will not properly rise. There is no Christmas feast in her cabin. Yet Lyman piously subordinates her own discomfort to that of friends who are on the trail with no shelter at all:

> 24th. Weather colder than ever, the dough freezes to the pan while we are mixing it.
> 25th. Christmas. Not a merry one for I can not think of any thing but the cold and my friends who are camped on the banks of the Colorado river with out houses or tents and exposed to the inclemency of the weather. May the Lord preserve them from suffering is my prayer continually.

The vulnerability of one's physical body to raw Nature is particularly apparent for women during childbirth, especially where interiors are described as squalid and crowded, or where one's location was remote and sparsely populated. Lyman's own daughter Carlie Lyman Callister suffered a difficult two-day labor in a remote Great Basin hamlet until a skilled midwife arrived from a larger town a day's ride away, and Callister died two weeks later of complications (Carter 1953, 266).

Nature is an essential ingredient of pioneer Mormon women's experiences and what they make of their experiences and their identities. Nature's harshness also molds women's characters, making them stronger and more reverent in the face of adversity. At times Nature's impacts are physically inscribed upon Mormon women's bodies. Older women's lined faces and hands are attributed to lifetimes of hard work and struggle on the frontier; deformities to walking the overland trail (Carter 1953, 262–63; Hafen 1983, 23–24).

As a child in southwestern Utah in the 1860s, Mary Ann Hafen's (1983, 42–44) parents were too poor to afford shoes for her until she was nearly grown up. Her bare feet blistered from the hot sand when she and her brother tended dairy cows in the common pasture above town. The first winter that she attended school, she developed hives (chilblains?) that "broke out in blisters" with an accompanying high fever from walking to school barefoot in the snow. "As I had no bed except a pile of straw covered with old clothes my back became raw and sore." Fortunately Hafen escaped the severe frostbite of Ellen and Maggie Pucell, two adolescent girls whose handcart company got trapped by snow in Wyoming. Maggie lost much of the flesh off her legs, and Ellen's had to be amputated at the knees (Hafen and Hafen 1992, 238).

The foregoing interpretations of women and Nature is miles apart from metaphors of the voluptuous female body, imperial domination of Nature, or blissful domesticity; and equally distant from popular historical caricatures of Old West frontierswomen as cowards in petticoats excluded by men from physical hardship. While such records further subvert masculinist generalizations about wilderness, they also subvert radical ecofeminism's idealized identification of women with an unfailingly supportive, beneficent Mother earth.[12]

Some contemporary Mormon women writers also include the theme of Nature's inscriptions on women's bodies, suggesting a resonant narrative tradition. Maureen Whipple's (1941) epic historical novel *The Giant Joshua* describes the intertwined lives of four pioneer plural wives in the Colorado Plateau country of southwestern Utah, with characters loosely based on real people.[13] Wilhelmina's elbows, knees, and feet are deeply scarred from crawling through the snow with frozen feet as a young handcart pioneer, permanently impairing her gait. Clorinda's kidneys are damaged from years of drinking muddy river water; with hands blistered from "salt rheum," she plays the organ in church. She has had several miscarriages and lost two young children to diphtheria exacerbated by malnutrition. Both women die of childbirth complications, but death ultimately ennobles them as they grow more confirmed in their religious faith. Whipple thus maps religion and environment onto the complex atlases of these women's anatomy and personality.

Terry Tempest Williams's (1991) autobiographical and fundamentally ecofeminist book *Refuge* describes the ecological deterioration of the Bear River Migratory Bird Refuge on the Great Salt Lake as an allegory for her mother's failing health. In her chapter entitled "The Clan of One-Breasted Women," she interprets her female relatives' breast and ovarian cancers as resulting from her family's exposure to above-ground nuclear testing in southern Nevada during the 1950s. In language reminiscent of Mormon pioneer women's belief in salvation through suffering, Williams's grandmother describes her mastectomy as a spiritual experience; her mother says following her own mastectomy: "I felt the arms of God around me" (Williams 1991, 252).

Implications

I have argued in this chapter for a fuller consideration of religion in the representation of Nature, identity, and difference, and for greater awareness of a variety of ways that gender, Nature, and the body may be mapped. While I do not claim that the texts of Tanner, Hafen, or Lyman are purely female-derived, given the patriarchal conditions in which the women lived and wrote, these women's representations of wild and rural landscapes nevertheless challenge masculinist conventions of Nature as female body. Although female body/ Nature imagery has been convincingly documented for other groups, such as eighteenth-century British landscape painters (Rose 1993) or Mediterranean agriculturists in pre-Christian times, my purposeful focus on historical writings by ordinary women, rather than by male intellectual elites (cf. Gregory 1994, 129–31) indicates alternative scriptings of Nature that exceed binary norms (see Nast and Kobayashi 1996).

This chapter might also be seen to extend the 1980s "Western women's history" project, with its faith in scholars' ability to interpret women's lived experience and its models of proto-feminist liberation (see, for example, Armitage and Jameson 1987). However, its exuberant interpretations of women's history, as opposed to gender studies or postcolonial studies, has been largely displaced in the academy by more sophisticated critical and theoretical approaches. (For examples, see McDowell, 1993.) To an unreconstructed liberal feminist, there is nevertheless something depressing about the sequential invalidation of research on ordinary women's lives, first by conservative male colleagues disinterested or even hostile toward female scholars or scholarship on women; and next by postmodern or postcolonial scholars who believed that focusing on women's lived experiences, particularly in the areas of mundane housewifery or spiritual growth, was tantamount to essentializing or valorizing women in naive isolation from binary patriarchal or colonial power relations. I argue, despite such potential pitfalls, that ordinary women's lives are "good enough" for serious study, as their neglect can lead to a needlessly elitist or masculinist scholarship of complex societies' representations of their environmental relationships. Marginalized women's letters, dairies, and memoirs may fundamentally challenge the current wisdom and assist in the construction of a broader representational frame within which to discuss geographies of difference. This chapter's focus on nineteenth-century Latter-day Saint women's domestic arrangements and masculinist religious beliefs may initially seem to be feminine, rather than feminist scholarship. However, I would argue that one of the underlying themes of feminist scholarship is women's ability to achieve significant personal growth and some level of economic self-sufficiency in the face of adversity and patriarchy.

Notes

The patience and helpful insights of Heidi Nast, Sue Roberts, and the New Horizons workshop participants, as well as the support of the Dean's Office staff at the University of Waterloo, are deeply appreciated.

    1. The concept "Nature" is problematic and will be here taken to mean undeveloped, rural, or largely vegetated land as interpreted through one's culture; with, however, the understanding that this definition has its own history and urban, ethnic biases inherent to it. Mormon texts include the word *nature* on occasion, but more commonly refer to individual features like weather, soil, or pasturage. I simply assume a reasonably close correspondence between their environmental experiences and current common usage of *nature*.

    2. "Pioneer" is defined here as the first or second generation of predominantly white settlers who immigrated to Utah or contingent territories. In the sense that this was a process of displacing indigenous people and significantly modifying their cultures, Mormon settlement can be interpreted as "colonial." However, pioneer Mormons were not an extension of American political control over the West, but rather a splinter religious sect viewed as a serious social problem and potentially seditious movement by mainstream America. When the federal government first established a military post, Fort Douglas, in Utah, its guns were trained on Salt Lake City.

    3. This chapter is part of a larger historical inquiry into Mormon women and Nature. For a sampling of representative primary sources see: Davis Bitton. *Guide to Mor-*

mon Diaries and Autobiographies Provo: Brigham Young University Press 1977; Kate B. Carter. comp. *Heart Throbs of the West*. 12 vols. Salt Lake City: Daughters of Utah Pioneers, 1939–1943; Kate B. Carter, comp. 1958–1963. *Our Pioneer Heritage*. Salt Lake City: Daughters of Utah Pioneers, 6 vols.; Kate B. Carter, comp. 1972. *Treasures of Pioneer History* . Salt Lake City: Western Epics. 6 vols; Madsen, Carol Cornwall and David J. Whittaker. 1979. History's Sequel. A Source Essay on Women in Mormon History. *Journal of Mormon History* 6: 123–45; Scott, Patricia Lyn. 1993. Mormon Polygamy: A Bibliography, 1977–91. *Journal of Mormon History* 19: 133–55. The Winter, 1991 issue of the *Utah Historical Quarterly* is a special issue on women.

4. The author is not a Latter-day Saint, but lived in Utah for thirteen years and retains a second home in a rural community in central Utah.

5. The literature on Mormon history and belief is voluminous and constantly expanding: see the *Journal of Mormon History*, *Brigham Young University [BYU] Studies*, and *Dialogue: A Journal of Mormon Thought*, particularly the latter's surveys of recent works, for more doctrinaire articles and books; *Sunstone* for a more liberal, even radical (and thus unsanctioned by the church) "insider" perspective; or the Utah *Historical Quarterly* for more secular approaches to Mormon history. The bibliographic sections of the *Western Historical Quarterly* are a useful reference guide. *Improvement Era*, the *Woman's Exponent*, and *Relief Society Magazine* provide church-approved or sponsored historical accounts. A sturdy classic overview of Mormon settlement in Utah is Leonard J. Arrington. 1966. *Great Basin Kingdom: An Economic History of the Latter-day Saints, 1830–1900*. Lincoln: University of Nebraska Press.

6. There are also accounts of the early LDS church by Mormon apostates that could be considered "Mormon" for a portion of the writers' lives. For example, see: Stenhouse (1971) or Young (1908). These also tend to have a standard narrative form (Victorian gothic) and to titillate with lurid anecdotes of dictatorial church leadership and polygamy and at its worst.

7. As a former geography professor at the University of Utah, I first became alerted to this emplotment when assigning standard family migration history projects to a third-year historical geography class. No matter how carefully I attempted to instruct the students to place their genealogies in the context of social science immigration theories, their chapters typically contained emplotments and anecdotes characteristic of Mormon historiography.

8. A surprising number of pioneer women wrote poetry, which shows more influence of Romantic conventions and an attempt to integrate concepts of the sublime with their workaday worlds.

9. Family heritage was Tanner's and Hafen's explicit rationale for setting down their life histories. Lyman's reasons are less clear: in her autobiography she cites extensively from her private journal. "It will perhaps not be very interesting to anyone but myself, but it shows more particularly how we were situated and the hardships we endured . . ." (Carter 1953, 220).

10. Hardship was not noticeably gender-specific: illness and death seemed exceptionally high for children of both sexes, partly due to malnutrition; to lack of immunization against diphtheria, whooping cough, measles; and to frequent accidents (scalding, drowning in an irrigation ditch, etc.) There are frequent references to specifically female health issues such as difficult births and nursing infants.

11. Redemption was surely in the mind of Lyman's editor (Carter 1953, 213) who

prefaced Lyman's autobiography with the note: "Her pattern of living exemplifies the pioneer woman who amid strife, persecution, sorrow and death, continued to live a full life gaining with each day's experiences a strength of character and soul which enabled her to bear the burdens of her everyday existence. She had a purpose in living and she fulfilled that purpose to the best of her ability."

12. This is not to deny Mormon women's other types of portrayals of Nature, without explicit reference to bodies, which were often quite positive and romanticized.

13. Whipple based the characters in her historical novel on oral history and the biographies and autobiographies of Mormon pioneer women of southwestern Utah, her native region. She writes (Whipple 1941, xi) ". . . it is natural for our generation to deify them. Perhaps because of the abuse they suffered for over half a century . . ." The novel begins with the tactile feel of the land—the rock surface and weather—on Clorinda's body.

References

Armitage, S., and Jameson, E. 1987. *The women's west*. Norman: University of Oklahoma Press.

Arrington, L. J. 1966. *Great Basin kingdom: An economic history of the Latter-day Saints, 1830–1900* Lincoln: University of Nebraska Press.

———. 1984. Rural life among nineteenth century Mormons: The women's experience. *Agricultural History* 58: 239–46.

Beecher, M. U. 1981. Women's work on the Mormon frontier. *Utah Historical Quarterly* 49: 276–90.

———. 1982. "The leading sisters": A female hierarchy in nineteenth-century Mormon society. *Journal of Mormon History* 9: 25–40.

Beecher, M. U. and Anderson, L. F. 1987. *Sisters in spirit: Mormon women in historical and cultural perspective*. Urbana: University of Illinois Press.

Blunt, A. 1994. *Travel, gender, and imperialism: Mary Kingsley and west Africa*. New York: The Guildford Press.

Blunt, A., and Rose, G., eds. 1994. *Writing women and space: Colonial and post-colonial geographies*. New York: Guildford.

Carter, K. B. 1953. Eliza Marie Partridge Lyman. In *Treasures of pioneer history,* ed., Kate B. Carter, vol.2, 213–84. Salt Lake City: Daughters of Utah Pioneers.

Diamond, I., and Orenstein, G. F., eds. 1990. *Reweaving the world: The emergence of ecofeminism*. San Francisco: Sierra Club Books.

duBois, P. 1988. *Sowing the body: Psychoanalysis and ancient representations of women*. Chicago: University of Chicago Press.

Duncan, J., and Duncan, N. 1988. (Re)reading the landscape. *Environment and Planning D: Society and Space* 6: 117–26.

Duncan, J. S. 1990. *The city as text: The politics of landscape interpretation in the Kandyan Kingdom*. Cambridge: Cambridge University Press.

Embry, J. L. 1987. *Mormon polygamous families: Life in the principle.* Salt Lake City: University of Utah Press.

Foster, L. 1991. *Women, family, and utopia: Communal experiments of the Shakers, the Oneida community, and the Mormons*. Syracuse: Syracuse University Press.

Frye, N. 1982. *The great code: The Bible and literature*. San Diego: Harcourt Brace Jovanovich.

Gaard, G., ed. 1993. *Ecofeminism: Women, animals, nature*. Philadelphia: Temple University Press.

Gregory, D. 1994. *Geographical imaginations*. Cambridge: Blackwell.

Hafen, L. H., and Hafen, A. W. 1992. *Handcart pioneers: The story of a unique western migration, 1856–1860*. Lincoln: University of Nebraska Press.

Hafen, M. A. 1983. *Recollections of a handcart pioneer of 1860: A woman's life on the Mormon frontier*. Lincoln: University of Nebraska Press.

Hampsten, E. 1982. *Read this only to yourself: The private writings of midwestern women, 1880–1910*. Bloomington: Indiana University Press.

Hardy, B. C. 1992. *Solemn covenant: The Mormon polygamous passage*. Urbana: University of Illinois Press.

Iverson, J. 1984. Feminist implications of Mormon polygyny. *Feminist Studies* 10: 505–22.

Kay, J. 1991. Landscapes of women and men: Rethinking the regional historical geography of the United States and Canada. *Journal of Historical Geography* 17: 435–52.

———. 1995. Mormons and mountains. In *The mountainous west: Explorations in historical geography*, eds., W. Wyckoff and L. Dilsaver, 368–96. Lincoln: University of Nebraska Press.

Kay, J., and Brown, C. J. 1985. Mormon beliefs about land and natural resources, 1847–1877. *Journal of Historical Geography* 11: 253–67.

Kimball, M. E. 1994 (1857–63). *Journal of Mary Ellen Kimball including a sketch of our History in this Valley*. Salt Lake City: Pioneer Press.

Kolodny, A. 1975. *The lay of the land: Metaphor as experience and history in American life and letters*. Chapel Hill: University of North Carolina Press.

———. 1984. *The land before her: Fantasy and experience of the American frontiers, 1630–1860*. Chapel Hill: University of North Carolina Press.

Lerner, G. 1980. The lady and the mill girl: Changes in the status of women in the Age of Jackson. In *Women's experiences in America: A historical anthology*, eds., E. Katz and A. Rapone, 87–99. New Brunswick, NJ: Transaction Books.

Limerick, P. 1987. *The legacy of conquest: The unbroken past of the American West*. New York: W. W. Norton & Co.

McDowell, L. 1993. Space, place and gender relations, Part II. Identity, difference, feminist geometries and geographies. *Progress in Human Geography* 17: 305–18.

Merchant, C. 1980. *The death of nature: Women, ecology, and the scientific revolution*. San Francisco: Harper and Row.

———. 1989. *Ecological revolutions: Nature, gender, and science in New England*. Chapel Hill: University of North Carolina Press.

———. 1995. *Earthcare: Women and the environment*. New York: Routledge.

Nast, H. J., 1996. Islam, gender, and slavery in west Africa circa 1500: A spatial archaeology of the Kano palace, northern Nigeria. *Annals of the Association of American Geographers* 86(1): 44–77.

Nast, H. J., and Kobayashi, A. 1996. *Re-corporealizing vision*. In *Body space: Destabilizing geographies of gender and sexuality*, ed. N. Duncan, New York: Routledge.

Neumann, E. 1963. *The great mother: An analysis of the archetype.*, 2d ed. New York: Bollingen Foundation Inc.

Norwood, V. 1993. *Made from this earth: American women and nature*. Chapel Hill: University of North Carolina Press.

Norwood, V., and Monk, J., eds. 1987. *The desert is no lady: Southwestern landscapes in women's writing and art* . New Haven: Yale University Press.

Ortner, S. 1974. Is Female to Male as Nature is to Culture? In Women, *Culture, and Society*, Michele Z. Rosaldo and Louise Lamphere, eds. 67–87. Palo Alto, CA: Stanford University Press.

Robertson, J. 1990. *The magnificent mountain women: Adventures in the Colorado Rockies*. Lincoln: University of Nebraska Press.

Rose, G. 1993. *Feminism and geography: The limits of geographical knowledge*. Minneapolis: University of Minnesota Press.

Said, E. 1978. *Orientalism*. London: Routledge and Kegan Paul.

Smith, G. D., ed. 1992. *Faithful history: Essays on writing Mormon history*. Salt Lake City: Signature Books.

Stegner, W. 1992. *The gathering of Zion: The story of the Mormon Trail*. Lincoln: University of Nebraska Press.

Stenhouse, Mrs. T. B. H. 1971 (1874). *Tell it all: The Tyranny of Mormonism or an Englishwoman in Utah*. New York: Praeger.

Swetnam, S. H. 1991. *Lives of the Saints in southeast Idaho: An introduction to Mormon pioneer life story writing*. Moscow: University of Idaho Press.

Townsend, J. G. 1991. Towards a regional geography of gender. *The Geographical Journal* 157: 25–35.

Van Wagenen, L. 1991. Sister wives and suffragists: Polygamy and the politics of women's suffrage, 1870–1895. Ph. D. diss., New York University.

Van Wagoner, R. S. 1992. *Mormon polygamy: A history*. 3d ed. Salt Lake City: Signature Books.

Ward, M. W., ed. 1980. *A fragment: The autobiography of Mary Jane Mount Tanner*. Salt Lake City: University of Utah Tanner Trust Fund.

Welter, B.. 1966. The cult of true womanhood, 1820–1860. *American Quarterly* 18: 151–74.

Whipple, M. 1941. *The giant Joshua*. Boston: Houghton Mifflin Company.

Williams, T. T. 1991. *Refuge: An unnatural history of family and place*. New York: Pantheon Books.

Young, A. E. W. 1908. *Life in Mormon bondage*. Philadelphia: Aldine Press.

18

The Cultural Construction of Rurality: Gender Identities and the Rural Idyll

Francine Watkins

Alice had always wanted to live in Pitcombe; everybody did, from miles around and if a house there was photographed for sale, in *Country Life*, the caption always read, "In much sought-after village." It was the kind of village long-term expatriates might fantasise about, a stone village set on the side of a gentle hill, with the church at the top and the pub at the bottom, by a little river, and the big house—baroque—looking down on it all with feudal benevolence. Sir Ralph Unwin, who owned the big house, three thousand acres and two dozen cottages still, was tall and grey-haired and an admirable shot. He drove a Range Rover through the village and waved regally from the elevated driving seat. He allowed Pitcombe Park to be used constantly for functions to raise money for hospices and arthritis research and the church *roof, though he drew the line at the local Conservatives*.

—Joanna Trollope *A Village Affair*

Through many representations in the media, in literature and in academic texts, English village life is mythologized.[1] The village represented in the passage above is a mythical place but for many represents a highly desirable reality, which they want to experience. The roots of this desirability lie in the historical creation of a symbolic distance between the city and the countryside. Raymond Williams (1973) documented the significance of the separation of the urban and rural landscapes with the advent of industrialization and subsequent developments over time.

Industrialization in England brought about urbanization, creating cities; in order for the city to exist as a superior society, an "other" was produced—the countryside (Williams 1973). While the city reflected the speed of change in industry and society, the countryside continued to be portrayed as a static, unchanging community embodying the "way things used to be" (Short 1992).

The countryside was seen as a place outside industrial society, a place that maintained the character of "old England," resisting the advance of progress in order to maintain its character—"The [rural] community . . . became perceived as essentially undifferentiated, harmonious and wholesome, fighting a rearguard action against external encroachment" (Newby 1986, 212). The countryside, represented as a form of community not existing in city society, was perceived as a supportive social network based on strong kinship relations and cooperation. The countryside was constructed as the place for city dwellers to escape the problems of industrialization, such as overcrowding, pollution, and squalor (Winstanley 1989).[2]

But more than just experiencing a cleaner way of life, those who moved to the countryside from the city expected to feel part of a supportive, strong village community. While there can be strong communities in urban areas (Pahl 1966), the quality of community life in the English countryside was imagined as being purer and more spiritual because of the physical and symbolic proximity to nature (Bell 1992). Life in rural villages in England continues to be depicted, in the media at least, as an idyllic community, with all inhabitants being enveloped in a warm, united society (Laing 1992). Life in the countryside is considered to have achieved a "truly human and supreme form of community . . . expressed through kinship, neighborhood and friendship, all these being closely related to space as well as time" (Tönnies 1955, 48; see Harper 1989). The myth that rural life in Britain is a "supreme form of community" has remained pivotal to representations of rural England in the media and in literature.

Many rural villages in England are not necessarily physically remote but are separated from other communities by open land. The separation is symbolic in that inhabitants of villages feel that they *should* unite and support each other, both because it is expected and necessary. Using Anderson's (1983) theory of imagined community, attention turns to the symbolic construction of rural space. Anderson argues that although members of a nation could never meet each other or know each other on a personal level, they imagined there was something that united them, so much so, that people would die for their country. It is this shared belief in a unity within a specific place (see Rose 1990) that needs further scrutiny in British rural studies.

This chapter illustrates, then, how a community in one rural area in England is not the coherent, supportive one that many expect to find and become part of, but a complex, fractured community that excludes those perceived as different. The argument presented in this paper reflects the experiences of women in a village in Oxfordshire, England, their multiple experiences of community, and the conflicts that exist between them. Based on research carried out using a variety of ethnographic research methods, this chapter will consider issues of marginalization within the imagined community and the representational practices that work to include and exclude those seen as "different."

Community in Rural England.

Studies of community life in rural England need to be more critical of the one-dimensional definition of community and instead understand the multiple experiences of persons living in them. The term "community," itself, assumes homogeneity, with all members sharing the same mutual identity (Young 1991). To achieve mutual identification, moral boundaries have to be constructed that include only those who share certain prescribed characteristics. Once these boundaries are in place as the "norm," transgressors are constructed as "other" and different. As Young argues with respect to people in the United States:

> Insofar as they consider themselves members of communities at all, a community is a group that shares a specific heritage a common self-identification, a common culture and set of norms. In the US today, identification as a member of such a community also occurs as an oppositional differentiation from other groups, who are feared or at best devalued. Persons identify only with some other persons, feel in community only with those, and fear the difference others confront them with because they identify with a different culture, history, and point of view on the world (Young 1993, 311).

Similarly, persons in English villages identify with those they feel they have something in common with and with whom they share a similar world view. A denial of difference between community members produces clique atmospheres that help maintain the particular accepted norms of the community. In previous academic studies and popular literature, the community is constructed as a very inflexible, static representation, one that assumes its members cannot control membership or moral boundaries (Newby 1979). Through various strategies, however, it is possible for members to keep boundaries flexible so as to exclude persons or minority groups who are "feared." Feminist geographers need to analyze how women can exclude and marginalize other women from communities by representing themselves as the "norm" vis-à-vis those who have an alternative culture or worldview. Living in rural areas is a multitude of women who have multiple identities. They are not just mothers or White or gay; rather they have many aspects of their identity that inform their ideas of community at different times. Multiple and changing identities across time and in any one space provide the potential for conflict within a community. As Aziz (1992, 302) states, "rooted as it is in complex layers of struggles and contexts, identity is not neat and coherent but fluid and fragmented."

Through representing themselves as the "norm," certain women can control access to a community, alienating others whom they construct as different. What follows is an analysis of a rural community in England that illustrates how the notion of community is mobilized to include those who share certain normative characteristics and to exclude those who are do not "fit" in.

Little Hatton: A Village in Oxfordshire, England.

Little Hatton epitomizes the type of rural village illustrated in the fictional quotation at the beginning of this chapter: the chocolate box image of an English rural village. Picturesque, with a population of approximately 450, there are several houses in the village dating back to the sixteenth and seventeenth centuries. In contrast to these Old World buildings is a modern executive estate with forty-five new family houses, located on the fringes of the village. A once thriving farm now employs only five people from the village. Thus, those employed generally work outside the village. The proximity of the village to the M40 motorway makes it popular with commuters who can be in the center of London in an hour. Many of the residents of Little Hatton enjoy the tranquillity of being surrounded by farmland in the heart of the English countryside. Since the village has its own post office, village school, church, and two public houses, residents can carry out basic day-to-day tasks in the village.

The research was carried out using ethnographic techniques. For three months I lived in the village, worked in the village public house, attended Women's Institute meetings, parish council meetings, mother and toddler groups, helped out at jumble sales, and tried to play an active part in the day-to-day activities in the village. In so doing, I was able to observe the operation of the community and the process of marginalization first hand, using personal observation to support information received through interviewing. The quotes are taken from twenty-two hour-long semistructured interviews. To recruit villagers, I employed a snowball technique.

Community Feeling in Little Hatton.

Many villagers interviewed for this study felt there was a very strong community feeling in Little Hatton, and many represented the village in romanticized terms. Their impressions of the imagined community in Little Hatton were often constructed prior to moving to the village. Their preconceived perception of village life embodied all the notions of community that Tönnies discussed (Harper 1989): friendship, cooperation, and a homogeneous existence, as these two quotes illustrate:

> The village has not only lived up to our perceptions of village life, it has beaten it. The trees, the color, no noise or traffic which are a way of life in the city. The views are fantastic, I only have to go out of my front door and I am in the country-

side. So it does live up to my perception and I find that everyone who has moved here seems to be of the same opinion.[3]

It's a lot more intimate here, I suppose. Most people in towns don't know who their neighbors are, or take a long time to get to know them. Here people tend to get to know each other a lot faster. I can't imagine going back to live in suburbia, its just a feeling you get in the country which you don't get in towns.[4]

The imagined village community was presented to outsiders in a very static, homogeneous way that neglected differences existing between women in Little Hatton. On the surface, the community in Little Hatton appeared very strong with supportive social networks but this assumed a uniformity of experience with all women in the village sharing the same identity based on gender alone. The remainder of this chapter considers identity aspects that transgress a dominant heterosexual community imagined by the majority of Little Hatton women.[5]

The Importance of the Family.

In Little Hatton, the center of imagined community life represented and supported the experiences and preferences of particular women namely, White, heterosexual, middle-class mothers. Their perception of village life made their experiences normative; anything outside their experience was considered marginal or at the extreme, transgressive. Women's notions of community were primarily informed by their ideals and experiences of the home, the family, and social networks. Within the village there were few places for women to meet informally, so there was little opportunity to escape traditional gendered spaces and roles. Ordinarily, women would meet in each other's homes. Part of the security of belonging to the imagined community, then, was being in the home and feeling secure and safe within the village environment. This experience was often contrasted to living in the city and feeling alone and isolated:

> I really like living here, it is a very safe place. I can sit here in, in the evening with the children while Peter is at the pub, and I can leave the doors unlocked and not worry about a thing. I wouldn't have dreamed of doing that before when we lived in Oxford.[6]

Being able to move about the countryside with much more freedom than in the city was also highly valued. To the women, the city was an isolating experience and the countryside offered freedom and security for the family that urban society could not:

> I don't think it would be a good idea to move the kids to the city, this is their home here and we would lose so much freedom, cooped up in a flat all day.[7]

Being part of strong social networks is another key element of community (Harper 1989). The social networks in Little Hatton centered on the family and participation in village activities with children. Many activities in the village involved the school and therefore many of the women in the village identified with each other through their children. The imagined community of Little Hatton was fundamentally tied into the family but a particular representation of the family: the strong, nuclear family, with a mother and father.

> I have a lot of friends here . . . yeah, they all have kids, I suppose it is because there is a lot to do here for families.[8]

As the research progressed it became clear that some women in the village transgressed the norms of this community and felt marginalized. For example, the supportive networks for mothers exclude women who do not have children and who cannot participate in many activities in the village because of the orientation of village life toward the needs of the family. This was made clear to me by one of the study participants, a young woman in her early twenties who is single:

> There is nothing of any interest here, for me. I think if you don't have children, you lose contact with what is going on in the village very quickly. It is very much people with children that keep the village going, but there is nothing for me here, especially since all my friends live outside the village.[9]

Single childless women were in fact treated as a threat and constructed as "man-eaters," that is, after someone else's husband. Young, single women epitomized the antithesis of rural community life in the minds of those "normative" women with families. The underlying fear appeared to be that young women without child-care responsibilities could socialize in the village pub where they would seduce other women's husbands. Older single women were not seen to be as threatening to the younger mothers and wives. The hostility toward young women on their own was tangible in the village public house. Although unspoken, women on their own in a public house were treated in a derogatory manner, as one woman alleged:

> Have you met Fay? She's single like me and as a single woman on her own she feels that other women are suspicious of her, that she is a threat and she has had women being nasty to her because they have thought she is after their husbands. She's seen women who have grabbed their husbands' arms when she's walked into the pub. Its never happened to me but I don't dye my hair or wear make-up like she does.[10]

Different perceptions of femininity existed side by side in the village but were often in conflict. In order to feel part of the community in Little Hatton, many women tried to identify with the "norm," denying any identity that would cause them to be associated with an excluded group. Individuals are identified by others within the community by those aspects of their character that signify their "normality." The next section considers the role of sexuality in representations of alternative femininities.

The Village Community and Sexuality.

Following on from the representation of village life as synonymous with the heterosexual nuclear family, there is a feeling among some women in the village that not having a husband or children suggests something odd about a woman's sexuality and femininity. Young women without husbands represented a "different" femininity, causing anxiety among other village women. This is because in Little Hatton representations of femininity are highly heterosexualized, with deviations from heterosexuality being seen as a threat to "norms of natural feminine behavior." As Valentine (1993, 396) argued,

> To be gay, therefore, is not only to violate norms about sexual behavior and family structure but also to deviate from the norms of "natural" masculine or feminine behavior. These norms change over space and time and hence sexuality is not defined merely by sexual acts but exists as a process of power relations.

The barman of the village pub was gay and while he was marginalized by some because of his sexuality, the vast majority of women in the village were very fond of Mark and treated him as an "honorary woman" in whom they could confide their marriage and sexual problems.

> When I found out about Mark, I didn't mind at all. He is just treated as one of the girls.[11]

While Mark's sexuality was accepted, many village women were hostile towards female homosexuality. The village community was constructed as heterosexual and heteropatriarchal with the family as central to the imagined community. Lesbianism did not belong in Little Hatton, it was part of city society, not part of village life:

> There is none of them [lesbians] here. It's a family village, there is lots for the family to do.[12]

The ability to construct the rural community through marginalizing "different" (female) sexual identities illustrates the power certain women have in making themselves the center of an imagined community and "others" peripheral. In this particular village, for example, the heterosexual nuclear family played a major role in social activities held in the village. There was a strong Mothers and Toddlers group and Women's Institute that promoted family values and perpetuated representations of the traditional nuclear family. Through such institutions, variations from the norm were constructed as threatening. One woman commented,

> It is not natural for a child to have parents of the same sex. It needs the male and female role models in its life or else when it goes to school, its life is made a misery. I can't believe that the authorities allow two women to have a child with no male influence, it is not right.[13]

The view that lesbian mothers are unnatural and therefore socially unacceptable illustrates how communities can unite against those who are perceived as different. The power of "community" can construct moral boundaries that centralize acceptable identities on the one hand and marginalize transgressive ones on the other. This is particularly the case when issues of motherhood and sexuality were involved. As Romans (1992, 99) claimed, a lesbian mother is particularly threatening because "she challenges the dominant ideologies of gender, motherhood and family which together are felt to contribute significantly toward the stability of society."

While homophobic women may be a minority within the village, they can unite other members of the village community by celebrating a common femininity informed by the image of the (heterosexual) mother and/or wife. By placing themselves at the center of the imagined community, heterosexual women control the representations of women, continuing to construct the "norm" as heterosexual. This representation was extremely powerful, so much so that members of the community were aware that to "belong" they must adhere to this identity or risk being associated with the excluded "other." Therefore, some women may play down aspects of their identity that they feel make them stand out. Obversely, others may play up aspects that they feel sets them aside from a community they do not want to belong to because they disagree with the "common" culture or hegemonic worldview. In rural communities, where the population is small and the individual cannot always be invisible among strangers, "place matters" in how identities are and can be played out.

Conclusion

The "rural" in England is an extremely powerful representation that influences constructions of imagined community life in villages across Britain. While the idea of a village "community" can be uniting, it is as likely to be divisive with its smallness allowing for a more forceful marginalization of those who are different. The many representations of rural life in the media, in literature, and in academia influence the imaginings individuals have about the nature of communities in rural villages in England. The assumption that village communities welcome everybody without question needs greater exploration. The role of women within rural communities should also be examined further to understand how certain women work to maintain the moral boundaries of their community by perpetuating idealized representations of "the rural woman." This chapter has focused on evidence from a particular village in England. Obviously the processes at work within rural communities vary depending upon the specific character of that community and the multiplicity of femininities that exist within it. Hierarchical power relations *between* women and the role this plays in constructions of village life, seem to me pivotal, given the centrality of the "home" in constructing a "rural" place. The "rural" is coded as static, traditional and feminine. As such the rural is one site where women exert an unusually large representational influence on the identity of a place. This is not to say that women realize this power or are conscious of it. Nonetheless, because it is through their bodies that rurality is defined (and vice versa), there is more potential for women to intervene and subvert the patriarchal order of things (see for example, Valentine, chapter 4).

Notes

1. This chapter will be concerned with issues regarding Englishness and will therefore not engage in the issues of Welsh or Scottish experiences.

2. For an overview of the development of the rural-urban continuum see Harper (1989).

3. Female, 30s, interview by author, tape recording. Little Hatton, Oxfordshire, England, 22 July 1994.

4. Female, 50s, interview by author, tape recording. Little Hatton, Oxfordshire, England, 18 July 1994.

5. There is insufficient space in this chapter to discuss all aspects of identity, such as lifestyle, class, and position in the lifecycle.

6. Female, 20s, interview by author, tape recording. Little Hatton, Oxfordshire, England, 4 August 1994.

7. Female, 30s, interview by author, tape recording. Little Hatton, Oxfordshire, England, 18 August 1994.

8. Female, late 20s, mother of three, interview by author, tape recording. Little Hatton, Oxfordshire, England, 25 July 1994.

9. Female, early 20s, interview by author, tape recording. Little Hatton, Oxfordshire, England, 8 August 1994.

10. Female, late 20s, single, interview by author, tape recording. Little Hatton, Oxfordshire, England, 29 July 1994.

11. Female, late teens, interview by author, tape recording. Little Hatton, Oxfordshire, England, 17 July 1994.

12. Female, mid 30s, interview by author, tape recording. Little Hatton, Oxfordshire, England, 21 August 1994.

13. Female, late 50s, interview by author, tape recording. Little Hatton, Oxfordshire, England, 21 July 1994.

References.

Anderson, B. 1983. *Imagined community: Reflections on the origin and spread of nationalism.* London: Verso.

Aziz, R. 1992. Feminism and the challenge of racism: Deviance or difference? In *Knowing women: feminism and knowledge,* eds. H. Crowley and S. Himmelweit. 291–305. Cambridge: Polity in association with Open University Press.

Bell, M. 1992. The fruit of difference: The rural-urban continuum as a system of identity. *Rural Sociology* 57 (1):65–82.

Harper, S. 1989. The British rural community: An overview of perspectives. *Journal of Rural Studies* 5 (2): 161–184.

Laing, S. 1992. Images of the rural in popular culture 1750–1990. In *The English rural community,* ed., B. Short. 133–47. Cambridge: Cambridge University Press.

Newby, H . 1979. *Green and pleasant land?* London:Hutchinson.

Newby, H. 1986 Locality and rurality—the restructuring of rural social-relations. *Regional Studies* 20(3): 209–15.

Pahl, R. 1966. The rural-urban continuum. *Sociologia Ruralis* 6: 299–327.

Romans, P. 1992. Daring to pretend? In *Modern homosexualities: Fragments of lesbian and gay experience,* ed., K. Plummer. London, New York: Routledge.

Rose, G. 1990. Imaging Poplar in the 1920s: Contested concepts of community, *Journal of Historical Geography* 16 (4): 425–437.

Short, B. 1992. Images and realities in the English rural community: An introduction. In *The English Rural Community,* ed., B. Short. 1–18. Cambridge: Cambridge University Press.

Trollope, J. 1989. *A village affair.* Great Britain: Black Swan.

Valentine, G. 1993. (Hetero)sexing space: Lesbian perceptions and experiences of everyday spaces. *Environment & Planning D: Society & Space* 11: 395–413.

Williams, R. 1973. *The country and the city.* London: Chatto and Windus.

Winstanley, M. 1989. The new culture of the countryside. In *The vanishing countryman.* ed., G. Mingay. 142–53. London: Routledge.

Young, I. 1991. The ideal of community and the politics of difference. In *Feminism/Postmodernism,* ed. L. Nicholson. 300–323. London: Routledge.

Conclusion

Crossing Thresholds

John Paul Jones III, Heidi J. Nast, and Susan M. Roberts

We hope this collection has provoked new ways of thinking about space and how it is integral to politics and to constructions of sexuality, "race," and gender. While the original three categories we used to organize and structure this book (difference, methodology, and representation) have practical and analytical value, we trust the collection has also encouraged readers to work "against the grain" of these divisions, to see other possibilities. Working against the grain not only foregrounds the interconnectedness of the book's parts and chapters, but helps us think about how feminist geography can speak to a wide range of contemporary political dilemmas.

As we assembled this collection, we were struck by what we saw as similar empirical and theoretical concerns, voiced across the book's three sections. We discuss these here, not to imply that there is one final reading, but to tease out some productive lateral connections across decidedly different sorts of empirical contexts and theoretical framings. In making such lateral connections, we arrive at different thresholds. Like those of difference, methodology, and representation, these new thresholds cannot be easily lined up or linearly categorized, but rather are nested and implicated, one in the other. We begin below, then, by identifying three "threads," or across-the-grain thresholds. These are focused around: first, the many ways in which discursive violence is wrought spatially; second, identities as fluid, varying with different spatial and bodily juxtapositions; and third, developing new ways of thinking *through* the body and *through* space/place. These new thresholds, in turn, speak collectively of, and creatively to, yet another: the "home." We begin, then, by discussing each of the first three, and end with a re-consideration of "home."

Discursive Violence as Spatial

Most chapters in this collection have called attention to interconnections between space and discursive violence, a relation not typically considered in feminist geography. We define discursivity as those processes and practices through which statements are made, recorded, and legitimated through institutional and other means of linguistic circulation. Discursive violence, then, involves using these processes and practices to script groups or persons *in* places, and in ways that counter how they would define themselves. In the process, discursive violence obscures the socio-spatial relations through which a group is subordinated. The end effect is that groups or persons are cast into subaltern positions.

This book's contributors have each, in one way or another, charted the spatial effects and means of such violence, or investigated the ways in which such violence can be ruptured through spatial practices. Laura Pulido (chapter 1), in her discussion of environmental activism in South Central and East Los Angeles, for example, speaks of an insistence by "White" women upon scripting some women of color activists as feminists, despite the fact that these women do not identify themselves as such. Moreover, few "White" feminists have taken up racism as a foundational part of their "feminist" agendas (cf., Russo 1991), leading many women of color to deem feminism a "White woman's movement." The latter is a discursive move that simultaneously opposes the spatial disavowal and marginalization of women of color by "White" women and records many "White" women's inabilities to work physically or intellectually against oppressively constructed socio-spatial categories other than those defined by gender (c.f. Mohanty, Russo, and Torres 1991; King 1994). Through both an historic marginalization of women of color and an attempt to re-claim women of color's successes as "feminist," many "White" feminists capitalize on struggles that were never their own and thwart possibilities for women of color to register their identities in their own terms.

Isabel Dyck (chapter 10), in her work with Indian Canadian women and the health care system in Canada, points to contradictions inherent in drawing upon discursive categories to help "others" (in this case, Indian women) who are excluded from, or ill-served by, mainstream "White" health care services. Drawing upon such terms as "Indian" or "Punjabi" to locate physically those who might need special services, a health care initiative paradoxically brings with it the assumption that those having certain geographical origins outside Canada are essentially—geographically and racially—different. Because such an initiative was undertaken in keeping with the Canadian government's official rubric of "multiculturalism," it also helped promulgate the notion that the only ones with "culture" are non-White immigrant others. Such discursive scriptings are violent to the extent that they obscure both differences within the Punjabi community and commonalities that work across place and "race." They additionally help establish highly racialized framings of space and culture. Thus, *geographically*-based identity categories, while perhaps politically effective and instrumental in improving services to recent immigrants or those of color, produce geographical essentialisms which reinforce racisms, making it appear that non-White "others" define what is multicultural. Moreover, such "others" are made to have an essentially different cultures and "races" which are depicted as bringing with them distinct sets of "problems."

Another kind of spatially wrought discursive violence is pointed out by Sherry Ahrentzen (chapter 5) in her study of women homeworkers in the contemporary United States. The prefix "home," she states, scripts women homeworkers in spatially denigrating ways, papering over, with a veneer of stasis and sameness, the complex and dynamic ways in which homeworkers are inserted spatially into a global capitalist economy. Homeworkers are metonymically identified with home, homemaker, housework and domesticity, terms which in the context of industrial capitalist societies are negatively feminized and associated with immobility, tradition, and unremunerative "reproductive" activities and places. Her chapter implies that this spatial violence, wrought in a distinctly post-industrial context, is a carryover from an earlier capitalism in which the home was coded culturally in terms of reproduction. The home has never been, however, a place of singular social dimensions; it has always been a variegated social field wherein many different kinds of activities are carried out. In an attempt to recuperate women's practical and contradictory experiences of the home, Ahrentzen documents the many functions of the home, drawing upon homeworkers' framings of, and feelings about, their space and their work.

Similarly, Vidya Samarasinghe (chapter 7) points to how spatial discursive violence is levied against rural Third World women through economic surveys of labor value which ignore labor accomplished in the home, whether these be national censuses or surveys carried out under the aegis of the World Bank, the United Nations, or the International Labor Organization. By ignoring the fact that the home is *the* major site wherein value is produced in rural economies of the Third World, rural women's lives are effectively effaced—statistically, nationally, economically, and hence, spatially, despite the fact that women are often the main producers of food and many goods and services. Samarasinghe offers practical suggestions for resisting such violence through transformations in surveying procedures and analyses.

Nikolas Huffman's work on feminist cartography (chapter 13) shows how dis-counting women has historically been a key practice in the subdiscipline of cartography. His work parallels that of architect Mark Wigley (1992) who shows that women (as passive, receptive objects) have historically been construed, through a series of metonymic equivalencies, as a kind of architectural flatness or paper upon which the ink of male pens (active, inscribing, erect) map out their message and agency. Huffman shows how cartography has typically been scripted by and for male interests, mapping the world in feminizing and subordinating ways, despite the relatively large presence of women professionals in the field. Drawing upon crosscultural and marginalized examples of mapping, Huffman produces concrete examples of new mappings that celebrate non-dichotomizing difference, mappings that do not require the denigration of an "other."[1] In so doing, he takes Donna Haraway's call to consider objects as "boundary projects" into the spatially discursive domain of maps (Haraway 1991).

Speaking from her position as a Latina immigrant to the United States,

Patricia Meoño-Picado (chapter 15) recounts a tale of spatial violence wrought discursively through radio broadcasts. Specifically, she discusses the highly racist, sexist, and homophobic shows aired by a Spanish language station in New York which, because the broadcasts were in Spanish, were "invisible" to federal regulators, thereby escaping scrutiny and prosecution under federal law. In part, her chapter tells how some Latina lesbians organized to make themselves and the violence of the broadcasts visible, physically asserting and mapping out an oppositional and legitimate public presence. For example, they marched in front of the radio station with placards, and they used alternative media such as Dyke TV and photographic exhibits. Because their invisibility fluctuated with the changing sentiments and coverage of mainstream media, such as news reports (or black outs) on television and radio stations and in newspapers, their spatial irruption into the circuits of discursive violence required continually changing spatial tactics. Her work shows how spatially transgressive acts can disrupt normative discursive circuits.

Last, Bronwen Walter (chapter 16) documents differences in racist representational framings of the Irish in nineteenth-century Britain and the United States, in the process showing how the framings served different nationalist ends. Whereas in Britain notions of "breeding" were (and still are) called upon to exclude the Irish in peculiarly biological ways, in the United States an emphasis on "citizenship" led eventually to assimilation of the Irish. By using two different national contexts to explore how racism is discursively and geographically wrought, Walter points not only to the politics of language, but to that of place. Like most other contributors, she offers spatial means of resisting such violence, in part, through calling attention to the power of the term "diaspora" in not only describing a globality of settlement patterns, but to possibilities for forging oppositional, transnational alliances for change. Other examples of the spatiality of discursive violence and spatial resistance to such violence are found throughout the collection.

Fluidity and Juxtaposition

One of the most exciting themes or thresholds threaded through the collection concerns not only how places and bodies shape identity, but more significantly, how identities derive from the ways in which places and bodies are relationally located or spatially juxtaposed. Because juxtapositions (of persons, places, things) are highly variable, *and* because who/what is juxtaposed is contingent, understanding how space and identity are shaped by or through them requires a theoretical framework altogether different from that which considers space as (an entirely finished) "text." Rather than conceptualizing spaces or bodies as symbolically decipherable and relatively stable, a view that permits key syntactical elements of a material assemblage (dress codes or landscape, for example) to be decoded, the chapters in this collection suggest that meanings are constantly dispersed, displaced, and spatially multiplied as objects are continually being re-placed next to others in often highly circumstantial ways.

Thus Mona Domosh (chapter 12) cautions feminist historical geographers against reading authorial intentions into spaces. She suggests, in keeping with a Foucaultian framework, that we consider spaces and bodies as parts of discursive webs of power through which meaning is produced only in relation to particular material contexts and, even then, only as effects; that is, certain socio-spatial configurations promote specific framings of and for practice and, hence, for experiences and feelings. We therefore need to understand how the construction of meaning is embedded within relations of power: things mean something different depending upon/against whom we (or our spaces) are juxtaposed.

Ahrentzen (chapter 5) tells us, for example, that when homeworkers' male clients enter their homes, the home often becomes (is felt to be) a site of potential danger, causing women to carry out a number of tactics they feel might ensure their safety, such as leaving men's clothing in view of visitors. Similarly, some homeworkers set apart a room in their home, giving it special design features so as to create a feeling of professional distance from the domestic. This setting apart inculcates feelings of enjoyment and freedom; the home becomes more valued through its differentiation. In contrast, neighbors who know that a homeworking woman is at home may, in an emergency, drop children off to be baby-sat by her, equating the woman's location in the home with a natural predisposition to be with a child. In each instance, the subject's body and "home" is transformed through juxtapositions which establish or resist cultural equivalences. This way of theorizing space points to the spatial fluidity of everyday political relations and identities and offers us imaginative possibilities for disrupting and transforming a highly heteropatriarchal world.

Imaginative possibilities are also evident in Gill Valentine's chapter on separatist lesbian re-appropriations of Nature (chapter 4). As she points out, the quality of separatist communities was (and is) highly variable, being contingent on a number of bodily and spatial factors. On the one hand, many separatists see rurality as a means of distancing themselves from urban-based heteropatriarchy and for achieving a certain level of material and economic self-sufficiency, something they see as impossible in urban frameworks. Yet within and amongst the communities Valentine discusses, identities are extremely fluid, a fluidity attained in part by spatial and bodily juxtapositions which bring different encodings into creative tension and contact: in one case the entry of sons into a commune disrupted notions of feminine purity, causing heated debates within at least some communities; the presence of disabled lesbians in another context raised issued not previously considered, such as how to define and negotiate divisions of labor; and, separatist communities made up of women of color were challenged by biracial same-sex marriages, children or friendships. As Valentine points out, "lesbian lands were not stable communities but were fluid with new women coming and going as different identities were maximized and minimized."

At a different scale, Karen Nairn (chapter 6) shows that where students place themselves in the classroom—both in relation to each other and to the teacher—makes a difference as to how they speak and feel in that context. The classroom periphery, for example, was defined by where the teacher was physically positioned: If the teacher had two desks, effectively defining the front and back of the classroom, quiet students clustered in seats around the classroom rim. "Front" and "back" also depended on where the teacher was positioned at any one moment and were felt to be sites of safety; in the first case (front) because no one could turn around to face you, and in the second case (back) because one could be present yet unnoticed by the students in the "front." In a similar vein, Nairn points out that the discipline of geography was itself gendered male or female depending upon juxtapositions within course schedules: geography was coded female if the only other course options given were math and chemistry, whereas it was coded male if read against art history and biology. Here, juxtaposition of context affected who took the classes.

At a larger geographical scale, Richa Nagar (chapter 11) talks about how her identity fluctuated (often dramatically) during her research into postcolonial political relations in Tanzania, fluctuations resulting from her insertion into very different sociospatial contexts. Nagar's differential juxtapositionings redefined her identity in relation to others and, perhaps more importantly, to herself. These identity fluctuations exceeded the norms used to define each ethnic and religious group and place, destabilizing her own and others' sense of herself and the world. For example, Nagar dressed in clothing that accorded with the most respectable conventions of the ethnic group with which she was scheduled to interact. Because each group generally lived in a circumscribed place, her decision produced anxieties and dilemmas concerning how she should dress *along the way* to those places. Wearing "traditional" Indian dress on the bus to her study sites seemed to her to provoke angry stares from black Africans who encoded and linked her Indian-ness to oppression. Ironically, bus travel was typically forbidden to local Indian women, as it was considered too "African" and, therefore, dangerous. Such scenarios of destabilization achieve almost comical dimensions when we realize that Nagar interacted with five different ethnic groups, each one requiring a specific dress code and regimented spatial forms of negotiation and comportment. Her ability to nonetheless traverse such a variegated domain with creativity and insight, while maintaining what she felt was a certain degree of personal, political and emotional integrity, points to our potential to deal bodily, productively, and intelligently with a world that—because we may be reluctant to inhabit "other" places and dress norms—can seem hopelessly, humorlessly, confusing.

Humor and playfulness were central to the success of Las Buenas Amigas in resisting a hostile public environment to create meaningful and legitimate places and identities for themselves (chapter 15). Patricia Meoño-Picado demonstrates how Las Buenas Amigas adopted Santería as a political and organizational model; Santería is a syncretic religious practice that calls for numerous creative and playful juxtapositions of traditional and modern spiritual forms. In so doing, they developed new representational imaginaries and fora better able to accommodate difference and facilitate a fluidity of identities conducive to productive change.

A fluidity of identity shaped by different representational imaginaries is likewise demonstrated by Bronwen Walter (chapter 16), albeit in very different contexts. She shows how Irish bodies were scripted as, and meant, something very different in the United States and England as a result of the quite different nationalistic ends toward which Irishness was deployed in the two countries. The two diasporic communities *and* the Irish in Ireland lived, were understood, and understood their own bodies differently in keeping with different nationalistic imaginaries. Thus, while nineteenth century Irish women in the United States were representationally cast as pillars of family strength at a time when domestic servants were in demand, those in Britain were denigrated as henpeckers after they took paid employment while their husbands were unemployed due to industrial lay-offs, simultaneously casting Irish husbands as docile men of little economic value.

Thinking *Through* Place and the Spaces of the Body

The production of fluid identities through juxtapositions of spaces, practices and performative norms, brings us to another common analytical thread found in many of the chapters—the importance of thinking with and *through* the actual materiality of place and of the body. Rather than divorcing the rational from the lived, and meaning from experience, most authors speak of the importance of bodily experiences as spatially lived. Nagar (chapter 11) did not assess political relations in Tanzania through reading texts or analyzing national and international data sets. Rather, she placed herself bodily and spatially within the communities she was studying, respecting and (at least for a moment) living out certain important cultural norms, especially those related to dress, food and religion. Her thinking was therefore bodily and spatial, not abstracted and disembodied. So too, Pulido (chapter 1) is not concerned to speak about racialized distances between "White" women and women of color in abstract terms, but rather how these distances were thought through and experienced in socio-spatial and political ways over time and in particular instances and neighborhoods, specifically East and South Central Los Angeles. Similarly, Ahrentzen (chapter 5), in her discussion of female homeworkers, is more concerned with how women experience and feel homeworking in bodily and spatial terms than with assessing the abstract economic contributions of such activity. Karen Nairn (chapter 6), in her discussion of girls' silences in the classroom, also focuses on understanding how girls experience, think, and feel space in a coeducational context, emphasizing that it is only when persons feel safe that they are, in fact, safe.

Demonstrating another sense of thinking through body and place, Melissa Gilbert (chapter 2) critiques the urban underclass thesis by mapping out everyday pathways through which poor African American and European American are economically marginalized. In the process she shows how spatial processes of economic marginalization extend far beyond individually ghettoized lives. In like fashion, through her investigation of income maintenance policies and spatial mobility, Glenda Laws (chapter 3) shows how state policies are caught up in the ways bodies are differently socially constructed and regulated.

This is not to say that thinking through the spaces of place and the body entails some "pure" phenomenological experience of the world, where we bracket our cultural predispositions. Rather, it is about uncovering, through places and bodies, the visceral spatial registers of knowledge and power. Accordingly, Meoño-Picado's chapter (chapter 15) speaks to how "mapping" can be reconceived in terms of Latina lesbian corporeality constructing itself spatially and through/in place and, obversely, as Latina lesbian spatiality and place constructing itself through the corporeal. As Huffman (chapter 13) points out, such mapping can either be ephemeral (the protest march) or more materially permanent (an anthology of Latina lesbian writing or a photography exhibit), the latter perhaps being more dangerous in that its permanence allows claims to legitimacy.

A concern for producing representational media which insist that the reader experience power's effects in bodily and spatial ways is one of the foci of Lydia Pulsipher's work (chapter 14) in community archaeological efforts to unearth a colonial slave village in Montserrat. An invitation to include her research in a Smithsonian exhibit led Pulsipher to develop several related exhibits, including a facsimile of a slaveship's hold. Exhibit-goers were forced to stoop in order to pass through the spaces of the ship, in the process experiencing bodily (even if in quite different contexts from the slaves) the material conditions of the ship's recesses. Through their bodily movements, any knowledge exhibit-goers may have had about the transport of slaves was re-known, transformed through corporeal experiences. Visitors to the exhibit also walked through a diorama of a slave village, a representational device that helped foreground slaves' bodily engagements with an oppressive landscape and slaves' creative resistance to oppression in everyday life. In addition, Pulsipher wrote and illustrated children's stories which strongly invoked bodily senses and which speak of the resilience and productivity of slave families in negotiating an otherwise oppressive place. Her forays into fiction allowed her license to attempt representations of the *lived* meaning of places, rather than restricting herself to representations of disembodied facts about morphological landscape features, for example. Through these and other endeavors, Pulsipher questions how we might imaginatively re-think, re-value, and re-present the lived spaces of bodies and places.

Jeanne Kay's (chapter 17) discussion of nineteenth-century Mormon women's experiences of particularly harsh environmental conditions, as recorded in diaries and letters, similarly awards primacy to the bodily and the spatial. In so doing, she recovers alternative, nongendered encodings of Nature that displace standard, hegemonic binary equations of nature/culture and female/male. Among the alternatives she re-presents is Nature as an agendered stage wherein God expresses his will and glory; alternatively Nature is scripted as a kind of agendered agent of God's will, bringing trials to women which forcefully map themselves onto the women's bodies through scarring, death (such as during childbirth), or bodily deformities. The body, then, visibly records one's ability to obey and/or submit to God's will, an agendered mapping essential to attaining redemption for all Mormons, and hence, a place in Zion (Utah).

The Threshold of Home

While geographers have had a long-standing interest in scale, it has tended to be taken as a rather unproblematic ordering principle, most often taking the form of a hierarchy of levels (local, regional, national, global, for example). The chapters in this collection, like other contemporary work in geography, demonstrate that core geographic concepts such as "space," "place," and "scale" are being rethought. Instead of seeing scale as a hierarchical ordering of self-evident "levels," these chapters, in various ways, move toward re-conceiving scale in terms of processes and flows that move across, between and among levels. These flows in part constitute and define what we think of as levels (such as "local" or "regional") themselves (see Massey 1994, 146–73; Smith 1992). Thus, no longer can the "national" be unproblematically assumed as a self-evident scale or level defining national space when flows of capital, people, ideas, and information are changing not only the nature of national boundaries but also anything called national identity. We might make similar claims regarding regional, local, or even global scales. Perhaps the scalar concept that has received the most explicit and implicit reworking in this collection, though, is that of "home."[5]

Several chapters point to a re-valuation and re-evaluation of home. On one level these chapters explode the notion of the home as a neatly bounded, unitary and necessarily coherent place. Rather, home is, like locality, a site which is variably constituted in relation to "stretched" social relations and flows of all sorts. On another level, seeing the home as a permeable site or nexus can reassess of what the home is, and what it means. The home's unproblematized associations with domesticity, femininity and motherhood and its emplacement in naturalized dualisms such as home/work, public/private, and so forth can therefore be challenged.

First, the home may be reconceptualized as a scalar concept situated in shifting scalar relations. Of course there is no such thing as *the* home; there are *homes*, homes situated in different ways within much wider spaces of flows (of people, goods, services, ideas, and so forth). The women homeworkers and telecommuters studied by Ann Oberhauser (chapter 9), Sherry Ahrentzen (chapter 5) and Karen Falconer Al-Hindi (chapter 8) experience home in changing ways as this space is entangled in, and constituted through, different webs of social relations and flows once the home becomes a site of paid employment. In the western contexts with which these authors deal, home is simultaneously a place where goods or services for sale are produced, where formal waged labor is undertaken, where enormous quantities of social services go unpaid, where social networking occurs, and where family life takes place. Samarasinghe (chapter 7) points out how homes in rural Third World economies are the nerve centers of socioeconomic life and need to be recognized and valued as such. Nagar (chapter 11) demonstrates the ways in which home can be a nexus of flows that cross and challenge the scalar levels of local to global. The home is perhaps a threshold, an entry way or exit way, to or from a wider world, from which it cannot be meaningfully separated. Indeed, in the English language "home" can shift scales: it can "refer with equal ease to house, land, village, city, district, country, or, indeed, the world" (Sopher 1979, 130). In other languages the meaning of the term "home" may not be as fluid.

Another way in which the home may be rethought is evident in the way many chapters in this collection move beyond a view of "home" as having forced associations that have *never* historically obtained (see also Johnston and Valentine 1995). The politics of associating home with a femininity tied to mothering, consumption, tradition, and stasis has in modern "Western" contexts nearly always been elitist and exclusionary. After reading this collection, it is hard to envision how anyone could work on the "home" without radically de-centering what it is politically or normatively made to mean. As Pulido (chapter 1) points out, for example, East and South Central Los Angeles is scripted as "home" to marginalized Latinos and African Americans and is staunchly defended as such. Perhaps it is for this reason that some Latino men have no problem becoming members of, or working with, the Mothers of East Los Angeles (MELA). That is, because the entirety of East Los Angeles is home (collapsing the divisions of male/public and female/private), men and women collectively feel called upon to maintain a territorial home/place. The home is claimed and defined differently again in Walter's study (chapter 16) wherein she shows how, because "public" space in nineteenth century Ireland was encoded as British colonial and oppressive, private homes became metonymic nationalist equivalents of a free Irish nation, the home serving as a site of colonial resistance. In similar fashion, Valentine (chapter 4) shows how "home" for separatist lesbians can be rural land itself, nuclear family homes often being sites of fear, marginalization and displacement. Watkins (chapter 18) demonstrates that rural villages can be encoded by village women as racially and heterosexually exclusive home/places, an encoding that requires a number of disciplinary procedures at the level of the body and place. In Meoño-Picado's chapter (15) it is clear that home can be a site of political empowerment; urban homes were used by lesbians in Las Buenas Amigas to organize for personal and social change. Last, the efforts of Pulsipher and others (chapter 14) to unearth the remains of a slave village (rather than the nearby industrial site of sugar cane production), speaks to a re-valuation of an entire location as a home/place of cultural creativity and survival.

Conclusion

The chapters in this collection, although addressing the key issues signaled by the three parts—difference, methodology, and representation—have clearly incorporated many other themes key to feminist inquiry. By pointing to a few salient thresholds cutting across the collection, we aimed to raise the possibilities of a range of new critical engagements. These thresholds lie at the intersection between a series of social relations—including those framed around "race," gender, sexuality, and space—and moments of discourse, fluidity/juxtaposition, the body, and the home. Re-working how these chapters may be understood is an unfinished project, one we trust that each reader will embark upon. More broadly, we hope this collection will stand as an important intellectual and political threshold, one that invites researchers and students alike to enter, crossover, and explore, so as to move beyond its present configuration. Crossing-overs of this sort promise to alter the boundaries of feminist geography, thereby transforming the relations between and the substance of both feminism and geography more generally.

Notes

1. Dichotomous dualisms are structured by the relation A/not-A, that is, they operate through negation of that/those which are different. See Massey (1993), Blum and Nast (1996), and Natter and Jones (1997) for discussions of different types of binaries and their sociospatial effects.

2. On the instability of identity, space, and their interrelations, see Natter and Jones (1997). Also, see Duncan (1990), Natter and Jones (1993), Mitchell (1996), Peet (1996) and Walton (1995, 1996) about the utility (or lack thereof) of the "text" metaphor. The text metaphor is also taken to task for different theoretical reasons in Lefebvre (1991) and Grosz (1995).

3. See, for example, the recent collection edited by Ruth Barnes and Joanne B. Eicher (1992), *Dress and Gender*.

4. We take this notion of juxtapositioning from the work of Deleuze and Guattari (1983) and, especially, its explication in more spatial terms by Grosz (1995) and Theweleit (1987).

5. Also see Sibley (1996).

References

Barnes, R., and Eicher, J. B., eds. 1992. *Dress and gender*. Providence: Berg Press/St. Martin's Press.

Blum, V. and Nast, H. 1996. Where's the difference? The heterosexualization of alterity in Henri Lefebvre and Jacques Lacan. *Society and Space* 14: 559–580.

Deleuze, G. and Guattari, F. 1983. *Anti-Oedipus. Capitalism and schizophrenia*. Minneapolis: University of Minnesota Press.

Duncan, J. 1990. *The city as text: The politics of landscape interpretation in the kandyan kingdom*. Cambridge: Cambridge University Press.

Grosz, E. 1995. *Space, time and perversion*. New York: Routledge.

Haraway, D. J. 1991. *Simians, cyborgs, and women: The reinvention of nature*. New York: Routledge.

Johnston, L. and Valentine, G. 1995. Wherever I lay my girlfriend, that's my home: the performance and surveillance of lesbian identities in domestic environments, In *Mapping desire: Geographies of sexualities*. D. Bell and G. Valentine, eds., 99–113. New York: Routledge.

King, K. 1994. *Theory and its feminist travels: Conversations in US feminist movements*. Bloomington: Indiana University Press.

Lefebvre, H. 1991. *The production of space*. Cambridge, Mass: Blackwell.

Massey, D. 1993. Politics and space/time, In *Place and the politics of identity*, M. Keith and S. Pile, eds., 141–61. New York: Routledge.

Massey, D. 1994. *Space, place, and gender*. Minneapolis: University of Minnesota Press.

Mitchell, D. 1996. Sticks and stones: The work of landscape. *The Professional Geographer* 48: 94–6.

Mohanty, C. T., Russo, A., and Torres, L., eds. 1991. *Third world women and the politics of feminism*. Bloomington: Indiana University Press.

Natter, W. and Jones, J. P. 1993. Signposts toward a poststructuralist geography, In *Postmodern contentions: Epochs, politics, space*, J. P. Jones, W. Natter, and T. Schatzki, eds., 165–203. New York: Guilford.

Natter, W. and Jones, J. P. 1997. Identity, space and other uncertainties, In *Space and social theory*, G. Benko and U. Strohmayer, eds., 141–161. Cambridge: Blackwell.

Peet, R. 1996. Discursive idealism in the "landscape-as-text" school. *The Professional Geographer* 48: 96–8.

Russo, A. 1991 'We cannot live without our lives': White women, antiracism, and feminism, In *Third world women and the politics of feminism*, C.T. Mohanty, A. Russo and L. Torres, eds., 297–313. Bloomington: Indiana University Press.

Smith, N. 1992. Geography, difference and the politics of scale, In *Postmodernism and the social sciences*, J. Doherty, E. Graham, and M. Malek, eds., 57–79. New York: St. Martin's Press.

Sopher, D. E. 1979. The landscape of home: Myth, experience, social meaning, In *The Interpretation of Ordinary Landscapes*, D.W. Meinig, ed., 129–49. New York: Oxford University Press.

Theweleit, K. 1987. *Male fantasies. Volume 1. Women floods bodies history*. Minneapolis: University of Minnesota Press.

Walton, J. 1995. How real(ist) can you get? *The Professional Geographer* 47, 1:61–5.

Walton, J. 1996. Bridging the divide—A reply to mitchell and peet. *The Professional Geographer* 48: 98–100.

Wigley, M. 1992. Untitled: The housing of gender, In *Sexuality and space*, B. Colomina, ed., 3278–89. Princeton: Princeton Architectural Press.

Index

About the Contributors

Sherry Ahrentzen is a professor of architecture at the University of Wisconsin-Milwaukee. Her research, focusing on new forms of housing to better address the social and economic diversity of the United States, has been published extensively in journals and magazines, including *Journal of Architecture and Planning Research, Environment and Behavior*, and *Progressive Architecture*. With Karen A. Franck, she edited the book, *New Households, New Housing*. Her research has been funded by the U.S. Department of Housing and Urban Development, the National Science Foundation, the National Endowment for the Arts, and the Graham Foundation for the Study of the Arts.

Mona Domosh teaches geography and women's studies courses at Florida Atlantic University. She is the author of *Invented Cities: The Creation of Landscape in Nineteenth-Century New York and Boston*, published by Yale University Press. Her recent research focuses on relationships between landscapes and gender, class, and racial identities in nineteenth-century cities.

Isabel Dyck is an associate professor at the School of Rehabilitation Sciences, University of British Columbia, Canada. She received her Ph.D. in geography from Simon Fraser University, British Columbia, following degrees in social anthropology from the University of Manchester, England. Her interests include women's domestic and paid labor, immigrant women and their health, and qualitative methodology. Her recent research concerns work issues for women with chronic illnesses, resettlement concerns of immigrant women with children, and student health professionals' development of cultural competencies.

Karen Falconer Al-Hindi is an assistant professor of geography at the University of Nebraska at Omaha. Her research focuses on gender and work. She also conducts research on feminist methodology and neotraditional community planning. She is currently studying gender and telecommuting in Omaha, Nebraska.

Melissa R. Gilbert is an assistant professor in the Department of Geography and Urban Studies at Temple University. Her research and teaching interests include gender, racism, and urban and economic restructuring. Currently, she is focusing on local labor markets, urban poverty, social networks, and the survival strategies of working poor women.

Susan Hanson is a professor of geography at Clark University. Her research and teaching interests focus on feminism and urban social and economic geography. She is coeditor of *Economic Geography*, a past president of the Association of American Geographers, a Fellow of the American Association for the Advancement of Science (AAAS), and a former Guggenheim Fellow.

Nikolas Huffman is a Ph.D. student in the Department of Geography at Pennsylvania State University. His M.S. thesis at Penn State focused on feminist cartography and postmodern map design theory. He previously worked as a freelance map designer for five years, including a three year affiliation with the National Geographic Society. His present research involves poststructuralist geographic visualization design theory and the historical geography of computing in the Nazi era.

John Paul Jones III is a professor of geography at the University of Kentucky. His research has examined the "feminization of poverty" in the United States and the social welfare program, Aid to Families with Dependent Children. His current work is situated at the intersection of contemporary social theory, critical human geography, and social science methodology. In 1996 he was appointed editor of the *Annals of the Association of American Geographers*.

Jeanne Kay is professor of geography and dean of the Faculty of Environmental Studies at the University of Waterloo in Ontario, Canada. She has published a number of journal articles and book chapters on the theme of religious beliefs and identities, examining how these related to societies' uses and representations of natural environments.

Audrey Kobayashi is a professor of geography and director of the Institute of Women's Studies at Queen's University in Kingston, Ontario, Canada. She has published extensively in the area of gender and racism, human rights, and critical legal studies and immigration, and is editor of *Women, Work and Place*.

Glenda Laws was an associate professor of geography at the Pennsylvania State University until her untimely death in 1996. After undergraduate studies at the University of Sydney in her native Australia, Glenda obtained her M.A. and Ph.D. degrees from McMaster University in Hamilton, Ontario, Canada. Her research and teaching covered social policy, gender relations, medical geography, urban geography, and issues of aging. Her publications can be found in such journals as the *Professional Geographer, Annals of the Association of American Geographers*, and *The Gerontologist*.

Patricia Meoño-Picado was born in San José, Costa Rica. She was trained as a geographer at Clark University and currently works as a book editor in New York City. She writes about film, the city, and Latin American popular culture.

Janice Monk began her formal geographic education forty years ago at the University of Sydney, Australia, but she crossed the threshold into geography as a small girl whose father took her for bus and train rides "to the end of the line." She is now executive director of the Southwest Institute for Research on Women and Adjunct professor of geography at the University of Arizona. She has been publishing and speaking on feminist geography since the late 1970s. Her works include the coedited book and coproduced video, *The Desert Is No Lady* (with Vera Norwood and Shelley Williams respectively). She is also the coeditor of *Full Circles* (with Cindi Katz) and *Women of the European Union* (with Maria Dolors García-Ramon).

Richa Nagar is an assistant professor of geography at the University of Colorado in Boulder. She received her Ph.D. from the University of Minnesota, where she was a Fellow in the MacArthur Interdisciplinary Program on Peace and International Cooperation. Her current research focuses on the intersections among social space, cultural politics, and the discourse and practice of development in India. She has written several articles on identity politics among South Asians in postcolonial Tanzania.

Karen Nairn is a doctoral student in the Geography Department at the University of Waikato, Aotearoa/New Zealand. Her doctoral research is titled, "Constructing Identities: Gender, Geography and the Culture of Fieldtrips." She is an experienced secondary teacher, having left a position as head of Department of Geography to take up her university work.

Heidi J. Nast is an assistant professor of international studies at DePaul University, Chicago. Her research addresses the interconnections between gender, "race," sexuality, and the state. Her work has been published in a number of venues, including *Africa*, the *Annals of the Association of American Geographers*, and *Society and Space*.

Ann M. Oberhauser is an associate professor of geography at West Virginia University. Her previous research examines regional development and restructuring of the automobile industry in France, the United States, and South Africa. Her current work focuses on gender and economic development in Appalachia, and includes intensive research on women's homework in West Virginia.

Laura Pulido is an assistant professor of Geography at the University of California where she teaches courses in environmental studies and Chicano studies. She is a member of the Labor/Community Strategy Center and is active in local struggles concerning social and environmental justice. Laura is also the author of *Environmentalism and Economic Justice: Two Chicano Struggles in the Southwest,* published by the University of Arizona Press.

Lydia Mihelič Pulsipher is a professor of geography at the University of Tennessee where she enjoys supervising the research of graduate students who are doing field work related to human ecology subjects in the Caribbean, Central America and the Pacific. She has two sons, who seem to share her interests in geography and culture, and is married to archaeologist, C. McCall Goodwin. They live on the edge of Knoxville in a house full of dogs, cats, friends, and family.

Susan M. Roberts is an assistant professor of geography at the University of Kentucky. Her research has focused on the geography of the contemporary international financial system, and currently she is pursuing a critical investigation of globalization. One of Sue's concerns is to integrate feminist theory with studies of the international political economy.

Vidyamali Samarasinghe is associate professor of international development in the School of International Service at the American University in Washington, D.C. She received her Ph.D. in geography from Cambridge University. Her research interests focus on women in development and the role of women in civil conflict. Much of her work focuses on women in her native country of Sri Lanka. She has been a Cornell Distinguished Visiting Professor at Swathmore College, a Research Fellow at Boston University, and has taught at the University of Maryland in College Park.

Gill Valentine is a lecturer in geography at the University of Sheffield, where she teaches courses on social geography and qualitative methods. She is coauthor, with David Bell, of *Consumption, Space and Identity: Cultural Geographies of Food* (Routledge, forthcoming), and coeditor, with David Bell, of *Mapping Desire: Geographies of Sexualities* (Routledge, 1995).

Bronwen Walter is senior lecturer in geography at Anglia Polytechnic University, in Cambridge, United Kingdom, where she helped establish an interdisciplinary program in Women's Studies. She has published in *Transactions of the Institute of British Geographers, Society and Space,* and *Feminist Review.* She contributes research on women's issues to Irish welfare and community groups. She also conducts research for the anti-racist program of Britain's Commission on Racial Equality.

Francine Watkins is a doctoral student at the University of Sheffield, United Kingdom. She is currently working on the completion of her thesis, titled *The Cultural Construction Of Imagined Rural Communities.*